Unfair Dismissal Handbook

OLD EDITION

Unfair Dismissal Handbook

Fourth Edition

M W T Mead, LL B, LL M

Partner, Bevan Ashford, Solicitors
Part-time Chairman of Industrial Tribunals

© Longman Group UK Ltd 1991

ISBN 0 85121 7621 ✓

Published by
Longman Law, Tax and Finance
Longman Group UK Ltd
21–27 Lamb's Conduit Street
London WC1 3NJ

Associated Offices
Australia, Hong Kong, Malaysia, Singapore, USA

A CIP catalogue record for this book is available from the British
Library.

0

Phototypeset by Intype, London
Printed and bound in Great Britain by
Mackays of Chatham PLC

Contents

Preface

The only right which the common law affords to a dismissed employee is an action for wrongful dismissal, which arises where the employer, without lawful cause, terminates a fixed-term contract during its term or a contract of indefinite duration with incorrect or no notice. The action of wrongful dismissal is not directly affected by the law of unfair dismissal. The common law has never been concerned with the concept of fairness of the employer's action in dismissing the employee. An employee who is dismissed by reason of redundancy is entitled to some financial redress under the provisions of Part VI (ss 81–96 and 98–120) of the Employment Protection (Consolidation) Act 1978, but redundancy is narrowly defined in the legislation and restrictively interpreted by the judiciary.

Before the introduction of the Industrial Relations Act 1971, many employees had little or no safeguard against arbitrary dismissals by their employer which were not in breach of contract. The employer may have had an internal procedure which required the employer to warn employees or gave the employees a right to explain their case before the dismissal or gave the employees a right of appeal, but few such procedures existed, and too many employees were subject to the vagaries of their employer. Some *de facto* protection might have been afforded if the employee were a union member, but union organisation in a workplace might be weak or non-existent, and it was rare to find a trade union participating in any procedure. It was exceptional that an independent arbiter would examine the dismissal to see that the employer had acted fairly.

In 1963 the International Labour Organisation recommended that termination of employment should not take place unless there was a valid reason connected with the capacity or conduct of the employee or based on an operational requirement of the employer. The government subsequently set up a committee of the National Joint Advisory Council to consider the problem and provide information. The Royal Commission on Trade Unions and Employers' Associations 1965–68, the Donovan Commission, concluded that 'In reality people build much of their lives around their jobs. Their incomes and prospects for the future are inevitably founded in the expectation that their jobs will continue.' For workers in many situations, dismissal is a disaster. It considered that existing voluntary procedures could be strengthened, but that they were insufficient. The Commission favoured legislation to give employees protection against unfair dismissal.

The legal concept that the employee should have the right not to be unfairly dismissed was first given statutory form in the Industrial Relations Act 1971. The law is now contained in the Employment Protection (Consolidation) Act 1978, which has been further amended as shown in the Table of Amendments.

Claims for unfair dismissal are considered in the first instance by industrial tribunals which claim as their characteristics informality and accessibility. Many of the claims for unfair dismissal which come before the industrial tribunals involve important issues for either the employer or the employee, even if, financially, the sums involved are not always large. Frequently there are complex issues of fact and/or law.

Employees bringing claims for unfair dismissal and employers faced with unfair dismissal claims, not surprisingly, increasingly rely upon professional advice. All those who are called upon to advise have to consider the application of the common law as well as the statutory provisions. Moreover, they are faced with a wealth of reported cases, often apparently conflicting, which may well be relevant.

This book has been written primarily for those who are required to advise upon the law of unfair dismissal, although it will be of interest to law students and others. It is a comprehensive examination of the law with particular reference to the reported cases.

The law is as stated as at October 1991.

Once again I would like to thank my publishers for all their advice, help and patience in the preparation of this fourth edition.

October 1991   Malcolm Mead

Table of Cases

xi

Table of Statutes

Table of Statutory Instruments

Table of Abbreviations

Employment Protection (Consolidation) Act 1978—EP(C)A 1978

Industrial Tribunal—the tribunal

Employment Appeal Tribunal—EAT

British Broadcasting Corporation—BBC

National Industrial Relations Court—NIRC

Employment Act 1980—EA 1980

Sex Discrimination Act 1975—SDA 1975

Trade Union and Labour Relations Act 1974—TULRA 1974

Race Relations Act 1976—RRA 1976

Table of Amendments to the Employment Protection (Consolidation) Act 1978

Sections 1–160 of the 1978 Act

Section 1(4) of the 1978 Act is amended by s 29(3) of and para 18 of Sched 6 to the 1989 Act.

Section 23 of the 1978 Act is amended by s 15(1) and (3), and s 20(3) of and Sched 2 to the 1980 Act: s 10(3) and (4) of the 1982 Act: ss 11(*a*) and 33 of and para 2(1) of Sched 3 and Sched 4 to the 1988 Act.

Section 27 of the 1978 Act is amended by s 14 of the 1989 Act.

Section 33 of the 1978 Act is amended by s 11 of the 1980 Act: s 23(4) of and para 31 of Sched 7 to the Nurses, Midwives and Health Visitors Act 1979: s 86 of and para 75 of Sched 10 to and Sched 11 to the Social Security Act 1986.

Section 45 of the 1978 Act is amended by s 23 of and para 15 of Sched 5 to the Social Security Act 1989 (this amendment is to take effect on a date to be appointed—probably 1 January 1993).

Section 47 of the 1978 Act is amended by s 11(3) of the 1980 Act.

Section 53 of the 1978 Act is amended by s 20 of and para 4 of Sched 2 to the 1982 Act: s 15(1) of the 1989 Act.

Section 55 of the 1978 Act is amended by s 21 of and para 1 of Sched 3 to the 1982 Act.

Section 56 of the 1978 Act is amended by s 20(2) of and para 11 of Sched 1 to the 1980 Act.

Section 56A of the 1978 Act is inserted by s 12 of the 1980 Act.

Section 57 of the 1978 Act is amended by s 6 of the 1980 Act.

Section 58 of the 1978 Act is amended by s 3 of the 1982 Act: s 11 of and para 2 of Sched 3 to and Sched 4 to the 1988 Act.

Section 59 of the 1978 Act is amended by s 21(2) of and para 17 of Sched 3 to the 1982 Act.

Section 62 of the 1978 Act is amended by ss 9 and 21(2) of and para 18 of Sched 3 to and Sched 4 to the 1982 Act: s 16(1) of and para 1 of Sched 2 to the 1990 Act.

Section 64 of the 1978 Act is amended by s 3(1) of the Sex Discrimination Act 1986: s 21(2) of and para 19 of Sched 3 to the 1982 Act:

The Unfair Dismissal (Variation of Qualifying Period) Order 1985 SI 1985/782.

Section 66 of the 1978 Act is amended by s 20(2) of and para 13 of Sched 1 and Sched 2 to the 1980 Act.

Section 67 of the 1978 Act is amended by s 9(5) of the 1982 Act.

Section 68 of the 1978 Act is amended by s 21(3) of and para 21 of Sched 3 to the 1982 Act.

Section 71 of the 1978 Act is amended by ss 5(1), and 21(2) and (3) of and para 22 of Sched 3 to and Sched 4 to the 1982 Act.

Section 72 of the 1978 Act is amended by ss 5(2) of the 1982 Act.

Section 72A of the 1978 Act is inserted by s 6 of the 1982 Act.

Section 73 of the 1978 Act is amended by ss 9 and 20 of and Sched 2 to the 1980 Act: ss 4, 20 and 21 of and para 5 of Sched 2 to and Sched 4 to the 1982 Act: s 3(2) of the Sex Discrimination Act 1986: the Unfair Dismissal (Increase of Limits of Basic and Special Awards) Order 1991 SI 1991/467.

Section 74 of the 1978 Act is amended by s 21(2) of and para 23 of Sched 3 to the 1982 Act.

Section 75 of the 1978 Act is amended by the Unfair Dismissal (Increase of Compensation Limits) Order 1991 SI 1991/466.

Section 75A of the 1978 Act is inserted by s 5(3) of the 1982 Act: the Unfair Dismissal (Increase of Limits of Basic and Special Awards) Order 1991 SI 1991/467.

Section 76A of the 1978 Act is inserted by s 7 of the 1982 Act.

Section 77 of the 1978 Act is amended by ss 8 and 21(3) of and para 24 of Sched 3 to and Sched 4 to the 1982 Act.

Section 80 of the 1978 Act is amended by s 1(3) of and para 30 of Sched 1 to the Education Act 1980.

Section 81 of the 1978 Act is amended by ss 20(1) and 21(2) of and para 6(2) of Sched 2 and para 2(1) of Sched 3 to and Sched 4 to the 1982 Act.

Section 82 of the 1978 Act is amended by s 16(1) of and para 3(1) of Sched 9 to the 1989 Act.

Section 134 of the 1978 Act is amended by s 20(2) of and para 18 of Sched 1 to the 1980 Act.

Section 138 of the 1978 Act is amended by s 28 of and Sched 5 to the Armed Forces Act 1981: s 157 of and Sched 9 to the Reserve Forces Act 1980: s 86(2) of and Sched 11 to the Social Security Act 1986: s 66(2) of and Sched 10 to the National Health Service and Community Care Act 1990.

Section 139 of the 1978 Act is amended by s 86(2) of and Sched 11 to the Social Security Act 1986.

Section 140 of the 1978 Act is amended by s 20 of and para 20 of Sched 1 and Sched 2 to the 1980 Act.

Section 141 of the 1978 Act is amended by the Insolvency of Employer (Excluded Classes) Regulations 1983 SI 1983/624.

Section 142 of the 1978 Act is amended by s 8(2) of the 1980 Act.
Section 144 of the 1978 Act is amended by s 57(4) of and Sched 6 to
the Merchant Shipping Act 1988.
Section 146 of the 1978 Act is amended by ss 20 and 21 of and para
8(5) of Sched 2 and para 6 of Sched 3 and Sched 4 to the 1982 Act:
the Insolvency of Employer (Excluded Classes) Regulations 1983 SI
1983/624.
Section 151 of the 1978 Act is amended by s 20 of and para 7(1) of
Sched 2 to the 1982 Act.
Section 153 of the 1978 Act is amended by s 23(4) of and Sched 7 to
the Nurses, Midwives and Health Visitors Act 1979: s 21 of and para
26 of Sched 3 to and Sched 4 to the 1982 Act: s 29(3) of and para 24
of Sched 6 to the 1989 Act: s 86(2) of and Sched 11 to the Social
Security Act 1986: s 33 of and Sched 4 to the 1988 Act.

Schedule 2 to the 1978 Act

Paragraph 2(1) is amended by s 20(2) of and para 23 of Sched 1 to
the 1980 Act.
Paragraph 2(4) is amended by s 20(2) of and para 24 of Sched 1 to
the 1980 Act: s 21 of and para 27(2) of Sched 3 to the 1982 Act:
s 7(4) of the Dock Work Act 1989.

Schedule 3 to the 1978 Act

Paragraph 3(3) is amended by s 10 of and para 13 of Sched 2 to the
Social Security and Housing Benefits Act 1982.

Schedule 5 to the 1978 Act

Schedule 5 is prospectively repealed by s 66(2) of and Sched 10 to the
National Health Service and Community Care Act 1990.

Schedule 9 to the 1978 Act

Paragraph 6A is amended by s 21 of and para 7 of Sched 3 to the
1982 Act.

Schedule 13 to the 1978 Act

Paragraph 1 is amended by s 20 of and para 7(2) of Sched 2 to the
1982 Act.
Paragraph 10 is amended by s 20 of and para 31 of Sched 1 to the
1980 Act.
Paragraph 11 is amended by s 20 of and para 32 of Sched 1 to the
1980 Act: s 21 of and para 29 of Sched 3 to the 1982 Act.

Paragraph 16 is amended by s 21 of and para 6 of Sched 4 to the Reserve Forces (Safeguard of Employment) Act 1985.

Paragraph 17 is amended by s 21 of and para 2(2) of Sched 3 to the 1982 Act.

Paragraph 18A is amended by s 21 of and para 2(3) of Sched 3 to the 1982 Act.

Schedule 14 to the 1978 Act

Paragraph 7(1) is amended by s 20(2) of and para 33 of Sched 1 to the 1980 Act: s 21 of and para 30(2) of Sched 3 to the 1982 Act: s 86(2) of and Sched 11 to the Social Security Act 1986.

Paragraph 8 is amended by s 21 of and para 30 (3) of Sched 3 to the 1982 Act: the Employment Protection (Variation of Limits) Order 1991 SI 1991/464.

References throughout the text to sections or paragraphs in Schedules to the 1978 Act are as amended.

Chapter 1

Persons Protected Against Unfair Dismissal

Section 54 of the Employment Protection (Consolidation) Act EP(C)A 1978 provides that every employee has the right not to be unfairly dismissed by his employer (except so far as is provided by ss 54–80 and 141–9 of the Act). Protection against unfair dismissal is thus afforded only to *employees*.

1 'Employee' defined

An 'employee' is defined as an individual who has entered into or works under (or, where the employment has ceased, worked under) a contract of employment. A 'contract of employment' is defined as a contract of service or apprenticeship, whether express or implied and (if it is express) whether it is oral or in writing: EP(C)A 1978, s 153(1). Whether an individual is an employee and thus protected against unfair dismissal depends upon the existence of a contract of service or apprenticeship with the employer. The phrases *contract of service* and *contract of employment* are treated by the courts and tribunals as interchangeable expressions; but, strictly, a contract of employment has a wider meaning than contract of service in that it includes a contract of apprenticeship.

1.1 Employees distinguished from independent contractors

A relationship which closely resembles that of the employer and the employee is that of hirer and independent contractor. This relationship has its foundation in a contract which is known as a *contract for services*. The independent contractor is not protected by the legislation when his contract is terminated. Therefore, the distinction between the contract *of* service and the contract *for* services is important. While it is easy to recognise the difference between the two, it is more difficult to say wherein that difference lies. The relationship of a chauffeur and his employer is that of employee and employer, and the contract is a contract of service. The relationship between a fare and his taxi driver is that of hirer and independent contractor, and the contract is a contract for services. The distinction

1

is apparent, but what are the differences? A contract under which a person provides services may be a contract *sui generis*: *Ironmonger v Movefield Ltd (t/a Deering Appointments)* [1988] IRLR 461.

In *WHPT Housing Association Ltd v Secretary of State for Social Services* [1981] ICR 737, Webster J thought that:

the difference between a contract of service and one for serices must reside, essentially, in the terms of the principal obligation agreed to be undertaken by the employee—a word which I use without begging the question. In a contract of service, it seems to me, the principal obligation undertaken by the employee is to provide himself to serve: whereas in a contract for services the principal obligation is not to provide himself to serve the employer but his services for the use of the employer.

Initially the courts attempted to solve the question by suggesting tests to be applied which would indicate the nature of the relationship. It has become apparent that rarely will these tests be determinative. However, the courts will take the tests into account as elements to be considered in determining the true nature of the relationship. In *WHPT Housing Association Ltd v Secretary of State for Social Services*, above, Webster J found that since the difference between the contract of service and the contract for services resided essentially in the terms of the principal obligation agreed to be undertaken by the employee, many of the tests suggested by the courts in earlier cases, which he described as secondary tests, were unlikely to be determinant one way or the other, in distinguishing between the contract of service and the contract for services.

The *control* test is the oldest test. It was based on the proposition that the employer had the right to control the employee, both as to the work to be done, but more importantly as to the manner in which that work was to be done. If the 'employer' did not have the right to control the manner in which the work was to be done then the contract was not a contract of service. This test has become difficult to apply with changing economic and social conditions. Where skills were simple, it might well be possible for the employer to control the employee. With the increase in specialist skills it is no longer possible for the employer to control the employee, particularly as to the manner in which the work is done, although it is quite clear that the relationship between the parties is that of employer and employee. The courts, recognising these problems, have modified the test so that the power or residual right to control the employee is an important factor in determining whether or not the relationship between the parties is that of employer and employee. Thus, except in exceptional circumstances the control test is unlikely to be determinative of the relationship between the parties, though control remains relevant as a factor in deciding whether an individual is an employee or not: see *Ready Mixed Concrete (South East) Ltd v Minister of Pensions and National Insurance* [1968] 2 QB 497 and *Warner Holidays Ltd v Sec-*

retary of State for Social Services [1983] ICR 440. In *Narich Pty Ltd v Commissioner of Pay-Roll Tax* [1984] ICR 286, Lord Brandon, giving the decision of the Privy Council, held:

while all relevant terms of the contract must be regarded, the most important, and in most cases the decisive, criterion for determining the relationship between the parties is the extent to which the person, whose status as employee or independent contractor is in issue, is under the direction and control of the other party to the contract with regard to the manner in which he does his work under it.

Although this Privy Council decision may appear to conflict with the decisions in cases decided in the English jurisdiction, it is none the less of considerable persuasive authority.

Even where the individual has agreed to be subject to the control of the 'employer' the relationship between the parties can still be one of hirer and independent contractor.

A second test, which has been little used, is the *organisation* or *integration* test. In *Stevenson, Jordan and Harrison v Macdonald and Evans* [1952] 1 TLR 101, Denning LJ said:

One factor which seems to run through the instances is that under a contract of service a man is employed as part of the business and his work is done as part of the business, whereas under a contract for services, his work, although done for the business, is not integrated into it but is only accessory to it.

This test was followed by Lord Denning in *Bank voor Handel en Scheepvaart NV v Slatford* [1953] 1 QB 248. This test may be of some assistance where, for instance, the control test is inapplicable because the employer is not able to control the employee in the way in which he performs his duties, but the employee is clearly an essential part of the organisation. It may be particularly relevant in the case of a doctor employed by a health authority (see *Cassidy v Ministry of Health* [1951] 1 All ER 574) or an employee who is a computer programmer within a commercial organisation.

Ungoed-Thomas J used this test in *Beloff v Pressdram Ltd* [1973] 1 All ER 241, to decide that Nora Beloff was an employee of the *Observer* newspaper.

More recently, the *economic reality* test has evolved; it was suggested by MacKenna J in *Ready Mixed Concrete (South East) Ltd v Minister of Pensions and National Insurance*, above. The issue before the court was whether or not the owner-driver of the lorry was an independent contractor. There was a complex agreement between the driver and the company which cast the driver as an independent contractor. Under the agreement the driver agreed to deliver the company's cement and not to haul for anyone else during the period of the agreement. The agreement provided that the driver should buy the lorry on hire-purchase from a company in the same group. The driver had to carry out orders given to him by the company as if he

were an employee. He was under obligations as to repairs and maintenance of the vehicle, but was not subject to the company's instructions in driving the lorry. There were no provisions as to the hours
of work, meal breaks and the times at which he took holidays; in
these matters he was not subject to the control of the company. The
driver could employ others who would be his employees, to drive the
vehicle. He could not be asked to do work other than drive for the
company, whereas drivers who were the company's employees could
be asked to do work other than drive lorries. Moreover, at the expiration of the agreement, the driver was free to work elsewhere. The
chance of profit from operating the vehicle and the risk of loss were
the driver's.

Following the decisions in *Montreal v Montreal Locomotive Works
and AG* (1947) IRLR 161, PC and *US v Silk* (1946) 331 US 704,
MacKenna J examined the economic realities, the ownership of tools,
investment, the use of skills, and particularly the chance of profit and
the risk of loss to answer the question suggested by the earlier authorities: whose business is it? Was the driver carrying on business on his
own behalf or on behalf of a superior, the company? It was held that
the driver was carrying on business on his own account. He was a
small businessman and not a servant.

A similar approach was adopted in *Market Investigations Ltd v
Minister of Social Security* [1969] 2 QB 173, where a social survey
worker for a market research company was held to be an employee.
She 'did not provide her own tools or risk her own capital, nor did
her opportunity of profit depend in any significant degree on the way
she managed her work'. This case was followed in *Lee v 1 Chung and
2 Shun Shing Construction and Engineering Co Ltd* [1990] IRLR 236,
where the employee had no responsibility for investment in or management of the work.

1.2 The need for mutual obligations

Some recent cases involving casual employees have highlighted the
need for mutuality of obligation between the employer and employee.
In *O'Kelly and Others v Trusthouse Forte plc* [1983] ICR 728, mutuality of obligation was treated as an important factor in deciding
whether or not the relationship was that of employer and employee.
It was found to be missing in the case of regular casual workers at
the Grosvenor Hotel.

In *Nethermere (St Neots) Ltd v Gardiner and Another* [1984] ICR
612, Kerr LJ, in a dissenting judgment, emphasised the need to determine at the outset whether or not there was a contract. He held:

The determination of . . . whether the [individuals] were 'employees' . . .
involves a two-stage process. The first stage requires the determination of the
question whether there was any contractually binding nexus between the
alleged employees and the alleged employer in relation to the 'employment'

in question. This must be a question of law. The existence or non-existence of a binding contract cannot be anything else. It cannot be a question of fact or of degree. The second stage, if some binding contract exists as a matter of law, is then to classify or define the nature of the contractual relationship.

Stephenson LJ emphasised the importance of mutuality of obligation. He found, quoting MacKenna J in *Ready Mixed Concrete (South East) Ltd v Minister of Pensions and National Insurance* above:

A contract of service exists if these three conditions are fulfilled. (i) The servant agrees that, in consideration of a wage or other remuneration, he will provide his own work and skill in the performance of some service for his master. (ii) He agrees, expressly or impliedly, that in the performance of that service he will be subject to the other's control in a sufficient degree to make that other master. (iii) The other provisions of the contract are consistent with its being a contract of service.
. . . I do not quote what he says of (i) and (ii) except as to mutual obligations:
'There must be a wage or other remuneration. Otherwise there will be no consideration, and without consideration no contract of any kind. The servant must be obliged to provide his own work and skill.'
There must, in my judgment, be an irreducible minimum of obligation on each side to create a contract of service. I doubt if it can be reduced any lower than in the sentences I have just quoted . . .

See also, *McLeod and Others v Hellyer Brothers Ltd* and *Wilson and Another v Boston Deep Sea Fisheries Ltd* [1987] IRLR 232.

1.3 Elements of the employer–employee relationship

Since no test is conclusive, the tribunals and courts will have to look at all the elements of the relationship. Each case must be considered on its own facts: see *Warner Holidays Ltd v Secretary of State for Social Services* [1983] ICR 440. The elements which may fall to be considered, depending upon the circumstances of the particular case, are set out below. The weight to be given to each of these elements will vary in each case. This is not an exhaustive list.

The employer's right of control   As a single test this is unlikely to be conclusive. It is likely to be important as indicative of but not conclusive evidence of a contract of service, where the skills are simple or the exercise of control is large.

The employee as an integral part of the business   It is unlikely that this test can be considered as more than a guideline.

The chance of profit and the risk of loss by the person who undertakes the work   If the person who undertakes the work has a chance of profit and a risk of loss, and has the responsibility for investment in the business, it is indicative of but not conclusive evidence that there is no contract of service. These factors are likely to be of increasing importance since the decision in the *Ready Mixed Concrete* case above.

Ownership of the instrumentalia and the onus to provide Where the instrumentalia belong to the person who undertakes the work and are complex, specialised or expensive, it is indicative of but not conclusive evidence that there is no contract of service. However, by custom employees may be obliged to provide their own tools: *Challinor v Taylor* [1972] ICR 129 and see *Hitchcock v Post Office* [1980] ICR 100. The provision of clothing by the 'employer' may also be indicative of a contract of service.

The entitlement to exclusive service Exclusive service is indicative of but not conclusive evidence of a contract of service.

The provision of substitutes If the person who agrees to undertake the work can substitute another to carry out the work, it is indicative of but not conclusive evidence that there is no contract of service. If the person who undertakes the work has to engage helpers at his expense, it is again indicative but not conclusive evidence that there is no contract of service.

The payment of wages, sickness pay and holiday pay, and by whom payment is made Payment of fixed remuneration for a specific period is indicative of but not conclusive evidence that there is a contract of service. The remuneration may be calculated in various ways, such as on a piece-work or day-work basis. Payment for holidays or for absences caused by sickness or injury will also be indicative of but not conclusive evidence that there is a contract of service. When payment is for a particular undertaking or task, it is indicative of but not conclusive evidence that there is a contract for services: see *O'Kelly and Others v Trusthouse Forte plc* [1983] ICR 728. Payment by tips received from others or payment by commission may be consistent with the existence of a contract of service.

The power of selection and appointment The courts and tribunals will pay particular attention to the circumstances at the time when the contract was made, and the way in which the individual was taken on. The unilateral imposition of contractual terms by one of the parties on the other may be indicative of but not conclusive evidence that there is a contract of service.

The power to suspend and dismiss In the contract of service it is usual for the employer to have the power to suspend the employee and to dismiss. In the contract for services there is no power to dismiss, but there may be a power to terminate the contract. In practice the effect may be the same, although the different nature of the provisions will be relevant. The power to dismiss is probably more important than the power of selection, although even where there is a power of dismissal, other elements may make the contract one for services.

The power to fix the place, time of work and the times at which holidays are taken These matters may be seen as an element of control and the existence of this power in the contract may be indicative of but not conclusive evidence of a contract of service.

The existence of the disciplinary and grievance procedure The existence of the disciplinary and grievance procedure may be indicative of but not conclusive evidence of a contract of service. The employer has an obligation to provide the employee with a statement specifying the disciplinary rules and a disciplinary and grievance procedure (see s 1(4) of the EP(C)A 1978), save that the employer need not provide the employee with disciplinary rules and a procedure if on the date when the employee's employment began there were less than twenty employees.

The right to decide whether or not to accept work If the person providing the work is under no obligation to provide work on a regular basis and the individual who undertakes the work has the right to decide whether or not to accept the work, it is indicative of but not conclusive evidence that there is no contract of service: see *O'Kelly and Others v Trusthouse Forte plc*, above.

The deduction of PAYE etc The deduction of income tax under the PAYE rules and the payment of national insurance contributions for an employed person may be indicative of but not conclusive evidence of a contract of service.

Mutuality of obligation This is considered above. If mutuality of obligation is simply an element for consideration (rather than a question which has to be considered at the outset: see the judgment of Kerr LJ in *Nethermere (St Neots) Ltd v Gardiner* [1984] ICR 612, above), the absence of mutuality of obligation while not determinative will be of importance: see *O'Kelly and Others v Trusthouse Forte plc*, above and also *Wickens v Champion Employment* [1984] ICR 365.

Intention of the parties The intention of the parties to the contract or the label which they use to describe their relationship cannot alter or indeed decide the true relationship. The expression of their true intention is relevant but not conclusive in determining the relationship. Thus a declaration by the parties in the contract that the person rendering the services is to be regarded as a self-employed person or as an independent contractor will be disregarded if the contract is consistent with the relationship of employer and employee. The legal relationship must be classified not by appearance but by reality: *Young and Woods Ltd v West* [1980] IRLR 201. In each case the tribunal will examine the agreement to discover its real nature. The intention of the parties may well be a relevant factor for consideration. While the parties cannot alter the true nature of the relationship between them by the label they give it, where there is doubt or ambiguity, their intentions and the agreement between them may be strong evidence as to the true nature of the relationship, or, in some cases, decisive: see *Massey v Crown Life Insurance Co* [1978] ICR 590, in which the Court of Appeal distinguished its earlier decision in *Ferguson v John Dawson and Partners (Contractors) Ltd* [1976] 1 WLR 1213. In *BSM (1257) Ltd v Secretary of State for Social Services* [1978] ICR 894, the High Court, following the case of *Massey*, held that effect should be given to the intentions of the parties unless the terms of the contract or the circumstances were inconsistent with their intentions.

The view of the ordinary person   In *Cassidy v The Ministry of Health* [1951] 2 KB 343, Somervell LJ quoting Buckley LJ in *Simmons v Heath Laundry Co* [1910] 1 KB 543, confirmed that a further element to be considered in determining whether the relationship between the parties was that of employer and employee was whether the contract was 'a contract of service within the meaning which an ordinary person would give to the words'. In *Thames Television Ltd v Wallace* [1979] IRLR 136, the Employment Appeal Tribunal (EAT) held that the tribunal in deciding whether or not there is a contract of service should consider whether, in the light of the members' own experience and qualifications, the contract is such that the ordinary person looking at it would say that it was a contract of service. This approach was applied in *Midland Sinfonia Concert Society Ltd v Secretary of State for Social Services* [1981] ICR 454.

A further variation was considered in *Withers v Flackwell Heath Football Supporters' Club* [1981] IRLR 307, where the issue was whether or not a steward was an employee or was self-employed. The EAT, following the decision of Cooke J in *Market Investigations Ltd v Minister of Social Security* [1968] 3 All ER 732, found that the ultimate question in deciding the relationship between the parties is to ask, 'Is he on his own business rather than the business of the party for whom the work is being done?' It considered that if Withers had been asked while acting as a steward of the club bar 'Are you your own boss?', then the answer would be 'No'. It followed he was an employee.

Addison v London Philharmonic Orchestra Ltd [1981] ICR 261; *Midland Sinfonia Concert Society Ltd v Secretary of State for Social Services* [1981] ICR 454; *Warner Holidays Ltd v Secretary of State for Social Services* [1983] ICR 440; and *O'Kelly and Others v Trusthouse Forte plc* [1983] ICR 728 provide examples of cases where most of the elements as set out above have been considered in determining the nature of the relationship between the parties. However, as these cases make clear, each of these elements has to be considered in the circumstances of each case and the importance to be attached to them will vary from case to case. Usually the presence or absence of one or more of these elements will not be conclusive as to the question whether there is or is not a contract of service.

Whose employee? It may be clear that an individual is an employee; but whose employee is he? Where one employer loans an employee to another employer, the elements set out above will need to be examined in relation to each potential employer in deciding who is the real employer. Some elements may be present in relation to both employers and the courts will have to decide the issue on balance. Some of the elements will be more appropriate than others as, for instance, who selected the employee and who may dismiss him?

Fact or law? 'Is a contract a contract of service or a contract for services?' a question of law alone or a question of fact and law? An appeal from the decision of the tribunal can only be made to the EAT on a question of law. If it is a question of law then it is open to the EAT to substitute its findings for the findings of the tribunal. However, even if it is a question of law, then for an appeal to be made successfully against the decision of the tribunal on the issue, the EAT must find that the tribunal has misdirected itself as to the law or has misapplied the law to the facts, or the decision was such that no reasonable tribunal properly instructed as to the law could have properly reached the conclusion that that tribunal reached on the evidence available to it.

There is a wealth of authority as to whether or not the question is one of law or fact, but regrettably the authorities are conflicting.

In *Young and Woods Ltd v West* [1980] IRLR 201, where Stephenson LJ inclined to the view:

that it is a question of law, in these cases of service or services as in the case of lease or licence, whether the true inference from the facts, the true construction or interpretation of a written agreement or of an agreement partly oral and partly written or of a wholly oral agreement, is a matter of law on which there is a right and a wrong view, and if an industrial tribunal comes to what in the view of this court is a wrong view of the true nature of the agreement, it can and should find an error in law on the part of the industrial tribunal and reverse its decision.

In the same case, Sir David Cairns found:

that this court should not reverse the decision of an industrial tribunal affirmed by the Employment Appeal Tribunal that a contract is a contract of service except in cases where that is clearly not its character; secondly, on balance, the matters pointing to its being a contract of service do outweigh the matters pointing in the other direction; thirdly, it is of great importance as a matter of public policy that an employer should not be able to avoid his statutory responsibilities as an employer—responsibilities for safety, redundancy payments, compensation for unfair dismissal and other matters—by offering to those who are, or are about to become, in substance employees a form of contract purporting to put them in another category and offering tempting fiscal advantages.

The view of Stephenson LJ was followed by the EAT in *Addison v London Philharmonic Orchestra Ltd* [1981] ICR 261, where the conflicting authorities were reviewed. In *Midland Sinfonia Concert Society Ltd v Secretary of State for Social Services* [1981] ICR 454, Glidewell J again reviewed the earlier authorities, and following the decision of Lord Radcliffe in *Edwards v Bairstow* [1956] AC 14, considered that he could interfere on appeal if 'the facts found are such that no person acting judicially and properly instructed as to the relevant law could have come to the determination under appeal', or to put it another way, 'the true and only reasonable conclusion contradicts the determination'. The powers of the appellant court to interfere with a decision at first instance were further considered in *WHPT Housing Association Ltd v Secretary of State for Social Services* [1981] ICR 737, where Webster J considered that an appellant court had jurisdiction to interfere only if it concluded that no reasonable body, on the facts found by it and the inferences reasonably to be drawn from those facts, and properly directing itself as to law, could have made the decision which was reached. 'In other words, if the validity of the decision in law depends on the nature of the inferences to be drawn from the primary facts found', then the appellant court 'should interfere with it only if it is wrong, as a matter of law, in the light of inferences which must inescapably be drawn'. The early authorities have been reviewed by the Court of Appeal in two recent cases.

In *O'Kelly and Others v Trusthouse Forte plc* [1983] ICR 728, the Court of Appeal found that the EAT had interpreted a passage in the judgment of Stephenson LJ in *Young and Woods Ltd v West* [1980] IRLR 201, as authority for the proposition that the question was one of pure law. Donaldson MR found that if this was the true interpretation of Stephenson LJ's judgment:

it represents a sudden and unexplained departure from what has been understood to be the law for over 70 years, for it was as long ago as that that this court went so far, in *Simmons v Heath Laundry Co* [1910] 1 KB 543, as to describe the issue as one of fact with which an appellate court could not interfere in the absence of reason to believe that the arbitrator had misdirected himself. . . .

The test to be applied in identifying whether a contract is one of employment or for services is a pure question of law and so is its application to the facts. But it is for the tribunal of fact not only to find those facts but to assess them qualitatively and within limits, which are indefinable in the abstract, those findings and that assessment will dictate the correct legal answer. In the familiar phrase 'it is all a question of fact and degree'.

It is only if the weight given to a particular factor shows a self-misdirection in law that an appellate court with a limited jurisdiction can interfere. It is difficult to demonstrate such a misdirection and, to the extent that it is not done, the issue is one of fact. This, I think, is what this court meant in

Simmons v Heath Laundry Co [1910] 1 KB 543 which, so construed, is consistent with *Edwards v Bairstow* [1956] AC 14.

In *Nethermere (St Neots) Ltd v Gardiner* [1984] ICR 612, Stephenson LJ accepted that in *Young and Woods Ltd v West*, above, he had suggested that whether a contract is a contract of service or for services was a question of pure law. That had been decided without reference to the case of *Simmons v Heath Laundry Co*, above. In the present case the Court of Appeal held that whether the contract is a contract of service or contract for services is a question of law, but the answer includes questions of degree and fact which it is for the industrial tribunal to determine. Applying the decision in *Edwards v Bairstow*, above, it was not open to the EAT 'to interfere with the industrial tribunal's decision unless the industrial tribunal had misdirected itself in law or its decision was one which no tribunal, properly directing itself on the relevant facts, could have reached'.

The conclusion which can be drawn from these two cases is that the answer to the question, 'Is a contract a contract of service or a contract for services a question of law or a question of fact and law?' is that it is a question of law, although it is for the tribunal to determine the facts and to decide the weight which will be attached to the tribunal's findings of fact.

1.4 Labour-only contracts

The distinction between the contract of service and the contract for services is of importance with the growth of the labour-only contract. Here the main contractor provides the plant and materials, and arranges with a subcontractor to find the labour. The subcontractor is given a lump sum to remunerate those he engages. The subcontractor may engage employees who will remain his employees, unless it is clear that in reality they are the employees of the main contractor, or he may engage independent contractors who may be independent contractors in relation to the main contractor and/or the subcontractor. In *Ferguson v John Dawson and Partners (Contractors) Ltd* [1976] 1 WLR 1213, a man taken on as a member of a 'lump' labour force was held by the Court of Appeal to be an employee.

1.5 Apprentices

A contract of apprenticeship is akin to a contract of service, but it has an essential difference. The apprentice agrees to serve his master for the purposes of learning and the master agrees to teach the apprentice. If these elements are not present or if they are incidental, the contract is not one of apprenticeship, but probably of service. If the apprentice is a minor, the contract must be substantially for his advantage, otherwise he may be free to repudiate it. As regards statutory protection the distinction is largely academic because an apprentice is afforded the rights given to employees.

1.6 A person on the government work experience programme

Whether a person on a work experience programme is an employee of the sponsoring company depends upon the nature of the relationship and this will be determined in the normal way. In *Hawley v Fieldcastle and Co Ltd* [1982] IRLR 223, the tribunal found the relationship between the parties was not that of employer and employee because the Manpower Services Commission (MSC) imposed some limitations or restrictions, which are not usually found in the employer–employee relationship, namely on recruitment, the work to be done, discipline, termination and remuneration. In *Daley v Allied Suppliers Ltd* [1983] IRLR 14, it was held that a person working under the MSC work experience scheme was not employed either by the MSC or by the 'sponsoring employer'. In so far as there was a contract between the sponsoring employer and the individual, it was not a contract of service. The object was to enable the individual to obtain some work experience.

1.7 Agents

In *Tyne and Clyde Warehouses Ltd v Hamerton* [1978] ICR 661, it was held that an agent expressly engaged as 'self-employed', who paid Schedule D income tax and self-employed social security contributions, was in fact an employee. It is unclear why *Massey*'s case was not regarded as applicable. See also *JC King Ltd v Valencia* (1966) 1 ITR 67.

1.8 Directors

Directors *qua* directors are not employees of the company, although they may be agents of the company or have a dual capacity of agent and trustee. However, most managing directors and directors with executive functions may well be employees of the company. In large companies it will usually be apparent from the circumstances and the existence of a service agreement that the director is an employee. Difficulties have occurred in the case of smaller companies, particularly 'one-man companies'. The question was considered in claims for redundancy payments where the tribunals regarded whether or not the director had a controlling interest as being important.

In *Ferguson v Telford Greir Mackay and Co Ltd* (1967) 2 ITR 387, Ferguson was a company director and also company secretary. He worked as a full-time executive and held 30 per cent of the share capital. The other director held 50 per cent of the share capital. It was held that Ferguson was an employee.

In *Robinson v George Sorby Ltd* (1967) 2 ITR 148, it was held that the managing director who held over 90 per cent of the shares and was in control of the board of directors was not an employee. The remainder of the shares were held by members of the family, and the director could devote such time and energies to the company as he thought fit. There was no control by the company over him because he was, in effect, the company. It is possible, however, for a controlling shareholder-director to be an employee if the position of the director *vis-à-vis* the company is consistent with that of an employee.

In *Margetts v Underwood (Zelah) Ltd* (1973) 8 ITR 487, directors were held not to be employees. The only functions they had were directional ones supervising the running of the business, and there was no evidence from which a contract of service could be inferred.

In *Albert J Parsons and Sons Ltd v Parsons* [1979] IRLR 117, the Court of Appeal held that a full-time working director who received no salary but had his remuneration voted to him by way of director's fees and emoluments, and who was treated as being self-employed for the purpose of national insurance contributions, was not an employee. See also *Eaton v (1) Robert Eaton Ltd and (2) Secretary of State for Employment* [1988] IRLR 83. In *Folami v Nigerline (UK) Ltd* [1978] ICR 277, the managing director of the respondents, a wholly owned subsidiary of a Nigerian company, was held by the EAT to be an employee of the respondents. It held that:

Where it is established that a person has been appointed managing director of a company, that his duties include effective management of the affairs of the company in all its respects, that he has discharged those duties, and that he has received a salary from the hands of that company, the prima facie conclusion to be drawn is that he is an employee of that company.

The position of a director who has some executive functions and whom it is alleged is an employee may be clarified by the existence of a service agreement between himself and the company. In marginal cases this may help to establish the director as an employee. See also *Stanbury v Overmass and Chapple Ltd* (1976) 11 ITR 7.

1.9 Office holders

In some circumstances, office holders may be both the holders of an office and also employees and, in the latter capacity, may gain the right not to be unfairly dismissed. In *Social Club (102) and Institute Ltd v Bickerton* (1977) 12 ITR 442, the EAT held that the fact that a club secretary held an office from which he was removable by a two-thirds majority of the members, was irrelevant to the consideration of the question of whether he was an employee. The EAT held that in deciding whether a secretary to a club is an employee the following factors should be considered:

(1) whether the individual's payment was contractual and whether it was an honorarium or a salary;
(2) whether payment was fixed in advance or whether it was voted at the end of the year in token of the individual's work;
(3) whether the arrangements conferred upon the individual a right to payment or whether what was paid was a mere bounty;

(4) the size of the payment;

(5) whether the individual was exercising the functions of an independent office (somewhat in the way that a curate or police officer does) or was subject to the control and orders of the club;

(6) the extent and weight of the duties performed—the smaller they are the less likely he is to be an employee;

(7) the description given to the payment in the Minute or Resolution authorising it, and its treatment in the accounts for tax and national insurance purposes.

1.10 Ministers of religion

In *President of the Methodist Conference v Parfitt* [1984] IRLR 141, it was held that a Methodist minister was not an employee. Even if the relationship between such a minister and the Methodist Church were to be contractual it would not be a contract of employment. Again in *Davies v Presbyterian Church of Wales* [1986] ICR 280, the House of Lords held that a pastor of the Presbyterian Church of Wales was not employed under a contract of service.

1.11 Partners

A partner is generally not an employee but a self-employed person: see *Cowell v Quilter Goodison Co Ltd and QG Management Services Ltd* [1989] IRLR 392. However, the circumstances may show that a salaried partner is an employee, as may be an associate partner. Someone who is not described as a partner may in law be a partner and not an employee. See *Burgess v O'Brien* (1966) 1 ITR 164.

1.12 Outworkers

An outworker working from home may be an employee and so entitled to claim unfair dismissal even though he or she is regarded as self-employed for the purposes of the Income and Corporation Taxes Act 1988, s 18.

In *d'Ambrogio v Hyman Jacobs Ltd* [1978] IRLR 236, the employee, a machinist, who had worked at the company's premises, agreed to work from her own home instead. She worked at least 40 hours a week on equipment provided by the company. She was visited daily by a director who supplied her with materials and took away the completed garments. He also instructed her as to the method of work. Following the *Ready Mixed Concrete* case, above, the tribunal held that the relationship was that of employer and employee.

In *Airfix Footwear Ltd v Cope* [1978] ICR 1210, the EAT also held that an employee who had worked for the company for seven years on work supplied to her on a daily basis five days a week and did her work in accordance with the company's instructions, was an employee.

There had grown up between the parties the relationship of a contract of service.

In *Nethermere (St Neots) Ltd v Gardiner and Others* [1984] ICR 612, it was held that the two individuals who were machinists working at home on machines provided by the company were employees. The Court of Appeal accepted that there was an 'overall' or 'umbrella' contract inviting the company to continue to provide work, and the individuals to continue to accept and perform the work provided.

There emerges from the evidence a picture of the applicants doing the same work for the same rate as the employees in the factory but in their own homes—and in their own time—for the convenience of the workers and the company . . . I cannot see why well founded expectations of continuing homework should not be hardened or refined into enforceable contracts by regular giving and taking of work over periods of a year or more, and why outworkers should not thereby become employees under contracts of service like those doing similar work and at the same rate as the factory.

See **1.2**, above, for the importance of mutuality.

1.13 Casual employees

In *O'Kelly and Others v Trusthouse Forte plc* [1983] ICR 728, it was held that individuals who were regular but casual waiters in the company's banqueting department were not employees.

1.14 Diplomats

The doctrine of sovereign immunity originally prevented an industrial tribunal from considering a claim for unfair dismissal brought by an employee at a diplomatic mission who was engaged in carrying out the work of that mission: see *Sengupta v Republic of India* (1982) *The Times*, 18 November. However, the State Immunity Act 1978 enables an employee to claim wrongful dismissal, provided the contract was made in the UK and the work is to be wholly or partly performed there; and to claim unfair dismissal; and also to take proceedings to enforce other statutory rights. The State Immunity Act 1978 does not apply to contracts made before the coming into force of that Act: see *Sengupta's* case.

1.15 Workers' co-operative

A workers' co-operative registered with the Registrar of Friendly Societies as a limited company is an employer capable of employing and dismissing its workforce, so that an employee who is a member of the co-operative and a member of the workforce is capable of bringing a claim against the co-operative: *Drym Fabricators Ltd v Johnson* [1981] ICR 274. Although the point was not in issue the EAT appears to have considered that an unregistered co-operative could have a legal personality as distinct from its members so that the co-operative could employ and dismiss, allowing an individual to bring a claim against it.

2 Employees excluded from protection

2.1 Employees who lack the qualifying period of employment

To claim unfair dismissal an employee must have been continuously employed for the requisite number of hours in each week for a period of not less than two years ending with the effective date of termination: s 64(1)(a) of the EP(C)A 1978, as amended by the Unfair Dismissal (Variation of Qualifying Period) Order 1985 (SI 1985 No 782) which had effect from 1 June 1985.

For the calculation of the continuous period of employment, see Chapter 2. Where the dismissal is for one of the reasons specified in s 58(1) of the 1978 EP(C)A (see generally Chapter 10), there is no qualifying period of employment: s 64(3) of the EP(C)A 1978. The qualifying period of employment is one month where the employee is dismissed on medical grounds by reason of any requirement imposed by law or any recommendation in a code of practice issued or approved under the Health and Safety at Work etc Act 1974, s 16: s 64(2) of the EP(C)A 1978.

2.2 Employees employed under illegal contracts

As a general principle the courts will not enforce illegal contracts entered into for purposes which are either forbidden by the law or which, while not forbidden by the general law, are immoral or contrary to public policy. It is for the tribunal to decide whether any illegality connected with the contract of employment renders it unenforceable. Where the contract is illegal then the employee is prevented from exercising his statutory rights: see *Tomlinson v Dick Evans 'U' Drive Ltd* [1978] ICR 639.

A contract may be illegal where it cannot be performed without illegality on the part of one or both of the parties to the contract, or it may be that the contract is on the face of it perfectly legal, but the parties intend or subsequently perform the contract illegally.

In *Corby v Morrison (t/a The Card Shop)* [1980] IRLR 218, the employee was paid in addition to his wages the sum of £5 a week which was not declared and upon which no tax was paid. This sum was roughly equivalent to the amount of tax and national insurance which was deducted from the employee's wage. The EAT held, following *Miller v Karlinski* (1945) 62 TLR 85, that the contract was a fraud on the Revenue and as such was illegal, and it made no difference whether or not the parties were ignorant that what they were doing was illegal. The EAT also held that if they were wrong in law and the contract was on the face of it legal so that 'the existence or otherwise of knowledge of its intended illegal performance by the employer and employee becomes relevant then the test must be subjective and not objective'. See also *Cole v Fred Stacey Ltd* [1974] IRLR 73, following *Napier v National Business Agency Ltd* [1951] 2 All ER 264. An agreement to understate earnings so as not to affect social security benefits will make the contract illegal: *Wilkinson v Lugg* [1990] ICR 599.

The employee as well as the employer must be guilty of an illegal act or intention: *Davidson v Pillay* [1979] IRLR 275. Failure by the employee, unknown to the employer, to declare to the Revenue a benefit which he has received from his employment does not necessarily render the contract illegal: *McConnell v Bolik* [1979] IRLR 422.

In *Newland v Simmons and Willer (Hairdressers) Ltd* [1981] IRLR 359, the EAT held:

We are all agreed, first, that a contract which is either illegal on its face, or one which cannot be performed by one or both parties otherwise than illegally, . . . is unenforceable by both parties to that contract whether or not they know the law. . . . ignorance of the law is no excuse.

It found that if the contract of employment is one which on the face of it is lawful and the illegality consists of an illegal performance by the employer it is necessary to consider whether the employee was aware at the time she entered into the contract or became aware during the continuance of the contract of that illegality. The EAT further found that if, viewed subjectively, although the employee ought to have appreciated that the contract was being performed illegally but as a matter of fact she did not, then the fact that the employee ought to have known but did not know is insufficient to deprive the employee of her right to rely upon the statutory employment provisions.

The illegal part of a contract which is a fraud on the Revenue cannot be severed from the remainder: *Corby v Morrison (t/a The Card Shop)*, above.

Illegality may be collateral to the contract in other ways. In *Coral Leisure Group Ltd v Barnett* [1981] IRLR 204, the employee alleged that after his employment commenced he was told by his employer that as part of his duties he was expected to obtain prostitutes for his employer's clients and pay for them out of funds provided by his employer. The EAT found that in deciding whether any taint of illegality affecting part of the contract necessarily rendered the whole contract unenforceable by a party who knew of the illegality, a distinction had to be drawn between '(a) cases in which there is a contractual obligation to do an act which is unlawful, and (b) cases where the contractual obligations are capable of being performed lawfully and were initially intended so to be performed, but which have in fact been performed by unlawful means'.

It found that in cases coming within category (a), it depends upon how far it is possible to separate the tainted contractual obligations from the untainted: in cases coming within category (b), it depends upon whether the performance of an unlawful act by a party to the contract precludes that party from further enforcing the contract. Where, in the course of performing a contract, an employee has committed an unlawful or an immoral act that does not by itself prevent him from further enforcing the contract, unless the contract was entered into with the purpose of doing an unlawful or immoral act, or the contract is prohibited by law. Since in this case the employee did not enter into employment with the intention of procuring prostitutes and there was no prohibition at law against the contract of employment, the employee was not precluded from asserting his contract against his employer. If an employee has been defrauding his employer, the employer cannot plead that the contract is therefore illegal: *Broaders v Kalkare Property Maintenance Ltd* [1990] IRLR 421.

An illegal contract cannot be taken into account in computing continuous employment. In *Hyland v JH Barker (North West) Ltd* [1985] IRLR 403, the employee received a tax-free lodging allowance for 4 weeks although he was not lodging away from home and this was known to his employer. The 4 weeks broke his continuous period of employment. Thus, although he had been employed for 16 years since the 4-week period had occurred 11 months before his dismissal, he could not establish a year's continuous employment (the then qualifying period).

2.3 Employees over retiring age

There is no lower age limit. However, an employee is precluded from bringing a claim for unfair dismissal if on or before the effective date of termination (see Chapter 4) he had attained the age which, in the undertaking where he was employed, was the normal retiring age for an employee holding such a position, and the age was the same whether the employee holding that position was a man or a woman, or where there is no normal retiring age in the undertaking, if he or she had attained the age of 65 (s 64(1)(*b*) of EP(C)A 1978). If there is a normal retiring age, the employee may bring a claim if he or she is under the normal retiring age, notwithstanding that he or she is over the age of 65. Conversely, if there is a normal retiring age which the employee has attained which is below 65, the employee is precluded from claiming unfair dismissal: *Nothman v Barnet London Borough Council* [1978] ICR 336 upheld on appeal to the House of Lords; *Nothman v Barnet London Borough Council* [1979] ICR 111.

There is no double barrier. In *Nothman*'s case, Lord Salmon held:

I do not agree that . . . [s 64(1)(*b*) of the EP(C)A 1978] erects a number of barriers under or over which every employee must successfully scramble in order to preserve his rights in respect of unfair dismissal. In my opinion [s 64(1)(*b*) of the EP(C)A 1978] sets up only one barrier to be overcome by the class of employee whose conditions of employment specify a normal retiring age, and another and entirely different barrier to be overcome by the class of employee whose conditions of employment specify no retiring age. The first class of employee preserves the right to claim in respect of unfair dismissal only if it is established that that dismissal took effect before the normal retiring age specified in the conditions of employment had been reached. The second class of employee preserves the right to claim in respect of unfair dismissal only if he or she establishes that that dismissal took effect before the employee . . . had reached the age of 65 years . . .

Where the employee has been taken on over the age of 65 and there is no normal retiring age, the employee will not be able to claim unfair dismissal: see *Dixon v (1) London Production Tools Ltd and (2) Phildon Instrumentation (London) Ltd* [1980] IRLR 385.

The interpretation of normal retiring age has given rise to a difference of judicial opinion. However, normal retiring age was considered by the House of Lords in *Waite v Government Communications Headquarters* [1983] ICR 653, where Lord Fraser held:

If the normal retiring age is to be ascertained exclusively from the relevant contract of employment, even in cases where the vast majority of employees in the group concerned do not retire at the contractual age, the result would be to give the word 'normal' a highly artificial meaning . . .

I therefore reject the view that the contractual retiring age conclusively fixes the normal retiring age. I accept that where there is a contractual retiring age, applicable to all, or nearly all, the employees holding the position which the appellant employee held, there is a presumption that the contractual retiring age is the normal retiring age for the group. But it is a presumption which, in my opinion, can be rebutted by evidence that there is in practice some higher age at which employees holding the position are regularly retired, and which they have reasonably come to regard as their normal retiring age. Having regard to the social policy which seems to underlie the Act—namely the policy of securing fair treatment, as regards compulsory retirement, as between different employees holding the same position—the expression 'normal retiring age' conveys the idea of an age at which employees in the group can reasonably expect to be compelled to retire, unless there is some special reason in a particular case for a different age to apply. 'Normal' in this context is not a mere synonym for 'usual'. The word 'usual' suggests a purely statistical approach by ascertaining the age at which the majority of employees actually retire, without regard to whether some of them may have been retained in office until a higher age for special reasons—such as a temporary shortage of employees with a particular skill, or a temporary glut of work, or personal consideration for an employee who has not sufficient reckonable service to qualify for a full pension. The proper test is in my view not merely statistical. It is to ascertain what would be the reasonable expectation or understanding of the employees holding that position at the relevant time. The contractual retiring age will prima facie be the normal, but it may be displaced by evidence that it is regularly departed from in practice. The evidence may show that the contractual retirement age has been superseded by some definite higher age, and, if so, that will have become the normal retiring age. Or the evidence may show merely that the contractual retiring age has been abandoned and that employees retire at a variety of higher ages. In that case there will be no normal retiring age and the statutory [alternative] of 65 . . . will apply.

The decision in *Waite*'s case was followed in *Mauldon v British Telecommunications plc* [1987] ICR 450, where the EAT held that the tribunal should have regard to both the statistical and the contractual situation. In *Whittle v Manpower Services Commission* [1987] IRLR 441, the EAT held that statistics are important. It further found that although Lord Fraser referred to the contractual retirement age as having been abandoned, this actually meant where there was evidence to show that the contractual retirement age had been regularly departed from in practice. See also *Secretary of State for Scotland v Meikle* [1986] IRLR 208.

However, there are still difficulties as the decisions in *Hughes v Department of Health and Social Security; Coy v Department of Health and Social Security* and *Jarnell v Department of Environment* [1985] ICR 419, illustrate.

In 1948 Hughes and Coy were transferred from local government to the civil service subject to a proviso that they could be retired at any time after reaching the age of 60. Service would not normally be prolonged after 65, although temporary employment might be permitted after that age. Because in 1948 there were staff shortages it was the intention that both should be employed to 65. The intention that both Hughes and Coy should be permitted to remain until the age of 65 was incorporated in a DHSS circular. There was a primary code applicable to civil servants which set out, *inter alia*, terms and conditions relating to retirement. This code made it clear that the contractual retirement age was 60, but retirement could be postponed in certain circumstances. In reliance upon the code in 1981 the DHSS changed its policy in relation to retiring ages and the changes were set out in a circular. This change in practice was to be operative in two stages from 1 April 1982 and 1 April 1983. This circular provided that:

officers aged 61 and over on 31 March 1982 will have to retire on that date; officers reaching age 61 between 1 April 1982 and 31 March 1983 will have to retire on their birthday in that year; officers over age 60 on 31 March 1983 will have to retire on that date and subsequently officers will retire on their 60th birthday.

Hughes, a senior executive officer, was retired on 31 March 1982 when he was aged just over 61. Coy, a higher executive officer, was retired on 2 May 1982, his 61st birthday. Had Hughes and Coy been dismissed before they reached normal retiring age? Lord Diplock held:

the Court of Appeal was also unanimously of opinion that the contractual retiring age, ie the age at which Mr Hughes and Mr Coy would be compelled to retire has been throughout their service in Crown employment the age of 60. No other conclusion is possible in view of those provisions of the primary code which I have cited earlier. But there is left to the head of each government department a discretion to permit a civil servant employed in his department to postpone the date of his retirement until he attains some higher age. Where as a matter of administrative policy a department decides that for the time being it is in the interests of departmental efficiency that a particular category of employees should, subject to continuing health and efficiency, be permitted if they so wish to remain in the employment of the department until they attain some specified age higher than 60, and such decision is communicated to employees in that category in a departmental circular issued pursuant to paragraph (iii) of the introduction to the primary code, employees in that category have a reasonable expectation that the higher age so specified has replaced the age of 60 as their 'normal retiring age', and the presumption of which Lord Fraser speaks in the *Waite* case [[1983] ICR 653] in favour of the contractual retiring age of 60 as constituting the normal retiring age of employees in that category (whatever the 'position' each may hold) is rebutted.

Lord Diplock recognised that there might be changes in administrative policy. Where these changes were communicated to the employees concerned their expectations were thereby altered. He continued:

The relevant departmental circular that was in force at the dates when Mr Hughes and Mr Coy respectively were required to retire was D76/81, issued on 3 June 1981. Thereafter any reasonable expectations that they held as to what constituted the normal age of retirement of employees of the DHSS in their respective positions of SEO and HEO was the age resulting from the application to them of the policy announced in D76/81. The dates on which the notices of termination of employment given to each of them expired were strictly in accordance with that policy.

Therefore neither Hughes nor Coy (nor Jarnell—the facts of his case were indistinguishable), was entitled to claim unfair dismissal because they had all attained normal retiring age.

Two other issues fell to be considered: first the relevant time for determining the normal retiring age and secondly, in ascertaining the normal retiring age, the 'group' of employees to be considered.

Lord Diplock, referring to the decision of the House of Lords in *Waite*'s case and the judgment of Lord Fraser (see **2.3** above) held:

Twice in this passage Lord Fraser uses the expression 'the group'. 'Group' is not a word that is used in the statute. Lord Fraser is clearly using it as a short way of referring to employees holding a similar 'position' to that held by the claimant, 'position' by statutory definition takes into account his status as an employee, the nature of his work, his terms and conditions of employment and nothing more. It is clear that the claimant's 'position' which, under s 64(1)(*b*) [of the EP(C)A 1978] falls to be ascertained at the date of termination of his employment, does not include the previous history of his employment whether by the employer by whom he was dismissed or any former employer; yet both Slade and Parker LJJ, who formed the majority of the Court of Appeal treated 'group' as if it were the relevant statutory expression and gave it an historical content confining it, in the case of Mr Hughes to

SEOs who had transferred from the local authority service to the government department that was the predecessor of the DHSS in 1948, and in the case of Mr Coy to HEOs who had done likewise. This was in my view wrong. There is no warrant for it in the language of the statute and it illustrates the danger of construing the words of a judicial pronouncement from however elevated a source as if they replaced the actual words used by the draughtsman of the statute. Sir John Donaldson MR fell into no such error in his dissenting judgment.

Lord Fraser also speaks of 'the relevant time' at which to ascertain the reasonable expectation or understanding of employees holding the same position as the claimant, if some other age or the statutory [age] of 65 . . . is to be capable of displacing the contractual retiring age as the 'normal retiring age' within the meaning of s 64(1)(b) [of the EP(C)A 1978]. The Court of Appeal were unanimously of opinion in my view rightly, that under the statute, what Lord Fraser was referring to as 'the relevant time' was the effective date of termination of the claimant's employment, or, to be strictly logical the punctus temporis [appointed time] immediately before that termination took effect.

Lord Diplock thus held that the relevant time for determining the normal retiring age is the effective date of termination and that the relevant employees were employees who were senior executive officers in the case of Hughes, and higher executive officers in the case of Coy. He did not accept that the relevant employees were restricted by reference to historical origin. The remainder of their Lordships concurred in the judgment of Lord Diplock. See also *Highlands and Islands Development Board v MacGillivray* [1986] IRLR 210.

When an employee was expected to retire between the ages of 62 and 63 it was held that there was no normal retiring age: *Swaine v Health and Safety Executive* [1986] IRLR 205.

In *Brooks and Others v British Telecommunications plc* [1991] IRLR 4, the EAT upheld the decision of the tribunal that there was no normal retiring age of 60 in the undertaking. It held in determining whether an employee is excluded from claiming unfair dismissal by s 64(1)(b)(i) of the EP(C)A 1978 because he was over normal retiring age, the tribunal has to identify the undertaking in which the employee was employed, and which of the employees in that undertaking held the position which the employee held. It must establish what, if any, was the normal retiring age for an employee holding that position. In establishing normal retiring age the starting point is the contractual retiring age, but if there is none, it may be that in practice there is a normal retiring age. This is a matter of evidence and statistical evidence may be of value. If there is no contractual age nor one established by practice there may be a policy retirement age, which is one established by a statement of policy. Evidence may show that the contractual retiring age or policy retiring age has been superseded by some definite higher age so that that becomes the normal retiring age. In *Waite*'s case above, it was held that the normal retiring age is to be established by ascertaining the age at which employees in the same undertaking, holding the same position as the employee in question, could reasonably expect to be compelled to retire. In Brooks's case this was interpreted as meaning the expectation or understanding of the relevant group of a future happening as it might affect a member of that group, in the light of the information reasonably within the contemplation of members of the group judged objectively. The enquiry is limited to what would have been within the knowledge of the hypothetical member of the group if he had thought about it. Such knowledge might come from what happened in practice to employees attaining the age of 60, ascertained from relevant statistics or from policy announcements made by the employers as to when members of the group would be compelled to retire, and what employees were told or led to believe during counselling sessions, if any. The EAT rejected the argument that it was the expectation of each member of the group. In identifying the undertaking the tribunal is a tribunal of fact. The position which the employee held may be decided by reference to the job rather than his grade. To equate position with grade would not give due regard to the nature of the work as required by the definition of position in s 153(1) of the EP(C)A 1978. In *Barber v Thames Television plc* [1991] ICR 253, the EAT held that a group could only be distinguished by the history of the employer's employment policy and not by the employee's terms and conditions.

2.4 Employees who ordinarily work outside Great Britain

Employees who, under their contracts of employment, ordinarily work outside Great Britain are excluded from protection against unfair dismissal: s 141(2) of the EP(C)A 1978. The phrase 'ordinarily works outside Great Britain' has given rise to difficulties.

In *Portec (UK) Ltd v Mogensen* [1976] ICR 396, the EAT held that under his contract of employment, an employee could ordinarily work both inside Great Britain and also ordinarily work outside Great Britain, and so could not claim unfair dismissal. The effect of this decision would have been to deprive many employees of their statutory rights.

In *Wilson v Maynard Shipbuilding Consultants AB* [1978] ICR 376, Wilson was employed by Maynard, a Swedish company, as a consultant from July 1973 until September 1975. His contract of employment contained no express provision as to where he was to work. It was found that he worked for 50 weeks in Italy and for 40 weeks in the UK. It was held that he could not ordinarily work both inside Great Britain and also outside Great Britain, and the decision in *Portec (UK) Ltd*, above, was wrong in law. The Court of Appeal gave some guidance in determining where the employee ordinarily works. It held:

By what criteria, then, is one to decide, looking at the contractual terms express or implied, where the employee 'ordinarily works' under that contract, where those terms do not themselves provide and require that the place of work is to be, wholly or substantially wholly, in Great Britain, or wholly or substantially wholly, outside Great Britain . . .

In such a case as the present it appears to us that the correct approach is to look at the terms of the contract, express and implied (with reference, it may be, to what has happened under the contract, for the limited purpose which we have expressed above) in order to ascertain where, looking at the whole period contemplated by the contract, the employee's base is to be. It is, in the absence of special factors leading to a contrary conclusion, the country where his base is to be which is likely to be the place where he is to be treated as ordinarily working under his contract of employment. Where his base, under the contract, is to be will depend on the examination of all relevant contractual terms. These will be likely to include any such terms as expressly define his headquarters, or which indicate where the travels involved in his employment begin and end; where his private residence—his home—is, or is expected to be; where and perhaps in what currency, he is to be paid; whether he is to be subject to pay national insurance contributions in Great Britain. These are merely examples of factors which, among many others that may be found to exist in individual cases, may be relevant in deciding where the employee's base is for the purpose of his work, looking to the whole normal, anticipated, duration of the employment.

The Court of Appeal accepted that the tribunal should not just look at the position at the time of dismissal but the whole of the employment—a view first propounded by the National Industrial Relations Court in *Maulik v Air India* [1974] ICR 528.

The decision in *Wilson*'s case was followed by the Court of Appeal in *Todd v British Midland Airways Ltd* [1978] ICR 959. Todd was employed by the company which was a British company as a first officer on aircraft flying on international routes. Although he worked outside Great Britain for 53 per cent of his time, his base was in Great Britain. The contract of employment did not provide where the employee ordinarily worked. The Court of Appeal was influenced by the fact that his base was in Great Britain in reaching its conclusion that he ordinarily worked in Great Britain and was thus entitled to claim unfair dismissal.

In *Wilson*'s case Lord Denning considered that the earlier case of *Claisse v Keydril Ltd* [1978] ICR 812, had been wrongly decided. In this case it was held that an employee who worked on an oil rig was based on that oil rig and not at Great Yarmouth where the company employing him had its base.

In *Janata Bank v Ahmed* [1981] ICR 791, the Court of Appeal again followed the decision in *Wilson*'s case above. Ahmed was employed by the United Bank in Bangladesh which was then taken over by the respondent. In 1972 he was posted to London although under the terms of his contract of employment he could be recalled to Bangladesh at any time. He was posted to Brussels for a short period of time and then returned to London. He was then ordered to transfer to the bank's head office in Dakar. He did not move to Dakar. His employment was terminated. The Court of Appeal held that in determining whether or not the employee ordinarily worked outside Great Britain under his contract of employment, 'a broad brush approach should be adopted'. The starting point was the contract of employment. Although the place where the employee has been working may be a strong indication of where he was required to work under his contract of employment it is not determinative. Donaldson LJ held: 'Any consideration of bases is simply an aid to answering the primary question of where [the employee] ordinarily worked.'

In *Wood v Cunard Line Ltd* [1989] IRLR 431, Wood, a seaman, was employed on a UK registered ship based in Puerto Rico, but which at no time entered UK territorial waters. His contract provided for each voyage to terminate in the UK. This did not happen in practice. The company's head office was at Southampton where he was recruited and from where he was paid. Wood argued that the proper test for determining where he ordinarily worked was the base test and his base was the company's head office in Southampton.

The EAT held that the proper test was where the employee would carry out his work under the contract rather than at the time of making the contract where it was contemplated his base would be. The base test is not the only test, nor is it always the appropriate test to determine where, under his contract, an employee ordinarily works.

In *Sonali Bank v Rahman, Same v Chowdhury* [1989] ICR 314, both employees worked in Great Britain. Both had contracts with a mobility clause which required them to work abroad. Both employees were based in and worked exclusively in Great Britain and the fact that they had a contract with a mobility clause did not mean that they were employees ordinarily working outside Great Britain.

An employee only ordinarily works under the contract subsisting at the time of the dismissal. It is that contract not the employment to which s 141(2) of the EP(C)A 1978 is directed. Thus, if under that contract the employee ordinarily works in Great Britain he is not excluded by s 141(2) of the EP(C)A 1978 Act, even if under a preceding contract he ordinarily worked outside Great Britain even within a period of two years prior to the dismissal: *Weston v Vega Space Systems Engineering Ltd* [1989] IRLR 429.

2.5 Employees on offshore installations

Pursuant to powers in the EP(C)A 1978, protection against unfair dismissal now applies to certain employees working on certain offshore installations: Employment Protection (Offshore Employment) Order 1976 (S1 1976 No 766) as amended by S1 1977 No 588, which, although made under earlier legislation, continues in force under the EP(C)A 1978 and is further amended by S1 1981 No 208 and S1 1984 No 1149. Employees working on offshore installations within British territorial waters are protected, provided they do not ordinarily work outside either those waters or Great Britain. Similarly, employees working on offshore installations in British designated areas of the continental shelf who are engaged on work connected with exploration of the sea bed or subsoil or the exploitation of their natural resources, are protected. Again those employees must neither be employed on other types of work in the British designated areas nor be ordinarily employed outside those areas, British territorial waters nor Great Britain. Under the 1981 Order employment for the purposes of activities connected with the exploration or exploitation of the Frigg Gas Field is covered if the employer is a company registered under the Companies Act 1985 or directs operations from Great Britain. The employment legislation may also be extended to cover activities relating to the exploration or exploitation of a cross-boundary petroleum field in a foreign sector of the continental shelf.

2.6 Specifically excluded employees

Certain categories of employee are specifically excluded from protection against unfair dismissal by the EP(C)A 1978 as follows:

Members of the armed forces Employment in the armed forces (other than employment by an association established for the purposes of the Reserve Forces Act 1980), although Crown employment, is specifically excluded from the statutory protection: s 138(3) of the EP(C)A 1978.

Police officers Persons engaged under contracts of employment in police service are excluded from protection against unfair dismissal: s 146(2) and (3) of the EP(C)A 1978. Police service means service as a member of any constabulary or service in any capacity 'by virtue of which the person has the powers or privileges of a constable'. Section 8 of the Prison Act 1952 provides that 'every prison officer while acting as such shall have all powers, authority, protection and privileges of a constable'. Therefore a prison officer could not claim unfair dismissal notwithstanding that the conduct complained of was while he was off duty and outside the prison: *Home Office v (1) Robinson and (2) Prison Officers Assocation* [1981] IRLR 524.

Share fishermen The master and crew members of a fishing vessel who are remunerated only by shares in the profits or gross earnings of the vessel are excluded from protection against unfair dismissal: s 144(2) of the EP(C)A 1978.

Seamen A person employed to work on board a ship registered in the UK, which is not registered at a port outside Great Britain, is regarded as a person who under his contract ordinarily works in Great Britain: s 141(5) of the EP(C)A 1978. To this provision there are exceptions where the employment is wholly outside Great Britain or the person is not ordinarily resident in Great Britain. See now *Wilson v Maynard Shipbuilding Consultants AB* [1978] ICR 376, which over-rules the decision of the EAT in *Portec (UK) Ltd v Mogensen* [1976] ICR 396.

The position of seamen was considered in *Royle v Globtik Management Ltd* [1977] ICR 552. Royle was an engineer who was employed by a shipping company which managed three tankers, two of which were registered in England and one overseas. By his contract Royle was obliged to work on any of the ships owned, managed or sub-managed by the employer, irrespective of the port of registry. Royle worked on the two tankers registered in London sailing between Japan and the Persian Gulf until he was dismissed. In a claim for unfair dismissal, the EAT held that for the purposes of what is now s 141(5) of the EP(C)A 1978, Royle was not employed only to work on board a ship registered in the UK and, further, that because he worked on a tanker registered in Great Britain, it was not sufficient to prevent him from ordinarily working outside Great Britain. A British ship was not part of Great Britain for these purposes. Thus what is now s 141(2) of the EP(C)A 1978 applied. See also *Wood v Cunard Line Ltd* at **2.4**, above.

3 Special categories of employee

3.1 Crown employees

The general rule is that Crown employees hold office at the pleasure of the Crown and can be dismissed at the Crown's pleasure. In *Riordan v War Office* [1960] 3 All ER 774, it was held that a Crown employee could not bring an action for wrongful dismissal. However, in *R v Civil Service Appeal Board ex parte Bruce* [1988] ICR 649, it was suggested that the Crown could enter into a contract of employment with its employees. Whatever the position, a Crown employee may claim unfair dismissal. The termination of Crown employment is treated as a dismissal for this purpose: s 138(1) of the EP(C)A 1978. The protection afforded may be removed where a Minister of the Crown issues a certificate certifying that the employment should be excepted from protection on the grounds of national security: s 138(4) of the EP(C)A 1978.

Section 49 of the EP(C)A 1978 (which relates to the minimum period of notice to which an employee is entitled) does not apply to Crown employees. Similarly, the provisions relating to redundancy payments (ss 81 *et seq* of the EP(C)A 1978) do not apply to Crown employees, but they are able to claim unfair dismissal in a redundancy situation, since the claim is one for unfair dismissal.

3.2 House of Commons staff

As with Crown employees, relevant members of the House of Commons staff may claim unfair dismissal, and the termination of their employment is treated as a dismissal: s 139(1) of the EP(C)A 1978. 'Relevant members of the House of Commons staff', are defined in s 139(3) as any person appointed by the House of Commons Commission or employed in the refreshment department, and any member of the Speaker's personal staff.

3.3 Teachers in aided schools

Where a teacher in an aided school is dismissed by the governors of the school as a result of a requirement of a local authority, pursuant to s 24(2) of the Education Act 1944, the statutory provisions as to unfair dismissal apply as if the local authority were the employer and it had dismissed the teacher for the reason or principal reason that it had required his dismissal: s 80(1) of the EP(C)A 1978.

4 Contracting out of statutory protection

There is no general power to contract out of the provisions affording protection against unfair dismissal. Thus, any provision in an agreement is void in so far as it purports to exclude or limit the operation of the unfair dismissal provisions or in so far as it precludes any person from presenting a complaint to, or bringing any proceedings before a tribunal for unfair dismissal: s 140(1) of the EP(C)A 1978. In *Council of Engineering Institutions v Maddison* [1977] ICR 30, Maddison was told he was to be dismissed by reason of redundancy and was given three months' notice. Subsequently, he received a letter together with a cheque for £1,600 which was described as being 'for severance . . . the acceptance of which is in final settlement leaving you with no outstanding claim . . .'. The EAT held that where any document or agreement purports to deprive the employee of his rights under what is now s 140(1) of the EP(C)A 1978, any uncertainty as to its meaning should be resolved in favour of the employee. Any agreement which deprived the employee of the right to claim unfair dismissal would be rendered void under s 140(1).

In *Naqvi v Stephens Jewellers Ltd* [1978] ICR 631, the EAT held that this section embraces an agreement to withdraw a complaint which has been made as well as to an agreement not to initiate proceedings. Where an employer settles a claim for unfair dismissal the settlement should be recorded on a form of settlement prepared by ACAS. The employer is thereby able to ensure that the employee is precluded from bringing a claim against the employer for unfair dismissal. See below, at **4.3**.

However, there are certain limited exceptions to this provision.

4.1 Fixed-term contracts

The employee's protection against unfair dismissal does not apply where the employee is employed under a contract entered into after 1 October 1980 for a fixed term of one year or more, provided that the dismissal consists only of the expiry of the term without its being renewed, where before the term expires the employee has agreed in writing to exclude his right to claim unfair dismissal in relation to that contract. Any agreement excluding any such claim must be contained either in the contract of employment or in a separate agreement. The agreement may be made at any time before the term expires, but since in many cases where the employee agrees to exclude his right to claim unfair dismissal after the contract has been signed there would be no supporting consideration from his employer, the contract will be unenforceable unless it is in the form of a deed: s 142(1) and (3) of the EP(C)A 1978.

A contract is for a fixed term if it fixes the maximum duration of the period of employment, whether or not the contract contains a power for either party to bring the contract to an end by giving notice to the other party before the expiration of the period certain: *BBC v Dixon* [1979] IRLR 114; *BBC v Constanti* [1979] IRLR 114. A contract may be a fixed-term contract where the employee has to make herself available for a fixed period even though during that period she is not called upon to perform the work for which she is employed: *Wiltshire CC v NATFHE and Guy* [1980] IRLR 198. But for the contract to be a fixed-term contract, it must have a defined beginning and end, so that a contract which is to come to an end upon the happening of an uncertain future event, eg for the life of the present sovereign, is not a fixed-term contract: *Wiltshire CC v NATFHE and Guy*, above. Similarly, a contract for a specific task which has no defined end is not a contract for a fixed term: *Ryan v Shipboard Maintenance Ltd* [1980] IRLR 16.

In determining if there is a fixed-term contract of sufficient length to include the statutory protection, it must be the final contract which is for a fixed term of one year or more. It is not possible to amalgamate the cumulative total of all contracts of a fixed term so as to achieve the one year: *Open University v Triesman* [1978] ICR 524. Arguably, a distinction must be drawn between the extension or renewal of an existing fixed-term contract and a re-engagement under a new contract, so that whereas the former would count as part of the fixed-term contract the latter would not. See the judgments of Stephenson and Lane LJJ in *BBC v Ioannou*, and compare the judgment of Denning MR.

4.2 *Dismissal procedures agreements*

A dismissal procedures agreement is an agreement in writing with respect to procedures relating to dismissal made by or on behalf of one or more independent trade unions and one or more employers or employers' associations: s 153(1) of the EP(C)A 1978. An application may be made jointly to the Secretary of State by all the parties to the agreement for an order designating the agreement as one which will have effect in place of the statutory protection against unfair dismissal. In such cases the provisions of the agreement shall apply where the employee is dismissed or is in the course of being dismissed (otherwise than on the grounds of pregnancy): ss 65(1), (3) and (4) and 140(2)(*c*) of the EP(C)A 1978. The Secretary of State must be satisfied that certain requirements have been fulfilled before he makes an order under s 65: see s 65(2) of the EP(C)A 1978. For revocation, see s 66 of the EP(C)A 1978.

4.3 *Conciliation*

It has already been noted that any provision in an agreement whether a contract of employment or not shall be void in so far as it purports to exclude or limit the operation of the unfair dismissal provisions or in so far as it precludes any person from presenting a complaint to or bringing proceedings before a tribunal for unfair dismissal: s 140(1) of the EP(C)A 1978. However, there are two relevant exceptions in the case of claims for unfair dismissal. Thus, s 140(1) does not apply to any agreement to refrain from presenting a complaint for unfair dismissal, where in compliance with a request under s 134(3) of the EP(C)A 1978 a conciliation officer has taken action in accordance with that subsection: s 140(2)(*d*) of the EP(C)A 1978; or to any agreement to refrain from proceeding with a complaint of unfair dismissal where a conciliation officer has taken action in accordance with s 134(1) and (2) of the EP(C)A 1978: s 140(2)(*e*) of the EP(C)A 1978. Thus, in these circumstances, an agreement not to present or pursue a claim for unfair dismissal will not be void.

Section 134(1) of the EP(C)A 1978 provides that where a complaint of unfair dismissal has been made to a tribunal, a copy of the originating application must be sent to the conciliation officer. It is the duty of the conciliation officer, if he is requested to do so by the employee and by the employer against whom it was presented, or in the absence of any such request, the conciliation officer considers that he could act with a reasonable prospect of success, to endeavour to promote a settlement of the unfair dismissal complaint without its being determined by the tribunal.

Section 134(2) of the EP(C)A 1978 provides that for the purpose of promoting such a settlement where the employee has ceased to be employed by the employer, the conciliation officer shall in particular seek to promote the reinstatement or re-engagement of the employee by the employer or by a successor of the employer or by an associated employer on terms appearing to him to be equitable, but where an employee does not wish to be reinstated or re-engaged or where reinstatement or re-engagement is not practicable and the parties desire the conciliation officer to act, he shall seek to promote agreement between them as to compensation to be paid by the employer to the employee.

Section 134(3) of the EP(C)A 1978 provides that where a person claims that action has been taken where a complaint for unfair dismissal could be presented to a tribunal and before a claim for unfair dismissal has been made, a request is made to a conciliation officer, whether by that person or by the employer, to make his services available, then the conciliation officer shall act in accordance with s 134(1) and (2) as if a complaint of unfair dismissal had been presented.

The conciliation officer is under an obligation, where appropriate, to have regard to the desirability of encouraging the use of other procedures available for the settlement of grievances: see s 134(4) of the EP(C)A 1978.

Anything communicated to the conciliation officer in connection with the performance of his functions under s 134 of the EP(C)A 1978 shall not be admissible in evidence before a tribunal except with the consent of the person who communicated it to the conciliation officer: s 134(5) of the EP(C)A 1978.

In *Duport Furniture Products v Moore and Another* [1982] IRLR 31, Moore was suspended by the employer on suspicion of theft. He was totally deaf but could read and write. At a meeting Moore was told by the employer that his job was at an end and he would not be re-employed. Under protest Moore accepted £300 and resigned. A conciliation officer was not present at that meeting but was then involved and asked to prepare a form of settlement on form COT3. He went through the form with both parties and they then signed it. Subsequently, Moore made a complaint of unfair dismissal. The House of Lords held that the duty of a conciliation officer to endeavour to promote a settlement does not necessarily involve any positive act. The words 'endeavour to promote a settlement' must be given a liberal construction capable of covering whatever action by way of such promotion is applicable in the circumstances of the particular case, so that ascertaining what the parties had agreed, and preparing a form of settlement recording the agreement, fell within the expression 'endeavouring to promote a settlement'. It was also held by the House of Lords that there is no obligation on the conciliation officer to see that the terms of settlement are fair for the employee.

Again in *Slack v Greenham (Plant Hire) Ltd* [1983] IRLR 271, the EAT held that there was no obligation upon a conciliation officer to advise or inform an employee of the framework of his rights under the relevant legislation:

There may well be many cases in which he deems it necessary, in his attempt to promote agreement of the payment of compensation, to give a brief description to an employee of the relevant framework of his statutory rights including, where appropriate, the liability of an employee to suffer a reduction of compensation for contributory fault. Plainly, he must never advise as to the merits of a case . . .

The EAT went on to hold that if a conciliation officer were to act in bad faith or adopt unfair methods when promoting a settlement the agreement might be set aside.

Likewise a conciliation officer will not have failed to comply with s 134(4) of the EP(C)A 1978 by not encouraging the use of a grievance procedure where it is obvious that the only area for negotiation was as to compensation: *Hennessey and Another v (1) Craigmyle and Co Ltd (2) ACAS* [1985] ICR 879.

Where an offer made by one of the parties in a claim for unfair dismissal has been accepted by the other through the intermediary of a conciliation officer, so that there is a binding agreement, the conciliation officer has undertaken his duties pursuant to s 134(1) of the EP(C)A 1978 and the employee will be prevented from claiming unfair dismissal: *Gilbert v Kembridge Fibres Ltd* [1984] IRLR 52.

It has been held that the expression 'where a person claims that action has been taken' enabling him to make a complaint of unfair dismissal is to be construed as 'not referring only to some express or formal claim, but as including also in its meaning an implied claim to be inferred from the overt acts or attitudes of the employee concerned in the particular circumstances of the case': *Moore v Duport Furniture Products Ltd and Others*, above. In *Hennessey and Another v (1) Craigmyle and Co Ltd (2) ACAS*, above, it was held that where the employee asserts that action has been taken and the evidence supports that assertion, the conciliation officer is required to act. The employee was told that if he signed an agreement prepared by a conciliation officer he would be treated as redundant and paid a sum of money. He saw his solicitor. The solicitor contacted ACAS and the employee had a discussion with them. He subsequently signed the agreement. It was held that the employee was plainly asserting that action had been taken in respect of which a complaint could be presented, and that the conciliation officer was entitled to act before a complaint had been presented.

Economic duress is capable of making a conciliated settlement voidable, but it is likely that this will only arise in the most exceptional circumstances: *Hennessey and Another v (1) Craigmyle and Co Ltd (2) ACAS*, above.

The provisions of s 140(1)(b) of the EP(C)A 1978 apply equally to an agreement which is reached between the employer and the employee after a tribunal has found that the employee's dismissal was unfair, but before the remedy had been determined. Section 140(1)(*b*) renders void any provision in an agreement which precludes an employee from bringing any proceedings before a tribunal. Bringing is not the same as beginning, and proceedings include a consideration of the employee's claim for reinstatement, re-engagement or compensation. Again, s 140(2) of the EP(C)A 1978 does not preclude a conciliation officer from taking action after proceedings have been commenced or after liability has been determined. There is a continuing duty on the ACAS officer until all questions of liability and remedy have been determined by the tribunal. Section 134(1) of the EP(C)A 1978 also makes it clear that the conciliation officer is under a duty to promote a settlement without the matter being determined by a tribunal: *Courage Takehome Trade Ltd v Keys* and *Keys v Courage Takehome Trade Ltd* [1986] IRLR 427. In this case, after the tribunal had determined liability, the employer paid the employee the sum of £9,500.50 which was expressed to be in full and final settlement of his unfair dismissal claim. After he had accepted the money the employee asked the tribunal to assess compensation. The agreement was found to be void under s 140(1) of the EP(C)A 1978, but the tribunal refused to award compensation on the grounds that it would not be just and equitable in all the circumstances to make a compensatory award to the employee. The EAT held:

We have come to the clearest possible conclusion that it would be unjust and inequitable in all the circumstances if this applicant were allowed to take advantage of the respondent. There may be situations in which a respondent has unduly persuaded an applicant to accept a figure by way of agreement, or brought pressure on him; it may be in that situation that an Industrial Tribunal would rule that the employer could scarcely be heard to say that it was unjust or inequitable if he were called on to pay a further sum. That question must, in the end, depend upon the particular facts of the case, but in the instant case we entirely agree with the Industrial Tribunal when they said: 'This was not what an ordinary man would regard as fair. It was taking advantage of a section of the statute and it is our view that justice and equity in this context imparts that it is not just and equitable to award any further compensation to the applicant.'

4.4 *Other agreements*

An agreement between the parties that an employee will not pursue his claim for unfair dismissal in consideration of a sum of money is void. Where there is such an agreement and payment is made, the agreement and payment cannot be pleaded as an accord and satisfaction in defence to a complaint for unfair dismissal. The tribunal will consider the case on its merits and may make an award accordingly. Depending on the nature of the payment, it may be taken into account by the tribunal if it makes an award of compensation. There are two exceptions to this rule, where the agreement to settle will not be void. The first is where agreement has been reached between the parties and the conciliation officer is involved as an intermediary, see s 140(2)(*d*) and (*e*) of the EP(C)A 1978, above. The second is where there is an agreement relating to the expiry of a fixed-term contract: s 140(2)(*h*) of the EP(C)A 1978, see above.

Chapter 2

The Qualifying Period of Employment

Subject to certain limited exceptions an employee cannot bring a claim for unfair dismissal unless he has been continuously employed for a period of not less than two years ending with the effective date of termination: s 64(1)(*a*) of the EP(C)A 1978.

There are certain exceptions to this provision, so that a claim for unfair dismissal can be brought by an employee with more than one month's continuous employment, where the employee is dismissed on medical grounds by reason of any requirement imposed by law or any recommendation in a code of practice issued and approved under s 16 of the Health and Safety at Work etc Act 1974: s 64(2) of the EP(C)A 1978. There is no minimum qualifying period of continuous employment where the reason or principal reason for dismissal is one of those specified in s 58(1) of the EP(C)A 1978. (See generally Chapter 10.)

1 Computation of the period of continuous employment

1.1 The general basis

Section 151(1) of the EP(C)A 1978 provides that references in the Act to a period of continuous employment, unless otherwise provided, are to a period of continuous employment computed in accordance with the provisions of s 151 of and Sched 13 to the EP(C)A 1978, and in any provision which refers to a period of continuous employment expressed in months or years, a month means a calendar month and a year means a year of 12 calendar months.

Schedule 13 to the EP(C)A 1978 provides a complete definition of what is meant by the term 'continuous employment': see *Wood v York City Council* [1978] ICR 840. Thus, it is not open to the parties to agree that one or more periods of employment shall be continuous employment within the meaning of continuous employment under Sched 13 to the EP(C)A 1978, unless the period or periods of employment are continuous periods of employment within Sched 13: see *Secretary of State for Employment v Globe Elastic Thread Co Ltd* [1979] IRLR 327. Conversely, it is not open to the parties to agree that a period of continuous employment shall not be continuous where continuity is preserved under Sched 13 to the EP(C)A 1978: see *Hanson v Fashion Industries (Hartlepool) Ltd* [1981] ICR 35.

It must be borne in mind that any agreement reached between the parties whereby employment is to be treated as continuous, even though it is not continuous under the provisions of Sched 13 to the EP(C)A 1978, may give rise to rights under the contract between the parties.

Section 151(2) of the EP(C)A 1978 provides that in computing an employee's period of continuous employment any question as to whether or not the employee's employment is of a kind counting towards a period of continuous employment or whether periods, consecutive or otherwise, are to be treated as forming a single period of continuous employment, is to be determined in accordance with Sched 13 to the EP(C)A 1978, that is to say week by week, but the length of an employee's period of employment is to be computed in months and years of 12 months. The qualifying period for unfair dismissal is now two years. However, the question whether or not a week counts as part of the employee's period of continuous employment, or whether it breaks the period of continuous employment, must be decided in terms of weeks. For these purposes a week is a week ending on a Saturday: para 24(1) of Sched 13 to the EP(C)A 1978. The effect of this provision is that a gap of up to 12 days will not operate to break the employee's continuity of employment. Thus, if an employee contracted to work 40 hours a week was dismissed on a Sunday, he may count that week as part of his period of continuous employment so that his continuity is preserved until midnight on the following Saturday. If he were re-engaged on the next following Saturday under a contract to work 40 hours in each week, he may count that week starting with the preceding Sunday as part of his period of continuous employment. Although in practice there has been a break in his continuity of employment, for the purposes of determining whether or not his employment has been continuous or whether or not there has been a break in the continuity of employment under Sched 13 to the EP(C)A 1978, there has for the purposes of the legislation been no break in his continuity of employment. *Roach v CSB Ltd* [1991] IRLR 200, which suggests otherwise it is submitted is wrongly decided.

Continuity of employment will be broken if, during what would otherwise have been a period of continuous employment, the contract has become illegal, that illegality will taint the whole of the contract of employment: *Hyland v JH Barker (North West) Ltd* [1985] ICR 861. Here the employee was employed by the company from September 1967 until he was dismissed on 11 May 1983. For a four-week period in May and June 1982 the employee was paid a tax-free lodging allowance in addition to his wages while working away from home, although in fact he returned to his home each night. He was not entitled to a tax-free lodging allowance and the EAT held that during the four-week period the contract of employment was an illegal contract. 'Continuously employed' means continuously employed under a legal contract of employment.

1.2 Date of starting and finishing work

Section 151(3) of the EP(C)A 1978 provides that an employee's period of continuous employment for the purposes of the Act begins with the day on which the employee starts work, and ends with the day by reference to which the length of his period of continuous employment falls to be ascertained for the purposes of the provision in question. In *General of the Salvation Army v Dewsbury* [1984] ICR 498, the EAT held that the phrase 'starts work' 'is not intended to refer to the undertaking of the full-time duties of the employment: it is intended to refer to the beginning of the employee's employment under the relevant contract of employment', so that in this case the employee who was offered a post as a teacher commencing on 1 May 1982, a Saturday, which she accepted, although she did not start work until Tuesday 4 May, had been continuously employed from Saturday 1 May.

The date upon which the employee starts work may be postponed if the employee is absent from work because he has been taking part in a strike or because he has been locked out by his employer. See **3.1**, below.

The period of continuous employment ends with the date by reference to which the length of the employee's continuous employment falls to be ascertained. For the purposes of unfair dismissal this is the effective date of termination. See Chapter 4.

The effect of this provision is that the employee cannot count the whole of the week in which his employment begins or ends for the purposes of calculating continuity of employment, but see above for the circumstances in which the whole week may count.

1.3 Presumption of continuity

Under para 1(3) of Sched 13 to the EP(C)A 1978, a person's employment during any period shall, unless the contrary is shown, be presumed to have been continuous.

In *Woolcott v Edwardes* (1966) 1 ITR 333, the employee claimed a redundancy payment. In order to establish his entitlement he had to show that he worked not less than 21 hours a week (the relevant period of continuous employment at the time). The employee argued that he worked 24 hours a week, the employer that he worked only 16 hours. The tribunal was left in substantial doubt as to where the truth lay, but found that the employee was entitled to rely on the presumption of continuous employment, and since the employer had not rebutted that presumption the employee was entitled to claim a redundancy payment.

The presumption of continuity was considered again in *Nicholl v Nocorrode Ltd* [1981] ICR 348, where the EAT held:

In our judgment
  (*a*) the employee has to show that he was employed under a contract of employment . . . and that he was dismissed;
  (*b*) he also has to establish for the purposes of . . . [what is now Sched 13 to the EP(C)A 1978 that there was a week or that there were weeks which counted and, so far as relevant here, this means that he or she was employed for 16 hours or more during those weeks;
  (*c*) in respect of subsequent weeks he can rely on the presumption of continuous employment . . . [in what is now para 1(3) of Sched 13 to the EP(C)A 1978 unless the contrary is shown;
  (*d*) the contrary may be shown by his evidence or that of his employer but the burden is not on him to show that he did 16 hours during every week of the period relied on once the period has begun to count. He may rely on the presumption of continuity.

The EAT assumed that it is for the employee to show that there were one or more weeks which counted. There is no statutory basis for such an interpretation, but as a matter of practicality the employee must be able to establish the circumstances upon which he relies. Under the present law continuity of employment must be examined on a week-by-week basis.

In *Secretary of State for Employment v (1) Cohen and (2) Beaupress Ltd* [1987] IRLR 169, Cohen was employed by company A which went into liquidation, but was succeeded as Cohen's employer by company B. Company B went into liquidation and was succeeded as Cohen's employer by company C. Company C went into liquidation. There was no evidence of any transfer within para 17(2) of Sched 13 to the EP(C)A 1978. The EAT, reversing the decision of the tribunal, held that the presumption of continuity of employment contained in para 1(3) of Sched 13 to the EP(C)A) 1978 only applied to employment with one employer (see para 17(1) of Sched 13 to the EP(C)A 1978) unless paras 17, 18 or 18A of Sched 13 applied, which in this case they did not.

1.4 Miscellaneous provisions

Schedule 13 to the EP(C)A 1978 applies to a period of employment notwithstanding that during that period the employee was engaged in work wholly or mainly outside Great Britain or was excluded by or under the Act from any right conferred by that Act: see para 1(2) of Sched 13 to the EP(C)A 1978. Schedule 2 to the Employment Act 1982 contains the detailed rules. See also *Weston v Vega Space Systems Engineering Ltd* [1989] IRLR 429.

2 Weeks which count

The method of calculating those weeks which count as continuous employment is prescribed by Sched 13 to the EP(C)A 1978. Two aspects of the calculation must be looked at separately; the weeks which count in computing continuous employment, and the events which do not break the continuity of employment.

Any week in which the employee is employed for 16 hours or more counts in computing the continuous period of employment: para 3 of Sched 13 to the EP(C)A 1978. If the employee works 16 hours in a week, that week will count even if the contract only requires him to work for fewer hours. Further, any week where during the whole or part of the week the employee's relations with the employer are governed by a contract of employment which normally involves employment for 16 hours or more a week will also count: para 4 of Sched 13 to the EP(C)A 1978. For the purpose of Sched 13 a week is any week ending with a Saturday: para 24(1).

Paragraph 3 of Sched 13 to the EP(C)A 1978 deals with the position where the employee actually works for 16 hours or more in any week, whether or not there is a contract requiring the employee to work 16 hours or more in any week. Paragraph 4 of Sched 13 deals with the position where there is a contract which requires the employee to work 16 hours or more in any week.

A change from one job to another job or the termination of one contract and the entry into a new contract, provided it is with the same employer under a qualifying contract with no break, will not break the continuity of employment: *Wood v York City Council* [1978] IRLR 228; *Tipper v Roofdec Ltd* [1989] IRLR 419.

2.1 Hours not governed by a contract of employment

The difference between the position where there is a contract which normally involves employment for 16 hours or more a week and the position where there is no such contractual obligation is important. In the latter case, subject to certain limited exceptions, only those weeks in which an employee is *actually* employed for 16 hours or more will count as part of the continuous period of employment: para 3 of Sched 13 to the EP(C)A 1978. Weeks in which the employee is not so employed will not count and will break the continuous period of employment. In the former case, where the contract subsists, periods of absence caused by holidays, sickness or otherwise, of whatever length, do not break the period of continuous employment and in fact form part of that period: para 4 of Sched 13 to the EP(C)A 1978.

The point is illustrated by taking as an example the two-year qualifying period for bringing a claim for unfair dismissal. If there is a contract which normally involves employment for 16 hours or more a week which subsists for two years, it does not matter that during the

2 years the employee takes holidays totalling 6 weeks. However, if there is no such contract, and the employee works for not less than 20 hours in each week during the first year, but then takes 3 weeks' holiday when he does not work at all, those 3 weeks do not form part of the continuous period of employment and will break the continuity. It does not matter that the employee then works a further year and in each week during that year works at least 20 hours in each week.

However, it will be seen that there are certain limited exceptions to the rule that, where there is no contract of employment, a week in which the employee does not work will not count as part of the period of continuous employment, and will break the continuity of employment. See **2.3**, below.

2.2 Hours governed by a contract of employment

In deciding whether or not the employee's relations with the employer are governed by a contract of employment which normally involves employment for 16 hours or more a week, the starting point is to examine the contract of employment. If the contract of employment expressly provides that the normal working week shall be 16 hours or more, para 4 of Sched 13 to the EP(C)A 1978 will apply. Even where the contract does not expressly provide for the employee to work 16 hours or more in each week, it may be an implied term of the contract of employment that the employee shall work for 16 hours or more in each week. It does not matter at what time those hours are worked during the week for this purpose; nor does it matter that there is a contractual obligation to work different hours in alternative weeks provided that the number of hours the employee has to work in each week are 16 or more.

Paragraph 4 of Sched 13 to the EP(C)A 1978 refers to a week during the whole or part of which the employee is employed under a contract normally involving 16 hours or more. If an employee works for only 4 hours during a week when he is contractually obliged to work 16 hours or more that week will count. In deciding whether the normal working week is 16 hours or more, overtime hours are to be disregarded unless the employer is contractually obliged to provide overtime hours and the employee is contractually obliged to work overtime hours. It must be borne in mind that overtime hours worked may count under para 3 of Sched 13 to the EP(C)A 1978.

In *ITT Components Group (Europe) Ltd v Kolah* [1977] ICR 740, the employee was unable to claim unfair dismissal unless she could establish that she was employed under a contract which normally involved employment for 21 hours or more weekly. Under her contract she was required to work 20 hours in each week together with over-time. She normally worked 3 hours' overtime in each week. The overtime hours were to be disregarded in determining the normal working week. Likewise, in *Lake v Essex County Council* [1979] ICR

577, where it again had to be decided whether or not the employee worked under a contract which normally involved employment for not less than 21 hours weekly, the employee, a teacher, worked 19 hours 25 minutes in each week, of which 15 hours 45 minutes were spent in the classroom and 3 hours 40 minutes were free time. The employee claimed that in addition she was required to do preparation and marking work at home outside school hours. The EAT held there was an implied term in the teacher's contract under which she was to do as much work outside the specified hours as was necessary for the proper performance of her duties as a teacher. The Court of Appeal rejected this argument, finding that if she did work at home 'it was a voluntary act on her part outside her contractual obligations'. A term requiring her to work outside the specified hours was too vague and unpredictable and could not be implied as a term of the contract.

See also *Girls Public Day School Trust v Khanna* [1987] ICR 339. In *Society of Licensed Victuallers v Chamberlain* [1989] IRLR 421, a teacher's contractual weekly hours of work were 15 hours 40 minutes made up of teaching and supervisory duties. He had three free periods a week when he was contractually required to undertake preparation and marking. It was felt that those periods could be treated as part of his normal weekly hours of work.

In *Society of Licensed Victuallers v Chamberlain* [1989] IRLR 421, a teacher's contractual weekly hours of work were 15 hours 40 minutes, made up of teaching and supervisory duties. He had three free periods a week when he was contractually required to undertake preparation and marking. It was held that those three periods could be treated as part of his normal weekly hours work. The cases of *Lake* and *Khanna* could be distinguished because in those cases the contracts provided time for preparation work to be done and any other time spent on preparation could not be included.

In deciding whether or not the employee's relations with the employer are governed by a contract of employment which normally involves employment of 16 hours or more each week, it is necessary to consider the contract as originally drawn and then to consider the normal working of that contract throughout its life in ascertaining what the contract of employment normally involved: see *Secretary of State for Employment v Deary and Others* [1984] ICR 413. Section 151(2) of the EP(C)A 1978 provides that in computing the employee's period of continuous employment, any question as to whether the employment is of a kind counting towards a period of continuous employment, or whether periods consecutive or otherwise are to be treated as forming a single period of continuous employment, shall be determined in accordance with Sched 13 to the EP(C)A 1978 on a week-by-week basis. Thus, if for the period under consideration, the contract provides that the hours worked in each week shall be less than the qualifying hours for each week, it would appear that those weeks must break the continuity of employment. This is subject to any other provisions contained in Sched 13 to the EP(C)A 1978. This interpretation was rejected in *Deary*'s case, above, because the EAT considered that it did not give effect to the word normally in para 4 of Sched 13 to the EP(C)A 1978. The employees had all worked for over five years for periods exceeding eight hours a week until, in 1980, one employee's hours were reduced to under eight hours a week and, in 1981, the other employees' hours were reduced to under eight hours. All of the employees were dismissed on the grounds of redundancy, the first in May 1981 and the others in the second half of 1982. The tribunal and the EAT held that the employees' contracts normally involved working for periods of eight hours or more.

The EAT held:

[para 4 of Sched 13 to the EP(C)A 1978] is dealing with a period terminating in the redundancy of the employee concerned which, in the nature of things, is likely to be an unusual period. Its terms are those of a contract of employment which normally involves employment for the requisite number of hours. Those terms, in our judgment, direct the mind to the contract as originally drawn, and to the normal working of that contract throughout its life. So applying them in the present case, one finds, as did the tribunal, that the contract of employment normally involved, in the case of each of these ladies during the life of the contract, a period which exceeded eight hours.

In two earlier cases a similar approach to that in *Deary*'s case, above, was followed. In *Dean v Eastbourne Fishermen's and Boatmen's Protection Society and Club Ltd* [1977] ICR 556, Dean was a part-time barman. He had no written contract of employment and his hours were never expressly agreed. It was held that it was an implied term of his contract of employment that he should work whatever hours he was asked to work. He worked 21 hours (the qualifying hours are now 16 hours) or more in 86 weeks and less than 21 hours in 18 weeks. During 5 of those he was away due to sickness. None the less it was held that his contract normally involved him in working for 21 hours or more.

In *Larkin v Cambos Enterprises (Stretford) Ltd* [1978] ICR 1247, Larkin had no written contract of employment and her hours were never expressly agreed. In deciding whether Larkin could bring a claim for unfair dismissal, the EAT examined the last 26 weeks of employment (the then qualifying period for bringing a claim for unfair dismissal). In 17 weeks she normally worked more than 21 hours (now 16 hours). In only 6 weeks did she work less than 21 hours, apart from 3 weeks when she was ill. If the whole period of employment were examined, out of 80 weeks in 47 weeks she worked 21 hours or more. If the 52 weeks immediately before she was ill were examined, in 37 weeks she worked more than 21 hours. In each of these cases she was ill for 3 weeks. It was held that her relationship with the employer was governed by a contract of employment which normally involved employment for 21 hours or more weekly. Even if the cases of *Dean, Larkin* and *Deary* were correctly decided under the law then applicable, it is open to argument that under s 151(2) and (2) of the EP(C)A 1978 the approach in these cases is now wrong. Each week has to be examined to see whether or not it counts part as a continuous period of employment or whether or not it breaks a period of continuous employment. Paragraph 4 of Sched 13 to the EP(C)A 1978 refers to a contract of employment which normally involves employment for 16 hours or more weekly. Does employment mean hours actually worked or hours when the employee can be required to work? In *Bromsgrove Casting and Machining Ltd v Martin* [1977] ICR 417, Martin was engaged as a 'consultant'. His contract of employment was silent as to the number of hours during which he was required to work. It was held he was only employed for those hours in which he was actually performing services under his contract by giving advice to the employer, not when he was retained but not performing services.

In *Suffolk County Council v Secretary of State for the Environment and Another* [1984] ICR 882, the House of Lords had to consider whether or not the hours of employment of a retained fireman consisted merely of the hours when he was on duty following a call, or those hours when he had to keep himself available for response to calls. It was held that while he was not on duty he was under a contract to make himself available for employment if a fire occurred and he was called. Such a contract was not a contract of employment and the fireman did not become an employee until he was called. The earlier case of *Bullock v Merseyside County Council* [1979] ICR 79, was therefore wrongly decided.

(a) Normal working weeks of 16 hours or more   Where the contract defines the number of hours which involve employment for 16 hours or more, it does not matter that the employee works less than the contracted number of hours. Therefore, periods of absence caused by holidays, sickness or otherwise of whatever length will count as part of the period of continuous employment, provided the contract subsists.

Where the employee is required by the contract of employment to live on the premises where he works, the hours of employment are those hours when he is on duty or when his services may be required: para 24(2) of Sched 13 to the EP(C)A 1978.

(b) Work for only part of a week   Any week during the whole or part of which the employee's relations with the employer are governed by a contract normally involving employment for 16 hours or more counts as a week for the purposes of computing the period of continuous employment. It has already been seen that an employee may be able to claim a week as part of the period of continuous employment even though, on the face of it, he might not appear to be entitled to it.

A gap of up to 12 days will not operate to break the employee's continuity of employment. If an employee contracted to work 40 hours a week was dismissed on a Sunday, he may count that week as part of his period of continuous employment, so that his continuity is preserved until midnight on the following Saturday. If he were re-engaged on the next following Saturday under a contract to work 40 hours in each week, he may count that week starting with the preceding Sunday as part of his period of continuous employment. In such circumstances the two periods of employment are linked together so as to give the employee continuity of employment.

(c) Concurrent contracts   It has been seen that where an employee has a series of contracts with an employer, then the employee may be able to establish continuity of employment under those contracts. It may be, however, that the employee has concurrent contracts with the same employer. In *Lewis v Surrey County Council* [1987] IRLR 509, the employee worked as a part-time teacher for the county council at three different establishments. She had a separate contract for her employment at each of the establishments, although the county council was the employer in every case. Taken separately, none of the contracts gave her the necessary period of qualifying employment to enable her to claim unfair dismissal. The employee sought to add the hours under each of the contracts to give her the necessary qualifying hours. The House of Lords held that Lewis was not entitled to add the hours which she worked under each of the contracts. The proper construction of the words 'a contract of employment which normally involves', contained in para 4 of Sched 13 to the EP(C)A 1978 precludes an entitlement to aggregate the hours worked under separate and distinct contracts. The House of Lords rejected a contention that the singular includes the plural. Schedule 13 to the EP(C)A 1978 focuses upon the particular contract of employment in respect of which relief is claimed. The total absence of any reference to aggregation provided the clearest indication that it was not permissible.

(d) Variation of contractual hours   Where the relations between the employer and employee cease to be governed by a contract which normally involves work for 16 hours or more weekly and become governed by a contract which normally involves employment for 8 hours or more but less than 16 hours weekly, those latter weeks where the contract provides 8 hours or more will not break the continuity of employment and may count as part of the period of continuous employment: para 5(1) of Sched 13 to the EP(C)A 1978. The contract is treated as if it normally involved employment for 16 hours or more a week. This is subject to the proviso that but for the reduction in hours those weeks would otherwise not break the continuity and would count: para 5(1) of Sched 13 to the EP(C)A 1978. For example, reduced hours worked for a different employer would not count as part of the period of continuous employment, save where for instance paras 17 and 18 of Sched 13 to the EP(C)A 1978 apply. The employee

must already have had a contract with his employer which normally involved work for 16 hours or more in a week. Only 26 weeks count; in computing 26 weeks under this provision no account is to be taken of any week which counts in computing a period of employment or does not break the continuity of a period of employment otherwise than by virtue of para 5 of Sched 13 for instance where 16 hours or more are worked in a week: para 5(2) of Sched 13 to the EP(C)A 1978.

Paragraph 5 requires that 16 hours or more are worked weekly and contemplates only an occasional shortfall. A normal working week is not the same as an average working week; and para 5 should not be applied at the end of each fortnight. This paragraph is intended to deal with the situation where, over a period of time, the hours of work each week regularly amount to 16 hours or more and this is followed by a period where the hours of work regularly amount to 8 hours or more: see *Opie v John Gubbins (Insurance Brokers) Ltd* [1978] IRLR 540. Thus, there will be no continuity under this paragraph if the employee works every other week for more than 32 hours, but does not work at all in the intervening week. The employee has a reserve of 26 weeks which count towards his continuous employment. If the hours are restored to 16 or more weekly before the expiration of the 26-week period the process starts again. If not, it is uncertain whether he can claim the 26 weeks because para 5(2) refers to a period between two contracts normally involving employment for 16 hours or more weekly. An exception would be where para 6 of Sched 13 to the EP(C)A 1978 applies. Because of the wording of para 5(2) it appears that para 5 may have the effect of simply preserving continuity, not only for 26 weeks, but indefinitely until his hours are restored to 16 weekly or he has been employed for more than 5 years (see para 6).

(e) Employees employed for five years Where the employee's relationship with the employer has been governed by a contract of employment which normally involves employment for 8 hours or more but less than 16 hours weekly and the employee, on the date when the continuous period of employment falls to be ascertained, has been continuously employed for a period of 5 years or more, then he is treated as if his contract normally involved employment for 16 hours or more weekly. Paragraphs 3 and 4 of Sched 13 apply as if 8 hours were substituted for 16: para 6 of Sched 13 to the EP(C)A 1978. Where there is a series of separate contracts for one or two days in each week, para 6 of Sched 13 to EP(C)A 1978 does not apply because it is impossible to show a normal pattern by reference to what happened weekly: *Letheby and Christopher Ltd v Bond* [1988] ICR 480.

2.3 Weeks which count where there is no contract of employment

It has been seen that where there is no contract of employment, a week in which the employee does not work will not form part of the continuous period of employment and will break the continuity. There are limited exceptions to this rule. Thus where there is no contract of employment and the employee is for the whole or part of the week:

(*a*) incapable of working in consequence of sickness or injury; or

(*b*) absent from work on account of a temporary cessation of work; or

(*c*) absent from work in circumstances such that by arrangement or custom he is regarded as continuing in the employment of his employer for all or any purpose; or

(*d*) absent from work wholly or partly because of pregnancy or confinement;

the whole of that week, although not caught under the earlier provisions, is counted as a week for computing a period of continuous employment: para 9(1) of Sched 13 to the EP(C)A 1978. Paragraph 9 will only apply when there is no contract of employment: *Ford v Warwickshire County Council* [1983] 1 All ER 753. Thus, para 9 covers a period between two contracts of employment.

In deciding whether or not there was no contract, and the reason why the employee was absent from work, the period has to be examined on a week-by-week basis.

(a) Incapacity due to sickness or injury Not more than 26 weeks will count under para 9(1)(*a*): para 9(2) of Sched 13 to the EP(C)A 1978. The employee must be incapable of doing work which he is obliged to do under the terms of his contract of employment; it does not mean that he must be incapable of any work at all: see *Collins v Nats (Southend) Ltd* (1967) 2 ITR 423. An absence for sickness arising out of a pregnancy or confinement is within this provision, but not the pregnancy or confinement itself. Under para 9(1)(*a*) of Sched 13 to the EP(C)A 1978, the absence must be connected with sickness: see *Scarlett v Godfrey Abbott Group Ltd* [1978] ICR 1106.

(b) Temporary cessation of work The test of temporary cessation has given rise to difficulties. In *Bentley Engineering Co Ltd v Crown and Miller* [1976] ICR 225, it was held that the decided cases have established that para 9(1)(*b*) of Sched 13 to the EP(C)A 1978 poses three questions:

Was there a cessation of the employee's work or job; was the employee absent on account of that cessation, and . . . was the cessation a temporary one?

The EAT considered that these questions were a helpful guide in considering the wording of the statutory provision. Having considered these questions the tribunal must still look at the question in the round to see whether or not an employee was absent from work on account of a temporary cessation of work.

(i) Absent from work   The employee must be absent from work because of a temporary cessation of work. Absent from work means away from work. The matter has to be considered retrospectively: *Fitzgerald v Hall, Russell and Co Ltd* [1970] AC 984; *Ford v Warwickshire County Council*, above. An employee may be absent on account of a temporary cessation of work notwithstanding that he obtains work with another employer where that employment is intended to bridge the gap during the temporary cessation. He is absent from work: *Thompson v Bristol Channel Ship Repairers and Engineers Ltd* (1970) 5 ITR 85. The position would be the same if, following the employment intended to bridge the gap, the employee returned to work not with the original employer, but with an associated employer. An employee may be absent on account of a temporary cessation of work where he takes a job elsewhere, even though he assumes that job will be permanent: *Bentley Engineering Co Ltd v Crown and Miller* [1976] ICR 225. This case was followed in *GW Stephens and Son v Fish* [1989] ICR 324, where it was held that absent from work does not necessarily mean physically absent. It means not performing in substance the contract that previously existed between the parties.

If, however, the employee leaves his employer and after a period of unemployment obtains a job with an employer which is an associated employer, the period of unemployment cannot be said to be an absence on account of a temporary cessation of work; rather it is an absence caused by the employee's resignation: *Wessex National Ltd v Long* (1978) 13 ITR 413. The position is the same if an employee is dismissed for misconduct and subsequently re-engaged: see *Clark v Blairs Ltd* (1966) 1 ITR 545.

(ii) Temporary   Whether or not the absence is caused by a temporary cessation of work is a matter of fact to be decided by the tribunal: see *Hunter v Smith's Dock Co Ltd* [1968] 2 All ER 81. Whether the cessation of work is temporary must be decided retrospectively. Broadly, temporary means a relatively short time compared with the period in work. In *Bentley Engineering Co Ltd v Crown and Miller* [1976] ICR 225, Phillips J, referring to *Fitzgerald v Hall, Russell and Co Ltd* [1970] AC 984, held:

The effect of that case is that the tribunal is enjoined to look at the matter as the historian of a completed chapter of events and not as a journalist describing events as they occur from day to day. The importance of that is this, that things are seen, as they unfold, quite differently from the way in which they are seen when one looks back and considers the whole of the chapter in its context. What at the time seems to be permanent may turn out to be temporary, and what at the time seems to be temporary may turn out to be permanent.

1   It is not possible to lay down what might be regarded as temporary but in *Bentley Engineering Co Ltd v Crown and Miller*, above, Phillips

J thought that two years could be temporary. See also *G W Stephens and Son v Fish*, above. In *Flack v Kodak Ltd* [1985] IRLR 443:

Mrs Flack had first been employed by the employer on 21 May 1979 for 215 days. She was then dismissed but re-employed 16 days later and worked for 19 days. She was then dismissed but re-employed 51 days later and worked for 264 days. She was then dismissed but re-employed 23 days later and worked for 26 days. She was then dismissed but re-employed 72 days later and worked for 234 days. On 27 November 1981 (that is to say just within the two years' period before her final dismissal on 25 November 1983) she was dismissed but re-employed 31 days later and worked for 18 days. She was then dismissed but re-employed 86 days later and worked for 17 days. She was then dismissed but re-employed 32 days later. She then worked for 542 days until her final dismissal.

The tribunal found that the cessation of work was not a temporary cessation but a cessation of a more substantial nature. In reaching this conclusion it confined itself to the purely mathematical approach of comparing each gap in employment falling within the two years preceding the final dismissal with the period of employment immediately before and the period of employment immediately after the gap. The EAT held that the tribunal:

ought to have regard to all the circumstances and should not confine itself to the purely mathematical approach of looking only to the gap and its immediately adjoining periods of employment. It may well be that in most cases that approach will be the decisive factor, but there may be cases where it is not.

It went on to find that the tribunal:

should look at the history of the whole period of intermittent employment including that part of the period which falls outside the two-year period, not for the purpose of seeing whether there were other periods which could be characterised as other than temporary cessations by applying the limited mathematical approach, but so that with the whole of the period of intermittent employment in mind the tribunal can conclude whether or not any gaps in the two-year period ought be called a temporary cessation.

The decision of the EAT was upheld on appeal: see *Flack v Kodak Ltd* [1986] IRLR 255. However, the Court of Appeal emphasised that in deciding whether or not there was a temporary cessation of work, regard must be had to all the circumstances over the whole period of employment, not simply the periods of work adjacent to the periods of absence. In *Sillars v Charrington Fuels Ltd* [1989] ICR 475, the Court of Appeal held that the tribunal was entitled to adopt the mathematical approach and to consider the length of the employee's last two periods of seasonal employment with the length of the last two periods of unemployment. The tribunal was not in error in failing to follow the broad approach of looking back over the entire period of the employment relationship. The last period was representative. See also *Berwick Salmon Fisheries Co Ltd v Rutherford and others* [1991] IRLR 203.

(iii) Cessation of work   A cessation of work may arise for a number of reasons, for instance, where the employer does not have orders; where the employer does not have supplies or where the employee cannot work at his employer's premises due to a serious fire, flood or explosion. In *Fitzgerald v Hall, Russell and Co Ltd* [1970] AC 984, the issue arose as to what was a cessation of work. Lord Morris posed the question:

Why in that period between the two contracts [of employment] was the employee absent from work? If it was a period during which he would have been at work but for the fact that his employer could not find work for him, but which period ended when the employer did find work for him, I consider that it could properly be said that he was absent from work on account of a cessation of work even though the employer's business, or the particular department of it, had not completely closed down.

In the same case Lord Upjohn equated a temporary cessation with the employee being laid off or dismissed and, following Lord Morris, found that the temporary cessation of work must refer to work available for a particular workman and not to workmen generally.

In *Ford v Warwickshire County Council* [1983] 1 All ER 753, the employee, a teacher, had been employed under a series of successive fixed-term contracts between September and July for eight years. Between July and September she was on holiday and had no contract of employment. The question which was raised was, was the holiday a temporary cessation of work? It was held that it was a temporary cessation of work, and it did not matter that the employers had foreseen the unavailability of work and had made arrangements accordingly by entering into fixed-term contracts with the employee. *Rashid v Inner London Education Authority* [1977] ICR 157 was overruled.

The cases suggest that there must be a cessation of work in that the employer cannot continue his normal operations due to circumstances outside his direct control.

In *Byrne v City of Birmingham DC* [1987] IRLR 191, the employee was a cleaner. He was a member of a 'pool' of casual cleaners. The Court of Appeal held that when he was not allocated work under the pooling arrangement he was not absent on account of a temporary cessation of work within the meaning of para 9(1)(*b*) of Sched 13 to the EP(C)A 1978. The expression cessation of work must denote that some 'quantum of work' had for the time being ceased to exist. Paragraph 9(1)(*b*) did not apply where work was available, but under the pooling arrangement it had been allocated by the employer to another employee. The decision was followed in *Letheby and Christopher Ltd v Bond* [1988] ICR 480.

Work means paid work for the employee to do: see *University of Aston in Birmingham v Malik* [1984] ICR 492, where it was held that the tribunal cannot consider the reason for the non-availability of work.

(c) Special arrangement or custom—absent from work   The meaning of the phrase absent from work has been considered above.

As in the case of para 9(1)(*a*) and 9(1)(*b*), para 9(1)(*c*) of Sched 3 to the EP(C)A 1978 only applies where there is no contract of employment. See above and *Ford v Warwickshire County Council* [1983] 1 All ER 753. In the light of the decision in *Ford*'s case the earlier decision in *Lloyds Bank Ltd v Secretary of State for Employment* [1979] ICR 258, must be considered wrong in law. The employee worked one week on, one week off and was held to be absent from work during each week that she had off. However it was held that the contract subsisted throughout. Notwithstanding the fact that the EAT seemed to suggest that the weeks off were not governed by a contract of employment, it is submitted that that cannot be so because there was clearly a contract defining what should happen both during the weeks on and the weeks off.

Likewise in *Corton House Ltd v Skipper* [1981] ICR 307, the employee worked for four hours on alternative evenings so that she worked 16 hours in one week and 12 hours in the next. Since there was a contract governing the arrangement, para 9(1)(*c*) of Sched 13 to the EP(C)A 1978 cannot now apply in such a case until the contract has come to an end, following the decision in *Ford*'s case, above. Although *Ford*'s case involved a consideration of para 9(1)(*b*), the same considerations must also apply to para 9(1)(*c*). However, the position is complicated by the fact that para 9(1)(*c*) refers to the employee being regarded as continuing in the employment of his employer. It may be difficult to establish an arrangement or custom where the employee is employed on a series of single separate contracts with no overall 'umbrella contract': *Letheby and Christopher Ltd v Bond* [1988] ICR 480. The reported cases show that whether or not there was a custom or arrangement, and whether or not the employee is regarded as continuing in employment during the period of absence, are matters of fact for the tribunal to decide.

It is probable that the parties cannot retrospectively agree that the absence from work is such that by arrangement or custom the employee is regarded as continuing in the employment; the arrangement must exist at the time when the absence began: *Murphy v Birrell and Sons Ltd* [1978] IRLR 458.

It may be possible for an employee to rely upon the terms of a collective agreement and have his employment treated as continuous: see *Taylor v Triumph Motors, British Leyland (UK) Ltd and Secretary of State for Employment* [1975] IRLR 369.

However, there are circumstances where an arrangement may be made retrospectively. In *Ingram v Foxon* [1984] ICR 685, the employee was dismissed and then reinstated by his employer without making a complaint to a tribunal. He was reinstated on the basis that his employment was regarded as having been continuous since the date when he first started work. It was held that this was an exception to the rule in *Murphy v Birrell and Sons Ltd*, above, and there was an arrangement, albeit retrospectively, that the employee's employment should be regarded as continuous. This provision is designed to cover a situation where an employee is loaned by one employer to another: see *Wishart v NCB* [1974] ICR 460.

It is necessary for the employee to establish the arrangement or the custom. Custom refers to a trade or professional custom going beyond the limits of a single employer's own practice. See the decision of the EAT in *Ford v Warwickshire County Council* (1980) (unreported).

It is open to argument that para 9(1)(*c*) of Sched 13 to the EP(C)A 1978 applies without limitation as to time, although in *Southern Electricity Board v Collins* [1969] 2 All ER 1166, there is some support for the argument that it applies only where there is a temporary absence.

Paragraph 9(1)(*c*) may apply to a period at the commencement of the employment, but it is essential that there should be clear evidence of such an arrangement: see *Brown v Southall and Knight* [1980] IRLR 130.
(d) Pregnancy or confinement The meaning of the phrase 'absent from work' has been considered. See above. Again, this provision only applies where there is no contract of employment, see below.

Not more than 26 weeks' absence can count under para 9(1)(*d*): para 9(2) of Sched 13 to the EP(C)A 1978. An example is where a woman is dismissed fairly because of pregnancy before she has completed two years' service. If the woman returns to work within 26 weeks from the date when she was dismissed, the whole period of absence will count as part of her continuous period of employment. There is therefore no break in the continuity of the employment. If the woman had been employed for two years or more, this provision would probably not apply to her, where in accordance with s 45(1) or in pursuance of an offer made in the circumstances described in s 56A(2) of the EP(C)A 1978, she exercises her right to return to work following a period of absence from work, occasioned wholly or partly by pregnancy or confinement. In this case every week during that period of absence counts in computing a period of employment. The situation is as if the employee had not been absent; further, there is no break in the continuity of employment: para 10 of Sched 13 to the EP(C)A 1978. If the employee does not return to work in accordance with s 45(1) or s 56A(2), para 9(1)(*d*), above, may apply.

Paragraph 9(1)(*d*) applies only to a period where there is no contract of employment. In *Mitchell v British Legion Club* [1980] IRLR 425, the applicant resigned her position 'due to personal reasons', namely her pregnancy, which was known to her employer. She returned to work following her pregnancy. The EAT held that if during a period when there is no contract of employment a woman is absent from work wholly or partly because of pregnancy then those weeks count in computing her period of employment and there is no break in continuity. It does not matter whether the contract comes to an end by resignation or dismissal.

In *Secretary of State for Employment v Doulton Sanitaryware Ltd* [1981] IRLR 365, the question arose whether the employee had been employed until immediately before the beginning of the 11th week before the expected week of confinement for the purposes of s 33(3)(*a*) of the EP(C)A 1978. The EAT held that under s 33(3)(*a*) and (*b*) the tribunal has first to consider if the employee was employed until the beginning of the 11th week before the expected week of confinement, and, secondly, if the employee had the requisite period of continuous employment. Paragraph 9(1)(*d*) does not apply where the contract of employment has come to and end, before the beginning of the 11th week before the expected week of confinement, so as to allow the employee to tack weeks on and extend the employment up to or beyond the beginning of the 11th week before the expected week of confinement to claim the benefits conferred by s 33 of the EP(C)A 1978. See Chapter 9 for more on maternity.

Where the employee is absent from work but the contract of employment continues, then the employee may be able to claim that the period of employment is continuous under one of the other provisions of Sched 13 to the EP(C)A 1978.

3 Events which do not break continuity

3.1 Industrial disputes

(a) *Strike* 'Strike' is defined in para 24(1) of Sched 13 to the EP(C)A 1978 as:

the cessation of work by a body of persons employed acting in combination, or a concerted refusal or a refusal under a common understanding of any number of persons employed to continue to work for an employer in consequence of a dispute, done as a means of compelling their employer or any person or body of persons employed, or to aid other employees in compelling their employer or any person or body of persons employed, to accept or not to accept terms or conditions of or affecting employment.

Under the EP(C)A 1978 a week will not count for the purposes of paras 3, 4, 5, 9 or 10 of Sched 13 if the employee is on strike for the whole or any part of that week: para 15(1) of Sched 13. However, a week beginning before 6 July 1964 will count if the employee was absent from work on strike for all or any part of the week: para 22 of Sched 13. The continuity of employment is not broken by a week which does not count under Sched 13 and which begins after 5 July 1964 if in that week, or any part of that week, the employee is on strike, whether or not the week would (apart from para 15(1) of Sched 13) have counted: para 15(2) and (3) of Sched 13.

The protection afforded by para 15 of Sched 13 extends to dismissed employees. In *Bloomfield v Springfield Hosiery Finishing Co Ltd* [1972] ICR 91, an employee was held to include an ex-employee. Note also that the definition of 'employee' contained in s 153(1) of the EP(C)A 1978 includes reference to a person whose employment has ceased. Thus a person or persons employed must, in relation to a strike, mean 'persons who, but for their action in ceasing or refusing to continue work, would be employees'. An employee has the benefit of this protection (per Sir John Donaldson):

unless and until [the employer] engages other persons on a permanent basis to do the work which the strikers had been doing or he permanently discontinues the activity in which they were employed.

It is clear from the decision in *Bloomfield*, that where strikers take temporary employment pending a settlement of the dispute, they may still claim they are on strike. Continuity of employment is not preserved under this provision where there is a break between the end of the strike and when the 're-employed' employee starts work. Where there is a shortage of work after the strike is over, an employee may be treated as being absent on account of a temporary cessation of work: *Clarke Chapman—John Thompson Ltd v Walters* [1972] ICR 83. Again it may be that an employee is absent from work, in circumstances that by arrangement or by custom mean he is regarded as continuing in the employment of his employer. In both cases the period of absence will count and continuity of employment is not broken.

Paragraph 15 of Sched 13 to the EP(C)A 1978 applies, even though during the strike the employee has been dismissed, if following the strike he is re-engaged. An attempt on re-engagement to contract out of the continuity provisions contained in para 15(2) and (3) of Sched 13 is void by virtue of s 140 of the EP(C)A 1978: see *Hanson v Fashion Industries (Hartlepool) Ltd* [1980] IRLR 393.

Section 151(5) and (6)(*b*) of the EP(C)A 1978 provides that if an employee's period of continuous employment includes one or more periods which under Sched 13 do not count in computing continuous employment but do not break the continuity of employment, the beginning of the period shall be treated as postponed by the number of days falling within that intervening period, or as the case may be by the aggregate number of days falling within those periods. Where para 15(2) of Sched 13 applies, the number of days falling within such an intervening period is the number of days between the last working day before the strike and the day on which work was resumed. The rationale for this provision is that only the days on which the employee was on strike are lost. However, on the wording of s 151(5) and

(6)(*b*) of the EP(C)A 1978, the period of continuous employment is postponed by the total number of days during which the strike lasted, even though the employee was not on strike for the whole of that period. The beginning of the period of continuous employment is postponed by the number of days for which the strike lasts. Presumably, for these provisions to apply, the employee must have participated in the strike at some stage. The provision is not restricted to working days.

The period is calculated from the last working day before the strike. Thus, if a strike takes place on a Monday, the number of days is calculated from the preceding Friday where the working week is Monday to Friday. This is so even if the strike finishes on the Monday. If, however, the strike starts and finishes on any other day of the week, no additional days are lost.

Paragraph 15 of Sched 13 only applies where an employee is actually taking part in a strike. (See Chapter 11 for a consideration of when an employee is taking part in a strike.)

It will be important for the employer to keep a record of when the strike started, when it finished and the names of employees involved in the strike.

(b) Lock-outs Lock-out is defined in para 24(1) of Sched 13 to the EP(C)A 1978 as:

the closing of a place of employment or the suspension of work, or the refusal by an employer to continue to employ any number of persons employed by him in consequence of a dispute, done with a view to compelling those persons, or to aid another employer in compelling persons employed by him, to accept terms or conditions of or affecting employment.

A week beginning before 6 July 1964 will count if the employee was absent from work due to a lock-out by the employer for all or any part of the week: para 22 of Sched 13.

The continuity of employment is not broken by a week which does not count under Sched 13 and which begins after 5 July 1964 if in that week, or any part of that week, the employee is absent due to a lock-out by the employer: para 15(4) of Sched 13 to the EP(C)A 1978. Further, such weeks may count in computing the period of employment. Unlike the position where the employee is taking part in a strike, there is no statutory exclusion akin to para 15(1) of Sched 13, applying only to strikes (see **3.1**(*a*), above), which prevents the employee who is locked out from counting a week where, during the week or part of the week, the employee is locked out.

Where the employee is locked out that period will count if it falls within one of the paragraphs of Sched 13. One example would be where the contract of employment still subsists. A lock-out does not automatically terminate the contract of employment: *E and J Davis Transport Ltd v Chattaway* [1972] ICR 267. If a week during which there is a lock-out is not caught by one of the other provisions of Sched 13 then continuity is preserved by para 15(4) of the EP(C)A 1978. Section 151(5) and (6)(*b*) of the EP(C)A 1978 apply, so that if an employee's period of continuous employment includes one or more periods which under Sched 13 do not count in computing continuous employment but do not break the continuity of employment, the beginning of the period shall be treated as postponed by the number of days falling within that intervening period, or as the case may be, by the aggregate number of days falling within those periods. Where para 15(4) of Sched 13 applies, the number of days falling within such an intervening period is the number of days between the last working day before the lock-out and the day on which work was resumed. (See (*a*) above for the way in which this provision operates.)

It follows that the employee who is locked out, and whose contract of employment is terminated, will find himself in a worse position than the employee whose contract of employment continues, because in the latter case the continuity of employment is not only preserved but increases.

3.2 *Absence on service with the armed forces*

An employee who is entitled to apply to his former employer under the Reserve Forces (Safeguard of Employment) Act 1985 to be reinstated may, provided he complies with the provisions of that Act, aggregate the periods before and after his service with the armed forces so that the continuity of employment is not broken: para 16 of Sched 13 to the EP(C)A 1978.

Section 151(5) and (6)(*c*) of the EP(C)A 1978 provides that if an employee's period of continuous employment includes one or more periods which under Sched 13 to the EP(C)A 1978 do not count in computing continuous employment but do not break the continuity of employment, the beginning of the period shall be treated as postponed by the number of days falling within that intervening period or, as the case may be, by the aggregate number of days falling within those periods. Where para 16(1) of Sched 13 applies, the number of days falling within such an intervening period is the number of days between the employee's last day of employment before service and the day on which he resumed employment: see the Reserve Forces (Safeguard of Employment) Act 1985.

4 An accrued right

Where the employee has, at any time during the relevant period of employment, been continuously employed for a period which qualifies him for a right, such as the right not to be unfairly dismissed or to claim a redundancy payment, he is regarded for the purposes of qualifying for that right, as continuing to satisfy the criteria for continuous employment until certain conditions occur: para 7(1) of Sched 13 to the EP(C)A 1978.

The relevant period of employment is the period of employment ending on the date by reference to which the length of any period of employment falls to be ascertained which would be continuous (under Sched 13) if, at all relevant times, the employee's relations with the employer had been governed by a contract of employment normally involving employment for 16 hours or more a week: para 7(2) of Sched 13 to the EP(C)A 1978. The preservation of an accrued right is lost where after the employee has qualified for the right, his relations with his employer are governed by a contract of employment which normally involves employment for less that 8 hours in each week and he is employed in a week for less than 16 hours: para 7(3) of Sched 13 to the EP(C)A 1978.

The employee has to acquire the right before he can preserve it. For example, an employee is taken on in employment for 10 hours a week. After a month he is asked to double his hours of work, and this continues for a period of 5 months. He then reverts to 10 hours a week. He continues in employment for 120 weeks and is then dismissed without notice. Here, the employee has been continuously employed for 16 hours or more in a week for 5 months, but he cannot claim unfair dismissal because he has not worked for 2 years for 16 hours or more in each week. However, he is entitled to the minimum period of notice under the EP(C)A 1978, since an employee is entitled to the minimum period of notice after being continuously employed for 1 month. Under s 49(1)(b) of the EP(C)A 1978 he will be entitled to 2 weeks' notice.

The amount of an employee's entitlement under any right under para 7(1) of Sched 13 will frequently depend upon his period of continuous employment. For the purposes of computing an employee's entitlement, he is treated as having been continuously employed up to the date by reference to which the period of continuous employment falls to be ascertained: para 7(4) of Sched 13 to the EP(C)A 1978. This means that, when an employee has qualified for a particular right which increases with further service, he will be allowed to build up his entitlement, provided his contracted weekly hours are not fewer than 8 hours. For example, suppose a woman has worked for 2 years under a contract for 20 hours a week. She has sufficient continuity of employment, *inter alia*, to claim unfair dismissal and also a redundancy payment, which depend on having 2 years' continuous employment. After the completion of 2 years, her contract is then varied to provide for 10 hours a week. She remains employed for the next 2 years at 10 hours a week and is then dismissed for redundancy. Even though the last 2 years do not count as part of her continuous employment, her rights have been protected and she will be entitled to 4 weeks' notice and a redundancy payment based on 4 years' service. She may also claim unfair dismissal in a redundancy situation. Using the same example, if the woman had been employed under a contract for 16 months at 16 hours and then her hours were reduced to 12, she would not be entitled to claim unfair dismissal and she would not be entitled to a redundancy payment on the dismissal, because at no time had she acquired the 2 years' continuous employment which is necessary for her entitlement. However, she would be entitled to 4 weeks' notice, because she would have fulfilled the minimum requirements for the prescribed statutory notice.

It must be remembered that para 7 of Sched 13 only preserves a statutory right which has been acquired by the employee, although once the right has been acquired, his entitlement under that right may be increased by virtue of para 7(4) of Sched 13. Again it must be remembered that para 7 does not bridge two periods of employment, thereby preserving continuity of employment.

5 Reinstatement or re-engagement

Continuity of employment may be preserved under the Labour Relations (Continuity of Employment Regulations 1976 (SI 1976 No 660). These Regulations apply to any action taken in relation to the dismissal of an employee which consists in the presentation of a complaint to a tribunal or making a claim under a designated dismissals procedure (see Chapter 1) or to any action taken by a conciliation officer under s 134(3) of the EP(C)A 1978. See Chapter 1. If, in consequence of any action to which these Regulations apply, a dismissed employee is reinstated or re-engaged by his employer or by a successor or associated employer of the employer, the continuity of that employee's period of employment shall be preserved and, accordingly, any week falling within the interval beginning with the effective date of termination and ending with the date of reinstatement or re-engagement, as the case may be, shall count in the computation of the employee's period of continuous employment. If a tribunal upon the hearing of a complaint makes an order for reinstatement or re-engagement, then clearly the employee's continuous employment is preserved. Again if the reinstatement or re-engagement is a consequence of the presentation of a complaint to tribunal, that will be sufficient to preserve the employee's continuity of employment. However, even where a complaint is made to the tribunal, not every reinstatement or re-engagement will be in consequence of that complaint. See *Gardener v NCB* (unreported EAT 375/82).

6 Change of employer

The general principle is that an employee will enjoy continuity of employment with only one employer. However, there are certain circumstances in which a change of employer will not break the continuity of employment and the employee's period of employment at the time of the change counts as a period of employment with a new employer. These exceptions are set out in para 17 of Sched 13 to the EP(C)A 1978. Unless an employee can show that a change of employer falls within one of the exceptions contained in para 17 of Sched 13, his continuity of employment will be defeated.

Paragraph 17 and particularly para 17(2) of Sched 13 often falls to be considered in conjunction with s 94 of the EP(C)A 1978, which deals with the employee's entitlement to a redundancy payment upon the change of ownership of a business or part of a business in which that employee is employed, whether the transfer comes about by sale or other disposition, or by operation of law. Under s 94, if the new owner renews the employee's contract of employment or re-engages him under a new contract, there is no dismissal by the original owner of the business and there will be no right to claim a redundancy payment. Section 94(1) and para 17(2) of Sched 13 are designed to deal with two aspects of the same transaction. If the employee is not entitled to a redundancy payment by virtue of s 94, then he can claim continuity of employment with his new employer under para 17(2) of Sched 13. Section 94(1) will be otiose if the Transfer of Undertakings (Protection of Employment) Regulations 1981 (SI 1989 No 1794) apply. These regulations have made a significant change in the law in so far as they affect the employee's rights upon the transfer of an undertaking. For a detailed account of the effect of these regulations see Chapter 12. Broadly the effect of these regulations is to provide that on a transfer of an undertaking which comes within the regulations, the employee's contract of employment is automatically transferred from the transferor to the transferee. Nothing in these regulations affects para 17 of Sched 13. It is arguable that since the employee's rights under the contract are transferred from the transferor to the transferee, the regulations operate to preserve continuity of employment. However, in any event, continuity will generally be preserved under Sched 13.

The exceptions contained in para 17 of Sched 13 to the EP(C)A 1978 are set out below.

Where a trade, business or undertaking is transferred from one employer to another Paragraph 17(2) of Sched 13 provides that if a trade, business or undertaking (whether or not it be an undertaking established by or under an Act of Parliament) is transferred from one person to another, the period of employment of an employee in the trade or business or undertaking at the time of the transfer shall count as a period of employment with the transferee, and the transfer, shall not break the continuity of the period of employment.

Section 153(1) of the EP(C)A 1978 provides that business includes a trade or profession and any activity carried on by a body of persons whether corporate or unincorporate. The use of the word activity in the definition of a business covers such operations as may be carried on by a charity and a college: see *Robinson v Council of the County Borough of Bournemouth* (1970) 5 ITR 100. To this extent it is wider than the provisions of the Transfer of Undertakings (Protection of Employment) Regulations 1981 (S1 1981 No 1794). See Chapter 12. Transfer in para 17(2) of Sched 13 is to be construed as if it involved a change of ownership. See *Lord Advocate v de Rosa* [1974] 2 All ER 849.

It is a question of fact whether or not there has been a transfer of a trade, business or undertaking. In *Kenmir Ltd v Frizzell and Others* [1968] 1 WLR 329, Widgery J held:

the vital consideration is whether the effect of the transaction was to put the transferee in possession of a going concern the activities of which he could carry on without interruption.

A transfer of the assets only is unlikely to amount to the transfer of a trade business or undertaking.

In *Woodhouse v Peter Brotherhood Ltd* [1972] 3 All ER 91, Crossleys manufactured diesel engines. This company sold its factory to Peter Brotherhood Ltd, together with some of the plant, machinery, equipment, fixtures and fittings. Peter Brotherhood Ltd purchased the factory to manufacture spinning machines and steam turbines. Some unfinished diesel engines remained in the factory and Peter Brotherhood Ltd agreed to complete the work on these diesel engines. It was held that the transfer was one of assets and not of a going concern. The Court of Appeal held that the fact that the employees continued to work in the same environment was not sufficient evidence of the transfer of a business. Buckley LJ held the test is simply whether B has become the proprietor of the trade, business or undertaking in succession to A.

In *Melon v Hector Powe Ltd* [1980] IRLR 477, where it was again held that there had been a transfer of assets, the House of Lords confirmed that it is for the tribunal to ascertain on the facts whether or not there has been the transfer of a business or part of a business or a transfer of physical assets. It did not matter that the individual employees may continue to do the same work in the same environment and that they are unaware that they are working in a different business.

In deciding whether or not there has been the transfer of a business as a going concern, the agreement between the transferor and the transferee will have to be considered. It is the substance of the agreement which will be determinative. Factors to be considered are has there been a transfer of assets, work in progress, the trading name, brand names or customer lists? The importance attaching to these factors will depend on the circumstances of each case. One aspect to consider is whether or not there has been a transfer of goodwill, perhaps supported by a restrictive covenant. In *Gibson v Motortune Ltd* [1990] ICR 740, Wood J, in a dissenting judgment, considered that there was no transfer of business since no lists of customers nor books of accounts were handed over and there was no restrictive covenant protecting the business connections. The absence of a transfer of goodwill will not be fatal. There may be little goodwill left in the business: see *Kenmir Ltd v Frizzell and Others* [1968] 1 WLR 329; see also *Jeetle v Elster* [1985] ICR 389. The transfer of goodwill on its own may be the transfer of a business or part of a business: see *Ward v Haines Watts and Another* [1983] ICR 231, where an accountant agreed with the transferee to sell to the transferee a list of clients. The clients were then informed by circular letter of the change of practice and were asked whether or not they were prepared to transfer their affairs to the transferee. About half of the clients circularized were prepared to do so. There was a transfer of the appropriate files, but there was no transfer of any physical assets. It was held that there was a transfer of part of a business as a going concern. See also *Secretary of State for Employment v Spence and Others* [1986] IRLR 248, where there was a transfer of the assets and goodwill of a business by a receiver. The employees had all been dismissed at the time of the transfer. The Court of Appeal found that although there were no employees, none the less the transfer of the assets and the goodwill of the business, where the transferee had the option to continue the business as a going concern, was a transfer of a business.

The sale of farmland has been held to amount to the transfer of a business as a going concern: see *Lloyd v Brassey* [1969] 2 QB 98. The transfer of licensed premises has also been held to be the transfer of a business as a going concern: see *Young v Daniel Thwaites and Co Ltd* [1977] ICR 877. Young surrendered the tenancy of his public house to Daniel Thwaites and Co Ltd who installed a manager to run the pub for them. There was no evidence of an assignment of goodwill or stock-in-trade or fixtures and fittings.

Paragraph 17(2) of Sched 13 to the EP(C)A 1978 may apply where there has been a transfer of part of a business: see *Melon v Hector Powe Ltd* [1980] IRLR 477. The part of the business may have been run separately before the transfer as in *Ault v Gregory* (1967) 2 ITR 301, but the part of the business transferred may not have been run as a separate entity before the transfer: see *Green v Wavertree Heating and Plumbing Co Ltd* [1978] ICR 928.

The transfer of part of the equity of a business by one of two partners to the other partner, whereby that other partner has the entire equity, was a transfer of a business within the meaning of para 17(2) of Sched 13 because two partners as joint proprietors transferred the whole business to one: *Allen and Son v Coventry* [1979] IRLR 399.

There may be a transfer at the time of the employee's dismissal even though further steps are to take place which do not take place and the merger is subsequently called off: *Dabell v Vale Industrial Services (Nottingham) Ltd* [1988] IRLR 439. There may be a transfer of a trade or business or undertaking within para 17(2) of Sched 13, if the business assets and goodwill of the transferor pass to the transferee, even though the transferor is insolvent at the time of the transfer and the business is no longer a going concern. The fact that the transferor is insolvent is a relevant factor, but it does not necessarily mean that there has been no transfer within this provision: *Teesside Times Ltd v Drury* [1978] ICR 822.

The meaning of the phrase 'at the time of the transfer' was considered in *Teesside Times Ltd v Drury* [1980] ICR 338. Drury worked for Champion Publications Ltd. A receiver was appointed on 15 October 1975. Drury was dismissed at 4pm on Friday 17 October. At 6.30pm on Friday 17 October the business of Champion Publications Ltd was transferred to Teesside Times Ltd. On Monday 20 October Drury went to work for Teesside Times Ltd. He was dismissed by Teesside Times Ltd that night. Teesside Times argued that continuity was broken because Drury was not employed at the time they took over. Goff LJ thought that phrase 'at the time of the transfer' meant moment (or as near as possible) of time. Stephenson LJ found that it meant the period of transfer, but that a gap which broke the continuity of employment under what is now Sched 13 to the EP(C)A 1978 would be fatal. Eveleigh LJ found that the length of the gap was not material.

In *Macer v Abafast Ltd* [1990] IRLR 137, Macer was employed by CTR Ltd (CTR). On 31 December 1986, Macer was told his employment with CTR had come to an end. It was intended to transfer the business to a subsidiary of Abafast, CTR (Recruitment) Ltd. The transfer took place in stages. On 21 January 1987 Abafast wrote to Macer offering him employment with effect from 12 January. Macer was subsequently dismissed. Did the gap between 31 December and 12 January break his continuous employment? The EAT held that para 17(2) of Sched 13 can be construed as having four essentials:

The first essential is the transfer and therefore the continuation of the business or undertaking. The second is employment by the owner before the transfer or change of ownership and by the owner after. The third essential is the period of service with the former must be continuous within paras 1 to 16 of Schedule 13, and likewise the periods of service with the latter. Fourthly, that the combined periods of service must satisfy the qualification period.

It construed para 17(2) of Sched 13 as meaning:

Provided that there has been a valid transfer of a business from A to B, then the continuous period of service of an employee with A may be added to the continuous period of service with B so as to establish a qualifying period of continuous employment . . .

The EAT rejected the view that the words 'at the time of the transfer' in para 17(2) referred to a moment in time. The decision of the EAT in *Brook Lane Finance Co Ltd v Bradley* [1988] IRLR 283, was not followed. Macer's continuity of employment was not broken. The EAT was influenced by the view of Eveleigh LJ in *Drury*'s case above and by the purposive approach of the House of Lords in *Litster v Forth Dry Dock and Engineering Co Ltd* [1989] IRLR 161.

There would appear to be a conflict with para 1 of Sched 13 which provides that a week which does not count breaks the continuity of employment. See the decision of Stephenson LJ in *Drury*'s case above. See also *Gibson*'s case, above.

If one body corporate is substituted for another body corporate as the employer Paragraph 17(3) of Sched 13 to the EP(C)A 1978 provides:

If by or under an Act of Parliament whether public or local and whether passed before or after this Act a contract of employment between any body corporate and an employee is modified and some other body corporate is substituted as the employer, the employee's period of employment at the time when the modification takes effect shall count as a period of employment with the second mentioned body corporate, and the change of employer shall not break the continuity of the period of employment.

If the employer dies and his personal representatives or trustees keep the employee on in employment Paragraph 17(4) of Sched 13 to the EP(C)A 1978 provides:

If on the death of an employer the employee is taken into the employment of the personal representatives or trustees of the deceased, the employee's period of employment at the time of the death shall count as a period of employment with the employer's personal representatives or trustees, and the death shall not break the continuity of the period of employment.

At common law the death of an employee automatically terminates the contract of employment. However, if the employee is employed by the deceased's personal representatives or trustees, continuity may be preserved.

The employee may be his deceased employer's personal representative. As the personal representative he has power to contract with himself as an individual and continuity of employment will not be broken: *Rowley, Holmes and Co v Barber* [1977] ICR 387. Where the employee, as well as being personal representative, is also beneficially entitled to the business, the position remains the same so long as the business remains part of the estate. If the employee sells the business as personal representative and continues in the employment of the purchaser, there will be no break under these provisions in the continuity of employment: *Rowley, Holmes and Co v Barber*, above.

If there is a change in the partners, personal representatives or trustees
Paragraph 17(5) of Sched 13 to the EP(C)A 1978 provides:

If there is a change in the partners, personal representatives or trustees who employ any person, the employee's period of employment at the time of the change shall count as a period of employment with the partners, personal representatives or trustees after the change, and the change shall not break the continuity of the period of employment.

At common law a change in the partnership is a change of employer.

Although a partner leaving a partnership or dying might not affect the contracts of employment of the partnership employees, a major change in the partnership may have the effect of terminating the employee's contract of employment: see *Tunstall and Another v Condon and Another* [1980] ICR 786, where the decision in *Brace v Calder* [1895] 2 QB 253 was considered.

Paragraph 17(5) of Sched 13 is intended to deal with the situation where there is a change in the partnership. Where there is a change from employment by a partnership to employment by a sole partner, continuity of employment is not preserved under para 17(5) of Sched 13: see *Harold Fielding Ltd v Mansi* [1974] IRLR 79. Where there is a change from employment by an individual to employment by a partnership where that individual becomes a partner, para 17(5) of Sched 13 does not preserve continuity: *Wynne v Hair Control* [1978] ICR 870.

In *Allen and Son v Coventry* [1979] IRLR 399, the employee was employed by a partnership of two solicitors. The senior partner retired, leaving the junior partner as the sole proprietor. The employee was subsequently dismissed and the EAT had to consider whether or not para 17(5) of Sched 13 preserved continuity. The EAT distinguished the cases of *Fielding v Mansi* and *Wynne v Hair Control*, above, finding that in each of these cases different businesses were involved, whereas this was the continuation of the same business. The EAT would have striven to interpret para 17(5) of Sched 13 as conferring continuity if it had been necessary to do so. However, the EAT found that there was a transfer of the ownership of the business within para 17(2) of Sched 13 and continuity of employment was preserved under that provision.

In *Jeetle v Elster* [1985] ICR 389, Elster was employed by a partnership of four doctors. The partnership was dissolved and Dr Jeetle set up as a sole practitioner in one of the surgeries previously operated by the partnership. He kept the majority of the patients who had previously attended that surgery and some others transferred to him from the other surgery previously operated by the partnership. He also acquired certain assets of the partnership. Elster joined Dr Jeetle. Did she have continuity of employment? Again, the EAT found that if necessary it would have interpreted para 17(5) of Sched 13 as preserving continuity. It found that the argument that ' "where one of two partners leaves the partnership, there are no partners but only a sole proprietor, after the change", . . . [was] correct in pure legal terminology . . . The expression "sole partner" is no doubt legally inaccurate but is extensively used and everyone knows what it means.' Again the EAT found that para 17(2) of Sched 13 preserved continuity because there was a transfer from one person to another within the meaning of para 17(2) of Sched 13, the other being a partner in the firm at the time of the transfer.

If the employee of one employer is taken into the employment of another employer Paragraph 18 of Sched 13 to the EP(C)A 1978 provides that:

if an employee of an employer is taken into the employment of another employer who, at the time when the employee enters his employment, is an associated employer of the first-mentioned employer, the employee's period of employment at that time shall count as a period of employment with the second-mentioned employer and the change of employer shall not break the continuity of the period of employment.

Section 153(4) of the EP(C)A 1978 provides, for the purposes of the EP(C)A 1978 Act, that any two employers are to be treated as associated if one is a company of which the other (directly or indirectly) has control, or if both are companies of which a third person (directly or indirectly) has control; and the expression 'associated employer' shall be construed accordingly.

Section 153(4) was considered in *Gardiner v London Borough of Merton* [1980] IRLR 472, where it was held that this section applies only where at least one of the employers concerned is a company with limited liability. For the purposes of para 18 of Sched 13, the definition of associated employer in s 153(4) is exhaustive. It follows that since a local authority is not a limited company local authorities could not be associated employers within s 153(4). See also *Southwood Hostel Management Committee v Taylor* [1979] IRLR 397.

Other forms of statutory bodies corporate are excluded: *Hasley v Fair Employment Agency* [1989] IRLR 106. A partnership of companies is within the definition: *Pinkney v Sandpiper Drilling Ltd* [1989] ICR 389. This case is difficult to reconcile with s 153(4) of the EP(C)A 1978. Likewise, a foreign company may be within the definition if it can be likened in its essentials to a company incorporated under the Companies Acts: *Hancill v Marcon Engineering Ltd* [1990] ICR 103.

'Control' in s 153(4) of the 1978 Act in the context of a limited company means control by the majority of votes attaching to shares exercised in general meetings. It is not control in the sense of how or by whom the enterprise is actually run: *The Secretary of State for Employment v (1) Newbold and (2) Joint Liquidators of David Arm-*

strong (Catering Services) Ltd [1981] IRLR 305; and see also *Umar v Pliastar Ltd* [1981] ICR 727. However, see *Secretary of State for Employment v Chapman and Another* [1989] ICR 771, where it was suggested that, exceptionally, factors other than voting control could be considered.

In *Zarb and Samuels v British and Brazilian Produce Co Sales Ltd* [1978] IRLR 78, it was held that 'person' may include a group of people exercising control, provided they act as one. This approach was followed in *Harford v Swiftrim Ltd* [1987] ICR 439.

In *South West Launderettes Ltd v Laidler* [1986] IRLR 305, South West Launderettes Ltd was controlled by S who held 94 per cent of the shares, the remainder being held by his son. There were other companies in which S had 50 per cent of the shares and his wife held the other 50 per cent. The Court of Appeal held that the persons controlling the companies were different and although S was the controller of South West Launderettes Ltd the other companies were controlled by Mr and Mrs S. Therefore, South West Launderettes Ltd and the other companies were not associated employers, because the third person was not the same person in each case. It also found that an alternative argument that S controlled all the companies failed because there was no evidence that S had any control over his wife's shares, or that he could exercise the voting powers which attached to his wife's shares. In this case the Court of Appeal cast considerable doubt on whether two or more individuals acting in concert could be a third person for the purposes of s 153(4) of the EP(C)A 1978.

In *Chapman*'s case above, it was held that where A held 50 per cent of the shares and B held 50 per cent of the shares as nominee for A, A had control. In *Hair Colour Consultants Ltd v Mena* [1984] ICR 671, it was held that a 50 per cent holding on its own did not give control. Negative control was not sufficient. *Laidler*'s case was followed in *Strudwick v Iszatt Brothers Ltd* [1988] ICR 796, where it was held that even if the third person can be more than one individual, the same individual, and not a varying combination, must have voting control over each relevant company. In this case Wood J expressed the view, *obiter*, that *Harford*'s case, above, would create an enormous problem and if necessary he would adopt the view of Mustill LJ in *Laidler*'s case, above, who did not accept the concept of plural control at all. See also *Poparm Ltd v Weekes* [1984] IRLR 388. In *Russell v Elmdon Freight Terminal Ltd* [1989] ICR 629, *Laidler*'s case was followed where no one person had voting control over two relevant companies and there was insufficient evidence to establish *de facto* joint control by two persons. A 'dormant' company may be an associated employer: see *Charnock and Another v Barrie Muirhead Ltd* [1984] ICR 641. Charnock was dismissed by company A and was not taken on by company B until some two weeks later. Company B had not previously had any employees. (The employee's continuity of employment was preserved by para 11 of Sched 13—when the employee was dismissed he was entitled to three weeks' statutory notice which meant that the effective date of termination with company A was postponed by three weeks thereby bridging the cap.) It was held that although company B had not previously been an employer it became an employer on the day when the employer entered its employment, and was an associated employer.

A gap between the employment with associated employers will not defeat the continuity of employment, provided it is preserved under Sched 13: see *Binns v Versil Ltd* [1975] IRLR 273 and *Charnock and Another v Barrie Muirhead Ltd*, above.

Continuity of employment in certain schools   Paragraph 18A of Sched 13 to the EP(C)A 1978 provides that where an employee of one employer is taken into the employment of another employer, and both those employers are governors of schools maintained by a local education authority and that authority, his period of employment at the time of the change shall count as a period of employment with the second employer and shall not break his continuity of employment.

Estoppel   At one stage it seemed that if, on a change of employer, the new employer promised the employee that he would honour the former employer's obligations to the employee, the new employer could be estopped from alleging a break in the continuity of employment and so defeating the employee's rights: *Evenden v Guildford City Association Football Club* [1975] ICR 367, and *Secretary of State for Employment v Globe Elastic Thread Co Ltd* [1978] ICR 1041. However, in *Secretary of State for Employment v Globe Elastic Thread Co Ltd* [1979] ICR 706, the House of Lords overruled the earlier decisions and held that continuity on a transfer of employment could only arise in accordance with the statutory provisions, and that nothing in the nature of an estoppel between the employer and the employee could confer jurisdiction on the tribunal beyond that given to it by statute. Where there is an enforceable agreement between the employer and the employee that the employer will honour the existing continuous period of employment, its failure to do so may give rise to an action in damages for breach of contract.

7 Effective date of termination

Where the contract of employment is terminated by the employer and the notice required by s 49 of the EP(C)A 1978 to be given by the employer would, if duly given on the material date, expire on a later date than the effective date of termination under s 55(4), that later date is to be treated as the effective date of termination in relation to the dismissal for certain purposes: s 55(5) of the EP(C)A

1978. The material date is the date when notice of termination was given by the employer, or where no notice was given, the date when the contract of employment was terminated by the employer: s 55(7)(*a*) of the EP(C)A 1978. This provision may prolong the period of continuous employment in certain circumstances: see para 11(1) of Sched 13 to the EP(C)A 1978.

Where the contract of employment is terminated by the employee and the material date does not fall during a period of notice given by the employer to terminate the contract, and had the contract been terminated not by the employee but by notice given on the material date by the employer, that notice would have been required by s 49 to expire on a later date than the effective date of termination under s 55(4), that later date is to be treated as the effective date of termination for certain purposes: s 55(6) of the EP(C)A 1978. Material date means the date when notice of termination was given by the employee or, where no notice was given, the date when the contract of employment was terminated by the employee: s 55(7)(*b*) of the EP(C)A 1978. This provision may prolong the period of continuous employment in certain circumstances: see para 11(1) of Sched 13 to the EP(C)A 1978. See also *Charnock and Another v Barrie Muirhead Ltd* [1984] ICR 641. See Chapter 4 for the effective date of termination.

8 Impact of Community law

The Equal Opportunities Commission has commenced proceedings against the government. In an application for judicial review it is seeking a declaration that the UK is in breach of its obligation under art 119 of the Treaty of Rome and Directive 75/117 (alternatively Directive 76/207), by providing less favourable treatment for part-time employees, most of whom are women, than for full-time employees, most of whom are men, in relation to, *inter alia*, the qualifying hours for claiming unfair dismissal.

However, it has not been successful in the High Court. See *R v Secretary of State for Employment ex parte Equal Opportunities Commission and another* (1991) *The Times*, 11 October.

Chapter 3

Dismissal

To claim unfair dismissal, an employee must have been dismissed. The onus of proving dismissal is on the employee.

1 The meaning of dismissal

The EP(C)A 1978 defines dismissal for the purposes of a claim for unfair dismissal in s 55(2). Dismissal may arise in the following cases.

1.1 Termination of employment by the employer

The employee is treated as dismissed where the contract under which he is employed is terminated by the employer whether with or without notice: s 55(2)(*a*) of the EP(C)A 1978. For the purpose of this provision, it is irrelevant that the contract is terminated by the employer with proper notice or with incorrect notice, or that it is terminated without notice whether with or without wages in lieu of notice.

(a) With notice The giving of notice by the employer or employee is a unilateral act, and once given, it can only be withdrawn with the agreement of the other, although, if the employer attempts to withdraw the notice, the withdrawal may be treated as an offer of new employment: *Riordan v War Office* [1959] 1 WLR 1046; see also *Harris and Russell Ltd v Slingsby* [1973] IRLR 221.

A possible exception arises where the employee is dismissed but successfully appeals against the decision to dismiss him under an internal disciplinary procedure resulting in an offer of reinstatement by the employer: see *Petch v Taunton Deane DC* (1977) (unreported), where the tribunal considered that the effect of the offer of reinstatement might be to render the notice null and void, because that was the intention of the parties under such an agreement, further, or in the alternative, that the notice in such a case is conditional, the employee impliedly agreeing that if his appeal is successful, the employer may withdraw the notice. See also *Savage v J Sainsbury Ltd* [1980] IRLR 109.

Notice, whether given by the employer or employee, must be specific. It should specify the date when it is to take effect, or if it does not specify the date, it must at least make it possible for the date to be deduced with certainty from what is said: *Morton Sundour Fabrics Ltd v Shaw* (1967) 2 ITR 84; see also *Hughes v Gwynedd Area Health Authority* [1978] ICR 161. It is not sufficient for the employer to tell the employee that the date of termination will be some specific date or such earlier date as the employer may select, whether or not it is coupled with a statement that the earlier date will not be earlier than the date upon which the contract could be brought to an end by the requisite period of notice: see *The Burton Group Ltd v Smith* [1977] IRLR 351.

In *Brown v Southall and Knight* [1980] IRLR 130, it was held that the summary dismissal of an employee by letter could not take effect until the employee had read the letter or had been granted a reasonable opportunity of reading it. In *Hindle Gears Ltd v McGinty and Others* [1984] IRLR 477, it was held that communication of a decision to dismiss an employee in terms which either bring it expressly to the attention of the employee, or give him at least a reasonable opportunity of learning of it, was essential.

An employee's contract of employment may be divisible into two distinct parts. The employer may by notice terminate part of the contract without bringing the contract to an end. In *Land and Wilson v West Yorkshire Metropolitan County Council* [1981] IRLR 87, the employee had initially been employed solely as a full-time fireman. Subsequently he had agreed to be available for work if required during his off-duty periods. The employer subsequently terminated with notice the arrangement under which the employee agreed to be available during his off-duty periods. It was held that it was open to the employer to terminate simply that part of the contract relating to his off-duty work.

Where an employer gives notice to an employee but tells the employee that he does not require the employee to continue to perform his duties, and the employee does not return to work, the employer and not the employee has brought the contract to an end: *Springbank Sand and Gravel Co Ltd v Craig* [1973] IRLR 278. Where an employer has given notice it is always open to the employer during the period of notice to dismiss the employee summarily before the expiration of the period of notice: *Stapp v The Shaftesbury Society* [1982] IRLR 326.

(b) The effect of warnings A warning of dismissal as opposed to notice will not operate to determine the contract of employment. Whether a warning or notice of dismissal was given is a question of fact. An example of a warning arises where, in a redundancy situation, employees are told that they may be dismissed for redundancy in the future: *Morton Sundour Fabrics Ltd v Shaw*, above: see also *International Computers Ltd v Kennedy* [1981] IRLR 28. An employer may

warn the employee against a repetition of a particular course of conduct or will seek through warnings to achieve an improvement in the employee's performance. Warnings of this nature will not amount to a dismissal in law except where the employer is not justified in giving a warning, or where the employer uses abusive language to the employee in administering the warning and the employer is thereby guilty of repudiatory conduct entitling the employee to resign and claim a constructive dismissal. See **1.3**, below.

In *Haseltine Lake and Co v Dowler* [1981] IRLR 25, the employee was told by a partner in the firm that he should seek a job elsewhere. When he asked what would happen if he failed to do so, he was told that he would have to be dismissed. No date for termination was given but the employee was told that he was expected to be gone by the end of the summer. It was held that there was no dismissal because the employer did not specify the date at which the employment was to come to an end, nor was a date positively ascertainable. Nor was this a case where the employers told the employee, 'resign or you will be dismissed forthwith or at a specified or ascertainable date'. *East Sussex County Council v Walker* (1972) 7 ITR 280, was distinguished because in *Walker's* case the employee was told that her job was to come to an end forthwith and she was invited to resign.

(c) Dismissal without notice The employer may terminate the contract without notice where he tells the employee that he is dismissed with immediate effect. The employer may also bring the contract to an end without notice by his use of words or actions.

(d) The problems of language It may not be clear from the language used by the employer whether or not the employer is terminating the employee's contract of employment. The use of abusive language by the employer may entitle the employee to resign and claim a constructive dismissal. Whether or not the words used by the employer terminate the contract of employment other than in a case involving a constructive dismissal has been considered by the tribunals, the EAT and the Court of Appeal.

The problem is illustrated by the following cases. In *Kendrick v Aerduct Productions* [1974] IRLR 322, an employee, having told his employer that he was hoping to take a tenancy of an off-licence, was told to 'fuck off and play with your shop'. It was held that he had been dismissed. In *King v Webbs Poultry Products (Bradford) Ltd* [1975] IRLR 135, it was held that the use of the words 'piss off' and 'fuck off' could only mean the employee was being dismissed where the employer took the initiative in terminating the contract of employment.

However, the employer's use of the expression 'fuck off' does not necessarily amount to a dismissal. Among the fish filleters of Hull, the use of the words, 'if you do not like the job, fuck off' means 'if you don't like the work you are doing, clock off. You will receive no pay after you clock off. You can come back to work the next day when you are disposed to do some work.' If a dismissal is imminent 'unexpected formality seems to descend upon the parties': *Futty v Brekkes (D&D) Ltd* [1974] IRLR 130. A similar conclusion was reached where the managing director of a building firm said to a building worker, 'If you are not satisfied, you can fuck off.' The tribunal found that in the circumstances, the manager was saying, 'If you don't like it, you can lump it.' The employee not liking it chose to lump it, and left the work never to return: *Davy v JE Collins (Builders) Ltd* [1974] IRLR 324.

What approach is to be adopted where ambiguous or indeed unambiguous words of dismissal are used? In *Tanner v DT Kean* [1978] IRLR 110, the employer had loaned Tanner a sum of money to enable him to purchase his own transport to stop him using the employer's transport. The employer discovered Tanner was still using his van and said, 'What's my fucking van doing outside? . . . I've just lent you £275 to buy a car and you are too tight to put juice in it. That's it; you're finished with me.' The EAT held when it is uncertain whether words or actions constitute a dismissal or resignation or not:

it is necessary to look at all the circumstances of the case, in particular to see what was the intention with which the words were spoken . . .

In our judgment the test which has to be applied in cases of this kind is along these lines. Were the words spoken those of dismissal, that is to say, were they intended to bring the contract of employment to an end? What was the employer's intention? In answering that a relevant, and perhaps the most important, question is how would a reasonable employee, in all the circumstances, have understood what the employer intended by what he said and did?

It further held that it was relevant to look at the events after the use of the words and before the employee's departure in order to establish the employer's intention. The EAT envisaged that 'in the case of ambiguous words, the test to be applied was a subjective one. *Gale (GB) Ltd v Gilbert* [1978] ICR 1149, gives some support to this approach. In *J and J Stern v Simpson* [1983] IRLR 52, there was a heated discussion during which one of the partners said to the employee 'go, get out, get out'. The EAT followed the decision of the Court of Appeal in *Sothern v Franks Charlesly and Co* [1981] IRLR 278, see below. It held that it was necessary to construe the words in all the circumstances to determine whether an employee has resigned or been dismissed, and that only where the words used are ambiguous after considering them in their context must a further test be applied; whether any reasonable employer or employee might have understood the words to be tantamount to a dismissal or resignation.

The following cases all involving a resignation by the employee, but relevant to cases involving a dismissal, are of assistance in establishing the principles to be applied where unambiguous words are used.

In *Gale (GB) Ltd v Gilbert*, above, Gilbert lost his temper and said to the employer, 'I'm leaving, I want my cards.' The EAT found that in the circumstances of this case the words were unambiguous and therefore the employee's resignation stood. It was not relevant to consider what a reasonable employer should have or would have understood.

In *Sothern v Franks Charlesly and Co*, above, Sothern again told the employer, 'I am resigning.' Fox LJ held that the words 'I am resigning' were unambiguous words of resignation so understood by her employer. Where unambiguous words are used, what a reasonable employer might have understood was not relevant. The natural meaning of the words and the fact that the employer understood them to mean that the employee was resigning could not be overridden by considerations of what a reasonable employer might have assumed. 'The non-disclosed intention of a person using language as to his intended meaning is not properly to be taken into account in determining what the true meaning is.' Fox LJ did not find it inconsistent with the conclusion which he had reached that the employee returned to work and stayed on for some weeks after she had said that 'I am resigning'.

In *Barclay v City of Glasgow District Council* [1983] IRLR 313, the EAT accepted that there might be exceptions to the principle that where unambiguous words of resignation were used the employer is entitled to accept the resignation. The exceptions included cases of an immature employee, or where a decision was taken in the heat of the moment, or where the employee was jostled into the decision by the employer, or where idle words were used under emotional stress which the employer knew or ought to have known were not meant to be taken seriously. In such cases a duty is imposed upon the employer to take into account the special circumstances of the employee before relying on the unambiguous words used by the employee.

In *Sovereign House Security Services Ltd v Savage* [1989] IRLR 115, the Court of Appeal, per May LJ, held:

. . . generally speaking, where unambiguous words of resignation are used by an employee to the employer . . . and are so understood by the employer, the proper conclusion of fact is that the employee has in truth resigned. In my view tribunals should not be astute to find otherwise. However, in some cases there may be something in the context of the exchange between the employer and the employee or, in the circumstances of the employee him or herself, to entitle the Tribunal . . . to conclude that notwithstanding the appearance there was no real resignation despite what it might appear to be at first sight.

It is difficult to extract guidelines from the reported cases. However, the following propositions can be put forward. The employer's intention will not generally be relevant, but see *Tanner*'s case, above. Unambiguous words must be construed at face value and given their ordinary meaning, unless the circumstances suggest otherwise. When ambiguous words are used, the question is what would a reasonable person have understood the words to mean. Thus, in interpreting the words used, whether the words used are ambiguous or unambiguous, an objective test must be adopted. There may be circumstances where unambiguous words are used which may not be binding on the employer, and he may be entitled to withdraw the same.

In *Martin v Yeoman Aggregates Ltd* [1983] IRLR 49, the EAT found that unambiguous words of dismissal or resignation used in the heat of the moment did not bring the contract to an end if they were immediately withdrawn. The party using the words should have the opportunity of recanting. It is a question of degree. Furthermore, it must be seen as an exception to the rule that once notice has been given by either the employer or the employee it cannot be withdrawn without the consent of the other party.

Just as the employer's words may operate to terminate the contract of employment, so the employer by his conduct may also bring about the termination of the contract of employment. The giving of a P45 does not of itself bring about the termination of the contract. Removing an employee's clock card may in certain circumstances amount to a dismissal, although where it is withdrawn pending investigation of some act of misconduct, it may be no more than an indication that management does not require the employee to work until the action has been investigated. Again the removal of the clock card may simply show that the employee is not wanted or is released from work for that particular day.

1.2 Expiration of fixed-term contracts

The employee is treated as dismissed when he is employed under a contract for a fixed term and that term expires without being renewed under the same contract: s 55(2)(*b*) of the EP(C)A 1978. A fixed-term contract is not defined by the legislation. If the contract is for a fixed term it fixes the maximum duration of the employment, whether or not the contract contains a power for either party to bring the contract to an end by giving notice to the other party before the expiration of the period certain: *BBC v Dixon* [1979] IRLR 114; *BBC v Constanti* [1979] IRLR 114. In *Wiltshire County Council v NATFHE and Guy* [1980] IRLR 198, the employee was engaged by the authority as a part-time teacher. It was held that she had a fixed-term contract starting at the beginning of the autumn term and ending on the last day of the summer term. The number of hours which she worked in each week fluctuated according to the number of students. It did not matter that through poor student attendance a course might stop and that she would not be paid. Her contractual obligation continued for the whole of the session. The Court of Appeal distinguished the contract where the employee was simply involved for a specific task which is not a contract for a fixed term: see *Ryan v Shipboard Maintenance Ltd* [1980] IRLR 16. In the case of a contract for the undertaking of a specific task it is not possible to ascertain the precise date in the future when the contract will come to an end.

In *Brown and Others v Knowsley Borough Council* [1986] IRLR 102, Brown's employment was to last only as long as sufficient funds were provided by the Manpower Services Commission (MSC) or any other firms or sponsors. When the MSC funding ceased, the contract of employment came to an end. It was held that she had not been dismissed. There was no fixed-term contract and so there was no dismissal.

1.3 Constructive dismissal

(a) General The employee is treated as dismissed where he terminates the contract with or without notice in circumstances such that he is entitled to terminate it without notice by reason of the employer's conduct: s 55(2)(c) of the EP(C)A 1978. The employee's termination of the contract in such circumstances is treated as a constructive dismissal.

In determining whether or not the employee is entitled to terminate the contract without notice by reason of the employer's conduct and have the termination treated as constructive dismissal, the test, which is commonly called the contract test, has to be applied—does the employer's conduct amount to a repudiation of the contract? See *Western Excavating (ECC) Ltd v Sharp* [1978] ICR 221.

For there to be a repudiation by the employer, the employer must by his act or omission be guilty of either a fundamental breach of the contract or a breach of a fundamental term of the contract. The term may be express or implied. The act or omission of the employer must go to the root of the contract. The employer must have evinced an intention no longer to be bound by the contract of employment: *London Borough of Camden v Pedersen* [1979] IRLR 377; see on appeal *Pedersen v London Borough of Camden* [1981] IRLR 173. A unilateral alteration by the employer of a minor or inconsequential term will not amount to a repudiation: *Gillies v Richard Daniels and Co Ltd* [1979] IRLR 457.

In *Western Excavating (ECC) Ltd v Sharp*, above, Sharp was found guilty of misconduct and suspended from work for five days without pay. Sharp did not dispute the justice of the company's decision. However, his financial plight forced him to ask the company for his accrued holiday pay or a loan. The company refused and he left claiming a constructive dismissal. The tribunal found that the company ought to have bent over backwards to help Sharp and found the dismissal unfair. The EAT felt it could not interfere. In reaching its decision the tribunal and the EAT had applied a test of reasonableness to the employer's conduct. The Court of Appeal rejected the application of any test of reasonableness. Lord Denning MR held:

If the employer is guilty of conduct which is a significant breach going to the root of the contract of employment; or which shows that the employer no longer intends to be bound by one or more of the essential terms of the contract; then the employee is entitled to treat himself as discharged from any further performance. If he does so, then he terminates the contract by reason of the employer's conduct. He is constructively dismissed. The employee is entitled in those circumstances to leave at the instant without giving any notice at all or, alternatively, he may give notice and say he is leaving at the end of the notice. But the conduct must in either case be sufficiently serious to entitle him to leave at once. Moreover, he must make up his mind soon after the conduct of which he complains: for, if he continues for any length of time without leaving, he will lose his right to treat himself as discharged. He will be regarded as having elected to affirm the contract.

Lord Denning adopted the common law test, Lawton LJ adopted a different approach he held:

For the purpose of this judgment I do not find it either necessary or advisable to express any opinion as to what principles of law operate to bring a contract of employment to an end by reason of an employer's conduct. Sensible persons have no difficulty in recognising such conduct when they hear about it. Persistent and unwanted amorous advances by an employer to a female member of his staff would, for example, clearly be such conduct.

Although recognising the need for a breach of a contractual term, Lawton LJ's approach was much wider and has enabled tribunals to find new implied terms in a contract of employment so that the result may sometimes be very little different from the application of a test of reasonableness. See (b), below.

This case firmly establishes that the test to be applied is one based on contract. In (1) Spafax Ltd v Harrison and (2) Spafax Ltd v Taylor [1980] IRLR 442, the Court of Appeal made it clear that in Western Excavating (EEC) Ltd v Sharp Lord Denning was not intending to distinguish between conduct which is a significant breach going to the root of the contract, and conduct which shows that the employer no longer intends to be bound by one or more of the essential terms of the contract, so that the latter course of conduct does not necessarily involve a breach of the contract. The Court of Appeal held that conduct which shows that the employer no longer intends to be bound by one or more essential terms will be a repudiation. Where the employer's action is lawful and does not involve a breach of contract it will not be a repudiation. The tribunal, having established the evidence, must decide whether or not there has been a constructive dismissal. There is no rule of law for determining whether a particular set of facts amounts to a fundamental breach of the contract by the employer entitling the employee to claim a constructive dismissal: *Woods v WM Car Services (Peterborough) Ltd* [1982] IRLR 413.

In deciding whether or not there has been a repudiation of the contract of employment by the employer, the fact that the employer neither intended to repudiate the contract nor that the employer did not reasonably believe that its conduct would be accepted as repudiatory, is not the proper test to apply. It is necessary to determine whether, viewed objectively, the employer's conduct evinced an intention no longer to be bound by the contract: *Lewis v Motorworld Garages Ltd* [1985] IRLR 465. See also *Post Office v Roberts* [1980] IRLR 347, where it was held that where the employer's conduct breaches the implied obligation of mutual trust and confidence, it does not matter that the employer did not intend his conduct to have that effect.

Again it is not relevant in deciding whether or not the employer has repudiated the contract of employment to examine whether or not the employer can justify the steps which it took. This will be relevant in considering whether or not the dismissal was fair or unfair under s 57(3) of the EP(C)A 1978: *Wadham Stringer Commercials (London) Ltd and Wadham Stringer Vehicles Ltd v Brown* [1983] IRLR 46. An earlier line of decisions which suggested a test based on reasonableness can be regarded as bad law. For an example of one of the earlier decisions: see *Scott v Aveling Barford Ltd* [1978] ICR 214. However, in *Dutton and Clark Ltd v Daly* [1985] IRLR 363, the EAT, in considering whether the employer had breached the contract by failing to take adequate safety precautions to protect a cashier against robberies, applied a modified test of reasonableness. It is submitted that the decision is wrong in law.

In *Courtaulds Northern Spinning Ltd v Sibson and Another* [1988] ICR 451, the employers required Sibson, an HGV driver, to transfer to a different depot a mile away to avoid conflict with the union. The Court of Appeal found there was an implied term that Sibson could be required to work at any place within reasonable daily reach of his home. This was sufficient protection for Sibson. There was no need or justification to import into the implied term a requirement that the request must be reasonable or for genuine operational reasons. In *Prestwick Circuits Ltd v McAndrew* [1990] IRLR 191, a case also involving a change in the workplace, the Court of Session accepted there was an implied term that McAndrew could be required to move but reasonable notice had to be given.

In *United Bank Ltd v Akhtar* [1989] IRLR 507, the bank insisted that Akhtar moved immediately under a contractual mobility clause. The EAT found that there was an implied term that reasonable notice would be given to Akhtar and that the employer's conduct in requiring an immediate move was a fundamental breach of the implied duty of trust. This implied duty may qualify a contractual right. Although this decision conflicts with the Court of Appeal's decision in *Sibson*'s case, none of these cases suggest that the test is other than a contractual test. The employer's failure to act responsibly may result in there being a breach of an implied term: see *White v Reflecting Road Studs Ltd* [1991] IRLR 331.

Whether there has been a repudiation, whether the employer has committed a fundamental breach of the contract or a breach of a fundamental term, might appear to be essentially a question of law. Initially that was the view of the EAT. However, in *Woods v WM Car Services (Peterborough) Ltd* [1981] IRLR 347, the EAT considered that in *Pederson v London Borough of Camden*, above, the Court of Appeal had found:

that the questions whether there has been a breach of contract and, if so, whether such breach is fundamental are both mixed questions of fact and law so that the Employment Appeal Tribunal cannot substitute its decision for that of the Industrial Tribunal if there was evidence which would justify the Industrial Tribunal's decision.

The decision of the EAT was upheld by the Court of Appeal: see *Woods v WM Car Services (Peterborough) Ltd* [1982] IRLR 413.

While a unilateral change by the employer in a fundamental term of the contract will be a repudiation, if the parties agree to the change then there is a consensual variation and no repudiation. The employer may have reserved the right to make a change in the contract. A change made in accordance with the contractual right will not be a repudiation. See above.

(b) Terms of the contract   To enable the employee to claim constructive dismissal the employer must fundamentally breach the contract of employment or breach a fundamental term of the contract of employment.

The terms of the contract may be express or implied, and may be oral or written. Certain implied contractual terms have long been recognised, such as the obligation to pay agreed wages promptly; or to take reasonable care for the employee's safety; but new implied contractual terms have been recognised by the courts and the tribunals coincidentally with the acceptance that the strict common law test should apply in determining whether the employer has constructively dismissed the employee although the process has not gone so far as to recognise an implied contractual term that the employer will behave reasonably (see *Post Office v Roberts* [1980] IRLR 347), because such a term was too wide and too vague.

In *FC Gardner Ltd v Beresford* [1978] IRLR 63, Beresford had not received any pay increases for two years, although other employees had received pay increases. The EAT held it was an implied term of the contract of employment that the employer will not treat the employee arbitrarily, capriciously or inequitably in matters of remuneration. In *Murco Petroleum Ltd v Forge* [1987] IRLR 50, it was held that where the contract of employment made no reference to pay increases it was impossible, as the tribunal had done, to imply a term in the contract of employment that there would always be a yearly pay rise so that a failure to give a pay rise in one year amounted to a constructive dismissal. The EAT further held that if the tribunal had considered whether or not the employer had acted arbitrarily or capriciously so as to be in breach of the implied duty of mutual trust and confidence, it would have reached the conclusion that the employer's action was neither arbitrary nor capricious.

In *British Aircraft Corporation Ltd v Austin* [1978] IRLR 332, Austin wore spectacles. She was required to wear safety goggles but because of her spectacles these were uncomfortable and unsatisfactory. Despite her complaints to management nothing was done and because she was concerned that she might suffer injury to her eyes she left her employment. The EAT held that the employers were in breach of a general obligation to take reasonable care for the safety of their employees. As part of that general obligation they were also under an obligation to act reasonably in dealing with matters of safety. Because they had failed to investigate complaints made by Austin promptly they had failed to take reasonable care. The EAT also found that if an employer behaves in a way which is not in accordance with good industrial relations practice to such an extent that the situation is intolerable or the employee cannot be expected to put up with it any longer, the employer will be in breach of an implied term of the contract of employment.

In *Palmanor Ltd (t/a Chaplins Night Club) v Cedron* [1978] ICR 1008, the manager used obscene language to the employee. The employee complained and the manager said, 'I can talk to you any way I like, you big cunt. . . . If you don't like it you can go.' The employee collected his things but the manager continued to be abusive; he threatened the employee that he would ensure that he did not get another job anywhere in London. While cautioning tribunals against attaching too much importance to words used in the heat of the moment, the EAT found that a time comes when, notwithstanding the fact that it is said in anger, an employee cannot be expected to tolerate it. The tribunal has to consider when the conduct was so unreasonable that it really went beyond the limits of the contract. In *Courtaulds Northern Textiles Ltd v Andrew* [1979] IRLR 84, an assistant manager told the employee who had had 18 years with the company, 'You can't do the bloody job anyway.' The EAT upheld the employee's claim that he had been constructively dismissed and found that any conduct which is likely to destroy or seriously damage the relationship of confidence and trust between employer and employee is something which goes to the root of the contract and is a fundamental breach.

In *Bliss v South East Thames Health Authority* [1985] IRLR 308, it was held that where the employer required Bliss, a part-time consultant in orthopaedics, to undergo a psychiatric examination where it had no reasonable cause to do so, the employer was acting in breach of a fundamental term of the contract of employment that the employer should not do anything calculated or likely to destroy the relationship of confidence and trust which ought to exist between employer and employee. In *Lewis v Motorworld Garages Ltd* [1985] IRLR 465, the Court of Appeal, following the decision of the EAT in *Woods v WM Car Services (Peterborough) Ltd* [1981] IRLR 347, held that it was now established that it was an 'implied term of the contract of employment that the employer will not, without reasonable and proper cause, conduct himself in a manner calculated or likely to destroy or seriously damage the relationship of confidence and trust between employer and employee'.

In *Wetherall (Bond Street W1) Ltd v Lynn* [1978] ICR 205, it was held that where a manager gave the employee a warning about his efficiency and performance, which the employee considered unfounded, and blackguarded him in the presence of his subordinates, there was a constructive dismissal.

Accusations made by the employer to the employee that the latter has been dishonest without any basis for the accusations will also be a breach of the implied term of mutual trust and confidence: *Robinson v Crompton Parkinson Ltd* [1978] ICR 401.

In *Wigan Borough Council v Davies* [1979] ICR 411, the EAT held it was an implied term of the contract of employment that the employer should take reasonable steps to ensure that the employee could do her job without harassment from fellow employees. No such steps had been taken, and, as it was in the employer's sphere of responsibility to take the appropriate action to remedy the situation, the onus was on them to show that there were no steps that they could reasonably have taken. They had not discharged that onus.

In *White v London Transport Executive* [1981] IRLR 261, it was held that there is an implied term in the contracts of employment of probationary employees that the employer will take reasonable steps to maintain an appraisal of the probationer during a trial period, giving guidance by advice or warning where necessary. The implied term is not so onerous that any employer is bound to support, assist, offer guidance to and train an employee during a probationary period.

The importance of implying new terms was considered by the EAT in *Woods v WM Car Services (Peterborough) Ltd* [1981] IRLR 347; see on appeal *Woods v WM Car Services (Peterborough) Ltd* [1982] IRLR 413. The EAT affirmed that there is implied in the contract of employment a term that the employer will not, without reasonable and proper cause, conduct itself in a manner calculated or likely to destroy or seriously damage the relationship of confidence and trust between the employer and employee. It held that if an employer persistently attempts to vary an employee's conditions of service, whether the conditions are contractual or otherwise, with a view to getting rid of the employee, or in varying the conditions of service acts in a manner which is calculated or likely to destroy the relationship of confidence and trust, he will have breached an implied term of the contract. The EAT recognised that one effect of the contract test as laid down in *Western Excavating (EEC) Ltd v Sharp*, above, is that an employer who wishes to get rid of an employee or to change the terms of the contract without paying unfair dismissal compensation or a redundancy payment, may try to squeeze out the employee. While not committing any major breach of the contract, the employer attempts to make the employee's life uncomfortable so that the employee resigns or accepts the changed terms. For this reason the implied term that the employer will conduct himself reasonably and not do anything calculated or likely to destroy or damage the relationship of mutual confidence and trust is of great importance.

In *Lewis v Motorworld Garages Ltd*, above, the Court of Appeal held:

it is now established that the repudiatory conduct may consist of a series of acts or incidents, some of them perhaps quite trivial, which cumulatively amount to a repudiatory breach of the implied term of the contract of employment, that the employer will not, without reasonable and proper cause, conduct himself in a manner calculated or likely to destroy or seriously damage the relationship of confidence and trust between employer and employee.

In *Hancox v David Strasburger Ltd* (1981) (unreported), the EAT held that there was an implied term in the contract of employment that neither the employer nor the employee should behave in a manner calculated or likely to destroy or seriously damage the relationship of mutual trust and confidence. In *Wood*'s case, above, the EAT were not able to interfere with the decision of the tribunal that there had been no breach of an implied term because the tribunal had considered the implied contractual term, and their decision was not perverse or based on an error of law. However, in *Hancox*'s case the tribunal had failed to consider an implied contractual term and the EAT was able to intervene. The cases of *Wood* and *Hancox* illustrate that in many cases there may be a series of incidents which result in the employee resigning. The particular incident which triggers the resignation, often called the 'last straw', need not in itself be a breach of contract. It is the cumulative series of acts taken together which must be examined to see whether or not there has been a breach of an implied term.

In *Bracebridge Engineering Ltd v Darby* [1990] IRLR 3, it was held that an employer's failure to treat allegations of sexual harassment seriously was a breach of the implied term of mutual trust, confidence and support towards a female employee.

In *Hilton International Hotels (UK) Ltd v Protopapa* [1990] IRLR 316, it was held that an unjustified reprimand given by the employee's supervisor which had the effect of humiliating, intimidating and degrading the employee was a breach of the implied term of trust and confidence which went to the root of the contract.

When new implied contractual terms are relied on, it will be for the employee to establish them. Thus, although there may be an express or implied term in some contracts allowing employees to have reasonable time off in an emergency, particularly where large employers are involved, there is no such term over the whole ambit of the employer and employee relationship, particularly where small employers are involved: *Warner v Barber's Stores* [1978] IRLR 109. If the new implied obligation has not been defined and established it is for the tribunal in the circumstances of each case to examine what would be reasonable in the general run of such cases: *Pepper and Hope v Daish* [1980] IRLR 13.

(c) Cases involving allegations of repudiatory conduct by the employer
The following are examples of cases where it was alleged the employer had breached a fundamental express or implied term of the contract and thus by his actions repudiated the same. Some of the cases were decided before *Western Excavating (ECC) Ltd v Sharp*, above, and although there is no specific reference to the contract test, the point in issue was whether or not there had been a fundamental breach of contract or a breach of a fundamental term by the employer.

Remuneration—non-payment Generally the employer's failure to pay the employee's wages in accordance with the terms of the contract agreed between them will be a repudiation by the employer. This may arise where the employee is suspended from employment where there is no right for the employer to suspend the employee without pay. Suspension without pay can only take place where there is a contractual term express or implied or an implied contractual right to suspend without pay arising from long usage or custom. Similarly the making of unauthorised deductions from wages may also amount to a repudiation of the contract of employment by the employer. In addition, the deduction may be in contravention of statute: see the Wages Act 1986. A unilateral reduction in the basic rate of pay, even for good reasons and even though it is small, may be a material breach of a fundamental term of the contract: *Industrial Rubber Products v Gillon* [1977] IRLR 389, where a reduction was made to regularise an inadvertent breach of the government's pay policy. However, not every reduction in remuneration will be a breach of a fundamental term. In *Gillies v Richard Daniels and Co Ltd* [1979] IRLR 457, the employer reduced payment made to Gillies for additional duties so that Gillies suffered a reduction of a maximum of £1.50 a week. It was held that although this was a unilateral change by the employer, it was not so fundamental as to strike at the root of the contract.

The employer's failure to give an employee overtime payment which was due to the employee, may also be a fundamental breach going to the root of the contract: *Stokes v Hampstead Wine Co Ltd* [1979] IRLR 298.

Remuneration—change in the method of computing wages   In *Graham v Glenrothes Time Switch Co* [1975] IRLR 43, a watchmaker was paid a basic wage plus overtime. He was told that he would be paid on a piece-work rate. He objected but the employer insisted. It was held that there was a repudiation of the contract by the employer.

The unilateral change by the employer of an express contractual term under which the employee was entitled to commission of 1 per cent on all sales to one which allowed him 1 per cent on sales over a target was a fundamental breach. It did not matter that subsequently the employer sought to justify it with figures which could not have been produced at the time of the change: *RF Hill Ltd v Mooney* [1981] IRLR 258.

A change which the employer is entitled to make which results in a reduction of commission may not be a fundamental breach of contract: see *(1) Spafax Ltd v Harrison* and *(2) Spafax Ltd v Taylor* [1980] IRLR 442.

Remuneration—failure to pay on the contractual date   In *Hanlon v Allied Breweries (UK) Ltd* [1975] IRLR 321, a barmaid was suspended with pay following a dispute with her superior. It was a term of her contract that she should be paid weekly on a Friday for work done in the week ending with the preceding Saturday. The employee was not paid while on suspension in accordance with her contract, that is, a weekly payment for the week worked up until the preceding Saturday. The tribunal held that this entitled the employee to resign and have her resignation treated as constructive dismissal because the employer had repudiated a term of the contract.

However, not every failure is a breach entitling the employee to resign and claim constructive dismissal: see *Adams v Charles Zub Associates Ltd* [1978] IRLR 551, where the employee was told when he enquired about payment that it depended upon payment being made by a foreign client.

Remuneration—failure to pay an increment   This may be a breach of an implied term of the contract of employment where everybody else has an increment or is to be given one and the employee is excluded: *Pepper and Hope v Daish* [1980] IRLR 13. The failure to pay may mean that the employer is treating the employee arbitrarily, capriciously or inequitably in breach of an implied term in the contract: see *FC Gardner Ltd v Beresford* [1978] IRLR 63. Alternatively, the non-payment may amount to victimisation which of itself may be a breach of an implied term.

Remuneration—change in fringe benefits In *Durrant and Cheshire v Clariston Clothing Ltd* [1974] IRLR 360, it was a term of the employment that both employees would receive free transport from their homes to their place of work. The company then discontinued the benefit, and although other proposals for transport were made, no agreement was reached. Free transport was an essential element of the contract, and since there were no other suitable means of getting to work, they resigned. The tribunal held that the decision to withdraw the free transport service was a breach of the employees' contracts of employment, entitling them to treat themselves as having been dismissed. The position may be different where the emoluments or fringe benefits are not fundamental terms of the contract.

Hours of employment A substantial unilateral change in the hours of work or the times at which such hours are worked may amount to a repudiation. An employer insisted that two female employees who worked respectively from 8.00am to 4.00pm and 8.30am to 4.30pm five days a week should change their hours of work to 8.30am to 4.30pm in one week, and from 9.30am to 5.30pm in the next week. Because of family commitments both refused. A tribunal held that by demanding a unilateral revision of the hours under which these ladies were employed, the employer had breached their contracts of employment: *Muggridge and Slade v East Anglia Plastics Ltd* [1973] IRLR 163. Similarly, altering the employee's shifts from night to day shifts is a breach of contract: *Simmonds v Dowty Seals Ltd* [1978] IRLR 211.

A ladies' hairdresser who did not usually work on Saturday afternoons, and was told that work on Saturday afternoons was to become compulsory, was entitled to claim that she had been dismissed: *Spencer Jones v Timmens Freeman* [1974] IRLR 325. In *Derby City Council v Marshall* [1979] IRLR 261, the employer repudiated the contract where it required the employee to be personally on call five days a week 24 hours a day.

Where the contractual terms on hours of work are varied by an agreement with the union, a change may be a repudiation of the individual's contract of employment. In *Singh v British Steel Corporation* [1974] IRLR 131, Singh was required to work a 15-shift system over a 5-day week. The employer then required the employee to work a 21-shift system over 7 days, which involved regular weekend working. The change in the system had been agreed with the union although there were no provisions in any agreement with the employee that the employer could change the system unilaterally. Singh had been a member of the union but ceased to pay union dues. After ceasing to pay union dues he no longer considered himself a member of the union, nor did he consider himself bound by its agreements. The agreement modifying the shift system was reached after Singh ceased to be a union member and was thus held not to be binding upon him. The tribunal was not prepared to imply a term in the contract of employment that the employee should be bound by agreements reached between the union and the employer, since there was no evidence establishing incorporation of the agreement in the individual's contract of employment.

There must be a firm proposal to alter the employee's hours of work. A mere suggestion by the employer as a basis for discussion, however, is not a repudiation of the contract of employment.

Where the employer has a contractual right to alter unilaterally the hours of work or to alter the pattern of shiftworking, the exercise of that power cannot be regarded as a breach by the employer of the contract of employment. See *Dal and Others v AS Orr* [1980] IRLR 413. The employer must have a contractual power and he must act in accordance with it.

Duties A substantial unilateral change in the work that the employee is required to do which involves a change of duties and loss of prestige is likely to amount to a repudiation. In *Coleman v S and W Baldwin (t/a Baldwins)* [1977] IRLR 342, the employee's duties as a buyer were an important part of his job. His employer took these away and left him with humdrum duties which involved a loss of job satisfaction and prestige. It was held there was a repudiation by the employer. A change in emphasis in an employee's duties from bar steward to catering assistant, where under the terms of the contract he was required to perform both duties, although the catering duties were subsidiary duties, was a breach of contract: *Pedersen v London Borough of Camden* [1981] IRLR 173. However, the removal of part of the contractual duties which the employee enjoys doing most is unlikely to be a breach. The employee cannot insist on doing those duties which he likes most: *Peter Carnie and Son Ltd v Paton* [1979] IRLR 260. A change in the employee's duties may be a breach of the contract by the employer even though the employee is leaving the employer and the change is to protect the employer's business interest: *Ford v Milthorn Toleman Ltd* [1980] IRLR 30.

Where an employer requires an employee to transfer to less skilled employment for an indefinite although temporary duration this may be a constructive dismissal: *Millbrook Furnishing Industries Ltd v McIntosh* [1981] IRLR 309. In this case it was not clear whether or not the employees were, in addition, going to suffer a reduction in their pay. The EAT considered that a temporary transfer to a different department for a specified or short fixed period was unlikely to be a constructive dismissal. In *McNeill v Charles Crimin (Electrical Contractors) Ltd* [1984] IRLR 179, it was held that where the employer required the employee, a foreman electrician, to do electrical work and work on tools under the supervision or direction of an ordinary electrician, there had been a breach of the fundamental term of the contract of employment. There was no evidence that this change was to be permanent. The tribunal had erred in finding that a breach can only be material where it involves a substantial alteration in the terms and conditions of employment on a permanent basis. It is sufficient if there is any substantial alteration in the terms and conditions of employment.

The change in duties may be accompanied by other changes. The demotion of an executive to the status of clerk, the deprivation of discretion in the way in which she performed her new duties, and the taking away of a car for her own exclusive use were held to be a repudiation of the contract: *Moore v Rowland Winn (Batley) Ltd* [1975] IRLR 16. Similarly, in *Middlemass v Greenwood Batley Ltd* [1972] IRLR 3, the demotion of Middlemass who had been employed as a sales manager to an ordinary representative with a probable reduction in pay and fringe benefits entitled the employee to claim a constructive dismissal.

A change of status unaccompanied by other changes may amount to a repudiation: see *Stephenson and Co (Oxford) Ltd v Austin* [1990] ICR 609.

The contract may provide for a change in duties and status following disciplinary action. Thus, under the disciplinary procedure of British Rail, a reduction in grade is one of the disciplinary measures which can be imposed. It is accepted custom and practice by both sides in the industry as an implied term of the contract. In *Theedom v British Railways Board* [1976] IRLR 137, a change in the employee's grade from signalman to leading railwayman as a disciplinary measure was not a repudiation of the contract of service, though it might be if the punishment were grossly out of proportion to the offence or were it imposed for improper motives. Similarly, in *Phillips v Glendale Cabinet Co Ltd* [1977] IRLR 307, demotion from charge hand to the workbench as a disciplinary measure for persistent lateness was not a repudiation.

In *BBC v Beckett* [1983] IRLR 43, it was held that Beckett's contract had been repudiated by the employer. There was a contractual power to demote an employee who had been guilty of a disciplinary offence. However, there was an obligation on the employer to act reasonably in exercising the power and, in the circumstances of the case, disciplinary demotion involving a loss of status and pay was outside the band of reasonable penalties which a reasonable employer might impose. The imposition of a penalty outside the range of reasonable penalties available to the employer under the employer's disciplinary procedure was held to be a constructive dismissal in *Cawley v South Wales*

Electricity Board [1985] IRLR 89. See also the approach in *McAndrew*'s case above.

Promotion   A failure to upgrade an employee where there is no express or implied contractual right to be upgraded will not entitle the employee to claim a constructive dismissal: *Bridgen v Lancashire County Council* [1987] IRLR 58.

Place of employment   A change in the place of the employee's employment may amount to a repudiation. Again the change will have to be fundamental.

In *Grace and Anderson v Northgate Group Ltd* [1972] IRLR 53, it was held that there was no repudiation when the two waitresses who worked in the directors' dining-room were asked to work in the executives' dining-room.

Where a more substantial move is involved, there may be a different result. A labourer who refused to transfer from King's Lynn to Roxton and resigned was held to be dismissed, although the employee had worked away from King's Lynn, which was his home, on a previous occasion. The terms and conditions of his employment were governed by a working rule agreement covering the company's operations and the employee was not a mobile operative within that agreement: *Aldridge v Dredging and Construction Co Ltd* [1972] IRLR 67.

A change in the employee's place of employment where it has been agreed that he shall not be moved out of a certain area, will amount to a repudiation of the contract: *Hawker Siddeley Power Engineering Ltd v Rump* [1979] IRLR 425. In *Little v Charterhouse Magna Assurance Co Ltd* [1980] IRLR 19, Little had a five-year fixed-term contract and was required to perform such duties as were necessary for the conduct and management of the company's affairs. There was no express term in the contract of employment as to location. It was held that there was an implied term that the employee could be required to move and there was no geographical limitation implied in the contract. Thus, there was no breach by the employer when the employee was required to move from Uxbridge to Bletchley. In *Jones v Associated Tunnelling Co Ltd* [1981] IRLR 477, it was held that the contract of employment cannot be silent on the place of work. If there is no express term then the term may be implied from the surrounding circumstances. In the circumstances of this case the employee could be required to work at any site within a reasonable daily commuting distance from his home. Since the employers required the employee to transfer from one site to another site which was within reasonable daily reach of his home, there was no constructive dismissal.

In *Sibson*'s case above, the Court of Appeal in approving the guidance given in *Jones*'s case above, held that there was no breach of an implied term where Sibson an HGV driver was required to transfer from one depot to another depot a mile away. Where the employee can be required under his contract to move there may be an implied term that reasonable notice should be given: see *McAndrew*'s and *Akhtar*'s cases above.

Assistance   The removal of assistance which the employee enjoys as a term of her contract may be a breach entitling the employee to claim constructive dismissal: *Seligman and Latz Ltd v McHugh* [1979] IRLR 130. In *Associated Type Specialists (Eastern) Ltd v Waterhouse* [1976] ICR 218, the employee, a supervisor, had complaints made against her by her subordinates because she was too strict and she was given a warning by her employer. The employer then failed to tell her about further complaints which were made. She was given no guidance by her employer as to whether or not her efforts to improve were successful. The subordinates walked out and she resigned. It was held that the employer had breached an implied term of the contract in not giving her management support and assistance in carrying out her duties on their behalf.

Provision of work   The employer's failure to provide the employee with work will not amount to a repudiation of the contract, except in certain cases, provided the employee is remunerated. If the employer suspends or lays-off the employee without pay where he has no contractual right to do so, it will amount to a repudiation of the contract of employment. In certain exceptional cases the employer's failure to provide the employee with work will amount to a repudiation of the contract. These exceptions arise where it is a term of the contract, express or implied, that the employer will provide work, as where it is a term of the contract that the employee shall have the opportunity of practising his skills, gaining experience, increasing his earnings or enhancing his reputation.

The overall circumstances of the contract may mean that the employer has to give the employee work, as where the employee is entitled to practise his skill etc. The contract must be looked at as a whole to decide whether the employer is obliged to provide the employee with work: *Breach v Epsylon Industries Ltd* [1976] ICR 316 and *Bosworth v Angus Jowett and Co Ltd* [1977] IRLR 374. The obligation to provide the employee with work may be greater where higher management is involved.

A variation of the traditional view was suggested by the remarks of Lord Denning MR in *Langston v Amalgamated Union of Engineering Workers* [1974] ICR 180, when he said, *obiter*, that there might be an implied term in every contract that an employee has a right to work.

Safety   At common law the employer is under a duty to take reasonable care to ensure that the plant, premises and system of work are safe. The Factories Act 1961, the Offices, Shops and Railway Premises Act 1963, and Health and Safety at Work etc Act 1974 and regulations made thereunder have imposed considerable obligations on the employer to ensure the health, safety and welfare of his employees. The employer's failure to take reasonable steps to ensure the safety of his employees may be a breach of an implied term of the contract which is fundamental either that the employer will take reasonable steps to ensure the safety of employees or a breach of an implied term that the employer will observe the law.

In *Pagano v HGS* [1976] IRLR 9, the employee was engaged as a gas converter, and to carry out his work he was allowed to drive one of the company's vans. Throughout his employment he had made numerous complaints about the condition of these vans. He was given a van to drive which he considered unsafe. This was checked and found to have faults in the braking system and a prohibition order was imposed on the van. At a meeting with the employer the employee made complaints about the van and the servicing. Following the meeting he resigned. The tribunal found that because of his concern about the state of the vans and the lack of concern by the employer, the employee was justified in terminating his employment with the employer.

In *Keys v Shoefayre Ltd* [1978] IRLR 476, the employer's failure to improve security following an armed robbery was held to be a breach of the employer's obligation to take reasonable care to operate a safe system of work and to take reasonable care to have reasonably safe premises. See also *Graham Oxley Tool Steels Ltd v Firth* [1980] IRLR 135.

It is likely that any serious failure by the employer to ensure his employee's safety will entitle the employee to resign and claim constructive dismissal: see *British Aircraft Corporation Ltd v Austin* [1978] IRLR 332; *Lindsay v Dunlop Ltd* [1980] IRLR 93; *Dutton and Clark Ltd v Daly* [1985] IRLR 363.

Rudeness and abuse   The employer's use of rude or insulting language where it amounts to a repudiation of the contract by the employer entitles the employee to terminate his employment and claim constructive dismissal: *Palmanor Ltd (t/a Chaplins Night Club) v Cedron* [1978] ICR 1008. In *Wares v Caithness Leather Products Ltd* [1974] IRLR 162 a female employee was constructively dismissed where foul language which was excessive and unreasonable was used in reprimanding her for taking time off. In *MacNeilege v Arthur Roye (Turf Accountants) Ltd* [1976] IRLR 88 a female assistant was constructively dismissed where a branch manager called her a 'bloody fat sod and stupid stuck up bitch', having earlier sworn at her in front of customers. In *Isle of Wight Tourist Board v Coombes* [1976] IRLR 413 a female secretary was constructively dismissed where her boss said of her in front of another employee 'She is an intolerable bitch on a Monday morning.' The mutual confidence and trust had been destroyed.

Disciplinary procedure The employer's failure to follow a contractual disciplinary procedure may be a repudiation of the contract as in *The Post Office v Strange* [1981] IRLR 515, where the employer's failure to allow an appeal against a disciplinary penalty to the proper level of management led to the imposition of a penalty which was a nullity and the employer's requirement that the employee comply with the penalty was a breach of contract. The lesson for employers is not to make the disciplinary procedure contractual.

Warnings The giving of a justified warning to an employee cannot amount to a breach of an implied term in the contract entitling the employee to resign and claim constructive dismissal. The giving of a warning, even though objectively unfair, will not necessarily amount to a repudiation of the contract. An unjustified reprimand given in an officious and insensitive manner was held to be a repudiatory breach in *Protopapa*'s case, above. Further, the EAT has expressed the view that the giving of an unjustified warning or a series of warnings without legitimate complaint, aimed not at improving the employee's conduct or performance but at disheartening him and driving him out of employment, might amount to a constructive dismissal: *Walker v Josiah Wedgwood and Sons Ltd* [1978] ICR 744. See also *Woods v W M Car Services (Peterborough) Ltd* [1981] IRLR 347; see on appeal *Woods v WM Car Services (Peterborough) Ltd* [1982] IRLR 413. The circumstances in each case have to be carefully investigated.

Strikes It has been suggested that if an employer provokes or engineers a strike or other industrial action in a gross manner, this may be misconduct amounting to a repudiation of the contract. It is interesting to speculate whether it is a repudiation requiring acceptance or whether the contract comes to an end automatically. If it is the latter, the action of the employee going on strike would occur after the contract came to an end and could not therefore amount to a termination of the contract: *Thompson v Eaton Ltd* [1976] ICR 336.

(d) Victimisation Victimisation of the employee by the employer will not entitle the employee to resign and claim a constructive dismissal, unless it is a fundamental breach of the contract of employment or a breach of a fundamental term.

Thus, failure to pay an award which the employer has undertaken to pay following a pay review; failure to include an employee in an annual pay review coupled with complaints about job performance; preferential treatment of other employees; warning of a redundancy situation with criticism of an employee's work; and advertising an employee's job while he is still employed, have been pleaded as acts of victimisation, but each have been held not to amount to a repudiation. For two cases where aggravation or victimisation were established see: *Bariamis v John Stephen of London Ltd* [1975] IRLR 237 and *Fanshaw v Robinsons and Sons Ltd* [1975] IRLR 165.

In both cases there was evidence on which the tribunal could find that the employer had breached a fundamental implied term of the contract.

(e) Repudiation and contracts generally It is a general principle that the repudiation of a contract does not in itself terminate the contract, unless the circumstances of the repudiation are such that the continuance of the contract is totally impossible. Save where performance is totally impossible upon a repudiation, the innocent party is entitled to ignore the breach and insist upon the performance of the contract or alternatively to accept the repudiation. In the former case each party remains bound by the contract, and the innocent party is entitled to sue for damages for loss caused by the breach. In the latter case the contract is terminated from the time the innocent party elects to accept the repudiation. The rights and obligations of the parties under the contract to that time are preserved and the innocent party is entitled to sue for damages.

(f) Repudiation and the contract of employment There has been a considerable division of judicial opinion upon the question whether or not the contract of employment comes within the general principles outlined above or whether, in this respect, it is a contract *sui generis*. One of the difficulties about the contract of employment in practical terms is that where the employer repudiates the contract by wrongfully dismissing the employee, it is difficult to provide a remedy which will keep the contract alive. It is this practical problem which has often led to the finding that a repudiation by the employer automatically brings the contract to an end, so that the employee cannot elect to keep the contract alive.

Repudiation and wrongful dismissal Apart from wrongfully dismissing the employee, the employer may repudiate the contract where he fundamentally breaches the contract of employment or breaches a fundamental term of the contract of employment, but the repudiation does not actually take the form of a dismissal. The need for acceptance has to be considered in relation to both cases involving wrongful dismissal and cases where the employer's repudiatory conduct does not take the form of a dismissal. Although this chapter is concerned with constructive dismissal for the purposes of unfair dismissal rather than wrongful dismissal, it is helpful to examine the way in which the courts have approached the problem of the need for acceptance in cases of wrongful dismissal.

Broadly, the traditional view has been that where the employer wrongfully dismisses the employee the employer's repudiation automatically terminates the contract of employment without the need for acceptance by the employee: see *Vine v National Dock Labour Board* [1956] 1 QB 658 and on appeal [1957] AC 488. It was recognised that the employee might suffer because wrongful dismissal brought the contract to an end without the need for acceptance and that the employee's remedy would usually be damages. However, the courts were undoubtedly influenced by the practical problems of adopting any other approach. Rarely can the employee keep the contract alive in practical terms whether or not the contract exists in theory. Furthermore, since the employee's claim, is for damages rather than remuneration under the contract because he has not performed further his obligations under the contract and he is obliged to mitigate his loss, he is usually well advised to treat the contract as being at an end as quickly as possible: see *Denmark Productions Ltd v Boscobel Productions Ltd* [1969] 1 QB 699.

In *Decro-Wall International SA v Practitioners in Marketing Ltd* [1971] 1 WLR 361, the Court of Appeal, doubted whether wrongful dismissal brought a contract of service to an end in law although no doubt in practice it does. It considered that the contract remained alive in principle although no action could successfully be brought to preserve the contract in practical terms. What was limited was not the employee's right to elect to preserve the contract but the range of remedies available to the employee. This view broadly accords with the general principles of contract law. Salmon LJ also doubted whether a contract of service could be unilaterally determined by the employer's breach.

Neither of the last two cases were concerned with a contract of employment.

In *Hill v CA Parsons and Co Ltd* [1972] 1 Ch 305, Hill, who was wrongfully dismissed by the employer, was granted an injunction against the employer preventing it from treating the contract as at an end. The vital element in this case was that the confidential nature of the relationship between the employer and the employee had not been affected by the dismissal, and so it was possible for the relationship to continue. There were special factors surrounding the introduction of the Industrial Relations Act 1971 which benefited Hill and because of this the Court of Appeal was anxious that the contract should be kept alive. The majority of the Court of Appeal, while accepting that where the employer wrongfully terminates the contract of employment the employment relationship comes to an end, found that in special circumstances the court may grant a declaration that the relationship still exists and an injunction to prevent the employer treating it as at an end. In this case the employee did not accept the repudiation, the notice was too short and damages were an inadequate remedy. See also *GKN (Cwmbran) Ltd v Lloyd* [1972] ICR 214.

In *Sanders v Ernest A Neale Ltd* [1974] ICR 565, a case which has been described as 'the high water mark of . . . automatic determination', the National Industrial Relations Court (NIRC) held that where the employer has wrongfully dismissed the employee, acceptance of the employer's repudiation by the employee is not necessary: the contract will come to an end without acceptance. The employee's refusal to accept the repudiation cannot keep the contract alive. The NIRC accepted that there might be rare exceptions such as *Hill v CA Parsons and Co Ltd*, above.

In *Brown v Southall and Knight* [1980] IRLR 130, the EAT held, in a case involving unfair dismissal, that wrongful dismissal brought the contract of employment to an end without the need for acceptance by the employee. There will be a dismissal within s 55(2)(*a*) of the EP(C)A 1978, whether or not the repudiation is accepted.

In *Gunton v The Mayor Aldermen and Burgesses of the London Borough of Richmond-upon-Thames* [1980] IRLR 321, Gunton was held to have been wrongfully dismissed where the authority failed to follow the terms of a disciplinary procedure incorporated in Gunton's contract of employment. Shaw LJ in a minority decision, followed the judgment of Sir John Donaldson in *Sanders v Ernest A Neale Ltd*, above. However, Buckley LJ and Brightman LJ held that a wrongful dismissal does not automatically terminate the contract of employment and the repudiation on the part of the employer needs acceptance by the employee. Buckley LJ recognised that because of the nature of the contract of employment, in many cases it would be very difficult for the employee to do other than accept the employer's repudiation. Indeed he found that in the case of wrongful dismissal, in the absence of special circumstances, the court 'should easily infer that the innocent party has accepted the guilty party's repudiation of the contract'. Brightman LJ found that where the employee did not accept the wrongful dismissal the contract remained alive even though it put an end to the status or relationship of the parties. See also *Dietman v Brent London Borough Council* [1987] ICR 737 where the High Court followed *Gunton's* case.

In *Robert Cort and Son Ltd v Charman* [1981] ICR 816, it was held that in determining the effective date of termination under s 55(4) of the EP(C)A 1978, wrongful dismissal brings the contract of employment to an end without the need for acceptance. The EAT found that it was of the greatest importance that there should be no doubt or uncertainty as to the effective date of termination. Uncertainty could result if the identification of the effective date of termination depended upon the law of repudiation and acceptance of repudiation. However, in *Shook v London Borough of Ealing* [1986] IRLR 46, the EAT appeared to accept that for the purposes of the statutory jurisdiction acceptance of the repudiation was required. Regrettably in this case many of the earlier authorities were not cited.

If wrongful dismissal does not bring the contract to an end without the employee's acceptance, once the employee has accepted the employer's repudiation, is it the employer's initial repudiation which terminates the contract or the employee's acceptance? There is authority for the proposition that it is the employee's acceptance that terminates the contract: see *Western Excavating (ECC) Ltd v Sharp*, above. This produces a strange result in that it is the employee rather than the employer who terminates the contract. The statutory provisions have been drafted on the basis that wrongful dismissal brings the contract of employment to an end without the need for acceptance.

However, recent cases suggest that wrongful dismissal does not bring the contract to an end without acceptance. Indeed, cases in which injunctions have been granted are inconsistent with a view that repudiation does not require acceptance. See *Dietman*'s case, above.

If the contract is brought to an end by repudiatory conduct without the need for acceptance, the guilty party may thereby relieve himself from performing his contractual obligations leaving the innocent party simply with a claim for damages: see *Evening Standard Co Ltd v Henderson* [1987] ICR 588.

Repudiation other than wrongful dismissal   Does a repudiation by the employer where there is no actual dismissal operate to determine the contract without the need for acceptance?

In *Thomas Marshall (Exports) Ltd v Guinle and Others* [1978] ICR 905, the employee was in breach of a term in his contract that during the continuance of his employment he was not to engage in any other business without the employer's consent. Megarry VC held:

If cases of master and servant are an exception from the rule that an unaccepted repudiation works no determination of the contract, and instead are subject to what I have called the doctrine of automatic termination, the result would be that many a contract of employment would be determined forthwith upon the commission of a fundamental breach, or a breach of a fundamental term, even though the commission of this breach was unknown to the innocent party, and even if, had he known, he would have elected to keep the contract in being.

In *Rasool and Others v Hepworth Pipe Co Ltd* [1980] IRLR 88, the EAT, following the tribunal in *Sealey and Others v Avon Aluminium Co Ltd* [1978] IRLR 285, found:

the cases support a cross division of fundamental breaches into (i) employer's and (ii) employee's breaches which:
  (a) being or entailing a deliberate curtailment of the contract, effectively terminate it without more, and those which
  (b) merely entitle the other party at his option to treat it as discharged, 'accepting' the repudiation, and thus lawfully terminating the contract without notice.

In *London Transport Executive v Clarke* [1981] IRLR 166, the majority of the Court of Appeal held that where there has been a repudiation of the contract, the contract does not come to an end unless and until repudiation is accepted by the innocent party, so the general rule of contract law applies to contracts of employment. Templeman LJ held:

I can see no reason why a contract of employment or services should be determined by repudiation and not by the acceptance of repudiation at common law. The argument has little practical importance at common law. The only difference which would exist at common law between 'self dismissal' and 'accepted repudiation' is that 'self dismissal' would determine the contract when the worker walked out or otherwise committed a repudiatory breach of the contract whereas 'accepted repudiation' determines the contract when the employer expressly or impliedly gives notice to the worker that the employer accepts the repudiation and does not wish to affirm the contract. But in practice, at common law 'self dismissal' and 'acceptance of repudiation' in contracts of service are usually simultaneous, both being implied rather than express where affirmation of the contract would be meaningless; in any event, they involve similar consequences in almost all cases. A difficulty, however, arises under the 1978 Act if . . . [Counsel's] argument of a special category of determination of a contract by self dismissal is correct. When a worker commits a breach of contract, neither he nor the employer nor in the final analysis, the Industrial Tribunal may be entirely clear whether the breach is repudiatory or not. Whatever the nature of the breach, the worker may seek expressly or impliedly to persuade the employer to affirm the contract and to allow the worker to continue in or resume his employment. If the employer does not allow the worker to continue or resume his employment, then if . . . [Counsel] is right an industrial tribunal must first decide whether the worker's breach of contract is repudiatory or not. If the breach of contract is so fundamental as to be repudiatory of the contract, then the Tribunal must decide whether the repudiatory act is of a special kind which amounts to self dismissal. If these matters are decided in favour of the employer, then the Tribunal is not authorised to consider whether in the circumstances the refusal of the employer to affirm the contract and to allow the worker to continue or resume employment is fair or unfair unless, despite the finding of self dismissal, the worker is able to establish conduct on the part of the employer which converts self dismissal into constructive dismissal. If the Tribunal decide that the breach of contract by the worker was not repudiatory or if the Tribunal decide that the repudiatory breach was not of the special kind which amounts to self dismissal, then they must conclude that the contract was terminated by the employer and they must then consider whether the employer satisfies the onus of proving that the termination of the contract which amounts to dismissal was in fact fair dismissal.

These complications arise, and only arise, if there is grafted on to the old common law rule that a repudiated contract is only terminated by acceptance, an exception in the case of contracts of employment. In my view any such exception is contrary to principle, unsupported by authority binding on this court and undesirable in practice. If a worker walks out of his job and does not thereafter claim to be entitled to resume work, then he repudiates his contract and the employer accepts that repudiation by taking no action to affirm the contract. No question of unfair dismissal can arise unless the worker claims that he was constructively dismissed. If a worker walks out of his job or commits any other breach of contract, repudiatory or otherwise, but at any time claims that he is entitled to resume or to continue his work, then his contract of employment is only determined if the employer expressly or impliedly asserts and accepts repudiation on the part of the worker. Acceptance can take the form of formal writing or can take the form of refusing to allow the worker to resume or continue his work. Where the contract of employment is determined by the employer purporting to accept repudiation on the part of the worker, the tribunal must decide whether the worker has been unfairly dismissed.

It is not clear from the judgment of Templeman LJ whether the employer who refuses to have the employee back dismisses the employee or not. In *Rigby v Ferodo Ltd* [1987] ICR 457, confirmed on appeal by the House of Lords [1988] ICR 29, it was held that a repudiatory breach of the contract of employment, being the employer's unilateral reduction in wages, did not bring the contract to an end without acceptance by the employee. Rigby continued in employment not accepting the breach and sued for the underpayment.

It is clear from these authorities that repudiation by the employer, in a case other than where he wrongfully dismisses the employee, as or indeed by the employee, requires accceptance by the other to bring the contract to an end, except perhaps in exceptional circumstances.

If the employer's repudiation needs acceptance by the employee, and the employee's repudiation needs acceptance by the employer to bring the contract to an end, by whom is the contract terminated? In *Western Excavating (ECC) Ltd v Sharp* , above, Lord Denning MR held that where the employer repudiates one or more essential terms of the contract and the employee accepts the repudiation, the employee's acceptance results in the termination of the contract. This is consistent with s 55(2)(*c*) of the EP(C)A 1978. It must be borne in mind that this was not a case where the repudiation consisted of wrongful dismissal. Conversely, if it is the employee who has been guilty of repudiatory conduct, it must be the employer's acceptance which terminates the contract. Thus, there will be a dismissal in law, see s 55(2)(*a*) of the EP(C)A 1978. See also *Sealey v Avon Aluminium Co Ltd*, above. If, however, the acceptance of the repudiation results in the termination of the contract by the party repudiating the same, then in the case of the employee who repudiated the contract, the employer's acceptance of the repudiation would mean that it was the employee who had terminated the contract.

Notwithstanding the decision in *Western Excavating (ECC) Ltd v Sharp* , above, the EAT has, on occasions, reached a different conclusion. Thus in *Kallinos v London Electric Wire* [1980] IRLR 11, the EAT found 'that where there is a fundamental breach of contract the person who is guilty of the fundamental breach so that it amounts to a repudiation of that contract is the party to the contract who is bringing the contract to an end'. In this case it was the employee who brought the contract to an end when he was discovered asleep in the rest room when he should have been on duty.

In *Rasool and Others v Hepworth Pipe Co Ltd* [1980] IRLR 88, the EAT followed the decision in *Western Excavating (ECC) Ltd v Sharp* , above, and found that attendance at an unauthorised mass meeting was a repudiation of the contract of employment by the employee and it was open to the employer to accept the repudiation which it did. The employer's acceptance of the repudiation terminated the contract of employment and so the employee was dismissed. In this case Waterhouse J held that:

it would be unfortunate if the impact of the unfair dismissal legislation were to depend in many cases on the whim of the employer (with or without legal advice) in deciding how to respond to a fundamental breach. . . . If a restrictive interpretation were to be applied to the word 'terminated' in . . . [s 55(2)(a) of the EP(C)A 1978] the result would be that a large category of decisions to 'dismiss' by employers would be excluded from scrutiny by Industrial Tribunals, and it is most unlikely that this was the intention of Parliament.

It is submitted that in the vast majority of cases the authority in *Rasool v Hepworth Pipe Co Ltd*, above, will be preferred, although there may be certain exceptional cases where there can be a self-dismissal. The tribunal recognised this in *Sealey v Avon Aluminium Co Ltd* above, and it was recognised in a dissenting judgment of Lord Denning MR in *Clarke*'s case, above, and also it seems in the judgment of Templeman LJ in that case. The view that an employee may, by his repudiatory conduct, bring the contract of employment to an end, is the antithesis of the view that wrongful dismissal brings the contract to an end without the need for acceptance by the employee. If wrongful dismissal needs acceptance, then it would seem unlikely that the concept of self-dismissal can survive in any form.

(g) The reason for leaving It has been seen that to enable an employee to claim that his contract of employment has been repudiated by the employer there must be a fundamental breach of the contract or a breach of a fundamental term. The breach must be sufficiently serious to entitle the employee to leave. The employee must leave as a result of the breach and not as a result of any other circumstances. In *Logabax Ltd v Titherley* [1977] IRLR 97, the EAT held that the employee was:

not entitled to claim benefit from an alleged repudiation because he did not treat the contract as repudiated. . . . An employee must signify his attitude in a clear unambiguous fashion . . . [he] . . . must indicate that he is exercising his entitlement to claim a constructive dismissal.

In *Walker v Josiah Wedgwood and Sons Ltd* [1978] IRLR 105, Arnold J held:

it is at least requisite that the employee should leave because of the breach of the employer's relevant duty to him, and that this should demonstrably be the case. It is not sufficient, we think, if he merely leaves. . . . And secondly, we think it is not sufficient if he leaves in circumstances which indicate some ground for his leaving other than the breach of the employer's obligations to him.

This dictum was approved by the EAT in *Norwest Holst Group Administration Ltd v Harrison* [1984] IRLR 419. Equivocal conduct which is consistent with the contract remaining in force will not amount to an acceptance: *Spencer v Marchington* [1988] IRLR 392.

(h) Waiver of the breach Where the employer has repudiated the contract of employment and the employee wishes to rely upon the repudiation, he must not do anything which amounts to a waiver of the repudiation. Where the employer, for instance, unilaterally alters a fundamental term of the contract, the employee may reject the unilateral alteration expressly or, without making any express statement, he may seek employment elsewhere. However, he may expressly accept the unilateral alteration and remain in the employment or without any express statement he may remain in the employment. If he remains in the same employment without demur he will acquiesce or waive the repudiation and he will have difficulty pleading the repudiation at a later date: *Betteridge v CA Parsons and Co Ltd and AUEW* [1973] IRLR 228; *Crapper v Butler Machine Tool Co Ltd* [1973] IRLR 194.

As Lord Denning said in *Western Excavating (ECC) Ltd v Sharp* [1978] ICR 221, 'he must make up his mind soon after the conduct of which he complains: for, if he continues for any length of time without leaving, he will lose his right to treat himself as discharged. He will be regarded as having elected to affirm the contract.'

Where the employee continues in the same employment, for any length of time he may, in exceptional circumstances, be taken not to have acquiesced in the change and therefore not to have affirmed the contract. However, he should make his position clear, otherwise it may be fatal. The position is illustrated by *Marriott v Oxford and District Cooperative Society Ltd (No 2)* [1970] 1 QB 186. Marriott was an electrical maintenance foreman. The side of the business in which he worked declined and his services were no longer required. He was told by the society that it would continue to employ him as a supervisor with a reduction in wages. Marriott complained and never accepted the transfer, although he continued to work for three or four weeks for the society following the change, and he looked for work elsewhere. He subsequently left and claimed a dismissal. It was held that he had been dismissed following the repudiation of the contract by the society. By remaining in employment for three to four weeks after the repudiation, he had not accepted the repudiation. He had never concurred with the changed terms. He had protested about the terms, but he remained in employment so that he would not be unemployed while he looked elsewhere. See also *Air Canada v Lee* [1978] ICR 1202.

Marriott's case may be regarded as an exceptional case, but in *Bashir v Brillo Manufacturing Co* [1979] IRLR 295, an employee who fell sick following a change in the terms of his contract and accepted sick pay for two and a half months, and had made it clear that the change was not accepted, was able to claim a constructive dismissal.

Here, the EAT distinguished the case where an employee actually performs his work from the case where he simply receives sick pay to which he might have been entitled in any event under the terms of his contract. See also *Sheet Metal Components Ltd v Plumridge and Others* [1974] IRLR 86 (although this is an early case decided before *Western Excavating (ECC) Ltd v Sharp* above), where it was held that a lapse of two months before resigning did not amount to a waiver of the employer's repudiatory conduct. The 'acceptance' of the change was on a trial basis. Compare *Grant v Shell Refining and Marketing UK Ltd* [1975] IRLR 150.

In *Hunt v British Railways Board* [1979] IRLR 379, Hunt, who claimed that he was constructively dismissed following disciplinary action taken against him by the Board, continued to report to work and was still reporting to work at the time of the tribunal hearing. It was held that he could not claim he had been constructively dismissed. By his subsequent conduct he had waived the breach. The concept of constructive dismissal does not allow the employee to go on acting as if he was employed when what the employee is trying to say is that he is no longer employed.

In *WE Cox Toner (International) Ltd v Crook* [1981] IRLR 443, the EAT held that Lord Denning's summary of the law in the *Western Excavating* case, above, was not intended to be a comprehensive statement of the whole law. It had to be seen in the context of the general principles of contract law which were that once there has been a repudiation of the contract the innocent party can either affirm the contract and insist on its further performance, or he can accept the repudiation and bring the contract to an end. Once he affirms the contract, his right to accept the repudiation is at an end. However, the innocent party is not bound to make an election either within a reasonable time or any other time. Delay by itself does not constitute an affirmation of the contract unless there is express or implied affirmation of the contract. Prolonged delay may be evidence of an implied affirmation. Implied affirmation may arise where the innocent party requires the guilty party to perform the contract further. It may arise if the innocent party himself does something which is only consistent with the continued existence of the contract unless the innocent party, while further performing the contract to a limited extent, makes it clear that he is reserving his rights to accept the repudiation or is only performing the contract so as to allow the guilty party to remedy the breach. The EAT recognised that there was an obvious difference between a contract of employment and most other contracts in that if the employee, following a repudiation of the contract by the employer, reports to work the next day, he will be acting in a way which in one sense is only consistent with the continued existence of the contract. Similarly, when he accepts his next pay packet there is strong evidence that he is affirming the contract. Much depends upon the evidence.

Delay in accepting the repudiation is only one factor which may be relevant.

In *Reid v Camphill Engravers* [1990] ICR 435, the employer failed to pay wages in accordance with a Wages Council Order for three years. It was held that this was a continuing breach, so that even if the employee had not reacted to the initial breach, he could refer to that initial breach where the employer committed further breaches. The facts were exceptional in that the employee could not in any event affirm a contract at a lower wage than that fixed by a Wages Council.

An employee will not be deemed to have acquiesced by waiting until the change takes place: *Simmonds v Dowty Seals Ltd* [1981] IRLR 211. Indeed there may be circumstances where the employee would be wise to await the change, particularly where changes in the contract are under negotiation. If an employee resigns and claims constructive dismissal before the results of the negotiations are clear, he may be unable to establish a constructive dismissal: *GC Machines Ltd v Forshaw and Malain* [1978] (unreported); see also *Genower v Ealing, Hammersmith and Hounslow Area Health Authority* [1980] IRLR 297.

Where the employer gives the employee an opportunity to make up his mind whether or not to accept the employer's repudiation or affirm the contract, and continues to pay the employee's salary while he is making up his mind, the employee cannot be taken to have waived the repudiation: *Bliss v South East Thames Regional Health Authority* [1985] IRLR 308. In this case Dillon LJ considered the case of *Payman v Lanjani* [1985] 2 WLR 154, a case not involving employment law, where May LJ found that:

I do not think that a party to a contract can realistically or sensibly be held to have made this irrevocable choice between rescission and affirmation unless he has actual knowledge not only of the facts of the serious breach of the contract by the other party which is the pre-condition of his right to choose, but also of the fact that in the circumstances which exist he does have that right to make that choice which the law gives him.

In *Bliss*'s case Dillon LJ commented that the acceptance of this formidable argument could have considerable repercussions in employment law. The acceptance of a new contract will not necessarily mean the employee has waived a breach of the original contract: *Hogg v Dover College* [1990] ICR 39.

The employee must be careful as to the language which he uses when notifying his employer that he is resigning because of the employer's repudiatory conduct. A request by the employee to the employer to leave which is answered in the affirmative may well be a termination by mutual agreement and will not be treated as the employee's acceptance of the employer's repudiation. Whereas in the case of a termination by mutual agreement the employee may seek and obtain the employer's consent, in the case of a constructive dismissal the employee tells the employer that because of the employer's conduct he is going without a by-your-leave from the employer: *Lipton (L) Ltd v Marlborough* [1979] IRLR 179.

(i) Anticipatory breach   The employer may give notice that he will not perform his obligations in the future or he may do something preventing the performance of the contract in the future. Such a breach is called an anticipatory breach. Generally, in the case of anticipatory breach, the innocent party may accept the repudiation and enforce the appropriate remedy, or wait until the time fixed for performance arrives. If the contract is then not performed the innocent party has the usual remedies. Where there is an anticipatory breach which is repudiatory of the contract of employment by the employer, the principles enunciated above as to acceptance apply. Where the employee does not accept the repudiation but waits until the time fixed for performance, the employer may perform the contract and, in effect, withdraw the repudiation. By so doing a constructive dismissal may be avoided.

In *Harrison v Norwest Holst Group Administration Ltd* [1985] IRLR 240, Harrison was employed as a director and manager of the company's design office in Derby. On 14 June 1982 the company wrote to him telling him that the design office would close on 30 June 1982, and that he would be based at Chesterfield but would no longer be a director. Harrison replied on 17 June 1982 in a letter headed 'without prejudice' pointing out that in view of the loss of his directorship and an apparent loss of salary he considered the letter to constitute a termination of his employment with effect from 30 June 1982. He requested 12 months' salary in lieu of notice and also a redundancy payment. He asked the managing director to contact him if he had misunderstood anything or if a further discussion would assist an amicable resolution of the matter. On 18 June the company told Harrison that his salary would not be reduced and on 24 June told him that he could continue as a director although based at Chesterfield. On 25 June Harrison was offered employment with another company and he ceased work with Norwest Holst Group on 30 June. It was held that the employer's action on 14 June amounted to a repudiation of the employer's contract of employment. However, the letter of 17 June did not amount to an unequivocal acceptance of the repudiatory conduct, since it was headed 'without prejudice', the effect of which was to communicate to the company that Harrison was prepared to enter into discussions. Cumming-Bruce LJ quoted from the decision of Buckley LJ in *Gunton v The Mayor Aldermen and Burgesses of the London Borough of Richmond-upon-Thames* [1980] IRLR 321:

where a party to a contract before the date of performance has arrived evinces an intention not to perform his part of the contract, he has committed no breach until the date for performance arrives. Nevertheless, the innocent party will be relieved of his obligations under the contract, if he so chooses, so to render him free to arrange his affairs unhampered by the continued existence of those obligations. It is for the innocent party to elect whether he wishes to be so relieved, which he does by accepting the repudiatory act of the guilty party as a repudiation of his, the guilty party's, obligations under the contract. In those circumstances the innocent party may treat the guilty party as having committed an entire breach of the contract, notwithstanding that the time for performance has not yet arrived. Where the time for performance of part of the guilty party's obligations has arrived but some of those obligations remain executory, the position is the same as regards those obligations which remain executory as it is in respect of all of the guilty party's obligations where none of them as yet become due for performance. If the guilty party has evinced an intention not to perform those obligations of his which remain executory, the innocent party may elect to treat himself as discharged from all obligations on his part to perform the contract any further. He does so by accepting the guilty party's repudiation of his outstanding obligations under the contract, in which case the innocent party may treat the guilty party as having committed an entire breach of all his outstanding obligations under the contract, notwithstanding that the time for performance of those obligations, or some of them, may not yet have arrived.

Cumming-Bruce LJ held that these principles applied to the contract of employment. It could not be held that the employer's actions constituted an immediate repudiation of the contract. Harrison had a reasonable period to make up his mind whether or not to accept the repudiation and the company had an opportunity of repentance because there was a sufficient anticipatory element in their breach to confer on them a *locus poenitentiae*.

It must be remembered that a contract of employment is not a contract for perpetual servitude. Thus if the employer tells the employee the contract will come to an end in the future, there is not necessarily an anticipatory breach by the employer. There must be evidence of an inevitable breach of the contract by the employer. Therefore, if there is no suggestion that the contract will not be terminated by the employer in accordance with the terms of the contract then there is no anticipatory breach: *Haseltine Lake and Co v Dowler* [1981] IRLR 25, following the decision in *Universal Cargo Carriers Corporation v Citati* [1957] 2 QB 401.

(j) The proper construction of a contract   It has been seen that where an employer repudiates the contract the employee may accept the employer's repudiation and claim a constructive dismissal. However, supposing the employer has repudiated the contract as a result of an erroneous interpretation or a genuine mistake of fact or law. The problem was considered in *Frank Wright and Co (Holdings) Ltd v Punch* [1980] IRLR 217. Punch resigned after the employer refused to pay him a cost of living increase which they were contractually obliged to pay. The employer argued that on their interpretation of

the contract they were not obliged to make such a payment. On appeal the employer argued that there was an error of interpretation or a mistake of both fact and law and that it was not to be taken as evincing an intention not to be bound by the contract of employment. The EAT, relying on *Chitty On Contracts* 24th edition vol 1 para 14.80, held:

In short, what is said there is that where there is a genuine dispute as to the construction of a contract, the courts are unwilling to hold that an expression of an intention by one party to carry out the contract only in accordance with its own, erroneous interpretation of it amounts to a repudiation, and the same is true of a genuine mistake of fact or law.

The case was remitted to the tribunal to see whether there was a genuine dispute as to the terms of the contract.

The EAT referred to two cases which supported this approach: *Sweet and Maxwell Ltd v Universal News Services Ltd* [1964] 2 QB 699 and *Woodar Investment Development v Wimpey Construction UK Ltd* [1980] 1 WLR 277. Neither of these cases involved employment law.

In *Financial Techniques (Planning Services) Ltd v Hughes* [1981] IRLR 32, there was a dispute between the parties as to the employee's entitlement under a profit sharing scheme. The Court of Appeal did not accept that there had been a repudiatory breach by the employer. While there was a dispute over the terms of the scheme, the employers were doing no more than arguing their point of view. The stage had not yet been reached where the employers had evinced an intention no longer to be bound by the contract. Templeman LJ expressed caution against holding that where a party to a contract has a plausible but mistaken view of his rights under the contract and insists upon his rights, that insistence cannot amount to a repudiation. He further expressed doubt about the decision in *Punch*'s case above, in so far as that case lends support to the view that a genuine but mistaken belief as to the terms of the contract may prevent repudiation.

In *Blyth v Scottish Liberal Club* [1983] IRLR 245, the Court of Session found that the decisions in the *Sweet and Maxwell* and *Woodar* cases, above, relied upon in *Punch*'s case, above, applied solely to anticipatory and not to actual breaches of contract. In *BBC v Beckett* [1983] IRLR 43, the EAT refused to follow *Woodar*'s case, above, where the employer believed that under the contract of employment it had the power to impose a particular disciplinary sanction where on an objective construction of the contract it did not.

In *Bliss v South East Thames Regional Health Authority* [1985] IRLR 308, the Court of Appeal again distinguished the decision in *Woodar*'s case, above, and found that it was not open to the authority to argue that by requiring Bliss to undergo a psychiatric examination which it genuinely believed it was entitled to do, its actions could not be repudiatory since the authority did not indicate any intention not to be bound by the contract. The authority was not purporting to exercise any power in the contract. It had to be judged not by its intentions, but by objective standards.

In *Millbrook Furnishing Industries Ltd v McIntosh* [1981] IRLR 309, the EAT appeared to accept the law as set out in *Punch*'s case, above, in so far as it related to the proper construction of a contract, but refused to extend the principle to cases when the employer genuinely did not intend to repudiate the contract. There was a repudiatory breach by the employer. The employer's contention that it did not intend to repudiate the contract of employment was held to be irrelevant. It was necessary to ascertain the nature of the breach and the impact of the breach on the contractual relationship without reference to the intention of the parties.

The effect of these decisions is greatly to reduce the import of the decision in *Punch*'s case, above. *Obiter* remarks by Lord Donaldson in *Bridgen v Lancashire County Council* [1987] IRLR 58, which suggest that to establish a repudiation it has to be shown that the guilty party did not intent to be bound by the contract, should be treated with caution.

1.4 Pregnant employee's right to return to work

Where an employee is entitled to return to work following a period of absence due to pregnancy or confinement and she is not permitted to return to work, she is treated as dismissed. The employee is treated as being employed until her notified date of return and treated as if she had been dismissed on that day for the reason for which she was not permitted to return to work: s 56 of the 1978 Act. The unfair dismissal provisions are modified to this extent. (See Chapter 10.)

2 Employee resignation

An employee who resigns whether with or without notice is not dismissed unless there is a constructive dismissal or there is a forced resignation. In certain circumstances the employee may not be able to rely upon the words of resignation and may find that in those circumstances there is a dismissal if the employment comes to an end: see *Gale (BG) Ltd v Gillbert* [1978] ICR 1149 and *Sothern v Franks Charlesly and Co* [1981] IRLR 278. Thus, where the employee resigns during the course of a heated argument or discussion, then it seems that provided he withdraws his words of resignation almost immediately, the resignation will not take effect: *Martin v Yeoman Aggregates Ltd* [1983] IRLR 49. Again, the employer may not be able to rely on the words of resignation if the employee is an immature employee, the decision was taken in the heat of the moment or the employee was jostled into the decision by the employer. The same applies where idle words are used under emotional stress which the employer knew or ought to have known were not meant to be taken seriously: *Barclay v City of Glasgow District Council* [1983] IRLR 313. See also *Sovereign House Security Services Ltd v Savage* [1989] IRLR 115.

3 Forced resignation

An employer may give an employee the option of resigning or being dismissed. If the employee then resigns, does this amount to dismissal? In *East Sussex County Council v Walker* (1972) 7 ITR 280, the NIRC held:

Suppose that the employer says to the employee, 'Your job is finished. I will give you the opportunity to resign. If you don't you will be sacked.' How, we would ask, is it possible to reach a conclusion other than that the employment is being terminated by the employer, even though the employee takes the first and more respectable alternative of signing a letter of resignation rather than being the recipient of a letter of dismissal? We feel that in such circumstances there really can be no other conclusion than that the employer terminated the contract.

Following this decision tribunals have consistently held that a forced resignation is a dismissal: see *Scott v Formica Ltd* [1975] IRLR 104; *Spencer Jones v Timmens Freeman* [1974] IRLR 325. In such cases the resignation is in form only and in substance the resignation will be treated as a dismissal: *Robertson v Securicor Transport Ltd* [1972] IRLR 70. The use of persuasion by an employer to obtain an employee's resignation may also be a dismissal. The element of persuasion by the employer is important: *Pascoe v Hallen and Medway* [1975] IRLR 116. However, an ultimatum to perform the contract or resign may not amount to a dismissal and each case will depend upon the circumstances. In *Chapple v Andrew Antenna Systems* [1975] IRLR 7, the employer told the employees that he did not intend to recognise their union, and they were told that if they did not want to accept the position and preferred to resign, they would be given a severance payment. The applicant resigned and it was held that he had not been dismissed either expressly or constructively. He had been given an opportunity to resign with severance pay or to continue in his employment, but with the knowledge that the employer did not intend to recognise the union. He had chosen to resign.

It may be that even though the employee has been given the option of resigning or being dismissed there is no dismissal in law because the employee resigns in consideration of the financial inducement or other terms offered to him to resign: *Sheffield v Oxford Controls Co Ltd* [1979] ICR 396. In this case Arnold J held:

It is plain, we think, that there must exist a principle . . . that where an employee resigns and that resignation is determined upon him because he prefers to resign rather than to be dismissed (the alternative having been expressed to him by the employer in the terms of the threat that if he does not resign he will be dismissed) the mechanics of the resignation do not cause that to be other than a dismissal. The cases do not in terms go further than that. We find the principle to be one of causation. In cases such as that we have just hypothesised, and those reported, the causation is the threat. It is the existence of the threat which causes the employee to be willing to sign, and to sign, a resignation letter or to be willing to give, and to give, the oral resignation. But where that willingness is brought about by other considerations, and the actual causation of the resignation is no longer the threat which has been made but is the state of mind of the resigning employee, that he is willing and content to resign on the terms which he has negotiated and which are satisfactory to him, then we think there is no room for the principle to be derived from the decided cases. In such a case he resigns because he is willing to resign as the result of being offered terms which are to him satisfactory terms on which to resign.

In *Staffordshire County Council v Donovan* [1981] IRLR 108, it was held that the employee's resignation was not arrived at under duress or threat of dismissal, where it resulted from negotiations during the course of the disciplinary procedure, the employee resigning on terms offered by the employer.

In *Martin v MBS Fastenings (Glynwed) Distribution Ltd* [1983] IRLR 198, the employee who drove to work each day in the company's minibus used the minibus on a Sunday to go and watch a company football match. After having consumed a quantity of liquor he was involved in an accident and was breathalysed with positive results. He was told by the company that there would be an inquiry which would probably result in his dismissal and that it would be in his own interests to resign rather than to face an inquiry. It was held that the employee had not been dismissed but had resigned. He had been presented with an option and had chosen voluntarily to resign. The question of whether or not in such circumstances there is a dismissal in law is a question of fact for the tribunal.

In *Caledonian Mining Co Ltd v Bassett and Steel* [1987] IRLR 165, the employees were 'inveigled' into resigning by the employer. Thus, since the employer really terminated the contract, the employees were in substance dismissed.

Again if an employee signs a letter of resignation as a result of a misrepresentation by the employer he may claim he had been dismissed: see *Makin v Greens Motors (Bridport) Ltd* (1986) *The Times*, 18 April.

An indication by the employer that the employee should look elsewhere for a job because his job would come to an end in the future would not in law amount to a dismissal. It is also not a case of enforced resignation: *Haseltine Lake and Co v Dowler* [1981] IRLR 25; see also *International Computers Ltd v Kennedy* [1981] IRLR 28.

4 Employee's resignation during notice

Where an employee gives notice to an employee to terminate the contract of employment, and within that period of notice the employee gives notice to the employer to terminate the contract of employment on a date earlier than the date on which the employer's notice is due to expire, the employee is nevertheless taken to have been dismissed by the employer. The reason for the dismissal is the reason which the employer originally gave in terminating the contract: s 55(3) of the EP(C)A 1978.

Where the employer gives notice, and during the currency of the notice the employee walks out and does not return, is he protected under this provision? The answer is, 'no'. The counter notice to terminate the contract by the employee must be a notice which, within reason, either specifies the date of termination or specifies sufficient facts from which the employer can reasonably work out the date of termination. While it is unlikely that this condition will be applied too strictly, some certainty is required: *Walker v Cotswold Chine Home School* (1977) 12 ITR 342. This case left open the question as to whether the notice had to be valid. However, in *Ready Case Ltd v Jackson* [1981] IRLR 312, the EAT found that it did not matter whether the notice given by the employee was shorter than the statutory minimum period or the contractual notice which the employee was required to give. In this case the EAT considered, but left open, the question whether notice could be immediate notice of termination.

5 Employee repudiation

As in the case of the employer, the employee may repudiate the contract where he fundamentally breaches the contract or breaches a fundamental term of contract. The employee must have evinced an intention to be no longer bound by the contract.

Examples of employee repudiation have arisen where an employee refused to work under a rota system agreed between the employer and the union and incorporated into the employee's contract of employment: *Dudar v Leys Malleable Castings Co Ltd* [1973] IRLR 51; where an employee refused to work on a construction site because of rain, although ordered to do so by the site foreman, as here there was a working rule agreement incorporated in the employee's contract that decisions as to stoppages for bad weather should only be made by the employer or his representative: *London v James Laidlaw and Sons Ltd* [1974] IRLR 136; calling a staff meeting during working hours despite the employer's instructions not to do so: *Johns and Bloomfield v Trust Houses Forte Ltd* [1975] IRLR 36. For disobedience to amount to a repudiation, it is likely that the disobedience must be wilful. Strikes, and possibly other industrial action, are further examples of employee repudiation. The essence of a strike is that the employee refuses to do any of the work which he is engaged to do. The employee is thus in breach of his contract: *Simmons v Hoover Ltd* [1977] ICR 61; *Wilkins v Cantrell and Cochrane (GB) Ltd* [1978] IRLR 483.

Does the breach of the contract by the employee bring the contract to an end immediately without further action on the employer's part, or does it give the employer the right to treat the contract as ended so that he can dismiss the employee, the act of acceptance (the dismissal) bringing the contract to an end? The cases suggest that the repudiatory conduct on the part of the employee does not bring the contract to an end, unless and until the employer accepts the employee's repudiatory conduct: see *Howard v Pickford Tool Co Ltd* [1951] 1 KB 417 and *Thomas Marshall (Exports) Ltd v Guinle* [1978] ICR 905. Usually the employer will in practice commit some act evidencing his acceptance of the repudiation, for instance, either by giving the employee notice or by forwarding to the employee his P45 or other employment documents. If the repudiation of the contract of employment by the employee does not need acceptance, then the contract is at an end without the need for further action. Therefore, the forwarding of the employee's P45 or other documents or property is not an act of dismissal, but a recognition of the fact that the employee has by his actions repudiated the contract and brought the employment to an end.

In *Rasool and Others v Hepworth Pipe Co Ltd* [1980] IRLR 88, the EAT, following the decision of the tribunal in *Sealey and Others v Avon Aluminium Co Ltd* [1978] IRLR 285, found that:

the cases support a cross division of fundamental breaches into (i) employer's and (ii) employee's breaches which:
- (*a*) being or entailing a deliberate curtailment of the contract, effectively terminate it without more, and those which
- (*b*) merely entitle the other party at his option to treat it as discharged, 'accepting' the repudiation, and thus lawfully terminating the contract without notice.

In *London Transport Executive v Clarke* [1981] IRLR 166, the Court of Appeal held that the contract of employment, like any other contract, is not brought to an end by an act of repudiation until the repudiation is accepted by the innocent party. See **1.3(*f*)**, above, for the judgment of Templeman LJ. Dunn LJ, while agreeing with Templeman LJ, conceived of circumstances where it was possible for the repudiation by the employee to bring about the termination of the contract without the need for acceptance. Referring to the decision in *Smith v Avana Bakeries Ltd* [1979] IRLR 423, he considered that where the company's rules were incorporated into the employee's contract of service and the rules provided that if an employee remained off work for more than three days without submitting a medical certificate he would dismiss himself, the failure to submit the medical certificate and remaining off work for more than three days would result in the contract being terminated by the employee in accordance with its terms. Denning MR, in a dissenting judgment, found there could be cases where the employee's conduct was completely inconsistent with the continuance of the contract of employment. The employee's misconduct was such as to evince an intention to bring the contract to an end without the need for acceptance. The decision of Templeman LJ, supported in the main by the decision of Dunn LJ, although permitting of some exceptions, is to be preferred to that of Denning MR.

If the employer wishes to rely on an act of repudiation by the employee, he must not do anything which amounts to a waiver of the repudiatory act: *Allders International Ltd v Parkins* [1981] IRLR 68.

Where there is a fundamental breach of the contract by the employee which is accepted by the employer, the contract is terminated by the employer and consequently there is a dismissal within s 55(2)(*a*) of the EP(C)A 1978. See the decision of *Western Excavating (ECC) Ltd v Sharpe* [1978] ICR 221 and the discussion above.

6 Constructive resignation

Associated with the repudiation of a contract by the employee and the need for acceptance by the employer is the concept of constructive resignation or self-dismissal. Implicit in this concept is the idea that the employee by his conduct 'dismisses' himself in that his misconduct is equivalent to giving his employer notice. The employee is repudiating the contract and the employer's acceptance of that repudiation is not required. The idea of constructive resignation arose in *Jones v Liverpool Corporation and Liverpool Polytechnic* [1974] IRLR 55. Jones refused to report to work when asked to do so, having been told that his failure would lead to the termination of his employment. It was argued that his conduct was equivalent to giving his employer notice and that the employer, by paying wages in lieu of notice, merely recognised the fact; so there was no dismissal but, rather, a constructive resignation. The NIRC held that the employee had by his conduct repudiated the employment and that, by paying wages in lieu of notice, the employer was in effect recognising that the employee had repudiated his contract by dismissing him. Support for the proposition was given by the cases of *Smith v Avana Bakeries Ltd* [1979] IRLR 423; and *Kallinos v London Electric Wire* [1980] IRLR 11. However, in *Rasool and Others v Hepworth Pipe Co Ltd* [1980] IRLR 88, another division of the EAT found that it is for the employer to decide whether or not to treat the employee's repudiation of the contract as discharging the employer from further performance. It is the employer rather than the employee who terminates the contract, although there may be circumstances where the employee's fundamental breach was such that it effectively terminated the contract without the need for anything more. If the employer accepts the repudiation so that the contract is terminated by the decision of the employer, then this is a dismissal: s 55(2)(*a*) of the EP(C)A 1978; see also *Fisher v York Trailer Co Ltd* [1979] IRLR 385, where the company required Fisher to sign an undertaking that he would work at normal speed. The employer told Fisher that if he failed to sign the undertaking the company would consider that he had repudiated his contract of employment. Fisher did not sign and his employment came to an end. It was held that although the employer regarded the conduct of the employee as repudiatory, since he had not indicated that he considered the contract to be at an end, the repudiatory conduct did not in itself determine the contract until it had been accepted by the employer. It was the acceptance which terminated the contract.

The line of reasoning in the cases of *Rasool* and *Fisher* was followed by the majority of the Court of Appeal (Denning MR dissenting) in *London Transport Executive v Clarke* [1981] IRLR 166, although whether Templeman LJ would have accepted that certain breaches effectively terminate the contract without more is open to doubt. In any event the ratio in the cases of *Smith* and *Kallinos* must be regarded as bad law, although see the views of Dunn LJ as to the decision in *Smith*'s case above.

7 Agreement

It is open to the parties to terminate the contract of employment by mutual agreement: *L Lipton Ltd v Marlborough* [1979] IRLR 179; but compare *Thames Television Ltd v Wallis* [1979] IRLR 136. It has been seen that where an employee leaves employment in consideration of a financial inducement, in law that will amount to a termination by mutual agreement: *Sheffield v Oxford Controls Co Ltd* [1979] IRLR 133; see also *Staffordshire County Council v Donovan* [1981] IRLR 108.

The issue of whether or not there has been a termination by mutual agreement may arise where the employee is under notice and seeks to leave his employment before the expiration of the period of notice. The employee may comply with the provisions of s 55(3) of the EP(C)A 1978. See **4**, above. The parties may agree that the employment shall come to an end on a date earlier than the date of the employer's notice. This may constitute an agreement to bring the contract to an end, or it may be an agreement that the effective date of termination shall be brought forward or that the employee may not be required to work out the balance of his notice period. In the first case dismissal by the employer is superseded by an agreement that the contract should be brought to an end. In the latter two cases the employer's notice remains effective so that there is a dismissal in law.

In *McAlwane v Boughton Estates Ltd* [1973] ICR 470, Sir John Donaldson held:

> it would be a very rare case indeed in which it could properly be found that the employer and the employee had got together and, notwithstanding that there was a current notice of termination of the employment, agreed mutually to terminate the contract, particularly when one realises the financial consequences to the employee involved in such an agreement. We do not say that such a situation cannot arise; we merely say that, viewed in a real life situation, it would seem to be a possibility which might appeal to a lawyer more than to a personnel manager.

See also *Lees v Arthur Greaves (Lees) Ltd* [1974] IRLR 93; and consider *Harman v Flexible Lamps Ltd* [1980] IRLR 418.

Where the employee offers to retire and his offer is accepted by the employer the contract is brought to an end by mutual agreement and not by dismissal: *Birch and Humber v University of Liverpool* [1985] IRLR 165. See also *Scott and Others v Coalite Fuels and Chemicals Ltd* [1988] IRLR 131. This situation must be distinguished from the case where the employee has no objection to being dismissed or even volunteers to be dismissed in a redundancy: *Burton, Allton and Johnson Ltd v Peck* [1975] IRLR 87. The judgment in this case did not encroach 'upon the distinction which exists in law between a contract which is terminated unilaterally (albeit without objection, and perhaps even with encouragement from the other party) and a contract which is terminated by mutual agreement'.

Where there is a clear agreement as to the termination of the contract of employment, then the employee cannot claim that he has been dismissed within the statutory definition and therefore is not able to claim unfair dismissal.

The problems of termination by mutual agreement have arisen in connection with employees who have failed to return from leave by an agreed date.

In *Midland Electric Manufacturing Co Ltd v Kanji* [1980] IRLR 185, the employer gave Kanji unpaid leave to go to India. Kanji was told that if she failed to return to work on the due date for whatever reason, including sickness, the company would consider that she had terminated her own employment. She was two weeks late in reporting to work because of ill health. The employer argued that the employment had been terminated by mutual agreement. It was held that a unilateral statement by the employer that the employee's employment could come to an end amounted to a dismissal and that there was no consensual agreement to termination.

In *Tracey v Zest Equipment Co Ltd* [1982] IRLR 268, the EAT held that an employee's employment had not come to an end by mutual consent where he overstayed a leave of absence having signed a document that if he did not return by a stipulated date the employer 'will assume that you have terminated your employment with us'. The employee wished to return to work. The EAT held that very clear words are required in such circumstances to constitute an agreement that, in the event of a failure to comply with such a requirement, there is a mutual consent to the termination of the employment. The employee's failure to return may be a repudiation by him of the contract.

In *Igbo v Johnson Matthey Chemicals Ltd* [1986] ICR 505, Igbo was granted extended leave to go to Nigeria. She signed a document which required her to work her normal shift immediately after her return from her leave of absence. The document which she signed went on to say 'you have agreed to return to work on 28 September 1983. If you fail to do this your contract of employment will automatically terminate on that date.' She returned to England but failed to return to work on 28 September 1983 due to ill health. The employers wrote to her advising her that her employment had come to an end in accordance with the terms of the agreement. The Court of Appeal held that agreement was intended to exclude or limit ss 54 and 55 of the EP(C)A 1978 and was therefore void by virtue of s 140. See Chapter 1. The earlier decision in *British Leyland (UK) Ltd v Ashraf* [1978] ICR 979, where it was held that the contract of employment had come to an end where the employee had agreed that if he did not return from overseas leave by a certain date is, it is submitted, wrongly decided. In that case the effect of s 140 of the EP(C)A 1978 was not considered.

8 Dismissal at common law

There are certain events which at common law amount to a dismissal. Historically these events have been regarded as a repudiation of the contract of employment by the employer because the employer has by his actions, albeit that the actions may be involuntary, rendered it impossible for the employer to continue with the employment.

8.1 Dissolution of a partnership

At common law the dissolution of a partnership by the retirement of one or more of the partners and the transfer of the business to the remaining partners, in the absence of an express or implied term in the contract of employment to the contrary, brought the contract to an end: *Brace v Calder* [1895] 2 QB 253. However, such a transfer is now likely to be within the provisions of the Transfer of Undertakings (Protection of Employment) Regulations 1981 (S1 1981 No 1794). In any event continuity of employment will probably be preserved under either para 17(2) or 17(5) of Sched 13 to the EP(C)A 1978. See Chapter 2, **6**, above.

The dissolution on the death of a partner will not automatically terminate the contract unless the contract is dependent upon the continued existence of that partner: see *Phillips v Hull Alhambra Palace Co* [1901] 1 QB 59. Again, if there is a transfer of the business to the surviving partners, the transfer will probably be within the 1981 Regulations and continuity will probably be preserved.

In a more recent case it was held where there is a major change in the partnership, the dissolution of the partnership will probably terminate the contracts of employment. A minor change may not have that effect: *Tunstall and Another v Condon and Another* [1980] ICR 786.

8.2 Bankruptcy and winding-up

The bankruptcy of an employer does not operate to terminate the contract of employment. As the contract is of a personal nature, it may be frustrated, although this is arguable.

The appointment of a receiver by the court will probably operate to terminate the contracts of employment: see *Re Foster Clark Ltd's Indenture Trust* [1966] 1 All ER 43 and *Reid v Explosives Co Ltd* (1887) 19 QBD 264, although the point is not free from all doubt. Where a receiver is appointed other than by the court, it will depend upon whether he is appointed as agent of the company or as agent for the creditors. If he is appointed as agent of the company his appointment will not necessarily be inconsistent with the continued existence of the contract of employment, unless it is clear from the circumstances that the contracts of employment must be terminated: *Deaway Trading Ltd v Calverley and Others* [1973] ICR 546; and *Re Mack Trucks (Britain) Ltd* [1967] 1 WLR 780. Where the receiver is agent for the creditors then it is more likely that the contracts of employment will be terminated.

A winding-up order has been held to operate as a termination of the contract of employment: *Golding and Howard v Fire Auto and Marine Insurance Co Ltd* (1968) 3 ITR 372; see also *McEwan v Upper Clyde Shipbuilders Ltd (in liquidation)* (1972) 7 ITR 296.

It has been held that a resolution for the voluntary winding-up of a company does not operate as a notice of dismissal of the company's employees: see *Midland Counties District Bank Ltd v Attwood* [1905] 1 Ch 357; but in *Reigate v Union Manufacturing Co (Ramsbottom)* [1918] 1 KB 592, it was held that although a voluntary winding-up will not always terminate the contract of employment, where it was not intended to carry on the business and therefore the contract, it would. Again a resolution for a voluntary winding-up may operate to terminate certain contracts: *Fowler v Commercial Timber Co Ltd* [1930] 2 KB 1, where it was held that a resolution for the voluntary winding-up was likely to result in the termination of the managing director's contract. In *Fox Brothers (Clothes) Ltd (in liquidation) v*

Bryant [1978] IRLR 485, it was held that the employees' contracts of employment did not automatically come to an end where the company went into voluntary liquidation. The EAT doubted if the employee could claim to have been unfairly dismissed.

9 Frustration

The common law doctrine of frustration applies to contracts of employment and is based upon the proposition that a contract of service is a contract of personal service. Consequently, it can only be performed by the contracting parties, and it will be discharged where either party is incapable of performing his contract due to circumstances beyond his control; ie the agreement as envisaged between the parties has become impossible and is frustrated. The contract is discharged and not avoided so that the parties' vested rights are preserved. In *Marshall v Harland and Wolff Ltd* (1972) 7 ITR 150, a case involving redundancy of a sick employee, the NIRC found:

there is nothing technical about the idea that a contract should cease to bind the parties if, through no fault of either of them, unprovided for circumstances arise in which a contractual obligation becomes impossible of performance or in which performance of the obligation would be rendered a thing radically different from that which was undertaken by the contract.

A contract which can be performed is not frustrated where there is a risk that it will not be performed in the future. Frustration is produced by events happening and not by the risk of such events: *Converfoam (Darwen) Ltd v Bell* [1981] IRLR 195. Frustration puts an end to the contract independently of the conduct or intention of the parties. Thus, where the contract is frustrated there is no dismissal, and an employee cannot claim unfair dismissal.

Incapacity due to sickness may be a frustrating event. In deciding whether the employee's incapacity renders future performance impossible or radically different from that which the parties envisaged when entering into the contract, the NIRC in *Marshall*'s case above, held that the tribunal should take into account the following:

(a) The terms of the contract, including the provisions as to sickness pay The whole basis of weekly employment may be destroyed more quickly than that of monthly employment and that in turn more quickly than annual employment. When the contract provides for sick pay, it is plain that the contract cannot be frustrated so long as the employee returns to work, or appears likely to return to work, within the period during which such sick pay is payable. But the converse is not necessarily true, for the right to sick pay may expire before the incapacity has gone on, or appears likely to go on, for so long as to make a return to work impossible or radically different from the obligations undertaken under the contract of employment.

(b) How long the employment was likely to last in the absence of

sickness The relationship is less likely to survive if the employment was inherently temporary in its nature or for the duration of a particular job, than if it was expected to be long term or even lifelong.

(c) The nature of the employment Where the employee is one of many in the same category, the relationship is more likely to survive the period of incapacity than if he occupies a key post which must be filled and filled on a permanent basis if his absence is prolonged.

(d) The nature of the illness or injury and how long it has already continued and the prospects of recovery The greater the degree of incapacity and the longer the period over which it has persisted and is likely to persist, the more likely it is that the relationship has been destroyed.

(e) The period of past employment A relationship which is of long standing is not so easily destroyed as one which has but a short history. This is good sense and, we think, no less good law, even if it involves some implied and scarcely detectable change in the contract of employment year by year as the duration of the relationship lengthens. The legal basis is that over a long period of service the parties must be assumed to have contemplated a longer period or periods of sickness than over a shorter period.

These factors are interrelated and cumulative, but are not necessarily exhaustive of those which have to be taken into account. The question is and remains: 'Was the employee's incapacity, looked at before the purported dismissal, of such a nature, or did it appear likely to continue for such a period, that further performance of his obligations in the future would either be impossible, or would be a thing radically different from that undertaken by him and accepted by the employer under the agreed terms of his employment?'

Any other factors which bear upon this issue must also be considered.

The ending of the relationship of employer and employee by operation of law is, by definition, independent of the volition or intention of the parties. A tribunal is, however, entitled to treat the conduct of the parties as evidence to be considered in forming a judgment as to whether the changed circumstances were so fundamental as to strike at the root of the relationship.

In *Egg Stores (Stamford Hill) Ltd v Leibovici* [1977] ICR 260, the EAT held:

one needs to know in what kind of circumstances can it be said that further performance of his obligations in the future will be impossible? It seems to us that an important question to be asked in cases such as the present—we are not suggesting that it is the only question—is: 'has the time arrived when the employer can no longer reasonably be expected to keep the absent employee's post open for him?' . . .

It is possible to divide into two kinds the events relied upon as bringing about the frustration of a short-term periodic contract of employment. There may be an event (eg a crippling accident) so dramatic and shattering that everyone concerned will realise immediately that to all intents and purposes the contract must be regarded as at an end. Or there may be an event, such as illness or accident, the course and outcome of which is uncertain. It may be a long process before one is able to say whether the event is such as to bring about the frustration of the contract. But there *will* have been frustration of the contract, even though at the time of the event the outcome was uncertain, if the time arrives when, looking back, one can say that at some point (even if it is not possible to say precisely when) matters had gone on so long, and the prospects for the future were so poor, that it was no longer practical to regard the contract as still subsisting. Among the matters to be taken into account in such a case in reaching a decision are these:

(1) the length of the previous employment;
(2) how long it had been expected that the employment would continue;
(3) the nature of the job;
(4) the nature, length and effect of the illness or disabling event;
(5) the need of the employer for the work to be done, and the need for a replacement to do it;
(6) the risk to the employer of acquiring obligations in respect of redundancy payments or compensation for unfair dismissal to the replacement employee;
(7) whether wages have continued to be paid;
(8) the acts and the statements of the employer in relation to the employment, including the dismissal of, or failure to dismiss, the employee; and
(9) whether in all the circumstances a reasonable employer could be expected to wait any longer.

This approach was followed in *Williams v Watsons Luxury Coaches* [1990] IRLR 164. It was held other factors to be considered were the contractual terms as to sickness pay, if any, and the prospects of recovery.

The *Marshall* and *Leibovici* cases were also followed in *Hart v A R Marshall and Sons (Bulwell) Ltd* [1977] ICR 539, where the EAT again emphasised the importance of examining why the employer did not dismiss the employee. If he did not think he could, this may well be important in establishing that the contract has not been frustrated. It may be that he has not put his mind to the question whether he can dismiss and this may be consistent with frustration of the contract.

In *Notcutt v Universal Equipment Co (London) Ltd* [1986] ICR 414, Dillon LJ held:

as a periodic contract of employment determinable by short, or relatively short, notice may none the less be intended in many cases by both parties to last for many years and as the power of the employer to terminate the contract by notice is subject to the provisions for the protection of employees against unfair dismissal now in the Act of 1978, I can see no reason in principle why such a periodic contract of employment should not in appropriate circumstances, be held to have been terminated without notice by frustration according to the accepted and long established doctrine of frustration in our law of contract. The mere fact that the contract can be terminated by the employer by relatively short notice cannot of itself render the doctrine of frustration inevitably inapplicable.

Notcutt suffered a coronary. His contract of employment was terminable by 12 weeks' notice. He was dismissed without notice and brought a claim for pay during the notice period under s 50 and para 3 of Sched 3 to the EP(C)A 1978. It was held that the contract had been frustrated and therefore the notice was unnecessary.

The contract of employment may also be frustrated by a period of internment where it is likely that the internment is of a permanent rather than a temporary nature.

Military service may also frustrate the contract of employment. An employee may be entitled to apply to his former employer to be reinstated: see the Reserve Forces (Safeguard of Employment) Act 1985.

In *Hare v Murphy Bros Ltd* [1974] ICR 603, the Court of Appeal appeared to find that a prison sentence of 12 months for unlawful wounding could be a frustrating event which brought the contract to an end. In *Harrington v Kent CC* [1980] IRLR 353, it was held that a prison sentence of 12 months imposed for offences of indecency operated to frustrate the contract of employment. The contract was frustrated from the moment the employee was sentenced, even though he was appealing against his sentence.

In *FC Shepherd and Co Ltd v Jerrom* [1986] ICR 802, the Court of Appeal held that a Borstal sentence of between six months and two years frustrated Jerrom's apprenticeship agreement, even though it arose as a result of fault on the employee's part. Thus, *Norris v Southampton CC* [1982] IRLR 141, where it was held that a contract is not frustrated by the deliberate conduct or fault of one party, would appear to be wrongly decided. However, in such cases, there is a thin dividing line between frustration and repudiation.

Chapter 4

The Effective Date of Termination

It is important to ascertain the effective date of termination for the following reasons:

(a) to decide whether the employee has brought his claim for unfair dismissal within the limitation period;

(b) to calculate the continuous period of employment;

(c) to calculate the employee's pay and the amount of the basic award of compensation; and

(d) to ascertain whether or not the employee is within the upper age limit.

1 Statutory definitions

Section 55(4) of the EP(C)A 1978 defines the 'effective date of termination' as follows:

(a) in relation to an employee whose contract of employment is terminated by notice, whether given by his employer or by the employee, the 'effective date of termination' means the date on which that notice expires;

(b) in relation to an employee whose contract of employment is terminated without notice, the 'effective date of termination' means the date on which the termination takes effect; and

(c) in relation to an employee who is employed under a contract for a fixed term, where that term expires without being renewed under the same contract, the 'effective date of termination' means the date on which the fixed term expires.

Where the employee is dismissed without notice the position is covered by s 55(4)(b) of the EP(C)A 1978. Where the employee is dismissed with less than the proper notice to which he is entitled the position is covered by s 55(4)(a) of the EP(C)A 1978. In both cases this is subject to the provisions of s 55(5) and (7)(a) of the EP(C)A 1978: see below.

Section 55(5) contains a provision designed to prevent employers defeating employees' claims to various statutory rights, by dismissing them with notice which is less than the statutory period of notice. It provides that where the contract of employment is terminated by the employer and the notice required by s 49 of the EP(C)A 1978 to be given by an employer would, if duly given on the material date, expire on a later date than the effective date of termination under s 55(4) of the EP(C)A 1978, then for the purposes of ss 53(2), 64(1)(a), 64A, 73(3) and para 8(3) of Sched 14 to the EP(C)A 1978, the later date shall be treated as the effective date of termination in relation to the dismissal. The material date for this purpose is the date when notice of termination was given by the employer or, where no notice was given, the date when the contract of employment was terminated by the employer: s 55(7)(a) of the EP(C)A 1978. Suppose that A is continuously employed until one week short of two years and is dismissed without notice one week short of two years. Apart from s 55(5) of the EP(C)A 1978, the day that he was dismissed would be the effective date of termination. Under s 55(5), however, the effective date of termination is treated as the date when statutory notice would have expired. A is entitled to one week's statutory notice, and so has two years' employment. Provided that the two years are made up of continuous weeks of employment, he may bring a claim for unfair dismissal.

Section 55(6) of the EP(C)A 1978 provides where the contract of employment is terminated by the employee and:

(a) the material date does not fall during a period of notice given by the employer to terminate that contract; and

(b) had the contract been terminated not by the employee but by notice given on the material date by the employer, that notice would have been required by s 49 of the EP(C)A 1978 to expire on a date later than the effective date of termination under s 55(4) of the EP(C)A 1978,

then for the purposes of ss 64(1)(a), 64A and 73(3) and para 8(3) of Sched 14, the later date shall be treated as the effective date of termination in relation to the dismissal. The material date means the date when notice of termination was given by the employee or, where no notice was given, the date when the contract of employment was terminated by the employee: s 55(7)(b) of the EP(C)A 1978.

The effect of this provision is to give the employee who is constructively dismissed the same protection as he would have enjoyed had he been actually dismissed by the employer.

Under s 55(5) and (6), and (7)(a) and (b) of the EP(C)A 1978, only the length of notice prescribed by s 49 of the EP(C)A 1978 can be considered and not the length of any contractual notice which the employee should have been given, so the effective date of termination can be postponed only by the length of the statutory notice: *Fox Maintenance Ltd v Jackson* [1978] ICR 110.

Does s 55(5) postpone the effective date of termination only where the employee has been lawfully summarily dismissed by the employer?

Arguably, s 55(5) does not protect an employee who has been lawfully summarily dismissed because s 49(5) of the EP(C)A 1978 does not affect the common law right of either party to terminate the contract without notice and so the statutory notice prescribed by s 49 of the EP(C)A 1978 need not be given. In *Lanton Leisure Ltd v White and Gibson* [1987] IRLR 119, it was held that the mere designation by an employer of the employees' conduct as gross misconduct did not preclude the operation of s 55(5). An employer could avoid the consequences of s 55(5) by simply designating the employees' conduct as gross misconduct. It is necessary to investigate the employees' conduct to see if it was gross misconduct.

Unlike s 55(5), s 55(6) does not apply to s 53(2) of the EP(C)A 1978 which deals with the qualifying period for a written statement of reasons for dismissal.

The effective date of termination and the need for acceptance of the employer's act of wrongfully dismissing the employee was considered in *Robert Cort and Son Ltd v Charman* [1981] ICR 816. Charman was summarily dismissed with one month's pay in lieu of notice and left his employment on the day on which he was given notice. If he had worked out his notice he would have had the necessary period of continuous employment to have brought a claim for unfair dismissal. The evidence established that Charman did not accept his dismissal. He argued that since he had not accepted his dismissal the effective date was not the date upon which he left work, but the date when he accepted the employer's repudiation of the contract of employment—a later date. Following the decision in *Gunton v The Mayor, Aldermen and Burgesses of The London Borough of Richmond-upon-Thames* [1980] 3 WLR 714, the tribunal found that the effective date of termination was postponed to the date when he accepted the employer's repudiation. The EAT rejected this approach. It found that s 55 had been drafted on the basis that wrongful dismissal terminated the contract of employment.

Thus, in s 55(4)(*a*) (dealing with the case of termination by notice) it is the date of the expiry of the notice served which is the effective date of termination: nothing in the subsection suggests that this is so only where the length of notice served complies with the contractual obligation. Again, s 49 of the [1978] Act lays down certain minimum periods of notice which have to be given. Section 55(5) provides that where either no notice or notice shorter than that required by s 49 is given, the effective date of termination is the date on which the notice required by s 49 would have expired. Such provision would have been unnecessary if the draftsman had considered that the contract would not otherwise have been terminated by an unlawful notice.

. . . Section 55(4)(*b*) defines the effective date of termination as being the date on which 'the termination takes effect'. The word 'termination' plainly refers back to the termination of the contract. But the draftsman of the section does not refer simply to the date of termination of the contract, but to the date on which the termination 'takes effect'. As we have pointed out, even on the acceptance view [where an employer repudiates the contract of employment, eg by wrongfully dismissing the employee, the contract is not thereby determined but will only be determined when the employee accepts the repudiation] the status of employer and employee comes to an end at the moment of dismissal, even if the contract may for some purposes thereafter continue. When dismissed without the appropriate contractual notice, the employee cannot insist on being further employed: as from the moment of dismissal, his sole right is a right to damages and he is bound to mitigate his damages by looking for other employment. We therefore consider it to be a legitimate use of words to say, in the context of s 55 [of the EP(C)A 1978], that the termination of the contract of employment 'takes effect' at the date of dismissal, since on that date the employee's rights under the contract are transformed from the right to be employed into a right to damages.

The EAT held it was 'of the greatest importance that there should be no doubt or uncertainty as to the date which is the "effective date of termination" '. A claim for unfair dismissal must be brought within three months of the effective date of termination and so it is important the employee knows when this is, free from the 'subtle legalities of the law of repudiation and acceptance of repudiation': see also *Brown v Southall and Knight* [1980] IRLR 130. The EAT followed the decision in *Dedman v British Building and Engineering Appliances Ltd* [1973] ICR 82 and on appeal [1974] ICR 53. See below.

Where an employee agrees to waive his right to statutory notice or to accept a payment in lieu thereof, this does not operate to defeat s 55(5) of the EP(C)A 1978 which still applies to postpone the effective date of termination until the date when the statutory notice would have expired had it been given in full: *Staffordshire County Council v Secretary of State for Employment* [1989] ICR 664. Nothing in s 55(5), (6) and (7) of the EP(C)A 1978 postpones the effective date of termination for the purposes of the statutory time limit.

2 Application of the statutory definitions

The statutory definition of the effective date of termination has given rise to difficulty in cases where: the employee is paid wages in lieu of notice; the employee is told during the period of notice that his services are no longer required; and the employee appeals against dismissal. In each case the question arises as to when the effective date of termination is.

2.1 The problem of wages in lieu of notice

A distinction must be drawn between those cases where an employee is dismissed immediately with wages in lieu of notice and those cases where an employee is dismissed with notice but is given wages in lieu of working out the notice. In the former case the effective date of termination will usually be ascertained in accordance with s 55(4)(b) of the EP(C)A 1978—the effective date of termination will be the date upon which the termination takes place. Thus, in *Dedman v British Building and Engineering Appliances Ltd* [1974] ICR 53, Dedman was given a letter on 5 May 1972 terminating his employment immediately. With the letter was his salary for the month of May, plus one month in lieu of notice. Lay members of the tribunal interpreted the payment for May as meaning that the employee was still employed but not required to work, although he had his card stamped only until 5 May and on that date his national insurance card and P45 were returned to him. The Court of Appeal found that the crucial words were 'terminate your employment immediately' and equally important was the fact that his national insurance card was only stamped up to 5 May. It held that the contract was terminated immediately, and the payment of salary was made as compensation for immediate dismissal and not by way of continuation of his employment. See also *Dixon v Stenor Ltd* [1973] ICR 157.

In *Hackwood v Benross Trading Co Ltd* [1975] IRLR 2, Hackwood was dismissed with one week's wages in lieu of notice and was given his P45 and his national insurance card, and ceased to work for the employer within 15 minutes of being handed his wages and cards. He argued that he was entitled to 4 weeks' wages in lieu of notice and later received a further 3 weeks' wages. It was held that the contract ceased as at the date the employee was dismissed with wages in lieu of notice and the payment of additional wages was not a continuation of the contract of employment.

Where an employee is given notice and during the notice period is told in a letter 'to relinquish your duties . . . with effect from today . . . and remove yourself and your belongings at the same time', that letter was a letter of summary dismissal and therefore the effective date of termination was the date upon which the employee finished work. The effective date of termination in s 55(4) of the EP(C)A 1978 meant the actual date of termination: *Stapp v The Shaftesbury Society* [1982] IRLR 326.

In *London Borough of Newham v Ward* [1985] IRLR 509, it was held that the content of form P45 is one of the factors to be taken into account in determining the effective date of termination, but it is of no more importance than that. The employee had been summarily dismissed on 9 February 1983; that was the effective date of termination, notwithstanding the fact that form P45 showed the effective date of termination as 27 June 1983.

Where an employee receives notice but is not required to work out the notice and is paid wages in lieu, the effective date of termination will usually be ascertained in accordance with s 55(4)(*a*) of the EP(C)A 1978.

In *Brindle v HW Smith (Cabinets) Ltd* [1972] IRLR 125, Brindle was given one month's notice, but during the notice was told that she need not come in to work and she was told to go on holiday. She indicated that she would prefer to work out her notice but she never returned to work again. Her national insurance card was stamped for the whole of the period of the notice. The Court of Appeal held that the effective date of termination was the date when the notice would have expired and not when Brindle was told that she need not come into work and could go on holiday. *Brindle*'s case was distinguished in *Stapp*'s case; there is a difference in that on the facts Brindle was not summarily dismissed whereas Stapp was.

In *Lees v Arthur Greaves (Lees) Ltd* [1974] ICR 501, Lees was given six months' notice orally on 1 October 1971 which was confirmed in writing on 7 October 1971 to expire on 31 March 1972. On 28 January 1972, it was alleged that the contract had terminated as at that date by agreement between the parties. As at that date Lees received all his monetary entitlements, his P45 and his national insurance card. The evidence was that Lees had agreed under pressure to leave on 28 January. The Court of Appeal, by a majority, refused to find an agreement whereby Lees consented to the termination of his employment as at that date, and concluded that after 28 January Lees was still employed but not required to work. As in the case of *Brindle*, Lees was not summarily dismissed and therefore this case may be distinguished on its facts from the case of *Stapp*. See above. Neither of these decisions is without its problems.

In both *Brindle* and *Lees*, notice had been given which straddled the introduction of the statutory protection against unfair dismissal. If the employee had been allowed to work out the notice it would have enabled the employee in each case to claim the benefit of the statutory protection and claim unfair dismissal.

In *Adams v GKN Sankey Ltd* [1980] IRLR 416, Adams was dismissed by letter dated 2 November 1979 which stated 'you are . . . given 12 weeks' notice of dismissal from this company with effect from Monday 5 November 1979.

'You will not be expected to work your notice but will receive monies in lieu of notice, and these, together with all other documentation, will be sent to you through the post.'

It was held on the evidence that this was a case where the employee was not required to work out the notice but would receive monies in lieu, and therefore the employment did not come to an end until the expiration of 12 weeks from 5 November 1979.

2.2 Appeals against dismissal

The effective date of termination, where the dismissed employee has a right of appeal against his dismissal under the provisions of a domestic appeal procedure, was first considered in *McDonald v South Cambridgeshire RDC* [1973] ICR 611. It was held that the exercise of the right of appeal did not affect the effective date of termination. In *High v British Railways Board* [1979] IRLR 52, it was held that in such circumstances the provisions of the contract of employment relating to the appeal procedure continue to apply to that extent only.

In *J Sainsbury Ltd v Savage* [1980] IRLR 109, Savage was instantly dismissed on 21 February 1978. He exercised his right of appeal against dismissal under the terms of the company's disciplinary procedure, where, pending the decision of an appeal against dismissal, the employee was suspended without pay, but if the employee was reinstated he would receive full back pay for the period of his suspension. However the exercise of the right of appeal did not affect the effective date of termination. On the failure of the appeal he was treated as dismissed from 21 February 1978, which was the effective date of termination.

An exception would arise where, under the provisions of the appeal procedure, the contract continues in full force pending the appeal so that the employee has the right to work and to be paid, and the employer can call upon the employee to work. See also *Crown Agents for Overseas Governments and Administration v Lawal* [1978] IRLR 542.

In *The Board of Governors, The National Heart and Chest Hospitals v Nambiar* [1981] IRLR 196, Nambiar was dismissed on 16 January. He exercised his internal right of appeal. His appeal was allowed to the extent of recommending that he should be found suitable alternative employment. The employer paid Nambiar his arrears of salary and continued to pay him until it became apparent that they could not find him suitable alternative employment. It was held that the effective date of termination was 16 January, notwithstanding the fact that he was paid arrears of salary and salary was paid to him while alternative employment was being sought. The contract of employment did not continue in force. If an employee's contract does continue in force pending the determination of an appeal the effective date of termination may thereby be postponed.

Where the employee is successful in having the decision to dismiss him overruled on appeal, then the effect upon his employment will depend upon the facts of the case and his contract of employment. Where the employee is reinstated his continuity of employment will not be broken whether or not there is a term to that effect in his contract of employment: see the cases of *High* and *Savage*, above, and also *Howgate v Fane Acoustics Ltd* [1981] IRLR 161. Where the employee is successful the initial notice may be rendered null and void: see *Petch v Taunton Deane District Council* (1977) (unreported).

In *BBC v Beckett* [1983] IRLR 43, Beckett was dismissed and appealed against the penalty of dismissal. Following the appeal he was demoted. Beckett argued that once notice of dismissal had been given by the employer it was not open to the employer to withdraw that notice unilaterally and therefore he was being offered alternative employment under a new contract. This contention was rejected by the EAT, which found that the employee was being offered the chance to continue his employment with the employer but in a different post.

In *Batchelor v British Railways Board* [1987] IRLR 136, Batchelor was dismissed with immediate effect on 5 February. She appealed. On 25 February she was told that an appeal against her dismissal had been disallowed. It was held that the effective date of termination was 5 February. The fact that the Board were not entitled under the disciplinary procedure to dismiss summarily for the conduct in question did not alter the effective date of termination. It might enable the employee to bring an action for breach of contract.

3 Miscellaneous matters

3.1 The effective date of termination — a matter of evidence

Where an employee is given wages in lieu, usually in a lump sum, it is a matter of evidence whether or not the employee is employed for the period of the notice, albeit that he is not required to work out the notice. It may be quite clear that the effective date of termination is the date when the notice would have expired, although the employee will not be required to work during the notice period. The employee may, for instance, be treated as still in employment for all or some purposes. However, it is open to argument that where the employer pays wages in lieu, particularly in a lump sum, unless there is clear evidence that the effective date of termination is not until the end of the notice period in practice, the relationship ceases on the day when the employee leaves the place of work, and in such cases the effective date of termination is likely to be the date when the termination takes effect, which will be when the employee is actually dismissed.

Whether a letter of dismissal brings the contract to an end immediately or at a future date depends upon the construction of the letter: see *Adams v GKN Sankey Ltd* [1980] IRLR 416. In *Chapman v Letheby and Christopher Ltd* [1981] IRLR 440, it was held that a letter of dismissal must be construed in accordance with what an ordinary reasonable employee would understand the words to mean in the light of the facts known to him at the time. In *Stapp v The Shaftesbury Society* [1982] IRLR 326, Stephenson LJ said:

a notice to terminate employment must be construed strictly against the person who gives it, the employer, and if there is any ambiguity it must be resolved in favour of the person who receives it, the employee.

Where an employee has received oral notification of dismissal followed by a confirmatory letter, the oral and written words have to be read and construed together in order to resolve any ambiguity: see *Leech v Preston Borough Council* [1985] ICR 192.

The importance of exercising care is illustrated by *Hammerton Shipping Co Ltd v Borg* (1977) 12 ITR 54, where the company wrote to Borg on 28 October 1975 terminating his employment on 31 January 1976. Borg accepted the notice and suggested that he should take his holidays on 15 November 1975 for two weeks. No reply was made to the letter, but on 14 November 1975 the employee notified the employer that he would be on holiday from 17 November to 30 November 1975. The company's response was that if he took his holiday then he should not return to work again. Borg took the holiday and did not return to work, but the employers continued to pay him until 31 January 1976. The EAT upheld the decision of the tribunal that the effective date of termination of the employment was 31 January 1976, the date when the notice expired. See also *Goldsmith v RIBA Services Ltd* [1974] IRLR 176.

Another example is *IPC Business Press Ltd v Gray* [1977] ICR 858, where the employers wanted to dismiss the employee summarily but were advised they could not do so. They gave notice to expire on 31 August, although the employee was later told that he was not required after 13 August. On 16 August he received his pay in lieu of notice until 31 August with his other entitlements and his P45. However, the accompanying letter told the employee that his last day of employment was 31 August. It was held by the EAT that the effective date of termination was 31 August. The employers thought that the employment could not be terminated before that date. Where an employee is sent a letter summarily dismissing him, the effective date of termination is the date when either the employee reads the letter or the date when he reasonably had the opportunity of knowing about it: see *Brown v Southall and Knight* [1980] ICR 617, see also *Hindle Gears Ltd v McGinty* [1984] IRLR 477.

3.2 An agreed change to the effective date of termination

In *TBA Industrial Products Ltd v Morland* [1982] IRLR 331, the employee was given a letter by his employer on 27 May terminating his employment on 2 August. At that date he was to be given a payment in lieu of the unexpired period of notice which would have continued until 30 August. He was told that if he wished to leave before 2 August he should fill in a blank letter and insert in that letter the date he wished to leave. The employee returned the letter and inserted 7 June. The employer accepted the employee's request and the agreed date when the employee was to leave was brought forward to 6 June. The majority of the Court of Appeal held that the effective date of termination was 2 August. Waller LJ held that, 'Termination by notice involves the notice being causative of the termination. The notice, in my opinion, has to be unconditional.' He found that the notice given by the employer was causative of the termination and unconditional and brought the employee's employment to an end on

2 August. The letter from the employee was simply an acceptance of the employer's invitation to leave before 2 August. Waller LJ also found that the letter did not produce a variation or waiver of the original notice. It was open to the employer if it wished to withdraw the original notice and serve a new notice complying with the date suggested by the employee. Support for this view was gained from the wording of s 55(4)(a) of the EP(C)A 1978. A variation would only be possible if after the words 'the date on which the notice expires' there were added 'or any variation thereof'.

In a dissenting judgment Ackner LJ clearly thought it was possible to vary by agreement the effective date of termination.

In *McAlwane v Boughton Estates Ltd* [1973] ICR 470, McAlwane was told in a letter that his employment was terminated with effect from 19 April. On 10 April he asked if he could leave his employment on 12 April to take up a new job and it was agreed that he could do so. It was held by the NIRC that in the circumstances the parties had agreed to vary the notice of dismissal by substituting an earlier date: that was the effective date of termination. The decision in *McAlwane v Boughton* was followed in *CPS Recruitment Ltd t/a Blackwood Associates v (1) Bowen and (2) Secretary of State for Employment* [1982] IRLR 54. As *TBA Industrial Products Ltd v Morland*, above, illustrates, much will depend on the facts. See also *Staffordshire County Council v Secretary of State for Employment* [1989] ICR 664.

However, in *Crank v Her Majesty's Stationery Office* [1985] ICR 1, the employers ceased trading at the premises where the employee worked. Crank was offered employment at the new premises. On 2 September 1983 he left the employers without telling them that he would not be moving to the new location. He subsequently obtained employment with different employers at the same premises. On 5 September he wrote to his employers asking for a redundancy payment. On 14 September in reply to a letter from his former employers asking why he was not working at the new location he wrote offering his resignation as from 2 September, which was accepted. It was held that it was open to the parties to agree retrospectively that 2 September was to be taken as the date of termination of the contract even though the contract was subsisting after that date. There was nothing in s 55(4) of the EP(C)A 1978 which required a later date to be taken.

3.3 The effective date of termination and the employee's counter notice

Section 55(3) of the EP(C)A 1978 enables an employee to whom an employer has given notice to terminate his contract of employment during the period of that notice to serve a counter notice upon the employer to terminate the contract of employment on an earlier date than that on which the employer's notice is due to expire. See Chapter 3. The Act is silent as to the effective date of termination in these circumstances. In *TBA Industrial Products Ltd v Morland* [1982] IRLR

331, it was argued before the EAT that the effective date of termination was the date specified in the employer's original notice. The EAT, while noting the force of the argument, did not reach any decision. An authoritative decision is therefore awaited.

3.4 Constructive dismissal and the effective date of termination

Where the employee is constructively dismissed (for the meaning of constructive dismissal see Chapter 3), the effective date of termination is the date when the employee accepts the employer's repudiation: see *Western Excavating (ECC) Ltd v Sharpe* [1978] ICR 221. Usually this will be the date of the employee's departure. It is clear from the decision in *Crank*'s case, above, that the parties may agree the effective date of termination and the date may be a specified date. But consider *TBA Industrial Products Ltd v Morland*, above.

3.5 Notice and effective date of termination

In *West v Kneels Ltd* [1986] IRLR 430, the employee was told on a Monday afternoon, 'We have made a decision: you are unsuitable for our kind of work and I am giving you a week's notice from now.' It was held that seven days' notice means seven days exclusive of the day on which work has been done. The EAT restricted its decision to cases where the notice of termination is given orally.

In *Octavius Atkinson and Sons Ltd v Morris* [1989] IRLR 158, Morris was summarily dismissed at lunchtime by reason of redundancy. He left the site on which he was working at 2.00pm. The Court of Appeal held that where an employee is summarily dismissed during the course of a working day and the employer's repudiation is accepted, the contract of employment and the status of employee cease at the moment when dismissal is communicated to the employee. The effective date of termination is determined in accordance with s 55(4)(*b*) of the EP(C)A 1978.

4 Strikes

Section 62(4)(*a*) of the EP(C)A 1978 contains special provisions dealing with the date of dismissal where the employee is dismissed by reason of a strike or other industrial action. The date of dismissal, where the employee's contract is terminated by notice, is the date on which the employer's notice is given. In any other case the date of the dismissal is the effective date of termination. This will apply where the contract is terminated summarily or where it is terminated by paying wages in lieu of notice.

Chapter 5

The Reason for Dismissal

In a claim for unfair dismissal, once the employee has established a dismissal or the employer has accepted that a dismissal has occurred, it is for the employer to show the reason for the dismissal and that it is a reason which is within the EP(C)A 1978, s 57(1) and (2). There are certain exceptions which are considered later. (See Chapters 9 and 10). The tribunal must then determine whether or not in the circumstances the employer has acted reasonably: s 57(3) of the EP(C)A 1978. Indeed, until the employer has established a reason, the tribunal should not consider reasonableness: *Post Office Counters Ltd v Heavey* [1989] IRLR 513. Before s 57(3) of the EP(C)A 1978 was amended by s 6 of the Employment Act 1980, the burden of proof was on the employer. Now it is sometimes described as a neutral burden. The tribunal must consider the whole of the evidence and satisfy itself on the evidence whether the employer acted reasonably.

1 Written reasons

Section 53(1) of the EP(C)A 1978, entitles every employee whose contract of employment is terminated by his employer, whether with or without notice or where his employment under a fixed-term contract expires without being renewed, to be given by his employer a written statement containing particulars of the reasons for his dismissal. The employee must ask the employer to give these written reasons and, once the request is made, the employer is obliged to supply the reasons within 14 days of the request.

If the employee claims constructive dismissal he is not entitled to a written statement. Further, a written statement need not be supplied unless, on the effective date of termination, the employee has been or will have been, continuously employed for a period of not less than two years ending with that date: s 53(2) of the EP(C)A 1978. This applies to any employee whose period of continuous employment commenced after 26 February 1990. Previously the period was six months ending with the last complete week before that date. The employee must have been continuously employed for a period of two years ending with the effective date of termination: see s 64(1)(*a*) of the EP(C)A 1978. The qualifying period for an employee to claim written reasons and unfair dismissal is now the same.

The requirement to give written reasons does not apply to an employee who under his contract of employment ordinarily works outside Great Britain: s 141(2) of the EP(C)A 1978 ; a share fisherman: s 144(2) of the EP(C)A 1978; and the police service: s 146 (2) of the EP(C)A 1978.

The employee has the right to make a complaint to a tribunal on the grounds that the employer has unreasonably refused to provide a written statement, or that the particulars of the reasons given by the employer are inadequate or untrue: s 53(4) of the EP(C)A 1978. If the tribunal finds the complaint well-founded it may make a declaration as to the employer's reasons for dismissing the employee and it must order the employer to pay to the employee a sum equal to two weeks' pay: s 53(4)(*a*) and (*b*) of the EP(C)A 1978. The period for making a complaint to the tribunal is the same as in the case of a complaint for unfair dismissal: s 53(5) of the EP(C)A 1978.

For the employer the problems are obvious. The statement is admissible in evidence in any proceedings (see s 53(3) of the EP(C)A 1978) and will be of particular value in proceedings for unfair dismissal. Thus, in giving the reasons in the written statement, the employer must ensure accuracy and consistency. Nothing will be worse for the employer than to inform the employee of one reason for the dismissal, to give another in the written statement and to give yet another reason in his notice of appearance in a claim for unfair dismissal. If the employer fails to give a reason, or gives the wrong reason, the tribunal may make a declaration as to the reason. The employer will then be fixed with that reason in any claim for unfair dismissal and he will have difficulty in seeking to put forward another reason.

A complaint can only be made to a tribunal if the employee has requested written reasons: *Catherine Haigh Harlequin Hair Design v Seed* [1990] IRLR 175.

The tribunal has to decide what amounts to a refusal and what is unreasonable.

In the early cases of *Joines v B&S (Burknall) Ltd* [1977] IRLR 83 and *Keen v Dymo Ltd* [1977] IRLR 118, the tribunals found that a failure to reply was in essence a refusal. However, these two cases must be considered in the light of more recent decisions of the EAT.

In *Daynecourt Insurance Brokers Ltd v Iles* [1978] IRLR 335, a failure to produce a written statement was treated as synonymous with a refusal. The EAT found that the employer must act reasonably and, however exceptional the circumstances, he should not simply ignore the employee's request. However this case needs to be considered in the light of later decisions.

In *Charles Lang & Sons Ltd v Aubrey (B)* [1978] ICR 168, the Scottish division of the EAT, referring to an earlier unreported case of a tribunal, accepted as a correct statement of the law and a proper interpretation of s 53(4) of the EP(C)A 1978 that in certain circumstances a stage must be reached where inaction on the part of the employer must be construed as a refusal. However, not every instance of inaction is equivalent to an unreasonable refusal. It also found that s 53 is penal in effect; therefore it should be rigidly construed and applied only where it is clear that there is an unreasonable refusal.

In *Lowson v Percy Main and District Social Club and Institute Ltd* [1979] IRLR 227, the EAT found that mere failure to comply with a request does not necessarily amount to an unreasonable refusal. There must be a refusal, which is either explicit or implied from conduct, to comply with the employee's request, and that refusal must be unreasonable. There had been a failure of communication between the employer and its solicitors. When the solicitors realised that a request for written reasons had not been complied with, they supplied them on behalf of the employer. The EAT considered that if the employee requested written reasons and on failing to obtain them pressed the employer but was stalled every time he asked, then there might well be a refusal to reply which would be unreasonable. It is a matter of degree so that the longer the period which elapses after the request the easier it is to construe the employer's unreasonable failure to comply with the request as an unreasonable refusal: see *Newland v Simons and Willer (Hairdressers) Ltd* [1981] IRLR 359.

The employer may deny that the employee has been dismissed. Where the employer reasonably believes that there is no dismissal it will be difficult for a tribunal although holding that there is a dismissal to find also that the employer unreasonably refused to give reasons for a dismissal where the employer genuinely believed that a dismissal had not occurred. It is a question of fact whether or not an employer genuinely and honestly believed that there had been no dismissal: see *Broomsgrove v Eagle Alexander Ltd* [1981] IRLR 127. A statement by the employer that there had been no dismissal is not a complete answer: see *Brown v Stuart Scott and Co* [1981] ICR 166, where the EAT held that the tribunal had to examine whether or not the employers were acting in bad faith in failing to produce written reasons relying upon an averment that there had been no dismissal.

No particular form is required for the written reasons but they must be adequate. The EAT in *Horsley Smith and Sherry Ltd v Dutton* [1977] ICR 594, suggested that:

The document must be of such a kind that the employee, or anyone to whom he may wish to show it, can know from reading the document itself why the employee has been dismissed. We do not mean to say that as long as the document satisfies that test it cannot also refer to other documents; it may sometimes be desirable to do so.

In *Marchant v Earley Town Council* [1979] IRLR 311, the EAT found that where in response to a request for written reasons the employer refers back to some other document and that document sets out the matters which should have been given in response to a request under s 53, then the employer cannot be held to have unreasonably refused to provide the written statement. They may have refused to provide a written statement, but they have not unreasonably refused. Much will depend upon whether the document to which reference is made clearly sets out what the EAT envisaged should be given to the employee in *Horsley Smith and Sherry Ltd v Dutton*, above. In *Gilham and Others v Kent CC (No 1)* [1985] ICR 227, the Court of Appeal held that where an employer, in response to a request for written reasons, writes to the employee's solicitor stating that the reasons for dismissal have been set out in two earlier letters and enclosing copies of those letters, and confirming that the contents of those letters contain the reasons for the employee's dismissal, the employer will have complied with his statutory obligations. The case of *Horsley Smith and Sherry Ltd v Dutton*, above, was not overruled, each case turning upon its own particular facts. In that case the letter did not contain written reasons. The employer cannot rely upon a notice of appearance filed by him in an unfair dismissal claim for the purposes of s 53(1) of the EP(C)A 1978. This section requires the employer to provide the employee with an independent and separate document: *Rowan v Machinery Installations (South Wales) Ltd* [1981] IRLR 122.

Section 53(4) of the EP(C)A 1978 requires an employer to state truthfully the reason that he was relying upon in dismissing the employee. This section is concerned with whether the employer is telling the truth. It does not involve an examination of the justification for the dismissal. Truth is concerned with the veracity of what the employer puts forward as the reason for the dismissal.

'A reason has two elements: it has a factual basis of events that have occurred and which the employer considers to be the foundation for the dismissal and it has the consequences of those factual events which the employer, rightly or wrongly, relies on to justify his dismissal': *Harvard Securities plc v Younghusband* [1990] IRLR 17.

2 Statutory reasons

Under s 57(1) and (2) of the EP(C)A 1978, the employer has to establish the reason for the dismissal or, if there was more than one reason, the principal reason, and that the reason:

(*a*) related to the capability or qualifications of the employee for performing work of the kind which he was employed by the employer to do; or

(*b*) related to the conduct of the employee; or

(*c*) was that the employee was redundant; or

(*d*) was that the employee could not continue to work in the position which he held without contravention (either on his part or on that of his employer) of a duty or restriction imposed by or under an enactment; or

(*e*) was some other substantial reason of a kind such as to justify the dismissal of an employee holding the position which that employee held.

2.1 General approach

Under s 57(1) of the EP(C)A 1978 it is for the employer to establish the reason or principal reason and it is for the tribunal to see whether or not there is a reason and if so whether it is a valid one: see *Shannon v Michelin (Belfast) Ltd* [1981] IRLR 505. The employer can rely upon more than one reason. In *Carlin v St Cuthbert's Co-operative Association Ltd* [1974] IRLR 188, it was held that an employee may be dismissed for a number of reasons, all of which are equally important in the mind of the employer. If the employer seeks to rely on more than one reason, he must establish those reasons or that the reasons which he can establish entitle him to dismiss: see *Smith v Glasgow City District Council* [1987] ICR 796. The employer must specifically plead each reason upon which he relies and he must adduce evidence in support of each of those reasons before the industrial tribunal: *Murphy v Epsom College* [1983] ICR 715, approved by the Court of Appeal [1985] ICR 80. If the employer only pleads one reason or only leads evidence in support of one reason he will fail if he cannot establish that reason, even if there is another reason which might have enabled the employer to succeed had it been pleaded or had evidence in support of it been adduced before the tribunal: *Barbar Indian Restaurant v Rawat* [1985] IRLR 57.

It is not sufficient for the employer merely to establish that the employee has committed a dismissible offence. The employer must also show the reason why he decided to dismiss: see *Adams v Derby City Council* [1986] IRLR 163. The reason for a dismissal is made up of all sorts of reasons and sub-reasons. 'A construction . . . which required one only to look at one reason would produce an absurdity': *Patterson v Messrs Bracketts* [1977] IRLR 137.

Neither the employer nor the tribunal is required to dissect the reason or reasons in excessive analytical detail. Generally it is not necessary for the employer to go into every reason, because in practice a reason and even a principal reason may be compounded of several elements which do not necessarily each in themselves constitute a separate reason: *Bates Farms and Dairy Ltd v Scott* [1976] IRLR 214.

In *Abernethy v Mott, Hay and Anderson* [1974] ICR 323, Cairns LJ held: 'A reason for the dismissal of an employee is a set of facts known to the employer, or it may be of beliefs held by him which cause him to dismiss the employee.'

Therefore, as a general proposition the employer must show that at the time of the dismissal he honestly believed that the employee was dismissed for the reason expressed. Additionally, the employer's belief should be based on reasonable grounds.

In *Ferodo Ltd v Barnes* [1976] ICR 439, a case involving the employee's vandalism, the EAT held that the tribunal should not ask, 'Are we satisfied the offence was committed?', but 'Are we satisfied that the employers had, at the time of the dismissal, reasonable grounds for believing that the offence put against the applicant was in fact committed?'.

In *British Home Stores Ltd v Burchell* [1978] IRLR 379, followed in *Weddel and Co Ltd v Tepper* [1980] IRLR 96, it was held that in the case of misconduct not necessarily involving dishonesty it is usually necessary for the employer to show that he:

entertained a reasonable suspicion amounting to a belief in the guilt of the employee of that misconduct at that time. That is really stating shortly and compendiously what is in fact more than one element. First of all, there must be established by the employer the fact of that belief; that the employer did believe it. Secondly, that the employer had in his mind reasonable grounds upon which to sustain that belief. And thirdly, we think, that the employer, at the stage at which he formed that belief on those grounds, at any rate at the final stage at which he formed that belief on those grounds, had carried out as much investigation into the matter as was reasonable in all the circumstances of the case.

See also *Pritchett and Dyjasek v J McIntyre Ltd* [1987] IRLR 18. In *The Distillers Company (Bottling Services) Ltd v Gardner* [1982] IRLR 47, the EAT considered *obiter* that this principle extended to cases of misconduct not involving dishonesty. However, the principle in *British Home Stores Ltd* and *Weddel and Co Ltd*, above, is not of universal application. In some exceptional cases a reasonable suspicion is sufficient: *Monie v Coral Racing Ltd* [1980] IRLR 464, a case where the employer had a reasonable suspicion that one of two employees or possibly both had been guilty of dishonesty.

In *Parr v Whitbread and Co plc* [1990] ICR 427, four employees had an equal opportunity of committing a theft. The employer found it impossible to identify which was guilty and dismissed all four. The EAT held that where a group of employees could have committed an offence the employer may be entitled to dismiss all four where the employer reasonably believes at the date of dismissal that one or more persons was guilty of theft and that that belief was based on solid and sensible grounds. In *Whitbread and Co plc v Thomas and Others* [1988] ICR 135, the employer dismissed three employees from a shop which had had serious stock losses for some years. The employer could not identify the cause of the stock losses or the persons responsible. It argued that its only option was to dismiss all three employees since they failed to prevent stock losses. The EAT found that the employers were able to establish a reason. The act or acts were committed by one or more of the group, all of whom were individually capable of having committed the act. The employers had been able to establish a reason at the time of the dismissal based upon conduct or capability.

Thus, the employer may be able to establish the reason notwithstanding the fact that the employer is mistaken in his belief, provided that the belief is genuinely held: *The Maintenance Co Ltd v Dormer* [1982] IRLR 491.

Where the employer relies upon a genuine belief, albeit mistakenly held, he may be in difficulty when it comes to considering the reasonableness of the dismissal: *The Maintenance Co Ltd v Dormer*, above, and see *Smith v City of Glasgow District Council* [1985] IRLR 79.

The approach in *Ferodo Ltd v Barnes*, above, has been adopted by tribunals in cases where the reason is a reason related to the employee's conduct, whether or not it involves the commission of a criminal offence, as well as cases where the reason is related to the employee's capability. In *Harper v National Coal Board* [1980] IRLR 260, the EAT held that where the reason for the dismissal was 'some other substantial reason' then:

Obviously an employer cannot claim that a reason for dismissal is substantial if it is a whimsical or capricious reason which no person of ordinary sense would entertain. But if the employer can show that he had a fair reason in his mind at the time when he decided on dismissal and that he genuinely believed it to be fair this would bring the case within the category of another substantial reason. Where the belief is one which is genuinely held, and particularly is one which most employers would be expected to adopt, it may be a substantial reason even where modern sophisticated opinion can be adduced to suggest that it has no scientific foundation.

Where the reason is 'some other substantial reason' of a kind such as to justify the dismissal of the employee under s 57(1)(*b*) of the EP(C)A 1978 the employer has to show that the reason is a justifiable one. The reason is one which can justify the dismissal but not necessarily one which does justify the dismissal. Thus if the employer is able to establish some other substantial reason the tribunal will still have to examine the reasonableness of the dismissal.

The relationship between the burden of proof imposed upon the employer and the burden which may be placed upon the employee if he seeks to rebut the employer's reasons was considered by the Court of Appeal in *Maund v Penwith District Council* [1984] ICR 143, where it was held that once the employer has produced evidence which appears to show the reason for the dismissal

then the burden passes to the employee to show that there is a real issue as to whether that was the true reason. The employee cannot do this by merely asserting in argument that it was not the true reason; an evidential burden rests upon him to produce some evidence that casts doubt upon the employer's reason. The graver the allegation, the heavier will be the burden. Allegations of fraud or malice should not be lightly cast about without evidence to support them.

But this burden is a lighter burden than the legal burden placed upon the employer; it is not for the employee to prove the reason for his dismissal, but merely to produce evidence sufficient to raise the issue or, to put it another way, that raises some doubt about the reason for the dismissal. Once this evidential burden is discharged, the onus remains upon the employer to prove the reason for the dismissal.

Where the reason for dismissal results from a corporate decision it may not always be sufficient to look at the reason recorded in the minutes of the corporate body: see *Smith v Hayle Town Council* [1978] IRLR 413; *Maund v Penwith District Council*, above. The minuted decision will be strong *prima facie* evidence of the reason for the dismissal; per Griffiths LJ in *Maund*'s case above. In *Smith*'s case the issue was whether Smith had been dismissed by reason of misconduct or because of union activities. Sir David Cairns felt that in reaching a decision as to the reason or principal reason '. . . it would be permissible to look at what was said at the meeting in order to see what actuated the minds of those who voted in favour of the resolution'. It was clear that there was no compelling evidence that the reason for dismissal was Smith's trade union activities. The fact that one of the councillors was influenced by anti-union prejudice and that his vote was decisive did not affect the reason or principal reason for the dismissal.

The hurdle of establishing a fair reason is designed to deter employers from dismissing employees for some trivial or unworthy reason. It is not a difficult hurdle to jump: *Gilham and others v Kent CC (No 2)* [1985] ICR 233.

Where the employer applies the wrong label   Where the evidence establishes that the employer has dismissed an employee but the employer has honestly although mistakenly given the wrong legal description to the reason, it will not prevent the tribunal from seeking the true reason and properly defining it. Thus, the employer is not estopped from relying on the true reason. It may be that the reason for the dismissal is clear and apparent in the employer's mind at the time of the dismissal, but that he is not aware of the correct legal description. In *Abernethy v Mott, Hay and Anderson* [1974] ICR 323, the employer thought that the reason for the dismissal was redundancy whereas there was no redundancy within the firm. The tribunal found that Abernethy was dismissed because of capability. There was work available, but Abernethy was not capable of doing it. In this case Lord Denning held:

I do not think that the reason has got to be correctly labelled at the time of dismissal. It may be that the employer is wrong in law as labelling it as dismissal for redundancy. In that case the wrong label can be set aside. The employer can only rely on the reason *in fact* for which he dismissed the man, if the facts are sufficiently known or made known to the man. The reason in this case was—on the facts—already known or sufficiently made known to Mr Abernethy. The wrong label of 'redundancy' does not affect the point.

The employer honestly thought that the facts constituted redundancy, but in law they did not.

See also *Land and Wilson v West Yorkshire Metropolitan County Council* [1979] IRLR 174.

In *Trust Houses Forte Leisure Ltd v Aquilar* [1976] IRLR 251, it was held:

the moment that his dismissal is complete the reason for the dismissal is a fact. It may be more difficult to ascertain. The employer's description of the reason for the dismissal is by no means conclusive. The tribunal . . . must look into the matter and determine what *was* the reason. But that reason, whatever it is, is something which exists at the moment of dismissal. Matters which happen subsequently are irrelevant to the ascertainment of what was the reason . . . they cannot . . . affect the identity of the reason.

It is necessary for a tribunal to distinguish those cases where the employer has applied an incorrect label and seeks to change the label, from those cases where the employer seeks to argue that the dismissal was for a reason other than that upon which the employer relied at the time of the dismissal.

In *Abernethy v Mott, Hay and Anderson*, above, Cairns LJ held:

A reason for the dismissal of an employee is a set of facts known to the employer or it may be of beliefs held by him which cause him to dismiss the employee. If at the time of his dismissal the employer gives a reason for it, that is no doubt evidence, at any rate as against him, as to the real reason, but it does not necessarily constitute the real reason. He may knowingly give a reason different from the real reason out of kindness or because he might have difficulty in proving the facts that actually led him to dismiss; or he may describe his reasons wrongly through some mistake of language or of law.

This view was approved by Lord Bridge in *West Midlands Co-operative Society Ltd v Tipton* [1986] IRLR 112. Cairns LJ had in mind more than a change of label. He had in mind a change of facts from those which the employer relied upon at the time of the dismissal. It is open to the employer at the hearing to rely upon a different set of facts from those which he gave to the employee at the time of dismissal. However, he may have difficulty in persuading the tribunal that the real reason is a different reason from that put forward at the time of the dismissal, although he may prove that the reason put forward before the tribunal is the real one. The employer cannot rely upon facts which were subsequently discovered and which were not known to him at the time of the dismissal: see *W Devis and Sons Ltd v Atkins* [1977] AC 931 and Chapter 6, **2**, below.

On an appeal from a tribunal to the EAT, the employer cannot rely upon reasons which were not pleaded by him in his notice of appearance to the tribunal and which were not canvassed by him before the tribunal: see *Nelson v BBC* [1977] ICR 649.

In that case an industrial tribunal had held a dismissal to have been on the grounds of redundancy. On appeal, this appeal tribunal doubted the correctness of the industrial tribunal's finding of redundancy but held that there was some other substantial reason for the dismissal. The Court of Appeal held that the reason for dismissal was not redundancy and that since redundancy was the only defence pleaded before the industrial tribunal the employers were not entitled to rely on a defence that there was some other substantial reason, nor was the appeal tribunal entitled to apply facts found in relation to the fairness of the dismissal for the purpose of holding that the dismissal was for 'some other substantial reason': per Browne-Wilkinson J in *Murphy v Epsom College* [1983] ICR 715.

In this case Browne-Wilkinson J felt bound to follow the decision in *Nelson's* case. He further held:

In *Gorman v London Computer Training Centre Ltd* [1978] ICR 394, this appeal tribunal held that it was not necessary to 'plead' some other substantial reason in the full technical sense of the word. However, in our judgment, in the light of the *Nelson* case it is probably necessary that the matter should be expressly ventilated in the industrial tribunal before it reaches a decision on the matter so that the parties can have a full and proper opportunity to deploy their case on the matter. Natural justice requires that the party should not have a case decided against him on a ground on which he has not had an opportunity to be heard.

The Court of Appeal approved the decision: see *Murphy v Epsom College* [1985] ICR 80.

In *Hotson v Wisbech Conservative Club* [1984] ICR 859, the club found that there was a considerable shortfall of cash compared with the amount invoiced. The employee was dismissed by reason of gross inefficiency. At the tribunal hearing, as the result of questioning by the tribunal chairman, the club added, or substituted as the reason for dismissal, suspected dishonesty.

On appeal the EAT held:

The position, according to authority, appears to be as follows. In satisfying the industrial tribunal as to the reason for the dismissal under s 57(1) of the Act of 1978, the employer is not tied to the label he happens to put upon the particular facts relied on. Thus he may say 'I made the employee redundant'. But he will not be prevented from saying later 'No, I have changed my mind. It was really a case of incapability'. Nor will he be prevented from running the two as alternatives: either redundancy or lack of capability. By the same token, the industrial tribunal may, it appears, of its own motion, declare that the reason relied upon by the employer was not the real reason; for the real reason may be something that he shrank from mentioning either through ignorance of the technicalities involved or perhaps through sheer kindness of heart or natural delicacy. In the same way, some other substantial reason under s 57(1)(*b*) [of the EP(C)A 1978] may be advanced by the employer or found by the tribunal to be the real reason for dismissal, differing from the sole or principal reason, such as redundancy or incapability, that may have been advanced by the employer himself.

That appears to us to be the effect of the decisions of the Court of Appeal in *Abernethy v Mott, Hay and Anderson* [1974] ICR 323 and of this appeal tribunal in *Gorman v London Computer Training Centre Ltd* [1978] ICR 394. What the employer may not do, however, is to change after the date of dismissal the facts upon which he relied at the time as the basis for dismissal. That is made plain by the decision of the Court of Appeal in *Monie v Coral Racing Ltd* [1981] ICR 109.

Finally, even in those cases where what is referred to in the authorities as no more than a change of label is involved—in the cases we have mentioned, for example, where lack of capability is treated as an alternative label for redundancy—great care must always be taken to ensure that the employee is not placed, as a result of the change in the label given to the reason for his dismissal, at a procedural or evidential disadvantage. That is made plain by the decision of this appeal tribunal in *Murphy v Epsom College* [see above].

In this case it is clear from the decision of the EAT that they did not feel that this was a case involving simply a change of label.

In *McCrory v Magee t/a Heatwell Heating Systems* [1983] IRLR 414, the tribunal following the approach in *Abernethy*'s case, above, found that the employer's reason for dismissing the employee was his belief or suspicion in the employee's dishonesty notwithstanding that the employer did not put forward that suspicion of dishonesty as the justification for the dismissal, either in his notice of appearance or in evidence. The Northern Ireland Court of Appeal held that although the tribunal could not 'pick out and substitute a reason which was neither given nor entertained by the employer merely because the tribunal thinks it a better reason or one which would justify dismissal (or summary dismissal) when the employer's stated reason would not' there was evidence to support the view that the employer's suspicion of dishonesty was the real reason for the employee's dismissal. Although the employer was not changing the label but relying upon a different reason the employee had been given the chance to deal with the allegations so that *Nelson v BBC*, above, is capable of being distinguished. None the less there is a difference in approach between the two cases.

In *Hannan v TNT-IPEC (UK) Ltd* [1986] IRLR 165, the EAT considered the earlier decisions. It held:

It seems to us that one can summarise the distinction between the two lines of authority to which we have referred in this way, that where the different grounds are really different labels and nothing more, then there is no basis for saying that the late introduction, even without pleading or without argument, is a ground for interference on appeal; but that where the difference goes to facts and substance and there would or might have been some substantial or significant difference in the way the case is conducted, then of course an appeal will succeed if the Tribunal rely on a different ground without affording an opportunity for argument. For the reasons which we have endeavoured to express, we are persuaded that [in this case] . . . the distinction is in truth one of labels and that there are no grounds for thinking the case would have been conducted in any significant way differently or more thoroughly investigated or the cross-examination or the evidence called would have been in any way significantly different had the case, as ultimately relied upon by the industrial tribunal, been pleaded or canvassed in evidence.

Facts discovered subsequent to the dismissal In a case of unfair dismissal the employer is only entitled to rely upon reasons which were known to him at the time of the dismissal. He cannot rely upon other grounds or reasons which were not then known to him, but which subsequently came to his knowledge after he dismissed the employee: *W Devis and Sons Ltd v Atkins* [1977] AC 931. The decision of the House of Lords in this case, makes it clear that the common law authorities *(Boston Deep Sea Fishing and Ice Co v Ansell* (1888) 39 ChD 339, and *Cyril Leonard and Co v Simo Securities Trust Ltd* [1972] 1 WLR 80) have no application to the statutory jurisdiction.

Subsequently discovered facts may entitle the employer to reduce the amount of compensation. See Chapter 13.

Following a dismissal, the employee may have the right to appeal against his dismissal under the employer's internal disciplinary procedure. The employer's failure to allow the employee to appeal against the dismissal notwithstanding that that is something which happens after the dismissal, may render the dismissal unfair: see *West Midlands Co-operative Society Ltd v Tipton* [1986] IRLR 112.

An internal appeal may show that the original reasons relied upon by the employer cannot be supported by the evidence. In *Monie v Coral Racing Ltd* [1981] ICR 109, the Court of Appeal held that the fairness or otherwise of the dismissal depends upon the sufficiency of the reason given by the employer at the time of the dismissal. The hearing of an appeal when the dismissal was confirmed was not the time of dismissal. Therefore, the employer was not entitled to rely upon a subsequent and different reason given to the employee for his dismissal following the hearing of an internal appeal.

In *West Midlands Co-operative Society Ltd v Tipton* [1986] ICR 112, the House of Lords held that in determining whether the employer acted reasonably or unreasonably in treating his real reason for dismissal as sufficient, both the original and appeal decisions are to be taken into account. Thus, it may be that on appeal the employer will realise that he is acting unreasonably in dismissing the employee because of circumstances established in the course of the domestic appeal procedure. If the employer could not take into account those facts discovered on appeal injustice would result. In giving judgment Lord Bridge approved a passage from the judgment of Waterhouse J in *The Board of Governors, The National Heart and Chest Hospitals v Nambiar* [1981] IRLR 196, where Waterhouse J held:

it is necessary to distinguish the case where an employee is dismissed for reason A and evidence at an internal appeal invalidates reason A but demonstrates that a different reason B would justify dismissal. It is clear that in such circumstances the original dismissal ought not to stand and the employer must look at the matter afresh in order to decide whether a later dismissal on the new information is appropriate. In the more usual case, however, where the employer confirms the decision to dismiss for reason A, following the appeal, we consider that it is right for an industrial tribunal to look at the information that came to light in the course of the appeal.

Lord Bridge went on to hold:

A dismissal is unfair if the employer unreasonably treats his real reason as a sufficient reason to dismiss the employee, either when he makes his original decision to dismiss or when he maintains that decision at the conclusion of an internal appeal.

Monie's case was not considered by the House of Lords in *Tipton's* case, above. The judgment of Lord Bridge does conflict with the decision in *Monie's* case, above; see also *Whitbread and Co plc v Mills* [1988] IRLR 501.

The statutory reasons are now considered in the light of reported cases. The cases referred to are simply illustrative of the statutory reasons. Because the employer can establish a reason, it does not necessarily mean that the dismissal was fair in all the circumstances.

2.2 Capability and qualifications

The reason for dismissal may relate to the employee's capability, or qualifications, and those grounds are defined by the EP(C)A 1978. 'Capability' means capability assessed by reference to skill, aptitude, health or any other physical or mental quality: s 57(4)(*a*) of the EP(C)A 1978. 'Qualifications' means any degree, diploma or other academic, technical or professional qualification relevant to the position which the employee held: s 57(4)(*b*) of the EP(C)A 1978. (As to dismissal for health see Chapter 7.)

(a) Skill Skills may be executive or manual. In the case of executive skills, it may be the total inability of the manager to perform competently the whole ambit of duties which are entrusted to him. In *Kendrick v Concrete Pumping Ltd* [1975] IRLR 83, Kendrick, a depot manager, was dismissed because he was not able to organise the repair or maintenance of vehicles, he had difficulties with the control of spares, with the organisation of the depot and with controlling personnel. In *Lewis Shop Groups v Wiggins* [1973] ICR 335, Wiggins, a shop manageress was dismissed because the shop was dirty and untidy, staff were allowed to be absent from the front of the sales area causing lack of security, the cash registers were not operating properly and receipts were not issued, stock was not put away properly and the

fitting rooms were crammed with stock which had not been put back for resale.

There may be criticism of a particular skill rather than the employee's overall capability. In *Duncan v Scottish Farmers Dairy Co Ltd* [1973] IRLR 48, Duncan's general performance as manager was good, but he had devised a system of banking which enabled someone to take £500 from the takings. He placed too much faith in his staff to the extent that he had allowed one person unsupervised to be responsible for the monies which had to be banked and so exposed his staff to temptations.

Capability may relate to manual skills. In *Davison v Kent Meters Ltd* [1975] IRLR 145, capability was the reason for dismissal where Davison failed to assemble components correctly; 471 out of 500 components were incorrectly assembled. In *Day v Diemer and Reynolds Ltd* [1975] IRLR 298, capability was the reason for dismissal where Day, who was employed by a firm of bookbinders as a gathering machine operator, failed to ensure that the sections of a book had been gathered together properly prior to binding.

Capability is assessed in relation to the employer's demands which may change.

In *Sutton and Gates (Luton) Ltd v Boxall* [1979] ICR 67, the EAT held that the tribunal, when dealing with a case involving dismissal on grounds of capability, should distinguish whether the case was one of sheer incapability due to an inherent incapacity to function, or one of failure to exercise to the full such talent as the employee possessed. Where a person has not come up to the standard through carelessness, negligence or idleness, the case should be dealt with as one of misconduct rather than incapability.

(b) Aptitude Lack of aptitude may be a failure to achieve a 'theoretical' or 'practical' standard. In *Blackman v Post Office* [1974] ICR 151, Blackman had been employed under a scheme negotiated between the Post Office and the Union of Postal Workers, whereby employees who did not possess the usual qualifications which were required could be employed on an unestablished basis. They were required to take an aptitude test and were given three attempts at the test which had to be taken and passed by a certain date. Additionally they had to have been satisfactory in practice. Blackman was capable at a practical level, but he had failed all three attempts at the test. The union was not prepared to waive the rule that the employee had to pass a written examination and so he was dismissed. It was held that the reason for his dismissal was one related to his capability.

In *Judge International v Moss* [1973] IRLR 208, lack of aptitude was the reason for the dismissal of a financial controller and group secretary. The employer felt in the long term he could not 'succeed in his job because we think the position is too big for him as he is not self-motivating and probably lacks leadership'. It had been the company's hope that the employee would one day become financial director.

In *Abernethy v Mott, Hay and Anderson* [1974] ICR 323, the employee's inflexibility and lack of adaptability was a reason which related to the employee's aptitude and his mental qualities for the job.

(c) Physical health Poor health (see Chapter 7) may be physical or mental health. In *Finch v Betabake (Anglia) Ltd* [1977] IRLR 470, Finch an apprentice motor mechanic was dismissed because of defective eyesight. A report by an ophthalmic surgeon stated he could not be employed without undue danger to himself or others.

Ill health may have been caused by the nature of the work, as where an employee contracts dermatitis and is no longer able to work a machine which exposes him to oil, or where an employee suffers with a skin complaint through using a chain-saw, or where he sustains a knee injury in the course of his work. See *Grootcon (UK) Ltd v Keld* [1984] IRLR 302. Physical incapacity may also be compounded by the anxiety and strain of employment.

Where a disabled worker is dismissed because of his disability, the reason is one related to his capability, even though the disability existed and was known to the employer when the employee was first employed. The reason for dismissal was one related to capability where a disabled worker was dismissed because of absences for prolonged periods which led to disruption in the employer's business: *Kerr v Atkinson Vehicles (Scotland) Ltd* [1974] IRLR 36; and also where the disability caused absences from work, particularly when the employee had to be sent to her doctor, which led to interruptions: *Pascoe v Hallen and Medway* [1975] IRLR 116.

In exceptional circumstances it may not be necessary for the disability to interfere with the employee's actual performance of his job. In *Harper v National Coal Board* [1980] IRLR 260, Harper, an epileptic, while in an epileptic fit attacked fellow employees. The EAT upheld the decision of the tribunal and found that if, because of ill health, an employee, however involuntarily, may be a source of danger to his fellow employees, this reflects upon his capability for performing work of the kind that he was employed to do. The tribunal held that in the alternative the dismissal of the employee was for 'some other substantial reason' of a kind such as to justify the dismissal of an employee holding the position which he held.

A novel point was raised in the case of *Shook v London Borough of Ealing* [1986] IRLR 46. Shook was appointed as a residential social worker in a home for handicapped children. She was dismissed due to problems with her back. It was contended that the tribunal had to look at 'the whole range of work not only being performed by the employee under the employment contract but which he or she might lawfully be required to do for the purpose of determining whether or not he or she has been dismissed for a reason relating to capability for performing such work'. It was contended on behalf of the employee that potentially she might have been obliged to work in a very wide range of activities and that she must be incapacitated from the performance of every such activity before the employer can establish that her dismissal was on the grounds of capability. The EAT held:

In our judgment this analogy is unsound. The scheme of s 57(2) [of the EP(C)A 1978] is to introduce four categories of reason. Two of them are couched in the language of actuality: the employee must be redundant or engaged under an unlawful contract, as the case may be. The other two are expressed in the language of relationship: the reason must *relate* to the capability for performing the work of the relevant kind or must *relate* to the conduct of the employee, as the case may be. The matter thus has to be looked at as an exercise in relation when one is dealing with questions of incapability.

Since Shook's disabilities related to the performance of her duties under the contract even though it may not have affected her performance of all of them, the tribunal had not erred in finding that the reason for dismissal fell within s 57(2)(*a*) of the EP(C)A 1978.

(d) Mental health This may include mental illness where the potential incapability is greater than the present. In *Singh-Deu v Chloride Metals Ltd* [1976] IRLR 56, an employee who worked in a lead smelting factory was diagnosed as having a susceptibility to paranoid schizophrenia. The job, although not skilled, was one which required him to have his wits about him and if he did not perform his duties properly it might cause serious consequences for his fellow employees. No assurances could be given by the doctor that he would not be subject to a recurrence of the illness. Although in the future the onset of an attack of paranoid schizophrenia might be so slow as to give a warning, it would generally only be apparent when his faculties were so impaired that it became obvious to his workmates. By then a catastrophic accident could have occurred.

Poor mental health may arise from the employment itself as where an employee suffers with a nervous breakdown due to the pressure and anxiety of his employment.

Where the reason for the dismissal is not merely the employee's mental illness but the fact that he has deliberately misled the employers by not disclosing the illness in order to obtain employment, the reason may be 'some other substantial reason' of a kind such as to justify the dismissal: *O'Brien v Prudential Assurance Co Ltd* [1979] IRLR 140.

(e) Qualifications Qualifications are widely defined in the legislation under s 57(4)(*b*) of the EP(C)A 1978. In *Blackman v Post Office* [1974] ICR 151, the NIRC commented: 'the passing of the aptitude test gives a technical or professional qualification relevant to the position' which the employee held. The court left open the question

of whether qualification is something analogous to degree, diploma or other academic qualification but held, 'One answer to that may be that "qualifications", in relation to the statute, has to be construed in the light of the particular position which the employee held.'

In *Singh v London Country Bus Services Ltd* [1976] IRLR 176, the tribunal considered that since Singh, a one-man bus driver, had been charged with theft, this accusation related to his trustworthiness, as 'One of the qualifications for performing such work is trustworthiness.' The EAT held that qualifications are more than personal characteristics. Trustworthiness was not a qualification within the statutory definition.

In *Blue Star Ship Management Ltd v Williams* [1979] IRLR 16, the EAT held that the employee's lack of authorisation as a registered seafarer was not a 'qualification' within s 57(4)(*b*). The EAT held:

It seems to us that 'qualification' as defined in . . . [s 57(4)(*b*) of the EP(C)A 1978] has in mind matters relating to aptitude or ability, and that a mere licence, permit or authorisation is not such a qualification unless it is substantially concerned with the aptitude or ability of the person to do the job.

In some cases the employee's lack of qualifications may mean that his continued employment will result in the infringement of legislative provisions.

2.3 Conduct

'Conduct' is not defined by s 57(2)(*b*) of the EP(C)A 1978 and it has been left to the tribunals and courts to decide what conduct includes.

(a) Timekeeping and absenteeism 'Conduct' includes bad timekeeping and unauthorised absenteeism in one of its various forms. Bad timekeeping may be lateness in arriving for work as in *Hallet and Want v MAT Transport Ltd* [1976] IRLR 5, where an employee was late for work on 12 out of 80 days following a final warning for lateness. He had been late on 65 occasions in 2 years, and on at least half of those occasions, he had been late by more than 15 minutes.

A reason related to the employee's conduct may arise obliquely out of timekeeping as when an employee falsifies another employee's clocking-in card by clocking-in for that employee: *Elliott Brothers (London) Ltd v Colverd* [1979] IRLR 92.

Absenteeism may arise when the employee leaves his place of employment during his working day without permission: see, for example, *Stewart v Western SMT Co Ltd* [1978] IRLR 553, where the employee was summarily dismissed for three incidents of leaving work early and claiming pay for hours not worked. Absenteeism may also arise where nightwatchmen absent themselves during the night from the building which they are employed to look after: *Ross v Aquascu-*

tum Ltd [1973] IRLR 107; *City of Edinburgh DC v Stephen* [1977] IRLR 135.

In *Maxwell v Grimwood Heating Elements Ltd* [1972] IRLR 81, Maxwell left the factory during a dispute about bonuses and was dismissed. It was held that the reason for his dismissal was one related to his conduct. In *Lindsay v Fife Forge Co Ltd* [1976] IRLR 47, a turner's labourer, whose duties included cleaning a lathe and keeping the surrounding floor clean, came on shift and alleged that the lathe was dirty because his opposite number on the earlier shift had not carried out his duties of cleaning the lathe. The employee clocked off and went home, refusing to clean the machine. He was dismissed. The reason was his conduct.

Absences may be for the best reasons. Thus an employee who absented himself on Saturdays to fulfil religious obligations without permission and in breach of contract was dismissed. It was held that the reason was one related to conduct: *Esson v London Transport Executive* [1975] IRLR 48. The employee was also failing to co-operate with his employer.

Absenteeism may follow annual or public holidays where the employee fails to return to work promptly, particularly where the holiday is abroad: *British Leyland (UK) Ltd v Ashraf* [1978] IRLR 330; *Midland Electric Manufacturing Co Ltd v Kanji* [1980] IRLR 185. Where an employee takes time off without securing permission or where permission has been refused and he is dismissed, the reason is one related to his conduct.

Lastly, absenteeism may result because the employee is in custody pending trial on criminal charges. If he is dismissed, the reason for his dismissal is one related to his conduct.

(b) Failure to co-operate The employee's failure or refusal to co-operate with the lawful requests or directions of his employer is a reason related to 'conduct'. There may be failure to co-operate by the employee arising out of one incident, as in *Lindsay v Dunlop Ltd* [1980] IRLR 93, where Lindsay was one of a number of employees whose jobs involved working in an area affected by hot rubber fumes. The employees decided not to work in the area in question where the fumes were emitted. The other employees then agreed to accept masks and resumed normal working as a temporary measure pending further action by the employer. Lindsay refused to work normally until the fumes were cleared, and was dismissed. Failure to co-operate may extend over several occasions or incidents and lead to a pattern of unwillingness to co-operate. That failure may arise in a broad sense as in *Rose v Leeds Metal Spinning Co Ltd* [1976] IRLR 142, where Rose refused to impart to the management any knowledge he had about offensive and derogatory graffiti which had been written on lavatory walls.

The failure or refusal to co-operate may arise because the employee has decided the way in which he will work irrespective of and in opposition to the way the management requires, or because the employee is unwilling to accept policy formulated by the employer and is prepared to make his dissension known: *Retarded Children's Aid Society Ltd v Day* [1978] ICR 437.

The employee's failure or refusal to co-operate with the employer may arise where he is requested to work overtime or to carry out special work or different duties, whether or not he is not contractually bound, so that where his refusal results in his dismissal, the reason for his dismissal is a reason related to his conduct. Thus, in *Martin v Solus Schall* [1979] IRLR 1, Martin was dismissed for refusing to comply with a contractual obligation to work overtime, the reason was his conduct.

The reason is one related to the employee's conduct if he is unwilling to accept a change in the terms of his contract of employment where the change is not a repudiation. In *Mordecai v Jacob Beatus Ltd* [1975] IRLR 170, an employee refused to move from a dispatch department in one factory to other operations in an adjoining factory owned by the company even though his contract contained a flexibility clause. The reason is conduct where an employee refuses to move from one site to another as in the building industry where his contract contains a mobility clause: *Wilson v IDR Construction Ltd* [1975] IRLR 260.

There may be no power in the contract to alter its terms, but if the employer seeks an alteration for good reason, as where he wishes to make the operation more economical to benefit the employee, and the employee refuses to accede to the change and is dismissed, the reason for the dismissal is conduct—his failure to co-operate. In *Coward v John Menzies (Holdings) Ltd* [1977] IRLR 428, the employer wished to transfer Coward from Letchworth to Swansea for training, which involved a loss of status, to improve his performance. Coward refused and was dismissed. The reason was his conduct.

Where the employee refuses to accede to a change in the terms of the contract and there is no contractual power to alter those terms, the reason for the dismissal may also be treated as 'some other substantial reason' within s 57(1)(*b*) of the EP(C)A 1978.

Where the employee's failure to co-operate arises from some lack of ability on the part of the employee, the reason for the dismissal may be one related to the employee's capability: *AJ Dunning and Sons (Shopfitters) Ltd v Jacomb* [1973] ICR 448.

(c) Refusal to obey an order 'Conduct' also includes the employee's failure to obey a lawful order given to him by his employer. Refusal to obey an order may also involve a failure to co-operate. The refusal may be a refusal to do a job, such as to work in a warehouse, to move concrete, to work in bad weather, to take out a loaded van, to undertake a night journey or to operate a new system. It may also relate to matters ancillary to the employment, for instance, a refusal

to have one's hair cut, to wear a uniform or to go on a course of instruction.

(d) Breach of the employer's rules The employee's breach of the employer's rules, whether the rules are written or oral, is a reason related to conduct. Breach of the employer's rules may cover a failure to obey the employer's orders or the commission of a criminal offence. Examples of such breach of rules are: drinking during working hours: *Gray Dunn and Co Ltd v Edwards* [1980] IRLR 23; failing to ring up purchases on a till: *Laws Stores Ltd v Oliphant* [1978] IRLR 251; disclosing confidential information belonging to the employer: *Archer v Cheshire and Northwich Building Society* [1976] IRLR 424; failing to follow procedures for the transfer of money from the employer's vehicles to customer's premises: *Rigden-Murphy v Securicor Ltd* [1976] IRLR 106; dealing in another company's products: *McCall v Castleton Crafts* [1979] IRLR 218; and a breach of the employer's rules relating to hygiene: *Unkles v Milanda Bread Co Ltd* [1973] IRLR 76.

There may be a breach of the employer's safety rules. In *Bendall v Paine and Betteridge* [1973] IRLR 44, the employee was dismissed because he smoked on the employer's premises, despite a warning to the contrary. The employer was a builder and his premises were constructed of matchwood and there were additional fire risks of paint, timber, wood shavings and refuse stored on the premises. Other cases have involved the removal of guards or safety devices on machinery: see *Martin v Yorkshire Imperial Metals Ltd* [1978] IRLR 440.

(e) Insubordination The employee's insubordination to his superiors is a reason related to 'conduct'. Insubordination may arise out of a failure to obey an order. It may also arise out of a failure to co-operate as in *Lambsdale v Her Majesty's Stationery Office* [1975] IRLR 239. Lambsdale refused to attend a meeting with his superior officers and failed to apologise for not attending. This failure was coupled with critical remarks about his employer.

Gross impertinence may be insubordination as in *McCabe v Ninth District Council of the County of Lanark* [1973] IRLR 75, where McCabe lost his temper on two occasions, and on the second occasion he was offensive and aggressive at an investigatory hearing.

Insubordination may involve or consist of the use of bad language. In *King v Motorway and Tyres Accessories Ltd* [1975] IRLR 51, King told his branch manager to 'fuck off', was argumentative and abusive; in *Chantrill v WF Shortland Ltd* [1974] IRLR 333, Chantrill an apprentice, on being told off by the managing director in front of two other apprentices, retorted, 'You couldn't have done any fucking better'; in *Rosenthal v Louis Butler Ltd* [1972] IRLR 39, the employee, a millinery trimmer and finisher, called the factory manager a 'stupid punk' when other staff were present.

(f) Employee relationships 'Conduct' also includes cases where the employee is dismissed because of his relationship with the other

employees. It may be potential, rather than actual, problems in the relationship which lead to the dismissal. Where there is a mere conflict or clash of personality leading to disharmony between employees and one employee is dismissed to restore harmony, the reason may be 'some other substantial reason' (within s 57(1)(b) of the EP(C)A 1978 Act), rather than one relating to the employee's conduct.

The problem may be of a general nature as where a foreman displayed an attitude to his fellow workers which was aggressive, unpleasant and created a bad atmosphere in the works: *McKinney v Bieganek* [1973] IRLR 311.

There may be a more specific incident which creates the difficulty, as where an employee has a violent argument with a colleague and subsequently the relationship is tense and quarrelsome, leading to further arguments. The tension may manifest itself in a violent fashion, as where one employee assaults another: *CA Parsons and Co Ltd v McLoughlin* [1978] IRLR 65; *Meyer Dunmore International Ltd v Rogers* [1978] IRLR 167. It does not matter that the violence arises outside the place of work if the tension arises within the place of work.

The reason for the dismissal may relate to the employee's sexual relationship with another employee. In *Newman v Alarmco Ltd* [1976] IRLR 45, Newman was dismissed because he formed an extra-marital relationship with his secretary and was living with her. The conduct was detrimental to the employer, was offensive and was something which was likely to be discussed to the detriment of the company. In *Grace v Harehills Working Men's Club and Institute* [1974] IRLR 68, a club steward was dismissed for his conduct when he formed a sexual liaison with a girl and allowed her to live with him on the club premises. In *Whitlow v Alkanet Construction Ltd* [1975] IRLR 321, Whitlow had a sexual relationship with the chief executive's wife and was dismissed. The reason was his conduct.

However, the employer may not be able to show a reason relating to the employee's conduct where the reason for the dismissal is extra-marital sexual activities carried on between the employee and another in private, but if sexual activities outside the place of employment involve a breach of criminal law resulting in dismissal, the reason is one related to the employee's conduct. In *Gardiner v Newport CBC* [1974] IRLR 262, a lecturer was convicted of an offence of gross indecency with another man in a public lavatory which followed other alleged incidents involving the employee and his sexual activities. The reason was his conduct.

Lawful sexual activities, for instance lesbianism, detrimentally affecting the employment, may be a reason relating to conduct. However, it is probable that such activities must actually detrimentally affect the employment.

(g) Criminal activities 'Conduct' is the reason where an employee is

dismissed because he is suspected of or has been found guilty of a criminal act connected with the employment. Where an employee is dismissed for a criminal offence unconnected with the employment which has an effect on the employment, the reason is one related to the employee's conduct: *Singh v London Country Bus Services Ltd* [1976] IRLR 176; *Nottinghamshire CC v Bowly* [1978] IRLR 252.

Examples of criminal activity which have been the reason for dismissal are theft: *Carr v Alexander Russell Ltd* [1975] IRLR 49; dishonesty: *Tesco Stores Ltd v Heap* (1978) 13 ITR 17; handling stolen property: *Jones v RM Douglas Construction Ltd* [1975] IRLR 175; vandalism: *Ferodo Ltd v Barnes* [1976] ICR 439; indecent assault: *Creffield v BBC* [1975] IRLR 23; incest: *Bradshaw v Rugby Portland Cement Co Ltd* [1972] IRLR 46; gross indecency: *Gardiner v Newport CBC* [1974] IRLR 262; and possession of cannabis: *Norfolk CC v Bernard* [1979] IRLR 220.

Even where no criminal proceedings are taken, conduct by the employee which might justify criminal proceedings would be a matter of conduct: *Hotson v Wisbech Conservative Club* [1984] IRLR 422, where a reason for the employee's dismissal was suspected dishonesty, and *Royal Society for the Protection of Birds v Crouche* [1984] IRLR 425, where the employee had dishonestly submitted private petrol bills for reimbursement by the society.

2.4 Redundancy

Redundancy is considered separately in Chapter 8.

2.5 Contravention of a statutory duty or restriction

The essence of this reason, under s 57(2)(*d*) of the EP(C)A 1978, is that the employee could not continue to work in the position which he held without contravention either by him or the employer of a duty or restriction imposed by or under an enactment. The contravention must affect the position which the employee held. In *Fearn v Tayford Motor Co Ltd* [1975] IRLR 336, Fearn, a vehicle supervisor, was required to drive vehicles as an essential and integral part of his duties. He was convicted of careless driving and failing to stop after an accident and was disqualified from driving for 12 months. The reason he was dismissed was that he could no longer legally do the job he was taken on to do.

However, in *Cordiner v Smith of Maddiston* (1975) (unreported), a yard foreman who was only required to drive occasionally was dismissed following his disqualification from driving. He was quite capable of carrying out his job without a driving licence, and so there need be no contravention of any legislation.

In *Tayside Regional Council v McIntosh* [1982] IRLR 272, McIntosh, a vehicle mechanic was disqualified from driving and dismissed. Although there was no specific provision in the contract, from the surrounding circumstances, the EAT considered it was an essential term of his contract that he should hold a driving licence, so he could not do his job without the contravention of legislation.

The continued employment itself may be a contravention of a statutory duty or restriction. It is for the employer to establish this. In *Myeza v Avon Area Health Authority* (1977) (unreported), Myeza was dismissed when it was discovered that her work permit had expired. However, at the date of dismissal, the Home Office were considering renewal of the permit and had intimated to the authority that until a final decision had been reached, it would not be in breach of the immigration regulations to continue to employ Myeza. Further, it was not possible to establish an offence on the part of the authority by the continued employment of Myeza. The authority had acted with haste and had not made sufficient investigations.

2.6 *Some other substantial reason*

'Some other substantial reason' within what is now s 57(1)(*b*) of the EP(C)A 1978, was considered by the NIRC in *RS Components Ltd v Irwin* [1973] ICR 535. The tribunal had interpreted the phrase 'some other substantial reason' as being *ejusdem generis* with the other reasons which the legislation prescribes as being reasons for dismissal, eg conduct, capability etc. The NIRC rejected this, finding that 'some other substantial reason' was not *ejusdem generis* with the other reasons now contained in s 57(2) of the EP(C)A 1978. It held:

There are not only legal but also practical objections to a narrow construction of 'some other reason'. Parliament may well have intended to set out . . . the common reasons for a dismissal but can hardly have hoped to produce an exhaustive catalogue of all the circumstances in which a company would be justified in terminating the services of an employee.

In *Priddle v Dibble* [1978] ICR 148, the EAT interpreted 'some other substantial reason' in the same way as the NIRC had done in *Irwin*'s case. This reason is intended as a safety net for the employer.

Further guidance was given by the EAT in *Harper v National Coal Board* [1980] IRLR 260. It held:

Obviously an employer cannot claim that a reason for dismissal is substantial if it is a whimsical or capricious reason which no person of ordinary sense would entertain. But if the employer can show that he had a fair reason in his mind at the time when he decided on dismissal and that he genuinely believed it to be fair this would bring the case within the category of another substantial reason. Where the belief is one which is genuinely held, and particularly is one which most employers would be expected to adopt, it may be a substantial reason even where modern sophisticated opinion can be adduced to suggest that it has no scientific foundation. *(Saunders v Scottish National Camps Association Ltd* [1980] IRLR 174, upheld on appeal [1981] IRLR 277.)

In *Dobie v Burns International Security Services (UK) Ltd* [1984]

IRLR 329, the Court of Appeal considered the meaning of s 57(1)(*b*) of the EP(C)A 1978. Sir John Donaldson MR held:

I construe it [s 57(1)(*b*)] as requiring the tribunal to consider the reason established by the employer and to decide whether it falls within the category of reasons which could justify the dismissal of *an* employee—not *that* employee but *an* employee—holding the position which that employee held. Thus different types of reason *could* justify the dismissal of the office boy from those which *could* justify the dismissal of the managing director.

It is not possible to give an exhaustive catalogue of instances which will fall within the category of 'some other substantial reason'. Some will suffice. For example, in *Gorfin v Distressed Gentlefolks' Aid Association* [1973] IRLR 290, and *Treganowan v Robert Knee and Co Ltd* [1975] ICR 405, the tribunals found that the reason for dismissal was 'some other substantial reason' where personality conflicts gave rise to hostility and tension between employees which were beginning to affect detrimentally the employer's business. In each case an employee was dismissed to stop dissension among the staff and to restore harmony.

The reason was 'some other substantial reason' where an employee was not prepared to abide by the terms and conditions generally prevailing for that category of employee within the company: *Tovey v F and F Robinson (Stockton-on-Tees) Ltd* [1975] IRLR 139.

Tribunals have also found that the reason is 'some other substantial reason' where the employee has been dismissed following his failure to accede to a request by the employer to work at times other than those provided in his contract. In *Knighton v Henry Rhodes Ltd* [1974] IRLR 71, Knighton was employed as a maintenance fitter. His contract of employment defined his normal working hours as day-time hours. He was asked by his employers to do a night shift working one week in six, but he refused and was dismissed. In *Martin v Automobile Proprietary Ltd* [1979] IRLR 64, a dismissal of three employees for refusing to accept a change in their contractual weekly hours of work from 31½ hours to 42 hours was a dismissal for 'some other substantial reason'. Even where the employee has a contractual right not to be asked to undertake additional duties but refuses to take on new duties the reason may be 'some other substantial reason': *Bowater Containers Ltd v McCormack* [1980] IRLR 50.

In *Moreton v Selby Protective Clothing Co Ltd* [1974] IRLR 269, Moreton who refused to accept the termination of one contract of employment and the substitution of another contract which would place her under a new obligation to work during school holidays, was dismissed. It was essential for the employer's business that the employee should work during the school holidays and other employees in the same position had accepted the change. See also *Muggridge and Slade v East Anglia Plastics Ltd* [1973] IRLR 163. Similarly a failure to agree new terms and conditions of employment following a reorganisation of the employer's business is 'some other substantial reason': *Hollister v National Farmers Union* [1979] ICR 542. Probably, for reorganisation to be 'some other substantial reason', the reorganisation must be such that there was some good sound business reason for it. Whether the reorganisation was such that the only sensible thing to do was to terminate the employee's contract unless he would agree to a new arrangement consequent upon the reorganisation, would depend upon the circumstances. Compare *Ellis v Brighton Co-operative Society Ltd* [1976] IRLR 419, see also *Genower v Ealing, Hammersmith and Hounslow Area Health Authority* [1980] IRLR 297, and consider *Evans v Elemeta Holdings Ltd* [1982] IRLR 143.

Again, where an employee is offered a more menial position following a reorganisation of the employer's business at the same salary as he enjoyed previously which he refuses to accept, the reason for his dismissal consequent upon his failure to accept the new position will be 'some other substantial reason': *Hannan v TNT-IPEC (UK) Ltd* [1986] IRLR 165.

The reason may be 'some other substantial reason' where the employee has breached his obligation of confidence to the employer. It may arise where the employee competes with his employer while his contract of employment subsists: see *Gray v Pembroke (CP) Ltd* (1972) (unreported); *Bergman v A Farr and Sons Ltd* (1972) (unreported), where an employee had an interest in another firm which might damage his employer's reputation for impartiality, and *Glendinning v Pilkington Bros Ltd* (1973) (unreported), where an employee refused to sign an undertaking that on leaving the employment he would not compete with the employer.

Although the reason may be 'some other substantial reason' where there is evidence that the employee is going to join some other firm: *Foster v Scaffolding (GB) Ltd* (1972) (unreported) (see also *Davidson and Maillov v Comparisons* [1980] IRLR 360); a dismissal simply because the employee is going to join another employer, albeit a competitor, or to set up on his own account in competition with the employer, is unlikely to make the dismissal unfair: see *Laughton and Hawley v Bapp Industrial Supplies Ltd* [1986] IRLR 245 and Chapter 6, **6.6**, below. However, a rumour that the employee is leaving to set up a rival business without evidence of an approach to customers was held not to be 'some other substantial reason' in *Betts v Beresford* [1974] IRLR 271. The fact that a member of the employee's family works for a rival firm is probably not 'some other substantial reason': *Cahill v Doulton Glass Industries Ltd* (1974) (unreported); *Ross v Holland House Electro Co Ltd* (1973) (unreported). But where an employee's wife is dismissed by the employer following her arrest on charges of theft from the employer, the dismissal of the employee on the grounds that consequent suspicions about the employee's involvement in the offence had resulted in the breakdown of the employer's confidence and trust in the employee was not some other substantial reason: *Wadley v Eager Electrical Ltd* [1986] IRLR 93. It was not an act of the employee which had caused the breakdown in confidence and trust, and the EAT considered that the act must be the act of the employee rather than of some third party. It expressed the view that the loss of confidence by customers in an employer if it continues to employ an employee might be 'some other substantial reason'. Marriage to an employee of a competitor may, however, constitute such a reason: *Foot v Eastern Counties Timber Co Ltd* [1972] IRLR 83; *Skyrail Oceanic Ltd (t/a Goodmos Tours) v Coleman* [1980] IRLR 226 overruled on appeal for different reasons, [1981] IRLR 398.

The reason may be 'some other substantial reason' where the employee is dismissed because the employer's best customers are not willing to accept him doing their work: *Scott Packing and Warehousing Co Ltd v Paterson* [1978] IRLR 166.

In *East African Airways Corporation v Foote* [1977] ICR 776, Foote, a white British citizen, was dismissed as a consequence of the employer's policy of 'Africanisation', which originated in a policy directive from the African governments (which had formed the airline corporation), that employees who were not citizens of one of these countries were to be replaced by those who were. The EAT held the tribunal should have asked itself whether this particular policy, and its adoption, was such as to constitute 'some other substantial reason'. It also held:

That involves a finding of what the policy is or what the policy was, consideration so far as necessary of the ingredients of the policy, the reasons for the policy and the circumstances in which the employer decides to apply the policy. Upon making such findings of primary facts it is then for the industrial tribunal to make a finding whether such facts constitute a substantial reason such as to justify dismissal.

The employee's failure to live within a reasonable distance of his work may constitute 'some other substantial reason' where it is important that the employee should live near the place of his employment: *Farr v Hoveringham Gravels Ltd* [1972] IRLR 104.

The dismissal of an employee following his conviction for indecently assaulting a 13-year-old girl was a dismissal for 'some other substantial reason'. Because of the conviction he was no longer regarded as fit to carry out his duties and represent his employer: *Creffield v BBC* [1975] IRLR 23. Similarly, in *Bell v The Devon and Cornwall Police Authority* [1978] IRLR 283, the employee was dismissed because of his admission that he was a practising homosexual. This was 'some other substantial reason'; see also *Saunders v Scottish National Camps Association Ltd* [1980] IRLR 174, confirmed on appeal by the Court of Session [1981] IRLR 277. In *Kingston v British Railways Board*

[1984] IRLR 146, the Court of Appeal upheld the decision of the tribunal that a sentence of three months' imprisonment was capable of being 'some other substantial reason'.

Failure to meet with the employer's requirements may also be 'some other substantial reason'. In *Flude v Post Office* [1975] IRLR 330, Flude was taken on for a trial period of one year. He received a written warning about being incapable of performing his duties because of drink. He was then involved in an argument with a colleague over the allocation of overtime and alleged that the other employee was given overtime because he purchased meals for the supervisor. The tribunal held that because of these incidents it was apparent from the trial period that the employee was not up to the employer's requirements. The employee's inability to obtain a fidelity bond may amount to 'some other substantial reason': *Moody v Telefusion Ltd* [1978] IRLR 311.

In the case of joint contracts of employment with the same employer, where it is a condition of the wife's employment that the husband should remain in employment or *vice versa*, the dismissal of the wife because the husband's employment has come to an end for whatever reason will be 'some other substantial reason': *Hendry and Hendry v Scottish Liberal Club* [1977] IRLR 5.

In *North Yorkshire County Council v Fay* [1985] IRLR 247, the Court of Appeal found that where an employee had been engaged under a fixed-term contract for a genuine purpose which was known to the employee, and the purpose for which the fixed-term contract was designed had ceased to exist, then the reason for the employee's dismissal on the expiry of the fixed-term contract may be 'some other substantial reason'. Fay's fixed-term contract had come to an end on the filling of a vacancy for which she was employed to provide cover.

There may be some overlap between the different statutory reasons.

3 Failure to show a statutory reason

Having heard the employer's evidence, the tribunal may make a finding that the employer has failed to establish one of the statutory reasons within s 57(1) and (2) of the EP(C)A 1978. It may decline to hear evidence from the employee. Thus the dismissal will be unfair without the need to consider the reasonableness of the dismissal. In *Coral Squash Clubs Ltd v Matthews and Matthews* [1979] IRLR 390, the EAT held that normally the tribunal will need to hear evidence from both the employer and the employee. However, in exceptional cases, the tribunal can stop a case at the end of the case of the party whose evidence and submissions come first and upon whom the onus lies, where that party has clearly failed in law or in fact to establish what he has to establish. See also *Ridley v GEC Machines Ltd* (1978) 13 ITR 195.

There may be a total failure of evidence as in *Yates v British Leyland UK Ltd* [1974] IRLR 367. Here the employer was not able to establish that the reason for the dismissal was that the employee had been urinating over the workshop floor as was alleged. The only evidence the employer could produce was that the employee 'indulged in certain gymnastic exercises . . . consistent with . . . urinating and restoring himself to what one might call his personal comfort'.

Similarly, in *Raynor v Remploy Ltd* [1973] IRLR 3, the employer was unable to show that the dismissal was due to incapability by the employee. The tribunal was left with:

the picture of a man who inherited a group which was not in good shape. Under his direction it maintained steady progress. It produced financial results which were good by any standards. His efforts were consistent with the main objects of the company, that is providing employment for disabled persons. His personal relations with his staff were good. There is no evidence of any serious blunders.

The burden imposed upon the employer is not an onerous one. Thus, where there is some evidence to support the reason given by the employer, the tribunal will only find that the employer cannot show one of the statutory reasons where the evidence is not sufficient to establish the employer's genuine belief in the reason and that he had reasonable grounds for honestly believing the reason existed. In some cases a suspicion may be sufficient: see *Monie v Coral Racing Ltd* [1980] IRLR 464.

In *Gilham and Others v Kent CC (No 2)* [1985] ICR 233, Griffiths LJ held:

The hurdle over which the employer has to jump at this stage of an inquiry into an unfair dismissal complaint is designed to deter employers from dismissing employees for some trivial or unworthy reason. If he does so, the dismissal is deemed unfair without the need to look further into its merits. But if on the face of it the reason *could* justify the dismissal, then it passes as a substantial reason, and the inquiry moves on to s 57(3) [of the EP(C)A 1978], and the question of reasonableness.

If the reason is not in dispute the tribunal will err in law in finding that the employer has failed to show a statutory reason: *Post Office Counters Ltd v Heavey* [1989] IRLR 513.

There may be a total failure of evidence where the evidence is not admissible, for instance where an employer seeks to rely on an employee's conviction which is a spent conviction under the Rehabilitation of Offenders Act 1974. Furthermore there is no obligation on the employee to disclose a spent offence: *Property Guards Ltd v Taylor and Kershaw* [1982] IRLR 175.

The employer will have difficulty in showing a reason where the reason for the dismissal is pressure brought about by a strike or other industrial action, or threats of a strike or other industrial action, because no account can be taken of such pressure in determining the reason or principal reason for a dismissal: s 63 of the EP(C)A 1978.

The employer will also be unable to establish a reason where he seeks to rely on facts relating solely to a prior employment. However, he may be able to rely on facts which predate the commencement of the employment where those facts affect the employment. In *Torr v British Railways Board* [1977] ICR 785, the employee made false statements in his application for employment. When asked if he had been found guilty of any offence, he replied, 'No'. After the employment had commenced the board discovered that in 1958 he had been convicted of a criminal offence and was sentenced to three years' imprisonment. He was successfully prosecuted for dishonestly obtaining a pecuniary advantage by deception and was dismissed. The board was able to establish a reason and it did not matter that the employee had discharged his duties as a guard satisfactorily for a period of 16 months.

The statutory reason where a dismissal is denied The employer may also be unable to establish a reason for the dismissal where dismissal is disputed. This may arise where the employee claims a constructive dismissal or where the employee alleges he was dismissed, but this is denied by the employer. The difficulties for the employer in showing a reason where the employee alleges he has been constructively dismissed and succeeds, were highlighted by the EAT in *Associated Tyre Specialists (Eastern) Ltd v Waterhouse* [1977] ICR 218. An employer who fights a constructive dismissal claim:

on the basis that there has been no dismissal at all is inevitably in the difficulty that it is really a very unhappy course to try to run in double harness with that [alternative] defence . . . if we did, this was our reason for the dismissal which we say we didn't do; and it was fair.

The problems were highlighted in the decision of Slynn J in *Savoia v Chiltern Herb Farms Ltd* [1981] IRLR 65. He held:

It is not entirely easy, as we have said recently in *Genower v Ealing, Hammersmith and Hounslow Area Health Authority* [1980] IRLR 297, to apply s 57 of the 1978 Act to the case of constructive dismissal. Where the employer dismisses, it is easy to understand how he is to show the reason for the dismissal under ss 57(1) and 57(2) of the Act. The employer, having done that, is entitled to go on to show that the dismissal was fair. [But see Chapter 6 as to the onus of proof since the passing of the 1980 Act.] But where it is the employee who has terminated the contract by accepting a repudiation of the contract, it is clearly not easy to apply the words of ss 57(1) and 57(2). The onus appears, if the words are read literally, still to require the employer to show what was the reason for the dismissal and that it was one of the reasons relating to conduct or capability or was some other substantial reason of a kind such as to justify the dismissal. But in a constructive dismissal situation, the employer has not determined the contract for one of these reasons, and so it seems to us that, in a case like the present one, the

Industrial Tribunal, having found that there was a fundamental breach, is entitled to consider the question posed in sub s 3 [of s 57] as adapted to a constructive dismissal situation and it must, applying those words to a constructive dismissal situation, ask itself whether, even though in fundamental breach of contract, the employer had, in all the circumstances, behaved fairly. It seems to us that that is the better approach rather than to seek to turn the words of ss 57(1) and 57(2) in such a way as to apply them to a constructive dismissal situation.

The decision of the EAT was upheld by the Court of Appeal: see *Savoia v Chiltern Herb Farms Ltd* [1982] IRLR 166, where Waller LJ held that under s 57 of the EP(C)A 1978 the onus is firmly put upon the employer to show what was the reason. He went on, 'This goes beyond the simple circumstances of the employer's conduct which amounted to dismissal and involves looking into the conduct of the employee and all the surrounding circumstances.'

In *Delabole Slate Ltd v Berriman* [1985] IRLR 305, the Court of Appeal held:

even in a case of constructive dismissal, s 57(1) of the 1978 Act imposes on the employer the burden of showing the reason for dismissal, notwithstanding that it was the employee, not the employer who actually decided to terminate the contract of employment. In our judgment, the only way in which the statutory requirements of the 1978 Act can be made to fit a case of constructive dismissal is to read s 57(1) as requiring the employer to show the reasons for his conduct which entitled the employee to terminate the contract thereby giving rise to a deemed dismissal by the employer. We can see nothing in the decision of *Savoia v Chiltern Herb Farms Ltd* [above] which conflicts with this view.

Where in a case involving a constructive dismissal the employer also puts forward a longstop defence that if the dismissal was for a particular reason it was fair, the tribunal must consider carefully the reason put forward for the dismissal: see *Derby City Council v Marshall* [1979] IRLR 261. In a case involving a constructive dismissal where the employer wishes to adopt the alternative defence that if there was a dismissal the dismissal was fair in all the circumstances, the employer must plead that defence: see *Post Office v Strange* [1981] IRLR 515.

In *Industrial Rubber Products v Gillon* [1977] IRLR 389, Gillon's basic rate of pay was unilaterally reduced to regularise a breach of the government's pay policy. It was a breach of a fundamental term of the contract enabling the employee to claim a constructive dismissal. However, it was held that the reduction to comply with the pay policy was 'some other substantial reason'. In *Genower v Ealing Hammersmith and Hounslow Area Health Authority* [1980] IRLR 297, there was a change in the employee's job which entitled him to claim he had been dismissed. The reason for the change was a reorganisation — 'some other substantial reason'.

Chapter 6

The Fairness of the Dismissal

1 General

The onus is upon the employer to show that the reason for the dismissal comes within the provisions of s 57(1) and (2) of the EP(C)A 1978. In addition the tribunal must be satisfied that the employer has acted reasonably.

Section 57(3) of the EP(C)A 1978 provides that:

The determination of the question whether the dismissal was fair or unfair, having regard to the reason shown by the employer, shall depend on whether in the circumstances (including the size and administrative resources of the employer's undertaking) the employer acted reasonably or unreasonably in treating it as a sufficient reason for dismissing the employee; and that question shall be determined in accordance with equity and the substantial merits of the case.

Before s 57(3) was amended by s 6 of the EA 1980, the burden of proof was on the employer. This is no longer the case. The burden of proof is sometimes described as being neutral so that there is a balance between the employer and the employee. The tribunal has to look at the whole of the evidence in deciding whether or not the employer has acted reasonably or unreasonably. In practice the employer presents his case first and the employee then presents his case. In *(1) Abbotts and (2) Standley v Wesson-Glynwed Steels Ltd* [1982] IRLR 51, the EAT held that the amendment of s 57(3) of the EP(C)A 1978 by s 6 of the EA 1980 neutralised the burden of proof, and it 'simply affects which way round the industrial tribunal has to look at its problem at the time of the hearing'. It is not wholly clear what the EAT meant by this. See also *Howarth Timber (Leeds) Ltd v Biscomb* [1986] IRLR 52, and for a case involving redundancy *Barratt Construction Ltd v Dalrymple* [1984] IRLR 385.

From an analysis of the reported cases it is clear that the difference in the burden of proof is only relevant in a few cases. In the majority of cases coming before the tribunals it will be clear whether or not the employer has acted reasonably or unreasonably.

Section 6 of the EA 1980 also amended the EP(C)A 1978 by requir-

158

ing tribunals in considering the circumstances to have specific regard to the size and administrative resources of the employer's undertaking. Thus what might be found to be unreasonable in the case of a large employer with perhaps a specialised personnel section might be reasonable in the case of a small employer with no more than, for instance, four employees.

However, the small size of the employer will not justify the employer's failure to carry out a proper investigation: see *Henderson v Granville Tours Ltd* [1982] IRLR 494. Conversely a large employer may not succeed in circumstances where a small employer may succeed.

In considering whether or not the employer acted reasonably or unreasonably the tribunal will have to consider whether the employer acted reasonably both 'procedurally' and 'substantively'. In deciding whether the employer acted reasonably or unreasonably a tribunal is entitled to have regard to equity and the substantial merits of the case.

In *UCATT v Brain* [1981] ICR 542, the Court of the Appeal held:

Whether someone acted reasonably is always a pure question of fact, so long as the tribunal deciding the issue correctly directs itself on the matters which should and should not be taken into account. But where Parliament has directed a tribunal to have regard to equity—and that, of course, means common fairness and not a particular branch of the law—and to the substantial merits of the case, the tribunal's duty is really very plain. It has to look at the question in the round and without regard to a lawyer's technicalities. It has to look at it in an employment and industrial relations context and not in the context of the Temple and Chancery Lane. It should, therefore, be very rare for any decision of a tribunal under this section to give rise to any question of law.

See also *Dillett v National Coal Board* [1988] ICR 218.

In considering the test of reasonableness the tribunal has to look and see whether or not the employer has acted reasonably or unreasonably. The fact that the employee may also have acted reasonably does not mean that the employer must have acted unreasonably. The point is illustrated by *Richmond Precision Engineering Ltd v Pearce* [1985] IRLR 179. Pearce was a foreman. His employer's business was taken over by the company. Pearce's employment continued but the company tried to integrate the terms and conditions of the two workforces. Discussions took place with Pearce about his terms and conditions, but ultimately the company offered Pearce less favourable terms and conditions of employment to which he refused to agree. The EAT found that the dismissal was fair. It held:

The task of weighing the advantages to the employer against the disadvantages to the employee is merely one factor which the Tribunal have to take into account when determining the question in accordance with the equity and the substantial merits of the case. Merely because there are disadvantages to the employee, it does not, by any manner of means, follow that the employer has acted unreasonably in treating his failure to accept the terms which they have offered as a reason to dismiss.

See also *Chubb Fire Security Ltd v Harper* [1983] IRLR 311.

However, injustice to the employee is one of the factors which has to be considered. In *Dobie v Burns International Security Services (UK) Ltd* [1984] IRLR 329, the Court of Appeal held:

In deciding whether the employer acted reasonably or unreasonably, a very important factor of which he has to take account, on the facts known to him at that time, is whether there will or will not be injustice to the employee and the extent of that injustice. For example, he will clearly have to take account of the length of time during which the employee has been employed by him, the satisfactoriness or otherwise of the employee's service, the difficulties which may face the employee in obtaining other employment, and matters of that sort. None of these is decisive, but they are all matters of which he has to take account and they are all matters which affect the justice or injustice to the employee of being dismissed.

The function of the tribunal is 'to decide, not what they would have done had they been the management, . . . [but] whether or not the dismissal was fair or unfair, which depends on whether the employer acted reasonably in treating it as a sufficient reason for dismissing the employee' *(Grundy (Teddington) Ltd v Willis* [1976] IRLR 118).

In deciding whether the dismissal was fair or unfair:

the Industrial Tribunal, while using its own collective wisdom, is to apply the standard of the reasonable employer: that is to say, the fairness or unfairness of the dismissal is to be judged not by the hunch of the particular Industrial Tribunal, which (though rarely) maybe whimsical or eccentric, but by the objective standard of the way in which a reasonable employer in those circumstances, in that line of business, would have behaved. It has to be recognised that there are circumstances where more than one course of action may be reasonable. In the case of redundancy, for example, and where selection of one or two employees to be dismissed for redundancy from a larger number is in issue, there may well be and often are cases where equally reasonable, fair, sensible and prudent employers would take different courses, one choosing 'A', another 'B' and another 'C'. In those circumstances for an Industrial Tribunal to say that it was unfair to select 'A' for dismissal, rather than 'B' or 'C', merely because had they been the employers that is what they would have done, is to apply the test of what the particular Industrial Tribunal itself would have done and not the test of what a reasonable employer would have done. It is in this sense that it is said that the test is whether what has been done is something which 'no reasonable management would have done'. In such cases, where more than one course of action can be considered reasonable, if an Industrial Tribunal equates its view of what it itself would have done with what a reasonable employer would have done, it may mean that an employer will be found to have dismissed an employee unfairly although in the circumstances many perfectly good and fair employers would have done as that employer did.

NC Watling and Co Ltd v Richardson [1978] IRLR 255; see also *Rolls*

Royce Ltd v Walpole [1980] IRLR 343. In *Neale v County Council of Hereford and Worcester* [1985] IRLR 281, the EAT held that:

as they [the tribunal] set about fixing the parameters of reasonable response to a given set of circumstances, that they should develop within their minds a picture of a hypothetical employer endowed with the attributes of reasonableness; and should ask themselves what range of response, in the same circumstances, would have been tolerable to him. The building up of that mental picture will normally be a gradual process to which many influences will have contributed—not least the impact made upon their minds by the experience (which is uniquely theirs) of seeing and hearing the parties and witnesses. The law protects that process by insisting that this delicately formed mental image is not to be shattered by applying to the case any less informed view of the facts or merits that may happen to occur to the minds or sympathies of an appellate tribunal.

In *British Leyland UK Ltd v Swift* [1981] IRLR 91, the Court of Appeal per Lord Denning MR held:

The correct test is: Was it reasonable for the employers to dismiss him? If no reasonable employer would have dismissed him, then the dismissal was unfair. But if a reasonable employer might reasonably have dismissed him, then the dismissal was fair. It must be remembered that in all these cases there is a band of reasonableness within which one employer might reasonably take one view: another quite reasonably take a different view. One would quite reasonably dismiss the man. The other would quite reasonably keep him on. Both views may be quite reasonable. If it was quite reasonable to dismiss him, then the dismissal might be upheld as fair: even though some other employers might not have dismissed him.

In *Swift's* case the issue was the employee's conduct. For a case involving a similar approach when the issue was capability, see *Bevan Harris Ltd (t/a The Clyde Leather Co) v Gair* [1981] IRLR 520.

In *Walton v TAC Construction Materials Ltd* [1981] IRLR 357, the employee, a heroin addict, was dismissed by the employer in accordance with their policy not to employ anybody who was a drug addict. The EAT found that although a more lenient employer might have continued the employee's employment it was within the range of reasonable responses for the employer to dismiss the employee, particularly since the tribunal found that the employer's policy of not employing drug addicts was a reasonable one. The dismissal in accordance with that policy was therefore fair.

In *Iceland Frozen Foods Ltd v Jones* [1982] IRLR 439, the EAT held that the correct approach for a tribunal when considering the test of reasonableness is as follows:

(1) the starting point should always be the words of s 57(3) [of the EP(C)A 1978] themselves;

(2) in applying the section a tribunal must consider the reasonableness of the employer's conduct, not simply whether they (the members of the tribunal) consider the dismissal to be fair;

(3) in judging the reasonableness of the employer's conduct a

tribunal must not substitute its decision as to what was the right course to adopt for that of the employer;

(4) in many (though not all) cases there is a band of reasonable responses to the employee's conduct within which one employer might reasonably take one view, another quite reasonably take another;

(5) the function of the tribunal, as an industrial jury, is to determine whether in the particular circumstances of each case the decision to dismiss the employee fell within the band of reasonable responses which a reasonable employer might have adopted. If the dismissal falls within the band the dismissal is fair: if the dismissal falls outside the band it is unfair.

The higher courts and the EAT have been reluctant to lay down guidelines for the tribunal to follow in applying the test of reasonableness. In *Thomas and Betts Manufacturing Co Ltd v Harding* [1980] IRLR 255, Eveleigh LJ held:

I myself deprecate the attempts that are made in these industrial relations cases to spell out a point of law developed upon precedent to create rules that have to be applied by the Tribunal in considering the straightforward question of fact which is provided for . . . [in s 57(3) of the EP(C)A 1978].

In *Rentokil Ltd v Mackin* [1989] IRLR 286, the EAT held that the tribunal, acting as an industrial jury, must determine whether the decision to dismiss falls within the band of reasonable responses which a reasonable employer might have adopted. 'That does not mean that such a high degree of unreasonableness be shown so that nothing short of a perverse decision to dismiss can be held to be fair. . . .'

See also *Bailey v BP Oil Kent Refinery Ltd* [1980] IRLR 287.

In *Anandarajah v Lord Chancellor's Department* [1984] IRLR 131, the EAT held:

The specialist law reports now contain an abundance of reported decisions documenting the application of the 1978 Act, by this Tribunal and by superior courts, to the circumstances of particular cases. They must be of great assistance to those concerned to observe the practical application of the jurisdiction from day to day. But there are dangers in giving such cases too general application. The authorities which will be found, in our view, to be the most helpful for the future are those recent decisions of the Court of Appeal— notably *O'Kelly v Trusthouse Forte plc* [1983] IRLR 369 and *Kearney and Trecker Marwin Ltd v Varndell and Others* [1983] IRLR 335—which have upheld the right of Industrial Tribunals to be their own guide on issues of reasonableness. Those cases have implicitly declared that the days are passing, if not already passed, when Industrial Tribunals were to be treated as dependent for the discharge of their fact-finding role upon judicial 'guidelines' sought to be extracted from reported decisions in other cases. Such dependency was understandable when the jurisdiction was in its infancy, but the Court of Appeal has now made it plain that for an Industrial Tribunal there can be no authority more persuasive than the language of Parliament. That must especially be so when parliament has directed an appraisal of the 'reasonableness' of a particular decision or action. In the infinite variety of circumstances, it can never be right to constrain the criteria by which a person's conduct is judged. Sometimes the judgment in a particular case will be found to express, in concise and helpful language, some concept which is regularly found in this field of inquiry and it becomes of great illustrative value. But reference to such a case can never be a substitute for taking the explicit directions of the statute as the guiding principle. This must be true even of authorities which, by frequency of citation, have attained a [hallowed] status . . . . Industrial Tribunals are not required, and should not in our view be invited, to subject the authorities to the same analysis as a court of law searching in a plethora of precedent for binding or persuasive authority.

The objective of Parliament, when it first framed the right not to be unfairly dismissed and set up a system of Industrial Tribunals (with a majority of lay members) to administer it, was to banish legalism and in particular to ensure that, wherever possible, parties conducting their own case would be able to face the Tribunal with the same ease and confidence as those professionally represented. A preoccupation with guideline authority puts that objective in jeopardy. It should seldom be necessary (and may sometimes even be unwise) for an Industrial Tribunal to frame its decision by reference to any direction other than the express terms of the statute.

See also *Siggs and Chapman (Contractors) Ltd v Knight* [1984] IRLR 83 and *Rolls Royce Motors Ltd v Dewhurst* [1985] IRLR 184.

Although there is a tendency illustrated by the foregoing cases to emphasise the importance of the statutory provisions without giving guidelines to the tribunal, this approach is by no means universal. In *Grundy (Teddington) Ltd v Plummer and Salt* [1983] IRLR 98, the EAT held:

It seems to us that it is a proper and useful part of our function in a limited number of cases to give guidance as to the general approach to what constitutes reasonable conduct by an employer . . . It may well be that in the past guidelines have been laid down too frequently and in too much detail. But to maintain uniformity of approach it should be proper in the absence of specific guidance in the statutory codes of practice for this Appeal Tribunal in a very limited number of cases to indicate in general terms how reasonable employers should approach the types of problems with which they are faced.

In deciding whether or not the employer has acted reasonably 'substantively', it is for the tribunal to reach a decision as an industrial jury having regard to all the circumstances in deciding whether or not the employer's response was within a range of reasonable responses. In deciding whether or not the employer has acted reasonably 'procedurally' the tribunal's approach will be the same. In addition, it is entitled to have regard to the guidelines laid down in the codes of practice. See below.

An appeal from a tribunal to the EAT can only be made on a point of law. The Court of Appeal has criticised dressing up points of fact so that they fall to be treated as points of law: see *Retarded Children's Aid Society Ltd v Day* [1978] ICR 437 and *Hollister v National Farmers Union* [1979] ICR 542. In *Kent County Council v Gillam* [1985] IRLR

18, it was recognised that since the question whether or not an employer has acted fairly is one of fact, different tribunals might reach a different conclusion on not dissimilar facts. There is judicial authority for the view that a tribunal has no obligation to provide an analysis of the facts and arguments on both sides with reasons for rejecting those they did reject, and for accepting those relied upon in support of their conclusion: see *Kearney and Trecker Marwin Ltd v Varndell and Others* [1983] IRLR 355, but see also *Iggesund Converters Ltd v Lewis* [1984] ICR 544, where the EAT found in cases of misconduct:

it will normally be desirable, and frequently essential, for the industrial tribunal to make specific findings as to what allegations were put by the employers at any accusatory interview preceding the dismissal, what opportunity the employee was given of learning the nature of the evidence relied on, what opportunity he was allowed of replying to it, and what his reply was.

If the tribunal has not asked the right question or the evidence does not support the conclusion the tribunal has reached, and the decision is perverse, the EAT will intervene: see *Day*'s case above; *Earl v Slater and Wheeler (Airlyne) Ltd* [1972] IRLR 115; *Spook Erection v Thackray* [1984] IRLR 116, and *Dillett*'s case, above.

2 Reasonableness and subsequently discovered misconduct

The question whether or not the employer acted reasonably or unreasonably has to be answered with reference to the circumstances known to the employer at the moment of dismissal: *Earl v Slater and Wheeler (Airlyne) Ltd* [1972] ICR 508. Moment of dismissal does not mean the effective date of termination, except in certain circumstances. The moment of dismissal is the time when the decision to dismiss was taken. The moment of dismissal and the effective date of termination will only coincide where the employee is dismissed instantly: see s 55(4) of the EP(C)A 1978. It follows that if the employer's action was unreasonable at the moment of dismissal, subsequently discovered facts which were unknown to the employer at the moment of dismissal cannot make the dismissal reasonable. For an interpretation of the moment of dismissal see *Stacey v Babcock Power Ltd (Construction Division)* [1986] IRLR 3 and see discussion below. The point was considered in *W Devis and Sons Ltd v Atkins* [1977] AC 931. Atkins was a manager of the employer's abattoir. He was dismissed because the employer was dissatisfied with the way in which he had made purchases. He was given salary in lieu of notice and offered £6,000 as an *ex-gratia* payment by way of compensation. Several weeks later the company discovered certain information which led it to believe Atkins was guilty of dishonesty and the *ex-gratia* payment was withdrawn. At the hearing before the tribunal the employer sought to adduce this evidence. The tribunal was not prepared to admit the evidence which was not known to the company at the time of the dismissal. It relied on the decision in *Earl v Slater and Wheeler (Airlyne) Ltd* [1972] ICR 508.

On appeal to the High Court, Phillips J referred to another decision of the High Court in *Merseyside and North Wales Electricity Board v Taylor* [1975] ICR 185, where it was held:

the circumstances . . . referred to are those applying at or prior to the date of dismissal. What happens subsequent to the date of dismissal cannot be relevant in considering whether the employer acted reasonably or unreasonably in treating the reason as sufficient for dismissing the employee.

Following this he found:

The Tribunal has to determine what was the real reason. Of necessity that must be something which existed at the date of dismissal, and so what the Tribunal has under consideration is whether the employer acted reasonably, in all the circumstances, in treating that reason as a sufficient reason for dismissing the employee. It is quite clear that the whole matter under consideration is the reasonableness of the behaviour of the employer at and leading up to the time of dismissal . . . there is an extremely powerful, almost an irresistible, argument in favour of holding . . . that the circumstances also are the circumstances as they existed at that time.

The decision of Phillips J was upheld by the Court of Appeal and the House of Lords. Both found that in applying the test of reasonableness the tribunal must decide whether the employer acted reasonably in treating his actual reason as a sufficient reason and not merely whether he acted reasonably in all the circumstances, so that circumstances after the dismissal could be taken into account.

In the High Court Phillips J did not accept that the common law principle as enunciated in *Boston Deep Sea Fishing and Ice Co v Ansell* (1888) 39 ChD 339, or *Cyril Leonard and Co v Simo Securities Trust Ltd* [1972] 1 WLR 80, applied to the statutory jurisdiction. At common law, where an employee has been guilty of uncondoned misconduct so grave that it justifies instant dismissal, the employer can rely on that misconduct to defend a claim for wrongful dismissal, even though he only becomes aware of it after the dismissal. Both the Court of Appeal and the House of Lords accepted that the common law authorities did not apply to the statutory jurisdiction. The approach in *Devis*'s case was followed in *Polkey v AE Dayton Services Ltd* [1988] ICR 142. It may happen that where there is an internal appeal by the employee against the employer's decision to dismiss, new evidence may emerge. In *Board of Governors, The National Heart and Chest Hospitals v Nambiar* [1981] IRLR 196, the EAT held that where the employee appeals against his dismissal under an internal appeals procedure, the fairness of the dismissal is to be judged by the tribunal on the basis of all the information available to the employer at the conclusion of the appeal. This may include information which came to the notice of the employer during the hearing of the appeal. It would be artificial to exclude any new material from consideration by the tribunal:

it is necessary to distinguish the case where an employee is dismissed for reason A and evidence at an internal appeal invalidates reason A but demonstrates that a different reason B would justify dismissal. It is clear that in such circumstances the original dismissal ought not to stand and the employer must look at the matter afresh in order to decide whether a later dismissal on the new information is appropriate. In the more usual case, however, where the employer confirms the decision to dismiss for reason A, following the appeal, we consider that it is right for an Industrial Tribunal to look at the information that came to light in the course of the appeal.

The date of the decision to dismiss and the principle reason for it are established before an internal appeal, but an Industrial Tribunal has to consider whether the employer can satisfy them that, [in the words of s 57(3) of the EP(C)A 1978] 'in the circumstances (having regard to equity and the substantial merits of the case) he acted reasonably in treating it as a sufficient reason for dismissing the employee'. In our judgment, these are words of broad application and we suggest that our interpretation does not do violence to the language. When an internal appeal body decides or recommends that a dismissal shall stand, it has to consider whether the reason is sufficient to justify confirmation of the dismissal in the light of any new information about it as well as the information available to the employer when the original decision was made; and it would be artificial to exclude the new material from consideration by an Industrial Tribunal adjudicating upon a decision to dismiss that the employer has confirmed.

The EAT distinguished the facts of this case where the appeal established and upheld the original reasons, and the case of *Monie v Coral Racing Ltd* [1980] IRLR 464, where the original reason was invalidated on appeal, although a new reason was established.

The employer cannot substitute a reason which was not in his mind at the time of the dismissal, for the reason which was in his mind at the time of the dismissal, to justify the original dismissal. In such a case the employer has to decide whether the new reason is one which can be a reason for dismissal.

The decision in *Board of Governors, The National Heart and Chest Hospitals v Nambiar*, above, was upheld in *Sillifant v Powell Duffryn Timber Ltd* [1983] IRLR 91, where Browne-Wilkinson J held:

The commonsense of industrial relations demands that in considering the reasonableness of the employer's conduct, account must be taken of information coming to his knowledge on the hearing of the appeal: the appeal is part of the procedural structure established by the employer to ensure fair treatment. . . . In our judgment this apparent exception to the rule that one can only look at facts known at the date of dismissal does not run contrary to the underlying principle of *Devis v Atkins*.

In *Greenall Whitley plc v Carr* [1985] IRLR 289, the EAT again found that the tribunal was entitled to take into account the circumstances considered at, and leading up to, the internal appeal hearing.

The earlier authorities were reviewed by the House of Lords in

West Midlands Co-operative Society Ltd v Tipton [1986] ICR 192, where Lord Bridge held:

Under s 57 of the Act of 1978 there are three questions which must be answered in determining whether a dismissal was fair or unfair: (1) What was the reason (or principal reason) for the dismissal? (2) Was *that* reason a reason falling within s 57(2) or some other substantial reason of a kind such as to justify the dismissal of an employee holding the position which that employee held? (3) Did the employer act reasonably or unreasonably in treating *that* reason as a sufficient reason for dismissing the employee?

As to question (1), Cairns LJ in *Abernethy v Mott, Hay and Anderson* [1974] ICR 323, in a passage approved by Viscount Dilhorne in the *Devis* case, said at p 330:

A reason for the dismissal of an employee is a set of facts known to the employer, or it may be of beliefs held by him, which cause him to dismiss the employee. If at the time of his dismissal the employer gives a reason for it, that is no doubt evidence, at any rate as against him, as to the real reason, but it does not necessarily constitute the real reason. He may knowingly give a reason different from the real reason out of kindness . . .

The reason shown by the employer in answer to question (1) may, therefore, be aptly termed the real reason. Once the real reason is established the answer to question (2) will depend on the application of the statutory criteria to that reason. Then comes the crucial question (3): did the employer act reasonably or unreasonably in treating the real reason as a sufficient reason for dismissing the employee? Conduct of the employee unrelated to the real reason for dismissal obviously cannot affect the answer to this question. This, and no more than this, is what the *Devis* case decided. But I can see nothing in the language of the statute to exclude from consideration in answering question (3) 'in accordance with equity and the substantial merits of the case' evidence relevant to show the strength or weakness of the real reason for dismissal which the employer had the opportunity to consider in the course of an appeal heard pursuant to a disciplinary procedure which complies with the statutory code of practice. The apparent injustice of excluding, in relation to this question, misconduct of the employee which is irrelevant to the real reason for dismissal is mitigated, as I have earlier pointed out, by the provisions relating to compensation in such a case. But there is nothing to mitigate the injustice to an employee which would result if he were unable to complain that his employer, though acting reasonably on the facts known to him when he summarily dismissed the employee, acted quite unreasonably in maintaining his decision to dismiss in the face of mitigating circumstances established in the course of the domestic appeal procedure which a reasonable employer would have treated as sufficient to excuse the employee's offence on which the employer's real reason for the dismissal depended. Adopting the analysis which found favour in *J Sainsbury Ltd v Savage* [1981] ICR 1, if the domestic appeal succeeds the employee is reinstated with retrospective effect; if it fails the summary dismissal takes effect from the original date. Thus, in so far as the original dismissal and the decision on the domestic appeal are governed by the same consideration, the real reason for dismissal, there is no reason to treat the effective date of termination as a watershed which separates the one process from the other. Both the original and the appellate decision by the employer, in any case where the contract of employment provides for an appeal and the right of appeal is invoked by the employee, are necessary elements in the overall process of terminating the contract of employment. To separate them and to consider only one half of the process in determining whether the employer acted reasonably or unreasonably in treating his real reason for dismissal as sufficient is to introduce an unnecessary artificiality into proceedings on a claim of unfair dismissal calculated to defeat, rather than accord with, the 'equity and the substantial merits of the case' and for which the language of the statute affords no warrant.

This is the conclusion I should reach as a matter of construction, taking due account of the decision in the *Devis* case, if there were no other authority to guide me. But the conclusion is powerfully reinforced by the series of decisions of the Employment Appeal Tribunal, to which I have earlier referred, with which it is in full accord. The relevant cases are *Rank Zerox (UK) Ltd v Goodchild* [1979] IRLR 185; *Quantrill v Eastern Counties Omnibus Co Ltd* (unreported), 30 June 1980; *National Heart and Chest Hospitals Board of Governors v Nambiar* [1981] ICR 441; *Sillifant v Powell Duffryn Timber Ltd* [1983] IRLR 91 and *Greenall Whitley plc v Carr* [1985] ICR 451.

In *Whitbread and Co plc v Mills* [1988] IRLR 501, the EAT held that it is possible to remedy defects in disciplinary and dismissal procedures on appeal, since appeal procedures form an important part of the process of ensuring that a dismissal is fair. An appeal hearing, if it is a rehearing, not just a review, may correct any earlier deficiencies in the procedure. The employer's original decision and its appellate decision are elements in the overall process of terminating the contract of employment. Fairness falls to be considered after the appeal procedure has been completed. There is nothing in *Devis*'s case which is inconsistent with this approach. The principle in *Devis*'s case is that information which comes to the knowledge of the employer after the decision to dismiss, and has no relevance to the real reason for dismissal, cannot be allowed to justify some other reason for the dismissal. It is clear from *Tipton*'s case that matters which come to light during the appeal procedure can be taken into account when considering equity and the substantial merits of the case.

Between the date when the employer gives the employee notice to terminate the employment and the date when the notice expires, certain facts may come to the attention of the employer.

In *Williamson v Alcan (UK) Ltd* [1978] ICR 104, Phillips J suggested that where an employer acquired information after the moment of dismissal and before the effective date of termination which indicated that they should not have dismissed the employee, the dismissal could well become unfair if they did not then do that which they obviously had the power to do, namely, to withdraw the notice. This, however, ignores one problem which can arise for the employer, namely that giving notice is a unilateral act and can only be withdrawn by consent. If the employee is unwilling to agree to the notice being withdrawn in these circumstances, will the dismissal still be unfair? In *Stacey v Babcock Power Ltd (Construction Division)* [1986] IRLR 3, the EAT found that where an employee is given notice of dismissal, the process of dismissal is not complete until the notice period has expired. 'Dismissal' in the EP(C)A 1978 is applied solely to cases where the contract is terminated by the employer and in the case of a dismissal on notice the contract does not terminate until the notice has expired. 'Dismissal' in s 57(3) of the EP(C)A 1978 is the whole process initiated by the giving of the notice and completed by its expiry. Although the language used in earlier authorities was consistent with the view that the date of notice rather than the effective date of termination, where the two were different, was the point at which the reasonableness of the dismissal fell to be determined, those cases were ones where either there was no or virtually no notice given and where it was immaterial to draw any distinction between the date of notice and the effective date of termination as representing the moment of dismissal, or the point was not raised. Therefore, since in this case there was a substantial period between the giving of the notice and the effective date of termination, the tribunal was entitled to take into account events occurring during the period of notice in deciding whether the employer's decision to dismiss was reasonable in all the circumstances. This case does not involve an exception to the rule in *W Devis and Sons Ltd v Atkins*, above. The EAT simply found that the dismissal was not complete until the notice expired.

It is arguable that if the employer acted reasonably at the moment of dismissal, subsequently discovered facts will not render the dismissal unreasonable. However, it is apparent from the decision in *Chrystie v Rolls Royce (1971) Ltd* [1976] IRLR 336, that there will be a greater degree of flexibility where facts are discovered subsequent to the dismissal, in deciding whether the decision to dismiss, which was reasonable at the moment of dismissal, is shown by subsequently discovered facts to be unreasonable.

3 Procedural fairness (1): introduction

In determining whether or not the employer has acted reasonably or unreasonably the tribunal is entitled to see whether the employer has followed a fair procedure. There may be an agreed procedure negotiated between the employer and the union, one which has been put forward by the employer unilaterally, or there may be no formal procedure. Guidance upon whether or not the formal agreed procedure or the procedure followed by the employer is fair can be obtained from the codes of practice.

The Industrial Relations Code of Practice came into effect on 28 February 1972, the day on which the unfair dismissal provisions of the Industrial Relations Act 1971 came into force. The Code of Practice — Disciplinary Practice and Procedures in Employment came into effect on 20 June 1977. As from that date this code supersedes the provisions of the 1972 Industrial Relations Code of Practice. The 1972 code ceases to have effect from 1 June 1991. Although repealed the principles of the 1972 Code are contained in case law. The 1977 code is referred to by that term in this chapter although it may be noted that, in 1977 codes of practice were also issued relating to the disclosure of information and to time off for trade union duties and activities.

In addition to the 1977 code ACAS has prepared an advisory handbook entitled Discipline at Work. This is simply for guidance and does not have the same weight attached to it as a code.

The principles in the 1972 Code may be relevant in claims for unfair dismissal particularly paras 45–6, giving guidance on dismissals for redundancy, paras 51–70, dealing with communication and consultation, and paras 120–9, dealing with grievance procedures. In a claim for unfair dismissal, the 1977 code will be the one which the tribunals will take into account where applicable. The 1972 code will be referred to by that term in this chapter.

The codes are a guide for the purposes of promoting good industrial relations, but are advisory only. The employer's failure to observe any provisions of the codes will not of itself render him liable to any proceedings, but when proceedings have been brought against him, the tribunal can take account of the codes' provisions: s 6(11) of the EPA 1975.

Although the 1977 code differs in certain respects from the 1972 code, the reported cases under the 1972 code are relevant to an examination of the way in which the tribunals and EAT will decide whether or not the dismissal was procedurally fair. The importance of the 1972 code of practice was considered in *Neefies v Crystal Products Ltd* [1972] IRLR 118, where the NIRC held:

we do not think that a failure to observe the detailed provisions of the code of practice is fatal to the employer in a claim for unfair dismissal, provided that the procedure which has in fact been followed is fair and equitable in the circumstances and is one which enables the substantial merits of the case to be considered. That is the overall objective of the code; and provided that that objective has been attained, we do not think that it matters that it has been attained without adherence to the detailed provisions of the code.

As a guideline, the same is true of the 1977 code.

The importance of following a proper procedure has recently been reaffirmed by the House of Lords in two cases. In *West Midlands Co-operative Society Ltd v Tipton* [1986] IRLR 112, Lord Bridge, quoted from the judgment of Viscount Dilhorne in *W Devis and Sons Ltd v Atkins* above, where he said:

It does not follow that non-compliance with the code necessarily renders a dismissal unfair, but I agree with the view expressed by Sir John Donaldson in *Earl v Slater and Wheeler (Airlyne) Ltd* [1972] IRLR 115, that a failure to follow a procedure prescribed in the code may lead to the conclusion that a dismissal was unfair, which, if that procedure had been followed, would have been held to have been fair.

In *Polkey v AE Dayton Services Ltd* [1988] ICR 142, the House of Lords further considered the importance of following a proper procedure. Before considering *Polkey*'s case, it is necessary briefly to consider the position before *Polkey*. As a result of cases such as *British Labour Pump Co Ltd v Byrne* [1979] ICR 347, the importance of following a proper procedure had been substantially undermined. The principle enunciated in *Byrne*'s case was as follows:

even if, judged in the light of circumstances known at the time of dismissal, the employer's decision was not reasonable because of some failure to follow a fair procedure yet the dismissal can be held fair if, on the facts proved before the industrial tribunal, the industrial tribunal comes to the conclusion that the employer could reasonably have decided to dismiss if he had followed a fair procedure.

This decision was supported by the Court of Appeal in *W and J Wass Ltd v Binns* [1982] ICR 486. The decision was binding on tribunals. It was criticised in *Sillifant v Powell Duffryn Timber Ltd* [1983] IRLR 91. The judgment of Browne-Wilkinson J in *Sillifant*'s case was approved by the House of Lords in *Polkey*'s case, above. In *Sillifant*'s case Browne-Wilkinson J held:

The only test of the fairness of a dismissal is the reasonableness of the employer's decision to dismiss judged at the time at which the dismissal takes effect. An industrial tribunal is not bound to hold that *any* procedural failure by the employer renders the dismissal unfair: it is one of the factors to be weighed by the industrial tribunal in deciding whether or not the dismissal was reasonable within s 57(3) [of the EP(C)A 1978]. The weight to be attached to such procedural failure should depend upon the circumstances known to the employer at the time of dismissal, not on the actual consequence of such failure. Thus in the case of a failure to give an opportunity to explain, except in the rare case where a reasonable employer could properly take the view on the facts known to him at the time of dismissal that no explanation or mitigation could alter his decision to dismiss, an industrial tribunal would be likely to hold that the lack of 'equity' inherent in the failure would render the dismissal unfair. But there may be cases where the offence is so heinous and the facts so manifestly clear that a reasonable employer could, on the facts known to him at the time of dismissal, take the view that whatever explanation the employee advanced it would make no difference: see the example referred to by Lawton LJ in *Bailey v BP Oil (Kent Refinery) Ltd* [1980] ICR 642. Where, in the circumstances known at the time of dismissal, it was not reasonable for the employer to dismiss without giving an opportunity to explain but facts subsequently discovered or proved before the industrial tribunal show that the dismissal was in fact merited, compensation would be reduced to nil. Such a approach ensures that an employee who could have been fairly dismissed does not get compensation but would prevent the suggestion of 'double standards' inherent in the *British Labour Pump* principle. An employee dismissed for suspected dishonesty who is in fact innocent has no redress: if the employer acted fairly in dismissing him on the facts and in the circumstances known to him at the time of dismissal the employee's innocence is irrelevant. Why should an employer be entitled to a finding that he acted fairly when, on the facts known and in the circumstances existing at the time of dismissal, his actions were unfair but which facts subsequently coming to light show did not cause any injustice?

In the same case Lord Bridge held:

In the case of incapacity, the employer will normally not act reasonably unless he gives the employee fair warning and an opportunity to mend his ways and show that he can do the job; in the case of misconduct, the employer will normally not act reasonably unless he investigates the complaint of misconduct fully and fairly and hears whatever the employee wishes to say in his defence or in explanation or mitigation; in the case of redundancy, the employer will normally not act reasonably unless he warns and consults any employees affected or their representative, adopts a fair basis on which to select for redundancy and takes such steps as may be reasonable to avoid or minimise redundancy by redeployment within his own organisation. If an employer has failed to take the appropriate procedural steps in any particular case, the one question the industrial tribunal is *not* permitted to ask in applying the test of reasonableness posed by s 57(3) [of the EP(C)A 1978] is the hypothetical question whether it would have made any difference to the outcome if the appropriate procedural steps had been taken. On the true construction of s 57(3) this question is simply irrelevant. It is quite a different matter if the tribunal is able to conclude that the employer himself, at the time of dismissal, acted reasonably in taking the view that, in the exceptional circumstances of the particular case, the procedural steps normally appropriate would have been futile, could not have altered the decision to dismiss and therefore could be dispensed with. In such a case the test of reasonableness under s 57(3) may be satisfied.

In *Hooper v British Railways Board* [1988] IRLR 517, the Court of Appeal followed the decision in *Polkey*'s case. It emphasised that it is for the tribunal to consider whether the employer acted reasonably notwithstanding the failure to follow a proper procedure and that depends upon the circumstances and the facts known to the employer at the time of making the decision. See also *McLaren v National Coal Board* [1987] ICR 370.

The tribunal may still need to consider what would have happened if a fair procedure had been followed. In *Polkey*'s case Lord Bridge held:

If it is held that taking the appropriate steps which the employer failed to take before dismissing the employee would not have affected the outcome, this will often lead to the result that the employee, although unfairly dismissed, will recover no compensation or, in the case of redundancy, no compensation in excess of his redundancy payment.

If the tribunal is in doubt whether or not the employee would have been dismissed if a proper procedure had been followed, then that doubt can be reflected in reducing the amount of compensation by a percentage representing the chance that the employee would have still lost his employment.

4 Procedural fairness (2): the 1977 code

4.1 General

The aim of the 1977 code is to give practical guidance to both employers and trade unions as well as individual employees. It is concerned with three aspects of disciplinary practice and procedure: the disciplinary rules; the penalties for the breach of them; and the procedures for enforcing the rules and imposing the penalties. It is designed to apply regardless of the size of the business although the code recognises that even in smaller establishments, although it may not be practicable to adopt all the provisions, most of the essential features of the disciplinary procedure could be adopted.

In practice it may be impossible for a small employer to observe the code in the same way as a larger employer. For instance, an appeals procedure may be impracticable because there is nobody to whom the employee can appeal. Although the letter of the code may not apply to a small employer the spirit of the code will: see *Earl v Slater and Wheeler (Airlyne) Ltd* [1972] ICR 508. The EAT has suggested that the code is drafted with industry and large enterprises in mind and it is not necessarily apt in the context of a small employer: *The Royal Naval School v Hughes* [1979] IRLR 383; and see also *MacKellar v Bolton* [1979] IRLR 59. However, the smallness of the employer's undertaking will not be an excuse for the failure by the employer to carry out a proper procedure: see *Henderson v Granville Tours Ltd* [1982] IRLR 494.

The code provides that disciplinary rules and procedures are necessary for promoting fairness and order in the treatment of individuals and in the conduct of industrial relations. Rules set standards of conduct; procedure helps to ensure that standards are adhered to, and also provides a fair method of dealing with alleged failures to observe them. Management is responsible for maintaining discipline and ensuring that there are adequate disciplinary rules and procedures. To be fully effective the rules and procedures need to be accepted as reasonable by both management and employees. Management should therefore aim to secure the involvement of employees and all levels of management when formulating new or revising existing rules and procedures. Although trade union officials may not wish to participate in the formulation of the rules, ideally they should participate fully with management in agreeing the procedural arrangements which will apply to their members and in seeing that these arrangements are used consistently and fairly.

Where the employer reaches an agreement with the union, it is sensible for the employer to ensure that the agreement has been brought to the attention of the work force. In *Gray Dunn and Co Ltd v Edwards* [1980] IRLR 23, the Scottish division of the EAT held, *obiter*, that where the employer had negotiated an agreement with a recognised trade union they were entitled to assume that those employees who were members of the union knew of and were bound by its provision. The rule related to conduct which any reasonable employee would realise would have as its consequence summary dismissal. In *W Brooks and Son v Skinner* [1984] IRLR 379, the English division of the EAT held that while the approach in *Edwards*'s case, above, may be a perfectly proper and reasonable approach in many cases, it did not follow that in every case an employer who reaches an agreement with the trade union will be justified in taking the view that the employees know what is agreed. In *Skinner*'s case there was clear evidence that Skinner did not know of the agreement, whereas in *Edwards*'s case no finding had been made as to whether or not the employee knew of the position. In *Skinner*'s case the agreement dealt with a specific occasion, namely that any employee who over-indulged at the Christmas party so that he was unable to attend for work would be instantly dismissed.

In addition to the employees' involvement in formulating new or revising existing rules, their involvement in formulating new or revising existing penalties should probably also be secured.

If the employer can show that the disciplinary rules, penalties and procedures have resulted from joint consultation, it suggests that due consideration has been given to the rules, penalties and procedures, and that the result is reasonable and mutually acceptable to both sides in the enterprise. Where the employer in reliance upon these rules, penalties and procedures, dismisses the employee there is a greater chance of the dismissal being found fair. In *Wells v E and A West Ltd* [1975] IRLR 269, the tribunal found:

We have had before us a document which represents the terms which have been agreed with the union by the respondents about dismissal and the Tribunal takes the view that if terms relating to dismissals are agreed with the unions and they are communicated to the workforce one cannot readily regard their unilateral abrogation as being reasonable.

Where a code is agreed between the parties, the employer cannot usually be accused of acting unreasonably if he follows the code and it is not for the tribunal to rewrite that code: *East Hertfordshire District Council v Boyten* [1977] IRLR 347. Where there is an agreed procedure which is fair, and has been properly developed and properly applied, it is not open to the tribunal to add a further step: *Donald Cook and Sons Ltd v Carter* [1977] IRLR 88.

4.2 Disciplinary rules and the proper penalty

The code recognises that disciplinary rules may not cover all circumstances that arise. The rules required will vary according to particular circumstances. The aim should be to specify clearly and concisely those rules necessary for the efficient and safe performance of work, and for the maintenance of satisfactory relations within the workforce, and between employees and management. Rules should not be so general as to be meaningless. Rules should be readily available and management should make every effort to ensure that employees know and understand them. Employees should be made aware of the likely consequence of breaking rules. They should be given a clear indication of the type of conduct which may warrant summary dismissal.

For the problem of defining gross misconduct, see **5.1(*a*)**, below, *et seq*.

Where the employer is unable to show a clear promulgation of the rule, or an amendment or variation of the rule, he will find himself in difficulty. In *Pringle v Lucas Industrial Equipment Ltd* [1975] IRLR 266, the employer tried to rely on a new rule which made certain misconduct an offence for which the employee could be instantly dismissed. This was a variation of an older rule incorporated in written rules given to the employee and acknowledged by him upon entering the employment. The variation had been agreed at a meeting of the shop stewards committee and promulgated by the chief shop steward at a mass meeting at which Pringle had not been present. He was summarily dismissed for breach of the rule, but it was held that the informal promulgation of the rule in this manner was an abdication of the management's responsibility, and that the employer could not rely on the new rule to dismiss instantly. See also the cases of *Edwards* and *Skinner* above.

Where an employer wishes to be able to dismiss an employee without imposing warnings for a certain course of conduct there must be a clear rule prohibiting that course of conduct and making it clear that the penalty will be dismissal. Ideally this should also be the position where the conduct is gross misconduct which might be considered sufficient to justify instant dismissal. In the latter case the employer may succeed even though there is no rule and/or penalty, but he may find himself in difficulties.

In *Pringle*'s case, above, the tribunal commented:

if employers wish to be able to dismiss automatically for certain misconduct which is short of inherently gross misconduct they must be able to show that management has unequivocally brought to the attention of the employees what the conduct is, and what its consequences will be. If they fail to do this, they can properly only dismiss an employee after due warnings and after giving the employee a chance to explain his conduct.

Dismissal in such circumstances must be within the bands of reasonable responses.

Both the rule and the penalty should be known to the employee. In *Rigden-Murphy v Securicor Ltd* [1976] IRLR 106, Rigden-Murphy breached the employer's rules dealing with the transfer of money from a bank to the employer's vehicle. Although the rule was known to

Rigden-Murphy, he was dismissed for the first breach. The tribunal found the dismissal was unfair because the employer had failed to make it clear what breaches of the employer's rules would be regarded as sufficient to justify dismissal without prior warning.

In *Dairy Produce Packers Ltd v Beverstock* [1981] IRLR 265, Beverstock worked as second man on one of the company's delivery vans. At 4pm the driver and Beverstock went into a public house. Beverstock went back to the factory. His supervisor believed that he was drunk. Next day he was dismissed because the company believed he had been drinking in a public house during the company's time. The tribunal accepted that he had been drinking while he should have been at work. However, other employees who were considered to be under the influence of drink while at work or had turned up late for work due to drink were only warned. The company argued that Beverstock had broken the duty of trust that existed because he worked away from the factory and so his conduct could not be monitored. It was held that, 'Where it is considered necessary to have specific penalties attached to the misuse of alcohol in a particular enterprise then it is proper . . . that this should be clearly laid down.'

Where the employer has a rule it should be clear. If it is not the employer may not be able to rely upon it. In *Trusthouse Forte (Catering) Ltd v Adonis* [1984] IRLR 382, the company had a rule that anyone caught smoking in a no-smoking area would be dismissed for gross misconduct. However, in the employee's particulars of employment, under the section headed 'Disciplinary Rules', smoking in a non-designated area was included in the list of examples of misconduct in respect of which the employee would be warned and only dismissed if, after warning, his standard of conduct fell below a level which was acceptable. The particulars were reissued after a notice containing the rule had been posted on a board by the company. It was held that the particulars of terms of employment set out the terms and conditions of his employment, and that the employer could not rely upon the notice posted on the board to the effect that smoking in a no-smoking area would be treated as gross misconduct, and his dismissal for that reason was treated as unfair.

Where both the rule and the penalty are known to the employee and the employer acts in reliance on the rule, his actions will usually be fair. In *Meyer Dunmore International Ltd v Rogers* [1978] IRLR 167, in considering a rule relating to fighting, the EAT said:

if employers wish to have a rule that employees engaged in, what could properly and sensibly be called fighting are going to be summarily dismissed . . . there is no reason why they should not have a rule, *provided* . . . that it is plainly adopted, that it is plainly and clearly set out, and that great publicity is given to it, so that every employee knows beyond any doubt whatever that if he gets involved in fighting in that sense, he will be dismissed . . . where there is a clear rule, it is well understood, the fighting is serious rather than unimportant, and the inquiry is properly and fairly conducted, it can be expected that industrial tribunals will ordinarily uphold the fairness of the dismissal for that reason.

In *Rowe v Radio Rentals Ltd* [1982] IRLR 177, Rowe, a television engineer, repaired a TV set for a woman, who was not one of the company's customers, for his own benefit, in contravention of a rule in the company staff handbook, that private trading for gain was gross misconduct. His dismissal was fair in all the circumstances. See also *Drym Fabricators Ltd v Johnson* [1981] ICR 274.

However, what is reasonable is a matter for the tribunal and the employer's rules and disciplinary penalties may not be reasonable. In *Taylor v Parsons Peebles NEI Bruce Peebles Ltd* [1981] IRLR 119, the EAT held that Parsons' dismissal for fighting was unfair notwithstanding that the company operated a policy where by any employee who deliberately hit another employee would be dismissed, because such a provision must always be considered in the light of how a reasonable employer would apply the rule and the penalty in the circumstances of each case. It considered that a reasonable employer having regard to the employee's 20 years' good conduct would not have applied the rigid sanction of automatic dismissal. See also *Ladbrooke Racing Ltd v Amott and Others* [1983] IRLR 154.

There may be cases where the employer has been lax in enforcing the rule and the prescribed penalty. In such cases he may not be able to rely on the rule and the penalty in the future.

In *Rennie v Eric Bemrose Ltd* [1974] IRLR 334, the employer had an unwritten rule, which was generally known among the employees, that absence from the factory without leave constituted gross misconduct. Rennie absented himself without leave and was instantly dismissed. In the past the employer had not treated every absence without leave as gross misconduct warranting instant dismissal. The tribunal found the dismissal unfair, *inter alia*, because the rule had not been treated as an absolute one in the past and had been applied in a discretionary way. The employee did not know what penalty would be applied because of the element of discretion.

In *Ayub v Vauxhall Motors Ltd* [1978] IRLR 428, the dismissal of an employee for sleeping on the night shift was held to be unfair. An employee who had committed the same offence three days earlier was suspended for three days following his internal appeal against the dismissal. In *Post Office v Fennell* [1981] IRLR 221, the Court of Appeal found that the idea of equity in the phrase 'having regard to equity and the substantial merits of the case' involves 'the concept that employees who misbehave in much the same way should have meted out to them much the same punishment'. So an employer who imposes a penalty in the form of dismissal in the case of one employee which is inconsistent with more lenient treatment of other employees is likely to have that dismissal found unfair.

In *Cain v Leeds Western Health Authority* [1990] IRLR 168, the EAT held that the employer's lack of consistency was something which had to be considered in determining the reasonableness of the dismissal.

Where an employee is dismissed and an employer subsequently imposes a different disciplinary penalty on another employee for the same offence, this may well be relevant in considering the fairness or otherwise of the dismissal: see *Eagle Star Insurance Co Ltd and Another v Hayward* [1981] ICR 860.

However, in *Hadjioannou v Coral Casinos Ltd* [1981] IRLR 352, the EAT found that there may be cases where it is not unfair to dismiss an employee for a breach of the rule, in this case prohibiting employees from socialising with customers, notwithstanding that in the past other employees had not been dismissed for a breach of the rule. The EAT found that the argument that a dismissed employee has not been treated in the same way as other employees is broadly relevant in determining the fairness of the dismissal in only three sets of circumstances:

Firstly, it may be relevant if there is evidence that employees have been led by an employer to believe that certain categories of conduct will be either overlooked, or at least will not be dealt with by the sanction of dismissal. Secondly, there may be cases in which evidence about decisions made in relation to other cases supports an inference that the purported reason stated by the employers is not the real or genuine reason for a dismissal . . . Thirdly . . . evidence as to decisions made by the employer in truly parallel circumstances may be sufficient to support an argument in a particular case, that it was not reasonable on the part of the employer to visit the particular employee's conduct with the penalty of dismissal and that some lesser penalty would have been appropriate in the circumstances.

See also *Securicor Ltd v Smith* [1989] IRLR 356.

Where the rule is known to the employee but the penalty is not prescribed, dismissal may be fair where the employee has been given an opportunity to comply with the rule and his failure to do so leaves the employer with no option but to dismiss him. In *Singh v Lyons Maid Ltd* [1975] IRLR 328, the employer had a rule 'Beards may not be worn by staff who work on the production line. Visitors must wear beard masks.' The rule was contained in a document that the employee acknowledged having received. He grew a beard in contravention of this rule, and although given an opportunity to comply with the rule, he failed to do so. The company had no work for him other than on the production line, and he was dismissed. The dismissal was fair. See also *Spiller v FJ Wallis Ltd* [1975] IRLR 362.

There may be exceptional cases where there is no rule and no penalty, but dismissal is nevertheless fair. In *CA Parsons and Co Ltd v McLoughlin* [1978] IRLR 65, the employer dismissed McLoughlin, a shop steward, for fighting with another employee. There was nothing in the employee's contract to prohibit fighting, but the dismissal was held to be fair. The EAT found that the dangers of fighting in the workplace are so well known as to enable an employer to dismiss without having the need for a rule: 'it ought not to be necessary for anybody, let alone a shop steward, to have to have in black-and-white in the form of a rule that a fight is something which is going to be regarded very gravely by management'.

Disciplinary rules are not and cannot be exhaustive. 'A catalogue of offences which carry the potential sanction of dismissal contained in company rules may occasionally be useful in assessing the quality of an offence but it does not follow that no offence which does not fall within it can ever merit dismissal': *Distillers Company (Bottling Services) Ltd v Gardner* [1982] IRLR 47, where the offence could easily have been catalogued as a gross neglect of duty.

However, the employer will not always succeed where he dismisses an employee for fighting where there is no clear rule: *Meyer Dunmore International Ltd v Rogers* [1978] IRLR 167, where the dismissal was held to be unfair. Other examples of analogous cases where the employer may succeed in dismissing fairly without a clear formal rule are theft, dishonesty and breach of safety rules.

Where there is a rule, the employer can only require the employee to do what is necessary under the rule. The employer will be in difficulty if he dismisses the employee for failing to go beyond what is required by the rule.

If the employer does not have a clear rule and/or a penalty then (apart from exceptional cases) although the employer wishes to dismiss he will have to warn the employee to desist from that course of conduct and further warn the employee that a repetition of the same course of conduct will result in his dismissal. In effect the employer is creating a rule by warning the employee of the penalty to be imposed.

The penalty must fit the offence, and must not be disproportionate and excessive. In deciding upon the penalty to be imposed the employer should consider the circumstances in which the offence has been committed and any mitigating circumstances which ought to be taken into account. There should be some discretion, but the discretion should be exercised in accordance with principles and within defined limits. A broad unfettered discretion may result in a finding of unfair dismissal: see *Lindsay v Fife Forge Co Ltd* [1976] IRLR 47.

In *Donson and Frudd v Conoco Ltd* [1973] IRLR 258, the tribunal concluded that a rule whereby an offence, whatever the degree of gravity, was punished by dismissal was too inflexible. Mitigating factors were not taken into account in the application of the rule. There was no provision enabling the employer to take into account the nature of the offence and whether it was grave or trivial.

In *Jones v London Co-operative Society* [1975] IRLR 110, the employer had a rule that 'incorrect recording of purchases for whatever reason would be treated as a serious offence and the employee will be summarily dismissed unless it can be proved the employee was justified in such incorrect recording'. Jones had an impeccable record but on one occasion rung up a wrong amount. The employer, while not suggesting dishonesty, dismissed her. Her dismissal was unfair. The rule failed to 'distinguish between genuine error on one occasion on the one hand and either a calculated act or a persistent failure to maintain adequate cash control standards on the other'. Further, the employer could not seek to rely on the rule and the penalty merely because the rule and penalty were known to the employee, and had been agreed with the union of which the employee was a member. The employer failed because the rule was harsh and unreasonable: see *Ladbroke Racing Ltd v Arnott and Others*, above.

5 Procedural fairness (3): the 1977 code in practice

The 1972 code contained provisions dealing with discipline and disciplinary procedures. These provisions are repeated in the 1977 code. Guidance for employers on the operation of the 1977 code can be gained from the way in which cases have been decided involving the provisions of the 1972 code.

There is some support for the view that the rules of natural justice have no application to internal disciplinary procedures: see the judgment of Lord Wilberforce in *Malloch v Aberdeen Corporation* [1971] 2 All ER 1278, where he reviewed the earlier authorities. However, in *Khanum v Mid-Glamorgan Area Health Authority* [1978] IRLR 215 the EAT held:

Some of the authorities are not easily reconciled and we do not think it would be helpful to try to do so, for in the end how nearly a domestic disciplinary inquiry, a statutory inquiry by a statutory body, a public statutory inquiry, or any other inquiry which has to make decisions must approach to the full-blown procedure of a court of justice in order to comply with the rules of natural justice is no doubt a matter of degree. But in our judgment as regards the sort of domestic tribunal with which we are concerned in this case the law is as it was expressed by Harman J in *Byrne v Kinematograph Renters Society Ltd* [[1958] 1 WLR 762] and approved and applied by the Privy Council to the context of a University Vice Chancellor's inquiry into cheating in examinations in . . . [*University of Ceylon v Fernando* [1960] 1 WLR 223].
What then are the requirements of natural justice in a case of this kind? First, I think that the person accused should know of the nature of the accusation made; secondly, that he should be given an opportunity to state his case; and thirdly, of course, that the Tribunal should act in good faith. I do not myself think that there is really anything more.

In *Bently Engineering Co Ltd v Mistry* [1978] IRLR 436, the EAT held:

natural justice does require not merely that a man shall have a chance to state his own case in detail; he must know in one way or another sufficiently what is being said against him. If he does not know sufficiently what is being said against him, he cannot properly put forward his own case. It may be, according to the facts, that what is said against him can be communicated to him in writing, or it may be that it is sufficient if he hears what the other protagonist is saying, or it may be that, in an appropriate case, for matters which have been said by others to be put orally in sufficient detail is an adequate satisfaction of the requirements of natural justice . . . it is all a question of degree.

In *Louies v Coventry Hood and Seating Co Ltd* [1990] IRLR 324, it was held that where statements had been given by witnesses upon which the employer is going to rely almost entirely the employee should have a sight of them or be told very clearly exactly what is in them. A failure to do so will be a breach of the rules of natural justice. See also *Spink v Express Foods Group Ltd* [1990] IRLR 320.

The employee's absence from a hearing does not necessarily involve a breach of the rules of natural justice provided the employee's representative is present: see *Pirelli General Cable Works Ltd v Murray* [1979] IRLR 190 and *Gray Dunn and Co Ltd v Edwards* [1980] IRLR 23.

It is apparent from these decisions of the EAT that the rules of natural justice apply to internal disciplinary procedures. The concept of fairness involves observance of the rules of natural justice.

In *Pritchett and Dyjasek v J McIntyre Ltd* [1986] IRLR 97, Waite J held that fairness and natural justice have a great deal in common. Referring to the judgment of Sir Robert Megarry in *John v Rees and Others* [1969] 2 All ER 274, he considered that the following remarks were apposite in the context of the fairness of dismissal. Sir Robert Megarry held:

It may be that there are some who would decry the importance which the courts attach to the observance of the rules of natural justice. 'When something is obvious,' they may say, 'why force everybody to go through the tiresome waste of time involved in framing charges and giving an opportunity to be heard? The result is obvious from the start.' Those who take this view do not, I think, do themselves justice. As everybody who has anything to do with the law well knows, the path of the law is strewn with examples of open and shut cases which, somehow, were not; of unanswerable charges which, in the event, were completely answered; of inexplicable conduct which was fully explained; of fixed and unalterable determinations that, by discussion, suffered a change. Nor are those with any knowledge of human nature who pause to think for a moment likely to underestimate the feelings of resentment of those who find that a decision against them has been made without their being afforded any opportunity to influence the course of events.

This decision was reversed on appeal on other grounds: see [1987] IRLR 18.

In *Moyes v Hylton Castle Working Men's Social Club and Institute Ltd* [1986] IRLR 482, Moyes was dismissed because of his alleged sexual harassment of a female employee. Two of the employer's officials were both witnesses and judges. The EAT held that this was a breach of the rules of natural justice and any reasonable observer would conclude that 'justice did not appear to be done nor was it done'. It was not necessary for the two of them to be both witnesses and judges, and it was impossible for them to disassociate their role as witnesses from that as judges. While there might be cases where it was inevitable that the person who was a witness was also a judge this was not the position here. The finding by the tribunal that, not-withstanding the dual position, the employer had acted reasonably, could not be supported either as a finding of fact or as a matter of law (see *Hannam v Bradford City Council* [1970] 2 All ER 690).

Generally the person who conducts an inquiry must be seen to be impartial. However, in *Slater v Leicestershire Health Authority* [1989] IRLR 16, it was held that a nurse's dismissal was not unfair because the manager who carried out the preliminary investigation also con-ducted the disciplinary hearing and took the decision to dismiss. It was further held that the rules of justice do not form an independent ground upon which a decision to dismiss may be attacked, although a breach of the rules of natural justice will be an important matter for a tribunal to take into account when considering reasonableness.

5.1 Conduct

At the outset of the jurisdiction, in determining reasonableness the tribunals placed great emphasis on procedural matters, including the need to give warnings so that a dismissal without a warning was likely to be unfair. Following cases such as *British Labour Pump Co Ltd v Byrne* [1979] ICR 347, tribunals then looked to see what effect a failure to follow a proper procedure had so that if it made no differ-ence the dismissal might still be fair. Thus, in the case of a warning the tribunal would look to see what effect a warning would have had and whether the employee would have benefited from the warning before finding that a failure to warn of itself made the dismissal unfair.

Greater importance now attaches to procedural matters since the decisions in *West Midlands Co-operative Society Ltd v Tipton* [1986] ICR 192 and *Polkey v AE Dayton Services Ltd* [1988] ICR 142, so that the employer will not be able to establish that he has acted reasonably unless he has taken the necessary procedural steps includ-ing the giving of warnings, save in exceptional circumstances.

(a) Warnings Warnings in relation to the reasons related to conduct are separately considered under conduct which may be classed as gross misconduct and conduct which is not gross misconduct.

Gross misconduct The 1977 code provides that a disciplinary pro-cedure should 'ensure that, except for gross misconduct, no employees are dismissed for a breach of discipline': para 10(h). The disciplinary rules may provide that the employee will be dismissed with or without notice where he has breached certain rules. In cases of gross misconduct such a rule and penalty may be reasonable. The employer should give the employee a clear indication as to the offences or type of offences which will fall into this category. Where the misconduct is not gross misconduct such a rule and penalty may still be reasonable. It is not possible to provide any legal definition of gross misconduct which will fit every case. The NIRC refused to accept an invitation to attempt any legal definition of gross misconduct: *Connely v Liverpool Corporation* (1974) 9 ITR 51. While at common law the phrase 'gross misconduct' is usually used to describe conduct which is repudiatory of the contract, the tribunals and the EAT have, in cases of unfair dismissal, avoided this concept of gross misconduct for the purposes of the application of the disciplinary provisions of the 1972 and 1977 codes. The use of the phrase 'gross misconduct' in these cases may well not be an apt description of what is covered. The EAT has sounded a note of caution against becoming involved in an exposition of what is and what is not gross misconduct: *CA Parsons and Co Ltd v McLoughlin* [1978] IRLR 65. Whether conduct is gross misconduct for these purposes will depend upon the nature of the business, the position held by the employee and the circumstances of the case.

Tribunals have been prepared to find dismissals for severe misconduct which may be gross, fair notwithstanding the fact that the employee has been dismissed for a first breach without any prior warning, and even though the employer's own disciplinary procedure has not been observed.

Thus, in *Stevenson v Golden Wonder Ltd* [1977] IRLR 474, Stevenson, a technical manager, was dismissed after he perpetrated a moderately serious and unprovoked assault on another employee at a social function held in the company's canteen, outside working hours. The employers failed to follow their own 'grievance procedure'. The EAT found the dismissal fair. The employer acted reasonably in dismissing Stevenson for blatant misconduct and the failure to follow the procedure was not fatal.

In some cases a dismissal has been held to be fair where the employer has no rule that the conduct for which the employee was dismissed would result in dismissal. In *McLoughlin*'s case above, McLoughlin, a shop steward, was dismissed following a fight with another employee who was also dismissed. The EAT found:

it ought not to be necessary for anybody, let alone a shop steward, to have to have in black-and-white in the form of a rule that a fight is something which is going to be regarded very gravely by management.

It went on to hold:

As the Court of Appeal pointed out [in *Retarded Children's Aid Society Ltd v Day* [1978] ICR 437], everybody has to recognise that the Industrial

Relations code of practice is not to be ignored; but at the same time it is not necessarily a code which has the force of law. The Court of Appeal, moreover, said that there were certain circumstances in which an employee could be dismissed without warning; in other words, that in some cases the employer is entitled to say, 'I cannot suspend, I cannot warn. This is in my view sufficiently serious for me to impose dismissal upon both the people who were involved in a fight in the factory.'

The EAT in *McLoughlin*'s case further held:

The mere fact of a fight, whoever starts it, is a very serious matter indeed . . . There was a very pragmatic and . . . sensible approach to this question expressed in the judgment of the Employment Appeal Tribunal . . . in *Greenwood v HJ Heinz and Co Ltd*. In that case the Employment Appeal Tribunal said 'These are essentially matters for the employer to make up his mind about, not necessarily in the heat of the moment but after pause for reflection and after investigation'. We cannot do better than use some of the words of Mr Justice Bristow towards the end of that judgment:

It seems to us it is quite wrong to say that a management faced with fighting, even of a very modest nature, in a workplace where there is a large amount of machinery would be perverse in deciding that whoever started the fight must be dismissed. The potential for danger which any degree of violence involves in close proximity to machinery is blindingly obvious. It is difficult enough sometimes to keep people who have to operate machines safe from hurting themselves in the machinery even in the absence of any violence at all. Add some violence; the risk of serious injury to other people, let alone severe interference with the work, is clearly great. Whilst circumstances must of course vary infinitely, in our judgment it certainly does not go without saying that to dismiss by reason of one blow, even by reason of the threat of a blow, is by itself plainly wrong. It may be in some circumstances wrong. It may well be a perfectly proper thing for management to do.

However, the foregoing approach is by no means universal. In *McPhail v Gibson* [1977] ICR 42, a farm manager was dismissed without warning where he gave an inaccurate reference about a farm labourer to a neighbouring farmer. The EAT considered that even in a case of gross misconduct a warning should usually be given. This case turned on its own facts.

It is for the tribunal to consider what is reasonable and a dismissal for a first offence of fighting may be unfair seen against 20 years' previous good service: see *Taylor v Parsons Peebles NEI Bruce Peebles Ltd* [1981] IRLR 119; see also *Dairy Produce Packers Ltd v Beverstock* [1981] IRLR 265.

Similar principles to those in *McLoughlin*'s case, above, may apply where the employee has been guilty of other acts which may be categorised as acts of gross misconduct: theft *Trust Houses Forte Hotels Ltd v Murphy* [1977] IRLR 186; or suspected dishonesty: *McCrory v Magee t/a Heatwell Heating Systems* [1983] IRLR 414.

In *Siraj-Eldin v Campbell Middleton Burness and Dickson* [1989] IRLR 208, the dismissal of an employee for taking alcohol on board an offshore rig justified dismissal for a first offence, even though the alcohol was kept in a locked suitcase. There was evidence that possession of alcohol on an oil rig was considered so serious that no mitigating circumstances could be accepted.

It has been seen that the employer may avoid the question whether or not a specific warning has to be given before dismissal in cases where the employee is guilty of severe misconduct where there is a clear and reasonable rule defining the conduct which will result in dismissal for the first offence.

The rule and the penalty must be reasonable and a tribunal may find it was not reasonable to impose dismissal as the penalty for an offence which was not severe.

However, a rule providing for dismissal where the conduct is regarded by the employer as gross misconduct may not be a reasonable rule when it is a first offence. In *Laws Stores Ltd v Oliphant* [1978] IRLR 251, Oliphant was guilty of a single lapse in operating the till. Technically the lapse fell within the definition of gross misconduct for which the penalty was instant dismissal under the company's agreed disciplinary procedure. However, the company did not act reasonably in dismissing her in the circumstances for a single lapse.

If the employer does have such a rule it is desirable that the rule should be clear, for if it is not, he may not be able to argue that the conduct is so gross as to justify dismissal in the absence of a clear rule and without any warning. In *Meyer Dunmore International Ltd v Rogers* [1978] IRLR 167, the EAT held:

if employers wish to have a rule that employees engaged in, what could properly and sensibly be called fighting are going to be summarily dismissed . . . there is not reason why they should not have a rule, *provided* . . . that it is plainly adopted, that it is plainly and clearly set out, and that great publicity is given to it so that every employee knows beyond any doubt whatever that if he gets involved in fighting in that sense, he will be dismissed.

See also *Trusthouse Forte (Catering) Ltd v Adonis* [1984] IRLR 382.

The employer should also ensure that the rule is made known to the employee, is fully understood by him and is consistently applied: *Richards v Bulpitt and Sons Ltd* [1975] IRLR 134. See also *Dairy Produce Packers Ltd v Beverstock* [1981] IRLR 265.

However, even where the employee has been guilty of misconduct which may be categorised as gross misconduct, the employer may be entitled to dismiss him without any prior warning, even if it is not clear whether that misconduct is a breach of the employer's rule. In *Martin v Yorkshire Imperial Metals Ltd* [1978] IRLR 440, Martin was dismissed after it was discovered he tied down a lever on an automatic lathe in the factory, in effect removing the safety device whereby the machine could be operated only if the employee used both hands. The EAT, while not reaching any conclusions on whether the conduct was gross misconduct, found that even though it was unclear whether the conduct was a breach of the employer's rule, the conduct was likely to endanger the well-being or safety of other employees and it was fair to dismiss for a first breach; compare *Trusthouse Forte (Catering) Ltd v Adonis*, above.

Even where there is a rule providing for dismissal for certain gross misconduct the employer should still investigate the circumstances and apply the rule reasonably so as to take into account any mitigating factors. See *Taylor*'s case, above. If the employer fails to apply the rule reasonably the tribunal may find the dismissal unfair and its discretion cannot be excluded: *Ladbroke Racing Ltd v Arnott* [1979] IRLR 192. The same applies to rules providing for dismissal in cases of misconduct other than severe or gross misconduct.

If the employee has not been guilty of severe or gross misconduct and if the employer does not have a rule (which is clear and fair) which provides that the employee shall be dismissed for a breach of the rule, the employer may be unable to justify the employee's dismissal in the absence of any warning. In *Retarded Children's Aid Society Ltd v Day* [1978] ICR 437, Lord Denning MR held: 'It is good sense and reasonable that in the ordinary way for a first offence you should not dismiss a man on the instant without any warning or giving him a further chance.'

See also *Atkin v Enfield Group Hospital Management Committee* [1975] IRLR 217.

Misconduct which is not gross   Where the employee has been guilty of misconduct which is not severe or gross, then the starting point is that it will be unfair to dismiss the employee in the absence of a clear and reasonable rule providing for dismissal for that offence, without prior warning. As it will appear there are qualifications to this premise.

In *MacKay v Robert Morton Temple Bakery* [1975] IRLR 57, MacKay's dismissal without warning was unfair where he failed to communicate with and send medical certificates to his employer over a period of ten days while he was away from work due to ill-health.

In *Greenslade v Hoveringham Gravels Ltd* [1975] IRLR 114, Greenslade's dismissal was unfair. He was told to wear a tie and have his hair cut. Two days later he had still not complied with the request and he was told to go home and carry out the instructions. He discussed the matter further with the employer from his home, but no conclusions were reached. Without warning he was dismissed.

Even where the conduct is of a more serious nature it may still be unfair to dismiss without prior warning. In *Young v E Thomas and Co Ltd* [1972] IRLR 40, Young, a lorry driver, deviated from his prescribed route for his own purposes and was dismissed. The dismissal was found to be unfair because at no stage had he been warned by the employer that he intended to dismiss employees for such conduct.

In *Newman v TH White Motors Ltd* [1972] IRLR 49, Newman was a foreman fitter. His attitude towards subordinates led to an altercation with the trainee storeman and he was dismissed. It was held the dismissal was unfair in the absence of a prior warning.

Where employers have condoned a course of conduct, then a warning becomes particularly necessary before dismissing for that course of conduct. In *Hackwood v Seal (Marine) Ltd* [1973] IRLR 17, a manager dismissed an experienced machinist for refusing to assist an inexperienced machinist. The order was a lawful one, and the employee should have obeyed it. However, in the past the manager had taken a more lax attitude to the employee's refusal to obey orders, and before dismissing her he should have warned her that in the future he would not tolerate her attitude.

Thus, where the incident is one of misconduct which is not gross misconduct it will be exceptional that dismissal for the first offence will be fair. In *Ayub*'s case, above, one offence of sleeping on the night shift did not justify dismissal.

Where, however, a clear warning or series of warnings have been given which the employee ignores, the employer is entitled to rely on the warnings and dismiss the employee: *Donald Cook and Sons Ltd v Carter* [1977] IRLR 88.

In *Hallett and Want v MAT Transport Ltd* [1976] IRLR 5, Want was given a second final warning that if he failed to improve his timekeeping significantly he would be dismissed. Following this warning he was late on 12 days out of 80 and was dismissed. It was held that after the warning the employer was entitled to a substantial improvement and the dismissal was fair.

Conversely, where following a warning there has been an improvement by the employee in his conduct, the employer may be acting unfairly if following that improvement he dismisses the employee. In *Hallett and Want v MAT Transport Ltd*, above, following the second final warning about lateness, the employer alleged that Hallett was late on 7 days out of 77 and was dismissed. On three occasions the late arrival was caused by industrial action on the railways and on a further day the employer could not show that the employee had arrived late. The tribunal found there was a substantial improvement following the warning and it was unfair to dismiss the employee.

There are exceptions to the general principle that it is unfair to dismiss the employee in the absence of a warning or indeed a clear and reasonable rule providing for dismissal which has been brought to the employee's attention. The first exception arises out of the purpose and nature of the warning. A warning is intended to give the employee a chance to improve. There may be cases where it is quite clear that a warning would not have made any difference. Thus, in *Farnborough v Governors of Edinburgh College of Art* [1974] IRLR 245, the employee, a lecturer, was dismissed without warning because he did not agree with a reorganisation. He became uncooperative and there was friction between him and the head of his department. He sought to involve the students in his dispute with the college and continually refused to carry out his employer's reasonable requirements. It was held the dismissal was fair. It made no difference that he argued he would have improved if he had received a warning where it is clear from evidence this is not likely to happen.

In *Retarded Children's Aid Society Ltd v Day* [1978] ICR 437, Day was employed at a home for retarded children and contrary to established practice required one of the children to do extra duties. When the employer discovered this, he was dismissed, notwithstanding there had been no prior warning. Day 'did not approve of the charity's methods and saw here an opportunity to apply his own methods. He thought he knew best. [He] showed that he remained out of sympathy with the Society's methods in fundamental respects and so presented the risk of further transgression.' It was held the dismissal was fair.

Similarly, it may be clear that the employee will not improve where he is prickly and self-opinionated, and a difficult man to work with: *Henderson v Masson Scott Thrissell Engineering Ltd* [1974] IRLR 98, or where he adamantly refuses to accept a new wage agreement: *Tovey v F&F Robinson (Stockton-on-Tees) Ltd* [1975] IRLR 139.

The second exception arises where the employee knew or was in such a position to know that by his act or conduct he was placing his job in jeopardy and ought not to have needed a warning. In *Newman v Alarmco Ltd* [1976] IRLR 45, Newman, the company's general manager, was living with his secretary. During office hours they showed their affection for each other. He was dismissed without any warning. It was held that the dismissal was fair. No warning was necessary because of his position. The conduct had persisted for some months, and he ought to have known that it was likely to discredit the company.

The third exception arises in cases where the interests of the business so dictate. In *James v Waltham Holy Cross UDC* [1973] ICR 398, Sir John Donaldson found the 'duty of fairness both to the employee and to the business is the only general rule. All else is but a particular application of that general rule'. The interests of the business must outweigh the interests of the employee for this exception to apply.

The fourth exception arises out of a recognition that the requirements of the 1977 code must be applied to the circumstances of the particular case. They are not rules of law; they are guidelines. Thus, what may be reasonable as between the foreman and the employee on the factory floor may not be reasonable in the case of a doctor and his receptionist, so a dismissal without a warning may be fair: *MacKellar v Bolton* [1979] IRLR 59.

(b) Warnings generally A warning should be sufficiently clear, so that the employee knows what will happen if he does not improve.

Circumlocutions like 'employment might be in jeopardy' should be avoided: *Wells v E&A West Ltd* [1975] IRLR 269. However, it may be unfair to dismiss an employee where he has been told he was liable for dismissal: *Elliott Brothers (London) Ltd v Colverd* [1979] IRLR 92.

Warnings should not be treated too technically: *Wood v Kettering Co-operative Chemists Ltd* [1978] IRLR 438. A warning may be sufficient even though it does not conform perfectly with the employer's disciplinary procedure.

A written warning has no particular magic. To an intelligent man a verbal warning may be just as good. The written warning is of course of evidential value: *McCall v Castleton Crafts* [1979] IRLR 218.

Ideally, warnings should be given to individuals rather than generally. However, the employer may give a general warning and it may well be fair to dismiss in reliance on a general warning: *Connely v Liverpool Corporation* (1974) 9 ITR 51, where the employer had given a general warning to employees against drinking during their lunch hour. The employee broke this rule and was dismissed. His dismissal was held to be fair.

There is no general rule as to how long a warning will remain in force. The disciplinary procedure may provide for the length of time that a warning will remain in force, although that it not necessarily binding upon a tribunal. In the absence of a provision it is for the tribunal to decide if the employer can rely upon the warning.

Where a warning has been given to the employee requiring an improvement within a specified period, the warning will not automatically lapse at the expiration of the period so that the employer can no longer rely on it at a later date. Whether a warning has lapsed will depend on the circumstances of each case: see *Kraft Foods Ltd v Fox* [1978] ICR 311.

(c) Investigation Where it is alleged that the employee has been guilty of misconduct the employer should investigate that allegation before taking any steps against the employee. The employer has to show the tribunal the reason for the dismissal and he must also put forward evidence to enable the tribunal to decide whether or not he acted reasonably in all the circumstances. It has been seen that in establishing the reason the tribunal does not have to ask itself the question 'Are we satisfied the offence was committed?' but to ask itself the question 'Are we satisfied that the employers had, at the time of the dismissal, reasonable grounds for believing that the offence put against the applicant was in fact committed?': *Ferodo Ltd v Barnes* [1976] ICR 439. In *British Home Stores Ltd v Burchell* [1978] IRLR 379, the EAT found that in a case involving the employee's conduct the employer had to establish a genuine belief based on reasonable grounds. It held:

What the tribunal have to decide every time is, broadly expressed, whether the employer who discharged the employee on the ground of the misconduct in question (usually, though not necessarily, dishonest conduct) entertained a reasonable suspicion amounting to a belief in the guilt of the employee of that misconduct at that time. That is really stating shortly and compendiously what is in fact more than one element. First of all, there must be established by the employer the fact of that belief; that the employer did believe it. Secondly, that the employer had in his mind reasonable grounds upon which to sustain that belief. And thirdly, we think, that the employer, at the stage at which he formed that belief on those grounds, at any rate at the final stage at which he formed that belief on those grounds, had carried out as much investigation into the matter as was reasonable in all the circumstances of the case. It is the employer who manages to discharge the onus of demonstrating those three matters, we think, who must not be examined further.

See *Pritchett and Dyjasek v J McIntyre Ltd* [1987] IRLR 18, where the Court of Appeal reffirmed the guidelines in *Burchell*'s case and *Scottish Midland Co-operative Society Ltd v Cullion* [1991] IRLR 261.

The establishment of the employer's belief based on reasonable grounds and the need for reasonable investigation are inextricably entwined. The amount of investigation required will depend on the circumstances. At one extreme there may be a case where the employee is virtually caught in the act and at the other extreme where the issue is one of pure inference: *ILEA v Gravett* [1988] IRLR 497.

In *Linford Cash and Carry Ltd v Thomson and Others* [1989] ICR 518, where the decision of the tribunal that the employer had not carried out a reasonable investigation was upheld, certain guidelines were laid down where allegations are made by an informant. In *Thomson*'s case there was an informant whose name was not disclosed. The EAT laid down the following guidelines:

(1) The information given by the informant should be reduced into writing in one or more statements. Initially these statements should be taken without regard to the fact that in those cases where anonymity is to be preserved, it may subsequently prove to be necessary to omit or erase certain parts of the statements before submission to others in order to prevent identification.

(2) In taking statements the following seem important: (a) Date, time and place of each or any observation or incident. (b) The opportunity and ability to observe clearly and with accuracy. (c) The circumstantial evidence such as knowledge of a system or arrangement, or the reason for the presence of the informer and why certain small details are memorable. (d) Whether the informant has suffered at the hands of the accused or has any other reason to fabricate, whether from personal grudge or any other reason or principle.

(3) Further investigation can then take place either to confirm or undermine the information given. Corroboration is clearly desirable.

(4) Tactful enquiries may well be thought suitable and advisable into the character and background of the informant or any other information which may tend to add to or detract from the value of the information.

(5) If the informant is prepared to attend a disciplinary hearing, no problem will arise, but if, as in the present case, the employer is satisfied that the fear is genuine then a decision will need to be made whether or not to continue with the disciplinary process.

(6) If it is to continue, then it seems to us desirable that at each stage of those procedures the member of management responsible for that hearing should himself interview the informant and satisfy himself what weight is to be given to the information.

(7) The written statement of the informant—if necessary with omissions to avoid identification—should be made available to the employee and his representatives.

(8) If the employee or his representative raises any particular and relevant issue which should be put to the informant, then it may be desirable to adjourn for the chairman to make further enquiries of that informant.

(9) Although it is always desirable for notes to be taken during disciplinary procedures, it seems to us to be particularly important that full and careful notes should be taken in these cases.

(10) Although not peculiar to cases where informants have been the cause or the initiation of an investigation, it seems to us important that if evidence from an investigating officer is to be taken at a hearing it should, where possible, be prepared in a written form.

See also *Morgan v Electrolux Ltd* [1991] IRLR 89.

In *W Devis and Sons Ltd v Atkins* [1977] ICR 662, Viscount Dilhorne held that an employer cannot be said to have acted reasonably if he reached his decision 'in consequence of ignoring matters which he ought reasonably to have known and which would have shown the reason was insufficient'. Again in *W Weddel and Co Ltd v Tepper* [1980] IRLR 96, Stephenson LJ held:

[employers] do not have regard to equity or the substantial merits of the case if they jump to conclusions which it would have been reasonable to postpone in all the circumstances until they had, ... 'gathered further evidence' or, . . . 'carried out as much investigation into the matter as was reasonable in all the circumstances of the case'. That means they must act reasonably in all the circumstances and must make reasonable enquiries appropriate to the circumstances. If they form their belief hastily and act hastily upon it, without making the appropriate enquiries or giving the employee a fair opportunity to explain himself, their belief is not based on reasonable grounds and they are certainly not acting reasonably.

In *Royal Society for the Protection of Birds v Croucher* [1984] IRLR 425, the EAT held that the kind of investigation referred to in *Burchell*'s case: '. . . that is to say, designed to confirm suspicion or clear up doubt as to whether or not a particular act of misconduct has occurred', was not appropriate where dishonest conduct was admitted. Whilst *Burchell*'s case was a helpful guideline it could not replace the soundness of an appraisal of all the circumstances of each particul case reviewed in accordance with s 57(3) of the EP(C)A 1978.

Certainty on the part of the employer is not the test to be applied. see *AEI Cables Ltd v McLay* [1980] IRLR 84.

The employer is under an obligation to carry out a real and thorough investigation of the facts and circumstances: *Johnson Matthey Metals Ltd v Harding* [1978] IRLR 248. But in a case involving dishonesty or a similar offence, the employer is not expected to carry out the sort of investigation that a police officer might carry out: see *British Home Stores Ltd v Burchell*, above. See also *Royal Society for the Protection of Birds v Croucher*, above, where, dishonesty was admitted. It is obviously in the employer's own interest to carry out a thorough investigation into any allegation of misconduct made against an employee. If he fails to do so he may be unable to put forward sufficient evidence to establish the reason for the dismissal. Again he may be unable to put forward sufficient evidence on which the tribunal can find that the dismissal was reasonable in all the circumstances. Reasonableness has to be judged on the basis of the position at the time of the dismissal: see *W Devis and Sons Ltd v Atkins* above, and 2, above.

In establishing reasonable grounds for the employer's belief an admission made by the employee may constitute evidence upon which the employer is entitled to rely in forming his belief, notwithstanding the fact that it would not be admissible in a criminal trial because the confession was obtained contrary to the Judges' Rules: *Morleys of Brixton Ltd v Minott* [1982] IRLR 270.

A failure to carry out a proper investigation is not simply a procedural question so that the dismissal will still be fair if the result would have been the same had a proper investigation been made, because in considering whether there has been an adequate investigation, the tribunal is concerned with the employer's state of mind at the moment of dismissal and the adequacy of the information to justify that state of mind: *Henderson v Granville Tours Ltd* [1982] IRLR 494.

Ideally any investigation should take place as quickly as possible as delay may be fatal. However, provided the delay is reasonable it will not necessarily be fatal to the employer: *Refund Rentals Ltd v McDermott* [1977] IRLR 59, where the delay was due to the company contacting customers as part of its investigation. In theory it is desirable that the investigatory procedure should be kept separate from the disciplinary procedure, but in practice this may not be possible. In exceptional circumstances following an investigation it may be that all the employer can establish is a reasonable suspicion short of actual belief. Thus, in *Monie v Coral Racing Ltd* [1980] IRLR 464, one or both of two employees were suspected of theft by the employer. The employer carried out an investigation but despite the investigation was not able to establish whether one or both of the employees had been guilty of theft. It was held that it was fair for the employer to dismiss on the basis of a reasonable suspicion short of actual belief.

This approach was followed in *Whitbread and Co plc v Thomas and Others* [1988] ICR 135, where one or more of three persons was suspected of being responsible for stock losses. Despite extensive investigations the employer could not determine which and dismissed all three. The EAT concluded that the approach in *Monie*'s case could be followed in cases of capability. In *Parr v Whitbread and Co plc* [1990] ICR 427, a similar approach was followed where four employees were dismissed. The EAT held:

In an attempt to analyse the *Monie* principles where dishonesty is involved together with the *Whitbread* principles where mere incapability was involved . . . a possible approach is as follows . . . If an Industrial Tribunal is able to find on the evidence before it: (1) that an act had been committed which if committed by an individual would justify dismissal; (2) that the employer had made a reasonable—sufficiently thorough—investigation into the matter and with appropriate procedures; (3) that as a result of that investigation the employer reasonably believed that more than one person could have committed the act; (4) that the employer had acted reasonably in identifying the group of employees who could have committed the act and that each member of the group was individually capable of so doing; (5) that as between the members of the group the employer could not reasonably identify the individual perpetrator; then provided that the beliefs were held on solid and sensible grounds at the date of dismissal, an employer is entitled to dismiss each member of that group.

See also *Whitbread and Co plc v Mills* [1988] IRLR 501. In cases involving a suspicion, a proper investigation is essential: see *Gravett*'s case, above.

(d) Opportunity for the employee to state his case   In *Earl v Slater and Wheeler (Airlyne) Ltd* [1972] ICR 508, in March 1972 while Earl was away ill, the company discovered certain matters of an unsatisfactory nature connected with his work and decided to dismiss him. The employee told the company that he would return to work on Monday, 27 March. On Friday, 24 March, he was summoned to attend the office the next day, Saturday, to see the works director. On his arrival he was confronted by the works director and the managing director who gave him a letter advising him that he had been dismissed and a replacement found. The NIRC found the dismissal was unfair as Earl was not given an opportunity to explain his conduct and any deficiencies in his work. Although he was unable to offer any

explanation, the employers had not taken any steps to discover this. The NIRC held:

> Whilst we do not say that in all circumstances the employee must be given an opportunity of stating his case, the only exception can be the case where there *can* be no explanation which *could* cause the employers to refrain from dismissing the employee. This must be a vary rare situation . . . The manner of his [Earl's] dismissal cannot possibly be justified, notwithstanding the fact that if a proper procedure had been adopted he would still have been dismissed and would then have been fairly dismissed.

The NIRC took the view that if an employer knows the employee can offer no explanation then a dismissal without giving the employee a chance to explain would be fair. If at the time of the dismissal the employer does not know whether or not the employee can offer any explanation but dismisses the employee the dismissal will be unfair.

In *W Devis and Sons Ltd v Atkins* [1977] 3 WLR 214, Viscount Dilhorne considered that:

> It does not follow that non-compliance with the code [the 1972 code] necessarily renders a dismissal unfair, but I agree with the view expressed by Sir John Donaldson in *Earl v Slater and Wheeler (Airlyne) Ltd* [1973] 1 WLR 51, that a failure to follow a procedure prescribed in the code may lead to the conclusion that a dismissal was unfair, which, if that procedure had been followed, would have been held to have been fair.

The above quotation was cited with approval by Lord Bridge in *West Midlands Co-operative Society Ltd v Tipton* [1986] IRLR 122; see also *UCATT v Brain* [1981] ICR 542.

In *Budgen and Co Ltd v Thomas* [1976] IRLR 174, the EAT held:

> whatever the circumstances, whatever the employee is alleged to have done, and however serious it may be, it is, in our judgment, always necessary that he should be afforded some opportunity of explaining himself to those persons in the management who will in the first instance take the decision whether or not he is to be dismissed.

The decision was criticised as overstating the need to give an employee an opportunity to put his case in *Parker v Clifford Dunn Ltd* [1979] IRLR 56, a case involving a criminal offence where it was held that there was no requirement on the part of the employer to give an employee an opportunity to explain, where the opportunity would have been of no use because it would have made no difference to the employer's decision. See, **5.3**, below as to criminal offences.

Recently, the importance of giving the employee an opportunity to put his side of the story has been re-emphasised. See *Polkey*'s case above. In *McLaren v National Coal Board* [1988] ICR 370, McLaren assaulted another miner during the miners' strike. He was convicted and dismissed. The Court of Appeal held that the standards of fairness, including giving the employee an opportunity of explaining his conduct, are immutable and applied notwithstanding the exceptional circumstances of the strike, although in a particular case the employer might be justified in not seeking an explanation that was for the tribunal to investigate.

A number of cases illustrate the need to give the employee an opportunity to explain.

In *Lees v The Orchard* [1978] IRLR 20, Lees was suspected of dishonesty when money went missing. The employer dismissed her without giving her sufficient opportunity to explain. The EAT accepted that there were a number of ways in which the money could have gone missing without necessarily involving dishonesty by the employee. It held that the tribunal was entitled to find, on the evidence, that the employer had not given the employee a reasonable opportunity of explaining her alleged dishonesty before the dismissal, which was unfair. A similar conclusion was reached by another division of the EAT in *Laws Store Ltd v Oliphant* [1978] IRLR 251, where Oliphant was found to have breached the employer's till procedures. The employer's rules provided that a breach of till procedure would be gross misconduct. There was no dishonesty involved but Oliphant was dismissed without being given a real opportunity to explain. The EAT upheld the tribunal's decision that in the circumstances the failure to give the employee a real opportunity to explain rendered the dismissal unfair. The EAT and the tribunal were clearly concerned that the employee was dismissed for a single lapse, notwithstanding that that lapse fell within the definition of what was technically gross misconduct.

In *John Crawford and Co (Plumbers) Ltd v Donnelly* [1979] IRLR 9, Donnelly, a plumber, was dismissed following a strike after he had been warned by the employer that a failure to return to work could result in his dismissal. He did not return to work because he was ill. Before he contacted the employer he was dismissed. The EAT upheld the decision of the tribunal that the dismissal was unfair. It found that if the company had given the employee an opportunity to explain his absence before they sent out the letter of dismissal, a satisfactory explanation might well have been given, and the employee would not have been dismissed. This is an illustration of the classic case where an opportunity to explain would have made a difference. Again, in this case the employer had acted unreasonably and precipitously in dismissing the employee and as in *Law's* and *Lee's* cases, above, the overall tenor of the dismissal was unfair.

Similarly in *Qualcast (Wolverhampton) Ltd v Ross* (1) and *Ross v Qualcast (Wolverhampton) Ltd* (2) [1979] IRLR 98, Ross, a gatekeeper, was found asleep by the employer's managing director and was dismissed. He was given no opportunity to explain before the decision to dismiss was taken. The EAT found that this case was not an exceptional case where the gravity of the matter was such that no explanation could make any difference, and because the employee was given no opportunity to explain or justify his conduct the dismissal was unfair.

The failure to give the employee an opportunity to explain will not inevitably render the dismissal unfair. There may be exceptional circumstances: see *Polkey*'s and *McLaren*'s cases, above, and *Hooper v British Railways Board* [1988] IRLR 517. Ideally, not only must the investigations be carried out as quickly as possible, but the employee should also be given the opportunity to state his case before recollections fade. See *Marley Homecare Ltd v Dutton* [1981] IRLR 380 and *Royal Society for the Prevention of Cruelty to Animals v Cruden* [1986] IRLR 83.

See **5.3(a)**, below, for the employee's opportunity to explain where the employee has been engaged in criminal conduct, and **5.2(e)**, below, for the employee's opportunity to explain where the employee's capability is in question.

(e) The nature of the opportunity In *Khanum v Mid-Glamorgan Area Health Authority* [1978] IRLR 215 the EAT set out guidelines to be followed by an internal disciplinary body. See **5**, above. The employer was a large local authority with a relatively sophisticated set of procedures. While a small employer, and indeed a medium-sized employer, may not have a procedure which is in any way as sophisticated, nonetheless the employer is expected to avoid what has been described as the fundamental breach of the rules of natural justice in determining disciplinary issues. What is reasonable will depend upon the circumstances in any particular case.

Where the employer gives the employee an opportunity to state his case or explain, he must ensure that opportunity is capable of being used by the employee if the employer is going to rely upon it. Thus, where the employee is given the opportunity to explain, it may be of little use if the employee is not in a fit state to give an explanation. In *Tesco Group of Companies (Holdings) Ltd v Hill* [1977] IRLR 63, Hill was under suspicion of dishonesty. She was asked for an explanation at a time when she was not well. The EAT held that the employer should have waited until she was in a position to give an explanation.

Where the police are present at a disciplinary hearing without the employee's prior knowledge and consent that will be wholly improper. If the police are present because they are conducting a police inquiry and have administered a caution, then the employee cannot be said to have had an opportunity of putting forward his side of the case. See *Read v Phoenix Preservation Ltd* [1985] IRLR 93.

The right of the employee to be given an opportunity to state his case must be considered in a broad and common-sense way. In *Ayanlowo v Commissioners of Inland Revenue* [1975] IRLR 253, the employee was dismissed because of his poor work. He was told of his right to make written representations against dismissal and he did so. He received no further communication from the Board and was dismissed. He complained that the Board had breached the provisions of natural justice in not giving him a hearing. The Court of Appeal did not refer expressly to the code, but made it clear that natural justice does not need 'an oral hearing of a complaint of this nature upon a matter of this kind'. The opportunity to make written representations was sufficient and the dismissal was held to be fair.

The opportunity for the employer to state his case involves knowing what is alleged against him and the factors being taken into account. The employee should be shown any documents or statements on which the employer intends to rely: *Bell v Devon and Cornwall Police Authority* [1978] IRLR 283. As an alternative to showing the employee a written statement the employer, before dismissing the employee, may ask those involved to outline to the employee the matters alleged against him. In either case the employee must know with sufficient certainty what is said against him. In addition it maybe that the employee should be given the opportunity of questioning any protagonist: *Bentley Engineering Co Ltd v Mistry* [1979] ICR 47. However, the employee is probably not entitled to be given written statements and to have the right of oral evidence: *Khanum v Mid-Glamorgan Area Health Authority*, above. There is no general obligation on an employer to carry out a quasi-judicial investigation, with confrontation of witnesses and cross-examination. There may be circumstances where it is necessary or desirable: *Ulsterbus Ltd v Henderson* [1989] IRLR 251. There is no absolute need for witnesses to be called if a procedure makes it optional whether or not to call them provided that justice is done: *East Hertfordshire District Council v Boyten* [1977] IRLR 347.

In *Louies v Coventry Hood and Seating Co Ltd* [1990] IRLR 324, the EAT held that where an employer relies almost entirely on witnesses' written statements the failure to make them available to the employee will be contrary to the rules of natural justice and so it will not be a fair procedure. In *Spink v Express Foods Group Ltd* [1990] IRLR 320, the EAT held that in general terms an employee should know the case he has to meet. He should hear or be told the important points of the evidence in support of that case and should have an opportunity to criticise or dispute the evidence, to adduce his own evidence and argue his case.

Where an employee fails to attend a disciplinary hearing and the employer proceeds in his absence this may well be fair: see *Mansard Precision Engineering Co Ltd v Taylor* [1978] ICR 44. However, when the employee is unable to participate because of ill-health then the employer, if he goes ahead on that basis, may be in difficulty: *Tesco Group of Companies (Holdings) Ltd v Hill*, above. If the employee fails to attend because of illness and writes to the employer explaining the position, the employer should consider the letter even though it arrives subsequently to the disciplinary hearing: *Chrystie v Rolls Royce*

(1971) Ltd [1976] IRLR 336; see also *John Crawford and Co (Plumbers) Ltd v Donnelly* [1979] IRLR 9.

It has been held there is no rule of natural justice which requires the employee to be present at a disciplinary hearing where his representative is present throughout and the employee has been given a chance to put his case: *Pirelli General Cable Works Ltd v Murray* [1979] IRLR 190.

However, it is important that the rights of the employee are safeguarded by his duly accredited representatives: *Gray Dunn and Co Ltd v Edwards* [1980] IRLR 23.

Generally, the person who conducts an inquiry must be seen to be impartial. In *Slater v Leicestershire Health Authority* [1989] IRLR 16, a nurse's dismissal was not unfair because the manager who carried out the preliminary investigation also conducted the disciplinary hearing and took the decision to dismiss; although the rules of natural justice do not form an independent ground upon which a decision to dismiss may be attacked a breach of the rules of natural justice will be for a tribunal to consider.

5.2 Capability

(a) Warnings It may be difficult to draw a clear distinction between a dismissal by reason of conduct and a dismissal by reason of capability. Where the lack of capability is due to fault on the employee's part such as carelessness or negligence, then the dismissal is probably better regarded as being a dismissal by reason of the employee's conduct rather than capability and so the need for warnings should be considered accordingly: *Sutton and Gates (Luton) Ltd v Boxall* [1979] ICR 67.

Both the 1972 and the 1977 codes in dealing with disciplinary procedures, rules and penalties refer only to conduct. Neither code suggests that the same requirements should be observed when the reason for the dismissal is capability (s 57(2)(*a*) of the EP(C)A 1978). None the less, warnings are of relevance where the employee's lack of capability is in issue. See *Polkey's* case above.

The NIRC held that the 'general concept of fair play inherent in the disciplinary procedure should also guide management in considering the dismissal for inefficiency': see *The Lewis Shops Group v Wiggins* [1973] IRLR 205; see also *Taylor v Alidair Ltd* [1978] ICR 445.

The approach to be followed in cases involving capability, including the need to give warnings, was set out by the NIRC in *James v Waltham Holy Cross UDC* [1973] ICR 398. It held:

If an employee is not measuring up to the job, it may be because he is not exerting himself sufficiently or it may be because he really lacks the capacity to do so. An employer should be very slow to dismiss upon the ground that the employee is incapable of performing the work which he is employed to do, without first telling the employee of the respects in which he is failing to do his job adequately, warning him of the possibility or likelihood of dismissal on this ground and giving him an opportunity of improving his performance.

The NIRC found there were two exceptions to this principle. The first arises where senior management 'may by the nature of their jobs be fully aware of what is required of them and fully capable of judging for themselves whether they are achieving that requirement. In such circumstances the need for warning and an opportunity for improvement is much less apparent.' The second exception arises where 'the inadequacy of performance is so extreme that there must be an irredeemable incapability. In such circumstances, exceptional though they no doubt are, a warning and opportunity for improvement are of no benefit to the employee and may constitute an unfair burden on the business'.

A similar approach was followed in *Winterhalter Gastronom Ltd v Webb* [1973] ICR 245, where a sales director was dismissed because of poor sales figures. The NIRC, while accepting that the disciplinary provisions of the code did not refer to warnings prior to dismissal for lack of capability, found they were appropriate, concluding 'many do not know they are capable of jumping the five-barred gate until the bull is close behind them'. While recognising this general principle the court differentiated between senior and junior personnel when considering the need for warnings. The court found:

there may be cases in which giving warning to a director would be neither necessary nor achieve any useful purpose. But, each case must depend upon its own particular facts and it is . . . quite impossible to say as a matter of law that there can never be circumstances in which it is necessary to give a warning to a director before dismissing him.

In *Cook v Thomas Linnell and Sons Ltd* [1977] ICR 770, the EAT held:

Where one is dealing with a breach of discipline the rules of procedure are of the greatest possible importance. They may be of less importance when one is dealing with alleged incapacity, provided—and this is most important— that the complaint has been brought to the attention of the employee concerned over a period of time. This remains a requirement even where the employee holds a position in which he can, within reason, be expected to monitor his own performance.

A dismissal for lack of capability without a warning may be unfair if there is some possibility that the employee might improve, following a warning.

Even though it is only a possibility, the employee should be given a chance to improve: see *Mansfield Hosiery Mills Ltd v Bromley* [1977] IRLR 301.

The employee may receive a warning by implication that his capability does not come up to the employer's requirements. Thus, in *Judge International Ltd v Moss* [1973] IRLR 208, it was found that a failure to review a salary might be sufficient warning that the employee was not carrying out his functions adequately: see also *Coward v John Menzies (Holdings) Ltd* [1977] IRLR 428.

Where the employee has been warned about his lack of capability he must be given sufficient opportunity to meet his employer's requirements before being dismissed. What is a reasonable period to give the employee will depend upon the circumstances of the case: see *Sibun v Modern Telephones Ltd* [1976] IRLR 81.

Where an employee has been dismissed for a lack of capability a warning may not be necessary and the dismissal may be found to be fair. Thus, a warning is not necessary where the employee is hopelessly incompetent so that no warning or suggestion to the employee that he should improve would alter the position. Similarly, a warning may not be necessary where the employee does not consider that he was performing badly and is not aware of any of his shortcomings so that a warning, even if given, would not have been heeded: see *Grant v Ampex Great Britain Ltd* [1980] IRLR 461.

Dismissal for capability may be fair where no warning has been given if the warning would have served no useful purpose. In *AJ Dunning and Sons (Shop Fitters) Ltd v Jacomb* [1973] ICR 448, the employee who was a contracts manager was dismissed because of a lack of capability. He was not warned before dismissal. The NIRC considered whether a failure to give a warning was a matter of procedure or whether it was a matter of substance. They concluded that it was a matter of substance. In this case the tribunal had to ask itself:

whether Mr Jacomb's incapacity as it existed at the time of dismissal was of such a nature and quality as to justify a dismissal, or whether it was of such a nature and quality that, were Mr Jacomb to receive a warning, he might or would be able to improve his performance. If the latter, then the mere fact that his performance had not been up to standard in the past would not, or might not, justify his dismissal.

The NIRC found that the lack of capability pointed to a constitutional inability on the employee's part so that a warning would have been of no use.

It may also be fair to dismiss an employee without a warning where the mistakes are serious. In *Lowndes v Specialist Heavy Engineering Ltd* [1977] ICR 1, the employee was dismissed after five costly mistakes without a warning or an opportunity to be heard. It was held that the dismissal was fair, for the circumstances 'were so egregious that dismissal was justified, despite the failure in procedure, and no injustice was done'. To have followed the proper procedure would have made no difference.

In *Alidair Ltd v Taylor* [1976] IRLR 420, confirmed by the Court of Appeal—*Taylor v Alidair Ltd* [1978] ICR 445, the EAT held that it may be fair to dismiss an employee where his lack of capability is so serious that an employer is not obliged to risk further serious errors. The Court of Appeal approved the judgment of Bristow J in the EAT where he found:

In our judgment there are activities in which the degree of professional skill which must be required is so high, and the potential consequences of the smallest departure of that high standard are so serious, that one failure to perform in accordance with those standards is enough to justify dismissal. The passenger-carrying airline pilot, the scientist operating the nuclear reactor, the chemist in charge of research into the possible effect of, for example, thalidomide, the driver of the Manchester to London express, the driver of an articulated lorry full of sulphuric acid, are all in the situation in which one failure to maintain the proper standard of professional skill can bring about a major disaster.

However, in *British Midland Airways Ltd v Gilmore* (1982) (unreported) EAT 173/81 the EAT found that in a case involving similar facts to those in *Taylor*'s case, the employer's failure to follow a proper procedure made the dismissal unfair.

The EAT has also recognised that where there is a close personal relationship between employees as between a managing director and his personal secretary it may not be necessary specifically to warn the employee that unless there is an improvement dismissal will follow: *Brown v Hall Advertising Ltd* [1978] IRLR 246, where the EAT emphasised that the code is not a mandatory document, the provisions of which fall to be applied rigidly to every employment situation. What is fair and good industrial practice for an employee on the shop floor will not apply in every situation. In this case the employee had at least been put on notice that her work was unsatisfactory and particular areas for improvement were pointed out to her.

As in the case of misconduct, a warning to the employee may be dispensed with when its need is outweighed by the interests of the business.

Where the employee has been taken on for a probationary or trial period a greater onus is placed on the employer to warn and aid the employee in his performance during that period: *Post Office v Mughal* [1977] IRLR 178. See also *Inner London Education Authority v Lloyd* [1981] IRLR 394. Similarly, in the case of young employees the employer's obligations may be greater. It has been suggested in the case of a young apprentice consideration should be given to consulting with his parents, as in *Small v Lex Mead Southampton* [1977] IRLR 48. However, compare *Finch v Betabake (Anglia) Ltd* [1977] IRLR 470. While each case will depend upon the circumstances, there is no general obligation on the employer to consult with the apprentice's parents, although it may be desirable to do so.

Although in cases such as *The Littlewoods Organisation Ltd v Egenti* [1976] ICR 516, the EAT has emphasised that the fairly strict requirement to follow a procedure which exists in a case of dismissal, where the reason is one relating to the employee's conduct, does not necessarily apply in cases of dismissal where the reason relates to capability, but see *Polkey*'s case, above.

The essential difference between cases involving conduct and cases involving capability is that in cases involving the employee's conduct the employee should be warned that if his conduct does not improve he will be dismissed. In cases involving incapability the employer should make it known to the employee that there is a need for the employee to improve. The warning should be seen more in terms of helping and encouraging the employee to achieve that improvement.

Where an employee has received a warning for lack of capability and, indeed, an opportunity to improve, there is no rule of law that an employer must attempt to fit the employee in elsewhere in the organisation. It will depend upon the circumstances in each case. It may be reasonable for a big employer but unreasonable for a small employer: see *Bevan Harris Ltd (t/a The Clyde Leather Co) v Gair* [1981] IRLR 520.

More recently there has been a recognition of the need to follow a proper procedure including the giving of warnings. Undoubtedly this is a result at least in part of the decision in *Polkey v AE Dayton Services Ltd* [1988] ICR 142.

(b) Warnings generally The nature of the warning has already been considered in relation to conduct, see **5.1(b)**, above.

(c) The need for assessment and help In cases involving substandard performance where the reason is a lack of skill in the broader sense on the employee's part, there is some obligation on the employer's part to assist the employee in reaching the required standard. That involves the employer in making an assessment.

It has already been seen that in cases involving probationary employees, there is an obligation on the employer to assess the employee's performance and to give advice and guidance: see *Post Office v Mughal* [1977] IRLR 178; *Inner London Education Authority v Lloyd* [1981] IRLR 394. Arguably similar guidelines apply where the employer has recently promoted the employee. In *Mansfield Hosiery Mills Ltd v Bromley* [1977] IRLR 301, the tribunal considered that the employee's dismissal was unfair where he had been promoted, because there had been insufficient supervision, warnings of his shortcomings and a lack of encouragement to improve. Although the EAT considered that it might have reached a different decision to that of the tribunal, none the less the tribunal had not erred in law.

The reported cases involve in the main new and probationary employees and employees who have been newly promoted. However, similar steps should be taken where an existing employee's work becomes substandard due to factors other than the employee's conduct. This may arise where there is a change in the level of the skill and other demands made upon the employee by the employer.

Again, a failure to give the employee appropriate guidance on training may lead or contribute to an unfair dismissal. In *Boobier v Johnsons Cleaners (Southern) Ltd* [1974] IRLR 329, complaints were made by the employer about the way in which Boobier managed the company's shop. He had never been given any advice or training on how the shop should be run. The tribunal found the dismissal was unfair. *Inter alia*, it found that the employer had not had regard to the guidance in para 35 of the 1972 code. Closely allied with the need for the employer to make the employee aware that his performance is not meeting the employer's requirements is the need for the employer to help the employee in achieving those requirements. See **6.1**, below.

It must be remembered that tribunals have found an employee's dismissal substantively unfair where the employer has failed to give training and assistance. See **6.1**, below.

(d) Investigation   The employer has to establish the reason for the employee's dismissal and that is a reason within s 57(1)(*b*) and (2) of the EP(C)A 1978. As in the case of conduct the employer must establish a genuine belief based on reasonable grounds that the employee is incapable: see *Taylor v Alidair Ltd*, above. In order that the employer might establish that belief he should carry out an investigation. See, generally, **5.1(*b*)**, above.

(e) Opportunity for an employee to state his case   *Polkey*'s case, above, is authority for the view that the proper procedural steps include, arguably, giving the employee an opportunity to state his case in appropriate cases before dismissing him for incapability. However, in practice, the failure by the employer to give the employee an opportunity to put his case may be less important than in the case of misconduct.

In *Sutton and Gates (Luton) Ltd v Boxall* [1979] ICR 67, Sutton, an electrician, was unfairly dismissed because of bad workmanship without being given the opportunity to explain. His lack of capability was affecting his employer's business. The tribunal found the employer's failure to give Boxall an opportunity to explain made the dismissal unfair. The EAT upheld the decision finding that if the employee had been given an opportunity of stating his case there was a possibility he would not have been dismissed.

There are exceptions, one of which may arise where the offence is so heinous and the facts so manifestly clear that the employer could on the facts known to him at the time of dismissal conclude that whatever explanation was offered it could make no difference. In *Earl v Slater and Wheeler (Airlyne) Ltd* [1972] ICR 508, the NIRC held that the employee must be given an opportunity of stating his case, except where there can be no explanation which would cause the employers to refrain from dismissing the employee.

In *Lowndes v Specialist Heavy Engineering Ltd* [1977] ICR 1,

Lowndes was dismissed for incompetence following five serious errors in his work. He was given neither a written warning nor an opportunity to explain his lapses prior to dismissal. While the EAT accepted that in principle there must be a fair procedure including an opportunity to explain, failure to follow a fair procedure does not always of necessity render a dismissal unfair. Although one element in deciding whether the dismissal is fair or unfair may be whether the employer has operated a fair procedure, in *Lowndes*'s case the tribunal had correctly found that the circumstances were so egregious that dismissal was justified and no injustice was done because there was a failure to observe a proper procedure. Although this case was decided before *Polkey*'s case, arguably this is the sort of case Lord Mackay had in mind.

Similarly, in *Taylor v Alidair Ltd* [1978] ICR 445, where an airline pilot made one single but serious mistake in landing his aircraft his dismissal was not unfair because he had been given no opportunity to explain prior to his dismissal. Lord Denning MR considered that the opportunity for an employee to state his case 'may be desirable in many cases: but it should not be regarded as of universal application'.

Another exception may arise where a reasonable employer can properly take the view that on the facts known to him at the time of dismissal no explanation or mitigation could alter his decision to dismiss, as where the employee has already made known his views and giving him the opportunity to explain would simply result in them being reiterated: see *James v Waltham Holy Cross UDC* [1973] ICR 398.

Further exceptions may arise where there is a close relationship between the employer and the employee: consider *Brown v Hall Advertising Ltd* [1978] IRLR 246, and where giving the employee an opportunity to explain might impose an unfair burden on the business: see *James*'s case, above.

(f) The nature of the opportunity This has already been considered in relation to conduct. See **5.1(e)**, above.

5.3 Criminal offences

(a) Criminal offences inside employment Exceptionally a criminal offence committed by the employee in his employment against the employer will not justify dismissal. It depends on the circumstances. However, usually the commission of such a criminal offence will justify the employee's dismissal, if not the employee's summary dismissal. This will be particularly so where the employer has a rule providing for dismissal or summary dismissal. The employer will not be absolved from following proper procedure: see *Fowler v Cammell Laird (Shipbuilders) Ltd* [1973] IRLR 72.

Where the criminal act is committed against a fellow employee as distinct from an employer, dismissal in those circumstances will usually be justified, although it must be remembered that whereas theft or some other act of dishonesty committed against the employer must almost inevitably involve a breach of the confidential relationship which exists between the employer and the employee, theft or some other act of dishonesty committed against another employee will not necessarily lead to such a breach: see *Johnson Matthey Metals Ltd v Harding* [1978] IRLR 248, where an employee with 15 years' service stole from a fellow employee and was dismissed. The dismissal was held to be unfair.

The onus is upon the employer to establish the reason. Even where the reason is the employee's alleged criminal conduct, the employer need only establish that at the time of the dismissal there were reasonable grounds for believing that the offence put against the employee was committed: *Ferodo v Barnes* [1976] ICR 439. In *British Home Stores Ltd v Burchell* [1978] IRLR 379, where Burchell was dismissed for dishonesty relating to staff purchases, the EAT held that where an employee is dismissed for misconduct the employer must show that he believed the employee to be guilty of that misconduct, he had reasonable grounds for his belief and, at the time he formed the belief on those grounds, he had investigated the matter to a reasonable extent in the circumstances. The employer must honestly or genuinely hold that belief. Where one, two or more employees are reasonably suspected of being guilty of misconduct but the employer cannot identify those responsible the employer may be entitled to rely upon a reasonable suspicion of dishonesty: see *Monie v Coral Racing Ltd* [1981] ICR 109; *Whitbread and Co plc v Thomas and Others* [1988] ICR 135 and *Whitbread and Co plc v Mills* [1988] IRLR 501, generally. See **5.1** (c) above. It is obviously important for the employer to carry out a proper investigation, particularly where he seeks to rely upon a reasonable suspicion. The employer may be entitled to rely upon an employee's admission of guilt: *British Gas plc v McCarrick* [1991] IRLR 305.

Investigation   If an employee is found in possession of stolen property belonging to his employer it may be fair to dismiss without further investigation. The employer must of course act fairly towards the employee: *Scottish Special Housing Association v Linnen* [1979] IRLR 265.

However, in any case involving the employee's criminal activities where there is any doubt, the employer should carry out an investigation. While this investigation may be limited by the need not to prejudice criminal investigation, such inquiry may be necessary to establish the employer's belief that he had reasonable grounds for dismissal: *Scottish Special Housing Association v Cooke* [1979] IRLR 264, or indeed a reasonable suspicion.

The need for investigation was illustrated in *Wm Low and Co Ltd v MacCuish* [1979] IRLR 458. MacCuish was dismissed for theft because she had taken pork chops from the employer without paying for them. She was not given a chance to explain and the employer, without having carried out an investigation and so without having reasonable grounds on which to base his belief that she was guilty of theft, jumped to the conclusion that she was guilty. See also *McLaren v NCB* [1988] ICR 370.

One of the difficulties for the employer in following a fair procedure prior to dismissal is that it may not be possible to interview the employee suspected of a criminal offence. Here, the employer will have to consider whether he has sufficient material on which to form his belief that the employee is guilty of a criminal offence in accordance with the approach in *Burchell*'s case, or in *Monie*'s case, above, a reasonable suspicion. However, wherever possible, it is essential that the employer should afford the employee an opportunity of giving an explanation and the employee should know that the employer in contemplating dismissal. If the employee chooses or is advised not to tell the employer anything it does not mean that the employer in forming his beliefs or suspicion in the employee's guilt has failed to carry out as much investigation into the matter as was reasonable in all the circumstances in accordance with the decisions in *Burchell*'s case and *Monie*'s case. He may have done all he can. However, it maybe that in these circumstances where the employer cannot hear the employee's version of events, he will be unable to form a belief or suspicion as to the employee's guilt. The employer may have to wait until the outcome of any criminal proceedings: see *Harris and Shepherd v Courage (Eastern) Ltd* [1981] IRLR 153, upheld on appeal, see [1982] IRLR 509.

The importance of following a proper procedure, including giving the employee an opportunity of explaining or offering some mitigation has been emphasised by the House of Lords in *Polkey*'s case, above. By giving the employee the opportunity to explain, the employer can listen to any representations which the employee has to offer and can communicate to the employee the action which it is proposed to take against him: see *Harris (Ipswich) Ltd v Harrison* [1978] ICR 1256. However, it is clear from the decision in *Polkey*'s case that there may be certain exceptions. The tribunal must consider whether the employer acted reasonably in not following a proper procedure. In rare cases an employer may act reasonably in taking the view that on the facts known to him at the time of the dismissal no explanation or mitigation could alter his decision to dismiss and so the failure to take this procedural step would not be fatal.

There are several early decisions where it has been held that the dismissal of an employee without an opportunity to explain was fair. In *Carr v Alexander Russell Ltd* [1976] IRLR 220, Carr, a labourer, was caught red-handed by the police in possession of his employer's property. He did not protest his innocence and did not exercise his rights under the employer's internal procedure. The police told the employer that he had been charged with theft of the employer's property. The employer dismissed him. Carr pleaded guilty to theft, he was convicted and fined. It was held that his dismissal was fair. The NIRC considered that Carr could offer no explanation and it would be unrealistic to expect the employer to accept any explanation offered. The decision in *Carr*'s case was followed in *Conway v Matthew Wright and Nephew Ltd* [1977] IRLR 89, where Conway, whose duties included those of a part-time watchman, was charged by the police with maliciously causing damage to the employer's property after a number of incidents in which windows were deliberately broken. The employer investigated the matter and discussed it with the police, but did not give Conway an opportunity to state his case before dismissing him. It was held that the dismissal was fair. Giving Conway an opportunity to state his case would not have advanced matters. In *Parker v Clifford Dunn Ltd* [1979] IRLR 56, Parker admitted to the police that he had stolen goods from his employer. The police told the employer's managing director who dismissed him without giving him an opportunity of explaining his conduct. It was held that the dismissal was fair. The opportunity would have been of no use because it would not have made any difference to the employer's decision. He admitted having stolen his employer's property. He made no protestations of innocence to the employer although he had the chance to do so and did not follow the employer's grievance procedure.

In *Kingston v British Railways Board* [1984] IRLR 146, Kingston's dismissal was fair following his imprisonment for three months for an assault committed in the course of his employment, notwithstanding that the employer had not followed a proper procedure.

In each of these cases, arguably the result would have been the same if they had been decided after *Polkey*'s case because they fall within the exceptions envisaged in *Polkey*'s case.

However, in the case of criminal misconduct as with other misconduct, the employer's failure to follow a proper procedure may mean the dismissal is unfair. In *Tesco Group of Companies (Holdings) Ltd v Hill* [1977] IRLR 63, a dismissal was held to be unfair because at the time when Hill was asked to give an explanation of her conduct she was not fit to do so. It may be unfair because pressure is put on the employee to extract a confession: *Goodwin v Fred Hartley and Sons Ltd* (1978) (unreported). Again a dismissal may be unfair where the employer fails to organise the disciplinary procedure properly. In *Tesco Stores Ltd v Heap* (1978) 13 ITR 17, Heap was charged with five offences of dishonesty. Prior to the hearing he was called to a café and questioned about two of the five offences which he was alleged to have admitted. There was no warning of the purpose of the meeting, no real effort was made to obtain the employee's side of the story and the employer failed to draw the employee's attention to a right of appeal. The dismissal was held unfair. In *Read v Phoenix Preservation Ltd* [1985] IRLR 93, the EAT held that where police officers are present at an internal disciplinary inquiry without the employee's knowledge and consent this will be wholly improper. The EAT also found that an employee will not have every opportunity of putting forward matters in his own defence where the police who are present at an internal disciplinary inquiry were conducting a criminal inquiry, and had administered a caution to the employee.

A subsequent conviction Since the employer need only show at most that he had reasonable grounds for believing that the employee was guilty of criminal conduct, it is not necessarily fatal that the employee is not subsequently convicted in criminal proceedings: *Davies v GKN Birwelco (Uskside) Ltd* [1976] IRLR 82. It also follows that the employer may dismiss the employee prior to any criminal proceedings being brought against the employee. There is no general obligation on the employer to await the outcome of criminal proceedings: *Tesco Stores Ltd v Heap* (1978) 13 ITR 17. There is no general obligation upon the employer to suspend the employee on full pay while awaiting the result of any criminal proceedings: *Conway v Matthew Wright and Nephew Ltd* [1977] IRLR 89. The employer may well be advised to suspend the employee with full pay until he has carried out his own investigations. In the circumstances envisaged in *Harris and Shepherd v Courage (Eastern) Ltd* [1981] IRLR 153, the employer might well be advised to retain the employee pending the outcome of criminal proceedings.

Fairness of the dismissal—general The tribunal is not able to substitute its decision for that of the employer. It is concerned to see whether or not the employer has acted fairly in all the circumstances judged by the objective standard, what would a reasonable employer in that line of business have done in those circumstances: see *Grundy (Teddington) Ltd v Willis* [1976] ICR 323 and *NC Watling and Co Ltd v Richardson* [1978] ICR 1049. There may be a range of reasonable responses and it is for the tribunal to see whether or not the employer's response was within that range of reasonable responses: see *Rolls Royce Ltd v Walpole* [1980] IRLR 343.

The tribunal must look to see what the employer could reasonably have done where the employee is alleged to have committed a criminal offence. In *Parkers Bakeries Ltd v Palmer* [1977] IRLR 215, Palmer, a bread salesman, was 20 loaves of bread short in his deliveries to a particular customer on four consecutive days. The EAT found there was abundant evidence on which the employer could conclude that the employee was responsible. At an interview Palmer made no outright acknowledgement of guilt but did agree to pay back certain moneys. In the circumstances this was considered to be approaching a tacit acknowledgement of guilt and the employer had acted reasonably.

Where the employer wishes to dismiss the employee by reason of an alleged criminal offence the employer must act swiftly. In *Allders International Ltd v Parkins* [1981] IRLR 68, an allegation of theft was made against Parkins, but nothing was done for nine days and he was allowed to work out the nine days. The tribunal found that the dismissal was unfair.

Activity which may lead the employer to suspect criminal conduct can also be a breach of the employer's rules or a breach of an implied term in the contract. Although an employer may not be able to show criminal conduct, the employer may be able to show other conduct which might justify a dismissal.

Other factors for consideration   Where the employee is in custody the contract of employment may be frustrated. See generally Chapter 3. Even if the contract is not frustrated, the employee's imprisonment may be sufficient to justify dismissal. Where an employee is convicted of a criminal offence so that his continued employment in a particular position may involve a contravention of a statutory duty or restriction—for instance his inability to drive a vehicle on the public highway—it may justify dismissal. See, generally, Chapter 5.

Where the procedure cannot be carried out immediately   Normally, when it is impossible or impracticable to follow the disciplinary procedure immediately, for whatever reason, the employee may be suspended with pay until the procedure can be followed.

(b) Criminal offences outside employment   The 1977 code provides that:

[Criminal offences committed outside employment] . . . should not be treated as automatic reasons for dismissal regardless of whether the offence has any relevance to the duties of the individual as an employee. The main considerations should be whether the offence is one that makes the individual unsuitable for his or her type of work or unacceptable to other employees. Employees should not be dismissed solely because a charge against them is pending or because they are absent through having been remanded in custody. (Paragraph 15(c).)

As a general proposition, if an employer wishes to dismiss an employee for a criminal offence committed outside employment, for the dismissal to be found fair the offence must have some detrimental effect upon the employer's interests in the wider sense. In *Robb v Mersey Insulation Co Ltd* [1972] IRLR 18, Robb, a shipwright securing cargoes on board ships, was convicted of theft. He was dismissed and it was held the dismissal was fair. The tribunal found 'the reputation of [the employer's] business would have been adversely affected if it had come to the knowledge of their customers that employees with convictions of this nature were working among cargo'. In *Richardson v City of Bradford Metropolitan Council* [1975] IRLR 296, the dismissal of a senior meat inspector following his conviction of taking money while working behind the bar of a local rugby club was fair because, 'It is only right that when the integrity of a public servant who is employed in a position where integrity is of prime importance is found to be wanting, the local authority which employs him should take necessary action to remove him from public service.' The same principle applies where criminal offences other than dishonesty are involved. In *Gardiner v Newport CBC* [1974] IRLR 262, a lecturer was dismissed following a conviction for gross indecency with other men in a public toilet. He was in charge of male and female teenage students. The tribunal found the dismissal fair holding, 'Both on the ground that such a person either cannot or will not control himself in public and should not be trusted with young persons, with the opportunities that a teacher has, and also having some respect for the feelings of parents we think that the decision to dismiss . . . was reasonable'. In *Nottinghamshire CC v Bowly* [1978] IRLR 252, the EAT made it clear that while there is no rule that following a conviction of gross indecency the employee must be automatically dismissed or that dismissal in such circumstances is automatically unfair, provided the employer has considered the case fairly and properly and directed itself properly it cannot be faulted in doing what in their judgment is just and proper. Putting it another way, was dismissal within the band of reasonable responses? In *Wiseman v Salford CC* [1981] IRLR 202, the EAT recognised that in cases involving teachers convicted of acts of gross indecency who come into contact with young male students, the tribunal has to assess the reasonableness of the employer's action in each case. There is no self-evident proposition that there is no risk attached to such an employee's continued employment. Wiseman's dismissal was held to be fair.

In *Creffield v BBC* [1975] IRLR 23, the dismissal of a film cameraman following his conviction of indecently assaulting a 13-year-old girl was held to be fair because the employer could not be selective in sending the employee on assignments and might be apprehensive about sending the employee on assignments in a responsible position in the future. Dismissal could be justified because Creffield was no longer able to do his job.

If it can be shown that the employee's criminal conduct is not detrimental to the employer's interest in the wider sense then the dismissal will not necessarily be fair. In *Bradshaw v Rugby Portland Cement Co Ltd* [1972] IRLR 46, Bradshaw's dismissal following his conviction for incest was unfair. The tribunal found:

This was an isolated incident, it had nothing to do with the applicant's work, his work did not bring him into contact with female staff, he was working with a gang of men, it did not, apparently, upset his relationships with his workmates in any way, it did not expose anyone to a moral danger from his presence in the works; and there must have been although we do not know what they were, very strong mitigating circumstances to enable a court to deal with the applicant in such a lenient manner [probation for three years].

In *Norfolk County Council v Bernard* [1979] IRLR 220, Bernard, a teacher, was convicted of possession and cultivation of cannabis and was dismissed. The EAT upheld the decision of the tribunal that dismissal was unfair. Following the judgment in *Bowley*'s case it found that a conviction for the possession of cannabis did not mean that the employee should be automatically dismissed or that the dismissal was automatically unfair.

The employee may be fairly dismissed because he dishonestly conceals from his employer a criminal conviction which was imposed before he commenced employment with that employer: see *Torr v British Railways Board* [1967] ICR 785.

As in the case of criminal conduct committed against the employer the employer need only satisfy himself at most that at the time of the dismissal he had reasonable grounds for believing that the offence put against the employee was committed, not that the employee in fact committed it: *Ferodo Ltd v Barnes* [1976] ICR 439; *British Home Stores Ltd v Burchell* [1978] IRLR 379. In exceptional circumstances a reasonable suspicion will be sufficient when the offence is committed outside the employment. See *Monie v Coral Racing Ltd* [1980] IRLR 464.

Before dismissing the employee for criminal offences outside employment the employer should follow a proper procedure. A failure to follow a proper procedure is likely to result in the dismissal being unfair: see *Tesco Group of Companies (Holdings) Ltd v Hill* [1977] IRLR 63. See **5.3**(*a*) above. However, a dismissal without following a proper procedure may mean in exceptional cases that the dismissal is not unfair: see *Carr v Alexander Russell Ltd* [1976] IRLR 220, and *Parker v Clifford Dunn Ltd* [1979] ICR 463 and the comments made thereon. The employer must not do anything to prejudice any criminal proceedings or interfere with the course of justice: *Carr v Alexander Russell Ltd*, above.

The 1977 code provides that an employee should not be dismissed solely because a charge has been brought against him or because he is absent while he is in custody.

5.4 Contravention of a statutory duty or restriction

The 1977 code does not specifically deal with cases where the employee is to be dismissed by reason of a contravention of a statutory duty or restriction. However, there is no reason why the employer's obligations as to investigation, consultation or giving the employee an opportunity to explain should not apply when appropriate.

Where the continued employment would be in contravention of a statutory duty or restriction, the dismissal will not always be fair. It is clear from the decision in *Myeza v Avon Health Authority* (1977) (unreported), see Chapter 5, **2.5**, above, that the employer still has to act reasonably. In this case Myeza's dismissal was unfair. The authority had acted with haste and without having carried out sufficient investigation. *Sutcliffe and Eaton Ltd v Pinney* [1977] IRLR 349, emphasises this point. Pinney was employed as a trainee hearing aid dispenser. He was dismissed when he failed to pass the examinations of the Hearing Aid Council within a prescribed period and on his failure, his name was removed from the register of hearing aid dispensers. Under the Hearing Aid Council Act 1968, it was an offence for anyone not on the register to dispense hearing aids or to be employed by a registered employer. However, it was possible for Pinney to obtain a further extension of the prescribed period, which he did after his dismissal. If the extension had been obtained prior to his dismissal the tribunal found that action against the employer was unlikely. However, the employer took no steps to ascertain the position or apply for an extension, but dismissed Pinney. The EAT found the dismissal unfair.

In cases where there is a contravention of a statutory duty or restriction, the tribunal must therefore examine whether or not it was reasonable to dismiss the employee. The fact that continued employment is in contravention of a statutory duty or restriction does not mean that the dismissal is therefore fair. Although it is improbable that the employee will obtain an order for reinstatement or re-engagement he is not precluded from claiming compensation: *Sandhu v (1) Department of Education and Science, (2) London Borough of Hillingdon* [1978] IRLR 208.

The need for the employer to act reasonably was emphasised in *O'Connor v Lothian Health Board* (1977) (unreported). O'Connor was employed as a dentist. He carried on private work without the board's consent in breach of the provisions of the National Health Service (Remuneration and Conditions of Service) (Scotland) Regulations 1974. These regulations rendered the board liable to prosecution by employing O'Connor. The board wrote to O'Connor on several occasions warning him to give up private practice, but he ignored these warnings. It was held that the dismissal was fair as the board had given O'Connor a chance to desist from private practice. It is clear from this decision that warnings are important before dismissing the employee where the employee is in breach of statute but could have remedied the situation. It would be different if the warning can be of no effect. The employer's genuine but erroneous belief that there has been a contravention is irrelevant in applying s 57(2)(d) of the EP(C)A 1978. The facts may provide the employer with 'some other substantial reason': *Bouchaala v Trust Houses Forte Hotels Ltd* [1980] IRLR 382.

For cases involving the contravention of a statutory duty or restriction under s 57(2)(d) of the EP(C)A 1978, see Chapter 5.

5.5 Some other substantial reason

Neither the 1972 code nor the 1977 code make reference to the need for warnings or the need for consultation with the employee, or giving the employee an opportunity to explain before dismissing the employee for 'some other substantial reason'. Where the reason for dismissal is 'some other substantial reason' the employer should investigate, warn the employee, consult with the employee, and give the employee an opportunity to explain before dismissing him. However, in exceptional cases, a failure to warn the employee or to consult with him or to give him an opportunity to explain before a dismissal will not be fatal. The tribunal must consider whether or not the employer has acted reasonably.

In *Hollister v National Farmers Union* [1979] ICR 542, Hollister was dismissed following a reorganisation of the employer's business. The Court of Appeal considered that consultation and negotiation were factors to be taken into account when considering whether the dismissal was fair or unfair. In this case the failure on the part of the employer to undertake consultation and negotiation did not mean that the dismissal was unfair. The tribunal had to look at all the circumstances in deciding whether or not what the employer did was fair and reasonable. It had done so and reached a proper conclusion. However, the lack of consultation may mean the employer is not aware of all the circumstances which, had he known them, would have led him to refrain from dismissing: *Ladbroke Courage Holidays Ltd v Asten* [1981] IRLR 59.

5.6 Appeals

The 1977 code provides that the disciplinary procedure should provide a right of appeal and specify the procedure to be followed: para 10(*k*) of the 1977 code. The need to provide a right of appeal is not confined to cases involving misconduct: *Lancaster v Anchor Hotels and Taverns Ltd* [1973] IRLR 13. The right is an important one and it should be brought to the attention of the employee or his representative: *Tesco Group of Companies (Holdings) Ltd v Hill* [1977] IRLR 63. Even if the employer's disciplinary procedure does not provide for a right of appeal, one should be given where possible: *Davison v Kent Meters Ltd* [1975] IRLR 145.

In *West Midlands Co-operative Society Ltd v Tipton* [1986] ICR 192, the House of Lords held that a failure to follow a proper procedure, including granting the employee a right of appeal, may render the dismissal unfair. This case underlined the importance of an appeal as part of a proper procedure. See **5.2** above. The nature and purpose of an appeal must be considered in determining the fairness of a dismissal where no appeal has been granted or the appeal procedure is defective. In *Post Office v Marney* [1990] IRLR 170, a failure to consider on appeal whether dismissal was an appropriate remedy was not a breach of Marney's contractual appeal procedure. The EAT held that not every breach of a contractual right of appeal rendered the dismissal unfair. It held that the appeal is a process whereby what has been done by an inferior official or tribunal is investigated to see whether it is something which ought to be disturbed or not. It considered that the principle in *Tipton*'s case that the employer activities right down to the end of the appeal process have to be considered should not mean losing sight of the fundamental question which is, 'was the dismissal fair or unfair?' Only if an appeal procedure is defective in that it should or could have demonstrated a flaw in the decision at 'first instance' will the dismissal be unfair. If the process leading to the decision to dismiss was a proper one, because on appeal the employer did not consider or review one of the parts of the process, it does not mean that the dismissal is unfair. Procedural defects may be remedied on an appeal where the appeal takes the form of a re-hearing and is comprehensive: see *Whitbread and Co plc v Mills* [1988] ICR 776.

It is more likely that a dismissal will be unfair where larger employers are involved and no right of appeal has been granted: *Lloyd v Scottish Co-operative Wholesale Society Ltd* [1973] IRLR 93, where the employer's failure to provide a right of appeal was a factor which contributed to the unfairness of the dismissal; see also *McConvey v British Steel Corporation* [1974] IRLR 196. Where larger employers have been involved, the tribunals have looked to see whether there is a level of management above that which took the step of dismissing the employee to whom the appeal could have been made: see *Davison*'s case, above, where the employer was a family concern with 250 employees and the failure to provide Davison with a right of appeal was found to contribute to a finding of unfair dismissal.

In practice, there may be difficulties in giving the employee an opportunity to appeal in particular where small businesses are involved. In *Tiptools Ltd v Curtis* [1973] IRLR 276. Curtis was dismissed by the managing director of a family company with some 45 employees. In finding the dismissal unfair, the tribunal relied upon the fact that the employee had been given no right of appeal against the imposition of dismissal. The NIRC overturned the tribunal's decision. It found that provisions of the code suggesting an appeal were designed for larger companies 'where the responsibility for dismissal may lie with a level of management below the top management'. Although it was desirable that there should be a right of appeal against dismissal, in this case this was clearly impracticable since the decision to dismiss was taken by the highest level of management within the company. The tribunal's suggestion that the employer should provide a right of appeal to an outside body was not accepted.

Where there is an appeal procedure it should conform with the code's guidance. In *Sewell and Francis v Ford Motor Co Ltd* [1975] IRLR 25, the appeal procedure provided that 'The appeal should be made in the first instance to the authority who administered the disciplinary action, rather than to any lower level of supervision.' The tribunal found this was not an appeal, but rather a reconsideration of the decision by those who had taken it. It did not accord with the guidelines laid down in the code and the provisions for appeal were sufficiently defective to make the dismissal unfair: but compare *Flude v Post Office* [1975] IRLR 330.

Where there is an appeal procedure, it should be followed and a failure to follow it may result in the dismissal being held unfair. In *Johnson Matthey Metals Ltd v Harding* [1978] IRLR 248, the EAT upheld the tribunal's criticism of the employer's appeals procedure. The manager, who considered an appeal, had already discussed the matter with other members of management who were involved and on a preliminary view decided on dismissal before the appeal was heard. The EAT commented that:

people can form a preliminary view and still be relied on to change it upon consideration; but if the situation is that the person to whom resort is being had by way of an appeal has already made a preliminary decision, it is surely desirable that that fact should be made known to the person under consideration for dismissal and to his adviser; and it is surely even more important that the person finally considering it . . . should fully inform himself of the whole circumstances.

Where the body hearing the appeal fails to consider the case properly, then the dismissal may be unfair: *McCabe v Ninth District Council of the County of Lanark* [1973] IRLR 75. However, compare *Rowe v Radio Rentals* [1982] IRLR 177.

On appeal the employee should be given an opportunity to state his case and, depending on the circumstances, either be given copies of statements, or when statements are not available the employer should ensure that the case against the employee is outlined orally to him: *Bentley Engineering Co Ltd v Mistry* [1979] ICR 47. Again on an appeal it is important that the employee knows what is alleged against him and the case he has to meet. In addition the employee may be given an opportunity to question any protagonist. Failure to give the employee the opportunity to state his case may lead to a finding that the dismissal is unfair.

Where the employee has a right of appeal against his dismissal his failure to exercise that right cannot be seen as an acquiescence by the employee in his dismissal: see *Chrystie v Rolls Royce (1971) Ltd* [1976] IRLR 336 and *Hoover Ltd v Forde* [1980] ICR 239.

However, as is clear from the decision in *Tipton*'s case, above, not every failure to provide an appeal, even where one could be provided, will be fatal. The right may be dispensed with where at the time of dismissal the employer reasonably decides there is no utility in an appeal and it could not have altered the outcome: see *Polkey*'s case, above. In *Gardiner v Newport CBC* [1974] IRLR 262, a lecturer was dismissed following a conviction for gross indecency. The employee had no right of appeal. The tribunal found the procedure unsatisfactory because there was no right of appeal when this was feasible, but in the circumstances of this case the procedure was fair because any reasonable employer would have dismissed, even if a right of appeal had been given. In *Tovey v F and F Robinson (Stockton-on-Tees) Ltd* [1975] IRLR 139, the employee, a lorry driver, was dismissed because he refused to work overtime hours unless he was paid for them, although other lorry drivers had accepted this position. It was held that the employer's failure to give the employee a right of appeal where this was possible did not render the dismissal unfair because a right of appeal would not have altered the employee's position. The employee was 'indicating that he was not prepared to abide by the terms . . . which covered all the other employees at the respondent's place of work'.

In *Rowe v Radio Rentals Ltd* [1982] IRLR 177, the EAT held that there was no conflict between the employer's disciplinary procedure and the rules of natural justice where the person who heard the appeal had been informed of the decision to dismiss before it took place, and further because the person who actually took the decision to dismiss was present at the appeal. He took no part in the appeal.

Disciplinary bodies should not become entrammelled in the net of legal procedure; provided that they have acted fairly and justly there can be no complaints. It recognised that it will often be difficult in practice to separate the 'dismisser' from the person hearing the appeal. Each case will depend on its own facts, and if it appears that the disciplinary body has acted unfairly or unjustly and it has prejudiced the employee, then the dismissal may be unfair: compare *Johnson Matthey Metals Ltd v Harding* [1978] IRLR 248, and see above.

Where the employer's disciplinary and dismissals procedure is agreed with the union concerned and entitles either party to call witnesses although neither is obliged to do so, the dismissal will not be unfair merely because the employer does not call witnesses and the committee which hears the appeal does not insist on the relevant witnesses being called by the employer: *East Hertfordshire DC v Boyten* [1977] IRLR 347.

There is no rule of natural justice that an employee must be present at an appeal when his representative is present: see *Pirelli General Cable Works Ltd v Murray* [1979] IRLR 90.

The fact that the employee's post has been advertised before the appeal does not necessarily mean that the appeal has been prejudiced: *Lambsdale v Her Majesty's Stationery Office* [1975] IRLR 239.

The fact that the right of appeal arises after the effective date of termination does not mean that the tribunal is precluded from considering a failure to allow an appeal in deciding the reasonableness of the dismissal: *Rank Xerox (UK) Ltd v Goodchild* [1979] IRLR 185. See **2**, above.

Finally, it should be noted that the existence of an appeals procedure does not justify the employer in dispensing with the obligation to consult the employee and invite an explanation from him when contemplating dismissal: *Qualcast (Wolverhampton) Ltd v Ross (1); Ross v Qualcast (Wolverhampton) Ltd (2)* [1979] IRLR 98.

5.7 The right of representation

The 1977 code provides that the employee should be given 'the right to be accompanied' either by a trade union representative or by a fellow employee of his choice: para 10(*g*).

The opportunity to be represented may be important. The employer's procedure may provide for representation. If in such circumstances the employee is denied representation either by a union representative or by a professional representative or by an 'employee representative', this may be an important factor, particularly where the employee is accused of a serious offence, in deciding whether or not a dismissal is fair or unfair: see *Rank Xerox (UK) Ltd v Goodchild*, above.

Where representation is allowed and the representative is present throughout the whole of the disciplinary hearing but the employee is not, and is only present when he gives his evidence, it is not contrary to the rules of natural justice if the employer proceeds in the absence of the employee, but in the presence of his representative: *Pirelli General Cable Works Ltd v Murray* [1979] IRLR 190; see also *Gray Dunn and Co Ltd v Edwards* [1980] IRLR 23.

Likewise, there is no rule of natural justice that the employee must be present at an appeal if his representative is present.

Where there has been a failure by the employer to allow the employee to be represented it does not necessarily mean that the dismissal will be unfair. Dismissal may be fair even though the employee is not represented if, at the time of the dismissal, the employer reasonably decides representation would be futile and would not have altered the decision to dismiss. It is for the tribunal to decide this and whether the dismissal was fair in all the circumstances.

5.8 Disciplinary action involving trade union officials

The 1972 code recommended that where shop stewards were involved no disciplinary action should be taken until the employer had consulted the full-time official of the union. This has been widened by the 1977 code. The 1977 code provides 'disciplinary action against a trade union official can lead to a serious dispute if it is seen as an attack on the union's functions. Although normal disciplinary standards should apply to their conduct as employees, no disciplinary action beyond an oral warning should be taken until the circumstances of the case have been discussed with a senior trade union representative or full-time official': para 15(*b*) of the 1977 code.

Some assistance from the way in which these provisions of the 1977 code will be interpreted can be gained from cases decided under the 1972 code.

In *Fowler v Cammell Laird (Shipbuilders) Ltd* [1973] IRLR 72, Fowler was convicted of theft from a fellow employee's car parked in the employer's car park in working hours. The employer's policy of instantly dismissing employees for dishonest acts, although not communicated to the employees in writing, had been made known to them. The employee's summary dismissal was not unfair. The tribunal found: 'The requirement as to discussion with a full-time official of the union in the case of the shop steward who is the subject of disciplinary procedure obviously does not contemplate the type of case with which we are concerned—so the fact that the applicant was a shop steward is irrelevant in this context.'

Similarly, in *Donald Cook and Son Ltd v Carter* [1977] IRLR 88 a shop steward was dismissed in accordance with the employer's disciplinary procedure. He had been issued with warnings in connection with bad language on two occasions, poor performance on two occasions and with leaving his place of work. The dismissal was found fair, even though there was no reference to a full-time union official.

In *CA Parsons and Co Ltd v McLoughlin* [1978] IRLR 65, a shop steward was dismissed following fighting with another employee. No reference was made to a full-time union official.

However, even where a dismissal is for a reason unconnected with the employee's union activities, it may well be advisable for the employer to consult with the full-time union official. Thus, in *Donnelly v London Brick Co Ltd* [1974] IRLR 331, the dismissal of a shop steward without consulting the full-time union official did not make the dismissal automatically unfair, however the tribunal held that if the full-time union official had been involved the decision to dismiss would not have been taken. Therefore, the decision was unfair.

In *British Labour Pump Co Ltd v Byrne* [1979] IRLR 94, a shop steward was dismissed because of his involvement in theft from the employer. The dismissal was held unfair. A proper procedure had not been followed; there had not been sufficient regard to the employee's position as a shop steward, and a full-time official of the union had not been in attendance. All these factors led the tribunal to find the dismissal unfair. For instance, the presence of the full-time union official might have resulted in representations being made on the employee's behalf which could have led to a lesser penalty.

However, the decision of the EAT upholding the tribunal's decision suggests that strict observance of the code may not be essential in a case of this nature.

5.9 *Other provisions of the 1972 code*

Failure to follow other provisions of the 1972 code may have contributed to a finding of unfair dismissal. Although the 1972 code has been repealed the precedent of case law remains.

Under para 40 of the 1972 code employers must use their best endeavours to ensure reasonable job security. Thus, where the employee has been away ill for a short period and the employer dismisses him, and engages a replacement, the dismissal may be unfair because the employer has not had regard to the need for job security: see *Moore v Central Electricity Generating Board (Midland Region)* [1974] IRLR 296. Again, failure to follow the guidance on training contained in para 35 of the 1972 code may have led to or contributed to an unfair dismissal. See *Boobier v Johnsons Cleaners (Southern) Ltd* [1974] IRLR 329. See **5.2(c)**, above. However, the provisions of the 1972 code, other than those dealing with redundancies, which are considered in Chapter 8, figured only exceptionally in cases of unfair dismissal.

6 Substantive fairness

A dismissal may be unfair in all the circumstances because the employer has not followed a proper procedure. It may also be substantively unfair, because no reasonable employer would have dismissed for that reason in all the circumstances. Substantive unfairness may result from a defect in the procedure where, for instance, the employer fails to give the employee an opportunity to explain before the dismissal and does not know all the facts and he would not have dismissed had he known those facts. Substantive unfairness may exist independently of a defect in the procedure.

The tribunal must consider whether or not the employer has acted reasonably or unreasonably. The tribunal must consider what a reasonable employer would have done in the circumstances. If the employer has acted reasonably in all the circumstances the dismissal will be fair, notwithstanding the fact that the employee has also acted reasonably. The tribunal is not entitled to substitute its views as to what should have happened in a particular case for those of the employer where the employer has acted reasonably albeit that the tribunal would have reached a different conclusion. There may be a range of options open to the employer, several of which are reasonable: the question for the tribunal is whether the option of dismissal is reasonable; or putting it another way, 'was the employer's action within a band of reasonableness?' It is not possible to categorise the instances of substantive unfairness. It will depend upon the circumstances of each case. It is possible though to give some guidance.

6.1 Deficiencies in the employer's organisation

A dismissal may be substantively unfair because the employer has failed to provide the employee with adequate training: *Boobier v Johnsons Cleaners (Southern) Ltd* [1974] IRLR 329, see also *Welsh v Associated Steels and Tools Co Ltd* [1973] IRLR 111; or where the employer has failed to provide a trained assistant: *Woodward v Bees-*

ton Boiler [1973] IRLR 7; or has failed to provide clerical help: *Cockcroft v Trendsetter Furniture Ltd* [1973] IRLR 6; or give proper instructions: *Newlands v J Howard and Co Ltd* [1973] IRLR 9; or has failed to define the management responsibilities: *Burrows v Ace Caravan Co (Hull) Ltd* [1972] IRLR 4.

6.2 Alternative vacancies

The employer's obligation to provide alternative employment where there is a redundancy situation or where the reason for dismissal is sickness is considered separately. Where the reason for dismissal is conduct or capability the dismissal may be unfair if the employer fails to consider whether there is an alternative vacancy. This obligation may be particularly relevant if the dismissal is a borderline case: *Henderson v Masson Scott Thrissell Engineering Ltd* [1974] IRLR 98. The obligation may arise where the employee has been convicted of a driving offence and has lost his licence, but there are other duties which he can perform: see *Fearn v Tayford Motor Co Ltd* [1975] IRLR 336. The obligation was held to exist where the employee was unable to get on with customers: *Scott Packing and Warehousing Co Ltd v Paterson* [1978] IRLR 166, or where the employee has been over-promoted: *Kendrick v Concrete Pumping Ltd* [1975] IRLR 83. In the majority of cases the circumstances will be such that the employer is not under any obligation to offer the employee alternative employment: see *Fitzpatrick v Holbourn Eaton (Manufacturing) Co Ltd* [1973] IRLR 17, and *Bevan Harris Ltd (t/a The Clyde Leather Co) v Gair* [1981] IRLR 520.

6.3 Long service

The length of the employee's service and any past lapses are matters which should be taken into account by the tribunal: see *Johnson Matthey Metals Ltd v Harding* [1978] IRLR 248, where Harding's length of service contributed to a finding of unfair dismissal. It was coupled with a failure by the employer to give sufficient consideration to the employee's misconduct, and to carry out a proper investigation. Long service with an employer may lead to a finding that a dismissal which would otherwise be fair is substantively unfair. Although at first glance it may seem that an employee with a short period of service should be more leniently treated than one with a longer period of service who may be presumed to know better, there is support for the view that weight must be given to the employee's length of service—the longer the service the more favourable the treatment that should be given to the employee, especially if it is coupled with other factors: see *O'Brien v Boots Pure Drug Co* [1973] IRLR 261, and see also *Sewell and Francis v Ford Motor Co Ltd* [1975] IRLR 25. However, in *AEI Cables Ltd v McLay* [1980] IRLR 84, the Court of Session held:

The length of service . . . is . . . in many cases a relevant consideration but . . . it would be wholly unreasonable to expect an employer who has been deceived by an employee in the way in which the respondent deceived the appellants, to have any further confidence in him and to continue him in his employ. The quality of the respondent's conduct was . . . of such gravity that the length of his prior service was of no materiality.

See *British Leyland (UK) Ltd v Swift* [1981] IRLR 91. In *Tiptools Ltd v Curtis* [1973] IRLR 276, Curtis, who had 19 years' service was dismissed for a lack of capability. The NIRC found: 'One would surely have expected that some special consideration would have been given to a man who had been employed with the company from the age of 15.' See also *Scottish Midland Co-operative Society Ltd v Cullion* [1991] IRLR 261.

In the case of a probationary employee a higher onus is placed upon the employer to assess and help the employee before he is dismissed. However, because an employee is on probation it does not mean that the employer is not able to dismiss the employee. In marginal cases it is easier to dismiss an employee on probation than one who is not: see *Hamblin v London Borough of Ealing* [1975] IRLR 354; *Bowden v Post Office* [1976] IRLR 169.

6.4 Consistency of the employer

A dismissal may be unfair because the employer has not acted consistently in following a particular course of action. Substantive fairness is closely allied with following a proper procedure and the need to give the employee adequate warning of any new standard of conduct or capability required: *Hackwood v Seal (Marine) Ltd* [1973] IRLR 17, where the employer had overlooked Hackwood's temperamental behaviour for two and a half years, and then dismissed her after she had been asked on three occasions to show another machinist how to undertake certain work and she refused. The dismissal was unfair because in the past the employer tolerated such temperamental outbursts. She was entitled to be warned that there was a change in attitude.

In *Field v Leslie and Godwin Ltd* [1972] IRLR 12, the employer asked the employee for an assurance that he would be returning to work in the near future following an absence due to ill-health. He gave the assurance but was dismissed unfairly. The employer could not seek an assurance and having received it dismiss. It was inconsistent.

In *Haspell v Rostron and Johnson Ltd* [1976] IRLR 50, Haspell was dismissed because she lacked capability, was prone to lateness and used the employer's telephone for personal calls. The employer gave her a reference which said 'her work has been completely satisfactory' and referred to her 'pleasant nature' and continued 'at all times she has been an agreeable member of the staff'. The tribunal pointed to the inconsistency and found that the employer could not 'blow hot and cold at one and the same time'.

For the position as to the employer's consistency in applying disciplinary rules, see **4.2**, above.

6.5 Other instances

Most of the cases of substantive unfairness do not fall within any of the foregoing categories. Some further examples will help illustrate the nature of substantive unfairness. In *Morrish v Henlys (Folkestone) Ltd* [1973] ICR 482, Morrish's dismissal because he refused to follow a common practice of falsifying records to cover up any deficiencies was held not reasonable in all the circumstances.

In *Wicks v Charles A Smethurst Ltd* [1973] IRLR 327, Wicks's dismissal because he refused to go to Newry and Belfast unless his employer provided insurance against death or injury was unfair. The employer did not even examine the problem before dismissing.

In *Grace v Harehills Working Men's Club and Institute* [1974] IRLR 68, it was held not reasonable in all the circumstances to dismiss Grace who had left his wife and who had formed a sexual liaison with a young girl who was living with him in the employer's premises. It might have become reasonable to do so, but it was not reasonable at the time of the dismissal.

In *Beard v The Governors of St Joseph's School* [1979] IRLR 144, Beard was engaged as a temporary assistant teacher of needlework. It was then decided to make a permanent appointment to the post. Beard applied but the employer overlooked the fact that she was qualified for the post, and she was not interviewed and was dismissed. The employer had acted unreasonably and the dismissal was unfair.

In *Kent County Council v Gilham and Others* [1985] IRLR 18, the employees were school-dinner ladies. Because of government restrictions on expenditure the local authority decided to effect savings in the education budget. The national conditions governing the school-dinner ladies provided that they should be paid half pay when they were not working in the school holidays and holiday pay was calculated on a basis that they worked 52 weeks in a year whereas in fact they only work 39 weeks. The local authority decided that they should only be paid for the 39 weeks they worked and their holiday pay should be reduced by calculating it on 39 weeks and not 52 weeks. Following negotiations the authority wrote to all the employees terminating their existing contracts of employment and offering them employment on the new terms and conditions. The Court of Appeal held that the decision of the tribunal that the employees' dismissals were unfair was not perverse. The Court of Appeal found that the tribunal had to balance the economic difficulties faced by the council on the one hand against the fact that the council had departed from the terms of the national agreement and had not deferred a decision until the matter had been considered at national level on the other. Since it was important for good industrial relations that the national agreement should not be breached unilaterally, it could not be said that no reasonable tribunal would have found that the dismissals were unfair.

Conversely, dismissals have been found substantively fair in the following cases.

In *Whitlow v Alkanet Construction Ltd* [1975] IRLR 321, it was held reasonable to dismiss Whitlow who had had sexual intercourse with the wife of the chief executive of the company when he had been invited to her home to work. This was so even though he had been subjected to temptation few men could resist.

In *James v Cory Distribution* [1977] IRLR 248, it was held reasonable to dismiss an employee who asked a fellow female employee, 'Is he shagging you or something?' because it was 'an imputation of promiscuity against [another employee] couched in offensive language'.

In *Saunders v Scottish National Camps Association Ltd* [1980] IRLR 174, the EAT held that the employers had acted reasonably in all the circumstances in dismissing a homosexual. The tribunal had not imposed their own criterion but had adopted that which they believed a reasonable employer would have adopted—that the employment of a homosexual should be restricted when required to work with children. This case was confirmed by the Court of Session [1981] IRLR 277.

In *Richmond Precision Engineering Ltd v Pearce* [1985] IRLR 179, the EAT found that Pearce's dismissal was fair when he refused to accept changes in his terms and conditions of employment which would bring him into line with other employees holding similar positions, notwithstanding the fact that he would be worse off under the new terms. The tribunal has to undertake the task of weighing the advantages to the employer against the disadvantages to the employee. However, this is merely one of the questions which has to be considered in deciding whether or not the employer has acted reasonably or unreasonably in all the circumstances, having regard to equity and the substantial merits of the case. Because there are disadvantages to the employee it does not mean that the employer has acted unreasonably: see also *Chubb Fire Security Ltd v Harper* [1983] IRLR 311.

6.6 Substantive reasonableness and the interests of the business

The interests of the business have already been considered in connection with procedural fairness: see *James v Waltham Holy Cross UDC* [1973] ICR 398.

The interests and needs of the business may make a dismissal substantively fair. In *Treganowan v Robert Knee and Co Ltd* [1975] ICR 405, there was a clash of personalities involving Treganowan and the other girls in the office where she worked, for which she was to blame.

There was a lack of co-operation between the girls and, after warnings, the employee was dismissed. The tribunal found, 'The atmosphere in this office had become so tense that it was unbearable and was seriously affecting the respondent's business.' The dismissal was fair. The employer was entitled to have regard to the continued interests of the business. However, where there is a breakdown in the working relationship and the employer fails to do all he can to see whether an improvement can be effected in the relationship, the dismissal may be unfair: *Turner v Vestric Ltd* [1981] IRLR 23.

In *Pascoe v Hallen and Medway* [1975] IRLR 116, Pascoe, a registered disabled worker, suffered with asthma. She had considerable periods away from work, but more importantly her attacks of asthma caused disruption during working hours and made her temperamental: 'the consequences of her ill-health were having a disrupting effect on [the employer's] factory'. Her dismissal was fair.

In *Mordecai v Jacob Beatus Ltd* [1975] IRLR 170, Mordecai refused to accept a transfer to a neighbouring factory pursuant to the provisions of a flexibility agreement negotiated between the employer and the union. The employer considered that it was essential that employees should accept the need for flexibility. The tribunal held that the dismissal was fair: 'the respondents were reasonably insisting on a term in the contract of employment, very necessary to them in running their business'.

In *Ali v Tillotsons Containers Ltd* [1975] IRLR 272, Ali was given an oral warning in April 1973 which was followed by a written warning in February 1974 advising him that if his attendance did not improve he would be dismissed. His absence was caused by poor health. After the written warning, his attendance improved, and management decided to review the matter after a further six months. In October 1974 the improvement was not sufficient, and the employer dismissed the employee. The tribunal found the dismissal fair, because the employer had to incur cost in hiring labour to replace Ali and such labour lacked the skills to achieve the output which would have resulted if Ali was more regularly present. Further, because Ali was a member of a team which was entitled to a bonus, the other members of that team were complaining to the employer that it was affecting the bonuses they earned.

In *Hollister v National Farmers Union* [1979] ICR 542, Hollister, a group secretary, was given new contractual terms following a reorganisation. He objected to the new financial provisions because he believed they were inadequate. The reason for his dismissal was some other substantial reason, namely a reorganisation of the employer's business which was essential for business reasons. The Court of Appeal accepted the decision of the EAT that a dismissal might well be justified where there was some sound business reason for reorganisation as in this case. Since Hollister would not accept the new contract the only sensible thing to do was to terminate his contract. The Court of Appeal did not accept that it would only be sufficient to justify the dismissal of the employee where he does not agree to reorganisation if the effect of his failure to agree would bring the whole business to a standstill. The court referred to *Ellis v Brighton Co-operative Society Ltd* [1976] IRLR 419, where the EAT suggested this might be the test. The Court of Appeal found in *Hollister*'s case that this test was too restrictive.

In *Genower v Ealing, Hammersmith and Hounslow Area Health Authority* [1980] IRLR 297, the EAT followed the decision in *Hollister*'s case, above. It found that a reorganisation or restructure of a business may well be some other substantial reason, even if the alternative to taking the course of action proposed by the employers is not that the business would come to a standstill but there would be some serious effect upon the business. In the circumstances of this case the employer was justified in moving the employee upon a reorganisation. However, in *Evans v Elementa Holdings Ltd* [1982] IRLR 143, the EAT found Evans's dismissal because of his persistent refusal to accept a new contract of employment which involved new and substantial obligations to work overtime to be unfair. The employer sought to impose the new contract because of the commercial need to rationalise the contract of employment. The EAT considered it was reasonable for Evans to have declined the new terms so that it was unreasonable for the employer to have dismissed him. The EAT was also much influenced by the fact that there was no need to change the provisions as to working overtime from a voluntary basis to a mandatory requirement.

An employee may work for a rival firm in his spare time or set up in competition with the employer either on his own account or with a competitor. The first problem was considered in *Nova Plastics Ltd v Froggatt* [1982] IRLR 146, where Froggatt was engaged by Nova Plastics Ltd as an odd-job man. He went to work for a rival company in his spare time. He was dismissed. The EAT upheld the decision of the tribunal that the dismissal was unfair. The EAT held that the tribunal were entitled to conclude that the nature of the work which the employee did for the rival company did not contribute seriously to any competition. It did not accept that there is a general implied term that 'an employer is entitled to expect from an employee total involvement in his employer's business, even outside normal working hours, and that any form of work done for a competitor, however small, must be regarded as a breach of trust and contrary to the implied term of loyal service'. The EAT accepted that if employment in employees' spare time is a breach of trust or of an implied term of loyalty then the dismissal might well be fair.

The second problem was considered by the EAT in *Laughton and Hawley v Bapp Industrial Supplies Ltd* [1986] IRLR 245. It referred to the decision of the NIRC in *Harris and Russell Ltd v Slingsby* [1973] IRLR 221. The NIRC held:

This court . . . would regard it as a wholly insufficient reason to dismiss a man, that he was merely seeking employment with a competitor, unless it could be shown that there were reasonably solid grounds for supposing that he was doing so in order to abuse his confidential position and information with his present employers. In the nature of things, when a man changes employment, it is more likely he will be seeking fresh employment with someone in the same line of business and therefore, a competitor of his present employers.

In *Laughton and Hawley*'s case, the EAT found that the tribunal had erred in holding that the employees' intention to set up in competition with the employer was in breach of the implied contractual duty of loyalty to the employer and the employees were therefore guilty of gross misconduct.

It held that:

An employee with experience in a particular industry who is intending to leave, whether to join a competitor as an employee or to set up in competition on his own account, commits no breach of contract in doing so unless either there is a specific term of his contract to that effect which does not fall foul of the doctrine against restraint of trade, or he is intending to use the confidential information of his employer otherwise than for the benefit of his employer. In general an employer is not entitled to protect himself against competition on the part of a former employee. The employee may in the course of his employment have acquired additional skills and knowledge of the trade in which he had been employed with the result that he is a more formidable competitor upon the termination of his service, but that additional skill and knowledge belong to him and their exercise cannot be lawfully restrained by the employer. It is only the trade secrets and other confidential information of the employer that the employee is not entitled to use or disclose. Not every piece of information which the employer regards as confidential will be protected by the court. The limits on the scope of confidential information have recently been expounded by the Court of Appeal in *Faccenda Chicken Ltd v Fowler* [1986] IRLR 69.

The EAT accepted that:

if at the time of dismissal the employer knew, or genuinely believed, on reasonable grounds that they were compiling confidential information such as by making lists of customers, or even memorising such lists, for use after their employment had ceased, then the employer could dismiss them for breaches of the implied term. The implied term was the duty or fidelity on the part of the employees. But in the circumstances of this case there was no such evidence.

In *Cook v Thomas Linnell and Sons Ltd* [1977] ICR 770, the EAT commented, 'It is important that the operation of the legislation in relation to unfair dismissal should not impede employers unreasonably in the efficient management of their business, which must be in the interest of all.'

Chapter 7

Dismissal for Sickness or Injury

When an employee is absent because of sickness or injury, his employer may wish to dismiss him because the employee's absence is incompatible with the employer's operational requirements. Again the employee's ill-health may raise doubts in the employer's mind as to his suitability for continued employment. Paragraph 40 of the 1972 code of practice required management, in so far as it is consistent with operational efficiency and the success of the undertaking, to provide stable employment including reasonable job security for employees absent through sickness. Thus, where the employee has been away ill for a short period, and the employer dismisses him and engages a replacement, the dismissal may be unfair because the employer has not had regard to the need for job security: see *Moore v Central Electricity Generating Board (Midland Region)* [1974] IRLR 296. Paragraph 41 required management, where practicable, to provide sick pay schemes. In considering the fairness of a dismissal by reason of sickness or injury tribunals have had regard to the guidelines laid down in para 40 of the 1972 code. In addition, some of the other provisons of the 1972 code and the 1977 code of practice may be relevant. Tribunals have tailored both the codes in cases of sickness and laid down practical requirements. It is desirable, if not essential, that in the employer's procedures there should be some provision for dealing with absences for sickness or injury; the employer's obligation and the employee's rights. Although the 1972 code has been repealed the precedents remain.

1 The dismissal

Frustration of the contract of employment has been considered in Chapter 3. In cases of sickness or injury it is relevant to enquire whether the contract still subsists so that there can be a dismissal. Under the doctrine of frustration, the contract of employment may be brought to an end by operation of law independently of any action or intention on the part of the employer or the employee.

227

1.1 The reason

Sickness is a reason related to the employee's capability: s 57(2)(*a*) of the EP(C)A 1978. The onus is upon the employer to establish the reason.

In *Shook v London Borough of Ealing* [1986] IRLR 46, Shook, a residential care officer, had a history of back trouble but when she was medically examined for the position she was certified as being fit. Within a few weeks of starting work she suffered with back trouble. She was then appointed as a residential social worker and allocated to a home for handicapped children. After three years at the home she again suffered with back trouble and was away from work for some eight months and then her employment was terminated. It was contended on Shook's behalf that in deciding whether or not the reason was one relating to her capability the tribunal had to 'look at the whole range of work not only being performed by the employee under the employment contract but which . . . she might lawfully be required to do . . .' Since Shook might potentially have been required to carry out a very wide range of activities, it had to be shown that she was incapacitated from performing every such activity if the employer was to discharge the burden of establishing the reason for her dismissal. The EAT held:

the reason must *relate* to the capability for performing the work of the relevant kind . . . The matter thus has to be looked at as an exercise in relation when one is dealing with questions of incapability. The Industrial Tribunal in the present case decided that the medical grounds leading to Miss Shook's dismissal constituted a reason which related to her capability for performing work of the kind which she was employed to do under her contract. However widely that contract is construed, her disabilities related to the performance of her duties thereunder even though it may not have affected her performance of all of them.

Therefore the tribunal's conclusion that the dismissal fell within s 57(2)(*a*) was correct in law.

However, in *Grootcon (UK) Ltd v Keld* [1984] IRLR 302, the employer was unable to establish that the reason for the employee's dismissal was a lack of capability. Keld, a plater on a North Sea Oil rig owned by British Petroleum Development Ltd, sustained a knee injury in the course of his work and was sent home three days before his tour of duty was due to end. His own doctor advised him he would be fit for duty at the end of his normal period of leave. The company telephoned him and told him that he was being made redundant, but then wrote to him telling him that the medical department of British Petroleum Development Ltd considered that he was not fit for duty and he would not be allowed to return to the rig. The EAT accepted that there was no medical evidence oral or written as to the employee's condition and therefore the employer could not establish the reason.

1.2 Fairness

In addition where the dismissal is for sickness, as in the case of any other dismissal which is not automatically unfair, the tribunal must be satisfied that the dismissal is fair under s 57(3) of the EP(C)A 1978.

Before s 57(3) was amended by s 56 of the Employment Act (EA) 1980 the burden of proof was placed on the employer. This is no longer the case. In *(1) Abbotts and (2) Standley v Wesson-Glynwed Steels Ltd* [1982] IRLR 51, the EAT held that the effect of s 6 of the EA 1980 was to neutralise the burden of proof so that it affects which way round the tribunal has to look at the problem at the time of the hearing. While it is not wholly clear what the EAT had in mind, in practice the change has not made any significant difference save that in some cases the employer may now succeed whereas previously he would not because he could not discharge the burden of proof placed upon him.

The general principles relating to reasonableness which are considered in Chapter 6 apply equally to dismissals by reason of ill-health. This chapter considers those additional matters which are relevant to dismissals by reason of ill-health.

What is reasonable conduct on the part of the employer where the reason for the dismissal is ill-health depends upon the circumstances of each case: see *Harman v Flexible Lamps Ltd* [1980] IRLR 418. Thus, it is not possible to lay down a period after which it will be fair for the employer to dismiss the employee. In *Chadwick v Rochdale Brick Co (1929) Ltd* [1972] IRLR 52, Chadwick's after 16 years' service following an absence of 3 weeks coupled with a request to work fixed hours for 3 to 4 weeks following his absence was unfair. In *Taylor v CG Southcott & Co Ltd* [1972] IRLR 78, dismissal after 6 months' absence for sickness after a period of nearly 7 years' employment was unfair. Prior to this period of absence Taylor had been absent on several occasions through her ill-health and the ill-health of her husband. However, in *Bowden v Post Office* [1976] IRLR 169 51½ days' absence in 1 year due mainly to illness where Bowden had been employed on a trial basis was held to be sufficient to justify dismissal. It was the employer's case that the employee's pattern of work is shown in the first 12 months of employment and that the absences were likely to continue, a view strengthened by the fact that he played rugby league and about half his absences were caused by injuries sustained in this sport.

It will not be fair to dismiss an employee because of a risk of illness in the future unless his employment is such that the risk makes it unsafe for the employee to continue in the job: see *Converfoam (Darwen) Ltd v Bell* [1981] IRLR 195. Again where the ill-health of one employee is a source of danger to his fellow employees it may be reasonable for the employer to dismiss: see *Harper v National Coal*

Board [1980] IRLR 260; see also *Jeffries v BP Tanker Co Ltd* [1974] IRLR 260 and *Singh-Deu v Chloride Metals Ltd* [1976] IRLR 56.

The employer's arrangements for sickness pay are not an indication of the length of time which an employee may be away from work due to ill-health. If the employer dismisses the employee during a period when, under his contract of employment, he is entitled to receive sickness pay, the dismissal will not necessarily be unfair. See *Coulson v Felixstowe Dock and Railway Co* [1975] IRLR 11. However, in *Hardwick v Leeds AHA* [1975] IRLR 319, it was found unfair to dismiss an employee whose entitlement to sick pay has been exhausted. See also *Kerr v Atkinson Vehicles (Scotland) Ltd* [1974] IRLR 36.

In deciding whether it is reasonable in all circumstances to dismiss an employee because of sickness or injury the tribunal has to consider s 57(3) of the EP(C)A 1978. The law is contained in that section and nowhere else. It has to consider whether or not dismissal was within the parameters of reasonableness. It cannot substitute its view for that of the employer. A failure to consider the factors enumerated in *Marshall v Harland and Wolff Ltd* [1972] ICR 101, which fall to be considered in deciding whether or not the contract has been frustrated does not mean that the tribunal has misdirected itself in reaching its decision. These factors are not necessarily relevant in deciding whether or not it is reasonable to dismiss an employee by reason of ill-health: see *Tan v Berry Bros and Rudd Ltd* [1974] ICR 586.

In *Spencer v Paragon Wallpapers Ltd* [1977] ICR 301, Spencer had been absent from work for two months and was likely to remain absent for another four to six weeks. He was dismissed and the tribunal found the dismissal was fair. On appeal, it was held that where an employee was dismissed through ill-health, the reasonableness of the dismissal will depend upon the circumstances of the case. 'The basic question which has to be determined in every case is whether, in all the circumstances, the employer can be expected to wait any longer and, if so, how much longer?' In deciding this, the tribunal has to consider the nature of the illness, the likely length of the continuing absence, the need of the employers to have the work done which the employee was engaged to do and the other circumstances generally. The tribunal has to maintain a balance between the need of the employer to carry on his business and the employee's need to return to work following a recovery. The EAT found that the questions as to whether the contract has been frustrated and whether dismissal for sickness is reasonable in the circumstances are distinct. There may be an overlap between the criteria to be applied in answering these questions, but the criteria are not identical.

The more important the position held by the employee the more likely it will be that a dismissal will be fair, even after a short period of absence. Tribunals recognise that temporary replacements of key employees are not usually acceptable or suitable.

There may be a provision in the contract of employment which provides for the dismissal of an employee who is frequently absent because of ill-health or which provides for the dismissal of an employee after a relatively short spell of absence where the robust health of the employee is essential for the proper performance of the employer's business: see cases such as *Leonard v Fergus and Haynes Civil Engineering Ltd* [1979] IRLR 235 and *Taylorplan Catering (Scotland) Ltd v McInally* [1980] IRLR 53. Where good health is important for the employer's business it is sensible for the employer to make that abundantly clear to the employee. This may well help the employer when it comes to the question of reasonableness.

Again, where it is clear from the evidence that the employee will be unlikely to cope in the future with the work, dismissal even after a short period of absence is likely to be fair.

Other factors may also be relevant in deciding whether or not the employer has acted reasonably in dismissing the employee. It may be reasonable to dismiss an employee where her illness has a disruptive effect upon other employees as in *Pascoe v Hallen and Medway* [1975] IRLR 116, where Pascoe was a registered disabled employee who suffered with severe asthma, and who required hospitalisation for asthma and depression. Again it may be fair to dismiss where absence imposes a considerable stain upon other employees: see *Ali v Tillotsons Containers Ltd* [1975] IRLR 272. Where at the time the employee is taken on it is known that he suffers with a disability, the employer can expect an increased level of absence. The obligations imposed upon the employer who takes on an employee in such circumstances may be increased: see *Kerr v Atkinson Vehicles (Scotland) Ltd* [1974] IRLR 36. Where the employee is a registered disabled worker the obligations imposed on the employer before dismissing the employee may be greater than in the case of an employee who is not disabled: see *Seymour v British Airways Board* [1983] IRLR 55 and s 9 of the Disabled Persons Employment Act 1944.

Illness arising out of the employee's employment   The employee's illness may result from his workplace. The employee's dismissal will not be unfair simply because ill-health results from the employment. This may arise out of an accident at work or where the employee is allergic to materials with which the employee comes into contact: see *Glitz v Watford Electric Co Ltd* [1979] IRLR 89. In *Jagdeo v Smiths Industries Ltd* [1982] ICR 47, Jagdeo was allergic to solder fumes. No other work was available and she was dismissed. However, as a result of negotiations attempts were made to overcome the allergy by the use of a mask and her dismissal was suspended. This proved to be unsuccessful and she was dismissed. However, before her dismissal took effect the employer was put on notice that the problem could have been overcome by the use of extractor fans. The tribunal found the dismissal was fair and the EAT remitted the case to the tribunal so that it could consider what response had been made by the company to that suggestion; it was a critical matter of fact which had not been considered by the tribunal in reaching its decision. While the case does not suggest that any greater burden is placed upon the employer not to dismiss the employee where the ill-health arises out of or in the course of the employee's employment, there is an obligation on the employer to ensure the health and safety of the employee and to act reasonably before dismissing the employee.

In *Rolls Royce Ltd v Walpole* [1980] IRLR 343, in the three years before Walpole's dismissal his absences averaged about 50 per cent. The company followed its internal procedure and since there was no reason to anticipate any improvement he was dismissed. The tribunal found the dismissal was unfair because the employee was not to blame as there was no up-to-date medical evidence. The EAT found that the decision of the tribunal was perverse and there was evidence upon which the tribunal could reach the conclusion that the dismissal fell within a range of reasonable responses on the part of the employer to Walpole's absenteeism record.

Where the employee is absent from work due to sickness there may be a range of possible reasonable responses on the part of the employer, one of which may be to dismiss the employee.

1.3 Warnings and consultations

In the early cases tribunals found that dismissal was unfair where the employer had not warned the employee that he was going to be dismissed because of his absence for sickness. The tribunals had in mind a warning akin to that given before the employee was dismissed for misconduct. They then expressed doubts about the need for warning. 'A warning would be irrelevant. The applicant could not help in that he was ill', held the tribunal in *Megennis v Stephen Austin and Sons Ltd* [1974] IRLR 357, and again 'persons cannot be warned to be well': *Case v Group 4 Total Security Ltd* [1974] IRLR 368. See also *Taylorplan Catering (Scotland) LTd v McInally* [1980] IRLR 53.

In *Spencer v Paragon Wallpapers Ltd* [1977] ICR 301, the EAT, when considering the need for warnings in dismissals for sickness, commented:

Obviously, the case of misconduct and the case of ill-health raise different considerations, but we are clearly of the view that an employee ought not to be dismissed on the grounds of absence due to ill-health without some communication being established between the employer and the employee before he is dismissed. The word 'warning', perhaps is not appropriate, for by its association with cases of misconduct it carries with it [the] suggestion that the employee is being required to change or improve his conduct. That is not the case where the absence is due to ill-health, and it is possible to imagine cases of ill-health where some damage could be done by a written warning unaccompanied by a more personal touch.

It held that what is required is a discussion between the employer and the employee so that the employer can ascertain the position.

The EAT expanded upon the need for discussion and consultation in *Patterson v Messrs Bracketts* [1977] IRLR 137. Patterson had been ill with a heart complaint and was given three months' sick leave on half pay. During that period he attended an office party where his behaviour convinced his employer that he was acting without due regard to his health, and they decided to dismiss him. A tribunal found the dismissal fair, but the EAT reversed the finding. It found the dismissal unfair because before dismissing the employee the employer had neither given careful consideration to the employee's health nor taken steps to ascertain all the facts. The tribunal said two steps should be taken prior to a dismissal. First, there should be discussion with the employee to ascertain the position; and secondly other steps should be taken by the employer to enable him to form a balanced view about the employee's health. The EAT considered that the employer must, where appropriate (and it usually will be appropriate), seek the employee's assistance in finding out the true medical position. It may be necessary to consult the employee's doctor, and in such a case the employee's permission must be obtained. If he refuses, the employer may ask him to be examined by the employer's own doctor, but he cannot be compelled to do so. If the employee is unwilling to co-operate the employer will have to make his decision on the basis of the information available to him. The lack of medical evidence may be prejudicial to the employee, but if the employer has done all it can reasonably do the employer should not be prejudiced by the employee's failure to co-operate.

The decisions in the earlier cases were further considered by the EAT in *East Lindsey DC v Daubney* [1977] ICR 566. Daubney, who was employed as principal assistant (building) surveyor, was dismissed because of ill-health. The employer had relied on a report of a district community physician who had been asked to state whether Daubney's health was such that he should be retired prematurely. The physician replied that Daubney 'is unfit to carry out the duties of his post and should be retired on the grounds of permanent ill-health'. On the basis of this report, Daubney was dismissed. However, the district community physician's conclusions were based upon the report of another doctor, Dr O'Hagan of the Lincolnshire Area Health Authority. This report was never before the Council although they knew of it. The tribunal found the dismissal was unfair because the employer had relied upon the general conclusions of the district community physician and had never obtained a full medical report. Further, the employee was dismissed without any form of consultation or communication. He was given no opportunity to provide and independent opinion.

The EAT upheld the decision of the tribunal. It did not accept that the employer should be required to obtain a full medical report. While the report of the district community physician verged on the inadequate, the employer might have been entitled to rely on it if he had consulted with the employee and given him an opportunity of discussing the position. The employer's decision to dismiss is not a medical one, but a decision to be taken in the light of medical evidence. In seeking medical evidence, the employer should have regard to the circumstances and ensure that proper advice is sought. If the advice is inadequate the employer may not be entitled to rely on it. However, the failure by the Council to consult with Daubney was a fatal one.

The EAT further held:

Unless there are wholly exceptional circumstances, before an employee is dismissed on the ground of ill health it is necessary that he should be consulted and the matter discussed with him, and that in one way or another steps should be taken by the employer to discover the true medical position. We do not propose to lay down detailed principles to be applied in such cases, for what will be necessary in one case may not be appropriate in another. But if in every case employers take such steps as are sensible according to the circumstances to consult the employee and to discuss the matter with him, and to inform themselves upon the true medical position, it will be found in practice that all that is necessary has been done. Discussions and consultations will often bring to light facts and circumstances of which the employers were unaware, and which will throw new light on the problem. Or the employee may wish to seek medical advice on his own account which, brought to the notice of the employers' medical advisers, will cause them to change their opinion. There are many possibilities. Only one thing is certain, and that is that if the employee is not consulted, and given an opportunity to state his case, an injustice may be done.

The need for consultation was described as 'well established' and as 'an elementary requirement of fairness' by the EAT in *Williamson v Alcan (UK) Ltd* [1978] ICR 104.

Where the employer has a medical report on which he intends to rely, there is no obligation on him 'to evaluate it as a layman in terms of medical expertise'. The employer is entitled to rely on it unless it is plainly erroneous: *Liverpool Area Health Authority (Teaching) Central and Southern District v Edwards* [1977] IRLR 471.

Where an employee is dismissed by reason of ill-health the employer does not have to decide, if there are conflicting medical reports, which one they will rely upon, because the employer does not have the expertise to weigh up the respective merits of the reports. The employer can rely upon medical advice. If the employer relies upon the advice of a medical expert who fails to investigate the matter properly the employer will be saddled with that expert's lack of investigation. Although they may proceed on the basis that they had reasonable grounds for believing the employee was unfit for work that belief must be based upon a proper investigation. The employer may be in difficulty in establishing that belief if there has been no proper investigation: *Ford Motor Company Ltd v Nawaz* [1987] IRLR 163.

Where the employer has obtained a medical report and has carried out consultations with the employee, he still has to make a decision in the light of the evidence whether to dismiss the employee. Provided he acts fairly in the light of the medical evidence available, he will avoid a finding of unfair dismissal.

Although the employer must consult with the employee, it has been suggested there is no obligation on him to make available to the employee confidential medical reports: *Crown Agents for Overseas Governments and Administration v Lawal* [1978] IRLR 542, but compare *Nawaz*, above.

The purpose of consultation with the employee must be borne in mind. It is to enable the situation to be assessed, to balance the employer's need to have the work done with the employee's need to recover his health, and to ensure that the employer takes proper steps to establish the true medical position.

The need for the employer to follow a proper procedure if the dismissal is to be fair has been emphasised in cases such as *Polkey v AE Dayton Services Ltd* [1988] ICR 142. See *A Links and Co Ltd v Rose* [1991] IRLR 353. However, if the tribunal is able to conclude that at the time of the dismissal the employer acted reasonably because of exceptional circumstances so that procedural steps which would normally have been appropriate would have been futile and could not have altered the decision to dismiss, and therefore could be dispensed with, the dismissal may be fair.

Where the employee is persistently absent for minor ailments so that his level of attendance is unacceptable, the employer should first of all review the attendance record and the reasons for it and, secondly, after the employee has been given an opportunity to make representations, assuming it is justified, should give the employee a warning that his level of attendance is unacceptable. If there is no adequate improvement in his record dismissal will normally be justified: See *International Sports Co Ltd v Thompson* [1980] IRLR 340 and *Rolls Royce Ltd v Walpole*, above.

Further guidance on the way to approach the dismissal of an employee with a poor attendance record due to intermittent illness is given in *Lynock v Cereal Packaging Ltd* [1988] IRLR 510. The EAT held that where there are intermittent periods of illness, each of which is unconnected, it is impossible to give a reasonable prognosis. While an employer may make enquiries there may be no obligation on him to do so because the results may produce nothing of assistance. Furthermore, the fact that at the time of dismissal the employee is fit will not render the dismissal unfair. In determining whether or not to dismiss an employee for intermittent periods of illness:

> The approach of an employer in this situation is, . . . one to be based on . . . sympathy, understanding and compassion. There is no principle that the mere fact that an employee is fit at the time of dismissal makes his dismissal unfair; one has to look at the whole history and the whole picture. Secondly, every case must depend upon its own facts, and provided that the approach is right, the factors which may prove important to an employer in reaching . . . a difficult decision, include perhaps some of the following—the nature of the illness; the likelihood of recurring or some other illness arising; the length of various absences and the spaces of good health between them; the need of the employer for the work done by the particular employee; the impact of the absences on others who work with the employee; the adoption and the carrying out of the policy; the important emphasis on a personal assessment in the ultimate decision and of course, the extent to which the difficulty of the situation and the position of the employer has been made clear to the employee so that the employee realises that the point of no return, the moment when the decision was ultimately being made may be approaching. These, we emphasise, are not cases for disciplinary approaches; these are for approaches of understanding . . .

Where the employee has frequent and persistent short-term absences it is always difficult for the employer to know whether the employee is genuinely ill or whether he is malingering or is guilty of some other misconduct. Where the employer suspects a warning should be given. Malingering is treated as essentially a matter of conduct.

Medical examination The employer's procedure or the employee's contract may provide for the employer or its doctor to obtain an independent medical report often from a specialist where there is doubt about the nature of the employee's illness or injury. Indeed from time to time employers have been criticised for relying upon a report of a general practitioner in reaching a decision to dismiss an employee particularly where there is doubt or uncertainty: see *Crampton v Dacorum Motors Ltd* [1975] IRLR 168. The employer may ask an employee to undergo a medical examination by a company doctor or a doctor or specialist nominated by the employer. Can an employer force an employee to submit to such an examination? In *Bliss v South East Thames Regional Health Authority* [1985] IRLR 308, Bliss was a consultant orthopaedic surgeon. The Court of Appeal held that in the absence of some relevant specific power in the employee's contract of employment, the employer has no general inherent power to require an employer to undergo a psychiatric examination. By analogy there is no general inherent power to require an employer to undergo any other form of examination. In *Bliss*'s case it was common ground that it was an implied term of his contract of employment that the employer was entitled to require him to undergo a medical examination if the employer had reasonable grounds for believing that he might be suffering from physical or mental disability which might cause harm to the patients, or adversely affect the quality of the treatment of the patients. This implied term depended very much upon the particular circumstances in *Bliss*'s case and it must not be taken as authority for the view that there is a general implied term in any employer's contract of employment that the employer can require the employee to undergo a medical examination. If the employee is asked by the employer to undergo a medical examination and unreasonably refuses, then the employer should point out to the employee the consequences of that refusal. If the employee still refuses to undergo a medical examination, then the employer who dismisses may well succeed in dismissing fairly if he has acted reasonably in all the circumstances on the evidence available to him, notwithstanding the fact that a further medical examination and the subsequent evidence in the form of a report, may have rendered it unfair for the employer to have dismissed.

Medical certificates In *International Sports Co Ltd v Thompson*, above, it was held that there is no rule of law which requires the employer to investigate the *bona fides* of the medical certificates issued. Although the employer is not required to establish the *bona fides* of the medical certificate the employer is entitled to go behind the sick note to discover whether or not his employees are engaged in activities which suggest they are fit for work: *Hutchinson v Enfield Rolling Mills Ltd* [1981] IRLR 318.

2 Employer's further obligations

There are two further problems for employers. First, are they obliged to find the employee a job elsewhere, and secondly, do they have to create a special job for the sick employee which he can manage to do?

In *Megennis v Stephen Austin & Sons Ltd* [1974] IRLR 357, it had been agreed with Megennis, a compositor's auxillary, that on his return to work following a period of illness, he should be employed as a storeman. However, before he returned to work, it was decided to dispense with the position of storeman, and he was dismissed. It was held that the dismissal was not unfair. There was no obligation on the employer to keep open another job for a sick employee which was outside the employee's contract of employment and which would not otherwise exist.

In *Case v Group 4 Total Security Ltd* [1974] IRLR 368, Case was absent from work with a heart condition. He was then certified as being 'perfectly fit for all ordinary office work or supervisory work but obviously shouldn't be expected to run after criminals, carry heavy weights or be exposed to sudden excessive physical strain'. The employer found these were vital elements in his job and he was dismissed. The tribunal found the dismissal fair because the employer was under no obligation to find other work for a sick employee. Even if there were such a requirement, on the facts of this particular case there was no job that Case could fill. Certainly the employer was not obliged to restructure the job which he was doing so that he could manage it, nor was he obliged to promote him to a higher position where he had more administration to carry out, nor to appoint him to a position for which he was not qualified. Equally, where the employee was required to have special physical and mental qualities for the job he was employed to do, there was no obligation on the employer to find the employee alternative employment suited to the employee's new state of health when that work was not available, in the sense of not being already in existence: *Leonard v Fergus and Haynes Civil Engineering Ltd* [1979] IRLR 235; *Taylorplan Catering (Scotland) Ltd v McInally* [1980] IRLR 53.

In *Merseyside and North Wales Electricity Board v Taylor* [1975] IRLR 185, the High Court held that there is no rule of law that an employer is obliged to create a job for a sick employee; conversely, neither is there a rule of law that the employer is not obliged to find alternative work for the employee. Each case depends on its circumstances so that if the employer has a light job available which the employer can do, it may be unreasonable if the employer fails to offer him the job even though it is at a lesser rate of pay than his old job. On the facts of this case it is apparent that the job must actually be available.

In *Spencer v Paragon Wallpapers Ltd* [1977] ICR 301, the EAT accepted that there was no obligation on the employer to create a job for the employee, but where there is an alternative suitable position for him which could await the employee's availability, it might be unfair to dismiss him. Where another vacancy does not exist, it might not be reasonable for the employer to keep that vacancy open until the employee is capable of doing the work.

The tribunal will consider whether the employer has sought to place the employee in any alternative available work at the date of dismissal. In *Todd v North Eastern Electricity Board* [1975] IRLR 130, the tribunal, accepting there was no obligation on the employer to create a job for a sick employee, found that the dismissal was unfair because the employer did not offer the employee a suitable job which was in existence and available. In *Garricks (Caterers) Ltd v Nolan* [1980] IRLR 259, Nolan was employed as a maintenance fitter on shifts. He suffered heart trouble, following which he was certified as fit for days but not for shifts. The company dismissed him because he refused to work shifts. The tribunal found that a day job could have been made available and rejected the employer's argument that it involved heavy lifting. It found that the employer could have reorganised matters without inconvenience to itself so that the employee could have been accommodated. The tribunal's decision was upheld on appeal.

3 Inactive registers and holding departments

Some employers operate an inactive register or holding department to which sick employees are transferred in accordance with the procedures thereof. Consideration has been given to the nature of these arrangements in the following cases.

In *O'Reilly v Hotpoint Ltd* (1970) 5 ITR 68, the tribunal and the High Court found that where an employee was transferred to a holding department, the contract of employment continued so that the rights and obligations of the parties were suspended, and the transfer did not operate as a dismissal.

In *Marshall v Harland and Wolff Ltd* [1972] ICR 101, the NIRC held that the effect of a transfer to a holding department was that the employee 'ceases to be employed in any legal sense', but is on a list of men with whom there is a voluntary arrangement that the employers will do their best to provide them with work as soon as they are fit again. The court envisaged that such an agreement might be reached between the employer and the union or with the employees direct. Such a transfer was applicable to long-term sickness. In the case of short-term sickness, the employees should 'be maintained in employment whether or not [they are] in receipt of full wages or sick pay'.

In *Normanton v Southalls (Birmingham) Ltd* [1975] IRLR 74, the tribunal found that where there is an inactive register or holding list, an employee can be transferred, particularly where he holds a key position and needs replacing, so that the employer will keep him on the list rather than dismiss him; and further found that where an employee is transferred to an inactive register or holding list, he will have those rights conferred on him under a scheme which will generally be negotiated with the union. The rights should be clearly defined. Normally the transfer will operate after a specified period. It does not preserve the employee's right on immediate recovery from illness to have his old job back, but the effect of an inactive register is to suspend the contract of employment so that the employee is retained and is not dismissed and his continuity of employment is preserved without interruption. During the period of sickness the employer is able to make arrangements for the work to be carried on without incurring any liability for unfair dismissal. Whether the employee is paid and has insurance contributions deducted during this period is a matter for agreement. There may be some limit on the length of time that the employee can remain on an inactive register or holding list. Where the employee reports back to work and the employer is not able to find him a job, the employee may then be dismissed for redundancy depending on the circumstances.

Other tribunals have reached different conclusions on the effect of the transfer to the inactive register or holding list in the circumstances of the particular cases. In *Burton v Boneham and Turner Ltd* (1976) (unreported), the employee was transferred to the holding department after receiving three warnings that he would be transferred unless he improved his record of absence for sickness. Once in the holding department his terms of contract were changed fundamentally. It was held that there was a termination of the existing contract of employment and a dismissal.

In *Parker v Westland Helicopters Ltd* (1976) (unreported), there were two holding departments. Employees transferred to one department continued in insurable employment and .pension contributions were paid; on recovery, by custom and practice, they returned to their old jobs. Employees in the other department were out of benefit with the company and had to wait for a suitable vacancy before restarting work. It was held that employees transferred to the first holding department continued in employment. Those who were transferred to the second holding department did not, and the transfer constituted a dismissal.

The employee's position on a transfer to a holding department or an inactive register should be defined. Where the matter is contractual, there can be little room for doubt. Transfers of sick employees to a holding department or an inactive register where the contract continues within defined time limits are beneficial for the employer.

4 The employee's obligations

Where the employee is absent from work due to ill-health there has to be some term implied in the contract limiting the employee's obligation to perform all the terms of his contract of employment during such time as he is sick. However as the EAT has held:

one does not imply into any contract any term wider than is necessary to give it business effect. In our view, business commonsense does not require that *all* obligations of an employee are suspended during sickness. The commonsense implication is that the employee is relieved of the obligation to perform such services as the sickness from which he is suffering prevent[s] him from carrying out

Thus, in this particular case, the EAT upheld the decision of the tribunal that the employer was entitled to require the employee to remove merchandise from her car standing on the public highway in accordance with the terms of her contract notwithstanding that she was away from work through ill-health at the time the request was made to her: *Marshall v Alexander Sloan and Co Ltd* [1981] IRLR 264.

Again it is important in cases where the employee is absent through sickness or injury that he should keep in touch with and inform the employer of developments. It may involve the need to provide the employee with medical certificates. Where the employee fails to do so, the employer should warn the employee of the consequences.

Chapter 8

Dismissal for Redundancy

An employee may be able to claim unfair dismissal where he has been dismissed for redundancy. Under s 81(2) of the EP(C)A 1978, an employee is dismissed for redundancy where the dismissal is wholly or mainly due to the fact that:

(a) his employer has ceased, or intends to cease, to carry on the business for the purposes of which the employee was employed by him, or has ceased, or intends to cease, to carry on that business in the place where the employee was so employed; or

(b) the requirements of that business for employees to carry out work of a particular kind, or for employees to carry out work of a particular kind in the place where he was so employed, have ceased or diminished or are expected to cease or diminish.

Redundancy has the technical meaning set out above and the question as to whether any dismissal is for redundancy will be decided in accordance with these provisions: see *Chapman v Goonvean and Rostowrack China Clay Co Ltd* [1973) ICR 310; and also *O'Hara and Rutherford v Rotaprint Ltd* [1980] ICR 94. To claim a redundancy payment, the employee must have completed two years' continuous employment ending with the relevant date: s 81(4) of the EP(C)A 1978. To claim unfair dismissal, the employee must also show that he has been continuously employed for a period of not less than two years at the effective date of termination: s 64(1)(a) of the EP(C)A 1978. There are certain transitional provisions. See, generally, Chapter 2.

Where the employee is dismissed for redundancy, the dismissal may be automatically unfair because it contravenes s 59 of the EP(C)A 1978, or it may be unfair because it is not reasonable in the circumstances (contrary to s 57(3) of the EP(C)A 1978). The fact that an employee has accepted a redundancy payment from the employer is not to be taken as an indication that he accepts that his dismissal is fair: see *Clarkson International Tools Ltd v Short* [1973] ICR 191.

241

1 Automatically unfair dismissal

Section 59 provides that dismissal will be automatically unfair where the reason or principal reason for the dismissal of an employee was that he was redundant, but it is shown that the circumstances constituting the redundancy applied equally to one or more other employees in the same undertaking who held positions similar to that held by him and who have not been dismissed by the employer, and either that:

(*a*) the reason (or, if more than one, the principal reason) for which he was selected for dismissal was one of those specified in s 58(1) of the EP(C)A 1978; or

(*b*) he was selected for dismissal in contravention of a customary arrangement or agreed procedure relating to redundancy and there were no special reasons justifying a departure from that arrangement or procedure in his case.

Where the employee can show that his case falls within one of the above provisions, the dismissal is treated as automatically unfair. This has the effect that it is not necessary to consider the question of reasonableness under s 57(3) of the EP(C)A 1978. See Chapter 10.

In the great majority of cases it has been difficult for the employee to establish that he has been selected for dismissal for one of those specified in s 58(1) of the EP(C)A 1978, or in contravention of a customary arrangement or agreed procedure where there are no special reasons justifying a departure.

1.1 The unit of selection

The statutory unit of selection is 'one or more other employees in the same undertaking'. The tribunal is left to decide whether the word 'undertaking' means the whole of the employer's business or particular departments or sections or just the department or section in which the employee was working. There are few cases and it is difficult to lay down clear guidelines.

In *Kapur v Shields* [1976] 1 All ER 873, Philips J found:

Where it is sought to show that the activities of separate persons together constitute an undertaking, it is not necessarily enough to show that the persons are connected and that the separate activities are similar. One would expect some evidence of organisational unity, eg common accounting, management, purchasing arrangements, insurance and so on.

In *Heathcote v North Western Electricity Board* [1974] IRLR 34, Heathcote, a driver's mate (in effect a labourer), was dismissed for redundancy after 18 years' employment because the Board decided there was no longer any need for drivers' mates. Selection for dismissal was made on the basis of last in, first out, but in making its selection, the Board looked only at the transport section and not at the remainder of its business. The tribunal found this was not the correct approach. If there were employees with specialist attributes within a department, they might form a group of persons who would form the unit of selection without reference elsewhere, but generally the selection should not be considered within specific departments or sections but throughout the whole concern, particularly where, as in this case, the employees involved were labourers. The tribunal found that the unit of selection was the whole concern. This case supports the proposition that the less skilled the employee, the wider the field which forms the unit of selection.   .

In *Simpson v Roneo Ltd* [1972] IRLR 5, where the tribunal proceeded on the basis that the case was within s 59 of the EP(C)A 1978, inspectors in one department only were considered as the unit of selection. The tribunal accepted that the test only applied in relation to the one department and not on the basis of the whole concern.

In *Dorrell and Ardis v Engineering Developments (Farnborough) Ltd* [1975] IRLR 234, the tribunal considered whether in selecting employees for redundancy pursuant to a customary arrangement providing for last in, first out, a company or section should be the basis. The tribunal thought this was an evidential point, but in so far as it had to decide the issue, it appeared to do so in favour of a company basis.

Much will depend on the evidence, and it may be that two separate entities are treated as an undertaking. In *Oxley v Tarmac Roadstone Holdings Ltd* [1975] IRLR 100, Oxley who had been employed at the Top Plant was transferred to the Vianova Plant. Other employees were transferred to the Vianova Plant from other plants. Redundancies were declared at the Vianova Plant and other plants including Top Plant, but employees with less service than Oxley were retained at Top Plant. Oxley claimed that the selection was in breach of a customary arrangement, but the company contended that selection under the customary arrangement was on a plant basis. On the evidence, the tribunal found that Top Plant and Vianova Plant were treated as one entity and in applying selection under the customary arrangement, the employer should have acted on that basis. For this reason Oxley's dismissal was held unfair.

In *Gargrave v Hotel and Catering Industry Training Board* [1974] IRLR 85, Gargrave, an office services manager, contended that she should not have been made redundant, *inter alia*, on the grounds that the wrong unit of selection was chosen. She was graded 10 in a scale of 1 to 12. She argued that the last employee in grade 10 should have been dismissed. The agreed procedure provided that selection should be 'within grades on the basis of last in, first out, in terms of total service with the board'. It was held that the terms of the agreed procedure could not be construed without reference to the department in which the redundancy had arisen or the category or description of the jobs affected. To dismiss an employee on the basis of grade alone might lead to an absurd situation whereby an employee was dismissed and his duties were taken over by another employee from a different department of the same grade, but whose skills were different. The dismissal was fair.

No help in the definition of 'undertaking' has been afforded by s 99 of the Employment Protection Act 1975, dealing with the procedure for handling redundancies. Here 'establishment' is the relevant unit; but again what is meant by 'establishment' is left for the tribunal to decide: *Barratt Developments (Bradford) Ltd v UCATT* [1978] ICR 319.

1.2 Positions similar

In the statutory unit of selection comparison can only be made with employees 'who held positions similar to that held by him'. In the EP(C)A 1978, 'position' in relation to an employee means the following matters taken as a whole: 'his status as an employee, the nature of his work and his terms and conditions of employment': s 153(1) of the EP(C)A 1978.

In *Heathcote*'s case, above, the tribunal accepted that employees who were interchangeable and who did almost the same jobs were employed in similar positions, even though they were employed in different departments. In *Gargrave*'s case, above, the problems of similar positions were also considered. The NIRC considered that comparison could only be made with employees in 'the department or field of activity directly affected by the redundancy situation and who are engaged in the same type or category of work'.

Different skills may mean that employees hold different positions. In *Simpson v Roneo Ltd* [1972] IRLR 5, there were five inspectors in one department. Four did the same work and the other did a more specialised job. He was the last to be taken on. The company had adopted a last in, first out, procedure for redundancy but retained the inspector who had been most recently taken on. It was held that the position held by that inspector was not the same as the others since he was engaged in more specialised work. Similarly, in *Selby and Teese v Plessey Company Ltd* [1972] IRLR 36, eight fitters in a department were divided into detail and assembly fitters. Detail fitters were more versatile than assembly fitters. The assembly fitters were declared redundant. Again, the differences in skill justified selection from the one group only. In *Powers and Villiers v A Clarke and Co (Smethwick) Ltd* [1981] IRLR 483, it was held that Class 1 drivers and Class 3 drivers did not hold similar positions, since although Class 1 drivers could drive four-wheeled vehicles as well as articulated lorries, this flexibility only worked one way and Class 3 drivers could not drive articulated vehicles.

1.3 Inadmissible reasons and s 58(1) of the 1978 Act as amended

The dismissal of an employee is regarded as automatically unfair if under s 58(1) of the EP(C)A 1978 the reason or principal reason is as follows: that the employee was, or proposed to become, a member of an independent trade union; or had taken part, or proposed to take part, in the activities of an independent trade union at an appropriate time; or was not a member of any trade union, or of a particular trade union, or of one of a number of particular trade unions, or had refused or proposed to refuse to become or remain a member.

Most of the cases were decided under the earlier legislation (when the reason was an 'inadmissible reason' which although similar to, was wider then s 58(1) of the EP(C)A 1978, but they are still of assistance.

In *Boorman and Kemp v Pickard and Beale Ltd* [1973] IRLR 135, a branch of the National Union of Funeral Service Operatives was formed in the company two years before the dismissals. A redundancy situation arose and a local union meeting was called by Kemp to discuss it. Three days later Boorman and Kemp, both members of the union, were dismissed. Boorman had been more ostentatious about his union membership than the other employees, and Kemp was a shop steward and had called the meeting. Kemp had originally been told by the company that two other employees less qualified and whose work was not good had been nominated for redundancy. Only after the union meeting did the management decide to dismiss these two instead of the two other employees. It was held that the dismissal was unfair because they had been selected on the grounds of their trade union membership and activities.

It may be difficult to decide whether the employee was selected in a redundancy situation for one of the reasons contained in s 58(1) of the EP(C)A 1978, or whether he had been selected for dismissal because of such a reason. *Taylor v Butler Machine Tool Co Ltd* [1976] IRLR 113 illustrates the point. Taylor was a committee member of the newly formed branch of the technical and supervisory section of the AUEW (TASS). The union tried to secure union recognition but protracted negotiations over a procedure agreement led to industrial action. On a return to work following a strike, the company reduced its staff by 22 employees of whom 18 left through a process of natural wastage. The 4 employees who were to be made redundant were all members of and active in the union. Other employees who were members of the union were redeployed. The tribunal accepted that there was a redundancy situation which affected the employee, but thought it was more than a coincidence that all the members of the staff chosen for redundancy were active in the formation of the union. Therefore the tribunal found that the dismissal was not wholly or mainly attributable to redundancy but, on the balance of probabilities, was attributable to union membership or activities which would now be a reason or reasons within s 58(1) of the EP(C)A 1978 (previously an inadmissible reason or reasons).

The relationship between a dismissal for one of the reasons contained in s 58(1) and selection for such a reason in a redundancy situation was considered in *Farmeary v Veterinary Drug Co Ltd* [1976] IRLR 322. The tribunal used the illustration of the employer who was antipathetic to trade union membership. Such an employer might dismiss an employee for becoming a member of a union or engaging in union activities. The dismissal will be for a reason with s 58(1), irrespective of the existence of a redundancy situation. Such a dismissal will be automatically unfair dismissal under s 58(1). Section 59 of the EP(C)A 1978 covers the same employer in a redundancy situation, who in that redundancy situation selects one employee in preference to another because the one was a trade union member and the other was not. In such a case, the principal reason for dismissal will be redundancy, not a dismissal for a reason within s 58(1), but the method of selection (which is for such a reason) renders the dismissal automatically unfair.

There is no presumption in such cases. Although the onus of showing the reason for dismissal is on the employer, if the employer alleges that the reason is, for instance, misconduct, it is for the employee to show that he was selected for one of those reasons specified in s 58(1) (and presumably where the point is in issue, in contravention of a customary arrangement or agreed procedure) at least on the balance of probabilities: *Bristol Channel Ship Repairers Ltd v O'Keefe and Lewis* [1978] ICR 691.

1.4 Contravention of customary arrangement or agreed procedure

Where there is a customary arrangement or an agreed procedure (ie within s 59(*b*) of the EP(C)A 1978), the onus is on the employer to show that he has observed it. Failure to discharge the onus may lead to a finding of unfair dismissal. In dealing with a customary arrangement or agreed procedure tribunals should not take too technical or too objective a view of the matter': *Wailes Dove Bitumastic Ltd v Woolcocks* [1977] ICR 817. Section 59(*b*) is concerned with the cases where the selection of the employee is in contravention of an agreed procedure or customary arrangement. It does not apply where the employer has failed to comply with the procedure requiring consultation with the union concerned or to consider volunteers for redundancy: *McDowell and Others v Eastern British Road Services Ltd* [1981] IRLR 482.

(a) Customary arrangement The legislation gives no guidance on what is meant by 'customary arrangement'. In *Bessenden Properties Ltd v Corness* [1973] IRLR 365, Corness was employed by a firm of estate agents and was laid off because of a reduction in business. The tribunal found the dismissal was due to redundancy and that it was unfair

because Corness was selected in contravention of a customary arrangement of last in, first out. The tribunal considered that 'the normal customary arrangement in industry in general proceeds on the principle of "last in, first out".' The NIRC found that this conclusion was erroneous. The tribunal had 'decided that what, within their knowledge, was a normal custom in industry amounted to a "customary arrangement".' The court concluded that what is contemplated by 'customary arrangement' (although the court was at pains to make it clear that it was not defining the phrase) 'is something which is so well known, so certain and so clear as to amount in effect to an implied "agreed procedure", as contrasted with the express "agreed procedure" which is the alternative contemplated by [s 59(*b*)]'. In this case the proper question was, 'Was there a customary arrangement applying to estate agents in Coventry (as part maybe of a wider field) under which it was so well known that the "last in" would be the "first out" that it amounted to an implied agreed procedure?'. The Court of Appeal upheld the decision of the NIRC: *Bessenden Properties Ltd v Corness* [1974] IRLR 338.

In *Henry v Ellerman Lines plc* [1985] ICR 57, the Court of Appeal considered the decision of Sir John Donaldson in *Bessenden Properties v Corness*, above. It reached the conclusion that an agreed procedure could be one that is made either expressly or by implication. Therefore, an implied agreed procedure was not a customary arrangement. Regrettably the Court of Appeal did not consider what was meant by customary arrangement. In *Bessenden Properties Ltd v Corness*, above, the NIRC had to consider whether or not there was a customary arrangement. It is open to argument that an arrangement which while not amounting to an implied agreement may be a customary arrangement, even though it may have some of the characteristics of an implied agreed procedure.

In *Kyle Stewart Contractors Ltd v Stainrod* (1977) (unreported), the EAT found that a 'customary arrangement' may exist, provided it is supported by suitable evidence even though there is only 'a measure of notoriety among the workforce'. The fact that it is not universally known will not defeat the customary arrangement. However, what is suitable evidence and what is sufficient notoriety are questions of fact which the tribunals will have to decide in each case.

Where there is a last in, first out principle, as part of a customary arrangement, it is important that the employer is clear which employees are to be dismissed and, in computing the length of employment, only those weeks which will count for continuity of employment in the legal sense will probably be considered unless there is some clear arrangement that the selection will be based upon cumulative service: *Dorrell and Ardis v Engineering Developments (Farnborough) Ltd* [1975] IRLR 234; and see *Sudders v Prestige Group Ltd* [1975] IRLR 367.

(b) Agreed procedure The 'agreed procedure' for the purposes of s 59(*b*) of the EP(C)A 1978 may be oral or in writing. It may be express or implied: see *Henry v Ellerman Lines plc* above. No particular form is required. Usually the procedure will be agreed between the employer and the employees, or their representatives. It should lay down criteria to be followed in the selection of employees in the event of redundancies.

There must be a clear morally or legally binding agreement. In *Jackson v General Accident Fire and Life Assurance Co Ltd* [1976] IRLR 338, the company undertook, in a letter dated 9 August 1974 sent to the union, that there would be no redundancies but a gradual run-down of staff over two years. In August 1975 the employee was told that he would be made redundant and was given notice which expired on 30 November 1975. The tribunal found that there was no agreed procedure between the employer and the employees, or their representatives. The EAT agreed. It did not accept that the letter of 9 August amounted to an agreed procedure. 'The letter however, was written to only one trade union and not all employees of the respondents were members of that union.' The letter was an expression of intent and was not intended to create a binding agreement.

An agreement between an employer and a union which is an *ad hoc* agreement covering a particular set of circumstances may be an agreed procedure: see *Evans and Morgan v AB Electronic Components Ltd* [1981] IRLR 111.

In *Camper and Nicholson Ltd v Shaw* [1978] ICR 520, the tribunal found that the employers had operated an agreed procedure of 'last in, first out, all other things being equal'. It was held by the EAT to have erred in substituting its own view of what was equal for that of the employers. The EAT said that 'equal' meant equal in the eyes of a fair and reasonable employer applying proper industrial considerations.

An agreed procedure may apply to the whole of the employer's concern or, alternatively, it may be negotiated with unions covering certain sections of the employer's labour force or certain departments in the employer's undertaking.

It is not unusual for an employer and a union to reach an agreement under which in the event of a redundancy non-union members will be selected for redundancy in preference to union members. See *Bygott v Woodall-Duckham Ltd* [1976] IRLR 168; and *Evans and Morgan v AB Electronic Components Ltd*, above. When an employee is selected for redundancy because he is not a member of the union, the dismissal will be automatically unfair. See Chapter 10.

It is possible to amend an agreed procedure. However, where it is intended to modify well-established and understood industrial procedures, that should clearly be made known by the employer to all concerned: see *International Paint Co Ltd v Cameron* [1979] ICR 429. A belief by one party to an agreed procedure that there has been some alteration will be insufficient unless the alteration has been agreed to by both sides either expressly or impliedly: *Tilgate Pallets Ltd v Barras and Others* [1983] IRLR 231.

(c) Special reasons justifying a departure Where an employer seeks to argue that there are special reasons justifying a departure from a customary arrangement or agreed procedure the onus is upon the employer to establish those reasons. This will usually involve the employer establishing that he used objective criteria: *Tilgate Pallets Ltd v Barras and Others* [1983] IRLR 231.

In *Wailes Dove Bitumastic Ltd v Woolcocks* [1977] ICR 817, the EAT suggested that in deciding whether there has been a departure from the procedure, the matter should not be looked at too rigidly but 'in the light of both sides trying to operate an agreed procedure as best they can'. Presumably, the same approach is to be adopted in the case of customary arrangements. It is for the tribunal acting as an industrial jury to decide whether or not there were special reasons justifying a departure from an agreed procedure. Therefore the decision of the tribunal cannot be overturned unless its decision is perverse: *Cross International v Reid and Others* [1985] IRLR 387.

Customary arrangements In *Best v Taylor Woodrow Construction Ltd* [1975] IRLR 177, the employers operated a normal practice whereby the last in would be the first to be dismissed in a redundancy situation. Best was selected for redundancy in preference to another employee with less service. During his employment Best had been given two oral warnings and four written warnings about his time-keeping. The other employee had only two time-keeping faults. The dismissal was held to be fair. The tribunal accepted that the employer is entitled to depart from the normal practice and select an employee with longer service where that employee's record is worse than one with shorter service.

In *Briers v ARC Marine Ltd* (1975) (unreported), the company had a customary arrangement of last in, first out. Briers had recently been incapacitated by an accident at work and was selected in preference to employees with shorter service. The tribunal held that the dismissal was fair. The job required fit employees and Brier's incapacity was a special reason justifying a departure from the customary arrangement.

In *Axe v British Domestic Appliances Ltd* [1972] IRLR 8, the company possessed a customary arrangement of last in, first out. Axe was selected for redundancy before four other employees with less service. These were retained on compassionate grounds put forward by the union and accepted by the company. The tribunal held that this agreement was in itself a special reason justifying a departure.

Agreed procedures In *Weston v Bentley Engineering Co Ltd* (1977) (unreported), the company possessed an agreed procedure that volunteers should be selected for redundancy first. The company refused to dismiss one of the volunteers because of his experience, and instead dismissed a non-volunteer. The tribunal held the dismissal was fair. The company was entitled to retain an employee with experience in the interest of the business. It was a special reason justifying a departure.

In *Green v Commercial Cable Co Ltd* (1976) (unreported), the company possessed an agreed procedure of last in, first out. The company retained an employee with less service than Green because he spoke fluent Spanish and had a knowledge of the trading area of South America. The tribunal held the dismissal was fair. Although it found the skills not essential to the company, they were certainly useful to the company's business and were a special reason for retaining him in preference to the dismissed employee.

In *Crump v Chubb and Sons Lock and Safe Co Ltd* [1975] IRLR 293, there was an agreed procedure providing for last in, first out. Crump was dismissed for redundancy and complained that the dismissal was unfair because another employee with less service had been retained. This had happened because that employee, and another employee with longer service, had agreed to change places. The agreement had the blessing of management and the senior shop steward. The tribunal therefore held that the dismissal was fair.

In *International Paint Co Ltd v Cameron* [1979] IRLR 62, the choice lay between Cameron and Boyle. The employers chose to make the former redundant because Boyle had greater cumulative service and, although there had been a break in his employment of four or five weeks in 1974 when he left to try to find a better job, it had been agreed when he returned that his service should be treated as continuous. The EAT said that these factors did not constitute special reasons justifying a departure from the agreed procedure. The EAT added that an agreement that, despite a break, the employee's service would be treated as continuous, would not serve to qualify the 'well-established principle of the last in, first out doctrine' unless the agreement had been made known to all who were likely to be affected by it. See also the cases of *Dorrell* and *Sudders*.

Where under an agreed procedure, selection under that procedure is an act of unlawful sex discrimination, this will be a good reason for departing from an agreed procedure: see *Clark and Powell v Eley (IMI) Kynoch Ltd* [1982] IRLR 131.

In *Cross International v Reid and Others* [1985] IRLR 387, the company, specialising in automated machine tools for the motor industry, found itself in a grave trading position. In 1981 there was a sharp downturn in the company's order book. In June 1982 an important order representing a substantial proportion of the anticipated turnover for the year was cancelled. This was coupled with a perilously low level of orders in a world recession with general over-capacity in the machine tool industry. Redundancies were necessary. The company concluded that because of the specialisation within the company it would have to depart from the agreed redundancy procedure of last in, first out, by substituting a policy of retaining those who would help to ensure survival of the company—selection on a merit basis. The company devised a rating system and each employee was separately assessed in accordance with this system. As a result 60 employees were selected for redundancy. The tribunal concluded that the company's situation was not so catastrophic or special as to justify departure from an agreed procedure and therefore the dismissals were unfair. The EAT while questioning whether or not they might have made a different decision to the tribunal, concluded that the tribunal had reached a decision which was reasonably open to it and so they could not interfere. The Court of Appeal by a majority upheld the decision. Before the Court of Appeal it was argued that it was for the employers to decide whether or not they had special reasons justifying a departure from the agreed procedure, and that provided their decision was within the range of reasonable responses of an employer in the particular situation the tribunal could not find the dismissal unfair. Neill LJ found:

The Industrial Tribunal acting as an industrial jury had to apply to the facts . . . the words '. . . and there were no special reasons justifying a departure from that procedure'. They had to consider and evaluate the 'reasons' which the parties put before them. I see no ground for putting a gloss on the words in the section [s 59(b) of the EP(C)A 1978] so as to introduce the concept of a range of possible options. The section [s 59(b)] does not say 'which could justify a departure'; the words are 'special reasons justifying a departure'.

(d) Reasonableness Where an employee is selected in accordance with a customary arrangement or agreed procedure, then his dismissal will usually be fair.

However, tribunals have from time to time examined customary arrangements to see that the arrangement in itself is fair. In *Norton v Chemidus Wavin Ltd* [1975] IRLR 294, the employee was selected in accordance with a customary arrangement. The tribunal found there was no contravention of s 59 of the EP(C)A 1978. However, the tribunal found that the customary arrangement conflicted with the recommendations of the 1972 code, in that it had been established without consultation. The dismissal was therefore held to be unfair under s 57(3) of the EP(C)A 1978, in that the employer had not acted reasonably. The fact that the customary arrangement results in personal hardship does not mean that the employer is acting unreasonably: *Forman Construction Ltd v Kelly* [1977] IRLR 468.

It is less likely that an agreed procedure will be found unreasonable than will a customary arrangement, except where the procedure discloses some manifest injustice: *Boothby v Kingston Craftsmen Ltd* [1975] IRLR 138.

An important decision is that in *Clarke and Powell v Eley (IMI) Kynoch Ltd* [1982] IRLR 131. The employer had an agreed procedure with the TGWU, whereby in a redundancy part-time employees would be dismissed before full-time employees and full-time employees would than be selected on the basis of last in, first out. Selection was on a unit basis. There was a proviso giving the employer some discretion as to selection where the agreed selection procedure would be harmful to the needs of the business. The tribunal held that the requirement or condition that an employee had to be employed full time before selection on a last in, first out basis applied was one with which a considerably smaller proportion of women than men could comply within the meaning of s 1(1)(*b*) of the Sex Discrimination Act (SDA) 1975 in that in practice a considerably smaller proportion of women than men could comply with the requirement to work full time. Powell could not comply because of domestic commitments, whereas Clarke had been in a position to work full time in the years before the dismissal and the requirement to be a full-time worker was not to her detriment. The employer, in operating the procedure, had been guilty of unlawful indirect sex discrimination against Powell and the requirement or condition could not be shown to be justifiable irrespective of the sex of the person to whom it applied. Therefore, under s 57(3) of the EP(C)A 1978 the dismissal of Powell, since it was an unlawful discriminatory selection under the SDA 1975, was not a fair selection. The tribunal considered that Powell should be taken back into employment. It accepted that this might necessitate the dismissal of a full-time employee with less service which would be in breach of an agreed procedure but none the less considered that it might well be a special reason justifying a departure from the agreed procedure. In the case of Clarke, since she could have avoided the dismissal by complying with the full-time requirement, her dismissal was not unfair under s 57(3) of the EP(C)A 1978.

The case was considered by the EAT in *(1) Clarke v Eley (IMI) Kynoch Ltd (2) Eley (IMI) Kynoch Ltd v Powell* [1982] IRLR 482. It dismissed the company's appeal against the tribunal's finding in the case of Powell, but upheld the appeal of Clarke, holding that the time at which the ability or inability of an employee to comply with a requirement or condition has to be shown is the date on which she suffered the detriment. This is the same point in time at which the requirement or condition has to be fulfilled. Clarke had shown that she suffered the detriment on dismissal because when she was dismissed she could not comply with the condition that she should be a full-time worker. It did not matter that at an earlier date she could have avoided the detriment by becoming a full-time worker. The EAT expressed the view, *obiter*, that the tribunal had erred in holding that a dismissal which is discriminatory is necessarily unfair under s 57(3) of the EP(C)A 1978, although the circumstances when such a dismissal could be fair would be very special.

Where there is an agreed procedure the fact that it causes hardship for an individual will not mean that the dismissal in accordance with the agreed procedure is unfair. There may be circumstances where an agreed procedure is fair to the majority of employees but an individual suffers. It is for the tribunal to consider whether or not either side has manipulated a situation unfairly to an individual: see *Wailes Dove Bitumastic Ltd v Woolcocks* [1977] ICR 817.

2 Reasonableness

Where the employee has been selected in contravention of s 59 of the EP(C)A 1978, the dismissal is automatically unfair and there is therefore no defence in this situation available to the employer. However, the employee may not be able to bring himself within the scope of this section. In this situation the dismissal must be reasonable in all the circumstances under s 57(3) of the EP(C)A 1978 which provides that the fairness or otherwise shall depend on whether in the circumstances (including the size and administrative resources of the employer's undertaking) the employer acted reasonably or unreasonably in treating redundancy as a sufficient reason for dismissing the employee; and that question shall be determined in accordance with equity and the substantial merits of the case.

Before s 57(3) of the EP(C)A 1978 was amended by s 6 of the Employment Act 1980, the burden of proof was on the employer. This is no longer so. In *(1) Abbotts and (2) Standley v Wesson-Glynwed Steels Ltd* [1982] IRLR 51, a redundancy case, the EAT found that the amendment of s 57(3) of the EP(C)A 1978 by s 6 of the EA 1980 'in no way affects the criteria by which the employer's decision to dismiss is to be judged, although it spells them out differently. What it does is to neutralise the burden of proof as far as the Act is concerned; that is, it simply affects the way round the industrial tribunal has to look at its problem at the time of the hearing.' It is not wholly clear what the EAT meant by this last remark. See also *Williams and Others v Compair Maxam Ltd* [1982] ICR 156, where the EAT considered that as a result of the amendments of s 57(3) of the EP(C)A 1978 by s 6 of the EA 1980, the employer has been relieved of the burden which was previously placed upon him, so that for instance it is no longer necessary for the employer to prove that selection criteria have been objectively and fairly applied—the burden is no longer on the employer—provided there was some evidence before the tribunal on which it could make a finding.

It was suggested by the Scottish division of the EAT in *Jackson v General Accident Fire and Life Assurance Co Ltd* [1976] IRLR 338, that where a redundancy dismissal passes the hurdle of s 59 of the

EP(C)A 1978, it was difficult to envisage a case where it would be unreasonable in the terms of s 57(3). See also *Robinson v Ulster Carpet Mills Ltd* [1991] IRLR 348. See also *Atkinson v George Lindsay and Co* [1980] IRLR 196, where the Court of Session held:

where the reason for a dismissal is redundancy and that dismissal has survived the tests prescribed in . . . [s 59] it will in most cases be extremely difficult for any tribunal to hold that in dismissing the particular individual, his employers acted unreasonably in the sense prescribed by . . . [s 57(3)].

This decision was relied upon in *Buchanan v Tilcon Ltd* [1983] IRLR 417. However, in *Lifeguard Assurance Ltd v Zadrozny* [1977] IRLR 56, the English division of the EAT was not prepared to accept this radical approach, but found this statement 'should put industrial tribunals on guard not lightly to find that a dismissal is unfair where it is admitted that the reason for dismissal' was redundancy. However, in *Valor Newhome Ltd v Hampson* [1982] ICR 407, the English division of the EAT followed *Atkinson v George Lindsay and Co*, above. The reported cases establish that while this may be a general guideline, dismissals for redundancy may still be unfair. Tribunals have been cautioned against finding that an employee has been unfairly dismissed so as to top up what they consider to be an inadequate redundancy payment: see *British United Shoe Machinery Co Ltd v Clarke* [1977] IRLR 297, and *Hinckley and Bosworth Borough Council v Ainscough* [1979] ICR 590.

2.1 Reasonableness—general principles

In *Williams and Others v Compair Maxam Ltd* [1982] ICR 156, the company's order book was falling off dramatically, and it was suffering losses. It called for voluntary redundancies, and short-time working was introduced. There were insufficient volunteers for redundancy and so the company, without reference to the union, drew up a list of employees whom the company considered it to be in their best interest to retain. Williams and others were dismissed by reason of redundancy.

The EAT laid down certain guidelines for tribunals in cases involving unfair dismissal in a redundancy. This case involved the selection of a number of employees where there was a recognised independent union, so that the guidelines must be considered in the light of the facts of this case. None the less the guidelines are of considerable relevance in other cases.

The EAT held:

For the purposes of the present case there are only two relevant principles of law arising from . . . [s 57(3)]. First, that it is not the function of the industrial tribunal to decide whether they would have thought it fairer to act in some other way: the question is whether the dismissal lay within the range of conduct which a reasonable employer could have adopted. The second point of law, particularly relevant in the field of dismissal for redundancy, is that the tribunal must be satisfied that it was reasonable to dismiss each of the applicants on the ground of redundancy. It is not enough to show simply that it was reasonable to dismiss *an* employee; it must be shown that the employer acted reasonably in treating redundancy 'as a sufficient reason for dismissing *the* employee', ie the employee complaining of dismissal. Therefore, if the circumstances of the employer make it inevitable that some employee must be dismissed, it is still necessary to consider the means whereby the applicant was selected to be the employee to be dismissed and the reasonableness of the steps taken by the employer to choose the applicant, rather than some other employee, for dismissal.

In law, therefore, the question we have to decide is whether a reasonable tribunal could have reached the conclusion that the dismissal of the applicants in this case lay within the range of conduct which a reasonable employer could have adopted. It is accordingly necessary to try to set down in very general terms what a properly instructed industrial tribunal would know to be the principles which, in current industrial practice, a reasonable employer would be expected to adopt. This is not a matter on which the chairman of this appeal tribunal feels that he can contribute much, since it depends on what industrial practices are currently accepted as being normal and proper. The two lay members of this appeal tribunal hold the view that it would be impossible to lay down detailed procedures which *all* reasonable employers would follow in *all* circumstances: the fair conduct of dismissals for redundancy must depend on the circumstances of each case. But in their experience, there is a generally accepted view in industrial relations that, in cases where the employees are represented by an independent union recognised by the employer, reasonable employers will seek to act in accordance with the following principles:

(1) The employer will seek to give as much warning as possible of impending redundancies so as to enable the union and employees who may be affected to take early steps to inform themselves of the relevant facts, consider possible alternative solutions and, if necessary, find alternative employment in the undertaking or elsewhere.

(2) The employer will consult the union as to the best means by which the desired management result can be achieved fairly and with as little hardship to the employees as possible. In particular, the employer will seek to agree with the union the criteria to be applied in selecting the employees to be made redundant. When a selection has been made, the employer will consider with the union whether the selection has been made in accordance with those criteria.

(3) Whether or not an agreement as to the criteria to be adopted has been agreed with the union, the employer will seek to establish criteria for selection which so far as possible do not depend solely upon the opinion of the person making the selection but can be objectively checked against such things as attendance record, efficiency at the job, experience, or length of service.

(4) The employer will seek to ensure that the selection is made fairly in accordance with these criteria and will consider any representations the union may make as to such selection.

(5) The employer will seek to see whether instead of dismissing an employee he could offer him alternative employment.

The lay members stress that not all these factors are present in every case and circumstances may prevent one or more of them being given effect to.

But the lay members would expect these principles to be departed from only where some good reason is shown to justify such departure. The basic approach is that, in the unfortunate circumstances that necessarily attend redundancies, as much as is reasonably possible should be done to mitigate the impact on the work force and to satisfy them that the selection has been made fairly and not on the basis of personal whim.

. . . A very large number of appeals on cases of alleged unfair selection for redundancy come before this appeal tribunal. In the experience of all of us, without exception hitherto, the approach of the industrial tribunals has reflected the canons of good industrial relations, set out above . . .

The EAT referred to the headnote of the case report setting out the decision of the tribunal in *Greig v Sir Alfred McAlpine and Son (Northern) Ltd* [1979] IRLR 372. In that case the tribunal found:

When so many employees are involved, and a basis of selection is to be used which is open to the possibility of being influenced by over-subjective assessments, or even sheer prejudice, on the part of the person making the choice, it is important that management be able to show that they took sufficient steps to make their decision as objective and unbiased as possible.

The approach of the EAT in *Williams and Others v Compair Maxam Ltd*, above, has been followed in other cases. See *Grundy (Teddington) Ltd v Plummer and Salt* [1983] IRLR 98, and *Robinson v Carrickfergus BC* [1983] IRLR 122, the latter case being a decision of the Court of Appeal in Northern Ireland.

However, the decision in *Williams and Others v Compair Maxam*, above, is not without its difficulties, as was recognised in *Grundy (Teddington) Ltd v Plummer and Salt*, above, where the EAT made it clear that it would welcome further guidance from the Court of Appeal. In *Williams and Others*, above, the EAT stressed that it was not seeking to lay down principles of law, simply standards of behaviour. Any finding that these were principles of law would have conflicted with decisions of the Court of Appeal. Thus, in *Hollister v National Farmers Union* [1979] ICR 542, the Court of Appeal held that reasonableness must be judged in the light of all the circumstances. In *Bailey v BP Oil (Kent Refinery) Ltd* [1980] ICR 642, the Court of Appeal emphasised that each case must depend upon its own facts, and Lawton LJ held:

In our judgment it is unwise for this court or the Employment Appeal Tribunal to set out guidelines, and wrong to make rules and establish presumptions for Industrial Tribunals to follow or take into account when applying . . . [s 57(3)].

Other divisions of the EAT have warned against tribunals applying the decision in *Williams and Others*, above, as a principle of law. Thus, the English division of the EAT in *Rolls Royce Motors Ltd v Dewhurst* [1985] IRLR 184, held:

To direct themselves, as the Tribunal has done — namely, that an act contrary to *any* of the principles enunciated in *Compair Maxam* leads to the conclusion, even *prima facie*, that the dismissals are unfair—is not, in our judgment, a proper direction.

The Scottish division of the EAT has also distinguished the decision in *Williams and Others*, above. In *A Simpson and Son (Motors) v Reid and Findlater* [1983] IRLR 401, it was held that the guidelines laid down in *Williams and Others*, above, apply only where substantial redundancies arise where there is an independent recognised union. It did not apply to the selection of two or three employees in a small business. Again in *Gray v Shetland Norse Preserving Co Ltd* [1985] IRLR 53, another division of the Scottish EAT emphasised that the guidelines were only appropriate where there were substantial redundancies and a recognised union was involved.

One helpful approach to the test of reasonableness was set out in *Dyke and Others v Hereford and Worcester County Council* [1989] ICR 800, see below.

In the light of these general guidelines there will now be considered substantive and procedural unfairness.

2.2 Substantive unfairness

(a) The necessity for redundancies As a first step the tribunal will decide whether or not the dismissal is for redundancy. The tribunal must be satisfied that the employee is redundant within the provisions of s 81(1)–(3) of the EP(C)A 1978 (see also para 5 of Sched 9 to the EP(C)A 1978). The tribunal cannot demand an 'excessively high standard of proof' of a redundancy. The employer is not obliged to produce 'accounts or figures to show the loss referred to, how it was sustained and how much it came to', nor does the employer have to show 'that the redundancy situation was so bad as to cause the dismissal'; nor is there any 'obligation on the employers to establish the existence of some economic or accountancy state of affairs which would, as it were, justify the declaration of a state of redundancy' in order to establish the necessary facts to show that the dismissal was because of redundancy: *H Goodwin Ltd v Fitzmaurice* [1977] IRLR 393.

Once a redundancy has been established then it is not open to the tribunal to consider the actions of the employer which led to the redundancy situation. Tribunals are not there to make findings about the way in which the employer has conducted the business: *Moon v Homeworthy Furniture (Northern) Ltd* [1977] ICR 117. In *Guy v Delanair (Car Heater) Ltd* [1975] IRLR 73, the company decided to do away with the whole of the night shift as a method of reducing production in a redundancy situation. The tribunal found it 'is not in a position to criticise the manner in which an employer decides its work must be cut down'. The tribunal was not prepared to consider whether the redundancies were necessary.

Sometimes there may be a thin dividing line between a consideration of the employer's business position and the question of reasonableness. In *Lloyd v The Standard Pulverised Fuel Co Ltd* [1976] IRLR 115, the company operated two shifts. It dismissed one shift and left the other shift doing overtime. The tribunal found the dismissal unfair because there would have been no dismissals for redundancy if the company had considered eliminating overtime and introducing a limited amount of short-time working. In a case such as this it used to be arguable that the employer had failed to have regard to para 45 of the 1972 code. Although this code has been repealed the precedent remains.

Again the tribunal may also find the dismissal unfair where it is likely that the employees could have been absorbed elsewhere within a short time. In *Allwood v William Hill (North East) Ltd* [1974] IRLR 258, there was a redundancy and the company decided to dismiss 12 of its betting-shop managers. The tribunal was not satisfied that the position was as desperate as the company thought. In the industry there was a high wastage of managers, and the employers had a large number of betting shops. The tribunal found that the company could have transferred employees, even temporarily, to other establishments until vacancies had occurred within the company through natural wastage or the expansion of the larger offices. Since the dismissals, vacancies had occurred. Additionally, the decision to dismiss had been taken with great haste; there was no warning or consultation. The dismissal was unfair. Again it used to be arguable that the employer had failed to have regard to the spirit of the 1972 code. It is still open to a tribunal to find that such a dismissal is unfair.

(b) Selection   Selection may be seen as either a matter of substance or procedure. Inevitably there will be many cases where selection is irretrievably bound up with the need for consultations. Although the onus of establishing reasonableness is no longer on the employer, when there is selection between employees, the employer will have to show the information he took into account and the criteria used for selection. He will have to go into some detail to satisfy the tribunal: *Bristol Channel Ship Repairers Ltd v O'Keefe and Lewis* [1978] ICR 691. In *Cox v Wildt Mellor Bromley Ltd* [1978] ICR 736, the EAT considered that this might be discharged by calling witnesses to explain the circumstances of the redundancy. The amendment of s 57(3) of the EP(C)A 1978 by s 6 of the EA 1980 will not alter the need for the employer to adduce evidence in support of these matters. See *(1) Abbotts and (2) Standley v Wesson-Glynwed Steels Ltd* [1982] IRLR 51. Only the employer will know the reasons for the selection and he must ensure that there is evidence before the tribunal.

In *Buchanan v Tilcon Ltd* [1983] IRLR 417, the Court of Session following the decision in *Cox v Wildt Mellor Bromley Ltd* above, held:

it is quite unrealistic and unreasonable for an industrial tribunal, which is prepared to accept that the senior official who made the selection reached his decision fairly upon the basis of company information, the reliability of which he had no reason to question, to demand of the employer for the purposes of s 57(3) that he should set up the accuracy of that information by direct evidence of other witnesses speaking, perhaps, to records for which they had responsibility. The industrial tribunal, in our opinion, set for the respondents in this case a standard which was much too high.

The way in which the tribunal is to consider the reasonableness of the employer's selection of the employee has given rise to some difficulty.

In *Bessenden Properties Ltd v Corness* [1974] IRLR 338, Bessenden a listing negotiator with a firm of estate agents was selected for redundancy in preference to the other listing negotiators although she had the longest period of service. She was selected because she was married and had the support of her husband, which was not the position of the other negotiators. There was no agreed procedure or customary arrangement. The tribunal found the dismissal unfair because the employer had not selected the employee on a last in, first out, basis. The Court of Appeal held that the tribunal was entitled to find the selection unfair because a last in, first out, procedure was not used. The tribunal, in deciding the issue of fair selection, was entitled to take everything into account and to act as 'an industrial jury'.

In *Grundy (Teddington) Ltd v Willis* [1976] ICR 323, Willis was a dispatch foreman. The company created a new post of finishing controller which absorbed the duties of several other persons. It decided to dispense with the services of one member of staff. Willis was preferred for dismissal because it was felt an alternative employee would do a better job and he had a longer total period of service with the company than Willis. The tribunal found that at the time of the dismissal, Willis was doing the job of the other employee. Because it seemed to the tribunal that consideration had not been given to this factor in selecting Willis, it held that the dismissal was unfair. The High Court upheld the company's appeal. It found the tribunal has to decide 'not what they would have done had they been the management', but whether or not management acted reasonably, so, 'provided the employers have applied their minds to the problem and acted from genuine motives, they cannot really be faulted, or be said to have acted unreasonably, in choosing one in preference to another'.

Comparing the decisions of the Court of Appeal in *Bessenden*'s case and the High Court in *Grundy*'s case, it would seem that there was a difference in approach between the two courts. In *Grundy*'s case the High Court did not accept that the judgment in *Bessenden*'s case meant that 'the decision as to who should be selected . . . is one ultimately to be left to the industrial tribunal'.

Clearly, if in *Bessenden*'s case the Court of Appeal was indicating that the tribunal was entitled to substitute its decision for that of the employer, *Bessenden* is wrong in law. However, if it is simply recognising that the tribunal in reaching its decision whether the employer has acted reasonably, is sitting as an industrial jury, then that is a correct interpretation of the law, and there is no difference between the decisions in *Grundy*'s case and *Bessenden*'s case.

In *NC Watling and Co Ltd v Richardson* [1978] IRLR 255, Richardson was employed as an electrician. He was transferred from a Watney Mann contract to a contract at Shaftesbury Avenue, was transferred back to the Watney Mann contract and was dismissed for redundancy when that contract came to an end. He argued that his dismissal was unfair, pointing out that the company had engaged two electricians at the Shaftesbury Avenue contract since he started employment and they were not dismissed. The tribunal held that the dismissal was unfair and the EAT dismissed the appeal. The EAT found that in deciding whether the dismissal was fair, the tribunal had to consider s 57(3) of the EP(C)A 1978 as a starting point.

It held that a dismissal for redundancy will be fair unless the case is one where the employer has acted in a way in which no reasonable employer would have done. Any higher degree of reasonableness which might have appeared to have been supported by cases such as *Vickers Ltd v Smith* [1977] IRLR 11, was not necessary. The EAT considered that the view that the decision in *Smith*'s case, above, supported a higher degree of reasonableness, was in fact misconceived.

In *Iceland Frozen Foods Ltd v Jones* [1982] IRLR 439, the EAT considered the earlier decisions and held:

Since the present state of the law can only be found by going through a number of different authorities, it may be convenient if we should seek to summarise the present law. We consider that the authorities establish that in law the correct approach for the Industrial Tribunal to adopt in answering the question posed by s 57(3) of the 1978 Act is as follows.

(1) the starting point should always be the words of s 57(3) themselves;
(2) in applying the section an Industrial Tribunal must consider the reasonableness of the employer's conduct, not simply whether they (the members of the Industrial Tribunal) consider the dismissal to be fair;
(3) in judging the reasonableness of the employer's conduct an Industrial Tribunal must not substitute its decision as to what was the right course to adopt for that of the employer;
(4) in many (though not all) cases there is a band of reasonable responses to the employee's conduct within which one employer might reasonably take one view, another quite reasonably take another;
(5) the function of the Industrial Tribunal, as an industrial jury, is to determine whether in the particular circumstances of each case the decision to dismiss the employee fell within the band of reasonable responses which a reasonable employer might have adopted. If the dismissal falls within the band the dismissal is fair: if the dismissal falls outside the band it is unfair.

Although the statement of principle in *Vickers Ltd v Smith* is entirely accurate in law, for the reasons given in *Watling v Richardson* we think Industrial Tribunals would do well not to direct themselves by reference to it. The statement in *Vickers Ltd v Smith* is capable of being misunderstood so as to require such a high degree of unreasonableness to be shown that nothing short of a perverse decision to dismiss can be held to be unfair within the section. This is how the Industrial Tribunal in the present case seems to have read *Vickers v Smith*. That is not the law. The question in each case is whether the Industrial Tribunal considers the employer's conduct to fall within the band of reasonable responses, and Industrial Tribunals would be well advised to follow the formulation of the principle in *Wating v Richardson* or *Rolls-Royce v Walpole*.

See also *Rolls Royce Ltd v Walpole* [1980] IRLR 343.

In *Williams and Others v Compair Maxam Ltd* [1982] ICR 156, the EAT emphasised that in considering the dismissal of an employee by reason of redundancy it is necessary to examine the reasonableness of the steps taken by the employer to choose the employees selected. The EAT laid down guidelines which included guidelines as to the criteria for selection. See **2.1**, above. The EAT accepted that the test under s 57(3) of the EP(C)A 1978 is 'was the dismissal an option which lay within the range of conduct which a reasonable employer would have adopted?' The EAT found that where more than one employee is being dismissed for redundancy, the tribunal should be satisfied it was reasonable to dismiss each of the employees so that the test of reasonableness must be applied to each of the employees who were dismissed. In deciding whether or not the decision to dismiss lay within the range of conduct which a reasonable employer could have adopted, it is necessary for the tribunal to know what principles a reasonable employer would have been expected to adopt in accordance with current industrial relations practice; hence the guidelines. In the case of selection this would involve the use of objective criteria in selecting that employee, so that the employer can demonstrate the reasonableness of choosing that employee rather than some other.

In *Buchanan v Tilcon Ltd* [1983] IRLR 417, the Court of Session following the decision in *Atkinson v George Lindsay and Co*, above, found that where the issue was the employees' selection, all that the employer had to do was 'to prove that their method of selection was fair in general terms and that it had been applied reasonably in the case of the appellant by the senior official responsible for taking the decision'. It is difficult to reconcile the differing approaches set out above. However, the test is contained in s 57(3). It is not open to the tribunal to substitute its own decision for that of the employer, the tribunal must simply be satisfied that the employer's decision was within the band of reasonable responses. There may be cases where the criteria suggested in *Williams and Others v Compair Maxam Ltd*, above, will be relevant although they are not to be regarded as principles or even guidelines applicable in each case. The tribunal must not be too ready to find that an employer has acted unfairly in its selection.

(c) The process of selection   Under s 59 of the EP(C)A 1978 the dismissed employee is only entitled to plead in his aid employees holding similar positions. There is no such restriction under s 57(3) of the EP(C)A 1978: *Thomas and Betts Manufacturing Co Ltd v Harding* [1980] IRLR 255. However, in *Thomas and Betts Manufacturing Co Ltd v Harding*, above, the Court of Appeal was not laying down a general principle that in selecting for redundancy the employer may not confine himself to an examination of employees holding similar positions in the same undertaking. There may be cases where it is not reasonable for the employer simply to restrict his attention to those employees who hold similar positions. In *Green v A and I Fraser (Wholesale Fish Merchants) Ltd* [1985] IRLR 55, it was held that Green was fairly selected as the driver to be made redundant on the basis of last in, first out, although there was another employee, a mechanic, who occasionally did some driving and had less service than Green. Where the work is unskilled it may be easier to fit in an employee of long standing at the expense of an employee who has been recently recruited. As *Green's* case makes clear there is no obligation to bump. It may be unfair to dismiss an employee for redundancy simply because there was a diminution in the employer's requirements for work which the employee was actually doing, if there is other work which the employee can be required to do under the terms of his contract. See *Cowen v Haden Carrier Ltd* [1982] IRLR 225; and *NC Watling and Co Ltd v Richardson*, above.

Length of service may be an important factor to be taken into account in determining the fairness of selection: see *Bessenden Properties Ltd v Corness* [1973] IRLR 365 and *Thomas and Betts Manufacturing Co Ltd v Harding*, above, but it is not a principle of law that selection must be on a last in, first out basis.

Where the criteria for selection are other than last in, first out, the employer must be able to show that the criteria are reasonable, and that they have been applied rationally and effectively where large numbers are involved. Selection should be on a structured and comparative basis and over-subjective assessments or bias should be avoided: *Grieg v Sir Alfred McAlpine and Son (Northern) Ltd* [1979] IRLR 372. This approach was confirmed in *Williams and Others v Compair Maxam Ltd* [1982] IRLR 83. The EAT recognised in this latter case that the burden of proof as set out in *Grieg's* case, above, has been amended by s 6 of the EA 1980. Although the burden of proof has been altered, in practical terms it is for the employer to show what criteria have been used and why he considered that these criteria are reasonable, as these are matters within his knowledge. The nature of the burden of proof may mean that the evidence which the employer has to adduce to enable the tribunal to reach its decision under s 57(3) of the EP(C)A 1978, as amended by s 6 of the EA 1980 may not be as great as previously: see *Williams and Others v Compair Maxam Ltd*, above.

In *Graham v ABF Ltd* [1986] IRLR 90, the EAT found that it was open to a tribunal to uphold a selection for redundancy based on the employee's attitude to his work as well as the employee's quality of work, and his efficiency in carrying it out. The EAT recognised that while an assessment of the employee's attitude to work involved personal and subjective judgments, and was dangerously vague, it was not so inherently nebulous and subjective a concept that it could play no part in any fair basis for redundancy selection. Nonetheless, the EAT hoped that so nebulous a criterion would not be found again in a negotiated agreement for redundancy selection. It found that the more vague and the more subjective the test used by the employer the greater should be the opportunity for personal consultation before the employee is judged by it.

Other factors may outweigh length of service. Examples are better management potential, administrative ability, stronger personality, more drive and greater cost-consciousness: *Lovie v Hugh Macrae and Co (Builders) Ltd* (1977) (unreported); or lesser expense: *Joines v B and S (Burknall) Ltd* [1977] IRLR 83; or greater skill and efficiency: see *Shaw v Garden King Frozen Foods Ltd* [1975] IRLR 98; a greater degree of experience in the operation of a particular piece of machinery: *(1) Abbotts and (2) Standley v Wesson-Glynwed Steels Ltd* [1982] IRLR 51; but it may not be fair to select a bachelor in preference to a married man who has less service: *Pickering v Kingston Mobile Units* [1978] IRLR 102.

In *BL Cars Ltd v Lewis* [1983] IRLR 59, it was held that there was no justification for attaching 'priority' to the employee's length of service so that there had to be major shortcomings in the employee's performance if this were to outweigh the length of service. Here, the employer's need was to retain a balanced workforce and in making the selection the employers were entitled to take into account length of service, occupation and skill without giving priority to length of service.

In *Noble and Others v David Gold and Son (Holdings) Ltd* [1980] IRLR 252, female employees were employed in a warehouse to do light work and men were employed to do heavy work. There was a reduction in the employer's need for the lighter work and six women were dismissed even though some had longer service than the men. There was a division in the work, based not on sex but on practical experience. The employer regarded the men's work as different. The Court of Appeal held the selection was fair.

In *Forman Construction Ltd v Kelly* [1977] IRLR 468, the EAT held that employers should take into account personal circumstances. It was unfair to select Kelly because he was a member of a particular squad of building workers whose work had run out without regard to his length of service compared with other employees and the fact that Kelly was disabled.

In *Paine and Moore v Grundy (Teddington) Ltd* [1981] IRLR 267, the employer selected employees for redundancy on the basis of their attendance records without looking at the reasons why they had been absent. The EAT held that the selection was not reasonable because the employer should have ascertained the reason for the absences before selecting the employees for redundancy.

In *Gray v Shetland Norse Preserving Co Ltd* [1985] IRLR 53, it was held that it was not incumbent upon an employer to warn an employee whose attendance record was unsatisfactory that in the event of redundancies he would be selected. It was necessary to distinguish a case where an employee was selected for redundancy because of a bad attendance record and the case where he was dismissed by reason of that bad attendance record. None the less if it is made clear to employees that a poor disciplinary record will affect selection, it may assist the employer in defending a claim for unfair dismissal based on selection for such a reason.

In selecting employees for redundancy, it seems that the employer is entitled to take into account the fact that the employees have been on strike. In *Cruickshank v Hobbs* [1977] ICR 725, six Newmarket stable lads went on strike. After the strike, five of these were selected for redundancy. It was held that the dismissal was fair. In selecting the employees the employer was entitled to rely on the fact that he would lose the loyalty of his remaining stable lads if he dismissed non-strikers. The EAT found that the particular factors of this case made the decision reasonable.

In establishing the fairness of selection the employer may show that the method of selection has been discussed with the union representative: see *Clyde Pipeworks Ltd v Foster* [1978] IRLR 313; and *Dutton v Hawker Siddeley Aviation Ltd* [1978] ICR 1057.

Where the employee is registered as disabled, special consideration must be given to him in the event of his prospective selection for redundancy: see *Seymour v British Airways Board* [1983] ICR 148 and *Hobson v GEC Telecommunications Ltd* [1985] ICR 777. See also s 9(5) of the Disabled Persons (Employment) Act 1944, which provides that an employer who employs a person registered as handicapped by a disablement shall not, unless he has reasonable cause for doing so, discontinue the employment of that person.

2.3 The 1972 code of practice

The 1972 code has been repealed. The precedent of earlier cases remains. The tribunal is entitled to consider these in deciding the fairness of the dismissal.

In determining whether the dismissal is unfair because it is not reasonable in all the circumstances, the tribunal was entitled to look at the 1972 code. Paragraphs 45 and 46 of the 1972 code gave specific guidelines on redundancies. As a first step the employer was required to possess a policy for dealing with redundancies.

Where redundancies became necessary, then the employer should ensure that restrictions were placed on recruiting, save in so far as recruiting was necessary. Where recruiting was necessary, the need should be made clear to the employees or their representatives. Employees should be given the opportunity of retaining to enable them to fill the vacancies. Transfer within the employer's organisation should be considered where possible. Overtime should be reduced save where overtime work was necessary to keep a particular process going, or particular skills or expertise were required. Short-time working to cover temporary fluctuations in manpower needs should be introduced. Where dismissals for redundancy were required, the retirement of employees beyond the normal retiring age should be the first step. If redundancies were necessary employers should again, where feasible, consider volunteers. Apart from the provisions of the 1972 code, an employer is still required to consult with trade union representatives over redundancies and to notify the Secretary of State under ss 99 and 100 of the Employment Protection Act 1975. Where redundancies took place, the employer should attempt a phased run-down of employment. The employer should establish which employees were to be made redundant and the order of discharge. Once he had decided he should give the employees or their representatives as much warning as was practicable and should also notify the Department of Employment. Where appropriate, in conjunction with the Department of Employment, the employer should co-operate in finding the employees other employment and give them time off for that purpose. (There is a statutory obligation: see s 31 of the EP(C)A 1978.) There may be situations where it was desirable to make the facts known to members of the general public. Where the employer did this, he should ensure that no announcement was made until the employees and their representatives had been told.

Redundancy dismissals may be substantially unfair which includes questions of selection, or procedural unfairness.

2.4 Procedural unfairness

(a) Warning and consultation   In *Short v Clarkson International Tools Ltd* [1973] IRLR 49, the tribunal found that Short's dismissal was unfair because of the 'unnecessarily abrupt and perfunctory manner' of the dismissal. There had been no warning and no consultation. The decision was upheld by the NIRC which found that warnings and consultation might only be dispensed with where 'the situation was truly exceptional'. The NIRC had in mind cases where 'a premature announcement of redundancy may shake confidence in the product

and excessively long notice . . . may be very damaging to morale'; *Clarkson International Tools Ltd v Short* [1973] IRLR 90. See also *Rigby v British Steel Corporation* [1973] ICR 160. Following these cases, tribunals were ready to find that a dismissal for redundancy was unfair where the code had not been observed. Where the employee had suffered no loss thereby, a nil award of compensation might result, as in *Clarkson International Tools Ltd v Short* [1973] IRLR 90.

There then followed a series of cases which placed less emphasis on the need for warnings and consultation. See *George M Whiley Ltd v Anderson* [1977] ICR 167; *Quinton Hazell Ltd v Earl* [1976] IRLR 296, and *Delanair Ltd v Mead* [1976] ICR 522. In *British United Shoe Machinery Co Ltd v Clarke* [1978] ICR 70 the EAT found that where there had been a lack of consultation it was necessary to consider what would have been the likely result if the employer had done what should have been done. If it would not have made the slightest difference it was open to a tribunal to find either that the dismissal was not unfair or that it was unfair, but there should be no compensation. Since the decision in *Polkey v AE Dayton Services Ltd* [1988] ICR 142, this approach can no longer be followed.

In *Williams and Others v Compair Maxam Ltd* [1982] ICR 156, the EAT referred to the code of practice (see paras 46 and 65–8 of the 1972 code of practice) and reminded tribunals that they are statutorily bound to take the code of practice into account.

The importance of the code of practice was re-emphasised in a number of cases. In *Freud v Bentalls Ltd* [1982] IRLR 443, the EAT held:

Turning now to considerations of industrial relations practice, consultation (as opposed to unilateral action by the employer) is one of the foundation stones of modern industrial relations practice. The statutory code of practice emphasises its importance in every aspect of industrial relations. In the particular sphere of redundancy, good industrial relations practice in the ordinary case requires consultation with the redundant employee so that the employer may find out whether the needs of the business can be met in some way other than by dismissal and, if not, what other steps the employer can take to ameliorate the blow to the employee. In some cases (though not this one) the employee may be able to suggest some re-organisation which will obviate the need for dismissal; in virtually all cases the employer, if he consults, will find out what steps he can take to find the employee alternative employment within the company or outside it. For example, in present day conditions when so many people are unemployed, many employees facing redundancy by reason of the disappearance of their existing job are prepared to take other jobs of lower status and commanding less pay. Only by consulting the employee can the employer discover whether such an option is open in any given case. Therefore good industrial relations practice requires that, unless there are special circumstances which render such consultation impossible or unnecessary, a fair employer will consult with the employee before dismissing him.

We must emphasise that we are not saying that good industrial relations practice *invariably* requires such consultation. There may well be circumstances (for example a catastrophic cash flow problem making it essential to take immediate steps to reduce the wages bill) which render consultation impracticable. We are only saying that we would expect a reasonable employer, if he has not consulted the employee prior to dismissal for redundancy in any given case, to be able to show some special reason why he had not done so.

In *Holden v Bradville Ltd* [1985] IRLR 483, the EAT held:

There is very little dispute these days as to what represents a fair industrial practice in such a context, because since 1972 the code of practice has provided that before taking the final decision to make any substantial reduction in their workforce, management should consult employees or their representatives and then, if redundancy becomes necessary, should among other things establish which employees are to be made redundant in consultation as appropriate with employees or their representatives. Consultation is defined by the code as meaning the joint examination and discussion of problems of concern to both management and employees and as involving a search for mutually acceptable solutions through a genuine exchange of views and information. The code of practice has never, as such, enjoyed statutory effect but s 6(11) of the Employment Protection Act 1975 provides that in any proceedings before an Industrial Tribunal the code of practice shall be admissible in evidence, and if any provision of the code appears to the Tribunal to be relevant to any question arising in the proceedings it becomes mandatory for the Tribunal to take that into account when determining the issue of fairness.

The implementation of the code has been reinforced by a series of decisions of our own Tribunal in which powerful emphasis has been laid upon the need for consultation as one of the fundamentals of fairness. The best known of those is *Williams v Compair Maxam Ltd* [1982] IRLR 83, but there have been many others. No court has ever gone so far, however, as to hold that consultation is so essential that the absence of it will render any dismissal unfair automatically. Each case has to be looked at upon its own particular merits and judged in its own special circumstances. Provided that Industrial Tribunals act upon the general premise that consultation will normally be necessary if a redundancy selection is to be demonstrably fair, it is entirely a matter for the individual Tribunal members to decide whether in the particular circumstances presented to them, the redundancy selection was a fair one, and to make that decision whether or not there had been prior consultation.

In *F Lafferty Construction Ltd v Duthie* [1985] IRLR 487, the Scottish division of the EAT also emphasised the importance of consultation. In *Graham v ABF Ltd* [1986] IRLR 90, the EAT held that in this case the failure to consult rendered the dismissal unfair and found that because of the nebulous nature of the criterion adopted in selection 'the more powerful . . . becomes the need that the employee should be given an opportunity of personal consultation', before he is selected in accordance with that criterion. It has already been seen that where a failure to warn and consult would have made no difference the dismissal may either be fair or unfair but nil compensation is awarded.

In *Polkey*'s case, [1988] ICR 142, the importance of following a proper procedure was reiterated. Lord Bridge held:

Employers contesting a claim of unfair dismissal will commonly advance as their reason for dismissal one of the reasons specifically recognised as valid by section 57(2)(*a*), (*b*) and (*c*) of the Employment Protection (Consolidation) Act 1978. These put shortly are; . . . (*c*) that he was redundant. But an employer having prima facie grounds to dismiss for [this reason] will in the great majority of cases not act reasonably in treating the reason as a sufficient reason for dismissal unless and until he has taken the steps, conveniently classified in most of the authorities as 'procedural', which are necessary in the circumstances of the case to justify that course of action . . . ; in the case of redundancy, the employer will normally not act reasonably unless he warns and consults any employees affected or their representative, adopts a fair basis on which to select for redundancy and takes such steps as may be reasonable to avoid or minimise redundancy by redeployment within his own organisation. If an employer has failed to take the appropriate procedural steps in any particular case, the one question the industrial tribunal is *not* permitted to ask in applying the test of reasonableness posed by section 57(3) is the hypothetical question whether it would have made any difference to the outcome if the appropriate procedural steps had been taken. On the true construction of section 57(3) this question is simply irrelevant. It is quite a different matter if the tribunal is able to conclude that the employer himself, at the time of dismissal, acted reasonably in taking the view that, in the exceptional circumstances of the particular case, the procedural steps normally appropriate would have been futile, could not have altered the decision to dismiss and therefore could be dispensed with. In such a case the test of reasonableness under section 57(3) may be satisfied.

Thus the fairness of the dismissal must be scrutinised at the moment of dismissal.

In *Walls Meat Co Ltd v Selby* [1989] ICR 601, the Court of Appeal approved the criteria in *Williams*'s case, above, and followed the approach in *Polkey*'s case.

In *Dyke and Others v Hereford and Worcester County Council* [1989] ICR 800, the EAT again emphasised the importance of consultation. It held:

The phases of redundancy would seem to be as follows: first, the consideration of the overall necessity for redundancies; secondly, the issuing of the section 99 notice; thirdly, the selection of individuals whom it is proposed to dismiss for redundancy; fourthly, the actual issue of the dismissal notice, action taken on the decisions earlier reached, and lastly, the period of notice before the employment is terminated. At each of the four stages, it is important that consultation should take place either with the trade union and (if the trade union will permit it—which it did not in the present case) with the employees individually or with both, and the importance of such consultation cannot be over-emphasised. Such consultation must necessarily be based upon sufficient information for them to be sensible.

It held that in a redundancy case the tribunal should examine the procedures up to the moment when the notice of dismissal was issued and decide on the facts whether the employer had acted reasonably. Then it should examine what had occurred during the period of notice for two purposes, first, if the employer had acted reasonably up to the issue of the notice to see whether he continued to do so up to the date of termination and, secondly, if he had acted unreasonably at the date of the issue of the notice to see whether that part of the procedure which had been criticised had, if it was capable of rectification had been rectified before the date of termination.

In *Selby*'s case, above, the Court of Appeal held that while in an appropriate case there should be a two-stage consultation, first with the union and then with the employees selected for redundancy, it was not always necessary to enter into such a two-stage process. Dismissal was held to be unfair because of the failure to consult with the individual even though the union had been consulted.

For a general discussion of procedural issues see Chapter 7.

Where the dismissal is unfair because the employer has failed to warn and consult with the employee, it may be that if the employer had warned and consulted, the employee would still have been dismissed. This may mean that the employee, though unfairly dismissed, will recover no compensation (other than a redundancy payment). However, as *(1) Abbotts and (2) Standley v Wesson-Glynwed Steels Ltd* [1982] IRLR 51, illustrates, even if there had been warnings and consultations but the employee would still have been dismissed there may still be a loss. The EAT found that had there been consultations with Abbotts he would have remained in employment for a longer period to enable consultations to take place, and awarded 14 days' remuneration as compensation. If, as a result of a failure to warn and consult the employee, he has been deprived of the opportunity of filling another vacancy, the losses will be more substantial. It is for the tribunal to assess the loss. It must compensate the employee for the financial loss suffered and should not award compensation out of benevolence or as a mark of disapproval of the employer's actions: *Lifeguard Assurance Ltd v Zadrozny* [1977] IRLR 56, or indeed as a topping up of the employee's redundancy payments. In *Polkey*'s case Lord Bridge, quoting the judgment of Browne-Wilkinson J, in *Sillifant v Powell Duffryn Timber Ltd* [1983] IRLR 91, held that:

There is no need for an 'all or nothing' decision. If the industrial tribunal thinks there is a doubt whether or not the employee would have been dismissed, this element can be reflected by reducing the normal amount of compensation by a percentage representing the chance that the employee would still have lost his employment.

The second consideration is perhaps of particular importance in redundancy cases. An industrial tribunal may conclude, as in the instant case, that the appropriate procedural steps would not have avoided the employee's dismissal as redundant . . . if . . . that conclusion does not defeat his claim for unfair dismissal, the industrial tribunal, apart from any question of compensation, will also have to consider whether to make any order under section 69 of the Act of 1978. It is noteworthy that an industrial tribunal may, if it thinks fit, make an order for re-engagement under that section and in so doing exercise a very wide discretion as to the terms of the order. In a case where an industrial tribunal held that dismissal on the ground of redundancy would have been inevitable at the time when it took place even if the appropriate procedural steps had been taken, I do not, as at present advised, think this would necessarily preclude a discretionary order for re-engagement on suitable terms, if the altered circumstances considered by the tribunal at the date of the hearing were thought to justify it.

Once unfair dismissal has been established, the onus of proof is on the employee to show his losses. The tribunal must not speculate, or guess, or top up, a redundancy payment. Equally, it must not attempt to apply the onus of proof 'so strictly that no claimant can hope to discharge it': *Barley v Amey Roadstone Corporation Ltd (No 2)* [1978] ICR 190. Once the employee puts forward some coherent, sensible suggestion as to what the loss is likely to be through the employer's failure the evidential burden will usually shift to the employer.

There may be situations where the employer has exceptional reasons why he did not warn and consult. Possible reasons may be in the interests of the other employees or the continuance of the business. In such exceptional circumstances the dismissal may be found fair: see *Polkey*'s case, above; consider *Clarkson International Tools Ltd v Short*, above; *James v Waltham Holy Cross UDC* [1973] ICR 398, where the decisions would arguably have been the same if they had been decided after *Polkey*'s case, above. Consultation with the employee's union without consulting the employee may be insufficient. See below.

The statutory obligation to consult and unfair dismissal A further obligation is introduced by s 99 of the Employment Protection Act (EPA) 1975. Section 99 requires the employer before dismissing for redundancy an employee of a description in respect of which an independent trade union is recognised, to consult with the representatives of that union. Consultation must start at the earliest opportunity. There are minimum prescribed periods depending upon the number of employees it is proposed to dismiss by reason of redundancy within certain periods. Where, due to special circumstances, it is not reasonably practicable for the employer to comply with his statutory obligations, he need only take such steps as are reasonably practicable in the circumstances. The employer's failure to carry out his statutory obligations may result in proceedings under s 101 of the EPA 1975 for a protective award. Only the appropriate trade union is entitled to make a complaint which is heard by a tribunal. The question which arises is, to what extent is the individual employee entitled to rely upon the employer's failure to consult under s 99 of the EPA 1975?

At first it seemed that the employee could rely upon the employer's failure to consult with the representatives of the union when claiming unfair dismissal. In *Kelly v Upholstery and Cabinet Works (Amesbury) Ltd* [1977] IRLR 91, the employee was dismissed without any warning or consultation either under the 1972 code or s 99 of the EPA 1975. There was a recognised union. The EAT found the dismissal was unfair. There should have been consultation under the 1972 code and also under s 99. The employer's failure under s 99 was something the employee could rely upon in claiming unfair dismissal.

In *North East Midlands Co-operative Society Ltd v Allen* [1977] IRLR 212, the approach in *Kelly*'s case was followed by another division of the EAT. It held that s 99 of the EPA 1975 makes warnings and consultations necessary in every case where there is a recognised union unless there are exceptional circumstances. Again, the employee could rely upon the employer's failure under s 99 in the claim for unfair dismissal.

In both the above cases there were particular circumstances where the dismissals had been carried out without warnings and consultations flagrantly in breach of both the obligation under s 99 of the EA 1975 and also the 1972 code.

In *Gorman v London Computer Training Centre Ltd* [1978] ICR 394, the EAT found that the approach in *Kelly v Upholstery and Cabinet Works (Amesbury) Ltd*, above, needed to be applied with care. This approach was confirmed by the Court of Sessions in *Atkinson v George Lindsay and Co* [1980] IRLR 196.

In *Forman Construction Ltd v Kelly* [1977] IRLR 468, the Scottish division of the EAT found that the right conferred by s 99 of the EA 1975 was a limited one. The remedy was provided by s 101 of the EA 1975, and no other rights are conferred on either the union or the employee for failure to follow the prescribed procedure. It is considered that this is the correct approach.

None the less a failure to consult with the recognised union may have a considerable bearing upon a claim for unfair dismissal. Thus in *Williams and Others v Compair Maxam Ltd* [1982] IRLR 83, the EAT confirmed that s 99 of the EA 1975 does not confer any legal rights other than those contained in s 101. Section 99 gives statutory confirmation of the approach to be followed in handling redundancies where there is a recognised union; a departure from this approach is justifiable only in special circumstances. Paragraph 46 of the code of practice indicates a similar approach and the tribunal is obliged by law to consider the code of practice in deciding what is good industrial practice which a reasonable employer will adopt. In this case there had been no consultation on the criteria to be followed in selecting employees for redundancy. The EAT considered that if there had been consultation reasonable management would not have insisted on the criteria that were followed. Furthermore, consultation with the recognised union might also have been relevant to the question of transfers within the organisation. These factors, *inter alia*, influenced the finding of the tribunal that the dismissals were unfair. See also

Grundy (Teddington) Ltd v Plummer and Salt [1983] IRLR 98. See also *Tilgate Pallets Ltd v Barras* [1983] IRLR 231.

Even where the employer has consulted with a recognised union it is not open to the employer to infer that an individual employee is privy to the negotiations. Notwithstanding that consultation has taken place with a recognised union, a failure to consult with an individual, where such consultation is likely to have produced a different result, may lead to the dismissal being unfair: see *Huddersfield Parcels Ltd v Sykes* [1981] IRLR 115. In *Pink v (1) White and (2) White and Co (Earls Barton) Ltd* [1985] IRLR 489, the EAT emphasised 'that it is not desirable for an employer to seek to discharge his duty by referring questions of redundancy solely to a trade union instead of consulting the employee as well'. The EAT found that the tribunal was justified in concluding that individual consultation would have made no difference. See also the guidance given in *Dyke and Others v Hereford and Worcester County Council*, above.

Even if the failure to consult under s 99 is relevant to the employee's claim for unfair dismissal, there is likely to be a limit upon the compensation which he can recover. In *Barley v Amey Roadstone Corporation Ltd (No 2)* [1978] ICR 190, the company failed to consult with the recognised union. The union complained to a tribunal and was granted a protective award for a period of 28 days. The employees successfully claimed unfair dismissal because of a failure to consult. The tribunal awarded compensation on the basis that if proper consultations had taken place the dismissals would have occurred 28 days later. It held that if consultations had taken place there was no probability that the employees would not have been dismissed.

(b) Alternative employment Under the 1972 code employers were obliged to consider transferring employees to other work or to other establishments within the undertaking.

In *Vokes Ltd v Bear* [1974] ICR 1, Bear was employed as a works manager by the company. The company was taken over by the Tilling Group and Bear was told that he was to be made redundant and was asked to leave forthwith. The tribunal found that the dismissal was unfair because no attempt had been made to see whether Bear could have been employed elsewhere within the group, which consisted of some 300 companies. Shortly after the dismissal another company within the group was advertising for persons to fill senior management positions. For the company it was argued that there was no centralised personnel system which could provide the information as to vacancies. The tribunal considered that it was practicable for the company to make enquiries to help Bear. The NIRC upheld the decision.

Following the decision in *Bear*'s case, in *Perks v Geest Industries Ltd* [1974] IRLR 228, the tribunal found that the employer was required to look not only at the transportation division of the company where the employee was employed, but throughout the company. In *Smith v*

Collinsons Precision Screw Co Ltd [1975] IRLR 196, the tribunal held that the company should have looked not only at companies within the same division but also at companies in other divisions.

More recent decisions of the EAT have suggested that the employer's obligations are not so strict as were suggested in *Bear's* case. In *Cliff v Reed Building Products Ltd* (1977) (unreported), the EAT applied the test of company law, holding that the company was under no obligation to look at separate companies within the goup.

In *Quinton Hazell Ltd v Earl* [1976] IRLR .296, it was held that employers are required to take reasonable steps to look for other employment but it may well be that they are not required to search for other employment. The EAT found that the dismissal might be unfair if the employer had not taken one single reasonable step to seek alternative employment, but it may be sufficient to show that consideration has been given to the employee's position. In making inquiries the employer should carry out proper investigations. He may fail to satisfy the tribunal if the evidence is exiguous or perfunctory. In addition, he must see that the employee has enough information about any alternative position, including financial prospects, to enable a realistic decision to be made. This obligation exists independently of any request by the employee: *Modern Injection Moulds Ltd v Price* [1976] ICR 370.

There may be an obligation on the employer to retain the employee if he would be able to relocate the employee in the near future: *Allwood v William Hill (North East) Ltd* [1974] IRLR 258.

In *Avonmouth Construction Co Ltd v Shipway* [1979] IRLR 14, the EAT held that the company had a duty to consider carefully whether they could transfer the employee to another vacancy within the undertaking but added that whether the vacant position involved demotion was something for the employee to worry about. Shipway's dismissal was unfair because the employer had not offered him a job which would have involved demotion for him.

Where the employee is employed under a fixed-term contract and his employment is brought to an end through redundancy during the continuance of the fixed term it may be fair to dismiss the employee if there is no other work for him to do. However the tribunal must be satisfied on the basis of credible evidence that enquiries about alternative work have been made without success: *Holliday Concrete (Testing) Ltd v Woods* [1979] IRLR 301. The fact that the dismissal is not unfair does not deprive the employee of his common law right to claim wrongful dismissal. The employer's obligation may probably be best described as an obligation to take such steps as a reasonable employer would consider important in an effort to find alternative employment: *Cox v Wildt Mellor, Bromley Ltd* [1978] ICR 736.

In *Thomas and Betts Manufacturing Co Ltd v Harding* [1980] IRLR 255, the employee, a packer, was dismissed by reason of redundancy.

The Court of Appeal rejected a contention that the employer is under no obligation to look among his other employees, other than those employed in similar positions to the dismissed employee to see if there were any alternative employment. However, the Court of Appeal held that a tribunal was entitled to conclude that the employer should have found work for the employee as a packer, notwithstanding the fact that that would have necessitated dismissing a recently recruited packer. The Court of Appeal approved the decision in *Vokes Ltd v Bear*, above.

In *Barratt Construction Ltd v Dalrymple* [1984] IRLR 385, the EAT found that the reasonable employer will not dismiss an employee by reason of redundancy if he can employ him elsewhere. Although under s 57(3) of the EP(C)A 1978, there is now a neutral burden of proof, this principle still holds good.

Since the decision in *Polkey*'s case, above, if the employer fails to follow a fair procedure which Lord Bridge considered included taking reasonable steps to avoid or minimise redundancy in the organisation, the dismissal will be unfair unless at the time of the dismissal the employer reasonably concluded in the exceptional circumstances of the case following a proper procedure would have been futile.

There is a difference of emphasis between *Bear* and *Harding* on the one hand and *Dalrymple* on the other. Although much will depend upon the facts of each case, the difference in part is due to the fact that the Scottish division of the EAT which considered *Dalrymple's* case, above, has expressed the view that if a dismissal is not automatically unfair under s 59 of the EP(C)A 1978 it is very difficult for it to be found unfair under s 57(3) of the EP(C)A 1978. The decision in *Dalrymple*'s case, above, was also reached after s 57(3) had been amended by s 6 of the EA 1980.

Finally, in *MDH Ltd v Sussex* [1986] IRLR 123, the EAT found that the tribunal had erred in law in finding an employee's dismissal for redundancy unfair primarily because the employers had failed to look for alternative employment amongst other companies within the same group. (MDH Ltd was in fact part of the Tilling Group, as was Vokes Ltd.) The EAT found that the decision in *Vokes Ltd v Bear*, above, did not lay down any principle of law.

Where, shortly after the dismissal, a job becomes available, then it is open to argument that since it was not available at the time of the dismissal, the failure subsequently to offer that job could not affect the fairness of the dismissal. Consider *Octavius Atkinson and Sons Ltd v Morris* [1989] IRLR 158, and *Labour Party v Oakley* [1987] ICR 178 (overturned on different grounds [1988] ICR 403).

Where the employer makes an offer of alternative employment on unreasonable terms that may result in the dismissal being unfair: see *Elliot v Richard Stump Ltd* [1987] ICR 579, where the employer had acted unreasonably in refusing the employee a trial period to which the employee was entitled as a matter of law.

2.5 Employer's other obligations

The 1972 code provided that the employer should consider short-time working to cover a temporary fluctuation in manpower needs. It also suggested that a scheme should be introduced by the employer for voluntary redundancies. When an employer is considering dismissals for redundancy there is still an obligation upon him to consider these matters. Failure to do so will not necessarily result in the dismissal being held unfair, but the tribunal may still take account of this factor. However, for it to be held unfair the tribunal must be satisfied that if these matters were considered the employer would have adopted a different solution: *Hassall v Fusion Welding and Construction (Birkenhead) Co Ltd* [1979] IRLR 12. It may be sufficient to defeat any argument that the employer should have considered a shorter working week if such a proposal is incompatible with his business requirements: *Atkinson v George Lindsay and Co* [1980] IRLR 196.

Chapter 9

Dismissal and Maternity

1 Pregnancy

An employee is unfairly dismissed if the reason or principal reason for her dismissal is that she is pregnant or any other reason connected with her pregnancy, except (a) that at the effective date of termination she is or will have become, because of her pregnancy, incapable of adequately doing the work which she is employed to do; or (b) that, because of her pregnancy, she cannot or will not be able to continue after that date to do that work without contravention (either by her or her employer) of a duty or restriction imposed by or under any enactment: s 60(1) of the EP(C)A 1978.

Where the employee is dismissed because she is pregnant or for any reason connected with her pregnancy the dismissal is treated as automatically unfair; it is not necessary for the tribunal to consider whether the employer acted reasonably or unreasonably under s 57(3) of the EP(C)A 1978. However, where the employer is able to show one of the exceptions set out above he may be able to avoid a finding of unfair dismissal if, under s 57(3) of the EP(C)A 1978, he acted reasonably in all the circumstances.

An employee is treated as unfairly dismissed if her employer dismisses her for either reason (a) or reason (b), above, but neither the employer nor any successor of his, where there is a suitable available vacancy, makes her an offer before or on the effective date of termination to engage her under a new contract of employment complying with certain conditions: s 60(2) of the EP(C)A 1978. Again the dismissal is automatically unfair so the tribunal will not have to consider whether the employer acted reasonably or unreasonably under s 57(3).

The new contract of employment must comply with the conditions set out in s 60(3) of the EP(C)A 1978. The conditions are that:

(a) the new contract must take effect immediately on the ending of employment under the previous contract (the intervention of a weekend will not defeat this provision);

(b) the work to be done under the new contract must be of a kind

276

which is both suitable in relation to the employee and appropriate for her to do in the circumstances; and

(c) the provisions of the new contract as to the capacity and place in which she is to be employed and as to the other terms and conditions of her employment must not be substantially less favourable to her than the corresponding provisions of the previous contract.

The onus is on the employer to show that he or his successor made an offer to re-engage the employee which conforms with these conditions. Alternatively, it is for him to show that there is no suitable available vacancy for the employee: s 60(4) of the EP(C)A 1978.

The application of the 1978 Act differs in cases of dismissal for pregnancy in the following respects:

(a) Section 55(3) does not apply where the employer gives notice to the pregnant employee for a reason contained in s 60(1)(a) or (b). Section 55(3) provides that the employee is treated as dismissed where during the period of notice she gives to her employer a counter-notice: s 60(5) of the EP(C)A 1978.

(b) Section 65(3) does not apply to a dismissal where the reason is one contained in s 60(1) or (2) so that a dismissal procedure agreement cannot exclude the statutory right to claim unfair dismissal in such cases: s 65(4) of the EP(C)A 1978.

To claim an unfair dismissal on the grounds of pregnancy, the employee must have two years' continuous employment: *Reaney v Kanda Jean Products Ltd* [1978] IRLR 427; *Singer v Millward Ladsky and Co* [1979] IRLR 217. See Chapter 2.

1.1 Automatic unfairness

A dismissal will be automatically unfair where the reason or principal reason is that the employee is pregnant, or is any other reason connected with the employee's pregnancy. This provision covers both the pre-natal and post-natal position. However, the pregnancy may be coincidental. It is not automatically unfair to dismiss a pregnant woman if the employer can show that she would have been dismissed even if she had not been pregnant. In such cases, the fairness of the dismissal will be considered in accordance with s 57(3) of the EP(C)A 1978. Where the employee is pregnant, and establishes a *prima facie* case that her dismissal was because of her pregnancy or a reason connected with it, the onus is on the employer to show that the dismissal is not automatically unfair within s 60(1) of the EP(C)A 1978. This may be difficult because poor attendance, illness or lack of capability may all stem from the pregnancy or be some other reason connected with the pregnancy.

In *George v Beecham Group* [1977] IRLR 43, George had been given a final warning, following frequent absences, that if she were absent again in the next six months she would be dismissed. She became pregnant, suffered a miscarriage and entered hospital. She was dismissed. It was held that the reason for her dismissal was the absence caused by her miscarriage—a reason connected with her pregnancy. The tribunal held that under s 60 of the EP(C)A 1978, there has to be a distinction between ill-health which is and ill-health which is not connected with the pregnancy.

If the employer did not know or believe that the employee was pregnant when he dismissed her the reason for the dismissal cannot be that the employee was pregnant nor can it be some other reason connected with her pregnancy. In *Del Monte Foods Ltd v Mundon* [1980] IRLR 224, Mundon had been away from work on several occasions because of gastro-enteritis or some other form of intestinal upset. She was again away from work due to some intestinal upset. The employer decided to dismiss her because of gastro-enteritis, although before they dismissed her they learned that she was pregnant. It was found that the reason for the dismissal was the gastro-enteritis.

The employer must show that because of her pregnancy the employee is incapable of adequately doing the work. However, the pregnancy may affect the employee's conduct. It remains to be seen whether tribunals will interpret 'incapable of adequately doing the work' (in s 60(1)(*a*) of the 1978 Act) as extending to the employee's conduct.

The phrase 'or any other reason connected with her pregnancy' has been broadly interpreted. In *Stockton-on-Tees Borough Council v Brown* [1988] ICR 410, Brown was employed on a temporary contract as a care supervisor in the Youth Training Scheme. The council were advised by the Manpower Services Commission that they were going to withdraw funding for the existing post after 31 March 1985. Three vacancies had arisen for the post of supervisor/instructor under a revised scheme. There were four applicants for the new post from among the staff who were to be made redundant and the employers applied selection criteria which included the applicants' ability to undertake their duties. Brown was pregnant. The employer considered that since she would require maternity leave at the end of April and would be away from work for between six to eight weeks, she would be unable to fulfil the contract and was not offered a position as a supervisor/instructor.

The House of Lords held that the selection of a woman for redundancy because she is pregnant and will require maternity leave is a dismissal for a reason connected with her pregnancy within s 60 of the EP(C)A 1978. Brown was unfairly dismissed. Redundancy is not one of the reasons for dismissing a pregnant woman which s 60 makes potentially fair. Her pregnancy was the reason why she is selected for dismissal on the grounds of redundancy. The reason for her dismissal was directly and intimately connected with her pregnancy. The House of Lords held that if an employer dismisses a woman because she is pregnant the dismissal is automatically unfair. The same principle should apply where the employee is selected for redundancy. In *Clayton v Vigers* [1989] ICR 713, Vigers was dismissed after the birth because the employer had been unable to employ a temporary assistant and had engaged a permanent replacement. It was held that her dismissal was automatically unfair under s 60(1) of the EP(C)A 1978. Following the decision in *Brown*'s case, the EAT found that the background to the dismissal was the pregnancy or its after-effects. It considered that the words, 'any other reason connected with her pregnancy', ought to be read widely so as to give full effect to the Statute.

Absence at the effective date of termination may mean that the employee is, because of her pregnancy, incapable of adequately doing the work which she is employed to do. If the employer can establish this he will be able to show a reason for the dismissal and provided that he acted reasonably under s 57(3), the dismissal will be fair.

Initially it was believed that to claim the benefit of this defence to automatically unfair dismissal the employer had to show that the employee was incapable of adequately doing the work because of the pregnancy and not for some reason connected with the pregnancy: see *Elegbede v The Wellcome Foundation Ltd* [1979] IRLR 383. However, in *Grimsby Carpet Co Ltd v Bedford* [1987] IRLR 438, the EAT did not accept that the defence only applies where the incapability is because the woman is pregnant and not for some other reason connected with her pregnancy. The phrase used in s 60(1)(a) of the EP(C)A 1978 is not 'because she is pregnant', but 'because of her pregnancy'. That phrase covers the phrase in the first part of s 60(1) that 'she is pregnant or is any other reason connected with her pregnancy'.

A case where the employer was able to claim the benefit of this provision is *Vaughan v Suede Club Co Ltd* (1977) (unreported). Vaughan, a secretary/receptionist, had been able to work for only 3 complete weeks in the 11 weeks preceding the dismissal because of her pregnancy. She was no longer capable of adequately doing the work because of her pregnancy. The company was a small employer and her absence had a detrimental effect upon its business. The dismissal was therefore held to be fair.

Pregnancy may result in the employee being absent thus affecting her capability. It may mean that the employee's overall capability to do her job is impaired. The onus is upon the employer to show that the employee is incapable of adequately doing the work. If he can establish the reason the tribunal must be satisfied that he acted reasonably.

In *Brear v Wright Hudson Ltd* [1977] IRLR 287, Brear was a shop assistant in a chemist's shop. Her job involved considerable lifting and carrying. The company's manager, a pharmacist, who had medical knowledge, concluded that because of difficulties surrounding her pregnancy she would not be able to carry out her duties. She was dismissed and the dismissal was held to be fair. While pregnancy might not in the normal case prevent a shop assistant from carrying out her duties, including some lifting, the element of lifting and carrying in this case was considerable. She would not be capable of doing this. The tribunal emphasised that, in this case, the employer's manager had some medical knowledge. The employer may be in difficulty if he has reached his conclusion as to the employee's capability unsupported by medical or some other evidence.

A dismissal for pregnancy will not be automatically unfair if the employee cannot continue in employment without contravention of a statutory duty or restriction. The onus is on the employer to establish this reason. The tribunal must be satisfied that he acted reasonably if the dismissal is to be fair. It remains to be seen whether a breach of a code of practice under the Health and Safety at Work etc Act 1974 will entitle the employer to claim the benefits of this provision. On balance it would seem that this is not the position.

1.2 'Suitable available vacancy'

In *Martin v BSC Footwear (Supplies) Ltd* [1978] IRLR 95, Martin was engaged in 'pulling and checking'. 'Pulling' involved taking a shoe-box from the shelf as well as pushing a trolley loaded with boxes. Martin was pregnant and her medical adviser told her she should continue with the 'checking' but not with the 'pulling'. This was not acceptable to the company who dismissed her with six weeks' notice. During the notice Martin did a lighter job of display packaging in place of a sick employee. The tribunal held that the dismissal was unfair because the employer had not discharged the burden of proving that there was no suitable available vacancy. Martin could have been kept on to do the job of display packaging until the sick employee returned or Martin left, whichever was earlier. The tribunal accepted that 'suitable available vacancy' (in s 60(2) of the EP(C)A 1978) is different from 'suitable alternative vacancy'. There is no obligation on an employer to create a job or modify a job description. 'Suitable' meant 'suitable to the lady's pregnant condition and health and, in relation to any vacancy, to her particular skill, experience and qualifications'. 'Available' meant 'the suitable job should exist or can be made to exist within the given complement of the employer's staffing and the employer's layout and organisation of operations'. 'Vacancy' meant 'a job vacancy existing in the organisation, structure and layout of the work and operations of and in the employer's business as they were at the effective date of termination'.

The employer must make reasonable attempts to see if there is a suitable available vacancy for a pregnant employee.

1.3 Constructive dismissal

In the case of pregnant employees, employers must ensure that changes, such as a change in the employee's hours, intended to be for the employee's benefit, are not in fact breaches of the employee's contract entitling the employee to resign and claim a constructive dismissal. Whether pregnancy gives rise to new implied terms in the contract to be observed by an employer, breach of which will entitle the employee to claim constructive dismissal is unresolved.

1.4 Remedies

An employee who is unfairly dismissed because of pregnancy has the same remedies available to her as in the case of any other employee who is unfairly dismissed: see s 68 of the EP(C)A 1978. An employee who has 2 years' continuous employment or more, at the beginning of the 11th week before the expected week of confinement has the statutory right to return to work: s 33(3)(b) of the EP(C)A 1978.

Where an employee has the statutory right to return to work, the tribunal may make an order for reinstatement or re-engagement. The order for reinstatement or re-engagement will reflect the statutory right to return to work. However the tribunal may only award compensation. Compensation will consist of a basic and compensatory award. The compensatory award will reflect the loss arising on the dismissal leaving the employee her right to return to work in accordance with the statutory principles. The compensatory award will probably be circumscribed by the time when the employee would have left work because of pregnancy. The employee will be entitled to a basic award. If she returns to work the continuity of her employment will be preserved: para 10 of Sched 13 to the EP(C)A 1978. Since continuity of employment is preserved, then arguably in the event of a future unfair dismissal the employee would be entitled to a basic award based on the then period of continuous employment although the employee has already claimed one basic award in respect of all or part of that period of continuous employment.

The employee's right to return to work may be excluded or it may be that the right to return is on less beneficial terms than those which she enjoyed before her absence.

Thus, by virtue of s 56A of the EP(C)A 1978, s 56 of the 1978 Act will not apply if immediately before her absence the number of employees employed by her employer added to the number employed by an associated employer did not exceed five and it is not reasonably practicable for the employer or his successor to permit the employee to return to work in accordance with s 45(1) of the EP(C)A 1978 or for the employer or an associated employer to offer her employment which fulfils the conditions contained in s 56A(3). Again, s 56 of the

EP(C)A 1978 will not apply if it is not reasonably practicable, other than on the grounds of redundancy, for the employer, or his successor to permit the employee to return to work in accordance with s 45(1), but he or an associated employer offers her employment under a contract of employment which fulfils the conditions specified in s 56A(3) and she accepts or unreasonably refuses that offer.

The conditions specified in s 56A(3) of the EP(C)A 1978 are that the work to be done under the contract is of a kind which is both suitable in relation to the employee and appropriate for her to do in the circumstances; and that the provisions of the contract as to the capacity and place in which she is to be employed, and as to the other terms and conditions of her employment, are not substantially less favourable to her than if she had returned to work in accordance with s 45(1) of the EP(C)A 1978. These conditions are the same as those which must be complied with where the employee cannot return in accordance with s 45(1) because of redundancy and the employee is offered a suitable available vacancy in accordance with s 45(3) the terms of which comply with s 45(4). See **3.1**, below. As to the onus of showing s 56A applies, see **3.4**, below.

The effect of s 56A is to deprive the employee of her right to return to work following an absence from work wholly or partly because of pregnancy or confinement, where an employer with five or fewer employees establishes that it is not reasonably practicable to reinstate the employee or to offer her other suitable work (a small employer exception); or where it is not reasonably practicable for a reason other than redundancy to reinstate her and he offers her suitable alternative employment (a more general exception). These exceptions may be relevant when considering the remedies.

1.5 Sex discrimination

In *Dekker v Stichting Vormingscentrum Voor Jonge Volwassen (VJV-Centrum) Plus* [1991] IRLR 27, the European Court of Justice held that to refuse to employ a woman or to dismiss her because she is pregnant was a breach of Directive 76/207 (the Equal Treatment Directive), since it was direct discrimination on the grounds of sex. It was not necessary to compare the treatment of a pregnant woman with that of a hypothetical man. The case involved a Directive and is as such enforceable by employees of the state. In applying national law a tribunal is required to interpret national law in the light of the wording and purpose of the Directive that the law was passed to implement. Although the Sex Discrimination Act (SDA) 1975 was not passed to implement the Equal Treatment Directive and the House of Lords has held in *Duke v GEC Reliance Ltd* [1988] ICR 339, that it has no obligation to distort the meaning of the SDA 1975 in order to enforce the Directive against an individual, there would be no distortion of the SDA 1975 Act as far as the provisions relating to pregnancy are concerned. First, the Act does not stipulate that there must be a comparator, and secondly, the Act allows positive discrimination in connection with pregnancy or childbirth. Arguably, national courts should interpret national law so as to give effect to the wording and purpose of any directive: see *Marleasing SA v La Comercial International de Alimentacion* 106/89 13 November 1990.

The Directive does not depend on any service qualification. It is submitted the potential defence to an automatically unfair dismissal available to the employer under s 60(1)(*a*) (and possibly s 60(1)(*b*)) of the EP(C)A 1978 can have no relevance to a claim based on sex discrimination.

In *Handels-Og Kontorfunktionaerernes Forbund i Danmark (acting for Hertz) v Dansk Arbejdsgiverforening (acting for Aldi Marked K/S)* [1991] IRLR 31, the European Court of Justice found that a woman is protected from dismissal because of absence for a reason connected with the pregnancy or confinement during pregnancy and any maternity leave to which she has a right under national law. If she is ill after her maternity leave there is no distinction under the Directive between illness which arises out of pregnancy or confinement and any other illness. Arguably, there is protection under s 60 of the EP(C)A 1978.

Clarification of the law is awaited by the Court of Appeal in *Webb v EMO Air Cargo (UK) Ltd*. In this case the EAT (see [1990] ICR 442) found that the pregnant woman complaining of dismissal or other detriment has to show less favourable treatment than a man in the same relevant circumstances.

2 Maternity absence

An employee may claim unfair dismissal where she is dismissed during a period of maternity absence, provided that:
(*a*) she is entitled under the provisions of the EP(C)A 1978 to return to work after maternity absence;
(*b*) her contract of employment subsists during the period of her absence; and
(*c*) she is dismissed by her employer during the period of absence, after the beginning of the 11th week before the expected week of confinement: para 6(1) of Sched 2 to the EP(C)A 1978.

An employee is not to be taken as dismissed during her period of maternity absence if the dismissal occurs in the course of the employee attempting to return to work in accordance with her contract, and the employee has a statutory right and also a contractual right to return, and is taking advantage of whichever right is in any particular respect more favourable: para 6(2) of Sched 2 to the EP(C)A 1978.

During the period of maternity absence she may claim that she is dismissed for redundancy and/or unfair dismissal. The onus of proving dismissal is on her. The onus of proving the reason for dismissal will be on the employer. In cases of unfair dismissal the tribunal will have to be satisfied that the dismissal is reasonable in all the circumstances: s 57(3) of the EP(C)A 1978. The dismissal during the employee's maternity absence does not affect her right to return to work: para 6(4) of Sched 2 to the EP(C)A 1978. If the tribunal finds the dismissal unfair it may make an order for reinstatement or re-engagement. Any order for reinstatement or re-engagement may have to be modified to take into account the employee's statutory right to return to work. If the tribunal awards compensation, that compensation shall be assessed without regard to the employee's right to return to work: para 6(4)(*a*) of Sched 2 to the EP(C)A 1978.

Further, her right to return to work is exercisable only on her repaying any redundancy payment or compensation for unfair dismissal paid in respect of that dismissal if the employer requests such repayment: para 6(4)(*b*) of Sched 2 to the EP(C)A 1978.

Where the employee is dismissed during her maternity absence she is entitled to notice equivalent to the statutory minimum under s 49 of the EP(C)A 1978.

If the dismissal during absence is fair it seems that the employee is still not precluded from exercising her right to return to work: ss 45–7 of the EP(C)A 1978. The employer may refuse to have the employee back. Such refusal amounts to a dismissal (see ss 56 and 86 of the EP(C)A 1978), unless the circumstances come within the provisions contained in s 56A of the EP(C)A 1978. Where there is a refusal within s 56 the tribunal will have to consider whether this dismissal is for redundancy, and whether it is unfair, or whether it is an unfair dismissal. In practice if the dismissal during absence is fair it will be difficult to envisage the circumstances in which an employee can claim that a dismissal because of a refusal to allow her to return can be unfair.

Where the employee has a contractual right to return to work, dismissal during the maternity absence may be a breach of that contract. This may be in addition to any rights which she has in respect of unfair dismissal.

Part V (the unfair dismissal provisions) is modified by para 6(3) of Sched 2 to the EP(C)A 1978. Thus in cases of dismissal during a period of maternity absence the following provisions do not apply;

(*a*) s 64—qualifying period and upper age limit;
(*b*) s 65—exclusion of the statutory protection against unfair dismissal when there is a dismissal procedure agreement;
(*c*) s 66—revocation of exclusion order under s 65;
(*d*) s 141(2)—employment ordinarily outside Great Britain;
(*e*) s 144(2)—employment as master or crew member of fishing vessel remunerated by share in profits or gross earnings.

3 Right to return to work

3.1 Generally

Section 33(1) of the EP(C)A 1978 provides that an employee who is absent from work wholly or partly because of pregnancy or confinement is entitled to return to work, provided that she fulfils certain conditions. These conditions are contained in s 33(3) of the EP(C)A 1978. The right to return to work applies whether or not a contract of employment subsists during the period of absence. Provided the employee fulfils the conditions contained in s 33(3), it does not matter that the employee resigns where the absence is wholly or partly because of pregnancy or confinement: see *Mitchell v British Legion Club* [1980] IRLR 425. The conditions contained in s 33(3) are as follows:

(a) she continues to be employed by her employer (whether or not she is at work) until immediately before the beginning of the 11th week before the expected week of confinement;

(b) she has at the beginning of that 11th week been continuously employed for a period of not less than 2 years; and

(c) . . . she informs her employer in writing at least 21 days before her absence begins or, if that is not reasonably practicable, as soon as reasonably practicable —

    (i) that she will be (or is) absent from work wholly or partly because of pregnancy or confinement,

    (ii) that she intends to return to work with her employer, and

    (iii) of the expected week of confinement or, if the confinement has occurred, the date of confinement.

Under s 33(3)(a) it is not necessary that the employee should work until immediately before the beginning of the 11th week before the expected week of confinement. The question is whether or not she is employed. See *Satchwell Sunvic Ltd v Secretary of State for Employment* [1979] IRLR 455, and *Secretary of State for Employment v Doulton Sanitaryware Ltd* [1981] IRLR 365. Compare *J Williams and Co Ltd v Secretary of State for Employment* [1978] IRLR 235. Although these are all cases on maternity pay they involve an interpretation of s 33(3)(a).

Section 33(3)(d) ((c) above) requires the employee to inform her employer in writing of her absence and the need for writing is not dependent upon the employer's request. In addition, the employee must notify the employer of the expected week of confinement or, if the confinement has occurred, the date of confinement. This condition is intended to cover the case where the employee gives birth prematurely.

Section 33(3A), provides that where not earlier than 49 days after the beginning of the expected week of confinement or the date of confinement which has been notified to the employer under s 33(3)(d) an employee is requested by her employer or a successor of his to give him written confirmation that she intends to return to work, she will not be entitled to exercise the right to return to work unless she gives that confirmation within 14 days of receiving the request. There is a saving provision in that where it is not reasonably practicable to give that written confirmation within 14 days of receiving the request the employee must give it as soon as reasonably practicable. A request made by the employer or his successor must be made in writing and must be accompanied by a written statement setting out the effect of the foregoing provision: s 33(3B) of the EP(C)A 1978.

An employee who has been dismissed by her employer for a reason falling within s 60(1)(*a*) or (*b*) of the EP(C)A 1978 (see **1**, above) and has not been re-engaged under that section, is entitled to exercise the right to return to work notwithstanding that she has thereby ceased to be employed before the beginning of the 11th week before the expected week of confinement if, but for that dismissal, she would at the beginning of the 11th week have been continuously employed for a period of not less than 2 years. To be entitled to the right to return, she must inform her employer in writing, if he so requests, before or as soon as is reasonably practicable after the dismissal takes effect that she intends to return to work with him: s 33(4) of the EP(C)A 1978. Continuous employment until immediately before the beginning of the 11th week before the expected week of confinement requires continuity of employment throughout the 12th week before the expected week of confinement. The requirement of employment until immediately before the beginning of the 11th week is strict. If the employee leaves before the beginning of the 11th week she will lose her right even though she leaves early because of a miscalculation: see *Hepworth v Teesside High School* (1978) (unreported).

An employee is not entitled to exercise her statutory right to return to work unless, if requested to do so by her employer, she produces for his inspection a certificate from a registered medical practitioner or a registered midwife stating the expected week of confinement: s 33(5) of the EP(C)A 1978.

The employee has an obligation to notify her employer, before her absence begins, if she wishes to exercise her statutory right to return: see s 33(3) of the EP(C)A 1978.

In addition the employer has a right to enquire after the confinement whether or not she intends to return to work. Where the employee, other than in pursuance of the statutory obligation to inform her employer 21 days before her absence begins, or if that is not reasonably practicable, as soon as reasonably practicable, makes a general statement that she will not be returning to work, this will not necessarily amount to a resignation disentitling her from claiming the statutory right to return to work. It may prevent the employee substantiating a claim for unfair dismissal if she allows the employer to act on this statement to his detriment, as for instance where he engages a replacement, before the employee notifies the employer that she wants to return: see *Hughes v Gwynedd Area Health Authority* [1978] ICR 161. Where after confinement the employer makes further enquiries of the employee about whether or not she intends to return to work such a general statement made to her employer may disentitle her from claiming the statutory right to return.

An employee who does not inform her employer in writing at least 21 days before her absence begins that she intends to return, or, where she informs him after 21 days, fails to show that it was not reasonably practicable for her to inform him within 21 days, will lose her right to return. Similarly, where the employer after the date of confinement requests the employee to give written confirmation of whether or not she intends to return to work and the employee fails to respond within the 14 days or responds outside the 14 days but fails to show that it was not reasonably practicable for her to have respond within the 14 days she will lose her right to return. The tribunal may have to consider the meaning of 'reasonably practicable'. In *Nu-Swift International Ltd v Mallinson* [1978] IRLR 537, an employee who knew of her rights and the obligation to give notice did not do so because she was concerned about the health of her baby. The EAT held it was reasonably practicable for her to have given notice.

It seems to us that this right which is given by . . . [s 33 of the EP(C)A 1978] is given to someone who, within the relevant time, and assuming she knows or reasonably ought to know of the provisions of the legislation and of the procedure, has decided that she intends to go back to work. It is not intended to protect the person who at the time does not intend to go back to work but who subsequently changes her mind outside the period and seeks to give a notice explaining that there were factors which have changed and which have caused her to change her mind. Nor, it seems to us, does it cover the case of an employee who really is not sure either way. There may, in very many cases, be factors of one kind or another which may make it doubtful whether the lady will go back to work or not. Taking into account not only the interests of the employee but also the difficulties of the employer and the difficulties of the replacement who is to be appointed, we do not think that Parliament here intended that the need to resolve difficulties of the kind involved here necessarily means that it is reasonably practicable for the applicant to delay giving a notice until she has resolved the difficulties. In a case where there are factors which make it doubtful whether the employee will go back to work the obviously sensible solution is for the employee to negotiate the matter with her employer, to discuss the possibility of coming back in certain eventualities, to clarify the position. And we have no doubt that all reasonable employers would seek to accommodate a woman who had problems of this kind so far as they were able to do. But we are quite satisfied on the findings here, sympathising as we do with this lady, that the resolution of these matters is not something which made it not reasonably practicable for her not to serve the notice.

In deciding what was reasonably practicable the EAT had regard to decisions of the Court of Appeal and the EAT in deciding what was reasonably practicable for the purposes of s 67(2) of the EP(C)A 1978 (where the complaint is not made within three months of the effective date of termination). The importance of complying with the statutory provisions is illustrated by the decision of the Northern Ireland Court of Appeal in *McKnight v Adlestones (Jewellers) Ltd* [1984] IRLR 453, where McKnight had no contractual right to return to work. She failed to give at least 21 days' notice in writing before her absence began that she intended to return to work. It was held that the only inference to be drawn from the parties' intention was that the contract of employment was to be suspended during the employee's absence and could only be revived if the employee complied with her statutory right to return. Since McKnight had no contractual right to return, her failure to comply with the statutory requirements resulted in her losing her statutory right to return and the employer's refusal to have her back was not a dismissal in law. See also *FW Woolworth plc v Smith* [1990] ICR 45. In *Lucas v Norton of London Ltd* [1984] IRLR 86, Lucas failed to give the prescribed notice and lost her statutory right. Since the contract subsisted the refusal to allow her back was a dismissal.

The employee's statutory right to return to work is a right to return to work with her original employer, or, where appropriate, his successor. The right may be exercised at any time before the end of the period of 29 weeks beginning with the week in which the date of confinement falls. Date of confinement is the actual not the expected date of confinement, see *Smith's* case, above. It is a right to return to the job in which she was employed under the original contract of employment, on terms and conditions not less favourable than those which would have applied to her if she had not been so absent: s 45(1) of the EP(C)A 1978.

The 'original contract of employment', in relation to an employee who is absent from work wholly or partly because of pregnancy or confinement, means the contract under which she worked immediately before the beginning of her absence or, if she entered into that contract during her pregnancy by virtue of s 60(2) of the EP(C)A 1978 or otherwise by reason of her pregnancy, the contract under which she was employed immediately before she entered into the later contract or, if there was more than one later contract, the first of the later contracts: s 153(1) of the EP(C)A 1978.

'Job', in relation to an employee, means the nature of the work she is employed to do in accordance with her contract, and the capacity and place in which she is so employed: s 153(1). 'Terms and conditions not less favourable than those which would have been applicable to her if she had not been so absent' means, as regards seniority, pension rights and other similar rights, that the period or periods of employment prior to the employee's absence are to be regarded as continuous with her employment following her absence: s 45(2).

In *Edgell v Lloyd's Register of Shipping* [1977] IRLR 463, the tribunal found that the employee's right to return to work is not a right to return to exactly the same job. She is entitled to return to a job of the same nature and capacity at the same place. During the period of maternity leave there may be a reorganisation or change in the employer's business. This may result in a change in the employee's job, but provided this change is not fundamental, the employer will have complied with s 45.

In *McFadden v Greater Glasgow Passenger Transport Executive* [1977] IRLR 327, the employee, before her maternity leave, was employed in an established clerical position. On her return to work she was given a non-established, supernumerary, clerical post. As a supernumerary, her terms and conditions of employment were less favourable and if for instance there were redundancy dismissals in the future, she would be more at risk than an established employee. Therefore, she had not been allowed to return on terms and conditions which were not less favourable to her than she had previously enjoyed.

Whereas in *Edgell*'s case there was no dismissal, in *McFadden*'s case the employee had not been permitted to return to work in accordance with s 45 and so under s 56 of the EP(C)A 1978 there was a dismissal which was held to be unfair.

It is the job under the original contract to which the employee is entitled to return, not any job which was given to her during her pregnancy, for instance, because that was a lighter job and she was more able to do it.

3.2 Right to return and redundancy

Where an employee is entitled to return to work, but it is not practicable by reason of redundancy (for the meaning of redundancy see s 81 of the EP(C)A 1978 and Chapter 8, 1, above) for the employer to permit her to return to work she is entitled, where there is a suitable available vacancy, to be offered alternative employment with her employer or his successor or an associated employer: s 45(3) of the EP(C)A 1978. The new contract of employment must comply with certain conditions (contained in s 45(4) of the EP(C)A 1978):

(*a*) the work to be done under the contract must be of a kind which is both suitable in relation to the employee and appropriate for her to do in the circumstances; and

(*b*) the provisions of the new contract as to the capacity and place in which she is to be employed and as to the other terms and conditions of her employment must not be substantially less favourable to her than if she had returned to work with her original employer (or, where appropriate, his successor) in the job in which she was employed under the original contract of employment, and on terms and conditions not less favourable than those which would have been applicable to her if she had not been so absent.

In *Community Task Force v Rimmer* [1986] IRLR 203, the EAT held that the test of availability in s 45(3) is not expressed to be qualified by considerations of what is economic or reasonable. If a suitable vacancy is available the consequences of the employer offering the job to the employee are not relevant to the consideration of s 45(3).

Suitability to the employee presupposes the application of the same tests as in the case of a dismissal for redundancy. This is a concept borrowed from the redundancy payments provisions where there is an offer of alternative employment. It is reasonable to assume this provision will be interpreted in broadly the same way. 'Appropriate for her to do in the circumstances' does not have its origin in the redundancy payments provisions. The phrase suggests that the tribunal can consider the particular problems of the employee following the confinement. Greater protection is therefore given to the redundant employee who is seeking to return to work following a pregnancy and/or confinement. The phrase 'not substantially less favourable' is also different to the corresponding provisions relating to redundancy payments: see s 82(6) of the EP(C)A 1978. It may well have the effect of extending the range of jobs that can be offered to the employee over and above the original contract as well as over and above what could have been offered to her were it a redundancy in the ordinary course of events without the intervention of a period of absence for pregnancy or confinement.

If the employee declines work which is suitable and appropriate for her to do she will not be entitled to a redundancy payment.

Where the employee is not permitted to return because of redundancy, she is treated as dismissed (see s 86 of the EP(C)A 1978) and she may have a claim under Part IV of the EP(C)A 1978. She may also be able to claim unfair dismissal. Where the employer fails to offer her alternative employment within s 45(3) of the EP(C)A 1978 where there is a suitable available vacancy, that failure shall be treated as an automatically unfair dismissal: para 2(2) of Sched 2 to the EP(C)A 1978.

Where the employee is not allowed to return to work because of a redundancy following an absence for pregnancy and/or confinement, the dismissal may also be automatically unfair under s 59 of the EP(C)A 1978 or it may be unfair where the employer has not acted reasonably: s 57(3) of the EP(C)A 1978.

Unless it is a case falling within para 5 of Sched 2, the employee will be regarded as having been continuously employed up to the notified day of return and her redundancy entitlement will be calculated accordingly.

3.3 *Exercise of the right to return*

An employee must exercise her right to return to work by giving written notice to her employer, who may be her original employer, or a successor of that employer, at least 21 days before the date on which she proposes to return, of her proposal to return on that day, which is referred to as the notified day of return: s 47(1) of the EP(C)A 1978. The requirement that the employee should give written notice to her employer 21 days before the date on which she proposes to return is a mandatory requirement. The giving of the notice is of critical importance, since all the employee's other rights flow from it. Unless 21 days' notice has been given which comply with the provisions of s 47(1), the employee cannot claim unfair dismissal under s 56 of the EP(C)A 1978 because the right only arises where the employee has exercised her right to return in accordance with s 47. It is also clear that the employee must also comply with the provisions of s 47(1), even where the employee's contract of employment subsists during the period of absence for maternity. By virtue of s 48(2) of the EP(C)A 1978, where an employee relies on a contractual right to return following a period of absence for maternity she is treated as exercising a composite right. However that right is subject to the provisions of s 47 and s 56 of the EP(C)A 1978. A failure to allow the employee to return where the employee exercises or seeks to exercise her composite right gives rise to a claim under s 56 for unfair dismissal. Once again the right to claim unfair dismissal under s 56 depends, *inter alia*, upon the employee having complied with the requirements of s 47(1). It might be different if the contract contained some express provision dealing with the right to return: see *Lavery v Plessey Telecommunications Ltd* [1982] IRLR 180, upheld on appeal [1983] IRLR 202; and *Kolfor Plant Ltd v Wright* [1982] IRLR 311, where the EAT held that if the employee cannot bring herself within the provisions of s 56, s 55 does not apply. See *Lucas*, above. This section can only apply if the employee was dismissed otherwise than in the course of exercising her right to return.

An employer may postpone an employee's return to work until a date not more than four weeks after the notified day of return if he notifies her before that day that for specified reasons he is postponing her return until that date, and accordingly she will be entitled to return to work with him on that date: s 47(2) of the EP(C)A 1978.

The employee may:

(*a*) postpone her return to work until a date not exceeding 4 weeks from the notified day of return, notwithstanding that the date falls after the end of the period of 29 weeks; and

(*b*) where no day of return has been notified to the employer, extend the time during which she may exercise her right to

return so that she returns to work not later than 4 weeks from
the expiration of the said period of 29 weeks;
if before the notified day of return or, as the case may be, the
expiration of the period of 29 weeks, she gives the employer a certificate from a registered medical practitioner stating that by reason of
disease or bodily or mental disablement she will be incapable of work
on the notified day of return or the expiration of the period as the
case may be: s 47(3) of the EP(C)A 1978. The employee may only
once exercise a right of postponement or extension in respect of the
same return to work: s 47(4) of the EP(C)A 1978. Again these provisions will be strictly interpreted. See *Dowuona v John Lewis plc*
[1987] IRLR 310 and *Kelly v Liverpool Maritime Terminals* [1988]
IRLR 310. If the employee does not comply with the statutory provisions the employment terminates.

If the employee has notified a day of return, but there is an interruption of work, whether due to industrial action or otherwise, which
renders it unreasonable to expect her to return to work on the notified
day of return, she may instead return to work when work resumes
after the interruption, or as soon as reasonably practicable thereafter:
s 47(5) of the EP(C)A 1978.

If no day of return has been notified and there is such an interruption of work, whether due to industrial action or otherwise, which
renders it unreasonable to expect her to return before the expiration
of the 29 weeks, or which appears likely to have that effect, and in
consequence she does not notify a day of return, she may exercise
her right of return so that she returns to work at any time before the
end of the period of 28 days (previously 14 days) from the end of
the interruption, notwithstanding that she returns to work outside the
period of 29 weeks: s 47(6) of the EP(C)A 1978.

Where the employee has either exercised her right under s 47(3)(*b*)
to extend the period during which she may exercise her right to return
to work, or has refrained from notifying the day of return under
s 47(6), the other of those subsections shall apply as if for the reference
to the expiration of the period of 29 weeks there were substituted a
reference to the expiration of the further period of 4 weeks or, as the
case may be, 28 days (previously 14 days) from the end of the interruption of the work: s 47(7) of the EP(C)A 1978.

Where an employee's return to work is postponed by her employer
under s 47(2) or by her under s 47(3)(*a*), above, or where the
employee returns to work on a day later than the notified day of
return in accordance with s 47(5), then references to the 'notified day
of return' are construed as references to the day to which the return
is postponed or, as the case may be, that later day: s 47(8) of the
EP(C)A 1978.

3.4 Right to return and unfair dismissal

For the purposes of unfair dismissal, a failure by an employer to permit an employee who is so entitled to return to work and exercises her right in accordance with s 47 is provided for by s 56, subject to s 56A of the EP(C)A 1978.

Under s 56 of the EP(C)A 1978 where an employee is entitled to return to work and has exercised her right to return in accordance with s 47 but is not permitted to return to work, she is treated as if she has been employed until the notified day of return and as having been continuously employed until that day (whether or not she would otherwise have been treated in that way); she is also treated as if she had been dismissed with effect from the notified day of return for the reasons for which she was not permitted to return. See also s 86 of the EP(C)A 1978 which contains similar provisions when the employee is redundant.

The employer will be in breach of s 56, where he allows the employee to return to work, but she does not return to the job which she was employed to do under the original contract of employment: see s 45(1); **3.1**, above. The failure to permit the employee to return to work may enable her to claim redundancy and unfair dismissal in a redundancy situation where the reason for the failure is redundancy (see **3.2**, above) or to claim unfair dismissal. The employee must have tried to exercise her right to return even though she may have been dismissed during her maternity leave. Certain dismissals will be automatically unfair (see **3.2**, above).

In a claim for unfair dismissal, where there is a failure to permit an employee to return to work after confinement, the provisions of s 57(3) of the EP(C)A 1978 are modified. Thus, determination of the question whether the dismissal was fair or unfair having regard to the reasons shown by the employer shall depend upon whether in the circumstances (including the size and administrative resources of the employer's undertaking) the employer would have been acting reasonably or unreasonably in treating it as a sufficient reason for dismissing the employee if she had not been absent from work; and that question shall be determined in accordance with equity and the substantial merits of the case: para 2(1) of Sched 2 of the EP(C)A 1978.

Section 56A of the EP(C)A 1978 provides for the exclusion of s 56 in certain cases. The first exclusion arises where immediately before the employee's absence began the number of employees employed by her employer added to the number employed by any associated employer of his did not exceed five, and it is not reasonably practicable for the employer or his successor to permit the employee to return to work in accordance with s 45(1) of the EP(C)A 1978 or for him or an associated employer to offer her employment under a contract of employment fulfilling the conditions set out in s 45(3): s 56A(1) of the EP(C)A 1978.

Secondly, s 56 shall not apply to an employee if it is not reasonably practicable, for a reason other than redundancy, for the employer or his successor to permit her return to work in accordance with s 45(1) and he or an associated employer offers her employment under a contract which satisfies certain conditions, and she accepts or unreasonably refuses that offer. The conditions are that the work to be done under the contract is of a kind which is both suitable in relation to the employee and appropriate for her to do in the circumstances, and that the provisions of the contract as to the capacity and place in which she is to be employed and as to the other terms and conditions of the employment are not substantially less favourable to her than if she had returned to work in accordance with s 45(1): s 56A(2) and (3) of the EP(C)A 1978. These latter provisions follow the provisions of s 45(4) (see **3.2**, above).

Where in a claim for unfair dismissal the question arises as to whether or not the operation of s 56 is excluded by s 56A(1) and (2), the onus is upon the employer to show that the provisions of those subsections were satisfied in relation to the employee: s 56A(4) of the EP(C)A 1978.

In a claim for unfair dismissal in relation to the failure to permit an employee to return to work after confinement, the provisions of the EP(C)A 1978 are modified by para 2(4) of Sched 2. The following provisions do not apply, with the exception of (b) which applies in a modified form:

(*a*) Section 55—the meaning of unfair dismissal and the effective date of termination. There is substituted therefore s 56 of the EP(C)A 1978 which deals with the question of dismissal where the employee is not permitted to return to work after confinement. Section 56 is subject to s 56A.

(*b*) Section 57(3)—the test of fairness. See above.

(*c*) Section 64(1)—the qualifying period and upper age limit.

(*d*) Section 65—exclusion of the statutory protection against unfair dismissal where there is a dismissal procedure agreement.

(*e*) Section 66—revocation of an exclusion order under s 65.

(*f*) Section 73(5) and (6)—the provisions relating to the upper age limit for the purposes of the basic award of compensation.

(*g*) Section 141(2)—employment ordinarily outside Great Britain.

(*h*) Section 142(1) as amended—exclusion of the statutory protection against unfair dismissal in contracts for one year or more.

(*i*) Section 144(2)—employment as master or crew member of a fishing vessel remunerated by a share in the profits or by gross earnings.

There are also consequential amendments for the purpose of computing the period of employment in that para 11(1) of Sched 13 to the EP(C)A 1978 does not apply, and for the purpose of calculating normal working hours and a week's pay in that paras 7(1)(*f*) to (*i*) and (2) and 8(3) of Sched 14, do not apply. Paragraph 10 of Sched 15 does not apply. This paragraph deals with the exclusions from protection against unfair dismissal where there are certain fixed-term contracts.

The phrase 'to return to work' in ss 33, 47, 56 and 61, and 86 of and Sched 2 to the EP(C)A 1978 means, unless the context otherwise requires, to return to work in accordance with s 45(1) of the EP(C)A 1978: s 153(3) of the EP(C)A 1978.

References to the effective date of termination in Part V of the EP(C)A 1978 and to the date of termination of employment in ss 69 and 70 are construed as references to the notified day of return: para 2(3) of Sched 2 to the EP(C)A 1978. Part II of Sched 14, in relation to ss 71 and 73, is also amended: see para 2(5) of Sched 2 to the EP(C)A 1978.

3.5 Contractual right to return

An employee who has a right both under the EP(C)A 1978 and under a contract of employment, or otherwise, to return to work, may not exercise the two rights separately, but may in returning to work take advantage of whichever right is, in any particular respect, the more favourable: s 48(1) of the EP(C)A 1978.

In *Bovey v Board of Governors of the Hospital for Sick Children* [1978] ICR 934, Bovey had a statutory right to resume full-time working in her original job but she wanted to return on a part-time basis. Her employers gave her the option of returning either to the previous position full-time or of taking a part-time position on a lower grade. Bovey claimed that the two rights could be composited to give her the right to return to her original job on a part-time basis. The EAT held that she could not form a composite right to return to work after maternity absence under s 48(1) of the EP(C)A 1978, by claiming that the offer of a part-time post on a lower grade allowed her to exercise her statutory right to return to her original job on a part-time basis in accordance with a contractual right. The legislation refers only to the contract of employment under which she is employed when she departs on maternity leave. It is under that contract that the right to return to work arises. It does not arise under an agreement under which she may have acquired a right to return to work on a part-time basis. She could not accept the offer and add to it her statutory right. Her claim for unfair dismissal therefore failed. Where the employee's contract subsists during a period of absence for maternity leave and the employee exercises her contractual right to return, then by virtue of s 48 she is treated as exercising a composite right. That right is subject to the provisions of ss 47 and 56 of the EP(C)A 1978. The only way in which the employee can claim unfair dismissal is in accordance with s 56 which involves the employee having to comply, *inter alia*, with the provisions of s 47(1). If the employee fails to comply with the latter provisions by not giving the appropriate length of notice then she can have no claim for unfair dismissal under the provisions of s 56. See s 48(2) of the EP(C)A 1978 and *Lavery v Plessey Telecommunications Ltd* [1982] IRLR 180, upheld on appeal [1983] IRLR 202, and *Kolfor Plant Ltd v Wright* [1982] IRLR 311, and *Lucas*, above. Likewise, if she fails to comply with s 47 of the EP(C)A 1978, she will have lost her right to return: see the cases of *Dowuona* and *Kelly*, above.

Sections 45, 46, 47, 56 and 86 of and paras 1, 2, 3, 4 and 6 of Sched 2 to the EP(C)A 1978 apply to this composite right as they apply to the right to return conferred solely by Part III (ss 33–48): s 48(2) of the EP(C)A 1978.

3.6 Replacements

Where an employee is absent from work because of pregnancy the employer may engage a replacement. If on engaging a replacement he informs that replacement in writing that his employment will be terminated on the return to work of the employee who is or will be absent wholly or partly because of pregnancy or confinement and he dismisses the replacement employee to make it possible to give work to the employee who returns following pregnancy then, for the purposes of s 57(1)(*b*) of the EP(C)A 1978 (see Chapter 5, **2.6**, above), the dismissal is regarded as having been for a substantial reason of a kind such as to justify the dismissal of an employee holding the position which the replacement held: s 61(1) of the EP(C)A 1978. The reasonableness of the dismissal will be considered under s 57(3): see s 61(1) of the EP(C)A 1978.

Chapter 10

Dismissal and the Trade Union Member

This chapter considers the dismissed employee's position as against his employer where the issues involved are the membership of an independent trade union or the non-membership of a trade union or taking part in the activities of an independent trade union.

1 Dismissal for trade union membership and activities

1.1 General

Section 58(1) of the EP(C)A 1978 provides that the dismissal of an employee by an employer shall be regarded as unfair if the reason or, if more than one, the principal reason was that the employee:

(a) was, or proposed to become, a member of an independent trade union, or

(b) had taken part, or proposed to take part, in the activities of an independent trade union at an appropriate time, or

(c) was not a member of any trade union, or of a particular trade union, or of one of a number of particular trade unions, or had refused or proposed to refuse to become or remain a member.

In such circumstances the dismissal is automatically unfair. The tribunal does not have to consider whether the dismissal was reasonable in all the circumstances under the provisions of s 57(3) of the EP(C)A 1978. The employer is given no opportunity of putting forward a potential defence.

Under s 58(1)(c) there is no qualification of a trade union and it is not restricted to an independent trade union.

Section 58(1)(a) and (b) will be interpreted strictly. In *Carrington and Others v Therm-A-Stor Ltd* [1983] ICR 208, the TGWU wrote to the company requesting recognition of the union by the company. Shortly thereafter the company decided to make 20 employees redundant. The selection of the employees was carried out by charge hands who were given no instructions as to the method of selection. The 20 employees dismissed were all TGWU members. Union membership played no part in selection by the charge hands. The Court of Appeal

297

found that the employees were dismissed by the company because of the union's request for recognition. It did not accept the submission put forward on behalf of the employees that s 58 should be construed so as to recognise a collective dimension; nor did it accept the contention that since the employees were members of the union and the reason for the dismissal was the activities of that union (the request for recognition), the reason for the dismissals was the employees' union membership or activities, albeit with others. The Court of Appeal held that s 58(1)(*a*) and (*b*):

is concerned solely with the dismissal of *an* employee and provides that it shall be regarded as unfair if the reason was that the (ie *that*) employee had done or proposed to do one or more specified things. The reason why each of the . . . employees was dismissed had nothing to do with anything which the employee concerned had personally done or proposed to do.

In *Crosville Motor Services Ltd v Ashfield* [1986] IRLR 475, Ashfield, a bus driver, was dismissed ostensibly because of a ticket irregularity. However, he had made it clear that unless there were changes in union policy and organisation he would leave the union, the TGWU, which had sole bargaining rights with the company. The tribunal held that the reason for his dismissal was his proposed refusal to remain a member of the union. The EAT upheld the decision of the tribunal and held that s 58(1)(*c*) could apply where the proposed refusal to remain a member of the union was conditional or contingent.

1.2 Onus of proof

The onus is placed upon the employer to show the reason for the employee's dismissal. Where the employee alleges that his dismissal was for one of the reasons set out in s 58(1) of the EP(C)A 1978 the burden of proof is not reversed. The onus is still upon the employer to establish the reason for the dismissal. If the employer produces evidence to show a reason for dismissal then the burden passes to the employee to show that there is a real issue as to whether that was the true reason. The burden is a lighter burden than that imposed upon the employer, but the employee cannot simply assert that the reason put forward by the employer was not the true reason. The evidential burden upon him is to produce some evidence that casts doubt upon the employer's reason. The graver the allegation by the employee, the heavier will be the burden: *Maund v Penwith DC* [1984] ICR 143: see also *Shannon v Michelin (Belfast) Ltd* [1981] IRLR 505.

However, where the employee does not have the necessary qualifying period of employment to bring a claim for unfair dismissal and argues that the reason for his dismissal is one falling within s 58(1), the onus is upon him to prove the reason for his dismissal: *Smith v The Chairman and Other Councillors of Hayle Town Council* [1978] IRLR 413. The dissenting judgment of Lord Denning in this case recognises the difficulties facing the employee in successfully proving that the reason or principal reason is one falling within s 58(1). Where there is more than one reason, a reason within s 58(1) has to be the principal reason so that, for instance, anti-union sentiment, which is not the principal reason would not be sufficient. See *Smith*'s case, above.

See also *The Marley Tile Co Ltd v Shaw* [1980] IRLR 25. Once the employee has presented his case, where the onus is on him because he does not have the qualifying period of employment, the employer has to present his case. It will only be in exceptional circumstances that the tribunal will be justified in not hearing the employer's evidence because, although the employee's allegations may at first instance appear weak, the evidence of the employer may also be weak and so bolster the employee's case: *H Goodwin Ltd v Fitzmaurice* [1977] IRLR 393.

In deciding whether or not the reason or principal reason for the dismissal is within s 58(1)(*b*), the Court of Appeal (in *The Marley Tile Co Ltd v Shaw*, above) suggested that the tribunal should determine the following:

(*a*) For what reason or reasons did the company dismiss the respondent and, if more than one, what was the principal reason?

(*b*) Was the conduct of the respondent which formed the only or principal reason for his dismissal, trade union activities?

(*c*) If so, was it with the consent, express or implied, of the company . . . ?

(*d*) If with implied consent only, then as a matter of construction of [s 58(2)(*b*) of the EP(C)A 1978] does consent include an implied consent or must it be expressed?

1.3 The statutory provisions

(*a*) Trade union   A trade union means an organisation (whether permanent or temporary) which either —

(*a*) consists wholly or mainly of workers of one or more descriptions and is an organisation whose principal purposes include the regulation of relations between workers of that description or those descriptions and employers or employers' associations; or

(*b*) consists wholly or mainly of —

(i) constituent or affiliated organisations which fulfil the conditions specified in para (a) above (or themselves consist wholly or mainly of constituent or affiliated organisations which fulfil those conditions); or

(ii) representatives of such constituent or affiliated organisations;

and in either case is an organisation whose principal purposes include the regulation of relations between workers and employers or between workers and employers' associations, or include the regulation of relations between its constituent or affiliated organisations: s 28(1) of the Trade Union and Labour Relations Act 1974.

(b) 'Independent trade union' An 'independent trade union' means a trade union which:

(*a*) is not under the domination or control of an employer or a group of employers or of one or more employers' associations; and

(*b*) is not liable to interference by an employer or any such group or association (arising out of the provision of financial or material support or by any other means whatsoever) tending towards such control;

and, in relation to a trade union, 'independent' and 'independence' are to be construed accordingly: s 153(1) of the EP(C)A 1978.

The phrase 'liable to interference by an employer . . . tending towards such control' has been interpreted as having the meaning 'vulnerable to interference' in that the union is exposed to the risk of interference. In deciding whether or not the union is independent it may be relevant to enquire whether there is a possibility of interference by the employer tending towards control of the union. If there is a risk which is recognisable and not insignificant, then it is likely that the union is not an independent trade union: *The Certification Officer v Squibb UK Staff Association* [1979] IRLR 75. See also *A Monk & Co Staff Association v Certification Officer* [1980] IRLR 431.

(c) Membership of an independent trade union Where an employee is dismissed because he refuses to transfer from one independent trade union to another independent trade union, this is not a reason within s 58(1) of the EP(C)A 1978: *Rath v Cruden Construction Ltd* [1982] ICR 60. In *Discount Tobacco and Confectionery Ltd v Armitage* [1990] IRLR 15, Armitage enlisted the help of her union official to obtain a written statement of her terms and conditions of employment. She then raised with her union official discrepancies between the terms which she was offered when she was taken on and terms set out in the written statement. The tribunal found that the reason she was dismissed was her union membership. The EAT held that the activities of the trade union officer in elucidating the terms of employment was simply the visible manifestation of trade union membership. It is an incident of union membership and no distinction should be drawn between membership of the union on the one hand and making use of the essential services of the union on the other. If such a distinction were drawn then s 58(1)(*a*) would have to be construed without regard to the consequences of union membership. To construe it so narrowly would be to emasculate the provision.

(d) Activities of an independent trade union Activities of a trade union are not defined in the legislation. Guidance can be obtained from reported cases which, although involving an interpretation of the earlier legislation, are still relevant. Activities of an independent trade

union in s 58(1)(*b*) of the EP(C)A 1978 means activities of a particular or specific union, not activities of trade unions generally: *Fitzpatrick v British Railways Board* [1990] ICR 674, following *National Coal Board v Ridgway and Another* [1987] ICR 641.

In *Brennan and Ging v Ellward (Lancs) Ltd* [1976] IRLR 378, the EAT held that in deciding whether an employee is taking part in the activities of a trade union the tribunal should make a list of all the acts and facts relied upon as constituting the activities and whether the employee is a union representative. If the common-sense view is that these factors constitute the activities of an independent trade union, then the tribunal must so find. It is not fatal that these acts are also for the employee's own benefit. The EAT did not accept that the activities must be those of a member of the union authorised to carry out those acts. The EAT gave the example of the union member who during his lunch-break sought to recruit further employees as members. He would be engaged in the activities of a trade union.

In *Lyon v St James Press Ltd* [1976] ICR 413, Lyon and another secretly organised the formation of a chapel of the National Union of Journalists among the company's employees. Not all the employees were invited to join, which led to unrest. The company was not consulted about the formation of the chapel. The EAT held that the acts done by Lyon and his associate were done in the course of taking part in the activities of a trade union, and their dismissal was unfair. However, the EAT commented that not 'every such act is protected. For example, wholly unreasonable, extraneous or malicious acts done in support of trade union activities might be a ground for dismissal which would not be unfair.'

In *Dixon and Shaw v West Ella Developments Ltd* [1978] ICR 856, the EAT held that the interpretation of activities of an independent trade union was not restricted 'to such matters as membership meetings and activities involving status as trade unionists'. The words are 'activities of an independent trade union' not 'trade union activities'. The EAT found that 'the words "trade union" are not being used in an adjectival sense; what is being looked for are the activities of a trade union'. It agreed with an example given in *Brennan and Ging v Ellward (Lancs) Ltd*, above: 'if a man were dismissed because he had sought the advice of a union representative on the shop floor, and had sought to apply approved union practice, such conduct could we think, in some circumstances, arguably at least fall within [s 58(1)(*b*) of the EP(C)A 1978]'. The EAT further found that 'arguably at least' could be expressed as 'strongly arguably'. Criticism of union policy by a group of union members can constitute an activity of a trade union: *British Airways Engine Overhaul Ltd v Francis* [1981] IRLR 9.

In *Chant v Aquaboats Ltd* [1978] ICR 643, it was held that organising a petition on safety standards which was the act of a single trade unionist was not within the phrase 'activities of an independent trade union'. The EAT held:

It is, of course, open to employees in any firm to make representations . . . to their employers about machinery which is unsafe. The mere fact that one or two of the employees making representations happen to be trade unionists, and the mere fact that the spokesman of the men happens to be a trade unionist does not make such representations a trade union activity.

In *Drew v St Edmundsbury BC* [1980] ICR 513, it was held that an individual's complaints about matters of health and safety were not activities of a trade union. The employee was carrying out his own activities and not the activities of a trade union. Similarly complaints about working conditions made by a dissatisfied employee who did not wish to involve her union in the complaints were not the activities of a trade union: *Gardner v Peeks Retail Ltd* [1975] IRLR 244; see also the *obiter* remarks of Eveleigh LJ and Stephenson LJ in *The Marley Tile Co Ltd v Shaw* [1980] IRLR 25, where they doubted whether an unaccredited shop steward calling a meeting in working hours was engaging in the activities of a trade union. Again, where two chapel officers were engaged in concerted resistance to management culminating in a breach of a collective agreement incorporated as a term of their contract they were not engaged in the activities of a trade union. They did not seek to raise their grievances in a proper manner. Despite the fact that they were chapel officers and acting in concert to promote what they considered to be the interests of members, they were acting on their own initiative without the endorsement of a chapel meeting. It was questionable whether their actions had the support of the majority of the chapel members and it was just as likely that they were representing only themselves in the action they took: *Stokes and Roberts v Wheeler-Green Ltd* [1979] IRLR 211; see also *Carrington and Others v Therm-A-Stor Ltd* [1983] ICR 208, from which it is clear the activities must be the activities of the employee who is dismissed.

From time to time the question has arisen as to whether the employee who is taking part in a strike or other industrial action is taking part or proposing to take part in the activities of an independent trade union. In *Winnett v Seamarks Brothers Ltd* [1978] ICR 1240, it was considered that the industrial action in this case was not synonymous with the activities of a trade union. Where the employee is dismissed because he is on strike the facts may show that he is dismissed for taking part in a strike rather than taking part or proposing to take part in the activities of a trade union. In *Drew v St Edmundsbury BC* above, the EAT went further and emphasised the difference parliament intended between cases where the employee is dismissed because he takes part in activities of a trade union and cases where he is dismissed while he is engaged in a strike or other industrial action.

See s 62 of the EP(C)A 1978 and Chapter 11 which deals with dismissal during a strike or other industrial action. The EAT considered it would be impossible for an employee to be both within s 58(1) and s 62.

In *Rasool v Hepworth Pipe Co Ltd (No 2)* [1980] IRLR 137, it was held that while an unauthorised meeting at the employer's premises in working hours to discuss wage negotiations, interrupting the manufacturing process of the employer, was not industrial action, it might be regarded as taking part in the activities of a trade union.

In *Fitzpatrick v British Railways Board* [1991] IRLR 376, it was held that s 58(1) did not apply to trade union activities which occurred before the employment commenced. Compare this with *Birmingham DC v Beyer* [1978] 1 All ER 910.

In practice, while action taken by a trade union official may fall within the definition of activities of an independent trade union, the same action taken by an individual member may not.

In determining what is meant by activities of a trade union, some assistance may be gained from s 23 of the EP(C)A 1978. This section provides that every employee shall have the right not to have action short of dismissal taken against him for the purposes of preventing or deterring him from being, or seeking to become, a member of an independent trade union or penalising him for doing so; or preventing or deterring him from taking part in the activities of an independent trade union at any appropriate time, or penalising him for doing so; or compelling him to be or become a member of any trade union or of a particular trade union or of one of a number of particular trade unions. In *Dixon and Shaw v West Ella Developments Ltd*, above, the EAT interpreted s 23 as pertaining to activities 'of a fairly varied kind'. See also s 27 of the EP(C)A 1978 which deals with the trade union official's right to time off for carrying out trade union duties and s 28 which deals with the employee's right to time off for trade union activities, as well as the Code of Practice, Time Off for Trade Union Duties and Activities, which came into force on 13 May 1991. In *Luce v Bexley London Borough Council* [1990] ICR 591, it was held that time off to attend a lobby of parliament to convey political or ideological objections to legislation was not taking part in trade union activities under s 28.

(e) 'Appropriate time' The 'appropriate time', in relation to an employee taking part in the activities of a trade union, means time which either:

(*a*) is outside his working hours; or

(*b*) is a time within his working hours at which, in accordance with arrangements agreed with or consent given by his employer, it is permissible for him to take part in those activities;

and 'working hours', in relation to an employee, means any time when, in accordance with his contract of employment, he is required to be at work: s 58(2) of the EP(C)A 1978.

The employee's right to take part in the activities of a trade union may be a contractual right: *Miller v Rafique* [1975] IRLR 70.

In *Post Office v Union of Post Office Workers* [1974] 1 All ER 229, Lord Reid considered what was meant by 'appropriate time'. He found:

The definition includes all time outside the worker's working hours and 'working hours' is defined as meaning time when in accordance with his contract with his employer he is required to be at work. I do not think that it was or can be disputed that 'at work' means actually at work and does not include periods when in accordance with his contract of employment the worker is on his employer's premises but not actually working. It is common knowledge, and Parliament was very well aware, that every day there are periods when a worker is on his employer's premises but is not expected or required to be actually working. He arrives at his employer's premises some time before he starts work. He leaves some time after his day's work is done. And I should think that in almost all cases he is not expected to work non-stop. There are recognised breaks for meals and perhaps other purposes during which he does and is expected to remain on his employer's premises. 'In accordance with his contract' does not I think mean in accordance with some formal condition, but rather in accordance with what the employer recognises to be customary. It cannot matter whether provision for dinner and other breaks in working time is written into his contract or is merely a recognised concession. So in my judgment the Act entitles a worker who is a member of a trade union to take part in the activities of his union while he is on his employer's premises but is not actually working.

The arrangements or the consent will usually be express. Depending upon the facts of the case it seems there may be circumstances where consent is implied. In *Zucker v Astrid Jewels Ltd* [1978] ICR 1088, the EAT found that conversation about trade union matters during working hours may be trade union activities within working hours undertaken in accordance with arrangements agreed with or consent given by the employer, since these might be informal and the employer had permitted employees to converse during working hours. Further it found, following the decision of the House of Lords in *Post Office v Union of Post Office Workers* above, that meal breaks might be times during which an employee although paid was not required to be at work and was not doing what she did during working hours. Thus meal breaks might be any appropriate time even if there were no arrangement or consent.

However, in *The Marley Tile Co Ltd v Shaw* [1980] IRLR 25, the Court of Appeal, reversing the decision of the tribunal and the EAT, held that a tribunal must be careful before finding that consent is implied. While recognising there may be circumstances where on the facts consent is implied, consent could not be implied in this case where an unaccredited shop steward called a meeting of the maintenance men in working hours to consider a problem which did not call for a desperately urgent solution. The employer remained silent; by so doing he was not deemed to have given consent. Nor could consent be implied by extension from other factories in the group, nor by custom and practice.

'Time' is not restricted to time with that employer. See *Fitzpatrick's* case, above but fraud in covering up earlier activities may be outside s 58(1). See *Beyer's* case above and see generally s 1 of the EA 1990.

If the activities have not taken place at any appropriate time or where it was proposed that they would not take place at any appropriate time, an employee's dismissal in such circumstances will be outside s 58(1) of the EP(C)A 1978, and the reason for and the reasonableness of the dismissal will be considered in the normal way.

1.4 The employers' objection

Section 58(13) of the EP(C)A 1978 provides that where the reason or one of the reasons for the dismissal of an employee was:

(a) his refusal, or proposed refusal, to comply with a requirement (whether or not imposed by his contract of employment or in writing) that, in the event of his failure to become or his ceasing to remain a member of any trade union or of a particular trade union or of one of a number of particular trade unions, he must make one or more payments; or

(b) his objection, or proposed objection (however expressed) to the operation of a provision (whether or not forming part of his contract of employment or in writing) under which, in the event mentioned in para (a), his employer is entitled to deduct one or more sums from the remuneration payable to him in respect of his employment;

that reason shall be treated as falling within s 58(1)(c) of the EP(C)A 1978.

References in s 58 of the EP(C)A 1978 to a trade union include references to a particular branch or section of the union.

2 Interim relief

An employee who presents a claim to a tribunal for unfair dismissal alleging that the reason or principal reason is one falling within s 58(1) of the EP(C)A 1978, may apply for interim relief: s 77(1) of the EP(C)A 1978. An application must be made to the tribunal before or within seven days of the effective date of termination and where the reason is the employee's actual or proposed membership of, or participation at, an appropriate time in the activities of an independent trade union it must be supported by a written certificate signed by an authorised official of the independent trade union in question and presented to the tribunal within the same time limit: s 77(2) of the

EP(C)A 1978. The certificate must contain the information set out in s 77(2)(*b*). The time limit is a strict one although the tribunal has a discretion to allow amendments after the expiration of the period: *Barley v Amey Roadstone Corporation Ltd* [1977] ICR 546. An authorised official is one authorised by the union to act in these cases. No form of certificate is prescribed and it appears that provided there is substantial compliance with the statutory provisions this will be sufficient. The certificate must clearly set out the reasons which must relate to trade union membership or activities: *Stone v Charrington and Co* [1977] ICR 248. A loosely worded application and certificate may not comply with the relevant provisions: *Farmeary v Veterinary Drug Co Ltd* [1976] IRLR 322. However, the EAT has warned against too great a concentration on technicality: *Bradley v Edward Ryde and Sons* [1979] ICR 488. The signatory need not state that he is an authorised official. In the absence of a challenge to the contrary, the tribunal is entitled to proceed on the basis that he is authorised. If the signatory's authority is challenged the onus is on him to establish his authority: *Sulemany v Habib Bank Ltd* [1983] ICR 60. Documents purporting to be an authorisation of an official by a trade union to act for these purposes shall be taken to be such an authorisation unless the contrary is proved: s 77(11) of the EP(C)A 1978.

No application can be made under this provision where it is contended that the employee has been unfairly selected for dismissal in a redundancy situation for one of those reasons specified in s 58(1) of the EP(C)A 1978: *Farmeary v Veterinary Drug Co Ltd*, above, nor where a claim is made under ss 99–101 of the Employment Protection Act 1975.

Where an application has been made the tribunal must hear the application as soon as practicable. It must at least seven days before the date of the hearing give the employer a copy of the application and certificate, together with notice of the date, time and place of the hearing: s 77(3) of the EP(C)A 1978. In the case of a request made under s 76A of the EP(C)A 1978 (that is to direct a person be joined as a party to the proceedings) made at least three days before the date of the hearing the tribunal must at the appropriate time, which in this case is as soon as reasonably practicable, give to the person to whom the request relates a copy of the application and certificate, if any, together with notice of the date, time and place of hearing. If, on hearing the application, it appears to the tribunal that it is likely that it will ultimately make a finding of unfair dismissal for the reasons set out above, then if the employer is willing, it shall order reinstatement or, if the employer is not willing to reinstate the employee but is willing to re-engage him in another job on terms and conditions not less favourable than those which would have been applicable to him if he had not been dismissed, then it shall order re-engagement on such terms provided the employee is prepared to accept the offer of re-engagement: see s 77(5) to (8) of the EP(C)A 1978. If the employee is not prepared to accept an offer of re-engagement and the tribunal considers the refusal is reasonable it shall make an order for the continuation of the contract of employment: s 77(8) of the EP(C)A 1978. If the employer is not present at the hearing or is not prepared to consent to reinstatement or re-engagement, the tribunal must make an order for the continuation of the employee's contract of employment: s 77(9) of the EP(C)A 1978. Where an order for the continuation of the contract is made the contract continues in force until the complaint of unfair dismissal has been determined or settled but for the purposes only of pay or any other benefit derived from the employment, seniority and pension rights, and other similar matters, and for the purposes of continuity of employment: s 78(1) of the EP(C)A 1978. Where the tribunal makes an order it shall specify the amount which is to be paid by the employer by way of pay and shall take into account any payment made by the employer to the employee under the contract or by way of damages for breach of contract, as well as wages in lieu of notice; the employee's pay is ascertained as if he had not been dismissed: see s 78(2) to (6) of the EP(C)A 1978. Where, following the order, there has been a change in the circumstances, either party may apply to the tribunal for the variation or revocation of the order: s 79(1) of the EP(C)A 1978. It does not have to be to the tribunal with the same personnel that made the order: *British Coal Corporation v McGinty* [1987] ICR 912. Where the order for reinstatement or re-engagement or for the continuation of the contract of employment has not been complied with the tribunal has power to award compensation: s 79(2) and (3) of the EP(C)A 1978.

The onus is upon the employer to establish the reason for dismissal. The onus appears to be on the employee in a claim for interim relief. It is sufficient for the employee to discharge the onus of proof in a claim for interim relief if he can show the tribunal that it is likely that the reason for his dismissal is trade union membership or activities. 'Likely' means that he has quite a good chance of succeeding in a claim for unfair dismissal. It is necessary for the employee to achieve a higher degree of certainty than showing that he has a reasonable chance of success: *Taplin v C Shippam Ltd* [1978] IRLR 450. Where the employee seeks to show that the reason for his dismissal is his union membership or activities, the employer, to defeat a claim for interim relief, must show a reason or principal reason for the dismissal other than trade union membership or activities. Where he alleges some other reason he must produce evidence to support it. It is not sufficient to show that the evidence was such that he could have dismissed for that reason.

3 Pressure on employer to dismiss

In determining the reason, or principal reason, why the employee was dismissed or whether the reason or principal reason is within s 57(1)(b) of the EP(C)A 1978 or whether the employer acted reasonably in dismissing the employee, no account should be taken of certain pressure put upon the employer. The reason for, or the fairness of, the dismissal is to be decided without regard to such pressure: s 63 of the EP(C)A 1978. Thus, the tribunal is not entitled to take into account any pressure put on the employer by calling, organising, procuring or financing a strike or other industrial action, or threatening to do so: s 63(a) of the EP(C)A 1978, and any such question shall be determined as if no such pressure had been exercised: s 63(b) of the EP(C)A 1978. The effect may be a fiction. The employer may dismiss because of a threatened strike and for no other reason. The tribunal is precluded from taking this into account in deciding the reason and so the employer will fail. In *McColm v Agnew and Lithgow Ltd* [1976] IRLR 13, the tribunal was unhappy with this fiction. However, in *Hazells Offset Ltd v Luckett* [1977] IRLR 430, the EAT found that although s 63 of the EP(C)A 1978 might produce a fiction, nonetheless it was bound by it and could not take into account industrial pressure.

Although the employer is not entitled to plead in his aid pressure placed upon him to dismiss, it may be open to him to argue that the pressure placed on him was due in part to the employee's fault and that he had contributed to his dismissal, for the purposes of a reduction in compensation: *Hazells Offset Ltd v Luckett*, above.

In *Ford Motor Co Ltd v Hudson* [1978] IRLR 66, the EAT in considering s 63 of the EP(C)A 1978, said that it was not necessary for the employee to show that those exerting pressure on the employers explicitly sought the employee's dismissal, but that conduct short of that might amount to pressure to dismiss. It suggested as an appropriate test:

A question which was canvassed upon the hearing of the appeal was 'whether pressure to dismiss can only be established by showing that dismissal was explicitly demanded'. We do not think that for a case to fall within . . . [s 63 of the EP(C)A 1978] it is necessary to be able to show that those exerting the pressure explicitly sought the dismissal of the employee; and conduct short of that may well amount to pressure to dismiss. It was suggested that if this were right, then in each case it would be a question of fact whether what had been done was pressure to dismiss. We agree; but some kind of guidance is necessary in order to determine whether such pressure has been exerted, and, without seeking to lay down a guiding principle for every case, we would say that the test to be applied should be on the following lines: Was the pressure exerted on the employers such that it could be foreseen that it would be likely to result in the dismissal of those employees in respect of whom the pressure was being brought?

It may be that the pressure exerted upon the employer results in the employer unilaterally changing the terms of the employee's contract: *Colwyn Borough Council v Dutton* [1980] IRLR 420.

Section 76A of the EP(C)A 1978 allows the employer who dismisses an employee because of pressure placed on him by a trade union or other person, to join that trade union or other person as a party to the proceedings. The pressure envisaged is referred to in s 76A and must have been exercised because the employee was not a member of any trade union, or of a particular trade union, or of one of a number of particular trade unions. Where the employer is ordered to pay compensation to an employee he may recover a contribution or indemnity from the third party: s 76A of the EP(C)A 1978.

In addition to the employer's rights the employee is given the power to join a trade union or other person as a party to proceedings where he alleges that the trade union or other person put pressure on the employer to dismiss him because he was not a member of any trade union or of a particular trade union or of one of a number of particular trade unions. The pressure is that referred to in s 76A. The third party may be ordered to pay the whole of any award, or part of any award, with the employer paying the other part, as the tribunal may consider just and equitable in the circumstances. For a more detailed consideration of these provisions see Chapter 13.

Chapter 11

Dismissals during Strikes and Lock-outs

1 General

Under the EP(C)A 1978, where an employee, who is referred to as the complainant, claims that he has been unfairly dismissed by his employer and at the date of dismissal the employer was conducting or instituting a lock-out, or the complainant was taking part in a strike or other industrial action, a tribunal has no jurisdiction to determine whether the dismissal was fair or unfair, unless it is shown that one or more relevant employees of the same employer have not been dismissed, or that any such employee has, before the expiry of the period of three months beginning with that employee's date of dismissal, been offered re-engagement and that the complainant has not been offered re-engagement: s 62(1) and (2) of the EP(C)A 1978. Section 62(5) of the EP(C)A 1978, as inserted by s 16(1) of and para 1 of Sched 2 to the Employment Act 1990, provides that s 62 does not apply to an employee who by virtue of s 62A has no right to complain of unfair dismissal. It confirms that nothing in s 62A affects the question 'who are relevant employees?' in relation to an employee to whom s 62 applies. The effect of this provision is that if the employee takes unofficial action and is dismissed he cannot bring an action for unfair dismissal even if he is selectively dismissed or if there is selective re-engagement.

Where the complainant claims unfair dismissal and shows that he has not been offered re-engagement where one or more other relevant employees have been offered re-engagement (see s 62(2)(*b*)) ss 57 to 60 of the EP(C)A take effect as if instead of referring to the reason or principal reason for which the complainant was dismissed they refer to the reason or principal reason for which the complainant has not been offered re-engagement: s 62(3) of the EP(C)A 1978.

For the purposes of s 62 'date of dismissal' means, where the employee's contract of employment was terminated by notice, the date on which the employer's notice was given, and in any other case the effective date of termination.

For the purposes of s 62 'relevant employees' means in relation to a lock-out, employees who were directly interested in the dispute in contemplation of furtherance of which the lock-out occurred, and in relation to a strike or other industrial action, those employees at the establishment who were taking part in the action at the complainant's date of dismissal. 'Establishment' means that establishment of the employer at or from which the complainant works: s 62(4) of the EP(C)A 1978.

The employer may treat each establishment as a separate unit thereby overcoming the problem where the employer has several establishments. Where there are different establishments it may be difficult for the employer to identify accurately which employees are taking part in a strike or other industrial action and who have to be dismissed.

No definition of establishment has been laid down in the EP(C)A 1978. Section 99 of the Employment Protection Act 1975 does refer to an establishment. The definition of establishment under this section has been considered: see *Barratt Developments (Bradford) Ltd v UCATT* [1978] ICR 319, but it is clear from this decision that it is difficult to lay down guidelines for what is essentially a question of fact and the meaning of establishment must be left to the tribunal to decide in the particular case.

Any reference to an offer of re-engagement is a reference to an offer made either by the original employer, his successor or an associated employer to re-engage an employee either in the job which he held immediately before the date of dismissal or in a different job which would be reasonably suitable in his case: s 62(4)(c) of the EP(C)A 1978.

The effect of s 62 is that a tribunal can only consider a dismissal where the employee is locked out, or is engaged in a strike or other industrial action, if it can be shown that the employee has been subjected to discriminatory treatment in the matter of dismissal or re-engagement. If the employee cannot establish that he has been subjected to discriminatory treatment in the matter of dismissal or re-engagement, then the tribunal has no jurisdiction to consider the merits of the unfair dismissal claim: see *Heath v JF Longman (Meat Salesmen) Ltd* [1973] 2 All ER 1228 and *Faust and Others v Power Packing Casemakers Ltd* [1983] IRLR 117.

2 Definitions

Although many of the following cases were decided under earlier legislation, they are none the less relevant in considering s 62.

2.1 'Lock-out'

Paragraph 24(1) of Sched 13 to the EP(C)A 1978 defines a 'lock-out' as the closing of a place of employment, or the suspension of work, or the refusal by an employer to continue to employ any number of persons employed by him in consequence of a dispute, done with a view to compelling those persons, or to aid another employer in compelling persons employed by him, to accept terms and conditions of or affecting employment. It should be noted that this definition is applied by statute only to Sched 13. However, the statutory definition was applied in *Fisher v York Trailer Co Ltd* [1979] ICR 834. In this case the company sought an undertaking from 34 employees that they would work normally. They were told that if they did not sign the undertaking they would be suspended from the start of the next shift. They did not sign, but the following day held a meeting to discuss the matter. All but seven of the employees signed. The seven were treated as suspended, and although they attended the factory they were not permitted to work. They were given another opportunity to sign an undertaking, they refused, and were dismissed. The EAT held that the dismissals had occurred during a lock-out. In *Express and Star Ltd v Bunday and Others* [1988] ICR 379, the majority of the Court of Appeal held that whether there has been a lock-out or a strike is a question of fact. Whether the presence of a particular element is necessary before there can be a lock-out may be a mixed question of law and fact or a question of pure fact. The Court of Appeal held that the definition of a lock-out contained in para 24(1) of Sched 13 affords guidance in determining what is meant by a lock-out. It is not a statutory definition of a lock-out to be applied generally throughout the Act. Whether the employer has breached the contract of employment is a relevant consideration in determining whether there has been a lock-out, but a breach is not an essential ingredient for there to be a lock-out. The statutory definition presupposes the continuance of the contract of employment between the parties. For earlier cases where the statutory definition contained in para 24(1) of Sched 13 was not followed: see *Rasool v Hepworth Pipe Co Ltd (No 2)* [1980] IRLR 137 and *McCormick v Horsepower Ltd* [1980] IRLR 182. See also the definition of a strike.

In *Brown v William Press and Son Ltd* [1975] IRLR 8, a tribunal having regard to the *Shorter Oxford English Dictionary* found a lock-out to mean 'a refusal on the part of an employer, or employers acting in concert, to furnish work to their operatives except on conditions accepted by the latter collectively'. A dictionary definition may be a useful indication of what is a lock-out, but it is not incorporated in the statute: see *Bunday*'s case, above.

2.2 'Trade dispute'

Under the EP(C)A 1978, relevant employees in relation to a lock-out means employees who were directly interested in the dispute in contemplation of furtherance of which the lock-out occurred: s 62(4)(*b*)(i) of the EP(C)A 1978. The definition of 'dispute' is wider than that of 'trade dispute', but it will include a 'trade dispute'.

The definition of a trade dispute is contained in s 29 of the Trade Union and Labour Relations Act (TULRA) 1974 and incorporated into the EP(C)A 1978 by s 153(1) of the Act. By virtue of these provisions a trade dispute is a dispute between workers and their employer which relates wholly or mainly to terms and conditions of employment or the physical conditions of work; engagement, non-engagement or termination or suspension of employment or duties of workers; allocation of work or duties; discipline; membership or non-membership of a trade union; facilities for officials of a trade union; and negotiating or consulting machinery or other procedures for dealing with the foregoing or with recognition issues: s 29(1) of the TULRA 1974. A worker in relation to a dispute with an employer means a worker employed by that employer, or a person who has ceased to be employed by that employer where his employment was terminated in connection with the dispute, or the termination of his employment was one of the circumstances giving rise to the dispute: s 29(6) of the TULRA 1974. A 'worker' means an employee, including the employees of government departments other than naval, military or air force personnel (or the police service), as well as any person who undertakes to perform personally any work or services for another party to the contract where the other party is not his professional client: s 30(1) of the TULRA 1974.

2.3 Strike and industrial action

(a) Strike   Paragraph 24(1) of Sched 3 to the EP(C)A 1978 defines a 'strike' as the cessation of work by a body of persons employed acting in combination, or a concerted refusal or a refusal under a common understanding of any number of persons employed to continue to work for an employer in consequence of a dispute, done as a means of compelling their employer or any person or body of persons employed, or to aid other employees in compelling their employer or any person or body of persons employed to accept or not to accept terms or conditions of or affecting employment. This definition also is applied only to Sched 13 to the EP(C)A 1978. In *McCormick v Horsepower Ltd* [1980] ICR 278, the EAT held that it was open to a tribunal to look to para 24(1) of Sched 13 for guidance in deciding what was meant by 'strike' in s 62, but the EAT by implication accepted that this paragraph did not define 'strike' for the purposes of s 62. In *Rasool v Hepworth Pipe Co Ltd (No 2)* [1980] IRLR 137, the EAT accepted that it was not permissible to import the definition of 'strike' in para 24(1) of Sched 13 into s 62 of the EP(C)A 1978. In *Coates and Venables v Modern Methods and Materials Ltd* [1982] IRLR 318, the majority of the Court of Appeal held that the words 'taking part in a strike' were ordinary words which a tribunal sitting as an industrial jury is best fitted to decide, an approach followed in *Bunday*'s case, above.

A strike must be more than a one-man withdrawal of labour. The essence of a strike is its collectivity. In *Tramp Shipping Corporation v Greenwich Marine Inc* [1975] 2 All ER 989, Lord Denning referred to a strike as a 'concerted stoppage of work'. In the same case Stephenson LJ found that there could not be a strike 'without a cessation of work by a number of workmen agreeing to stop work'. It is arguable that as in the case of a lock-out, a strike is not restricted to a strike in contemplation or furtherance of a trade dispute. It extends to any dispute.

In *Hindle Gears Ltd v McGinty and Others* [1984] IRLR 477, the EAT held that the tribunals are sole arbiters of what does or does not amount to taking part in strike action. While the question whether or not the employer was aware of any particular conduct on the part of an employee would be relevant to determining whether that conduct amounted to taking part in a strike, it was not a principle of law that the employee's participation in strike action had to be known to the employer before it could be capable of constituting conduct amounting to taking part in the action, for the purposes of s 62(4)(*b*)(ii) of the EP(C)A 1978.

Although s 62 does not make it clear whether or not the strike must be in breach of the employee's contract of employment the provisions of s 62 will operate when a strike is not in breach of the employee's contract of employment: consider *Power Packing Casemakers v Faust and Others* [1981] IRLR 120 (upheld on appeal see [1983] IRLR 117). In most cases a strike would be in breach of the employee's contract of employment but it will not operate to terminate the contract unless the repudiation is accepted by the employer: *Simmons v Hoover Ltd* [1976] IRLR 266, and see generally Chapter 3.

(b) Other industrial action It may be difficult to decide whether particular action amounts to a strike. However, the phrase is 'strike or other industrial action' and where there is doubt the tribunal is likely to find in the alternative. In many cases it may be difficult to decide whether the employees are engaging in a strike or other industrial action. Thus, in *Thompson v Eaton Ltd* [1976] ICR 336, employees left their place of work to stand around a machine which the employer wished to install and so were physically preventing their employer from operating the new machine. The EAT found there was an element of picketing in addition to the withdrawal of labour. If the action was not a strike it was certainly 'other industrial action'.

Industrial action may include the following; an overtime ban: see *Power Packing Casemakers v Faust and Others* [1981] IRLR 120 (upheld on appeal [1983] IRLR 117); a decision to impose an immediate overtime ban; see *Naylor and Others v (1) Orton and Smith Ltd (2) MD Tweddell Engineering Ltd* [1983] IRLR 233; a go-slow: see *Drew v St Edmundsbury BC* [1980] IRLR 459; a work to rule: see *Secretary of State for Employment v ASLEF (No 2)* [1972] ICR 19; as well as picketing: *Thompson v Eaton Ltd*, above and possibly sit-ins, but in *Rasool and Others v Hepworth Pipe Co Ltd (No 2)* [1980] IRLR 137, it was held that where employees attended an unauthorised mass meeting at the employer's premises during working hours, such action did not constitute 'other industrial action'.

In *Power Packing Casemakers v Faust and Others*, above, the EAT found that the industrial action did not have to be in breach of contract. This finding was upheld by the Court of Appeal, Stephenson LJ posing the question 'why . . . should the . . . tribunal have to embark on an enquiry into the terms of a claimant's contract of employment, express and implied, in order to decide whether he was taking part in industrial action when he was dismissed?'. Whether or not action amounted to 'other industrial action' was a matter for a tribunal to decide. The words must be given their plain and ordinary meaning. In this case the employees were dismissed for refusing to work overtime hours at a time when wage negotiations were in progress. When the employees were threatened with dismissal all but three agreed to work overtime hours. The three who refused to work overtime hours were dismissed. The tribunal held that they were not in breach of their contracts of employment and were therefore unfairly dismissed. The EAT held that they were engaging in 'other industrial action' and therefore the tribunal had no jurisdiction to hear the claim.

In *Winnett v Seamarks Brothers Ltd* [1978] ICR 1240, it was held that employees who agreed at a meeting to stop work from the time of the meeting may be on strike or engaging in 'other industrial action' from the time of the decision, notwithstanding that at the time of the decision they are not contractually due to work, but they have made it clear that when asked to work they will not do so: see *Naylor*'s case, above.

In *Midland Plastics v Till and Others* [1983] IRLR 9, the employees advised their employer that they were going to engage in industrial action at 11 o'clock. Before they engaged in industrial action they were dismissed. It was held that they were not on strike at the time of the dismissal, nor were they engaging in other industrial action.

It is often not clear whether employees are engaging in a strike or other industrial action or whether they are taking part or proposing to take part in the activities of an independent trade union. The difference is important as the EAT emphasised in *Drew v St Edmundsbury BC* [1980] IRLR 459. If the employee is dismissed for taking part or proposing to take part in the activities of a trade union then the dismissal is automatically unfair. See Chapter 10, and consider s 58 of the EP(C)A 1978. However, if the employee is taking part in a strike or other industrial action then the tribunal does not have jurisdiction to hear the claim under s 62 of the EP(C)A 1978, unless the employee can prove that the employer has been selective in dismissing or re-engaging.

(c) Strikes or other industrial action 'engineered' by the employer   The legislation draws no distinction between a strike or other industrial action which is initiated by the employees of their own volition and a strike or other industrial action which results from conduct on the part of the employer, for instance where the employer seeks unilaterally to alter working conditions. In *Wilkins v Cantrell and Cochrane (GB) Ltd* [1978] IRLR 483, the employers on a number of occasions sent out lorries in an overloaded condition. Following the dismissal of employees who went on strike because of this, the EAT found that the tribunal was entitled to conclude that the instances of overloading which occurred were insufficient to constitute a fundamental breach. It added that even if the employers had been in breach of contract by requiring the employees to drive overloaded vehicles, the act of going out on strike could not be held to be a sufficient indication by the employee that he was treating the contract as not only capable of being repudiated, but as one which has been broken and which he regarded as at an end. The employee was therefore dismissed whilst on strike since the contract still continued. Further, there was no jurisdiction to hear the claim even though the strike was caused by the employer's actions. This case was followed by the EAT in *Marsden v Fairey Stainless Ltd* [1979] IRLR 103, in which it was held that where a strike is 'engineered' by the employers, the provisions of s 62 of the EP(C)A 1978 will continue to operate. Consider also *Faust and Others v Power Packing Casemakers Ltd* [1983] IRLR 117, where the Court of Appeal held that motive on the part of the employer in dismissing the workers is entirely irrelevant.

3 Date of dismissal

Where the employee's contract of employment is terminated by notice, the date of dismissal is the date on which the employer's notice was given: s 62(4)(*a*)(i) of the EP(C)A 1978. In any other case the date of dismissal is the effective date of termination: s 62(4)(*a*)(ii) of the EP(C)A 1978. Where the claim is based upon a failure to offer re-engagement to one or more employees where other relevant employees have been offered re-engagement, the complainant's date of dismissal within the meaning of s 62(4) is substituted for a reference to the effective date of termination for the purposes of s 67(2) (period of time for bringing a complaint of unfair dismissal): s 67(3) of the EP(C)A 1978.

For s 62 to apply, the employer must have been conducting a lockout or the employee must have been taking part in a strike or other industrial action at the date of dismissal. In both cases 'date', in effect, means 'time': *Heath v JF Longman (Meat Salesmen) Ltd* [1973] 2 All ER 1228. For example, if a strike takes place in the morning and finishes at noon, an employee who was on strike and who was dismissed at 2 o'clock is not on strike at the date of the dismissal. The tribunal has jurisdiction to hear his claim. If the employer does not know that the strike or industrial action has been called off, and could not have known other than by a communication from those involved, it is open to argument whether the tribunal has jurisdiction under s 62: *Heath v JF Longman (Meat Salesmen) Ltd*, above. However, to claim the benefit of this argument it is likely that the employer must honestly believe and have good grounds for believing that the strike or other industrial action is still continuing. Thus, if the employees act in a manner consistent with the discontinuance of the strike, the employer may be unable to rely on this argument.

In *Midland Plastics v Till and Others* [1983] IRLR 9, the employees told their employer that they were going to take part in a strike at 11 o'clock. They were dismissed before 11 o'clock. It was held that they were not taking part in a strike at the date of the dismissal, see above. A warning of possible dismissal when industrial action ceases is not a notice of dismissal: *Bolton Roadways Ltd v Edwards and Others* [1987] IRLR 392.

4 Taking part in a strike or other industrial action

In *Coates and Venables v Modern Methods and Materials Ltd* [1982] IRLR 318, the Court of Appeal held that a tribunal was entitled to find that an employee who went to her place of work but who was unwilling to pass the picket line because she did not wish to suffer abuse, and who stayed for an hour at the gate and then went home, was taking part in the strike. The Court of Appeal considered that an employee's participation in a strike had to be judged by what the employee did and not by what he thought or why he did it. Since the employee did not say or do anything to make plain any disagreement with the strikers, or anything which could amount to a refusal to join them, she was held to be on strike in this case.

Eveleigh LJ, in a dissenting judgment, held that for a person to be participating in a strike he must act jointly or in concert with those who withdrew their labour. This was not the position here. Stephenson LJ held that whether or not an employee was taking part in a strike or other industrial action was a matter of fact for the tribunal to decide.

This approach was the subject of criticism by the EAT in *Naylor and Others v (1) Orton and Smith Ltd and (2) MD Tweddell Engineering Ltd* [1983] IRLR 233. The EAT found that since the question whether or not an employee was taking part in a strike or other industrial action was not a point of law, they could not interfere with the decision of the tribunal. The EAT held:

We therefore conclude that the Court of Appeal have decided that there can be no error of law by the Industrial Tribunal in making a decision under s 62 [of the EP(C)A 1978] unless upon the evidence of the Industrial Tribunal reached a conclusion which the words of the section could not reasonably bear . . .

If we have correctly formulated our function, in our judgment a decision to impose an immediate overtime ban could reasonably be considered as not constituting taking industrial action, as the Industrial Tribunal held: it could also reasonably be considered to constitute industrial action. Since both views are reasonable, we cannot interfere with the industrial tribunal decision . . .

As it seems to us, on the primary facts as found by the Industrial Tribunal in this case, another Industrial Tribunal could reasonably have found that the imposition of the immediate ban on overtime itself constituted industrial action and that those who voted for it took part in it. If so, a diametrically opposite, but equally correct, conclusion would have been reached. In cases to which s 62 of the Act of 1978 apply, it is of great importance to employers that they should, so far as possible, know the consequences of their acts before they decide who to dismiss and who to retain or re-engage. If both views can properly be held, an employer confronted with an overtime ban who asks for advice can only be advised to dismiss everyone who could conceivably have taken part in the industrial action. If he follows that advice, the consequences to the employees who might be considered not to be taking part are that they lose their jobs. Whether such employees have a claim for unfair dismissal will depend on whether or not the Industrial Tribunal they chance to come before takes the view that they were taking part in industrial action. The present case illustrates the quandary facing employers. These employers are small companies. If the Industrial Tribunal had reached the opposite conclusion, the employers' liability to pay compensation for unfair dismissal to those dismissed could easily reach six figures, a sum which would effectively put them out of business. In our view it is not in the best interests of orderly industrial relations that such severe consequences to both employers and employees should depend on which of two, equally correct but diametrically opposite, views is subsequently adopted by the Industrial Tribunal before which the case may come.

It may be that the employee is away from work on holiday at the time of the strike. If the employee is away because he is on holiday, and not because he is on strike, the employer cannot claim the benefit of s 62 of the EP(C)A 1978. Where the employee is on strike and then becomes sick the employer is protected if the employee would have been on strike in such circumstances unless he expressly notifies the employer that he is no longer on strike but is away sick and would return if he was not sick: *Craig v JD Welding Construction and Engineering Co* (1975) (unreported). In *Williams v Western Mail and Echo Ltd* [1980] ICR 366, the employee, with others, had taken part in industrial action. He then went on a one-day strike. All the employees were told that unless they resumed normal working they would be dismissed. Notwithstanding this ultimatum the other industrial action continued. Williams did not attend work following the strike due to ill-health. He was dismissed. The tribunal found that since he had not indicated to his employers that he no longer intended to take part in industrial action, he was still taking part in the industrial action and s 62 applied. The EAT, upholding the decision of the tribunal, found:

once men have stated that they will apply sanctions and do so they may be regarded as applying the sanctions either until they are discontinued or until they indicate or state an intention of stopping them.

Indeed, were it to be otherwise it would cause immense problems for the employer. In *Hindle Gears Ltd v McGinty and Others* [1984] IRLR 477, Smith had been away from work due to ill-health when his colleagues were engaged in strike action. He visited the factory regularly for the sole purpose of handing in medical certificates. In the course of those visits he spent time with his colleagues who were pickets at the factory gate and talked to them. The tribunal found that he was participating in the strike. The EAT found that the tribunal's decision was perverse and that no reasonable tribunal could have found that such fleeting encounters between a sick employee and his striking colleagues was participation in strike action. Whereas Williams had been engaged in industrial action and had then become ill, Smith had never engaged in industrial action and had been away during the whole of the period when his colleages were on strike.

Whether an employee is taking part in a strike is to be determined by evidence. If his actions and omissions justify an inference that he was participating in a strike that cannot be invalidated simply because his employer was unaware of his actions or omissions: *Bolton Roadways Ltd v Edwards* [1987] IRLR 392. The emphasis placed on the employer's knowledge by Waite J in *McGinty*'s case, above, was not accepted.

In *McKenzie v Crosville Motor Services Ltd* [1989] IRLR 516, a strike was in progress. McKenzie was absent from work, allegedly for various reasons. He did not keep his employers informed of the reasons for his absence. The EAT found that where there is a strike and an employee who does not continue to work, then in the absence of some reasonable explanation, the employer is reasonably entitled to assume that the employee is withholding his labour. It is incumbent on the employee as an implied contractual obligation that if he is away from work he should provide his employer with information and a reason for so doing. If a strike is taking place, it is for the employee to ensure that the employer is aware that he is not taking part in the strike. Whereas in *Edward*'s case the employer's knowledge was not relevant, in *McKenzie*'s case the employer's knowledge was material. In *Manifold Industries v Sims and Others* [1991] IRLR 242, the EAT held that the employer does not need to know that the employees are taking part in a strike of other industrial action for s 62 of the EP(C)A 1978 to apply. The approach in *McKenzie*'s case was preferred.

If the employee leaves the place of employment not because he is on strike but because he is afraid for his health or safety during the strike then it may well be that he is participating in the strike: see *Coates and Venables v Modern Methods and Materials Ltd* [1982] IRLR 318. In this case Kerr LJ found that in deciding whether or not an employee was engaging in a strike or other industrial action, regard must be had to the employee's actions. His reasons or motives were not relevant; likewise it was irrelevant whether the employee's utterances or actions, his silence or inaction showed support, opposition or indifference in relation to the strike. Stephenson LJ also found that participation had to be judged by what the employee did, not by what he thought or why he did it. While recognising that the line between unwilling participation and not taking part may be difficult to draw, he considered that those who stayed away from work with the strikers without protest, for whatever reason, were to be regarded as having crossed that line and to be taking part in the strike. Eveleigh LJ dissenting considered that the employee's intention was vital.

5 Relevant employees

A tribunal cannot consider whether a dismissal is fair or unfair where the complainant was locked out or was engaging in a strike or other industrial action unless it can be shown that relevant employees of the same employer have not been dismissed or have been offered re-engagement and the complainant has not been offered re-engagement: see s 62(1) and (2) of the EP(C)A 1978.

In the cases of a lock-out relevant employees are those employees who are directly interested in the dispute in contemplation or furtherance of which the lock-out occurred: s 62(4)(*b*)(i) of the EP(C)A 1978. The definition is not confined to employees locked out to the end. The question, 'Which employees are directly interested in the dispute in contemplation of the furtherance of which the lock-out occurred?' involves enquiry as to 'when the lock-out occurred and what was the . . . dispute in contemplation or furtherance of which the lock-out was put into effect': *Fisher and Others v York Trailer Co Ltd* [1979] IRLR 385.

In deciding who were 'relevant employees' for the purposes of s 62(4)(*b*)(i) of the EP(C)A 1978, the test is a retrospective one. What has to be looked at is the date at which the lock-out occurred. The tribunal has to consider who, at that date, were the employees directly interested in the dispute in contemplation or furtherance of which the lock-out occurred. Employees who return to work before the lock-out ceases may also be relevant employees: *H Campey and Sons Ltd v Bellwood and Others* [1987] ICR 311.

In *Presho v DHSS* [1984] ICR 463, a case involving the interpretation of the Social Security Act 1975, as amended, it was held that the words 'directly interested' in relation to a trade dispute meant that if, whatever the outcome of the trade dispute, it would be applied to all employees whether or not they were members of the union in dispute. They were directly interested.

In the case of a strike or other industrial action relevant employees are the employees at the establishment who are taking part in the action at the complainant's date of dismissal: s 62(4)(b)(ii) of the EP(C)A 1978. In *Hindle Gears Ltd v McGinty and Others* [1984] IRLR 477, employees were on strike. The employer decided to dismiss them and wrote to each of them dismissing them with immediate effect. Before the letter had been received two employees returned to work. The employer only took them back once it had obtained their assurances that they had not received the letters. The EAT held that the dismissal could not take effect until the employees had been told of the decision to dismiss them. Since the employees were not dismissed and they were no longer taking part in the strike when the other employees were dismissed they were not relevant employees for the purposes of s 62(4)(b)(ii). Thus, only those employees who are on strike or are engaging in other industrial action will have to be examined in determining whether or not there has been any discrimination, and not those who have returned to work. Selective dismissal or re-engagement in the case of a strike or other industrial action is easier than in the case of a lock-out.

In *P and O European Ferries (Dover) Ltd v Byrne* [1989] ICR 779, the Court of Appeal held that the words 'unless it is shown' in s 62(2) of the EP(C)A 1978 means unless it is proved on the evidence and shown to the satisfaction of the tribunal. These words unambiguously direct attention to the conclusion of the relevant hearing before the tribunal. This may be the substantive hearing or the preliminary hearing at which the jurisdictional point is considered. See *Sims's* case above. *Obiter* remarks contained in *McCormick*'s case, above, which suggest the words mean the beginning of the hearing, were not applied.

Section 62(2)(b) of the EP(C)A 1978 provides that a tribunal shall not have jurisdiction unless it is shown that any relevant employee has, before the expiry of the period of three months beginning with that employee's date of dismissal, been offered re-engagement and that the complainant has not been offered re-engagement. After three months have elapsed from the date of the last dismissal of any relevant employee the employer can start to re-engage selectively the former employees without affecting the protection afforded by s 62. This applies if it is the employer conducting or instituting a lock-out, or if it is the employee who is engaging in a strike or other industrial action.

There is no obligation to offer re-engagement to all the employees at the same time. In *Highlands Fabricators Ltd v McLaughlin* [1984] IRLR 482, 2,000 employees went on strike. On 17 August they were dismissed. On 21 August 1,600 employees were offered re-engagement. McLaughlin was not one of them. On 16 September the remaining 400, including McLaughlin, were offered re-engagement. The chairman of the tribunal found that since all the striking employees, including McLaughlin, had been offered re-engagement within the appropriate period, neither of the exceptions in s 62(2) of the EP(C)A 1978 applied and the tribunal had no jurisdiction to entertain the application. The EAT upheld the decision of the tribunal chairman. It found:

> For a variety of reasons offers of re-engagement may be made to striking employees in differing numbers and at different times. It would wreck all chance of negotiation in what is frequently a delicate and tense industrial situation if a limited offer of re-engagement were to confer immediately on employees to whom the offer was not directed a vested right to complain of unfair dismissal. Certainly if at the date of the Tribunal hearing such an employee can show that the terms of s 62(2)(a) or (b) have been complied with, the Tribunal will have jurisdiction to entertain the application. We regard the three month period . . . as something of a 'cooling off' period, designed to achieve the very objective which was reached in the present case, viz settlement of a strike on terms acceptable to management and workforce alike, on sensible and honourable terms. To interpret s 62(2)(b) in the manner in which the majority of the Tribunal have done would make it impossible to attain this objective and we do not consider it was the intention of Parliament that it should be construed in this way.

6 The reason for dismissing or not re-engaging a relevant employee

What is the position of a relevant employee who has been dismissed or not offered re-engagement, not because he was participating in a strike or other industrial action, but for some other reason? The matter was considered in *McCormick v Horsepower Ltd* [1980] IRLR 182, by the EAT. B was employed as a fitter's mate. The boilermakers, of whom McCormick was one, employed at the employer's premises, went on strike. B refused to cross a boilermakers' picket line, although subsequently he did cross the picket line. After he had recommenced work and while the strike was continuing, B was dismissed for redundancy. It found that B had withdrawn his labour to aid the strikers against their common employer so he was a relevant employee. The EAT also held that an employee who took part in a strike and was dismissed for whatever reason could not be a relevant employee who took part in the strike and was not dismissed. It did not matter that he was not dismissed for taking part in the strike or other industrial action and that the reason for his dismissal was, for instance, redundancy. The Court of Appeal (see [1981] IRLR 217) disagreed with the EAT's view that B took part in the strike. Although he refused to cross the picket line he did not have any common purpose with the strikers or any interest in their dispute and was not acting in concert with them, and therefore was not a relevant employee. The

Court of Appeal, however, held that there was no requirement that a relevant employee had to be dismissed while he was taking part in the strike and he could be dismissed for other reasons.

7 Re-engagement

Where following a lock-out, strike or other industrial action one or more employees have been offered re-engagement within the prescribed period and the complainant has not been offered re-engagement, the unfair dismissal provisions contained in ss 57–60 of the EP(C)A 1978 must be interpreted as if for any reference to the reason or principal reason for which the employee was dismissed there were substituted a reference to the reason or principal reason for which he has not been offered re-engagement: s 62(3) of the EP(C)A 1978.

It may be that following a strike or other act of industrial action all the relevant employees are dismissed but subsequently one or more are offered re-engagement. If a claim for unfair dismissal is brought by one or more employees who have not been offered re-engagement it has been held that the test of reasonableness under s 57(3) of the EP(C)A 1978 is 'the determination of the question whether the dismissal was fair or unfair, having regard to the reason shown by the employer for not offering re-engagement to the applicant, shall depend on whether the employer can satisfy the tribunal that in the circumstances (having regard to equity and the substantial merits of the case) he acted reasonably in treating the reason for which the applicant has not been offered re-engagement as a sufficient reason for' not offering re-engagement. Thus, the tribunal must look at the situation which exists at the time of the failure to offer re-engagement. The facts at the time of the initial dismissal may well be relevant but the question of reasonableness cannot be answered by restricting consideration to those facts: *Edwards v Cardiff City Council* [1979] IRLR 303. With effect from 1 October 1980 the test of reasonableness is modified so that the test of reasonableness suggested in *Edwards v Cardiff City Council*, above, will depend upon whether in the circumstances (including the size and administrative resources of the employer's undertaking), the employer acted reasonably or unreasonably in treating the reason for which the applicant has not been re-engaged as a sufficient reason for not offering re-engagement; and that question shall be determined in accordance with equity and the substantial merits of the case: s 57(3) of the EP(C)A 1978. Any reference to an offer of re-engagement is construed as a reference to an offer made either by the original employer, or by a successor of that employer or an associated employer to re-engage an employee, either in the job which he held immediately before the date of dismissal or in a different job which would be reasonably suitable in his case: s 62(4)(c) of the

EP(C)A 1978. In *Williams and Others v National Theatre Board Ltd* [1981] IRLR 5, the EAT had to consider the position where some employees on strike were offered re-engagement on condition they would be treated as being on a second warning under the employer's disciplinary procedure, whereas another employee had been offered re-engagement without any such condition. It held that s 62(4)(c) defines an offer of re-engagement as an offer to re-engage an employee either in the job which he held immediately before the date of dismissal or in a different job which would be reasonably suitable in his case. Section 153 of the EP(C)A 1978 defines job to mean 'the nature of the work which he is employed to do in accordance with his contract and the capacity and place in which he is so employed'. The EAT did not accept that a change in capacity was the same thing as a change in the security of employment so that the offer was not the offer of the employees' jobs. The jobs which they were offered were those which they held immediately before the dismissal. This decision was upheld by the Court of Appeal: see [1982] IRLR 377. An offer of re-engagement need not be in writing. Nor is there any need for a communication to each individual employee: *Marsden v Fairey Stainless Ltd* [1979] IRLR 103. An offer of re-engagement does not require some positive offer; a tacit acceptance of continuity of employment may be sufficient: *Bolton Roadways Ltd v Edwards* [1987] IRLR 392.

8 Fairness of selection

Where the employer dismisses some employees but not others who are directly interested in the dispute in contemplation or furtherance of which the lock-out occurred, or who took part at the establishment in a strike or other industrial action, or re-engages some but not others, the tribunal may consider any claim for unfair dismissal made by any of those who are dismissed or not re-engaged, as the case may be. In deciding the fairness or otherwise of the dismissal or failure to re-engage, the tribunal will consider the fairness of the selection — the employer's reasons for selecting those who were dismissed or not re-engaged, and those who were retained or re-engaged. The tribunal must be satisfied that the employer acted reasonably in making the selection. It follows that in practice the employer must be able to show the tribunal the criteria which he used in making the selection for dismissal or the failure to offer re-engagement. Thus, if during the course of the strike or other industrial action some employees are re-engaged but others are not because of redundancy, the relevant criteria for the employer to consider are those which would have applied in a redundancy situation: *Laffin and Callaghan v Fashion Industries (Hartlepool) Ltd* [1978] IRLR 448; see also *Cruickshank v Hobbs* [1977] ICR 725. The reasonableness must be judged at the time of the dismissal or the failure to offer re-engagement: *Edwards v Cardiff City Council*, above.

Where selection for redundancy is made after the date of the strike, s 62 of the EP(C)A 1978 will not apply and either s 59 of the EP(C)A 1978 will apply, or the fairness or otherwise of the dismissal will have to be considered under s 57(3) of the EP(C)A 1978.

9 The limitation period

Under s 67(2) of the EP(C)A 1978, a claim for unfair dismissal must be brought before the end of the period of three months beginning with the effective date of termination or within such further period as the tribunal considers reasonable in a case where it is satisfied that it was not reasonably practicable for the complaint to be presented before the end of the period of three months. By virtue of s 67(3) of the EP(C)A 1978, s 67(2) shall apply in relation to a complaint to which s 62(3) applies, as if for a reference to three months there is substituted a reference to six months: s 67(3)(*a*) of the EP(C)A 1978. Section 67(3)(*b*) of the EP(C)A 1978 provides that s 67(2) shall apply to a complaint under s 62(3), as if for a reference to the effective date of termination there is substituted a reference to the complainant's date of dismissal, within the meaning of s 62(4) of the EP(C)A 1978.

10 Dismissal and unofficial industrial action

The EP(C)A 1978 draws no distinction between an employee taking part in official and unofficial industrial action. Section 9 of the EA 1990 inserts s 62A into the EP(C)A 1978, which applies where the employee is engaging in an unofficial strike or other industrial action. Section 62A(1) of the EP(C)A 1978 provides that an employee has no right to complain of unfair dismissal if at the time of the dismissal he was taking part in an unofficial strike or other industrial action.

A strike or other industrial action is unofficial in relation to an employee unless:

(*a*) he is a member of a trade union and the action is authorised or endorsed by that union; or

(*b*) he is not a member of a trade union but there among those taking part in the industrial action members of a trade union by which the action has been authorised or endorsed,

provided that a strike or other industrial action shall not be regarded as unofficial if none of those taking part in it are members of a trade union: s 62A(2) of the EP(C)A 1978.

Whether industrial action is taken or has been authorised or endorsed by a trade union shall be determined in accordance with s 15(3) to (7) of the EA 1982. Section 15(3) of the EA 1982 provides that an act shall be authorised or endorsed by a trade union if it was done, authorised or endorsed by any person who had the power under the rules to do, authorise or endorse acts of the kind in question; or by the principal executive committee, president or general secretary of the union; or by any committee of the union being a group of persons constituted in accordance with the rules of the union or any other official (whether employed or otherwise) of the union. An act shall be deemed to have been done, authorised or endorsed by an official if it was done, authorised or endorsed by, or by any member of any group of persons of which he was at the material time a member and the purposes of which include organising or co-ordinating industrial action. It does not matter that the principal executive committee, president, general secretary or other committee or official were acting contrary to any union rules, contract or rule of law. However, the actions of a committee or official of the union may be repudiated by the principal executive committee, president or general secretary, provided that it is done as soon as reasonably practicable after coming to their knowledge. If the repudiation is to be effective, written notice of the repudiation must be given to the committee or official without delay and the union must do its best to give individual written notice of the repudiation and the date thereof without delay to every member of the union who the union has reason to believe is taking part or might take part in industrial action, and to the employer of every such member. The notice, which must contain a statement in a prescribed form, shall inform members that the union has repudiated the call for industrial action and is not supporting such action so that any member dismissed while taking part in such action will have no right to complain of unfair dismissal. An action will not be treated as repudiated if, after the purported repudiation, the principal executive committee, president or general secretary has behaved in a way which is inconsistent with the purported repudiation. Behaviour is to be regarded as inconsistent if upon a request made to any of them within three months of the purported repudiation by a person who is a party to a commercial contract which has been or may be interfered with as a result of the action and who has not been given written notice by the union of repudiation, does not have written confirmation forthwith that the action has been repudiated.

Thus, where a strike has been called by a shop steward, it does not matter that the action is unsupported by a ballot, it is still official action. Even if the action is repudiated by the union it does not become official immediately. Industrial action shall not be treated as unofficial before the end of the next working day after the day on which the repudiation takes place: s 62A(4) of the EP(C)A 1978. A working day means any day which is not a Saturday or a Sunday, Christmas Day, Good Friday or a bank holiday under the Banking and Financial Dealings Act 1971: s 62A(5) of the EP(C)A 1978. Whether industrial action is official or unofficial is a question of fact to be determined at the time of the dismissal: s 62A(4) of the EP(C)A 1978.

Time of dismissal means:

(a) where the employee's contract of employment is terminated by notice, when the notice is given;

(b) where the employee's contract of employment is terminated without notice, when the termination takes effect, and

(c) where the employee is employed under a contract for a fixed term which expires without being renewed under the same contract, when that term expires: s 62A(5) of the EP(C)A 1978.

The interrelationship of s 62A(4) and (5) means that it is possible for an employee to be dismissed before he has been told that the industrial action has become unofficial and thereby protection removed.

Membership of a trade union for purposes unconnected with the employment in question is disregarded. However, an employee who is a member of a trade union when he began to take part in industrial action continues to be treated as a member for the purpose of determining whether that action is unofficial in relation to him or another, notwithstanding that he may in fact have ceased to be a member: s 62A(6) of the EP(C)A 1978.

Section 62A of the 1978 Act applies to the dismissal of an employee if the time of his dismissal falls after 31 December 1990. Industrial action shall not be regarded as unofficial for the purposes of s 62A if the action is taken in response to a call for industrial action made before the 1 January 1991 or the action started before 1 January 1991.

Chapter 12

The Transfer of Undertakings and the Employee

1 General

The Transfer of Undertakings (Protection of Employment) Regulations 1981 (SI 1981 No 1794) provides for a significant change in the law to safeguard the employee's rights in the event of the transfer of an undertaking. The regulations are made to implement the EEC Council Directive 77/187. References in this chapter are to the 1981 regulations, unless otherwise stated.

Under the regulations an employee means any individual who works for another person whether under a contract of service or apprenticeship or otherwise but does not include anyone who provides services under a contract for services and references to a person's employer shall be construed accordingly, a contract of employment means any agreement between an employee and his employer determining the terms and conditions of his employment: reg 2(1). The definition of an employee is wider than under the EP(C)A 1978. It does not include an equity partner: see *Cowell v Quilter Goodison Co Ltd and QG Management Services Ltd* [1989] IRLR 392.

A transfer within the regulations is a relevant transfer: reg 2(1).

These regulations apply to a transfer from one person to another of an undertaking situated immediately before the transfer in the UK or a part of one which is so situated: reg 3(1). They apply whether the transfer is effected by sale or by some other disposition or by operation of law: reg 3(2).

'Undertaking' includes any trade or business but does not include any undertaking or part of an undertaking which is not in the nature of a commercial venture: reg 2(1). Thus, local government is excluded, although nationalised industries operating on a commercial basis would appear to be within the regulations. The regulations apply to the transfer of part of an undertaking provided that it is being transferred as a business. The transfer of a ship without more is expressly excluded: reg 2(2).

The regulations apply notwithstanding that the transfer is governed or effected by the law of a country or territory outside the UK; that persons employed in the undertaking or part transferred ordinarily work outside the UK (but see Chapter 1, **2.4**, above); that the employment of any of those persons is governed by any such law: reg 3(3).

A transfer of an undertaking or part thereof may be effected by a series of two or more transactions between the same parties. In deciding whether or not such a series of transactions constitutes a single transfer regard must be had to the extent to which the undertaking or part thereof was controlled by the transferor and transferee respectively before the last transaction, to the lapse of time between each of the transactions, to the intention of the parties and to all other circumstances: reg 3(4). For the position of seamen on the transfer of a UK registered ship: see reg 3(5).

The meaning of an undertaking The regulations apply only where there is a change in the legal identity of the employer. They do not apply where what is transferred is the share capital of a company, so that a transfer by a sale and purchase of shares is not a transfer within the regulations. Undertaking includes any trade or business but does not include any undertaking which is not in the nature of a commercial venture. Whether or not there has been a relevant transfer of an undertaking is a question of fact for the tribunal to determine. In *Hadden v University of Dundee Students' Association* [1985] IRLR 449, Hadden was the manageress of the association's catering facilities. The association was a non-profit making organisation but incurred losses on its catering activities. It entered into an agreement with outside caterers under which they would provide management, supervision and control of catering services at no cost to the association. They were remunerated by a commission on net sales. They provided the food and services of a manageress. The association provided other catering staff, accommodation and equipment and were responsible for other costs. Hadden was dismissed by the association and was engaged by the outside caterers as their manageress. The agreement between the association and the outside caterers expired and Hadden was told that she was not going to be re-engaged by the association. The catering services reverted to the association. Had there been a relevant transfer of an undertaking? The EAT held that there was no transfer of a commercial undertaking when the catering services reverted to the association. Hadden could not claim unfair dismissal against the association. Although the expression 'commercial undertaking' is a wide one and may include in certain circumstances an undertaking deliberately run at a loss, the outside caterers were not trading in the full commercial sense. See also *Stirling v Dietsmann Management Systems Ltd* [1991] IRLR 368.

In *Woodcock and Others v (1) Committee for the Time Being of the Friends School Wigton (2) Genwise Ltd* [1987] IRLR 98, it was held that a school which had originally been set up by the Society of

Friends (Quakers) and had charitable status, although a trade or business was not in the nature of a commercial venture. The intention was simply to break even rather than make a profit. If any profit was made it was transferred to an accumulated fund which was the subject of the charitable trust. Thus it was not an undertaking.

In *Expro Services Ltd v Smith* [1991] IRLR 156, it was held that a catering and cleaning activity contracted out by the Ministry of Defence to the company was not a commercial venture when carried on by the Ministry of Defence and was therefore not a business, albeit that it was a commercial venture when carried on by the company.

The regulations do not apply where there is merely a sale and purchase of the physical assets of an undertaking or part thereof without anything more. In determining whether or not there has been a transfer of an undertaking as distinct from an asset sale the earlier cases involving redundancy or continuity of employment (see Chapter 2) are of assistance. In *Woodhouse and Another v Peter Brotherhood Ltd* [1972] 2 QB 520, there was a transfer of the factory and some of the plant machinery, equipment, fixtures and fittings in the factory. However, the transferor and transferee carried on different businesses and there was no transfer of the goodwill. The Court of Appeal held that there was no transfer of the ownership of the business or undertaking, in that the transferee had not become the proprietor of the business or undertaking in succession to the transferor. In *Kenmir Ltd v Frizzell* (1968) 3 ITR 159, there was no transfer of the stock in trade and goodwill of the business. The Divisional Court held that in deciding whether the transaction amounted to a transfer of a business:

regard must be had to its substance rather than its form, and consideration must be given to the whole of the circumstances, weighing the factors which point in one direction against those which point in another. In the end the vital consideration is whether the effect of the transaction was to put [the] transferee in possession of a going concern the activities of which he could carry on without interruption. Many factors may be relevant to this decision though few will be conclusive in themselves. Thus, if the new employer carries on business in the same manner as before this will point to the existence of a transfer, but the converse is not necessarily true because a transfer may be complete even though the transferee does not choose to avail himself of all the rights which he acquires thereunder.

It was held that although the assignment of goodwill is strong evidence of the transfer of a business it is not conclusive and found that there had been a transfer of a business.

In *Melon and Others v Hector Powe Ltd* [1981] 1 All ER 313, Lord Fraser referring to the criteria applied by Lord Denning in *Lloyd v Brassey* [1969] 2 QB 98, held that:

the essential distinction between the transfer of a business or part of a business, and a transfer of physical assets, is that in the former case the business is transferred as a going concern 'so that the business remains the same business but in different hands' . . . whereas in the latter case the assets are transferred to the new owner to be used in whatever business he chooses. Individual employees may continue to do the same work in the same environment and they may not appreciate that they are working in a different business, but that may be the true position on consideration of the whole circumstances.

The existence of a workforce is not vital to the existence of an undertaking and there may be a transfer of an undertaking within the regulations even though at the time of the transfer there was no workforce: see *Secretary of State for Employment v Spence and Others* [1986] IRLR 248. For factors which should be taken into account in determining whether or not there has been a transfer of an undertaking as a going concern see Chapter 2.

The following may be transfers of an undertaking: the transfer of land and farm buildings: see *Lloyd v Brassey* [1969] 2 QB 98; the surrender of a pub by the tenant to the brewery which then carried on the business: see *Young v Daniel Thwaites and Co Ltd* [1977] ICR 877; where the licensee of a petrol station gives up the licence to the petrol company: see *Premier Motors (Medway) Ltd v Total Oil Great Britain Ltd and Others* [1984] ICR 58. There was a sale of the business of a petrol station by Premier Motors to Total Oil. Premier Motors continued to run the business as licensees. When they gave up the licence there was a transfer of a business as a going concern to Total Oil. Total Oil then granted a licence to a third party. It appears that it was accepted there was a further transfer of a business as a going concern to the third party.

In *Norris (t/a Littlebrickhill Service Station) v Bedwell* EAT (1983) (unreported), the EAT found that there was a transfer of a business as a going concern between the outgoing tenant of a petrol station and the incoming tenant. The fixtures and fittings, and stock-in-trade were sold by the outgoing tenant to the incoming tenant. Under the terms of the lease the outgoing tenant could not assign the lease to the incoming tenant and had to surrender it to the petrol company which then in turn granted a new lease to the incoming tenant. The transfer of a franchise may not be the transfer of an undertaking; see *Robert Seligman Corporation v Baker and Another* [1983] ICR 770. Robert Seligman Corporation had a concession to carry on the business of a ladies' hairdresser in a store belonging to Debenhams plc. Debenhams terminated Seligman's concession and granted it to Roband Investments Ltd with effect from 21 June. Baker was employed by Seligman. On 29 June Baker was told there was no job with Roband. Under the terms of the concession Seligman was responsible for installing shop fittings. On the termination of the concession the position was obscure but it was found that Debenhams reimbursed Seligman for the cost of the fixtures and made them available to Roband. A crucial question in deciding whether there had been a transfer of a business was whether or not the goodwill belonging to Seligman had been transfered to Roband. The essential element of goodwill attributable to the skills of Seligman's staff was not transferred to Roband. It was open to Seligman to set up in competition next door using the same staff. It was held that there had been a transfer of physical assets and not the transfer of a business. Therefore, Baker's contract of employment was not transferred to Roband under the 1981 Regulations. In *Mannin Management Services Ltd v Ward* (1989) *The Times*, 9 February, the Court of Appeal was reluctant to interfere with the decision of the tribunal (since it was not perverse) that the transfer of a contract to manage a shopping centre was the transfer of a trade business or undertaking.

In other cases the transfer of a business which involves a franchise may be a transfer of an undertaking as a going concern, eg 'a Wimpey': see *Lane v Dynorod* (1985) (unreported).

Four cases heard by the European Court of Justice illustrate the scope of the Directive upon which the 1981 Regulations are based. In *Foreningen af Arbejdsledere i Danmark v Daddy's Dance Hall A/S* [1988] IRLR 315, it was held that the Directive applied where, after the termination of a non-transferable lease of restaurants and bars, the owner leased the restaurant and bars to a new lessee who continued to run the business without any interruption using the same staff. It was held that the Directive applied as soon as there was a change of the natural or legal person responsible for operating the undertaking. In *Landsorganisationen i Danmark v Ny Mølle Kro* [1989] IRLR 37, it was held that the Directive applied where the owner took back the running of a leased business following a breach of the lease by the lessee. It was held the objective of the Directive is to safeguard the rights of workers in the event of a change of employer and it applies whenever, as a result of a legal transfer or merger, there is a change in the natural or legal person responsible for running the undertaking and who because of this enters into contractual obligations as an employer towards the employees in the undertaking regardless of whether ownership of the undertaking has been transferred. In *P Bork International A/S v Foreningen af Arbejdsledere i Danmark* [1989] IRLR 41, it was held that the Directive applied where the owner of an undertaking, after giving notice terminating the lease or after forfeiting the same, retakes possession of the undertaking and then sells it to a third party who thereafter continues operations which had ceased on the termination of the lease with one-half of the staff previously employed in the undertaking by the former lessee, provided the undertaking retained its identity. There had to be an economic entity still in existence which was continued by the new employer carrying on the same or a similar business. This was a question of fact which depended upon whether the tangible and intangible assets had been transferred as well as the major part of the staff, the degree of similarity between the activities before and after the transfer, and the period of interruption. In *Berg and Busschers v Besselsen* [1989] IRLR 447, it was held that the Directive applied to the transfer of an undertaking under a lease purchase agreement as well as to the re-transfer of the undertaking where the lease purchase arrangement had been dissolved.

The transfer of part of an undertaking is covered by the regulations if it is being transferred as a business. It is a question of fact whether or not what is being transferred is part of a business. It need not be self-contained: *GD Ault Ltd v Gregory* (1967) 2 ITR 301. In *Melon and Others v Hector Powe Ltd*, above, Lord Fraser held 'a change in the ownership of part of a business will, I think, seldom occur, except when that part is to some extent separate and severable from the rest of the business, either geographically or by reference to the products, or in some other way'.

However, where staff are redeployed and there is no transfer of assets or goodwill then the regulations will not apply: *Banking Insurance and Finance Union v Barclays Bank plc and Others* [1987] ICR 495. Staff were redeployed from subsidiaries of Barclays Bank to a service company established to provide staff for an international investment bank which was to be formed. This case illustrates a defect in the regulations in that an employer may redeploy employees without any transfer of assets or goodwill.

Regulation 3(4) provides that a transfer of an undertaking may be effected by a series of two or more transactions between the same parties. Whether or not such a series constitutes a single transfer is a question of fact. Regard must be had to the extent to which the undertaking or part of it was controlled by the transferor and transferee respectively before the last transaction, to the lapse of time between each of the transactions, to the intention of the parties and to all the other circumstances. In *Forth Estuary Engineering Ltd v Litster and Others* [1986] IRLR 59, the EAT, *obiter*, considered that reg 3(4) was declaratory and permissive. It did not make it essential that the transaction must be between the same parties. It merely declared that where there is a series of transactions between the same parties that may amount to a relevant transfer.

2 Transfers by receivers and liquidators

Where the receiver of the property or part of the property of a company or the administrator of a company appointed under Part II of the Insolvency Act 1986 or, in the case of a creditors' voluntary winding up, the liquidator of the company transfers the company's undertaking, or part of the company's undertaking (the relevant undertaking) to a wholly owned subsidiary of the company, the transfer shall be deemed not to have been effected until immediately before:

(*a*) the transferee company ceases (otherwise than by reason of its being wound up) to be a wholly owned subsidiary of the transferor company; or

(*b*) the relevant undertaking is transferred by the transferee company to another person;

whichever first occurs, and, for the purposes of the regulations, the transfer of the relevant undertaking shall be taken to have been effected immediately before that date by one transaction only: reg 4(1). For these purposes 'creditors', 'winding up' and 'wholly owned subsidiary' have the same meaning as in the Companies Act 1985: reg 4(2).

The Transfer of Undertakings (Protection of Employment) (Amendment) Regulations 1987 (SI 1987 No 442) amend reg 4 of the 1981 Regulations to reflect changes in the law made by the Insolvency Act 1986.

This regulation is intended to deal with a hiving-down operation. Before the regulations became law it was frequently the practice where a receiver or liquidator contemplated a sale of an undertaking for the receiver or the liquidator to separate the business from the employees. To achieve this the receiver or liquidator would transfer the 'undertaking' or part of the 'undertaking' to a wholly owned subsidiary. The purchaser would either acquire the wholly owned subsidiary or the purchase would be made from the wholly owned subsidiary. The employees would not become employees of the subsidiary, although their services would be made available. Often it was essential that the business was hived off as quickly as possible. The purchaser would be relieved of the obligation to make a decision immediately, whether or not he would take on some or all of the employees and could make a decision at a later date. If he did take some of these employees on he could do so after the transfer of the 'undertaking' and in the meantime the employees remained employees of the original employer. The original employer became liable for any claim to notice and/or redundancy pay. The purchaser thereby avoided liability for any claims for redundancy and/or unfair dismissal. Regulation 4 is designed to preserve the flexibility of a hive down, but to protect the employees in such circumstances.

Regulation 5 provides that on a relevant transfer the employees become the employees of the transferee. The effect of reg 4 is that the transfer of the employees' employment is delayed until immediately before the transferee company ceases to be a wholly owned subsidiary of the transferor company or the undertaking is transferred by the transferee company to another person.

Under reg 4(1)(*a*) the number of shares acquired by the transferee is therefore irrelevant. The transfer takes place when the subsidiary is no longer wholly owned.

There is deemed to have been only one transaction and the workforce will be transferred to the ultimate purchaser via the subsidiary at the time that the real transfer takes place.

If the transferee insists that the employees are dismissed then the liability may pass to the transferee if the employees were employed immediately prior to the transfer. See below. If they were not employed immediately prior to the transfer, the liability will of course remain with the transferor. In practice this will mean that the Secretary of State will become liable.

3 Automatic transfer of the contract of employment

A transfer within the regulations shall not operate so as to terminate the contract of employment of any person employed by the transferor in the undertaking or part transferred, but any such contract which would otherwise have been terminated by the transfer shall have effect after the transfer as if originally made between the person so employed and the transferee: reg 5(1).

Without prejudice to reg 5(1), on the completion of the relevant transfer all the transferor's rights, powers, duties and liabilities under or in connection with any such contract will be transferred to the transferee, and anything done before the transfer is completed by or in relation to the transferor in respect of that contract for a person employed in that undertaking or part shall be deemed to have been done by or in relation to the transferee: reg 5(2).

Any reference in reg 5(1) or (2) to a person employed in an undertaking or in part of one, transferred by a transfer within the regulations, is a reference to a person so employed immediately before the transfer, including, where the transfer is effected by a series of two or more transactions, the person so employed immediately before any of those transactions: reg 5(3).

Regulation 5(2) shall not transfer or otherwise affect the liability of any person to be prosecuted for, convicted of and sentenced for any offence: reg 5(4).

Regulation 5(1) is without prejudice to any right of an employee arising apart from the regulations to terminate his contract of employment without notice if a substantial change is made in his working conditions to his detriment; but no such right shall arise by reason only that, under reg 5(1), the identity of his employer changes unless the employee shows that, in all the circumstances, the change is a significant change and to his detriment: reg 5(5).

At common law the effect of a transfer of a business was to bring the employee's contract of employment to an end with the transferring employer. Where this was without notice the employee was wrongfully dismissed by the employer. The common law position was set out in *Nokes v Doncaster Amalgamated Collieries Ltd* [1940] AC 1014, where it was held that an employee is entitled to choose the employer whom he promises to serve, so that the right to his services cannot be transferred from one employer to another without his assent.

There is nothing in the regulations which prevents the employer from terminating the employee's contract. However, such a termination may have certain consequences for the employer which are considered later. The regulations also confirm the employee's right to resign and claim a constructive dismissal, except perhaps in very exceptional circumstances. This will be considered later.

Regulation 5 has given rise to difficulties. In the main the difficulties have surrounded the interpretation of the phrase 'immediately before the transfer'. What was meant by 'immediately before'? Was it to be interpreted literally or was the employee employed immediately before the transfer where there was a gap between his dismissal and the transfer? In *Apex Leisure Hire v Barratt* [1984] IRLR 224, it was held that the employee was employed by the transferor immediately before the transfer, notwithstanding that he was dismissed on a Friday and the business was not transferred until a Monday. See also *Secretary of State for Employment v Anchor Hotel (Kippford) Ltd* [1985] ICR 724, *Fenton v Stablegold Ltd (t/a Chiswick Court Hotel)* [1986] IRLR 64 and *Bullard v Marchant* [1986] ICR 389, where the decision in *Apex Leisure Hire v Barratt* was followed.

Other decisions of both the tribunals and the EAT suggested a different approach. In *Premier Motors (Medway) Ltd v Total Oil Great Britain Ltd and Others* [1984] ICR 58, the EAT held that 'immediately before' meant at the time of, or moment of the transfer. In *Bullard's* case, above, the EAT felt obliged to follow *Barratt's* case, above, but recognised the problems of the conflicting interpretations.

In *Secretary of State for Employment v Spence and Others* [1986] IRLR 248, the Court of Appeal considered reg 5. Spence and Sons (Market Harborough) Ltd went into receivership on 16 November. The company's main customer was British Telecom (BT). BT told the receiver that unless the business was sold by 24 November, BT would withdraw from the contract and would place its business elsewhere. On Monday 28 November at 11.00am the workforce was told that they were dismissed with immediate effect. At 2.00pm on the same day there was a transfer by the receiver to Econ Atkinson. It was a condition precedent to the purchase by Econ Atkinson that a new contract should be concluded with BT. A new contract with BT was concluded about the same time. The purchasers purchased the plant, stock, work in progress, and intangible assets, the vendor's rights against third parties and the goodwill of the business. After consideration Econ Atkinson decided to retain the business as a going concern. The employees were told to report for work the following morning when they were re-employed under fresh contracts of employment. Spence and others claimed a redundancy payment. The Secretary of State refused to pay a redundancy payment on the basis that there had been a transfer of the undertaking and that the employees had been employed immediately before the transfer. Therefore there was no redundancy. The effect of reg 5 was to transfer their employment to Econ Atkinson without a break.

The Court of Appeal held that there was no contract in existence at the time of the transfer. Since there was no contract, there was nothing on which the regulations could bite. Balcombe LJ held:

[reg 5(1)] has two effects: first, that a relevant transfer does not terminate a contract of employment; and the second effect . . . is that there is a statutory novation of the contract. That provision can clearly only relate to a contract of employment which is subsisting at the moment of transfer; otherwise there is nothing on which the regulation can operate.

Balcombe LJ concurred with the judgment of Browne-Wilkinson J in *Premier Motors (Medway) Ltd v Total Oil Great Britain Ltd and Others*, above. He accepted that immediately before meant at the time or moment of transfer. Conversely, he found *Apex Leisure Hire v Barratt*, above; *Secretary of State for Employment v Anchor Hotel (Kippford) Ltd*, above; *Fenton v Stablegold (t/a Chiswick Court Hotel)*, above and *Bullard v Marchant*, above, were wrongly decided.

Although the decision in *Spence*'s case, above, clarified the law, it has meant a loss of protection for an employee whose contract is brought to an end before the business is transferred because of the transfer.

In *Bork*'s case, above, the European Court of Justice held that where the employment relationship has been terminated before the transfer in breach of art 4(1) of the Directive (which provides that the transfer of an undertaking shall not itself constitute grounds for dismissal by the transferor or transferee), the employee must be considered as still employed at the date of the transfer so that the obligations of the employer are transferred from the transferor to the transferee. Regulation 8 gives effect to art 4(1) of the Directive.

The matter was put beyond doubt in *Litster v Forth Dry Dock and Engineering Co Ltd* [1989] ICR 341. The company went into receivership. At 3.30pm on 6 February the entire workforce was dismissed with immediate effect. At 4.30pm the business was transferred by the receivers. Within 48 hours the transferee was recruiting employees. Three former employees were re-engaged. The House of Lords held that the purpose of the Directive and the regulations was to protect employees where there was a transfer of the business in which they were employed. If the words 'immediately before a transfer' were read literally it was possible to circumvent the purpose of the Directive and the regulations by dismissing the employees a short time before the transfer took effect. Following the decision in *Bork*'s case, above, the House of Lords held that the words 'a person employed immediately prior to the transfer' in reg 5(3) must be construed as meaning a person employed immediately prior to the transfer or who would have been so employed if he had not been unfairly dismissed within reg 8(1) before the transfer where the transfer or a reason connected with it was the reason or principal reason for his dismissal. Regulation 8(1) which provides where the reason or principal reason for a dismissal is the transfer, or a reason connected with it, the dismissal shall be automatically unfair, was giving effect to art 4 of the Directive in that the transfer is not to be a good ground for dismissal. If it is possible to show that the employee has been dismissed for an economic, technical or organisational reason entailing changes in the workforce within the meaning of reg 8(2), then the dismissal is not automatically unfair under reg 8(1) and if such an economic, technical or organisational reason can be shown then *Spence*'s case, above, will apply. Thus, if it can be shown that the reason is an economic, technical or organisational reason and the employee is not employed immediately prior to the transfer, his contract of employment will not transfer. The House of Lords held that the expression 'immediately before' takes its meaning from the context, but ordinarily it involves the notion that between the two relevant events there is no intervening space, lapse of time or event of any significance. Where an employee has been dismissed prior to the transfer, but is deemed to have been employed immediately prior to the transfer is the dismissal ineffective or does it simply pass the liabilities to the transferee? It is submitted that the liabilities pass but the dismissal remains effective. Where *Litster*'s case, above, applies then arguably all the liabilities, not just the liability for unfair dismissal, become the liabilities of the transferee. However, where the dismissal is not unfair under reg 8(1) it may be unfair under s 57(3) of the EP(C)A 1978. Following *Litster*'s case, above, the liability would be that of the transferor.

Although the cases of *Spence* and *Litster*, above, support the view that employment must exist at the time or moment of the transfer, the acquired rights Directive refers to the date of the transfer: see also *Wendelboe v LJ Music Aps* [1985] ICR 457.

Under reg 5(4) the transferee is not liable for the criminal offences of the transferor. However, he would appear to be liable for most civil as distinct from criminal wrongs, including tortious liability: see *Spence*'s case, above.

In *Angus Jowett and Co Ltd v National Union of Tailors and Garment Workers* [1985] ICR 646, it was held that liability under a protective award where an employer has failed to consult with a recognised trade union under s 99 of the Employment Act 1975, would not transfer from the transferor to the transferee. Regulation 5(2)(*a*) provides that on a transfer all the transferor's rights, powers, duties and liabilities under, or in connection with, any such contract shall be transferred to the transferee. The EAT held that although the words 'in connection with' were extremely wide, the employer's duties or liabilities which lead to the making of a declaration that the employer has not complied with the requirements of s 99 of the 1975 Act, arise under the Act and not in connection with any contract with an individual employee but by reason of the failure to consult a recognised union.

The transfer of the business may take place at a single moment. However, it may be spread over a period of time as, for instance, where there is an exchange of contracts with completion taking place at a later date. In *Kestongate Ltd v Miller* [1986] ICR 672, the EAT thought that transfer could be on exchange of contracts where completion took place later. However, in *Spence*'s case, above, the Court of Appeal appeared to assume that transfer meant completion. In *Wheeler v Patel* [1987] ICR 631, doubt was cast upon whether the decision in *Kestongate* was right, particularly since it was decided before *Spence*'s case. In *Brook Lane Finance Co Ltd v Bradley* [1988] IRLR 283, further support was given to the view that transfer takes place on completion. However, in *Macer v Abafast Ltd* [1990] IRLR 137, the EAT seems to have assumed that exchange could be a transfer, or indeed that possibly an offer and acceptance prior to exchange could be a linked transaction and therefore a transfer. Regulation 3(4) provides that linked transactions may be regarded as one. In *Wheeler*'s case, above, it was held that exchange and completion could not be construed as a linked transaction. Regulation 3(4) only applies to a series of two or more transactions between the same parties and thus cannot apply where more than two parties are involved.

A further issue which remains to be determined is whether or not continuity of employment is preserved under the regulations. Even if it is not it is preserved under para 17 of Sched 13 to the EP(C)A 1978. The problem was considered in *Keabeech Ltd v Mulcahy* [1985] ICR 79. The better view is that continuity is preserved under para 17 of Sched 13 to the EP(C)A 1978 rather than the regulations. Continuous employment is neither a right nor a liability. It is simply a question of calculation based upon facts: see *Macer*'s case, above. It is open to argument that the transfer of an undertaking within the regulations is wider than the transfer of a business within the EP(C)A 1978.

There may be a transfer of a business, notwithstanding that a proposed merger is subsequently called off: *Dabell v Vale Industrial Services (Nottingham) Ltd* [1988] IRLR 439. Dabell was employed by the company which became technically insolvent. An agreement was reached in principle to transfer the business to Nofotec. Orders, machines and other items or materials were transferred, together with a list of the company's debtors. Dabell and others were sent to premises under Nofotec's control. Subsequently negotiations between the respondent and Nofotec failed and the merger did not take place. Nonetheless there was a transfer.

Regulation 5(5) provides that the transfer of the contract of employment is without prejudice to any right of an employee arising other than by virtue of the regulations to terminate his contract of employment without notice if a substantial change is made in his working conditions to his detriment. This regulation further provides that no right shall arise by reason only that under this regulation the identity of the employer changes unless the employee can show that in all the circumstances the change is a significant change and is to his detriment. This regulation has two parts. The first part of the regulation confirms the employee's right to resign and claim a constructive dismissal where there is a substantial change in his working conditions to his detriment. The second part deals with the change in the identity of the employer. The change in identity of the employer of itself is not sufficient to enable the employee to terminate his contract without notice and claim a constructive dismissal, unless the change is a significant change and is to the employee's detriment. It is difficult to envisage circumstances in which a change of employer's identity is likely to be a significant change and to be to the employee's detriment. Where the employee can bring himself within this provision it seems that he can claim a constructive dismissal. Presumably, the use of the word detriment is intended to suggest a change which strikes at the root of the contract and so is fundamental.

4 Collective agreements

Regulation 6 provides that where at the time of a relevant transfer there is a collective agreement made by or on behalf of the transferor with a recognised union (not necessarily an independent trade union) covering an employee whose contract is automatically transferred under reg 5(1), then broadly the effect is to transfer the obligations arising out of the collective agreement to the transferee. Regulation 6 is without prejudice to s 18 of the Trade Union and Labour Relations Act 1974 which provides that collective agreements are conclusively presumed to be unenforcable, unless the agreement is in writing and contains a proviso that it is intended to be legally enforceable. Where the terms of a collective agreement have been incorporated into the individual's contract of employment, reg 5 will apply. Regulation 6 is concerned with the transferee's liability under a collective agreement. A collective agreement will cover terms such as disputes procedures, collective grievance procedures or redundancy procedures. It may provide for union recognition.

Where a collective agreement is transferred the transferee is not under any obligation to observe the terms in respect of employees who are not in the undertaking at the time it was transferred: see *Ny Mølle Kro*, above. Regulation 9 applies where, after a relevant transfer, the undertaking, or part thereof, maintains an identity distinct from the remainder of the transferee's undertaking. Where before such a transfer an independent trade union is recognised to any extent by the transferor in respect of employees of any description who in consequence of the transfer become employees of the transferee, then, after the transfer, the union shall be deemed to have been recognised by the transferee to the same extent in respect of employees of that description and any agreement for recognition may be varied or rescinded accordingly.

There is a potential overlap between regs 6 and 9. A collective agreement may provide for union recognition. Under reg 6 this obligation will pass to the transferee even though the undertaking does not maintain a separate identity in the hands of the transferee. If the agreement is not legally enforceable it is open to the transferee to terminate the same. The transferee may enter into negotiations with the union after the transfer.

A collective agreement has the same meaning as in the 1974 Act and a recognised trade union has the same meaning as in the EP(C)A 1978: see reg 2(1).

5 Exclusion of occupational pension schemes

Regulations 5 and 6 do not apply to a contract of employment or collective agreement which relates to an occupational pension scheme or to any rights, powers, duties or liabilities under or in connection with any such contract, or subsisting by virtue of any such agreement and relating to such a scheme or otherwise arising in connection with the person's employment and relating to such scheme. An occupational pension scheme is one within the meaning of the Social Security Pensions Act 1975: reg 7.

6 Dismissal of an employee because of a transfer

Regulation 8(1) provides that where either before or after a relevant transfer any employee of the transferor or transferee is dismissed that employee shall be treated for the purposes of Part V of the 1978 Act as unfairly dismissed if the transfer or a reason connected with it is the reason or principal reason for his dismissal. Under reg 8(1) a dismissal is automatically unfair. However reg 8(2) provides that where an economic, technical or organisational reason entailing changes in the workforce of either the transferor or the transferee before or after a relevant transfer is the reason or principal reason for dismissing an employee, reg 8(1) shall not apply. However the dismissal shall for the purposes of s 57(1)(b) of the EP(C)A 1978 be regarded as having been for a substantial reason of a kind such as to justify the dismissal of an employee holding the position which that employee held. Thus, reg 8(2) provides that the dismissal will not be automatically unfair if the employer can establish an economic, technical or organisational reason. It will then be for the tribunal to determine whether the employer acted reasonably in dismissing the employee under s 57(3) of the EP(C)A 1978: see *McGrath v Rank Leisure Ltd* [1985] ICR 527.

Regulation 8(3) provides that the regulations apply whether or not the employee in question is employed in the undertaking or part thereof transferred or to be transferred.

Regulation 8(4) provides that reg 8(1) shall not apply where the dismissal of an employee was by reason of the application of s 5 of the Aliens Restriction (Amendment) Act 1919 to his employment.

The onus is upon the dismissing employer to establish an economic technical or organisational reason entailing changes in the workforce: see *Forth Estuary Engineering Ltd v Litster*, above.

In *Anderson and Another v Dalkeith Engineering Ltd* [1985] ICR 66, the EAT held that the words 'economic', 'technical', and 'organisational' were not mutually exclusive and a reason may 'at the same time be economic and organisational, technical and organisational, or all three together'. In *Wheeler*'s case, above, the EAT held that economic had to be construed *ejusdem generis* with the adjectives technical and organisational. This justified giving a limited meaning to the word economic.

One issue involving reg 8(2) is its impact upon the employee's entitlement to a redundancy payment. There is a division of opinion between the Scottish EAT and the English EAT. In *Meikle v McPhail (Charleston Arms)* [1983] IRLR 351, the Scottish division of the EAT held that where a dismissal is for an economic, technical or organisational reason, it is treated as a substantial reason of a kind such as to justify the dismissal of the employee holding the position which that employee held under s 57(1)(*b*) of the EP(C)A 1978. Therefore, the dismissal cannot be described as being a dismissal by reason of redundancy because that is a reason within s 57(2)(*c*) of the EP(C)A 1978. This approach was followed in *Canning v (1) Niaz (2) McLoughlin* [1983] IRLR 431. However, in *Gorictree Ltd v Jenkinson* [1985] ICR 51, the English division of the EAT held:

we are unable to accept that regulation 8(2) creates, for the purposes of s 57 [of the EP(C)A 1978], a category of reasons from which redundancy is necessarily excluded. As a matter of fact, we suppose that redundancy is one of the most common of the economic, technical or organisational reasons entailing changes in the workforce to which regulation 8(2) applies. If the reasons comprised in regulation 8(2) commonly include redundancy as a matter of fact, we feel that clear words would be required to exclude redundancy as a matter of law; and the words used do not appear to us to satisfy that requirement . . . the position would be different if reg 8(2) required the reasons to which it applied to be regarded as falling within the category of some 'other' substantial reason, for that would imply that it had to be regarded as a reason other than redundancy.

. . . we attach much importance to the fact that regulation 8(2)(*b*) applies 'for the purposes of s 57(1)(*b*)'. The function of s 57(1) is to determine 'for the purposes of this Part'—that is, Part V of the Act—whether the dismissal of an employee was fair or unfair. The right to a redundancy payment, on the other hand, is created by s 81 which introduces Part VI of the Act.

In *Anderson*'s case, above, the Scottish division of the EAT preferred the decision in *Gorictree Ltd v Jenkinson*, above, to that in *Canning v (1) Niaz (2) McLoughlin*, above, and suggested that it was open to tribunals to follow the reasoning in *Gorictree Ltd v Jenkinson*, above, if they preferred it to that in *Canning v (1) Niaz (2) McLoughlin*, above.

Another issue arising out of reg 8(2) is whether or not a pre-transfer dismissal can be an economic, technical or organisational reason. A pre-transfer dismissal may be at the request of the transferee. There may be a contractual obligation to that effect in the agreement. In *Anderson*'s case the Scottish division of the EAT came to the conclusion that a contractual stipulation that the transferor should dismiss the employees prior to the transfer was for an economic reason and in this case the dismissal was unfair. In *Litster*'s case, the EAT also appeared to accept that a pre-transfer dismissal could be for an economic technical or organisational reason. However, more recent cases throw doubts on this.

Thus, in *Wheeler v Patel*, above, the EAT held that the word economic had to be construed *ejusdem generis* with the words technical and organisational. Economic had to be given a limited meaning relating to the conduct of the business. It did not include broader economic reasons such as the achievement of a sale or the achievement of sale at an enhanced price. In *Gateway Hotels Ltd v Stewart* [1988] IRLR 287, the hotel was sold by Gateway to Lytpark. Lytpark insisted as a condition of the sale that the employees should be dismissed before the sale. The employees were dismissed by reason of redundancy prior to the sale. Some were subsequently taken on by the purchaser. It was argued that the reason for the dismissal was redundancy and that that was a reason within reg 8(2). The EAT, upholding the decision of the tribunal, found that the principal reason for the dismissal was the condition in the contract of sale and this did not amount to an economic, technical or organisational reason. Thus, following this case, any agreement between the parties that the employees should be dismissed prior to the transfer will not be a reason within reg 8(2). Likewise, some tribunals have found that where a receiver dismisses employees prior to the transfer simply to gain an enhanced price even though not expressly asked by the purchaser, the reason is not one in reg 8(2).

Regulation 8(2) will apply if the reason for the dismissal is an economic reason relating to the conduct of the business. A genuine redundancy unconnected with the transfer will fall within reg 8(2).

Liability for automatically unfair pre-transfer dismissals will pass to the transferee under the principle in *Litster*'s case, above.

The economic, technical or organisational reason must entail changes in the workforce: reg 8(2). In *Berriman v Delabole Slate Ltd* [1985] ICR 546, Berriman was a quarryman. He had a guaranteed weekly wage of £100. The undertaking in which he was employed was transferred. After the transfer the transferee told Berriman that his remuneration would be altered to an hourly rate of £1.94 (£77.60 a week) with an anticipated weekly bonus of around £22.00. The transferee wished to ensure that the employees transferred enjoyed standard rates of pay with existing employees. Berriman resigned and claimed a constructive dismissal. The EAT found that the dismissal was unfair. An economic, technical or organisational reason must entail changes in the workforce. There were no changes in the workforce, the only change was in terms and conditions of employment—the rate of pay. The fact that Berriman had been constructively dismissed was not sufficient to constitute a change in the workforce for the purposes of reg 8(2). The Court of Appeal affirmed the decision of the EAT and held it:

First, the phrase 'economic, technical or organisational reason entailing changes in the workforce' in our judgment requires that the change in the workforce is part of the economic, technical or organisational reason. The employers' plan must be to achieve changes in the workforce. It must be an objective of the plan, not just a possible consequence of it.

Secondly, we do not think that the dismissal of one employee followed by the engagement of another in his place constitutes a change in the 'workforce'. To our minds, the word 'workforce' connotes the whole body of employees as an entity: it corresponds to the 'strength' or the 'establishment'. Changes in the identity of the individuals who make up the workforce do not constitute changes in the workforce itself so long as the overall numbers and functions of the employees looked at as a whole remain unchanged.

The Court of Appeal was not persuaded by the argument that if this construction was adopted it would mean that after a transfer of an undertaking the employer would not be able to impose on the employees taken over changes in the terms and conditions of employment which, if the transfer had not taken place, they could have imposed upon the existing workforce. See *Hollister v National Farmers Union* [1979] ICR 542, where it had been recognised that employers may be able to make changes in the terms and conditions of employment where commercial considerations so dictate. The Court of Appeal recognised that one of the intentions of the regulations was to safeguard employee's rights. Among the employees' most important rights are the existing terms and conditions of service. See also *Bullard and Another v Marchant and Another* [1986] ICR 389.

In practice the transferee who wishes to change the terms and conditions of employment may be better off in dismissing the employees, and then offering new terms and conditions to such of the employees as are prepared to return on those new terms and conditions. This would appear to be within reg 8(2).

In *Crawford v Swinton Insurance Brokers Ltd* [1990] ICR 85, Crawford worked as a typist and clerk. When the business was transferred she was told that after the transfer the nature of her job would change from secretarial work to selling insurance. Instead of working from home she would have to attend the office and work normal office hours, and would lose the use of her company car. She resigned and claimed a constructive dismissal. The tribunal found that she had been constructively dismissed, but that the dismissal was not automatically unfair under reg 8(1) because the reason was an organisational one entailing changes in the workforce within reg 8(2). The tribunal found the dismissal was fair. The EAT held that there could be a change in the workforce under reg 8(2) where the same people are retained but undertake different functions.

Once the employer has been able to establish that reg 8(2) applies, it is then necessary for the tribunal to consider the test of reasonableness in the normal way. As the EAT held in *McGrath v Rank Leisure Ltd* [1985] ICR 527:

[the case] . . . is thrown back into the main stream of s 57 [of the EP(C)A 1978], by which it is then carried on to the filter through which in the end every reason is required to pass—the test of the reasonableness of its treatment by the employer as a sufficient reason for dismissal determined in the accordance with equity and substantial merit under s 57(3).

Where the dismissal is held to be unfair then the tribunal must assess damages in the normal way. However, where the employer seeks to limit his liability by arguing that even if the employees had not been dismissed at the time when they were, they would have been dismissed within a short time thereafter, the onus is upon the employer to establish the evidence limiting its liability.

7 Duty to inform and consult trade union representatives

Regulation 10 deals with the obligation to inform and consult trade union representatives. It relates to an affected employee. An affected employee is any employee of the transferor or transferee whether or not employed in the undertaking or part to be transferred who may be affected by the transfer or measures taken in connection with it and references to the employer shall be construed accordingly: reg 10(1). Thus, the regulations apply, unless they otherwise provide, to both the transferor's and transferee's employees. Regulation 10(2) provides that long enough before a relevant transfer to enable consultations with the union representatives to take place the employer of any affected employees in respect of whom an independent trade union is recognised by him must inform the representatives of (a) the fact that the relevant transfer is to take place, when approximately, it is to take place and the reasons for it; and (b) the legal, economic and social implications of the transfer for the affected employees; and (c) the measures which he envisages he will, in connection with the transfer, take in relation to those employees or, if he envisages that no measures will be so taken, that fact; and (d) if the employer is the transferor the measures which the transferee envisages he will, in connection with the transfer, take in relation to such of those employees as, by virtue of reg 5 above, become employees of the transferee after the transfer or, if he envisages that no measures will be so taken, that fact. Under reg 10(3) the transferee must give the transferor such information at such time as will enable the transferor to perform his duties for this latter purpose. Regulation 10(5) provides that where the employer of any affected employees envisages that he will, in connection with the transfer, be taking measures in relation to such employees in respect of whom an independent trade union is recognised by him he must consult with representatives of that union. During the course of consultations the employer must consider any representations made by the trade union representative and reply to those representations with reasons if he rejects any representations made: see reg 10(6). As under s 99 of the Employment Protection Act 1975, if there are special circumstances which render it not reasonably practicable for an employer to perform any of the obligations he must take all such steps as are reasonably practicable in the circumstances: see reg 10(7).

The obligation to consult only arises where it is envisaged that measures will be taken in connection with the transfers: *Institution of Professional Civil Servants and Others v Secretary of State for Defence* [1987] IRLR 373, where it was suggested that the regulations envisage that there may be voluntary consultations. Further it was held that information must be given in a form that would enable the employer to comply with its statutory obligations. Thus it cannot be supplied under the cover of commercial confidentiality. Where the information is based on the employer's judgment there is no obligation to disclose the calculations on which that judgment is based. In this case it was held that the word 'measures' is of the widest import.

Under reg 11(1), in the event of failure to inform or consult, a complaint may be presented by the trade union to the tribunal. If on a complaint a question arises whether or not it was reasonably practicable for an employer to perform a particular duty or what steps he took to perform it, the onus is upon him to show there were special circumstances which rendered it not reasonably practicable for him to perform the duty, and he took all such steps towards its performance as were reasonably practicable in the circumstances: see reg 11(2).

On any complaint against a transferor that he failed to comply with reg 10(2)(d) or, in so far as it relates thereto, reg 10(7), the transferor may not show that it was not reasonably practicable for him to perform the duty in question because the transferee has failed to give him requisite information at the requisite time in accordance with reg 10(3), unless he has given the transferee notice of his intention to show that fact; giving such notice makes the transferee a party to the proceedings: see reg 11(3).

Where a tribunal finds a complaint well founded, it must make a declaration to that effect and may order the employer to pay appropriate compensation to such affected employees as may be specified or if the transferee did not inform the transferor (see above), then it may order the transferee to pay appropriate compensation to those affected employees as may be specified: see reg 11(4).

Appropriate compensation is such sum not exceeding two weeks' pay for each of the employees affected as the tribunal considers just and equitable having regard to the seriousness of the failure of the employer to comply with his duty: see reg 11(11). If the employer fails to pay compensation, an employee can make a claim to the tribunal: see reg 11(5) and (6). There is a time limit of three months (or such further period as the tribunal considers reasonable where it is satisfied that it was not reasonably practicable to bring the complaint before the end of three months) for bringing a claim beginning with the date on which the relevant transfer is completed, in cases of failure to consult, and the date of the tribunal's order in cases of failure to pay compensation: see reg 11(8).

Nothing in this regulation affects the employer's obligation under s 99 of the EPA 1975 nor the requirement under any code of practice.

If the employer has also failed to comply with the provisions of s 99 of the EPA 1975, awards to employees under this regulation go towards reducing the amount payable under a subsequent protective award and any damages for breach of contract for a period within the protected period. The converse situation also applies: see reg 11(7).

The position of these regulations is likely to be akin to the effect of s 99 of the EPA 1975 in claims for unfair dismissal. See Chapter 8.

For regs 10 and 11 to apply there must be a relevant transfer: see *Banking Insurance and Finance Union v Barclays Bank plc and Others* [1987] ICR 495.

8 Restrictions on contracting out

Regulation 12 provides that any provision of any agreement whether a contract of employment or not shall be void in so far as it purports to exclude or limit the operation of regs 5, 8 or 10, or to preclude any person presenting a complaint to a tribunal under reg 11.

9 Exclusions

Regulations 8, 10 and 11 do not apply to employment where under his contract of employment the employee ordinarily works outside the UK. A person employed to work on board a ship registered in the UK shall, unless the employment is wholly outside the UK or he is not ordinarily resident in the UK, be regarded as a person who under his contract ordinarily works in the UK: reg 13. See Chapter 1, **2.6** above.

10 Coming into force of the regulations

Regulations 1–3 and 10–13 came into operation on 1 February 1982. Regulations 4–9 and 14 came into operation on 1 May 1982.

Chapter 13

Remedies

Where the tribunal makes a finding of unfair dismissal it may make a recommendation for reinstatement, re-engagement or it may make an award of compensation: s 68 of the EP(C)A 1978. An order for either reinstatement or re-engagement is the principal remedy.

Having found the dismissal unfair and before considering the remedies, the tribunal must explain to the employee that it can make an order for reinstatement or re-engagement, and explain the circumstances in which these orders can be made. It must also ask the employee whether he wishes to be reinstated or re-engaged: s 68(1) of the EP(C)A 1978. See also *Pirelli General Cable Works Ltd v Murray* [1979] IRLR 190, where it was held that the tribunal's obligation to explain its power to the employee is mandatory even if the employee is professionally represented. If the employee is not seeking reinstatement or re-engagement the tribunal must consider compensation: s 68(2) of the EP(C)A 1978.

1 Reinstatement

An order for reinstatement has the effect of putting the employee in the same position which he would have enjoyed had he not been dismissed: s 69(2) of the EP(C)A 1978. In deciding whether it will make an order for reinstatement the tribunal, under s 69(5) of the EP(C)A 1978, has to take into account the following considerations:

(*a*) Does the employee wish to be reinstated?

(*b*) Is it practicable for the employer to comply with an order for reinstatement?

(*c*) Where the employee has caused or contributed to some extent to the dismissal, would it be just to order his reinstatement?

In assessing the practicability of reinstatement the tribunal must, under s 70(1) of the EP(C)A 1978, ignore the fact that the employer has engaged a permanent replacement for the dismissed employee unless the employer can show:

(*a*) that it was not practicable for him to arrange for the dismissed employee's work to be done without engaging a permanent replacement; or

(b) that he engaged the replacement after the lapse of a reasonable period, without having heard from the dismissed employee that he wished to be reinstated or re-engaged, and that when the employer engaged the replacement it was no longer reasonable for him to arrange for the dismissed employee's work to be done except by a permanent replacement.

Where the tribunal decides to make an order for reinstatement, on making the order it must, by s 69(2) of the EP(C)A 1978, specify:

(a) any amount payable by the employer in respect of any benefit which the employee might reasonably be expected to have had but for the dismissal, including arrears of pay, for the period between the date of termination of employment and the date of reinstatement;

(b) any rights and privileges, including seniority and pension rights, which must be restored to the employee; and

(c) the date by which the order must be complied with.

In addition, the order for reinstatement must also reflect any improvement in the terms and conditions which the employee would have enjoyed but for the dismissal: s 69(3) of the EP(C)A 1978.

The amount of any benefit payable by the employer to the employee under para (a), above, is to be reduced by any sums received by the employee between the date of termination and the date of reinstatement by way of:

(a) wages in lieu of notice or ex gratia payments paid by the employer; and

(b) remuneration paid in respect of employment with another employer.

In addition, the tribunal must take into account, so as to reduce the amount, any other benefits it thinks appropriate in the circumstances: s 70(2) of the EP(C)A 1978. There is no limit to the amount of any benefit which the tribunal may order to be deducted under this provision.

Where the employee has been guilty of any contributory fault the tribunal must consider whether it is just to make an order for reinstatement: s 69(5)(c) of the EP(C)A 1978. However, the order for reinstatement cannot reflect any element of contributory fault because of the effect of s 69(2) of the EP(C)A 1978.

In *Boots Company plc v Lees-Collier* [1986] IRLR 485, Lees-Collier, a shift chemist, was dismissed following an incident which led his employers to believe that he had stolen a packet of Sweetex from the shop from which he worked. The dismissal was found to be unfair and the tribunal ordered him to be reinstated. The employers appealed against the tribunal's finding. The EAT found that the wording of s 69(5)(c) of the EP(C)A 1978 echoed the words of s 74(6). It provides that where the employee caused or contributed to some extent to the dismissal the tribunal has to consider whether it would be just to order his reinstatement. Section 74(6) of the EP(C)A 1978 provides that where the tribunal finds that the dismissal was to any extent caused or contributed to by the action of the employee, it shall reduce the amount of compensatory award by such proportion as it considers just and equitable having regard to that finding. Thus, once the tribunal had reached the conclusion that the employee's conduct had not caused or contributed to his dismissal, in the sense that it would justify a reduction in the compensatory award, there was no rule for finding that he had caused or contributed to some extent to his dismissal for the purposes of s 69(5)(c) of the EP(C)A 1978.

If the employee has a contractual right to be promoted then that is something which the tribunal must take into account in making an order for reinstatement: *O'Laoire v Jackel International Ltd*, [1991] IRLR 170.

2 Re-engagement

The tribunal may make an order that the employee should be re-engaged by the employer or by a successor of the employer or by an associated employer in employment comparable to that from which he was dismissed, or other suitable employment: s 69(4) of the EP(C)A 1978. In deciding whether to make an order for re-engagement the tribunal under s 69(6) of the EP(C)A 1978, has to take into account the following considerations:

(a) What are the employee's wishes as to the nature of the order to be made?

(b) Is it practicable for the employer, successor, or associated employer to comply with an order for re-engagement?

(c) Where the employee caused or contributed to some extent to the dismissal, would it be just to order his re-engagement and if so on what terms?

Except where the tribunal takes into account contributory fault, where it orders re-engagement it must do so on terms which are, so far as is reasonably practicable, as favourable as an order for reinstatement: s 69(6) of the EP(C)A 1978.

In deciding whether it is practicable for the employer to comply with an order for re-engagement the tribunal has to ignore a permanent replacement, except in the same limited circumstances as in the case of reinstatement: s 70(1) of the EP(C)A 1978. (See **1**, above.)

Where the tribunal makes an order for re-engagement it must specify the terms on which re-engagement is to take place including (s69(4) of the EP(C)A 1978):

(a) the identity of the employer;

(b) the nature of the employment;

(c) the remuneration for the employment;
(d) any amount payable by the employer in respect of any benefit which the employee might reasonably be expected to have had but for the dismissal, including arrears of pay, for the period between the date of termination of employment and the date of re-engagement;
(e) any rights and privileges, including seniority and pension rights, which must be restored to the employee; and
(f) the date by which the order must be complied with.

Section 70(2) applies to computing (d), above. Again, there is no limit on the amount the tribunal can deduct. (See 1, above.)

Where the tribunal makes an order for re-engagement it writes a new contract for the parties. A direction to the employer to offer re-engagement within a stated period upon terms specified by the tribunal (which is sometimes called an 'offer direction'), merely directs the employer to make an offer to the employee without specifying as to whether and if so in what circumstances or upon what terms the employee should be bound in law to accept it. An offer direction does not discharge the obligations of the tribunal under s 69(4) of the EP(C)A 1978: *Lilley Construction Ltd v Dunn* [1984] IRLR 483.

Where the tribunal finds that the employee has contributed to his dismissal to the extent of 75 per cent, an order for re-engagement may be appropriate: see *Nairne v Highland and Islands Fire Brigade* [1989] IRLR 366.

There is no power to reduce the arrears of pay for the period between the date of termination of employment and the date of re-engagement because a tribunal considers that if the employee had pursued her complaint more vigorously or expeditiously she would probably have been re-engaged at an earlier date. An order for reinstatement requires the employer to treat the employee in all respects as if she had not been dismissed and an order for re-engagement must be on terms which are, so far as is reasonably practicable, as favourable as an order for reinstatement: see s 69(6) of the EP(C)A 1978. The discretion given to the tribunal in s 69(1) of the EP(C)A 1978 is not capable of overriding these mandatory provisions. The reference in s 69(2)(a) and (4)(d) to a benefit which the employee might have had but for the dismissal does not confer a discretion of the tribunal to increase or decrease what the employee would otherwise have had: *City and Hackney Health Authority v Crisp* [1990] IRLR 47.

Where a tribunal orders re-engagement at a lower salary, in assessing arrears of pay up to the date of re-engagement, the relevant salary is the salary at the date of dismissal and not the new salary: see *Electronic Data Processing Ltd v Wright* [1986] IRLR 8.

3 Non-compliance with order for reinstatement or re-engagement

Although s 69 of the EP(C)A 1978 refers to an order for reinstatement or re-engagement, tribunals have no power to enforce the order. Where an employee fails to comply with an order the matter must be dealt with under s 71(2) of the EP(C)A 1978. The tribunal will make an award of compensation calculated in the usual way together with an additional award or special award. Only one order can be made under s 69 of the EP(C)A 1978: see *Mabirizi v National Hospital for Nervous Diseases* [1990] IRLR 133.

The monetary provisions of a re-instatement or re-engagement order do not create a cause of action enforceable through the county courts: *O'Laoire v Jackel International Ltd* [1990] IRLR 70. The remedy is contained in s 71 of the EP(C)A 1978.

3.1 Partial compliance

Where the employee is reinstated or re-engaged, as the case may be, but the terms of the order are not fully complied with, the tribunal must make an award of compensation to be paid by the employer to the employee of the amount the tribunal thinks fit, having regard to the loss sustained by the employee through the employer's failure to comply fully with the order: s 71(1) of the EP(C)A 1978. The provision is a compensatory one and follows the wording of the section providing for the compensatory award. An award under this heading is based upon the employee's loss subject to a maximum of £10,000: See **5.2**, below.

3.2 Non-compliance

Where the employee is not reinstated or re-engaged, the tribunal must make an award of compensation calculated on the same principles which apply where the tribunal awards compensation only. Except in a case in which the dismissal is unfair by virtue of s 58 of the EP(C)A 1978 (dismissal for membership of or non-membership of, or taking part in the activities of a trade union), or s 59(*a*) of the EP(C)A 1978 (selection for redundancy for membership of, non-membership of, or taking part in the activities of a trade union), or in which the employer is able to satisfy the tribunal that it was not practicable to comply with the order, the tribunal must make an additional award of compensation the amount of which will be (i) not less than 26 weeks' pay nor more than 52 weeks' pay, or (ii) not less than 13 weeks' pay nor more than 26 week's pay: s 71(2) of the EP(C)A 1978. Under s 71(3), the higher band will only apply where the employer has dismissed the employee:

(*a*) where the dismissal is an unlawful act of discrimination within the meaning of the Sex Discrimination Act 1975, or (*b*) where the dismissal is an unlawful act of discrimination within the meaning of the Race Relations Act 1976.

Where the employee is unfairly dismissed because of membership of or non-membership of a trade union, or for taking part in the activities of a trade union or further is selected for any such reason in a redundancy situation and an order for reinstatement or re-engagement is not complied with, a special award will be made: see s 72 of the EP(C)A 1978 and see **5.4**, below. The amount of a special award in this case is either one week's pay multiplied by 156 or £19,735 whichever is the greater: s 75A(2) of the EP(C)A 1978, which applies where the effective date of termination falls on or after 1 April 1991. Previously the limit was £18,795. Where it is not practicable to comply with an order for reinstatement or re-engagement the employee will still be entitled to the special award which in such cases is either one week's pay multiplied by 104 or £13,180, whichever is the greater, but shall not exceed £26,290: s 75A(1) of the EP(C)A 1978 which applies where the effective date of termination falls on or after 1 April 1991. Previously the figures were £12,250 and £25,040. For the assessment of the special award see **5.4**, below.

In determining whether it is practicable for the employer to comply with an order for reinstatement or re-engagement the engagement of a permanent replacement must be ignored, unless the employer can show that it was not practicable for him to arrange for the dismissed employee's work to be done without engaging a permanent replacement: see s 71(4) where the award is an additional award and s 75A(6) where the award is a special award.

3.3 Additional award

Although the additional award is referred to as an award of 'compensation' it is not compensation in the sense that it compensates the employee for specific losses suffered by him. The side note to s 71 of the EP(C)A 1978 (which provides for the additional award) is 'enforcement of s 69 order and compensation'; the s 69 order is an order of reinstatement or re-engagement. Section 71(2) provides for the tribunal to make an additional award which is fixed by an upper and lower limit. The tribunal has a discretion as to what award it should make within these limits and no reference is made to assessing losses. It is impossible to see how it could be argued that these limits reflect the employee's losses. The view that an additional award is a penalty is strengthened by a comparison between the wording of s 71(1) and (2)(*b*) of the EP(C)A 1978. Subsection (1), which deals with assessment of compensation where the employer has not fully complied with the order for reinstatement or re-engagement, refers to 'loss' and has its origin in the compensatory provision. Subsection (2)(*b*) makes no reference to 'loss'.

Where a week's wages exceed £198, the excess is ignored: para

8(1)(*a*) of Sched 14 to the EP(C)A 1978 which applies where the date by which an order for reinstatement or re-engagement must be complied with is a date after 1 April 1991. Previously the limit was £184. This further supports the view that an additional award is intended to be a penalty. A week's pay for the purposes of an additional award is a week's pay gross; this is again different from the assessment of a compensatory award where a week's pay net is the basis for assessment: *George v Beecham Group* [1977] IRLR 43.

Tribunals have a wide discretion as to the matters which can be taken into account in deciding where in the range the additional award should fall. In exercising their discretion some assessment and balancing must take place. The tribunal is entitled to have regard to the conduct of the employer in refusing to comply with the order: see *Morganite Electrical Carbon Ltd v Donne* [1988] ICR 18, followed in *Motherwell Railway Club v McQueen and Another* [1989] ICR 418. See also *George*'s case, above, where the tribunal found it regrettable that a national employer of the size and responsibility of the respondent should be unable to comply with an order for reinstatement of a modest production line employee. It may be material for the tribunal to take into account where the statutory limit results in compensation being reduced, the extent to which the compensatory award has met the actual loss suffered by the employee: see *Donne*'s case, above. It may also reflect the fact that the employer's failure to reinstate was neither a wilful refusal nor a device to save money, although culpability attached to the employer's non-compliance: see *Mabirizi*'s case, above.

In making an additional award it is incumbent on the tribunal to act with care and scrupulous fairness: *Enessy Co SA (t/a The Tulchan Estate) v Minoprio* [1978] IRLR 489.

Again, the assessment of a special award is not made on the basis of the employee's losses: see **5.4**, below.

4 Practicability and orders for reinstatement or re-engagement

What is 'practicable' may have to be considered by the tribunal first in deciding whether to make an order for reinstatement or re-engagement and, secondly, where it has made such an order which has not been complied with, whether it was practicable for the employer to comply with it.

Guidance was given to the tribunal as to the way in which it must approach practicability in these two applications in *Freemans plc v Flynn* [1984] ICR 874, where the EAT held:

a very clear distinction is advisedly drawn by the statute between the two stages at which practicability will fall to be considered for the purposes of making a re-engagement order on the one hand and assessing the consequences of non-compliance with it on the other. The differences in language between s 69(6)(*b*) on the one hand and s 71(2)(*b*) [of the EP(C)A 1978] upon the other are striking. In the first instance, practicability of compliance is described as a 'consideration' which, among others, the tribunal has to take into account. In the second instance, there is a burden of proof thrown upon the employer (if he is to escape the consequence of non-compliance) of satisfying the tribunal that it was not practicable to comply with the order. This distinction of language led this appeal tribunal in *Timex Corporation v Thomson* [1981] IRLR 522, to state that at the earlier stage of considering whether or not to grant a re-engagement order, the tribunal is not required to make any definite finding that it would be practicable to comply with such an order, whereas at the later stage the tribunal would have to decide, looking at the matter in the knowledge of the actual facts which have occurred whether or not it was practicable to carry out the order. We respectfully follow that reasoning . . .

See *Timex Corporation v Thomson*, below.

4.1 Making the order

In deciding whether or not to make an order for reinstatement or re-engagement the tribunal is exercising an independent discretion. See s 69 of the EP(C)A 1978. What is practicable depends upon the context.

In *Meridian Ltd v Gomersall* [1977] ICR 597, where two employees were unfairly dismissed for clocking offences, and reinstatement was ordered, the EAT, in deciding whether reinstatement was practicable, referred to *Dedman v British Building and Engineering Appliances Ltd* [1974] ICR 53, where Scarman LJ had considered the word 'practicable'. He found:

The word 'practicable' is an ordinary English word of great flexibility: it takes its meaning from its context. But, whenever used, it is a call for the exercise of common sense, a warning that sound judgment will be impossible without compromise. Sometimes the context contemplates a situation rarely to be achieved, though much to be desired: the word then indicates one must be satisfied with less than perfection . . . Sometimes . . . what the context requires may have been possible, but may not for some reason have been 'practicable'. Whatever its context, the quality of the word is that there are circumstances in which we must be content with less than 100 per cent: and it calls for judgment to determine how much less.

Applying this to the question of reinstatement, the EAT held that the tribunal will fall into error 'if it approaches the question of reinstatement on the basis of general objective rules, guidelines and principles'; it has 'to look at the circumstances of the case where reinstatement is being considered and not try to analyse in too much detail the application of the word "practicable" but to take a broad common-sense view'. In this case reinstatement was not practicable because a redundancy situation had overtaken the company.

Expediency has nothing to do with what is practicable. It describes the state of things which is favourable to the fulfilment of some objective which is in mind and is not a relevant matter for consideration by the tribunal when exercising its discretion as to whether to order reinstatement or re-engagement: (1) *Qualcast (Wolverhampton) Ltd v Ross* and (2) *Ross v Qualcast (Wolverhampton) Ltd* [1979] IRLR 98. 'The legislation is not designed to enable complainants to re-establish their reputation or vindicate their reputation or anything of that kind.' So that once a finding of unfair dismissal has been made the tribunal must see 'how reasonably and most sensibly to compensate the . . . employee': *Nothman v London Borough of Barnet (No 2)* [1980] IRLR 65.

In *Timex Corporation v Thomson* [1981] IRLR 522, where it was argued that re-engagement of a senior manager was not practicable, the EAT held:

Section 69(6) [of the EP(C)A 1978] only requires the Industrial Tribunal to 'have regard' to matters of practicability. In our judgment there is no need for an Industrial Tribunal to reach a final conclusion that re-engagement is practicable before making any such order. If, having made an order for re-engagement, it proves not to be practicable to perform it there are no adverse consequences for the employer. If the employee asks for compensation by reason of the failure of the employers to re-engage, no order for additional compensation can be made under s 61(2)(*b*) [of the EP(C)A 1978] if the employer satisfies the Tribunal that it was not practicable to comply with the order. Therefore at that stage the Industrial Tribunal will have to decide, looking at the matter in the knowledge of the actual facts which have occurred, whether or not it was practicable to carry out the order. At the stage when the order to re-engage is being made, it is not in our judgment necessary for the Industrial Tribunal, looking at future possible events, to make a definite finding that the order for re-engagement was practicable. They must have regard to the question of practicability and if they are satisfied that it is unlikely to be effective, they will no doubt not make an order. The only strict requirement is that they should have regard to practicability.

See also *Boots Company plc v Lees-Collier*, above.

In looking at the practicability the tribunal is entitled to consider the industrial reality. In *Coleman v Magnet Joinery Ltd* [1974] ICR 25, Coleman and another employee had stopped paying union dues. The union and company sought to persuade them to continue payment but failed. A stoppage of work resulted and the company was threatened with a strike if nothing was done about the employees. The company therefore dismissed the employees and the tribunal, finding the dismissal unfair, held that re-engagement was not practicable. Before the NIRC it was argued for the employees that 'practicable' had to be given 'a very restricted construction closely equated to "possible" '. The court considered that such an interpretation could lead to unfortunate results. The court held:

The tribunal in making a recommendation are exercising an entirely independent discretion to which one would hope the parties to the dispute will give the most careful consideration, and which they will not lightly reject. If, because of a restrictive construction of 'practicable' which precludes the tribunal from considering the consequences of a re-engagement, they are led into making recommendations which have no hope of being acted upon, or which if they were would only lead to industrial strife, the result will be that their recommendations will fall into disrepute and carry no weight. When considering whether a recommendation is 'practicable' the tribunal ought to consider the consequences of re-engagement in the industrial relations scene in which it will take place.

In *Coleman*'s case it was likely to lead to industrial unrest and so it was not practicable. The decision was affirmed by the Court of Appeal: *Coleman v Magnet Joinery Ltd* [1975] ICR 46.

In *Bateman v British Leyland (UK) Ltd* [1974] ICR 403, Bateman refused to join a union and was dismissed following consequent industrial unrest and the threat of a stoppage of work. Before the NIRC it was argued on Bateman's behalf that since he was not to blame and was anxious to be re-employed an order should be made for re-engagement. It was further argued that the tribunal had erroneously held that because a recommendation for re-engagement would have been resented on the shop floor it would not be practicable; the tribunal should have assumed that its recommendations would be complied with. The NIRC upheld the view of the tribunal emphasising the importance of preserving tribunals' discretion in deciding whether re-engagement was practicable. See also *Langston v Amalgamated Union of Engineering Workers (No 2)* [1974] ICR 510.

Friction may arise because a reinstatement or re-engagement would cause dissension within the place of employment either generally: *see Coleman v Tolemans Delivery Service Ltd* [1973] IRLR 67, or with a particular person or persons: see *Wood v Louis C Edwards and Sons (Manchester) Ltd* [1972] IRLR 18; *Thornton v SJ Kitchin Ltd* [1972] IRLR 46.

It may not be practicable to order re-engagement because the employee has made allegations during the course of the proceedings about her fellow employees: see *Nothman v London Borough of Barnet (No 2)* [1980] IRLR 65, where Nothman alleged that her fellow employees had conspired to oust her from her employment.

In *Goodbody v British Railways Board* [1977] IRLR 84, the tribunal considered that reinstatement was practicable. Goodbody had refused to join a union because of his membership of 'The Brethren'. The tribunal found the dismissal unfair and ordered reinstatement because both parties to the application accepted that there would be no difficulty in a reinstatement and were able to agree the terms.

In addition to what may be described as industrial realities the tribunal is also entitled to look and see if there is a suitable vacancy. It may not be possible to make an order for reinstatement or re-engagement where at the time of the hearing the place of work had closed: *Mawson v Leadgate Engineering Ltd* [1972] IRLR 105, or where a redundancy situation has arisen at the place of employment: *Trusler v Lummus Co Ltd* [1972] IRLR 35. Again an order for reinstatement or re-engagement may place an undue burden upon the employer: *Perks v Geest Industries Ltd* [1974] IRLR 228.

It is also relevant for the tribunal to consider whether the employee can in fact return to employment. It may be that it is not practicable to order reinstatement or re-engagement because the employee is no longer fit: *McAulay v Cementation Chemicals Ltd* [1972] IRLR 71.

Reinstatement or re-engagement will be difficult where there was a close personal relationship between the employer and the employee, as in the case of a small employer. It is probable that an order for reinstatement or re-engagement in such circumstances will be exceptional and should only be made where the tribunal is clear that there is powerful evidence that it will succeed: *Enessy Co SA (t/a The Tulchan Estate) v Minoprio* [1978] IRLR 489.

4.2 Enforcing the order

Where an employer fails to comply with an order for reinstatement or re-engagement he will only escape an additional award if he can show that it was not practicable to implement the order: s 71(2)(*b*) of the EP(C)A 1978. In *George v Beecham Group*, above, the tribunal did not accept that reinstatement was not practicable because of the long history of the affair and the effect on other employees, and the resultant undermining of management's authority. In its view these were all exaggerated fears which, although bound to arise to some extent, should be overcome by competent management. Redundancy arising after the tribunal hearing may be an example of where it is not practicable to implement the order.

Where the tribunal makes an order for reinstatement or re-engagement which the employer does not follow, the tribunal may still make an additional award of compensation, even though, following the order, the employee decides not to return if the employer has reached his decision in ignorance of the employee's change of heart: *Cullen v Neilly* (1977) (unreported).

5 Other awards of compensation

Where the tribunal makes an order for reinstatement or re-engagement which is not complied with, then in addition to any additional award of compensation (see **3.3** above), it must make a basic award and a compensatory award. Where it finds the dismissal unfair but makes no order for reinstatement or re-engagement it must make a basic award and a compensatory award. Where the dismissal is regarded as unfair by virtue of s 58 of the EP(C)A 1978 (dismissal for membership of or non-membership of a trade union, or for taking part in the activities of a trade union), or s 59(*a*) of the EP(C)A 1978 (selection for redundancy for membership of, or non-membership of a trade union, or for taking part in the activities of a trade union), it must make a special award, where an order for reinstatement or re-engagement is not complied with when it takes the place of an additional award in such cases, or where an order for reinstatement or re-engagement is made but it is not practicable for the employer to comply with the order, or it may be made where the employee seeks an order for reinstatement or re-engagement but no such order is made: see s 72 of the EP(C)A 1978. No special award will be made unless the employee asks the tribunal to make an order for reinstatement or re-engagement. The special award is in addition to a basic award and a compensatory award. A special award will not be made in a case coming within s 73(2) of the EP(C)A 1978. See **5.4**, below.

5.1 Basic award

A basic award will be made even though the employee has suffered no financial loss other than his accrued rights, eg redundancy entitlement: see *Cadbury Ltd v Doddington* [1977] ICR 982. The amount of the basic award depends upon the length of continuous employment. Starting with the effective date of termination and working backwards, the number of complete years of continuous employment is calculated: s 73(3) of the EP(C)A 1978. Under this section the employee is entitled to:

(a) 1½ weeks' pay for each year of employment in which the employee was not below the age of 41;

(b) 1 week's pay for each year of employment not falling within para (a) above in which the employee was not below the age of 22; and

(c) ½ week's pay for each such year of employment not falling within either of paras (a) and (b).

The effect of para (c) is that an employee who at the effective date of termination is aged between 16 and 18 can claim a basic award calculated in accordance with that paragraph. Employees who have a year of employment in which their 41st or 22nd birthdays fall may count that year in the higher bracket for the purpose of calculating the basic award.

Where the effective date of termination is after the 64th birthday, the amount of the basic award will be reduced by 1/12 for each complete calendar month after the 64th birthday, and before the effective date of termination: s 73(5) and (6) of the EP(C)A 1978. An employee whose contractual age of retirement is in excess of 65 may claim unfair dismissal: *London Borough of Barnet v Nothman* [1979] IRLR 35. However he cannot recover a basic award.

Where by virtue of s 55(5) to (7) of the EP(C)A 1978, a date is treated as the effective date of termination which is later than the effective date of termination as defined by s 55(4) the period falling between the two dates counts as a period of employment for the purposes of computing the basic award: para 11(1) of Sched 13 to the EP(C)A 1978. Section 55(5) to (7) of the EP(C)A 1978 has the effect of extending the effective date of termination as defined in s 55(4) by the length of notice prescribed in s 49 in cases where the employee is dismissed without the notice prescribed by s 49 or is constructively dismissed.

In reckoning back the number of years of continuous employment no account is to be taken of years of employment prior to 20 years from the effective date of termination: s 73(4) of the EP(C)A 1978.

Section 73(4A) of the EP(C)A 1978 provides that where the dismissal is to be regarded as unfair by virtue of s 58 or by s 59(a) of the EP(C)A 1978, the amount of the basic award before any reduction under the provisions of s 73 of the EP(C)A 1978, shall not be less than £2,650. This increase applies where the effective date of termination falls on or after 1 April 1991. Thus, where the dismissal is found unfair on the grounds of trade union membership, non-membership or participation in trade union activities or where the employee is selected for any of those reasons in a redundancy situation the basic award shall be a minimum of £2,650, unless for instance the employee is found to have contributed to his dismissal. See **8**, below. The figure of £2,650 may be increased by the Secretary of State: see s 73(4B) of the EP(C)A 1978.

The amount of the basic award is limited to two weeks' pay (s 73(2) of the EP(C)A 1978) where the reason, or principal reason, for dismissal is redundancy and the employee:

(a) unreasonably refuses to accept a renewal of the contract or suitable alternative employment or where the employee during a trial period unreasonably terminates the contract under s 82(5) or (6); or

(b) is not dismissed on the ending of his employment under the old contract under s 84(1) (on a renewal of employment or re-engagement).

The basic award may be reduced because of contributory fault on the part of the employee: see **8**, below. See also **7**, below. The amount of the basic award is reduced or further reduced by the amount of any redundancy payment awarded by the tribunal under Part VI of the EP(C)A 1978 for the same dismissal or any payment made by the employer on the ground that the dismissal was by reason of redundancy whether in pursuance of Part VI or otherwise: s 73(9) of the EP(C)A 1978.

Section 73(1)(e) of the EP(C)A 1978 provides that the calculation of the basic award shall be subject to s 76 which prohibits compensation being awarded under the EP(C)A 1978 for unfair dismissal and the Sex Discrimination Act 1975 or the Race Relations Act 1976 in respect of the same matter.

For the purposes of the basic award a week's pay is the gross amount: *George v Beecham Group* [1977] IRLR 43. Nevertheless, monies emanating from someone other than the employer should be excluded in calculating the basic award: *Palmanor (t/a Chaplins Night Club) v Cedron* [1978] ICR 1008 (tips). Payment in excess of £198 is ignored: para 8(1)(*b*) of Sched 14 to the EP(C)A 1978, where the effective date of termination falls on or after 1 April 1991. Previously the limit was £184. Pay for voluntary overtime should not be included in the calculation of the basic award, though net overtime pay should be included when the compensatory award is calculated: *Brownson v Hire Service Shops Ltd* [1978] ICR 517. See Chapter 14.

Where an employer makes an *ex gratia* payment in excess of the total of the maximum compensatory award and the appropriate basic award, the employer is entitled to set off the *ex gratia* payment against the basic award. The tribunal is not obliged to order a further basic award. Although the amount of a basic award can only be reduced in the manner prescribed by statute, where the employer has paid an *ex gratia* payment, including an amount in respect of the basic award, a defence of payment is not reducing the amount of the basic award; it is accepting the amount and putting forward payment as an answer. This is the position whether or not the employer admits liability: *Chelsea Football Club and Athletic Co Ltd v Heath* [1981] IRLR 73.

Whereas the payment in full of a statutory redundancy payment breaks the continuity of employment, (see para 1 (1) and (2) of Sched 13 to the EP(C)A 1978) there is no corresponding provision relating to the basic awards.

5.2 Compensatory award

The amount of a compensatory award is the amount the tribunal considers just and equitable in all the circumstances having regard to the loss sustained by the employee in consequence of the dismissal in so far as that loss is attributable to the action taken by the employer: s 74(1) of the EP(C)A 1978. This is subject to the proviso that the amount of the compensation should not exceed £10,000: s 75(1) of the EP(C)A 1978 where the effective date of termination is on or after 1 April 1991. Previously the limit was £8,925. For the operation of this limit see s 75(3) which provides that the limit applies to the amount which the tribunal would, apart from this section, award after taking into account any payment made by the employer in respect of the dismissal and any reduction required by statute. The loss (referred to in s 74(1)) includes any expenses reasonably incurred by the employee in consequence of the dismissal and (subject to the next paragraph) any loss of benefit that he might reasonably be expected to have had but for the dismissal: s 74(2) of the EP(C)A 1978.

The loss in so far as it is a loss of any entitlement, potential entitlement or expectation of, a payment on account of dismissal by reason of redundancy, whether under Part VI of the EP(C)A 1978 or otherwise, includes the loss by which the amount of that payment exceeds the amount of the basic award for that dismissal; any reduction in the basic award under s 73(7A) to (9) of the EP(C)A 1978 in respect of the same dismissal is ignored for these purposes: s 74(3) of the EP(C)A 1978.

If the amount of any payment made by the employer to the employee on the grounds that dismissal was by reason of redundancy, whether under Part VI of the EP(C)A 1978 or otherwise, exceeds the basic award which would be payable but for s 73(9), the excess goes to reduce the amount of the compensatory award: s 74(7) of the EP(C)A 1978. Thus, the payment for redundancy is first set off against the basic award and any excess is then set against the amount of the compensatory award.

The employee is under an obligation to mitigate his loss. See **7**, below. The amount of the compensatory award may be reduced because of contributory fault on the part of the employee. See **8**, below.

5.3 Calculation of compensatory award

Guidance on calculating compensation was given by the NIRC in *Norton Tool Co Ltd v Tewson* [1972] ICR 501. The court rejected the application of the common law principles, holding that the measure of compensation for unfair dismissal was to be found in statute law and nowhere else. It found that a tribunal has an element of discretion in assessing compensation in that it is not necessary to adopt 'the approach of a conscientious and skilled cost accountant or actuary', but the tribunal has to exercise its discretion judicially on the basis of principle. Compensation must be assessed in an amount which is just and equitable and 'there is neither justice nor equity in a failure to act in accordance with principle'. The court recognised that tribunals are often faced with unaided litigants who cannot be expected to prepare precise details of their losses. If any other approach were adopted it would burden the parties with the expense of 'adducing evidence . . . which is disproportionate to the sums in issue'.

Where the compensatory award has been calculated on the basis of principle, nonetheless the tribunal may reduce the amount of the compensatory award where it would not be just and equitable for the employee to receive either the whole or part of the compensatory award. See *W Devis and Sons Ltd v Atkins* [1977] ICR 662.

In *Townson v The Northgate Group Ltd* [1981] IRLR 382, the EAT held that when assessing the compensatory award, the tribunal must calculate the actual losses and must then consider all the circumstances. Then acting as an industrial jury it must decide what is just and equitable compensation in all the circumstances. The circumstances include a consideration of the employee's conduct and how unfair was the unfair dismissal? It is submitted that the employer's conduct is not a proper consideration under s 74 of the EP(C)A 1978 and is a matter for the tribunal to take into account in assessing contributory fault on the part of the employee, otherwise the compensatory award will be reduced twice: see *Morris v Acco Co Ltd* [1985] ICR 306.

Tribunals are concerned with awarding compensation for financial loss. They cannot make an award of compensation to express disapproval of any industrial relations policies: *Clarkson International Tools Ltd v Short* [1973] ICR 191; *British United Shoe Machinery Co Ltd v Clarke* [1978] ICR 70. They must not act in 'a general, benevolent manner according to their conception of what they think would be fair in the circumstances': *Lifeguard Assurance Ltd v Zadrozny* [1977] IRLR 56.

It may be just and equitable for the employee to receive compensation where she has been unfairly dismissed notwithstanding that the employer could have dismissed her fairly for another reason: see *Trico-Folberth Ltd v Devonshire* [1989] IRLR 396.

In *Tewson*'s case, above, the NIRC considered loss under the following heads:

(*a*) immediate loss of wages;
(*b*) manner of dismissal;
(*c*) future loss of wages;
(*d*) loss of protection in respect of unfair dismissal and dismissal by reason of redundancy.

These categories are not exhaustive. If necessary, the tribunal should itself raise each of these heads: *Tidman v Aveling Marshall Ltd* [1977] ICR 506.

The tribunal should set out its reasoning when awarding compensation. In *Blackwell v GEC Elliott Process Automation Ltd* [1976] IRLR 144, Phillips J held:

it is absolutely essential that Industrial Tribunals, when determining the amount of compensation, should explain and set out, in the manner prescribed in . . . [*Norton Tool Co Ltd v Tewson*, above], the details of the individual heads under which compensation is awarded and, briefly, at all events, the manner and reasoning by which they have arrived at those figures. It is necessary to do that for a number of reasons. First of all, if it is not done, the parties cannot see whether the amounts awarded are correct. Secondly, if they wish to consider an appeal, they cannot decide whether it is an appropriate case in which to appeal. Thirdly, the Appeal Tribunal, if it is not done, cannot see whether the order appealed from was right. And there is perhaps a more important point than any of those: that, fourthly, the very discipline of having to set down in orderly manner the heads under which the compensation is awarded, and the brief reasons for it, ensures that the Tribunal does not make a mistake, does not omit anything and arrives at a reasonable figure.

Depending on the circumstances the tribunal may also have to consider loss of fringe benefits, loss of pension and expenses incurred in seeking other employment.

(a) Immediate loss of wages This is the loss suffered between the date of dismissal and the date of the tribunal hearing. In assessing the immediate loss of wages the tribunal must look to see what has actually occurred between the date of dismissal and the date of the tribunal hearing. In *Gilham and Others v Kent CC* [1986] IRLR 56, the tribunal, in awarding compensation to dinner ladies who had been unfairly dismissed, imposed an arbitrary cut-off point of 12 months in assessing their losses, regardless of what actually had happened. In fixing this period of 12 months the tribunal found that if the county council had not terminated the existing contracts of employment and offered new contracts of employment on less advantageous terms, the school meals service would have closed down within a year. The EAT held that the tribunal had fallen into an error of law in examining the future prospects of the school meals service instead of looking at what had actually happened.

Thus, in assessing this loss the tribunal must make its assessment in the light of facts known to it at the date of the assessment. Where the employee has obtained other employment between the date of dismissal and the date when compensation falls to be assessed, the earnings of that employment will normally have to be brought into account either to reduce or to extinguish any ongoing losses of the employee: see *Ging v Ellward Lancs Ltd* (1978) 13 ITR 265. However, it may be that the employer's liability for compensation terminates once the employee has found other employment, even though the employee subsequently loses that job before compensation falls to be assessed: *Courtaulds Northern Spinning Ltd v Moosa* [1984] IRLR 43. Moosa's dismissal by the new employer was not attributable to action taken by Courtaulds and therefore they were not liable after the date when he obtained employment with a new employer.

(b) Wages in lieu of notice In an action for wrongful dismissal the employee has to give credit for anything which he earned or could have earned during the period of notice with another employer. In *Norton Tool Co Ltd v Tewson*, above, the NIRC held that the employee need not give credit for any sums which he earned or could have earned elsewhere during the notice period:

> In the context of compensation for unfair dismissal we think that it is appropriate and in accordance with the intentions of Parliament that we should treat an employee as having suffered a loss in so far as he receives less than he would have received in accordance with good industrial practice.

In *J Stepek Ltd v Hough* (1973) 8 ITR 516, it was held that an employee who receives some wages in lieu of notice, but not his full entitlement, may claim the balance without deduction even though he works elsewhere for that part of the notice period for which he seeks to claim from his former employer.

In *Hilti (Great Britain) Ltd v Windridge* [1974] ICR 352, it was held that where the employer makes a payment in lieu of notice but bases this on gross pay rather than net and makes a payment which is short of the number of weeks' entitlement, the excess of the gross pay over the net pay can be set off against the liability of the employer to make payment for the weeks of the notice for which no payment was made. In *Everwear Candlewick Ltd v Isaac* [1974] ICR 525, it was held that any sums over and above the net pay for the notice period must be brought into account. See also *Blackwell v GEC Elliott Process Automation Ltd* [1976] IRLR 144.

In *Vaughan v Weighpack Ltd* [1974] ICR 261 the NIRC held:

[The tribunal shall] bring into the equation on one side the wages and other benefits the employee would have received had he not been dismissed and on the other side all sums which he has received as a direct consequence of the dismissal, including any sums paid in lieu of notice, any wages earned since the dismissal, unemployment benefits, training grants and so forth. It may occasionally happen that the result of this arithmetic will produce a figure lower than the wages he should have received in lieu of notice. If this be the case the compensation assessed should be equivalent to wages in lieu of notice. If, however, as will probably more often be the case, it produces a larger figure, then that is the figure to which he is entitled.

However, in *Tradewinds Airways Ltd v Fletcher* [1981] IRLR 272, the EAT refused to accept that where an employee gets another job during the notice period, wages in lieu of notice was the irreducible minimum to which the unfairly dismissed employee is entitled.

However, in *TBA Industrial Products Ltd v Locke* [1984] IRLR 48, the EAT held that an employee dismissed with pay in lieu of notice does not have to give credit to his former employer for any earnings from a new employer during the period covered by the payment in lieu of notice.

In *Babcock FATA Ltd v Addison* [1987] IRLR 173, the Court of Appeal upheld the principle established in *Norton*'s case. Gibson LJ held:

The first step in the reasoning of the court in *Norton*'s case is that when a payment is made of wages in lieu of notice at the time of the dismissal the employee would not have to make any repayment upon obtaining further employment during the notice period. That is in accordance with the normal intention of both sides when such a payment is made without stipulation of any special terms. The next step in the reasoning is . . . of a different nature: because good industrial practice requires that the employer either give the notice or pays six weeks' wages in lieu, the employee, who is given neither notice nor payment, should not be worse off and therefore he also should not have to give credit for wages earned from another employer during the period of notice notwithstanding the direction that the rule as to the duty to mitigate shall be applied. I do not doubt that the industrial practice referred to was a good practice and right to be applied in a case such as *Norton Tool* and such a case must be typical of a very large proportion of the cases coming before industrial tribunals. In such a case the employer, if he was acting fairly, would pay the sum due in lieu of notice. It is usually convenient for the employer if the dismissed employee leaves the premises and if the wages for the whole . . . period are paid in advance; and it is convenient for the employee to be released to look for other work; and the immediate receipt of wages for the period of notice, coupled with the chance of getting other employment during that period, may soften a little the blow of losing employment . . . however . . . circumstances may arise in which, having regard to the length of notice required, and the known likelihood of the employee getting new employment within a short period of time, or for other sufficient reason, an employer may show that a payment less than the wages due over the full period of notice did not offend good industrial practice. . . . I am unable to accept that any rule of law exists which requires that in all circumstances, irrespective of the terms upon which a payment in lieu of notice was made, and of any justification for not making payment in full of wages in advance for the full period of notice, the employee is entitled in claiming a compensatory award under s 74 to disregard wages earned from another employer during the notice period. The number of cases in which an employer will be able, in the view of an Industrial Tribunal, to justify departure from the general practice would probably be small. But in my view no rule of law exists to prevent the Industrial Tribunal from considering such case or from giving effect to it if it is established.

. . . The employee is to be treated as having suffered a loss in so far as he recovers less than he would have received in accordance with good industrial practice . . . the principle, when applicable on the basis of good industrial practice, secures to the dismissed employee the opportunity to earn during the period of notice without giving credit for earning from another employer against wages due during the period of notice. It does not secure to him anything in addition to the amount of wages due during the period of notice: he can only get the extra if he gets the new job and thereby earnings from another employer. If the employer has paid the wages due in lieu of notice at the time of dismissal, the employer has complied with good industrial practice. If the employee does not get employment during the period of notice, no principle of good industrial practice can secure to the employee any further payment by way of lost wages in respect of the period of notice: he has received the wages for that period and if he is to recover the same amount again it must be by reference to some rule of law outside the provisions of the 1978 Act and in my view no such rule exists.

The effect of this decision is to give tribunals considerable discretion to decide what good industrial practice demands.

However, in *Isleworth Studios Ltd v Rickard* [1988] ICR 432, Rickard, who had a fixed-term contract, was unfairly dismissed. He earned more in his new business than he would have done had he continued to work under the fixed-term contract. The EAT reduced the compensatory award to nil. It held to provide compensation where there was no loss was inconsistent with s 74 of the EP(C)A 1978. Contrary to the view in *Addison*'s case, it found that *Norton*'s case was laying down a rule of law of limited scope. From the judgment it was difficult to see when *Norton*'s case might apply. *Rickard*'s case should be regarded as confined to its own facts in the light of the decision in *Addison*.

The employee has to give credit to the former employer for any wages in lieu of notice paid by him: *Addison*'s case, above.

Apart from wages in lieu of notice the employee is entitled to claim compensation for the loss of other benefits which he has suffered. Since these losses may fall to be considered under both this and the next heading, they are for convenience considered under the next heading.

Since tribunals are concerned with assessing loss in calculating the loss of wages, whether past or future, the tribunal should work on the difference between the net wage enjoyed by the employee in his former employment and the net wage in the new employment: *Tradewinds Airways Ltd v Fletcher*, above.

(c) Future loss of earnings '[T]here must be some evidence of future loss and the scale of future loss to enable the tribunal to make any award under that head': *Adda International Ltd v Curcio* (1976) IRLR 425.

Whereas the calculation of the immediate loss of wages is based upon fact, the calculation of future loss of wages must be speculative. Where, at the date of the hearing before the tribunal, the employee has obtained other employment at a wage equal to or higher than that which he earned with his former employer there is no future loss; however, where the employee has obtained other employment at a wage less than that enjoyed with his former employer, the tribunal has to consider when it is likely that the employee will be restored to the position which he held with his former employer.

Where the employee has not secured new employment at the date of the hearing the calculation of future loss becomes even more speculative. There is no specified period as to the length of future loss that should be allowed, nor is there any normal period despite a suggestion to this effect in *Tidman v Aveling Marshall Ltd* [1977] ICR 506. Parties may or may not lead evidence as to when the employee is likely to obtain other employment. If the employee wishes to adduce evidence as to the period of future loss he should do so, otherwise he will have no cause for complaint about the period of future loss fixed by the tribunal, provided that it acts properly: *UBAF Bank Ltd v Davis* [1978] IRLR 442. Tribunals in reaching their conclusions are entitled to draw on their knowledge of local conditions and their knowledge of the local employment situation and common sense in assessing future loss. Where the tribunals exercise their discretion properly it is unlikely that an appellate body will interfere with their decision: *Moncur v International Paint Co Ltd* [1978] IRLR 223. The uncertainties and the imponderables which surround the assessment of future loss may be reflected in the multiplier chosen by the tribunal to assess future loss: *Cartiers Superfoods Ltd v Laws* [1978] IRLR 315.

Where the tribunal allows future loss over a period of time it must make clear its reasoning behind the period chosen: (1) *Qualcast*

(Wolverhampton) Ltd v Ross (2) Ross v Qualcast (Wolverhampton) Ltd [1979] IRLR 98.

The current employment position and the availability of particular jobs are not the only factors which the tribunal must take into account.

It must consider the circumstances of the employee. In *Fougère v Phoenix Motor Co Ltd* [1976] ICR 495, Fougère was 58 and in poor health. He was unfairly dismissed. The tribunal in calculating the future loss ignored the employee's age and his health. Instead they considered the length of time it would take a man of average health to find other employment. The EAT held that the employer must take the employee as he finds him. The personal characteristics of the employee are important in deciding the future loss. In this case 'they unfairly dismissed an employee who, at the date of his dismissal and before, was elderly and in poor health'. The tribunal had to look at that employee and decide how long it would take for him to find employment elsewhere. Compensation is compensation for the loss sustained by the employee because of the dismissal. The loss must be a consequence of the dismissal and must be attributable to the action taken by the employer.

Where, at the date of the dismissal, although it is not the reason for dismissal, the employee suffers from an illness or disability the tribunal must take that into account in assessing future loss and the likelihood of the employee obtaining other employment. It must also consider whether the employer would have been entitled to dismiss the employee in the future because of that illness or disability. It may also be relevant to consider in such circumstances whether the employer instead of dismissing the employee for illness or disability in the future would have kept the employee on in some alternative position, possibly at a reduced wage: *Brittains Arborfield Ltd v Van Uden* [1977] ICR 211.

Another factor which may affect the amount of the loss is the proximity of pension age. In *Penprase v Mander Bros Ltd* [1973] IRLR 167, Penprase was 3½ years from retirement when he was unfairly dismissed. The tribunal found that but for the dismissal he would have continued to be employed until he was 65. They assessed his losses over 3½ years, taking the view that it was unlikely that he would obtain other employment.

Again, in *Isle of Wight Tourist Board v Coombes* [1976] IRLR 413, a female employee aged 58, who was unfairly dismissed, had her losses assessed on the basis that she was two years from retirement and unlikely to get another job.

Normally compensation will not be awarded for losses occurring after the employee has attained the age of 65 or if in that employment there is a normal retiring age that age. However, if the employee can establish that but for the dismissal he would have continued in employment after 65 or the normal retiring age as the case may be, then compensation for such losses may be awarded.

In *Wood v Louis C Edwards and Sons (Manchester) Ltd* [1972] IRLR 18, it was held there was nothing in the legislation which limited the loss of earnings to those accruing before the 65th birthday. See also: *Barrel Plating and Phosphating Co Ltd v Danks* [1976] ICR 503.

Redundancy may also affect the assessment of future loss. In *Marcus v George Wimpey and Co Ltd* [1974] IRLR 356, Marcus was unfairly dismissed for redundancy. Between the date of the dismissal and the date of the tribunal hearing, four months had elapsed. During this period there had been a worsening of the employment situation and the employer's work had further reduced. Dismissal at the time of the hearing would have been fair. Thus, the employee was not entitled to any future loss. A similar decision was reached in *Costello v United Asphalt Co Ltd* [1975] IRLR 194. The burden is on the employer to show that even if the employee had not been dismissed then, he would have been dismissed in the future for redundancy. The tribunal must not speculate and should not calculate that the employee was likely to be redundant in the future unless there is evidence to support that conclusion: *Young's of Gosport Ltd v Kendell* [1977] ICR 907; but compare *Tidman v Aveling Marshall Ltd* [1977] ICR 506.

It is not open to a tribunal to award compensation for an 'unfair declaration' of redundancy unless the dismissal is unfair, for instance, because an employee has been unfairly selected or a proper procedure has not been followed. Although a tribunal is entitled to consider whether the closure of a business is genuine it is not open to it to investigate the commercial and economic reasons for a closure. Where the closure is genuine compensation cannot be awarded beyond that date: *James W Cook and Co (Wivenhoe) Ltd (in liquidation) v Tipper and Others* [1990] IRLR 386.

The issue of redundancy is one which must be raised by the employer before the tribunal and cannot be introduced *de novo* on an appeal: *Kunz Engineering Ltd v Santi* [1979] IRLR 459.

Another factor affecting the assessment of future loss may arise when following the dismissal, the employee decides to undertake a course of training or study: *Pagano v HGS* [1976] IRLR 9.

A problem which may fall to be considered in relation to both present and future loss is what losses should be allowed when the dismissal is unfair because the employer has failed to follow proper procedure. In *(1) Abbotts and (2) Standley v Wesson-Glynwed Steels Ltd* [1982] IRLR 51, Abbotts was dismissed without consultation. The tribunal considered that consultation would have made no difference and the employee would still have been dismissed, a view upheld by the EAT. The EAT reversed the decision of the tribunal that Abbotts was not entitled to any compensation and instead awarded two weeks' pay. It considered that if there had been consultation it would have resulted in Abbotts remaining in employment for a further two weeks.

The decision in *Abbott's* case, above, was followed in *Mining Supplies (Longwall) Ltd v Baker* [1988] IRLR 417. The EAT held that a tribunal had not erred in awarding compensation where Baker was unfairly dismissed because of the failure to follow a proper procedure. Even if a proper procedure had been carried out Baker would still have been dismissed. If there had been consultation the date of dismissal would have been postponed by one week.

The tribunal acting as an industrial jury has considerable discretion over what period it will allow future losses. It will have regard not only to the circumstances of the individual employee, but also to the economic climate: see *Perks v Geest Industries Ltd* [1974] IRLR 228; and *MacNeilage v Arthur Roye (Turf Accountants) Ltd* [1976] IRLR 88.

The tribunal may assess compensation on the basis that the employee will be unable to obtain another job for a considerable time. However, after the tribunal hearing the employee may obtain another job. The compensation may be well in excess of the loss which the employee has suffered. In such circumstances what redress has the employer? Where the tribunal has erred in law the employer may appeal against its decision. This must be done within 42 days from the date of the decision: r 3 of the EAT Rules 1980 (SI 1980 No 2035). If there is no error in law the employer may ask the tribunal to review its decision on the grounds that a review is necessary in the interests of justice. The application must be made not later than 14 days from the date the decision was sent to the parties: r 10 of the Industrial Tribunals (Rules of Procedure) Regulations 1985 (SI 1985 No 16). In deciding whether to allow a review:

The tribunal must ask itself whether the forecasts which were the basis of its decision have been falsified to a sufficiently substantial extent to invalidate the assessment and whether this occurred so soon after the decision, that a review was necessary in the interests of justice. There must be some finality . . . but . . . if very shortly after a tribunal has reached a decision it comes to its notice, upon an application for review, that the facts are so different from those which it had assumed, that the whole substratum of its award has gone, then, subject to such consideration as whether the party applying could have obtained that evidence before the hearing, there is manifestly a case for review: *Yorkshire Engineering and Welding Co Ltd v Burnham* [1974] ICR 77.

Again, in *Help the Aged Housing Association (Scotland) Ltd v Vidler* [1977] IRLR 104, the tribunal assumed that Vidler, who was 60, would be unlikely to find new employment. It awarded £4,700 compensation. Thirteen days after the hearing he obtained new employment and the Association asked for a review. The tribunal refused and the Association appealed. The EAT accepted that the tribunal's assumption was a reasonable one to make, but found that because Vidler had obtained other employment so quickly the substratum of the award had gone. It reduced the compensation to £3,000.

Future loss where the employee starts his own business The employee must act reasonably and try to mitigate his loss. If he has made a reasonable attempt to find other employment but has been unsuccessful, the tribunal may find that he then acted reasonably in setting up in business on his own account. However, if he has not sought other employment then he may not be able to hold his former employer responsible for the losses flowing from the dismissal. The employer may argue that compensation should be restricted to the loss which the employee would have incurred had he made reasonable attempts to obtain comparable employment: *York Trailer Co Ltd v Sparkes* [1973] ICR 518.

In *Gardiner-Hill v Roland Berger Technics Ltd* [1982] IRLR 498, it was held that the employee who became self-employed had not failed to mitigate his loss simply because he did not look for salaried employment. He had acted reasonably in setting up his own business and was entitled to compensation, including the cost of setting up.

In *Lee v IPC Business Press Ltd* [1984] ICR 306, it was held that Lee, who became self-employed, was entitled to compensation for any losses he suffered following his unfair dismissal. He had an obligation to mitigate his losses but simply because he became self-employed he was not thereby prevented from claiming compensation. There was no finding that he had not mitigated his losses.

Where the tribunal considers that the employee has acted reasonably it will have to assess the loss he has suffered. The period which the tribunal allows will depend on how long it thinks it will be before the employee can make the new venture viable. The tribunal may take into account that the compensation for those losses which may make up the deficit between the first year's trading and the employee's former salary is an accelerated receipt of capital: *York Trailer Co Ltd v* Sparkes, above. However, the fact that the employee may have a capital asset in the business which he is establishing will usually be ignored.

In *Lee*'s case, above, Lee was entitled to a contractual redundancy payment from his employer in the event of his dismissal by reason of redundancy. This was something which he lost as a result of the unfair dismissal. If Lee took another job he would have to requalify for the right not to be unfairly dismissed and also the right not to be made redundant and, if he were dismissed by reason of redundancy, the chances were that he would not have been entitled to an enhanced redundancy payment under the terms of his new contract. The EAT held that in assessing compensation, these were matters for the tribunal to consider. Compare *Sparkes*'s case and *Gardiner-Hill*'s case, above, where it was held that the employee was not entitled to compensation for the loss of his accrued statutory employment rights.

(d) Manner of dismissal   An award will be made under this head only in exceptional circumstances. The manner and circumstances of the dismissal must give rise to a risk of loss in the future, as for instance, where the employee is less acceptable to a potential employer or likely to be selected for dismissal in the future. There must be cogent evidence that the manner of the dismissal caused financial loss: *Vaughan v Weighpack Ltd* [1974] ICR 261, confirmed in *Brittains Arborfield Ltd v Van Uden* [1977] ICR 211.

In *Wiggins v Lewis Shops Group* [1973] IRLR 114, Wiggins, a manageress, had been dismissed in distressing circumstances without a reference. This resulted in her being unable to obtain another management job. The tribunal took this into account in assessing future loss. The circumstances of the dismissal had contributed to the loss. The case was overturned on other grounds.

However, in *John Miller and Sons v Quinn* [1974] IRLR 107, the NIRC confirmed that nothing should be awarded for emotional upset on its own. Distress following dismissal could only be taken into account if it were likely to affect the employee's chances of securing other employment. In *Vaughan's* case, above, the fact that an employee lived in a small community and was sacked on a Sunday which, it was argued, increased his disgrace, did not warrant any increase in compensation.

(e) Loss of statutory rights   In *Norton Tool Co Ltd v Tewson* [1972] ICR 501, the NIRC awarded compensation for the loss of the employee's accrued redundancy entitlement. This element of loss has now been replaced by the basic award. In this case the sum of £20 was awarded to the employee to compensate him for the loss of his accrued statutory rights. The loss of the employee's statutory rights includes his loss of protection against unfair dismissal. He will have to be employed for a continuous period of two years before he will be able to claim unfair dismissal in the future.

Tribunals award a nominal sum for loss of accrued statutory rights, for instance, to claim unfair dismissal because the employee has to requalify for those rights. In *SH Muffett Ltd v Head* [1986] IRLR 488, the EAT held that the sum of £20 was now inappropriate and that the sum of £100 should be regarded as appropriate in all the circumstances. It rejected the view that the sum of £20 was fixed and immutable. The sum of £100 had been reached after consultation with the President of the EAT and the EAT commented that this figure would need to be reconsidered in three to four years' time. It has not been increased.

In addition, the tribunal may make an award because the employee has lost his entitlement to a longer period of notice under Part IV of the EP(C)A 1978. Again, the employee has to requalify for this right. This may be a speculative matter although in principle it is a permissible head of loss. In *Hilti (GB) Ltd v Windridge* [1974] IRLR 53, it was held that it should not attract other than a very small award in the average case. However in *Daley v AE Dorsett (Almar Dolls Ltd)* [1981] IRLR 385, the EAT suggested that the loss of entitlement to a longer period of notice may now be more valuable in view of the economic conditions than previously. In this case a sum of half the employee's statutory notice entitlement was awarded. The EAT held:

this . . . is not a claim in respect of lost earnings over a period . . . It is a claim for compensation for the loss of an intangible benefit, namely that of being entitled, in the course of one's employment, to a longer notice than might otherwise be the case.

Some tribunals award the sum of £100 for this element of loss of protection. See also *Lee v IPC Business Press Ltd* [1984] ICR 306.

However, as the EAT pointed out in *SH Muffett Ltd v Head*, above, compensation for loss of the longer period of notice depended upon a double contingency, first that the dismissed employee will get a new job and secondly that he will be dismissed from that job before building up the same entitlement to the period of notice applicable to the first job. It also involves a possible loss of accruing further notice. The EAT accepted that this was a matter for the tribunal to consider, but a tribunal will not err simply because it makes no award where it considers the double contingency is extremely unlikely.

In *Arthur Guinness Son and Co (GB) Ltd v Green* [1989] IRLR 288, the EAT found that while it is the practice in a proper case to award a sum calculated by multiplying net take home pay by a fraction of the statutory maximum period of 12 weeks' notice, the multiplier should not be more than 6 weeks.

(f) Fringe benefits, past and future The employee is entitled to claim compensation for the loss of fringe benefits, pension and expenses. These losses form part of past or future losses but for convenience are dealt with separately.

Remuneration Where commission and other payments in the nature of commission form part of the employee's emoluments, he will receive compensation for the loss as part of the compensatory award. The employee may also lose bonuses and gratuities by virtue of his dismissal. Where these are part of his remuneration, he will be compensated for their loss. Allowances which are chargeable to tax and therefore form part of the remuneration will be compensated. Allowances which are paid to reimburse expenses actually incurred and which are tax free will not be remuneration, so no compensation will be received: see *Tradewinds Airways Ltd v Fletcher* [1981] IRLR 272.

Loss of car Before the tribunal can award compensation for the loss of a car it must know what benefit the employee enjoyed. If the employee was only entitled to use the car for business purposes, he will have suffered no loss on that account from the dismissal. However, contractually he may be entitled to use the car for his own purposes. Thus, where the employee has made contributions towards the purchase of the car either by a lump sum payment or by hire-purchase contributions, he is entitled to compensation for the loss of capital involved. However, the employee may have made no capital contribution but be contractually entitled to use the car for his own purposes, with or without the obligation to provide petrol. Here the tribunal will have to assess the loss to the employee of the use of the car.

There is a divergence between the amounts allowed by the tribunals as representing the loss to an employee of the car. Usually a tribunal will award a specific sum per week. It will also have to decide the number of weeks for which the loss will continue. This need not be the date when the employee obtains other employment since he may not have a car in that employment, or the terms upon which the vehicle is made available to him may not be so advantageous. Instead of awarding a weekly payment for loss, the tribunal may award a capital sum as in *Sparks v ET Barwick Mills Ltd* (1977) (unreported), where the employee had to make a down payment on a new car of £1,000. The tribunal allowed this sum as his loss. Guidance on the value of a car can be obtained from figures produced by the AA. These figures give a breakdown between the fixed costs of a car and the running costs of a car. Tribunals may have regard to these figures when fixing the figure of compensation.

Housing   Where the employee is entitled to free housing because of employment which is lost to him upon his dismissal, the tribunal will have to assess the value of the free housing: *Butler v J Wendon and Sons* [1972] IRLR 15. Where the employee has found other accommodation for which he has to pay rent, the loss will be the new rent: *Scottish Co-operative Wholesale Society Ltd v Lloyd* [1973] ICR 137. Where he has not obtained other accommodation, the tribunal will have to consider what it will cost him to obtain premises which are suitable for him.

Where the housing which the employee enjoyed through his job was not free but subsidised, the difference will be the difference between the payment which he made and the rent which he will have to pay in the future. The employee may decide not to rent accommodation but to purchase his own with a mortgage. It seems the tribunal then has two courses from which it may choose. First, it may award the difference between the payments he was making for the property occupied by virtue of his employment and any weekly mortgage payment on a similar property. The second course is to pay the difference between any former rent and the open market rent for the former or other similar property.

Food and board   By virtue of employment the employee may be entitled to free food or board and accommodation, for example, farm workers. The employee is entitled to claim compensation for such losses. Compensation will be assessed on the basis of the loss to him. Again the tribunal will have to determine the length of the continuing loss.

(g) Stock options   The employee may be entitled to be compensated for the loss of stock options; see *O'Laoire*'s case, above.

(h) Holiday leave   Loss of holiday leave may also be a loss for which the unfairly dismissed employee can be compensated: *Tradewinds Airways Ltd v Fletcher* [1981] IRLR 272.

(i) Removal expenses   In looking for new employment the employee may be able to show that he was unable to find new work in the area and that he is moving elsewhere where he will be able to find employment. In such cases the tribunal may allow the costs of removal, legal costs and estate agents' fees. In *Co-operative Wholesale Society v Squirrell* (1974) 9 ITR 191, Squirrell decided that his prospects of employment were better in an urban area rather than in the rural area where he had been employed. He decided to sell his house and move. He incurred legal fees and removal expenses of £800. The tribunal allowed these sums and the decision was upheld by the NIRC. See also *Yeats v Fairey Winches Ltd* [1974] IRLR 362.

Tribunals may assess compensation on the basis that the employee will have to move in the future to obtain other employment thus restricting the period of future loss which it would otherwise award if the employee did not move but awarding in lieu the costs of moving to another area.

(j) The assessment of loss and tax   Where the employee has been dismissed and has not obtained new employment, he is likely to receive a repayment of income tax. Where he obtains other employment at a lesser wage his liability to tax for the remainder of the year may be reduced and result in a repayment. In assessing the loss a tribunal may take this repayment into account, particularly where the loss is large. Tribunals have deducted it from the total amount of the compensatory award. However, it is clear from the decision in *Norton Tool Co Ltd v Tewson*, above, that where the sums involved are small such calculations may be inappropriate to the broad common-sense assessment of the compensation. This approach was confirmed by the EAT in *Adda International Ltd v Curcio* [1976] ICR 407.

However, in *Lucas and Others v Laurence Scott and Electromotors Ltd* [1983] IRLR 61, it was held that a compensatory award could include a sum to represent a loss of income tax rebates. In this case the employer had failed to follow a redundancy procedure which, if used, would have resulted in the employees being dismissed on 14 July rather than 27 March. If the employees had continued in employment up to 14 July they would have received their wages less tax. In the ensuing financial year each of the employees was totally unemployed. At the end of that financial year, bearing in mind the tax allowances and the notional earnings from 27 March to 14 July, the employees would probably have received a tax rebate. The EAT held that this was an element of loss of wages which the employees should recover.

But, in *MBS Ltd v Calo* [1983] ICR 459, the EAT held that the tribunal was correct in ignoring a tax rebate. It recognised that the assessment of future earnings is based upon the employee's net wage rather than gross wage. Certain assumptions are made which may prove to be false, for instance, that the employee will be taxed in the future at the same rate as he has been in the past. It is the obligation of the tribunal to assess compensation in such amounts as it considers just and equitable in all the circumstances. The EAT held:

Where the sums are of the order normally coming before industrial tribunals, it does not seem to us that it is 'just and equitable' to take into account rebates on past earnings without taking into account possible tax repercussions as to the future. In our judgment, it is just and equitable in the ordinary case for the tribunal to ignore the tax repercussions on both sides, balancing the one against the other.

(k) Pension Guidelines as to the way in which tribunals should assess compensation for loss of pension rights is contained in a booklet prepared by a committee of chairmen of tribunals in consultation with the Government Actuary's Department. The burden of proof is on the employee. There is no right way of assessing the loss. A broad common-sense approach should be adopted. The tribunal has to award a just and equitable sum. It is open to the tribunal to use a rough and ready system if necessary: *Manpower Ltd v Hearne* [1983] IRLR 281.

The retirement pension payable by the State can be made up of a basic pension, a graduated pension (based on contributions paid between April 1961 and April 1975) and an additional pension payable pursuant to the State Earnings Related Pension Scheme (SERPS) which varies according to an individual's earnings since April 1978. It is possible to contract out of SERPS where there is an occupational pension scheme, provided certain criteria are fulfilled. The guidelines recommend that the assumption should be made that there is no loss where an employee is unfairly dismissed if he is not in an occupational pension scheme. That assumption is, of course, capable of being rebutted by evidence.

An occupational pension scheme may be either a final salary scheme or a money purchase scheme. A final salary scheme is where the amount of the employee's pension is based not on the contributions made but on a proportion of the salary when he retires—eg 1/60 of his final salary for each year of service. Occupational pension schemes differ as to the fraction. Some schemes take an average of the employee's salary over a number of years. Some schemes use the best of a number of years' salary. In a final salary scheme the employer's contributions are not earmarked for a particular employee. They are a contribution to the fund. What the employee receives is not necessarily proportionate to the contributions that he and his employer have made. It is usually possible to ascertain the contributions made by the employer as a percentage of the total pay roll, although this may depend on what is required for funding the scheme. The guidelines suggest that where there is a lack of accurate evidence, or when the pension contribution position is anomalous, on average the overall contribution for a good scheme is 15 per cent of the pay roll made up in a contributory scheme, as to 10 per cent from the employer and 5 per cent from the employee. In a final salary scheme which is non-funded (such as is found in the public sector), there are no contributions as such. However, the notional contributions are fixed by the scheme's actuary and should be easily attainable. Non-funded schemes should be treated in the same way as other final salary schemes. Some publicly financed schemes do have the advantage in that they are index-linked to the cost of living index, both from the date of leaving until retirement and after retirement without any top limit.

Where additional voluntary contributions (AVCs) are made they usually operate on a money purchase basis (see below), even though the main scheme is a final salary scheme and they should be treated as an employer's money purchase scheme. Where a scheme allows an employee to purchase extra years, those years should be put into the equation as if the employee had actually worked those years. AVCs which are made by the employee alone must be distinguished from 'free standing additional voluntary contributions', which are in effect separate money purchase plans and should be dealt with as personalised plans.

A money purchase scheme is where the pension is directly related to contributions made by the employer and employee. These have the advantage that the employer knows exactly how much he will have to pay in each year. They do not have the open-ended commitment of a final salary scheme. Closely allied with the money purchase scheme is a personalised plan where the employer and the employee pay a contribution to a pension policy in the name of the individual employee. On retirement the employee receives an annuity based on the value of his personal fund. The employee decides where the money should be invested.

The employee who leaves pensionable employment before retirement is known as an early leaver. This expression will include an employee who is unfairly dismissed. The tribunal has to consider his position, depending upon whether he is in a final salary scheme or money purchase scheme. Where the employee is a member of a final salary scheme he will be entitled to a pension payable as from what would have been his retirement date as an annuity for the rest of his life. In the guidelines this is referred to as a deferred pension. Usually when an employee retires he will receive 1/60 of his final salary for each year he has worked. For an employee retiring at 60 there is a maximum 40/60ths. The early leaver will receive a deferred pension representing 1/60th of his final salary for each year that he worked. It follows that if he had worked until his retiring age the final salary would be more than the salary which he actually receives at the date he left (unless this was close to his retirement age). The Social Security Act (SSA) 1985 provides that in respect of service after 1 January 1985 the deferred pension should increase by 5 per cent per annum up to retirement or by the annual price rises if lower than 5 per cent. The SSA 1990 provides that as from 1 January 1992 all preserved pension rights will be increased in accordance with this formula, and it will not be necessary to distinguish between pre- and post-1985 service.

The unfairly dismissed employee might not have remained in the employment until retirement. Equally if he had not been unfairly dismissed he might have remained in the employment but in a better position earning more and with a better pension. These are factors which have to be taken into account. Under the SSA 1985 an ex-employer can be required to transfer the value of his accrued pension either to a similar scheme run by a new employer or the employee can make other arrangements meeting the statutory requirements. The transfer value is calculated in accordance with the Occupational Pensional Schemes (Transfer Values) Regulations 1985 (SI 1985 No 1931).

The employee's losses will depend upon the nature of the pension scheme. While many schemes have a degree of commonality there are considerable variations, but the broad approach to the way the employee's losses are to be calculated are now considered.

Loss of pension rights from the date of dismissal to the date of hearing If the employee had not been dismissed, and he and his employer had continued to make contributions to the pension fund, this would have secured additional pension benefits. Although there is a difference between a final salary scheme and a money purchase scheme the guidelines suggest that in both cases the tribunal should include a sum to represent what the employer would have contributed notionally to the employee's pension, had he still been employed. Although it recognises that in a final salary scheme this is not strictly the correct method of assessing the employee's loss, since the benefit which accrues to the employee by remaining in employment does not necessarily correspond to the figure, it is fair to both parties. In a money purchase scheme or personalised plan it will be easy to ascertain the employer's contribution and calculate it on a weekly basis. In a final salary scheme, the guidelines suggest that the normal cost of the scheme to the employer is usually given as a percentage in the actuary's report. This percentage should be applied to the employee's gross pensionable pay to produce a weekly figure for loss of pension rights. It may be necessary to adjust this sum to take account of the circumstances, for instance if the pension fund is over-funded and the employer is having a pension contribution holiday. In the case of a non-contributory pension scheme, then it may be necessary to impute a notional contribution. If the figure for the employer's contribution is not readily ascertainable, then the guidelines suggest that the tribunal should assume the employer's contribution is 10 per cent (or 15 per cent in the case of non-contributory schemes). In each case the employer's contribution should be treated as a weekly loss in the same manner as a weekly loss of earnings. If the employee has obtained other employment with a scheme which provides the same or better benefits the date when he joined that scheme will be the date up to which losses will be calculated.

Loss of future pension rights   This is the loss of benefits which the employee would have had if he had continued in employment beyond the date of the hearing. The guidelines suggest that the same principles should apply as in the case of the loss of pension rights from the date of dismissal to the hearing. It is for the tribunal to decide what multiplier to use, reflecting the time when the employee will be in the position in which he would have been if he had not been dismissed. The guidelines suggest that the multiplier should be the same as the assessment for future loss of earnings, so if the tribunal assumes that the employee will obtain fresh employment in one year and his earnings in the new employment are likely to be comparable with the old, then it is reasonable to assume that the pension scheme will also be comparable. However, it may be that that is not appropriate, where the employee gains employment and there is no loss of earnings but simply a loss of pension rights. The guidelines recognise that it is unlikely that there will be a substantial qualifying period before an employee can benefit from the new employer's pension scheme. If there is a qualifying period benefits may be backdated once the qualifying period has been met. The guidelines suggest that if the qualification period is two years or less and if once the qualification period has been met the entitlement is backdated to the beginning of the employment, there is no loss.

Where the pension scheme in the new employment is as beneficial as in the old employment there will be no loss, but if it is not as beneficial the guidelines suggest that the difference in contributions can be regarded as the weekly loss of future pension rights and the tribunal should apply the appropriate multiplier.

If in the new employment there is no pension scheme the loss of the employer's contributions will be assessed as a weekly or other periodic loss and the employee will be included in SERPS. Any contribution made to SERPS by the new employer should be deducted. If the SERPS contribution is now known then it can be assumed that the employer is contributing 3 per cent of the employee's gross pay to SERPS.

Loss of enhancement of accrued pension rights If the employee had not been unfairly dismissed there might have been further enhancement of the rights which have already been secured. In some cases accrued rights may be forfeited. The guidelines suggest that the tribunal should assume there is no loss of enhancement of accrued pension rights unless the contrary is proven in money purchase schemes or personalised plans. Similar principles apply to public sector schemes, both funded and non-funded, and also to private sector final salary schemes where the employee has less than five years to go until retirement and where all the service is after 1 January 1985, or the trustees of the pension fund indicate that service prior to 1 January 1985 is to be index-linked in the same way as service after 1 January 1985.

Where there is a final salary scheme in ascertaining the loss of enhancement of accrued pension rights the guidelines suggest that the tribunal should ascertain the deferred pension the employee will receive. Any anticipated increases or additional benefits should be ignored. The employee's age and his anticipated date of retirement should be ascertained. An appropriate multiplier should be applied. The multipliers are set out in Appendix 4 to the guidelines. The figure obtained should be reduced, if appropriate, by a percentage representing the likelihood that the employee would have lost his job before retirement even if he had not been unfairly dismissed.

It is up to the tribunal to make a reasonable assessment of the appropriate reduction.

The guidelines can be no more than guidelines. The facts of a particular case may indicate that they are not appropriate. The starting point is the statute.

Compensation may be reduced because there is a high degree of probability that the employee would have been dismissed due either to a continuation of his unsatisfactory performance or to redundancy, and further reduced because his poor performance contributed to his dismissal. In *TBA Industrial Products Ltd v Locke* [1984] IRLR 48, the tribunal reduced the compensation for loss of pension rights by 70 per cent because of the employee's unsatisfactory performance to reflect the fact that he might have been dismissed fairly for this reason in the future or by reason of redundancy and then reduced the compensation again by a further 70 per cent, because by his poor performance he had contributed to his dismissal. Locke was not being penalised twice for the same reason, the poor performance was taken into account twice for different reasons.

(l) Expenses The employee is under an obligation to mitigate his loss and look for other employment. In so doing he will probably incur

Table 13.1 Table of multipliers to be applied to the deferred annual pension to assess compensation for loss of enhancement of accrued pension rights.

Age last birthday	Normal retirement age 60	Normal retirement age 65
Under 30	2.6	1.9
30–34	2.6	2.1
35–39	2.6	2.2
40–44	2.6	2.3
45–49	2.6	2.4
50	2.4	2.4
51	2.2	2.4
52	2.1	2.4
53	1.8	2.3
54	1.6	2.2
55	1.4	2.1
56	1.2	1.9
57	0.9	1.8
58	0.5	1.6
59	0.2	1.4
60	NIL	1.1
61		0.9
62		0.6
63		0.4
64		0.2

expenses. He may have to take additional newspapers or trade journals or professional papers where jobs are advertised. He may have to write to or telephone employers. He may have to travel for interviews. This is a loss for which compensation can be recovered: *Mathieson v Noble and Son Ltd* [1972] IRLR 76. Credit will have to be given for anything received from employers by way of expenses for interviews or from the Department of Employment. Generally, these expenses will be small, but they can be considerable where the employee has been out of work for some time and has made substantial efforts to obtain other employment. Legal costs are not included. To award compensation to cover such costs would be to circumvent r 11 of the Industrial Tribunals (Rules of Procedure) Regulations 1985 (SI 1985 No 16): see *Raynor v Remploy Ltd* [1973] IRLR 3; and *Nohar v Granitstone (Galloway) Ltd* [1974] ICR 273.

(m) Ex gratia payments *Ex gratia* or similar payments made by the employer will normally be set off against the compensatory award: see *Finnie v Top Hat Frozen Foods* [1985] ICR 433; *Addison v Babcock FATA Ltd* [1987] ICR 805; and *Horizon Holidays v Grassi* [1987] ICR 851. In certain cases however an *ex gratia* payment may not be deducted as where the employee would have received it in any event: see *Roadchef Ltd v Hastings* [1988] ICR 142.

Where the compensation award exceeds the statutory maximum of £10,000 the EAT held in *McCarthy v British Insulated Callenders*

Cables plc [1985] IRLR 94, that s 75(3) of the EP(C)A 1978 makes it clear that the amount of *ex gratia* payments must be deducted from the compensatory award before the statutory maximum for compensatory awards is applied: see *Morris v Gestetner Ltd* [1973] ICR 587; but compare *Powermatic Ltd v Bull* [1977] ICR 469.

Where the employer makes an *ex gratia* payment, that *ex gratia* payment may be set off against any basic award for which the employer is liable: see *Chelsea Football Club and Athletic Co Ltd v Heath* [1981] IRLR 73.

(n) Industrial pressure In assessing the compensatory award and determining how far the loss sustained by the employee was attributable to action taken by the employer, no account is to be taken of any pressure which, by calling, organising, procuring or financing a strike or other industrial action, or threatening to do so, was exercised on the employer to dismiss the employee: s 74(5) of the EP(C)A 1978. The employer may be able to recover the whole or part of any compensation awarded from the person exercising the pressure: see more particularly **6**, below.

In such circumstances it may be possible for the employee to have contributed to the dismissal. However, such a finding is more likely where there are factors other than the pressure to dismiss which the tribunal may take into account: *Ford Motor Co Ltd v Hudson* [1978] ICR 482. In this case it was held:

No doubt there are many cases where if the pressure is put out of mind as the result of a compliance with . . . [s 63 of the EP(C)A 1978 which directs a tribunal where an employer dismisses an employee because of a threat of industrial action to determine the fairness or otherwise of the dismissal as if there had been no such industrial pressure] it will be found that the pressure so excluded was the sole cause of the dismissal, and in such a case no doubt a contribution by the employee to the dismissal is out of the question. We do not think that such is necessarily the case. For example, assuming that the Industrial Tribunal came to the conclusion that this case was one to which . . . [s 63] applied, and further came to the conclusion that the dismissal was unfair, it would be open to them to find (if they thought it was the fact) that the applicants had been unduly unco-operative in a difficult situation, and not wholly reasonable in refusing to move.

Thus in *Sulemanji v Toughened Glass Ltd* [1979] ICR 799, following industrial action with which Sulemanji did not agree, he ceased paying his union subscriptions. When he started work he knew he would have to be a member of the appropriate union. His colleagues refused to work with him. Despite attempts to persuade him to pay the subscriptions he refused to do so and was dismissed. The tribunal concluded that the dismissal was unfair and it was not entitled to take account of the pressure put upon the employer. However, because the dismissal was solely the result of the employee's own conduct the tribunal reduced the compensatory award by 100 per cent and this was upheld by the EAT. The compensatory award and the basic award may be reduced: see *Colwyn BC v Dutton* [1980] IRLR 420. Dutton was a dustcart driver. His colleagues refused to work with him because they believed that he was a dangerous driver. Industrial action was threatened if they were disciplined for refusing to travel with him. He was dismissed. His driving had contributed to his dismissal and the EAT held that therefore Dutton's compensation should be reduced.

5.4 Special award

Section 72 of the EP(C)A 1978 provides that where the tribunal makes an award of compensation under s 68(2), where an order for reinstatement or re-engagement is not made, or under s 71(2)(*a*), where an order for reinstatement or re-engagement is made but the order is not complied with, the award shall consist of a basic award, a compensatory award and in certain circumstances a special award. A special award will only be made where the dismissal is unfair under s 58 or s 59(*a*) of the EP(C)A 1978; that is where the employee is unfairly dismissed because of trade union membership, non-membership, or trade union activities, or where he is selected for any such reason in a redundancy situation. No special award will be made unless the employee requests the tribunal to make an order for reinstatement or re-engagement and shall not be made in any event in a case within s 73(2) of the EP(C)A 1978; that is where the reason for dismissal is redundancy and the employee unreasonably refuses to accept a renewal of the contract or suitable alternative employment or where the employee during a trial period unreasonably terminates the contract under s 82(5) or (6) of the EP(C)A 1978; or is not treated as dismissed on the ending of his employment under the old contract under s 84(1) of the EP(C)A 1978 (on a renewal of employment or re-engagement): s 72 of the EP(C)A 1978.

A special award is calculated in accordance with the provisions of s 75A of the EP(C)A 1978.

If the award of compensation is made under s 68(2) of the EP(C)A 1978 (that is where no order for reinstatement or re-engagement is made), the amount of the special award shall be either (*a*) one week's pay multiplied by 104 or (*b*) £13,180 whichever is the greater, but shall not exceed £26,290: s 75A(1) of the EP(C)A 1978.

If the award of compensation is made under s 71(2)(*a*) of the EP(C)A 1978 (where an order for reinstatement or re-engagement is not complied with and compensation is calculated in the normal way for unfair dismissal in accordance with ss 72 to 76 of the EP(C)A 1978) then, unless the employer satisfies the tribunal that it was not practicable to comply with an order under s 69 of the EP(C)A 1978 (an order for reinstatement or re-engagement) the amount of the special award shall be increased to (*a*) one week's pay multiplied by 156 or (*b*) £19,735, whichever is the greater: s 75A(2) of the EP(C)A

1978. Where the employer can show that it was not practicable to comply with an order for reinstatement or re-engagement a special award shall still be made under s 75A(1) of the EP(C)A 1978. The amount will be either one week's pay multiplied by 104 or £13,180, whichever is the greater, but shall not exceed £26,290. An award under s 75A(2) of the EP(C)A 1978 is made instead of an additional award of compensation in those circumstances of an additional award would otherwise be made. The cases in which a special award of compensation can be made are wider than those in which an additional award can be made. For the circumstances in which an additional award can be made see **3.3**, above. Section 75A(2) of the EP(C)A 1978 is subject to the following provisions.

Section 75A(3) provides that where the amount of the basic award is reduced under s 73(5) of the EP(C)A 1978 (where the effective date of termination is after the employee's 64th birthday) the amount of the special award shall be reduced by the same fraction. That fraction is ¹⁄₁₂ for each complete calendar month after the 64th birthday and before the effective date of termination.

Where the employer has engaged a permanent replacement for the employee the tribunal shall not take that fact into account in determining for the purposes of s 75A(2) whether it was practicable to comply with an order under s 69 of the EP(C)A 1978 (an order for reinstatement or re-engagement) unless the employer shows that it was not practicable for him to arrange for the employee's work to be done without engaging a permanent replacement: s 75A(6) of the EP(C)A 1978.

The Secretary of State is given power to increase the sums of £13,180, £26,290 and £19,735, respectively. The sums apply where the effective date of termination falls on or after 1 April 1991. Previously the limits were £12,550, £25,040 and £18,795: see s 75A(7) of the EP(C)A 1978.

There is no provision limiting the amount of a week's pay that can be taken into account in calculating the special award.

The special award, although referred to as an award of compensation, is not compensation in the sense that it compensates the employee for a specific loss suffered by him.

The amount of the special award can be reduced by the employee's contributory conduct: see **7** and **8**, below.

6 Contribution and pressure on the employer

Section 76A of the EP(C)A 1978 provides that if in proceedings for unfair dismissal the employer or the employee claims that the employer was induced to dismiss the employee because of pressure which a trade union or other person exercised on the employer, either the employer or the employee may request the tribunal to direct that the person who he claims exercised the pressure be joined as a party to the proceedings. The pressure is pressure which is exercised on the employer by calling, organising, procuring or financing a strike or other industrial action, or by threatening to do so, and which is exercised because the employee was not a member of any trade union, or of a particular trade union or of one of a number of particular trade unions: s 76A(1) of the EP(C)A 1978.

A request to join a person exercising the pressure as a party to the proceedings shall be granted if it is made before the hearing of the complaint of unfair dismissal begins, but it may be refused if it is made thereafter. No request may be made after the tribunal has made an award under s 68(2) of the EP(C)A 1978 (an award of compensation for unfair dismissal) or under s 69 of the EP(C)A 1978 (an order for reinstatement or re-engagement): s 76A(2) of the EP(C)A 1978. Where any person has been joined as a party to the proceedings and the tribunal makes an award of compensation under s 68(2) of the EP(C)A 1978 or s 71(2)(a) of the EP(C)A 1978 (ie whether a compensatory award, basic award, additional award or special award), but the tribunal also finds that such pressure has been exercised against the employer, the tribunal may make an award against that person instead of the employer, or partly against that person and partly against the employer, as the tribunal may consider just and equitable in the circumstances: s 76A(3) of the EP(C)A 1978. In assessing the employee's losses, no account however is to be taken of any such pressure put upon the employer to dismiss the employee: s 74(5) of the EP(C)A 1978.

7 Mitigation

In ascertaining the loss which the employee has suffered in consequence of the dismissal, for the purpose of calculating the compensatory award, the tribunal must apply the same rule concerning the duty of the person to mitigate his loss as applies to damages recoverable under the common law: s 74(4) of the EP(C)A 1978. There is a statutory obligation to consider mitigation in relation to both past and future loss: *Morganite Electrical Carbon Ltd v Donne* [1987] ICR 18.

The obligation to mitigate at common law was considered in *Yetton v Eastwoods Froy Ltd* [1966] 3 All ER 353. Yetton was a joint managing director of a company under a five-year contract. After he had completed just over a year's service he was offered a post as assistant managing director at the same salary but with loss of status. He refused. Blain J held:

The basic principle of damages is restitutio in integrum: the plaintiff should have what he has lost through the defendants' fault; but, of course, if a plaintiff in fact, in the case of a contract of service, earns something elsewhere through being at liberty so to do, then he has lost that much less as the consequence of the default. Moreover, if he can minimise his loss by a reasonable course of conduct, he should do so, though the onus is on the defaulting defendant to show that it could be, or could have been, done and is not being, and has not been, done. Thus, the opportunity to reduce damages by finding reasonable (I repeat reasonable) alternative employment, should be taken and, indeed, sought, whether such employment is by the same defaulting employer or by someone else; in either case the test being whether it is reasonable to refuse it or not in the circumstances of each case.

In this case Blain J referred to the judgment of Bankes LJ in *Payzu Ltd v Saunders* [1919] 2 KB 581. Bankes LJ held:

It is plain that the question what is reasonable for a person to do in mitigation of his damages cannot be a question of law, but must be one of fact in the circumstances of each particular case. There may be cases where as a matter of fact it would be unreasonable to expect a plaintiff, in view of the treatment he has received from the defendant, to consider any offer made. If he had been rendering personal services and had been dismissed after being accused in the presence of others of being a thief, and if after that his employer had offered to take him back into his service, most persons would think he was justified in refusing the offer, and that it would be unreasonable to ask him in this way to mitigate the damages in an action for wrongful dismissal. But that is not to state a principle of law, but a conclusion of fact to be arrived at on a consideration of all the circumstances of the case.

In the same case Scrutton LJ held:

In certain cases of personal service it may be unreasonable to expect a plaintiff to consider an offer from the other party who has grossly injured him:

The court held that Yetton had not unreasonably refused the offer of alternative employment.

Section 71(5) of the EP(C)A 1978 provides that in making an award of compensation where the tribunal finds that the employee has unreasonably prevented an order of reinstatement or re-engagement being complied with, it shall take that conduct into account as a failure by the employee to mitigate his loss. This is without prejudice to the generality of s 74(4) of the EP(C)A 1978.

7.1 Alternative employment

The duty to mitigate arises when the employee has been dismissed. The employee cannot be expected to suspect in advance that his employment will come to an end. An employee who has been unfairly dismissed does not have to show that he took steps in mitigation before he was actually dismissed: *Savoia v Chiltern Herb Farms Ltd* [1981] IRLR 65, and on appeal [1982] IRLR 166, where this point was not considered. See also *Prestwick Circuits Ltd v McAndrew* [1990] IRLR 191.

The essence of mitigation is that the employee cannot recover losses which he could have avoided by taking reasonable steps. The employee must seek suitable alternative employment. If the employee mitigates his loss by taking such reasonable steps he cannot recover any of the losses which he has avoided, even though the steps which he has taken have been more than were reasonably required of him. If in looking for other employment he incurs any expense or cost in taking reasonable steps, he can recover this expense or cost from the employer. The employee cannot recover compensation for losses arising because he failed to mitigate his loss by seeking other employment.

In *AG Bracey Ltd v Iles* [1973] IRLR 210, the NIRC held:

The law is that it is the duty of a dismissed employee to act reasonably in order to mitigate his loss. It may not be reasonable to take the first job that comes along. It may be much more reasonable, in the interests of the employee and of the employer who has to pay compensation, that he should wait a little time. He must, of course, use the time well and seek a better paid job which will reduce his overall loss and the amount of compensation which the previous employer ultimately has to pay.

In *Bessenden Properties Ltd v Corness* [1973] IRLR 365, the NIRC found:

The proper test is to consider whether the person who is said to have failed to mitigate his damage acted reasonably in all the circumstances. In deciding whether he acted reasonably, a useful test is . . . to ask . . . 'If the complainant had had no hope of recovering compensation from anybody else and if he had consulted merely his own interests and had acted reasonably in all the circumstances, would he have accepted the job in mitigation of the loss which he had suffered?' If the answer is 'Yes' then he should have taken the job and the fact that he is able to look towards the respondent for compensation provides him with no excuse for not doing so.

This decision was affirmed by the Court of Appeal: [1974] IRLR 338. The approach was followed in *Archbold Freightage Ltd v Wilson* [1974] IRLR 10. The onus is on the employer to show that the employee ought reasonably to have mitigated his loss by taking certain steps: *Fyfe v Scientific Furnishings Ltd* [1989] ICR 648; see also *Corness's* case, above.

What constitutes reasonable steps is a question of fact for the tribunal to decide on the evidence available. It may be reasonable for the employee not to accept the first job which is offered to him: *McKinney v Bieganek* [1973] IRLR 311. It has been seen that it may be in the interests of both the employer and the employee that the employee should wait until a better job is offered, provided that the employee is making efforts to secure a better job. Conversely, it may be reasonable for the employee to suffer a drop in status and to accept less pay; and any failure to do so may be regarded as a failure to mitigate. This may arise because of the difficulties of obtaining suitable employment due to the economic situation or due to the employee's age. It is not reasonable to make only one application for a job in a period of eight weeks: *O'Reilly v Welwyn and Hatfield DC* [1975] IRLR 334.

Although it should be slow in so finding, it is open to the tribunal to find that an employee has acted reasonably in failing to accept subsequent employment where the remuneration he would receive would be less than any benefit he was receiving from the State. The employer would therefore be liable for compensation even after the date when the employee could have accepted such other employment: see *Daley v AE Dorsett (Almar Dolls Ltd)* [1981] IRLR 385.

In determining reasonableness regard must be had to all the surrounding circumstances: see *Fyfe*'s case, above, where it was held that Fyfe's failure to accept an offer of early retirement the benefit of which outweighed unfair dismissal compensation was not a failure to mitigate.

Following the dismissal, the employee may obtain other employment which he subsequently loses. He will not have failed to mitigate his loss if he has not been culpable in losing the second job: *Barrel Plating and Phosphating Co Ltd v Danks* [1976] ICR 503, but see *Moosa*'s case, **5.3(a)**, above.

Where an employee following his dismissal chooses to set up his own business rather than looking for employment he will not necessarily have failed to mitigate his loss. While there is an onus on the employee to take reasonable steps to mitigate his loss becoming self-employed may be reasonable in all the circumstances. See *Gardiner-Hill v Roland Berger Technics Ltd* [1982] IRLR 498; *Lee v IPC Business Press Ltd* [1984] ICR 306.

7.2 Reinstatement or re-engagement

The EAT has held that an employee's failure to accept an offer of employment made by the employer to the employee during the period of notice may be a failure by the employee to mitigate his loss if he has not acted reasonably: *Gallear v JF Watson and Son Ltd* [1979] IRLR 306; *Kendrick v Aerduct Productions* [1974] IRLR 322; and *Sweetlove v Redbridge and Waltham Forest Area Health Authority* [1979] IRLR 195. Not every failure to accept an offer of reinstatement or re-engagement will be a failure by the employee to mitigate his loss: see *How v Tesco Stores Ltd* [1974] IRLR 194. Where the tribunal makes an order for reinstatement or re-engagement, it must consider the employee's unreasonable refusal to comply with the order as a failure on the part of the employee to mitigate his loss. This is without prejudice to the generality of s 74(4) of the EP(C)A 1978: see s 71(5) of the EP(C)A 1978.

Where the tribunal finds that the employee has unreasonably refused an offer by the employer which if accepted would have had the effect of reinstating the employee, the tribunal shall reduce or further reduce the amount of the basic award to such extent as it considers just and equitable having regard to its findings: s 73(7A) of the EP(C)A 1978. The provision appears to envisage the situation where the employer of his own violation makes an offer, rather than where he is ordered to reinstate by the tribunal. It is clear that this provision applies only to reinstatement and not re-engagement. Although this provision applies only to the basic award the tribunal still has its existing power to reduce the compensatory award under s 74(4) of the EP(C)A 1978: see for example *Gallear v JF Watson and Son Ltd v* [1979] IRLR 306. A similar approach will be adopted by the tribunals in considering whether or not the basic award should also be reduced. The tribunal's power to make a reduction under this provision is in addition to its power to make a reduction under any other provisions.

Section 75A(5) of the EP(C)A 1978 provides that where the employee has unreasonably prevented an order of reinstatement or re-engagement from being complied with the tribunal shall reduce or further reduce the amount of the special award to such an extent as it considers just and equitable. This is similar to the provision contained in s 71(5) of the EP(C)A 1978 (a failure to mitigate his loss). Section 75A(5) of the EP(C)A 1978 further provides that if an employee unreasonably refuses an offer by the employer made otherwise than in compliance with an order of the tribunal which, if accepted, would have had the effect of reinstating the employee in his employment in all respects as if he had not been dismissed, the tribunal shall reduce or further reduce the amount of the special award to such an extent as it considers just and equitable having regard to that finding. This is similar to the provision contained in s 73(7A) of the EP(C)A 1978 (reduction of basic award). The only difference is that s 75A(5) of the EP(C)A 1978 makes it quite clear that the offer is an offer made by the employer of his own violation and not made pursuant to an order of the tribunal.

7.3 Failure to utilise the employer's disciplinary procedure

In *Seligman and Latz Ltd v McHugh* [1979] IRLR 130, McHugh was constructively dismissed. She did not utilise the employer's 'grievance procedure'. It was held that the fundamental breach of contract by the employer brought the contract to an end and it was not open to the employer to claim that the employee had failed to mitigate her loss by not following the 'grievance procedure'.

In *Hoover Ltd v Forde* [1980] ICR 239, the EAT found that the failure by an employee to appeal internally against his dismissal might amount to a failure to mitigate. However, in *William Muir (Bond 9) Ltd v Lamb* [1985] IRLR 95, the EAT again considered whether a failure by an employee to pursue an internal appeal procedure within the company amounted to a failure to mitigate her loss. It held:

there is no obligation upon an employee who is dismissed to follow up an internal appeal procedure before making application to an industrial tribunal. This in our opinion is clear from the case of *Chrystie v Rolls Royce (1971) Ltd* [1976] IRLR 336 and *Hoover Ltd v Forde* [1980] ICR 239. It is true that in the latter case an industrial tribunal had found that had the dismissed employee availed himself of the appeal procedure the decision to dismiss him might have been rescinded and on that ground apparently his compensation was reduced by 50 per cent. We are bound to say we have great difficulty in accepting the reasoning in that case. It seems to us to be purely speculative to attempt to assess what would have happened in the event of an appeal being taken. There are many imponderable factors. One is the manner in which the appeal is handled. Another is the person or persons to whom the appeal lies. In an industrial situation it may very often happen than an employee who has been dismissed considers that there is no point in him following up the internal appeal procedure because he does not have confidence in the persons who would hear that appeal. It would therefore be quite wrong in our view to penalise an employee who has been unfairly dismissed by reducing her compensation because she did not follow through whatever internal appeal procedure may have existed.

7.4 Mitigation and compensation

In assessing the deduction to be made from the employee's compensation because of his failure to mitigate his loss, tribunals usually disallow any claim beyond the time when they think the employee could have reasonably secured other employment.

In *Smith, Kline and French Laboratories Ltd v Coates* [1977] IRLR 220, the tribunal assessed losses for a period of 16 months but, because the employee had not mitigated his loss, ordered that compensation should be reduced by 50 per cent. The EAT criticised this approach. The failure to mitigate should be expressed in terms of weeks or months. The tribunal's approach might be a useful preliminary investigation into the proper allowance to be made for the mitigating factor but, having decided that the failure to mitigate was 50 per cent, it should have looked at the likely period of unemployment which was 16 months and then halved the period of loss. By halving the total compensation the employee may be deprived of benefits to which he is entitled and which are unaffected by his failure to mitigate. This case was followed in *Peara v Enderlin Ltd* [1979] ICR 804.

In *Gardiner-Hill v Roland Berger Technics Ltd* [1982] IRLR 498, the EAT again held that where a tribunal finds that an employee has failed to mitigate his loss it is not open to the tribunal to make a percentage reduction in the compensation. It held:

it is well-established that it is inappropriate in dealing with failure to mitigate damages to reduce the amount of the compensation by a percentage. In order to show a failure to mitigate, it has to be shown that if a particular step had been taken, Mr Gardiner-Hill would, after a particular time, on balance of probabilities have gained employment; from then onwards the loss flowing from the unfair dismissal would have been extinguished or reduced by his income from that other source. In fixing the amount to be deducted for failure to mitigate, it is necessary for the Tribunal to identify what steps should have been taken; the date on which that step would have produced an alternative income and, thereafter, to reduce the amount of compensation by the amount of the alternative income which would have been earned. Since that is the principle of mitigation, a reduction of a percentage of the total sum representing compensation for the whole period is inappropriate.

In *Sturdy Finance Ltd v Bardsley* [1979] IRLR 65, it was held that Bardsley who took a refund of his pension contributions rather than taking a deferred pension, did not fail to mitigate his loss of pension rights. There is no rule of law that an employee must take a deferred pension rather than a refund of contributions, and the onus was on the employer to establish that it was wholly unreasonable for the employee to elect to take a refund of his pension contributions.

One exception to the principle of mitigation in claims for unfair dismissal arises in that no deductions may be made from sums awarded for wages in lieu of notice when the employee has obtained, or could have obtained, other employment during the notice period. See **5.3**, above.

8 Contributory fault

The doctrine of contributory fault applies to the basic award, compensatory award and special award.

8.1 Basic award

Section 73(7B) of the EP(C)A 1978 provides that where the tribunal considers that any conduct of the employee before the dismissal or, where the dismissal was with notice, before the notice was given, was such that it would be just and equitable to reduce or further reduce the amount of the basic award to any extent the tribunal shall reduce or further reduce that amount accordingly. This section specifically refers to conduct and not to capability.

Section 73(7B) of the EP(C)A 1978 allows the tribunal to reduce or further reduce the amount of the basic award as will be just and equitable because of the employee's conduct. Subsequently discovered conduct may make it neither just nor equitable that the employee should receive the whole or part of the basic award. This section would also appear to allow the employer to adduce before the tribunal evidence of the employee's conduct generally, even where it was known to the employer at the time of the dismissal, although that conduct may not have been relied upon by the employer as the reason or principal reason for the dismissal, so that if the tribunal considers that any conduct of the employee before the dismissal, or where the dismissal was with notice, before the notice was given, was such that it would be just and equitable to reduce or further reduce the amount of the basic award to any extent, the tribunal shall reduce or further reduce that amount accordingly.

Section 73(7C) of the EP(C)A 1978 provides that s 73(7B) shall not apply where the reason or principal reason for the dismissal was that the employee was redundant unless the dismissal is unfair under s 59(*a*) of the EP(C)A 1978—selection for trade union membership, or non-membership or trade union activities—and in that event shall apply only to so much of the basic award as is payable because of s 73(4A). Section 73(4A) of the EP(C)A 1978, where the effective date of termination falls on or after 1 April 1991, provides, *inter alia*, that in such cases the amount of the basic award before reduction under the other provisions of s 73 of the EP(C)A 1978 shall not be less than £2,650, so that the reduction will in effect only apply to the excess of the basic award over what would otherwise be the basic award, which will usually be the same as the redundancy payment.

Where a tribunal reduces the amount of the compensatory award to take account of the employee's contributory conduct must it make the same reduction in the basic award as in the compensatory award? In *G McFall and Co Ltd v Curran* [1981] IRLR 455, the Northern Ireland Court of Appeal held that the same deduction ought to be made in respect of both compensatory and basic awards to take account of the employee's contributory conduct. However, in *Les Ambassadeurs Club v Bainda* [1982] IRLR 5, the EAT held that it was open to the tribunal to reduce the compensatory award by 70 per cent while leaving the basic award untouched.

This difference in approach was considered in *RSPCA v Cruden* [1986] ICR 205. The EAT held that it would only be in exceptional circumstances that a tribunal should treat a reduction in the basic award differently from the reduction in the compensatory award to reflect the employee's contributory conduct. It held:

Section 73(7B) [of the EP(C)A 1978] provides that in cases where the tribunal considers that the complainant's *conduct* before the dismissal was such that it would be just and equitable to reduce the amount of the basic award it 'shall reduce . . . that amount accordingly.' Section 74(6) [of the EP(C)A 1978] provides that where the tribunal finds that the dismissal was to any extent caused or contributed to by any *action* of the complainant it shall 'reduce the amount of the compensatory award by such proportion as it considers just and equitable having regard to that finding'. Common to both sub-sections are the words 'just and equitable': but it may well be that the difference in emphasis between the words 'shall reduce . . . that amount *accordingly*' and the words 'such proportion as it considers just and equitable having *regard* to that finding' justifies adopting somewhat different approaches under the two sub-sections. Moreover, one refers to conduct of the complainant, the other to his actions. The difficulty is to divine precisely what difference is intended. Unhappily, the conflicting decision in *Les Ambassadeurs Club v Bainda* above, was given at a time when the wording of both sub-sections was significantly different from what it is now. Moreover, the point there argued by the appellant was not that there must be consistency between the compensatory and the basic awards, but rather that the tribunal, having found that the employee had contributed to the extent of 70 per cent to his own dismissal, should have reduced the basic award by that precise percentage.

Plainly both sub-sections involve the exercise of a discretion, and the wording of each, while sufficiently different to admit differentiation in cases where the tribunal finds, on the facts, that it is justified, is sufficiently similar to lead us to conclude that it is only exceptionally that such a differentiation will be justified. In the present case we revert once again to the tribunal's finding that the employers would have been failing in their duty had they not dismissed the employee, who had very clearly been shown to be guilty of a grave neglect of duty. They were amply justified in reducing the compensatory claim to nothing, and on the facts of the present case we cannot see how a proper exercise of their discretion would have enabled them to take any different course in relation to the basic award.

8.2 Special award

Under s 75A(4) of the EP(C)A 1978, where the tribunal considers that any conduct of the employee before the dismissal, or where the dismissal was with notice, before the notice was given, was such that it would be just and equitable to reduce or further reduce the amount of the special award to any extent the tribunal shall reduce or further reduce that amount accordingly. This provision follows s 73(7B) of the EP(C)A 1978. For a consideration of s 73(7B) see **8.1**, above.

8.3 Compensatory award

Under s 74(6) of the EP(C)A 1978 where the tribunal finds that the dismissal was to any extent caused or contributed to by any action of the employee, then it shall reduce the amount of the compensatory award by such proportion as it considers just and equitable having regard to that finding.

In deciding whether the dismissal is fair or unfair the tribunal is not entitled to take into account reasons which only came to the employer's knowledge after dismissal. It is clear from the judgment of the House of Lords in *W Devis and Son Ltd v Atkins* [1977] ICR 662 that the employer cannot rely on s 74(6) to reduce the assessment of the compensatory award to take account of reasons discovered after the dismissal. The tribunal has to find that the dismissal was to some extent caused or contributed to by the actions of the employee. Where these actions were not known until after the dismissal, they cannot have been factors relevant to the dismissal. However, it is equally clear from the judgment that the assessment of the compensatory award must be just and equitable in the circumstances: see s 74(1) of the EP(C)A 1978. Thus, subsequently discovered conduct may make it neither just nor equitable that the employee should receive compensation, so that under this provision the compensatory award may be reduced, and may be a nil or nominal award.

In *Tele-Trading Ltd v Jenkins* [1990] IRLR 430, Jenkins's compensation was not reduced under s 74(6) where his dismissal for alleged dishonesty was found to be unfair, because at the time of the dismissal the employer did not have reasonable grounds for believing that he was guilty. The Court of Appeal accepted the argument that the compensatory award could be reduced under s 74(1) if a thorough investigation would or might have resulted in the employee still being dismissed.

8.4 General

The onus of proving contributory fault is upon the employer. Whether or not the employee has contributed to his dismissal and the extent are questions of fact for the tribunal: *Associated Tyre Specialists (Eastern) Ltd v Waterhouse* [1977] ICR 218. In *Hollier v Plysu Ltd* [1983] IRLR 260, the Court of Appeal held that the apportionment of responsibility 'is so obviously a matter of impression, opinion and discretion' so that the EAT is not entitled to interfere with the decision of the tribunal unless there is 'either a plain error of law, or something like perversity'. In *Warrilow v Robert Walker Ltd* [1984] IRLR 304, the EAT held that in deciding whether or not the tribunal's findings as to the apportionment of contributory fault can stand, the principles of law to be applied are precisely the same as the principles which apply and which bind an appellate court in relation to appeals under the Law Reform (Contributory Negligence) Act 1945. In *Maris v Rotherham County BC* [1974] IRLR 147, the NIRC held that in exercising its discretion the tribunal should ignore technicalities. The tribunal had to look at all the circumstances and take a broad common-sense view.

8.5 Conduct of the employee

Section 73(7B) (reduction of the basic award) and s 75A(4) of the EP(C)A 1978 (reduction of the special award) expressly refer to the employee's conduct. It is doubtful whether conduct will include a lack of capability. It seems that it will not. Section 74(6) of the EP(C)A 1978 refers merely to the employee's action.

Only where the employee has by his fault caused or contributed to his dismissal will there be any reduction; otherwise it would not be just and equitable: see *Morrish v Henlys (Folkestone) Ltd* [1973] 2 All ER 137, where an employee was dismissed because he failed to falsify certain records. Although there is no reference in the statute to culpability or blameworthiness the conduct on the part of the employee must be culpable or blameworthy.

In *Nelson v BBC (No 2)* [1980] ICR 110, Brandon LJ held:

an award of compensation to a successful complainant can only be reduced on the ground that he contributed to his dismissal by his own conduct if the conduct on his part relied on for this purpose was culpable or blameworthy. This conclusion can be arrived at in various ways. First, it can be said that the epithet 'culpable' or 'blameworthy' should be implied before the word 'action'. Or, secondly, it can be said that the expression 'caused or contributed' impliedly incorporates the concept of culpability or blameworthiness. Or, thirdly, it can be said that, in any case, it could never be just or equitable to reduce a successful complainant's compensation unless the conduct on his part relied on as contributory was culpable or blameworthy. For my part, I prefer the third way of arriving at the conclusion to either the first or the second, and would approach the application of . . . [s 74(6) of the EP(C)A 1978] on that basis.

It is necessary, however, to consider what is included in the concept of culpability or blameworthiness in this connection. The concept does not, in my view, necessarily involve any conduct of the complainant amounting to a breach of contract or a tort. It includes, no doubt, conduct of that kind. But it also includes conduct which, while not amounting to a breach of contract or a tort, is nevertheless perverse or foolish, or, if I may use the colloquialism, bloody minded. It may also include action which, though not meriting any of those more pejorative epithets, is nevertheless unreasonable in all the circumstances. I should not, however, go as far as to say that all unreasonable conduct is necessarily culpable or blameworthy; it must depend on the degree of unreasonableness involved.

In *Morrison v Amalgamated Transport and General Workers Union* [1989] IRLR 361, it was held that in determining contributory fault the tribunal must take a broad, common-sense approach, which should not necessarily be confined to a particular moment, even the terminal moment of employment. What the tribunal has to look for over a period is conduct on the part of the employee which is culpable, blameworthy or otherwise unreasonable, which contributed to or played a part in the dismissal.

In *Gibson and Others v British Transport Docks Board* [1982] IRLR 228, the EAT held that where an employee has been guilty of improper conduct of a blameworthy nature which led to his dismissal, the tribunal may find that the conduct contributed to the dismissal.

The action or conduct of the employee must have caused or contributed to the dismissal and the amount of the reduction is the amount which is just and equitable having regard to that finding. For the purposes of s 74(6) of the EP(C)A 1978 there must be a causal link between the actions or conduct of the employee and the dismissal: *Hutchinson v Enfield Rolling Mills Ltd* [1981] IRLR 318, but general bad behaviour may result in a reduction: see s 73(7B) and s 75(A)(4) of the EP(C)A 1978.

It is the employee's conduct alone which is relevant: *Allders International Ltd v Parkins* [1981] IRLR 68.

However, blameworthy conduct of a person acting on behalf of the employee as his agent may be taken into account. Thus, in *Allen v Hammett* [1982] IRLR 89, Allen was employed on Hammett's farm. He was away from work due to a minor accident but was paid his wages in full by Hammett. Hammett had an insurance policy in respect of his liability for sick pay for a period of 52 weeks and made a claim. The insurers sent a cheque for the wrong amount to Allen not Hammett. Allen told Hammett that he had received the cheque but Hammett expressed doubts as to Allen's entitlement. Allen immediately cashed the cheque and spent some of the money. Hammett told the insurance company of the error and they wrote to Hammett asking for the money to be returned. He passed the letter to Allen. Allen went to see his solicitors who advised him not to repay the money until they had looked into the matter. The insurers continued to write to Hammett asking that Allen return the money, but Allen never did so. Hammett was informed by the insurers that until the money was returned Allen could not be included in the accident policy. This led to Allen's dismissal. Allen's dismissal was unfair, but the tribunal went on to find that his failure to repay the money, albeit on the advice of his solicitors, was a matter contributing to the dismissal and reduced his compensation by 60 per cent. The EAT held that in law a man is responsible for the acts of his agent. The course taken by Allen's solicitors was contributory to the dismissal and was blameworthy.

In the somewhat unusual case of *Ladup Ltd v Barnes* [1982] IRLR 7, an employee was dismissed after being arrested and charged with growing and possession of cannabis. It was held that the dismissal was unfair because a proper investigation had not been carried out. Compensation was awarded. After the hearing he was convicted. On a review the tribunal refused to reduce the compensation because of the employee's conduct. On appeal the EAT reduced the compensation by 100 per cent because of the employee's conduct. It is to be hoped that this case does not set a precedent enabling an employer who unfairly dismisses an employee to rely upon subsequent events to avoid the consequences of his actions.

Failure by an employee to disclose a spent criminal conviction under the Rehabilitation of Offenders Act 1974 will not mean he has contributed to his dismissal because there is no obligation upon him to disclose a spent conviction and therefore there is no blameworthy conduct: *Property Guards Ltd v Taylor and Kershaw* [1982] IRLR 175.

Where the employee is dismissed because of lack of capability rather than misconduct it may be difficult to argue that he has caused or contributed to his dismissal. In *Kraft Foods Ltd v Fox* [1978] ICR 311, the EAT held that:

If an employee is incompetent or incapable and cannot, with the best will in the world, measure up to the job, it seems to us to be wrong to say that that condition of incapacity is a contributory factor to his dismissal. The whole point about contribution is that it is something by way of conduct on the part of the employee over which he has control. Thus a man may be guilty of misconduct, he may misbehave . . . In the case of a man who falls short, he may not try. He may not be doing his best. That is something over which he has control. However, if he is doing his best and his best is not good enough, it does not seem to us to be proper to say that in those circumstances he has contributed and therefore a finding in his favour should be reduced by whatever proportion the industrial tribunal has decided.

In *Slaughter v C Brewer and Sons Ltd* [1990] IRLR 426, it was held that in cases of ill-health there will rarely be a reduction in the compensatory award on the grounds of contributory fault because there will be no act or omission on the part of the employee which was culpable or blameworthy. In a case of ill-health it may be possible to reduce the amount of compensation under s 74(1) of the EP(C)A 1978 where, for instance, a dismissal is unfair on procedural grounds, but the employee is incapable of doing the job: see *Nelson*'s case, above.

The approach in *Fox*'s case is by no means one of universal application. In *Patterson v Messrs Bracketts* [1977] IRLR 137, the EAT found the tribunal was entitled to take into account in assessing contributory fault not only the employee's conduct but 'the whole of [the employee's] work record . . . to the extent that his dismissal was contributed to by his lack of ability at work.' Similarly, in *Moncur v International Paint Co Ltd* [1978] IRLR 223, another division of the EAT doubted whether the decision in *Kraft Foods Ltd v Fox*, above, was attempting to lay down a proposition of law, see also *Finnie v Top Hat Frozen Foods* [1985] ICR 433.

In *Sutton and Gates (Luton) Ltd v Boxall* [1978] IRLR 486, the EAT found that it was necessary to distinguish between the case where the employee's lack of capability was due to his own fault in the sense that he was lazy, negligent or idle, or did not try to improve, as distinct from the case where the employee tries desperately hard but cannot cope. In the first case the degree of contribution would be considerable.

Where an unfair dismissal involves the selective re-engagement of employees who have taken part in a strike or other industrial action, the issue of contributory fault must be considered in relation to the dismissal. Did the employee contribute to his dismissal? It is neither necessary nor proper to consider whether he has contributed to his failure to be re-engaged. Where the employee is dismissed because he took part in a strike or other industrial action can the taking part in such strike or other industrial action be characterised as contributory fault? It has been held that:

it is not possible for an Industrial Tribunal to hold under s 74(6) [of the EP(C)A 1978] that the industrial action in which the employee was taking part (whether or not it was in breach of contract) in itself justifies a reduction in compensation, since an Industrial Tribunal is unable to determine whether or not, and to what extent, it is just and equitable to make such reduction (*Courtaulds Northern Spinning Ltd v Moosa* [1984] IRLR 43).

8.6 Amount of deduction

The amount of the deduction for contributory fault is a matter for the tribunal. Tribunals have first to assess the amount of the basic, compensatory or special award. They then have to decide whether or not there should be a reduction because of contributory fault. Any reduction will be expressed in percentage terms. In assessing the degree of contribution it is the gravity of the action rather than the state of mind of the employee which is relevant: *Ladbroke Racing Ltd v Mason* [1978] ICR 49. In assessing the deduction to be made for contributory fault the tribunal must first ascertain the extent to which the employee's action brought about his dismissal; and secondly it must decide by 'what proportion should what the award would otherwise have been, be reduced considering justice and equity? Justice and equity means justice to both sides and fair treatment of both sides': *Parker and Farr Ltd v Shelvey* [1979] IRLR 434.

The reduction may not be from the whole of the award. The tribunal must examine what the employee would have received by way of earnings if he had not been dismissed, and must then take into account any wages in lieu of notice or *ex gratia* payment which has been paid to the employee by the employer. These sums will be deducted before applying the appropriate proportion for contributory fault. Thus, if the employee has a net loss of wages of £2,000 but has been paid £1,500 wages in lieu of notice and has contributed to his dismissal by 25 per cent, a 25 per cent reduction will be made from the £500 which remains after deducting £1,500 from £2,000 and not by applying it to the £2,000 leaving £1,500 and then reducing this to a nil figure by deducting the £1,500: *UBAF Bank Ltd v Davis* [1978] IRLR 442; *Clement-Clarke International Ltd v Manley* [1979] ICR 74; *Parker and Farr Ltd v Shelvey*, above.

In *TBA Industrial Products Ltd v Locke* [1984] IRLR 48, Locke suffered a reduction of 70 per cent in the assessment of his compensation for loss of pension rights because there was a very high degree of probability that he would have left the employment, either due to a continuation of his unsatisfactory work performance, or because of a redundancy. He suffered a further 70 per cent reduction of his total compensation, including the compensation for loss of pension rights, because his unsatisfactory work had contributed to his dismissal. The EAT held that he had not been improperly penalised twice.

The contributory fault deduction will be made from total losses awarded and not from the maximum permitted by statute. Thus, if the employee has a compensatory award of £12,000 and is found 25 per cent to blame, £2,500 will be deducted from the £12,000 and not from the statutory maximum of £10,000: see *Morris v Gestetner Ltd* [1973] ICR 587 and *Walter Braund (London) Ltd v Murray* [1991] IRLR 100. Confirmation of this approach is provided by s 75(3) of the EP(C)A 1978.

There is nothing incompatible with a finding of unfair dismissal by making a nil award of compensation or an award of nominal compensation: *W Devis and Sons Ltd v Atkins* [1977] ICR 662; see also *Allders International Ltd v Parkins* [1981] IRLR 68.

A reduction by 100 per cent may be logical where the only reason the dismissal is unfair is due to a procedural irregularity: *Nairne v Highland and Islands Fire Brigade* [1989] IRLR 366.

In *Hollier v Plysu Ltd* [1983] IRLR 260, the EAT suggested that there should be a tariff for contributory conduct of 25 per cent, 50 per cent, 75 per cent or 100 per cent. In *Yorke v Brown* (1982) (unreported) EAT 262/82, it was suggested that a reduction of 10 per cent on account of the employee's contribution was almost *de minimis*.

8.7 Constructive dismissal

There may be a deduction for contributory conduct where the employee has been constructively dismissed: *Western Excavating (ECC) Ltd v Sharp* [1977] IRLR 25, overruled by the Court of Appeal on other grounds at [1978] ICR 221.

It is for the tribunal to decide whether the employer's actions amount to a constructive dismissal. Where the employer has repudiated the contract the behaviour of the employee must be examined in deciding upon contributory conduct. The tribunal is entitled to take into account the circumstances of the dismissal, but these may be completely or largely irrelevant in assessing compensation or any reduction. The proper approach is for the tribunal to look broadly over the whole period of time prior to the dismissal: *Garner v Grange Furnishing Ltd* [1977] IRLR 206. See *Morrison*'s case, above.

In *Holroyd v Gravure Cylinders Ltd* [1984] IRLR 259, the EAT distinguished the case of *Garner v Grange Furnishing Ltd*, above, on the grounds that it was 'a last-straw incident' following a course of conduct which gave rise to the fundamental breach of contract by the employer. Although it held that it was 'exceptional to have a situation where there is a genuine constructive dismissal due to the employer's breach of contract which at the same time has been contributed to by the employee', there may be such cases.

8.8 Failure to appeal

Where an employee fails to appeal against his dismissal under an internal procedure he is not thereby guilty of contributory fault: *Hoover Ltd v Forde* [1980] ICR 239. The EAT held:

in order to find that an applicant contributed to his dismissal by his own fault it is necessary to find that it was culpable or blameworthy and that it contributed to, and therefore preceded or was contemporaneous with, the act of dismissal. With the exception of the failure by the employee to make use of the appeal procedure, all the matters referred to by the industrial tribunal . . . were matters which could properly be taken into account in coming to a conclusion as to whether or not his dismissal had been contributed to by his own fault. However, having regard to our decision that the employee did not have any duty in law after dismissal to apply the appeal procedure, it cannot be said in our view, that his failure to do so can be something which contributed to his own dismissal.

In *William Muir (Bond 9) Ltd v Lamb* [1985] IRLR 95, the EAT found that the employee's failure to appeal against dismissal under the company's internal appeal procedure did not mean that the employee had contributed to the dismissal.

8.9 *Factors which cannot be taken into account*

Section 72A of the EP(C)A 1978 restricts the power of the tribunal in determining contributory fault by providing that certain matters shall be ignored. This section applies where the tribunal makes an award of compensation under s 68(2) (where an order for reinstatement or re-engagement is not made but there is an award of compensation), or under s 71(2)(*a*) of the EP(C)A 1978 (where an order for reinstatement or re-engagement is made but the order is not complied with) and the dismissal is regarded as unfair under s 58 or s 59(*a*) of the EP(C)A 1978, that is where the employee is unfairly dismissed because of trade union membership, non-membership or trade union activities, or where he is selected for any such reason in a redundancy situation.

In such a case the tribunal in considering whether it would be just and equitable to reduce or further reduce the amount of any part of the award, shall disregard any conduct or action of the employee in so far as it constitutes:

(*a*) a breach or proposed breach of any requirement falling within s 72A(3) of the EP(C)A 1978,

(*b*) a refusal or proposed refusal, to comply with the requirement of a kind mentioned in s 58(13)(*a*) of the EP(C)A 1978 (a refusal or proposed refusal to comply with a requirement that in the event of the employee's failing to become or ceasing to remain a member of any trade union, or a particular trade union or one of a number of particular trade unions he must make one or more payments), or

(*c*) an objection or proposed objection however expressed to the operation of a provision of a kind mentioned in s 58(13)(*b*) of the EP(C)A 1978 (an objection or proposed objection to a provision enabling the employer to deduct money from remuneration in the event of the employee failing to become or ceasing to remain a member of any trade union, or a particular trade union or one of a number of particular trade unions):

s 72A(2) of the EP(C)A 1978. This section provides that there may be a reduction in the basic award (see s 73(7B)), the compensatory award (see s 74(6)) or the special award (see s 75A(4)).

A requirement for the purposes of s 72A(3) of the EP(C)A 1978 is one imposed upon the employee by or under any arrangement, or contract of employment, or other agreement and requires him:

(*a*) to be or become a member of any trade union or of a particular trade union or of one of a number of particular trade unions;

(*b*) to cease to be, or refrain from becoming a member of any trade union or of a particular trade union or of one of a number of particular trade unions; or

(*c*) not to take part in the activities of any trade union or of a particular trade union or of one of a number of particular trade unions:

s 72A(3) of the EP(C)A 1978.

This section has been inserted to prevent the employer relying upon any contractual arrangement entered into by the employee for reducing the amount of the award of compensation on the grounds of contributory fault.

9 Compensation and state benefit

9.1 Past benefit

Unemployment benefit or income support paid to the employee by the State between the date of the dismissal and the date of the tribunal hearing are not deducted from the immediate loss of earnings: reg 5(1) of the Employment Protection (Recoupment of Unemployment Benefit and Supplementary Benefit) Regulations 1977 (SI 1977 No 674) as amended. Instead, when giving a decision, the tribunal must, under reg 5(3) of the 1977 Regulations, set out the following particulars:

(a) the monetary award;

(b) the amount of the prescribed element, if any;

(c) the dates of the period to which the prescribed element is attributable; and

(d) the amount, if any, by which the monetary award exceeds the prescribed element.

The monetary award is the total amount of the compensation awarded. The prescribed element is the immediate loss of wages. Where the monetary award is reduced to take account of the employee's contributory fault or because it exceeds the statutory maximum, a proportionate reduction has to be made in the amount of the prescribed element: reg 5(2) of the 1977 Regulations.

Where the tribunal makes a monetary award at the hearing it must then (and in any case in the written decision) explain to the parties the amount of the prescribed element and the provisions as to recoupment: reg 5(4) of the 1977 Regulations. The prescribed element is not payable by the employer until the Department of Employment has either notified the employer that it does not intend to serve a recoupment notice or serves a recoupment notice. The Department of Employment must serve either of these notices where the tribunal announces its decision at the hearing, 21 days after the hearing, or 9 days after the decision has been sent to the parties, whichever is the later; or in any other case 21 days after the decision has been sent to the parties: reg 9(5) and (6) of the 1977 Regulations. A recoupment notice requires the employer to pay to the Department the lesser of the following sums: either the amount of the prescribed element; or the amount paid as on account of unemployment benefit or supplementary benefit to the employee for any period that coincides with the period for which the prescribed element is attributable: reg 9(1) and (2) of the 1977 Regulations.

Payment to the Department of Employment is a complete discharge for the employer in favour of the employee, although the employee is not prejudiced thereby in appealing against the recoupment notice: reg 9(10) of the 1977 Regulations. Where the employer pays the recoupable amount to the employee before the time for serving the recoupment notice he will still be liable to the Department of Employment: reg 9(9) of the 1977 Regulations.

9.2 Future benefit

The position of future benefits is governed by the Social Security (Unemployment, Sickness and Invalidity Benefit) Regulations 1983 (SI 1983 No 1598) as amended. References in this section to the '1983 Regulations' are references to those regulations as amended.

The employee is not treated as being unemployed and so is not entitled to benefit for any day where a tribunal following an order for reinstatement or re-engagement awards an amount for non-compliance with such an order of reinstatement or re-engagement or as compensation for unfair dismissal and the payment represents remuneration which the tribunal considers the employee might have earned for that day but for the dismissal: reg 7(1)(*k*)(iii) of the 1983 Regulations.

These provisions only apply within a year from the date of registration of the tribunal's decision: reg 7(1)(*k*)(iii) of the Regulations. The compensation awarded by the tribunal must be payable to the employee. Payable means due and owing rather than has been or will be paid so it is immaterial that the employer does not or cannot pay: *Marton v Chief Adjudication Officer* [1988] IRLR 444.

In cases where the employer and employee settle a case without going to the tribunal, there is no liability to recoupment. Further, in such circumstances, the employee will not necessarily be disentitled to unemployment benefit in the future. Where the employee receives a capital sum there may be a redetermination of his entitlement to benefit.

10 Death of the employee

Where the employee has died tribunal proceedings for unfair dismissal may be instituted or continued by a personal representative of the deceased employee. If the employer has died proceedings for unfair dismissal may be defended by a personal representative of the deceased employer: para 2 of Sched 12 to the EP(C)A 1978. Where there are no personal representatives of a deceased employee the claim for unfair dismissal may be instituted or continued on behalf of the estate of the deceased employee by such person as the tribunal may appoint, being either a person authorised by the employee before his death to act or a close relative: see para 3(1) of Sched 12.

If either the employee or the employer dies during the notice period the unfair dismissal provisions shall apply as if the contract had been terminated by the employer by notice expiring on the date of death: para 8 of Sched 12.

Paragraph 9 of Sched 12 applies where, by virtue of s 55(5) and (6) of the EP(C)A 1978, the notice period has been extended so that if either the employer or the employee dies before the later date s 55(5) and (6) takes effect as if the notice would have expired on the date of death. Where an employee has died and no order for reinstatement or re-engagement had already been made, the tribunal can award compensation only: para 10 of Sched 12. It follows that the award of compensation will be circumscribed by the date of the employee's death. If an order for reinstatement or re-engagement has been made and the employee dies before the order is complied with, but the employer before the employee's death has refused to carry out the order, the tribunal will assess compensation in the normal way and an additional award will become payable unless the employer can show that it was not practicable at the time of the refusal to comply with the order: para 11(a) of Sched 12. Because of the wording of para 11 of Sched 12 it is doubtful if a special award can be made. If there has been no refusal by the employer to comply with the order but the employer fails to comply with any ancillary terms of the order which remain capable of fulfilment after the employee's death the tribunal shall assess compensation as if the employee had been reinstated or re-engaged, but the employer has not fully complied with the terms of the order (see s 71(1) of the EP(C)A 1978): para 11(b) of Sched 12.

11 Discrimination

Where compensation is awarded for an act both under the Sex Discrimination Act (SDA) 1975, and/or the Race Relations Act (RRA) 1976, and under the EP(C)A 1978 for unfair dismissal, compensation in respect of any loss can only be awarded once for that act: s 76(1) of the EP(C)A 1978. The aggregate limit of compensation for loss is £10,000: ss 75(1) and 76 of the EP(C)A 1978, where the effective date of termination falls on or after 1 April 1991. Previously the limit was £8,925.

Where an unfair dismissal is also an act of discrimination under either the SDA 1975 or the RRA 1976 or both, in addition to a compensatory award for unfair dismissal or compensation for other losses awarded under the provisions of the Acts, the employee will receive a basic award, or, if a recommendation for reinstatement or re-engagement is made but not complied with under s 71(2) of the EP(C)A 1978, an additional award (see s 71(2)(*b*)(i) of the EP(C)A 1978 for the amount): s 76 of the EP(C)A 1978.

12 Interest

Under the Industrial Tribunals (Interest) Order 1990 (SI 1990 No 479) where the whole or any part of a sum of money awarded by a tribunal remains unpaid, the sum of money remaining unpaid on the calculation day carries interest. The calculation day is the day immediately following the expiry of the period of 42 days, beginning with the relevant decision day. The decision day is the day signified by the date recording the sending of the document to the parties recording an award or other determination of a tribunal. There are separate definitions where the decision of a tribunal is reviewed, an appellate court remits a matter to the tribunal for reassessment or if there is an appeal from the decision of the tribunal. The rate of interest is the rate specified in s 17 of the Judgments Act 1838 on the decision day. The order came into force on 1 April 1990.

Chapter 14

Normal Working Hours and a Week's Pay

In calculating the amount of the employee's compensation for unfair dismissal the tribunal will have to ascertain the amount of a week's pay. This will be necessary for the purposes of the additional and basic awards: see ss 71(2)(*b*) and 73 of the EP(C)A 1978. It is also going to be necessary to ascertain the amount of a week's pay for the purposes of the special award: see s 75A of the EP(C)A 1978. As a preliminary the tribunal will have to decide whether or not the employee has any normal working hours.

1 Normal working hours

The employee's normal working hours may be ascertained from collective agreements, national or local, the written contract of employment, the statutory statement served pursuant to Part I of the EP(C)A 1978 or an oral agreement and subsequent practice.

The express terms of the contract of employment may subsequently be varied either expressly or impliedly: see *Armstrong Whitworth Rolls Ltd v Mustard* [1971] 1 All ER 598. However, the evidence must establish that there has been a variation. In *Friend v PMA Holdings Ltd* [1976] ICR 330, the EAT held that there had been no variation in the employees' contracts of employment. The employees' contracts provided they should work 40 hours a week. In early 1974 the employees went on to a three-day week due to a national fuel crisis. Subsequently it was arranged with the employees that they would be told on a weekly basis how much work would be available for them. This temporary arrangement did not operate to vary the existing contracts. But compare *Lowe v East Lancashire Paper Mill Ltd* (1970) 5 ITR 132.

Where an employee signs a contract of employment which clearly sets out the normal working hours that agreement will be conclusive evidence of the terms of the contract as to normal working hours in the absence of any variation or waiver of its terms: see *Gascol Conversions Ltd v Mercer* [1974] ICR 420. In this case the Court of Appeal was not prepared to accept that the national agreement which was reflected in the contract of employment had been varied by a local agreement. Whether or not the national agreement incorporated into the employees' contracts of employment can be varied by a local agreement, depends upon the circumstances, and whether or not the local agreement has become incorporated into the employees' contracts of employment: see *Barrett v NCB* [1978] ICR 1101.

Do the employee's overtime hours form part of the normal working hours? Paragraph 2 of Sched 14 to the EP(C)A 1978 provides that where the contract of employment fixes the number, or the minimum number of hours in a week or other period, whether or not those hours can be reduced in certain circumstances, and even though those hours exceed the number of hours without overtime pay, those hours are the normal working hours. Thus, in practice, it does not matter that some of those hours are regarded as overtime hours, nor that they are remunerated at overtime rates. If the employer has contracted to provide a fixed number of hours' overtime and the employee to work it, so that the overtime is compulsory on both sides, those fixed hours form part of the normal working hours. Conversely, where the employee works additional hours to those which are fixed by the contract, and the additional hours are voluntary on both sides, those hours do not form part of the normal working hours. Where, under the contract, overtime hours are compulsory for the employee only, as where the employer is entitled but not bound to call on the employee to work overtime, but the employee is bound to work overtime when called upon by the employer to do so, those hours are not normal working hours: *Tarmac Roadstone Holdings Ltd v Peacock* [1973] ICR 273; *Gascol Conversions Ltd v Mercer* [1974] ICR 420; and *Lotus Cars Ltd v Sutcliffe and Stratton* [1982] IRLR 381.

2 A week's pay

The legislation specifies four categories of employee, who may be classified as: employees on time work; employees whose pay varies with the work done; employees on a rota or shift; and employees who have no normal hours of work. Each category of employee is treated separately and each section of the legislation dealing with these separate categories has its own peculiar wording. However, in each case it is necessary to ascertain what is meant by the word 'remuneration' for the purposes of computing a week's pay. There is no statutory definition of remuneration. Guidance is available from the reported cases. Although it was at one stage considered that remuneration might differ for each of the categories of employee (consider *S and U Stores Ltd v Lee* [1969] 2 All ER 417), the practice among tribunals is to interpret the word 'remuneration' in the same way for each of the four categories of employees.

In *S and U Stores Ltd v Wilkes* [1974] ICR 645, the NIRC held:

In our judgment the test for determining the 'average' weekly rate of 'remuneration' is as follows:

(i) any sum which is paid as a wage or salary without qualification is part of the employee's remuneration;

(ii) the value of any benefit in kind (eg free accommodation) or paid in cash by someone other than the employer (eg the Easter offering) is to be disregarded as not forming part of the remuneration;

(iii) any sum which is agreed to be paid by way of reimbursement or on account of expenditure incurred by the employee has to be examined to see whether in broad terms the whole or any part of the sum represents a profit or surplus in the hands of the employee. To the extent that it does represent such a profit or surplus it is part of the employee's remuneration.

This is not a matter which calls for an involved accountancy exercise. It is for the tribunal of fact to form a broad common sense view of the realities of the situation as revealed by the evidence assessed in the light of their expert knowledge and experience.

Remuneration includes wages and salaries. It is the wage or salary payable under the contract of employment in force on the calculation date. Therefore, if the employee has agreed to a reduction in his wage or salary before the calculation date, it is that reduced wage which must be taken into account: see *Valentine v Great Lever Spinning Co* (1966) 1 ITR 71. Any future increase cannot be taken into account. Whether or not any increase awarded under an agreement made after the calculation date, but having retrospective effect, can be taken into account is not beyond doubt. On balance it is unlikely that such an increase can be included: see *Leyland Vehicles Ltd v Reston and Others* [1981] ICR 403, where such an increase was discounted; but compare *Carrod v Pullman Spring Filled Co Ltd* (1967) 2 ITR 650; see also *Tsoukka v Potomac Restaurants Ltd* (1968) 3 ITR 259, a case involving the operation of a Wages Council Order.

Where an employee is paid a basic wage together with commission, remuneration will include commission: see *Weevsmay Ltd v Kings* [1977] ICR 244. Where commission is payable at the end of an accounting period it may be apportionable under the employee's contract of employment: *J and S Bickley Ltd v Washer* [1977] ICR 425. This case is some support for the proposition that commission can be apportioned similarly under the statutory provisions. Remuneration includes a contractual bonus: see *Mole Mining Ltd v Jenkins* [1972] ICR 282, and a regular bonus: see *A and B Marcusfield Ltd v Melhuish* [1977] IRLR 484. A site bonus may also be included where it is an implied term of the contract that the employee shall receive the same: see *Donelan v Kerrby Constructions Ltd* [1983] ICR 237.

Remuneration will not include payments in kind, for instance the provision of a car including maintenance and petrol: see *Skillen v Eastwoods Froy Ltd* (1966) 2 ITR 112; board and lodging: *British Transport Hotels Ltd v Minister of Labour* (1966) 2 ITR 165. Nor will it include a lodging allowance: *AM Carmichael Ltd v Laing* (1972) 7 ITR 1.

Remuneration will not include any payment made by a third party. Thus, a waiter cannot claim tips or gratuities as part of his remuneration for the purposes of the statutory provisions: see *Palmanor Ltd t/a Chaplins Night Club v Cedron* [1978] IRLR 303; although where customers of a restaurant were contractually obliged to pay a 10 per cent service charge, which was then distributed to employees in fixed proportions, the payment (known as tronc) to an employee did form part of remuneration for statutory purposes: *Tsoukka and Others v Potomac Restaurants Ltd* (1968) 3 ITR 259. See also *Keywest Club Ltd v Choudhury* [1988] IRLR 51.

A week's pay for the purposes of Sched 14 to the EP(C)A 1978 is a week's pay gross: see *Secretary of State for Employment v John Woodrow and Sons (Builders) Ltd* [1983] IRLR 11. The case of *Secretary of State for Employment v Jobling* [1980] ICR 380, which held that a week's pay was net of tax is wrong in law.

In assessing the employee's compensation for the purposes of the compensatory award the tribunal may take into account losses which would not form remuneration for the purposes of Sched 14. A week's pay to which the employee is entitled: see *Cooner v P S Doal & Sons* [1988] ICR 495.

2.1 Employees on time work

If an employee's remuneration for employment in normal working hours, whether by the hour or week or other period, does not vary with the amount of work done in the period, the amount of a week's pay is the amount which is payable by the employer under the contract of employment in force on the calculation date if the employee works throughout his normal working hours in a week: para 3(2) of Sched 14.

2.2. Employees whose pay varies with work done

Where the employee is not on time work, the amount of a week's pay is the amount of remuneration for the number of normal working hours in a week, calculated at the average hourly rate of remuneration payable by the employer to the employee in respect of the period of 12 weeks ending, where the calculation date is the last day of the week, with that week or, in any other case, with the last complete week before the calculation date: para 3(3) of Sched 14. References to remuneration varying with the amount of work done include references to remuneration which may include any commission or similar payment which varies in amount: para 3(4) of Sched 14; see also para 5 of Sched 14. (See **2.3**, below.)

2.3 Employees on shifts or rotas

Where there are normal working hours for an employee when employed under the contract of employment in force on the calculation date, and he is required under that contract to work during those hours on days of the week, or at times of the day, which differ from week to week or over a longer period so that the remuneration payable for or apportionable to any week varies according to the incidence of those days or times, the amount of a week's pay is the amount of remuneration for the average weekly number of normal working hours at the average hourly rate of remuneration: para 4(1) and (2) of Sched 14.

The average number of weekly hours is calculated by dividing by 12 the total number of the employee's normal working hours during the period of 12 weeks ending, where the calculation date is the last day of the week, with that week, or, in any other case, with the last complete week before the calculation date: para 4(3) of Sched 14. The average hourly rate of remuneration is the average hourly rate of remuneration payable by the employer to the employee for the same 12 weeks: para 4(4) of Sched 14.

In computing the average hourly rate of remuneration (for the purposes of para 3 or para 4) only hours worked and only payment made for those hours can be considered. This may cause hardship for the employees, hence the averaging formula. If in some of the 12 weeks no remuneration was payable, those weeks are ignored and the next preceding weeks are taken into account: para 5(1) of Sched 14. See also para 5(2) of Sched 14 which provides for work done other than in normal working hours at a greater remuneration than work done in normal working hours to be treated as work done in normal working hours at a rate of remuneration adjusted accordingly. See *British Coal Corporation v Cheesborough* [1990] ICR 317. No account is to be taken of any overtime premium even if the overtime hours are compulsory: see para 5(3) of Sched 14.

2.4 Employees with no normal working hours

If there are no normal working hours for an employee when employed under the contract of employment in force on the calculation date, the amount of a week's pay is the amount of the employee's average weekly remuneration in the period of 12 weeks ending, where the calculation date is the last day of the week, with that week or, in any other case, with the last complete week before the calculation date: para 6(1) and (2) of Sched 14.

In arriving at the average weekly rate of remuneration no account is taken of a week in which no remuneration was payable. Those weeks are ignored and the next preceding weeks are taken into account so as to bring the number of weeks up to 12: para 6(3) of Sched 14.

2.5 The calculation date

The calculation date for the purposes of determining a week's pay varies according to the circumstances.

Failure to give a written statement of the reasons for dismissal   Where the dismissal was with notice the calculation date is the date on which the employer's notice was given: para 7(1)(*f*) of Sched 14. In any other case, the calculation date is the effective date of termination: para 7(1)(*g*) of Sched 14.

The basic or additional award for the employee who is unfairly dismissed in breach of her right to return after maternity   The calculation date is the last day on which she worked under the original contract of employment: para 2(5) of Sched 2.

The basic award for unfair dismissal   Where s 55(5) or (6) of the EP(C)A 1978 does not apply the calculation date is the date on which notice would have been given had certain conditions been fulfilled whether or not they are, in fact, fulfilled: para 7(1)(*i*) of Sched 14. The conditions are those set out in para 7(2) of Sched 14. The conditions are that the contract was terminable by notice and was terminated by the employer giving notice which complied with s 49 of the EP(C)A 1978 and that the notice expired on the effective date of termination. This paragraph will include unfair dismissals where the contract is terminated by proper notice or, being a fixed-term contract, expires without being renewed, and in certain circumstances includes cases of constructive dismissal. Where s 55(5) or (6) of the EP(C)A 1978 applies, so that the effective date of termination is treated as being the date when the contract would have ended had proper notice been given, rather than the effective date of termination as defined in s 55(4), the calculation date is the effective date of termination in s 55(4): para 7(1)(*h*) of Sched 14.

Additional award of compensation where there is a failure to comply with an order for reinstatement or re-engagement   Where the dismissal was with notice the calculation date is the date on which the notice was given. In any other case, it is the effective date of termination: para 7(1)(*f*) and (*g*) of Sched 14.

The calculation date for the basic award can cause problems in certain cases of constructive dismissal or where a fixed-term contract expires without being renewed. The calculation date has to be determined by ascertaining the date when the employment actually ended—the effective date of termination—and, when the actual date has been found, it is necessary to take away the number of weeks' notice to which the employee is entitled under the statutory provisions. The date which is then reached is the calculation date. Where the employee is dismissed with notice which is less than the statutory minimum, the employee is credited with the additional weeks and the effective date of termination is later than the date when the employment actually ended. Were there no provision for calculating a week's wages, since the effective date of termination will be later than the actual date when the employment terminated, weeks would be taken into account when the employee had not worked. To overcome this difficulty the calculation date for these purposes is the effective date of termination—ie when the contract actually ends and not the date when the contract would have ended if proper notice had been given.

2.6 Supplemental

Where the employee has not been employed for a sufficient period to enable a calculation to be made, the amount of a week's pay is the amount which fairly represents a week's pay. In ascertaining this, the tribunal must apply as nearly as possible the provisions contained in Sched 14: para 9 of Sched 14. It may have regard to remuneration offered by the employer to the employee and the amount received by the employee for the work. It may also have regard to remuneration received by other persons engaged by the same employer, or other employers for relevant comparable employment: para 9(a)–(d) of Sched 14.

Account may be taken of remuneration earned by the employee with a former employer, where that counts as part of the employee's continuous employment: para 10 of Sched 14.

The tribunal has power to make apportionments in computing the rate of remuneration: para 11 of Sched 14.

Twelve weeks means the last 12 calendar weeks. It does not mean the last 12 working weeks or the last 12 weeks of employment: see *Sylvester v Standard Upholstery Co Ltd* (1966) 2 ITR 507.

For the purposes of this chapter, a week means, in relation to an employee whose remuneration is calculated weekly by a week ending with a day other than Saturday, a week ending with that other day, and in relation to any other employee, a week ending with Saturday: s 153(1) of the EP(C)A 1978.

Index